# THE REAL HISTORY

## OF THE

## A NEW LOOK AT THE PAST

### Alan Axelrod

STERLING

New York

STERLING
New York

An Imprint of Sterling Publishing
387 Park Avenue South
New York, NY 10016

ISBN 978-1-4027-6390-8

Library of Congress Cataloging-in-Publication Data

Axelrod, Alan, 1952-
 The real history of the Civil War : a new look at the past / Alan Axelrod.
   pages cm
 Includes index.
 ISBN 978-1-4027-6390-8
 1. United States--History--Civil War, 1861-1865. I. Title.
 E468.A95 2012
 973.7--dc23
                    2011049409

Distributed in Canada by Sterling Publishing
c/o Canadian Manda Group, 165 Dufferin Street
Toronto, Ontario, Canada M6K 3H6
Distributed in the United Kingdom by GMC Distribution Services
Castle Place, 166 High Street, Lewes, East Sussex, England BN7 1XU
Distributed in Australia by Capricorn Link (Australia) Pty. Ltd.
P.O. Box 704, Windsor, NSW 2756, Australia

For information about custom editions, special sales, and premium and corporate purchases,
please contact Sterling Special Sales at 800-805-5489 or specialsales@sterlingpublishing.com.

Printed in China

2  4  6  8  10  9  7  5  3  1

www.sterlingpublishing.com

# For Anita and Ian

"Light it with every lurid passion,
the wolf's, the lion's lapping thirst for blood;
the passionate, boiling volcanoes of human revenge
for comrades, brothers slain;
with the light of burning farms, and heaps of smutting,
smouldering black embers—
and in the human heart everywhere
black, worse embers—
and you have an inkling of the war."

*Walt Whitman, "A Glimpse of War's Hell Scenes,"* Specimen Days (1882)

# CONTENTS

# THE REAL HISTORY OF THE CIVIL WAR

## PART ONE

## TITLE PAGE TO A GREAT TRAGIC VOLUME

## PART TWO

## FIRE-EATERS

## PART THREE

## HELL BEFORE NIGHT

## PART FOUR

## BROKEN GENERALS

# DRAMATIS PERSONAE

**Adams, Charles Francis** (1807–86) U.S. minister to Great Britain 1861–68; Adams attempted to prevent British shipyards and munitions factories from supplying the Confederacy.

**Anderson, Robert** (1805–71) Maj. Gen. USA; Commandant who surrendered Fort Sumter to Confederate forces.

**Banks, Nathaniel P.** (1816–94) Maj. Gen. USA; Massachusetts governor 1858–60; went on to commands in the Army of the Potomac (corps cdr.) during Shenandoah Valley campaign, 1862; Army of Virginia (corps cdr.) during battle of Cedar Mountain; Dept. of the Gulf (cdr.) during battle of Port Hudson and the Red River campaign.

**Barton, Clara** (1821–1912) Pioneering volunteer battle-field nurse who went on to found (in 1881) the American Red Cross.

**Beauregard, P. G. T.** (1818–93) General CSA; received surrender of Fort Sumter; had field command at first battle of Bull Run; Army of Mississippi (cdr.) at battle of Shiloh; Departments of South Carolina, Georgia, and Florida (cdr.), Aug. 1862–April 1864; Departments of North Carolina and Southern Virginia (cdr., April 1864–March 1865) at Petersburg campaign.

**Benjamin, Judah P.** (1811–84) Confederate attorney general, Feb.–Sept. 1861; secretary of war, Sept. 1861–March 1862; secretary of state, March 1862–May 1865.

**Booth, John Wilkes** (1838–65) Pro–Confederate actor who assassinated President Lincoln, April 14, 1865.

**Bragg, Braxton** (1817–76) General CSA; Army of Mississippi (corps cdr.) at battle of Shiloh; Army of Mississippi (cdr.) at battle of Perryville; Army of Tennessee (cdr.) at battles of Murfreesboro and Chickamauga and Chattanooga campaign; military adviser to President Jefferson Davis, Feb.1864–Jan. 1865.

**Breckinridge, John C.** (1821–75) Maj. Gen. CSA; U.S. vice president, 1857–61; presidential candidate, 1860; Army of Mississippi (corps cdr.) at battle of Shiloh; Army of Tennessee (div. cdr.) at battles of Murfreesboro and Chickamauga; Army of Tennessee (corps cdr.) at Chattanooga campaign; Army of Northern Virginia (div. cdr.) at battle of Cold Harbor; Confederate secretary of war, Feb. 1864–May 1865.

**Buchanan, Franklin** (1800–74) Admiral CSN; first superintendent of U.S. Naval Academy (Annapolis), 1845–47; commanded CSS *Virginia* (ex–*Merrimack*) at battle of Hampton Roads, March 8, 1862, and ironclad ram CSS *Tennessee* at battle of Mobile Bay, Aug. 5, 1864.

**Buchanan, James** (1791–1868) Fifteenth U.S. President, 1857–61, who did nothing to avert the Civil War.

**Buckner, Simon Bolivar** (1823–1914) Lt. Gen. CSA; surrendered Fort Donelson to U. S. Grant; Army of Mississippi (div. cdr.) at battle of Perryville; Army of Tennessee (corps cdr.) at battle of Chickamauga.

**Buell, Don Carlos** (1818–98) Maj. Gen. USA; Dept. of the Ohio (cdr., Nov. 1861–March 1862); Army of the Ohio (cdr.) at battles of Shiloh and Perryville; relieved of command, Oct. 1862; resigned commission, June 1864.

**Buford, John** (1826–63) Maj. Gen. USA; Army of Virginia (cav. brigade cdr.) at second battle of Bull Run; Army of the Potomac (chief of cav.) at battles of Antietam and Fredericksburg; Army of the Potomac (cav. div. cdr.) at battle of Gettysburg.

**Burnside, Ambrose E.** (1824–81) Maj. Gen. USA; brigade cdr. at first battle of Bull Run and battle of Roanoke Island; Army of the Potomac (corps cdr.) at battle of Antietam; Army of the Potomac (cdr.) at battle of Fredericksburg; Army of the Ohio (cdr.) at battle of Knoxville; Army of the Potomac (corps cdr.) at battles of the Wilderness, Spotsylvania, and Cold Harbor, and at Petersburg campaign; relieved of command, Aug. 1864.

**Butler, Benjamin F.** (1818–93) Maj. Gen. USA; commanded occupations of Baltimore and New Orleans; Army of the James (cdr.): battles of Bermuda Hundred and Fort Fisher; relieved of command, Jan. 1865.

**Cameron, Simon** (1799–1889) Lincoln's corrupt U.S. secretary of war, March 1861–Jan. 1862, who was "promoted" to minister to Russia, 1862.

**Canby, Edward R. S.** (1817–73) Maj. Gen. USA; Dept. of New Mexico (cdr.) at battle of Valverde; Military Div. of West Mississippi (cdr.) at battle of Mobile Bay; received surrender of the last Confederate armies.

**Chase, Salmon P.** (1808–73) Ohio governor, 1855–61; U.S. secretary of the treasury, March 1861–June 1864; chief justice of the U.S. Supreme Court, 1864–73.

**Crittenden, George B.** (1812–80) Maj. Gen. CSA; son of Senator John J. Crittenden (below); defeated at battle of Mill Springs; resigned commission, Oct. 1862.

**Crittenden, John J.** (1787–1863) U.S. senator from Kentucky, 1854–61; authored the Crittenden Compromise intended to avert war, Dec. 1860; U.S. congressman, 1861–63; father of a Confederate general and a Union general.

**Crittenden, Thomas L.** (1819–93) Maj. Gen. USA; son of Senator John J. Crittenden (above); Army of the Ohio (div. cdr.) at battle of Shiloh; Army of the Cumberland (left wing cdr.) at battle of Murfreesboro; Army of the Cumberland (corps cdr.) at battle of Chickamauga; resigned commission, Dec. 1864.

**Custer, George A.** (1839–76) Maj. Gen. USA; first battle of Bull Run; Army of the Potomac (cav. brigade cdr.) at Peninsula campaign through Petersburg campaign; Army of the Shenandoah (cav. div. cdr.) at Shenandoah Valley campaign and Appomattox campaign; killed with his entire command at the battle of the Little Bighorn, 1876.

**Davis, Jefferson** (1808–89) U.S. senator (Mississippi), 1847–51 and 1857–61; U.S. secretary of war, 1853–57; president of the Confederacy.

**Early, Jubal A.** (1816–94) Lt. Gen. CSA; brigade cdr. at first battle of Bull Run; Army of Northern Virginia (brigade cdr.) at Peninsula campaign and second battle of Bull Run; Army of Northern Virginia (div. cdr.) at battles of Antietam, Fredericksburg, Chancellorsville, Gettysburg, the Wilderness, Spotsylvania; Army of Northern Virginia (corps cdr.) at battle of Cold Harbor and Shenandoah Valley campaign.

**Ericsson, John** (1803–89) Architect and builder of USS *Monitor* and inventor of the rotating gun turret.

**Ewell, Richard S.** (1817–72) Lt. Gen. CSA; Army of Northern Virginia (div. cdr.) at Shenandoah Valley and Peninsula campaigns and second battle of Bull Run; Army of Northern Virginia (corps cdr.) at battles of Gettysburg, the Wilderness, and Spotsylvania, and commanded the Richmond defenses.

**Farragut, David G.** (1801–70) Vice Adm. USN; West Gulf Blockading Squadron (cdr.); led the capture of New Orleans, the bombardment of Vicksburg and Port Hudson, and the capture of Mobile Bay.

**Foote, Andrew** (1806–63) Rear Adm. USN; Upper Mississippi River fleet (cdr.), Aug. 1861–May 1862, at the capture of Forts Henry and Donelson and Island No. 10.

**Frémont, John C.** (1813–90) Maj. Gen. USA; Western Dept. (cdr., May–Nov. 1861); Mountain Dept. (cdr., March–June 1862) at Shenandoah Valley campaign (1862).

**Gibbon, John** (1827–96) Maj. Gen. USA; Army of Virginia (brigade cdr.) at second battle of Bull Run; Army of the Potomac (brigade cdr.) at battle of Antietam; Army of the Potomac (div. cdr.) at battle of Fredericksburg; Army of the Potomac (corps cdr.) at battle of Gettysburg; Army of the Potomac (div. cdr.) at battles of the Wilderness, Spotsylvania, and Cold Harbor and Petersburg campaign; Army of the James (corps cdr.) at Appomattox campaign.

**Gordon, John B.** (1832–1904) Maj. Gen. CSA; Army of Northern Virginia at Peninsula campaign and battle of Antietam; Army of Northern Virginia (brigade cdr.) at battles of Chancellorsville, Gettysburg, the Wilderness, and Spotsylvania; Army of Northern Virginia (div. cdr.) at Shenandoah Valley campaign, 1864; Army of Northern Virginia (corps cdr.) at Petersburg and Appomattox campaigns.

**Grant, Ulysses S.** (1822–85) Lt. Gen. USA; commanding officer at battles of Belmont, Fort Henry, and Fort Donelson; Army of the Tennessee (cdr.) at battle of Shiloh and Vicksburg campaign; Military Div. of the Mississippi (cdr.) at Chattanooga campaign; general-in-chief of Union armies, from March 12, 1864, with direction of Army of the Potomac in the Overland campaign, 1864–65; received Lee's surrender of the Army of Northern Virginia at Appomattox, April 9, 1865, for all practical purposes ending the Civil War.

**Greeley, Horace** (1811–72) Abolitionist editor of the *New York Tribune*, 1841–72.

**Halleck, Henry Wager** ("Old Brains") (1815–72) Maj. Gen. USA; Dept. of the Missouri (cdr., Nov. 1861–March 1862); Dept. of the Mississippi (cdr., March–July 1862); general-in-chief of Union armies, July 1862–March 1864; chief of staff under Grant, March 1864–April 1865.

**Hamlin, Hannibal** (1809–91) U.S. vice president, 1861–65.

**Hancock, Winfield Scott** (1824–86) Maj. Gen. USA; Army of the Potomac (brigade cdr.) at Peninsula campaign; Army of the Potomac (div. cdr.) at battles of Antietam, Fredericksburg, Chancellorsville; Army of the Potomac (corps cdr.) at battles of Gettysburg, the Wilderness, Spotsylvania, and Cold Harbor and at Petersburg campaign.

**Hardee, William J.** (1815–73) Lt. Gen. CSA; Army of Mississippi (corps cdr.) at battle of Shiloh; (left wing cdr.) at battle of Perryville; Army of Tennessee (corps cdr.) at Murfreesboro, Chattanooga and Atlanta campaigns, and in the Carolinas; Dept. of South Carolina, Georgia, and Florida (cdr., Sept. 1864–April 1865).

**Heth, Henry** (1825–99) Maj. Gen. CSA; Army of Mississippi (div. cdr.) at battle of Perryville; Army of Northern Virginia (div. cdr.) at battles of Chancellorsville, Gettysburg, the Wilderness, and Spotsylvania and the Petersburg and Appomattox campaigns.

**Hill, Ambrose Powell** (1825–65) Lt. Gen. CSA; Army of Northern Virginia (div. cdr.) at the Peninsula campaign and first and second battles of Bull Run, battles of Antietam, Fredericksburg, and Chancellorsville; Army of Northern Virginia (corps cdr.) at battles of Gettysburg, the Wilderness, and Cold Harbor and at Petersburg campaign (in which he was killed, April 2, 1865). No relation to Daniel Harvey Hill.

**Hill, Daniel Harvey** (1821–89) Lt. Gen. CSA; Battle of Big Bethel; Army of Northern Virginia (div. cdr.) at Peninsula campaign and battle of Antietam; Army of Tennessee (corps cdr.) and battle of Chickamauga; Army of Tennessee (div. cdr.) in the Carolinas. No relation to Ambrose Powell Hill.

**Hood, John Bell** (1831–79) Lt. Gen. CSA; Army of Northern Virginia (brigade cdr.) at Peninsula campaign; Army of Northern Virginia (div. cdr.) at second battle of Bull Run and battles of Antietam, Fredericksburg, and Gettysburg; corps (cdr.) at battle of Chickamauga; Army of Tennessee (corps cdr.) at Atlanta campaign; Army of

Tennessee (army cdr.) at Atlanta campaign and battles of Franklin and Nashville.

**Hooker, Joseph** ("Fighting Joe") (1814–79) Maj. Gen. USA; Army of the Potomac (div. cdr.) at Peninsula campaign and second battle of Bull Run; Army of the Potomac (corps cdr.) at battle of Antietam; Army of the Potomac (Center Grand Div. cdr.) at battle of Fredericksburg; Army of the Potomac (cdr.) at battle of Chancellorsville; Army of the Cumberland (corps cdr.) at Chattanooga and Atlanta campaigns.

**Howard, Oliver O.** (1830–1909) Maj. Gen. USA; brigade cdr. at first battle of Bull Run; Army of the Potomac (brigade cdr.) at Peninsula campaign; Army of the Potomac (div. cdr.) at battles of Antietam and Fredericksburg; Army of the Potomac (corps cdr.) at battles of Chancellorsville and Gettysburg; Army of the Cumberland (corps cdr.) at Chattanooga and Atlanta campaigns; Army of the Tennessee (cdr.) at Atlanta campaign, Sherman's March to the Sea, and in the Carolinas.

**Jackson, Thomas J.** ("Stonewall") (1824–63) Lt. Gen. CSA; brigade cdr. at first battle of Bull Run; cdr. at Shenandoah Valley campaign (1862); Army of Northern Virginia (div. cdr.) at Peninsula campaign; Army of Northern Virginia (left wing cdr.) at second battle of Bull Run; Army of Northern Virginia ("Jackson's Command" cdr.) at battle of Antietam; Army of Northern Virginia (corps cdr.) at battles of Fredericksburg and Chancellorsville, where he was mortally wounded by friendly fire, May 2, 1863, and died on May 10, 1863.

**Johnson, Andrew** (1808–75) Governor of Tennessee, 1853–57; U.S. senator, 1857–62; military governor of Tennessee, 1862–65; U.S. vice president, 1865; became president on death of Lincoln, April 15, 1865; impeached and acquitted, 1868.

**Johnston, Albert Sidney** (1803–62) General CSA; Western Dept. (cdr., September 1861–April 1862); Army of Mississippi (cdr.) at Shiloh, where he was killed, April 6, 1862.

**Johnston, Joseph E.** (1807–91) Gen. CSA; cdr. at first battle of Bull Run and battle of Fair Oaks; Div. of the West (cdr., November 1862–December 1863); Army of Tennessee (cdr., Dec. 1863–July 1864) at Atlanta campaign; Army of Tennessee (cdr., Feb.–April 1865) in the Carolinas.

**Lee, Fitzhugh** (1835–1905) Maj. Gen. CSA; son of Robert E. Lee; Army of Northern Virginia (cav. cdr.) at Peninsula campaign; Army of Northern Virginia (cav. brigade cdr.) at battles of Antietam, Chancellorsville, and Gettysburg; Army of Northern Virginia (cav. div. cdr.) at battle of Spotsylvania and Shenandoah Valley campaign (1864); Army of Northern Virginia (cav. corps cdr.) at Appomattox campaign.

**Lee, Robert E.** (1807–70) General CSA; cdr. of Virginia troops, April–Nov. 1861; Dept. of South Carolina, Georgia, and Florida (cdr., Nov. 1861–March 1862); military adviser to Jefferson Davis, March–June 1862; Army of Northern Virginia (cdr., June 1, 1862–April 9, 1865): from Peninsula to Appomattox campaign; named Confederate general-in-chief, Feb. 6, 1865; surrendered Army of Northern Virginia to Grant, April 9, 1865.

**Lincoln, Abraham** (1809–65) Sixteenth president of the United States, 1861–65; assassinated April 14, 1865, and died the following day.

**Longstreet, James** ("Old Pete," "Gloomy Pete") (1821–1904) Lt. Gen. CSA; brigade cdr. at first battle of Bull Run; Army of Northern Virginia (div. cdr.) at Peninsula campaign; Army of Northern Virginia (right wing cdr.) at second battle of Bull Run; Army of Northern Virginia, "Longstreet's Command" at battle of Antietam; Army of Northern Virginia (corps cdr.) at battles of Fredericksburg and Gettysburg; Army of Tennessee (left wing cdr.) at battle of Chickamauga; Confederate cdr. at Knoxville; Army of Northern Virginia (corps cdr.) at the battle of the Wilderness and Petersburg and Appomattox campaigns.

**Magruder, John B.** (1810–71) Maj. Gen. CSA; cdr. at battle of Big Bethel; Army of Northern Virginia, "Magruder's Command" cdr. at Peninsula campaign; district cdr., Texas and Arkansas, Oct. 1862–May 1865.

**Mallory, Stephen R.** (1813–73) Confederate secretary of the navy, 1861–65.

**Mason, James M.** (1798–1871) Confederate commissioner to Great Britain and France, Aug. 1861; captured in Trent Affair, Nov. 8, 1861.

**McClellan, George B.** (1826–85) Maj. Gen. USA; Dept. of the Ohio (cdr., May–July 1861) at battles of Philippi and Rich Mountain; District of the Potomac (cdr., July–Aug. 1861); Army of the Potomac (cdr., Aug. 1861–Nov. 1862) at Peninsula campaign and battle of Antietam; Union army general-in-chief, Nov. 1861–July 1862; Democratic candidate for president, 1864.

**McDowell, Irvin** (1818–85) Maj. Gen. USA; Army of the Potomac (div. and corps cdr., Oct. 1861–April 1862) at first battle of Bull Run; Army of the Rappahannock (cdr., April–June 1862); Army of Virginia (corps cdr.) at second battle of Bull Run; relieved of command, Sept. 1862.

**McPherson, James B.** (1828–64) Maj. Gen. USA; chief engineer at battles of Forts Henry and Donelson and battle of Shiloh; Army of the Tennessee (brigade cdr.) at battle of Iuka; Army of the Tennessee (div. cdr., Oct. 1862–Jan. 1863); Army of the Tennessee (corps cdr.) at Vicksburg campaign; Army of the Tennessee (cdr.) at Atlanta campaign, during which he was killed at the battle of Peachtree Creek, July 22, 1864.

**Meade, George Gordon** (1815–72) Maj. Gen. USA; Army of the Potomac (brigade cdr.) at Peninsula campaign and second battle of Bull Run; Army of the Potomac (div. cdr.) at battles of Antietam and Fredericksburg; Army of the Potomac (corps cdr.) at battle of Chancellorsville; Army of the Potomac (cdr., June 1863–April 1865) at battle of Gettysburg through Appomattox campaign.

**Morgan, John Hunt** (1825–64) Brig. Gen. CSA; Battle of Shiloh; leader of Kentucky raids, July, October, Dec. 1862, and the Ohio Raid, July 1863; killed at Greeneville, Tennessee, Sept. 4, 1864.

**Mosby, John S.** ("The Gray Ghost of the Confederacy") (1833–1916) Col. CSA; First battle of Bull Run; Shenandoah Valley campaign (1862); cdr. of Partisan Rangers, Jan. 1863–April 1865.

**Pickett, George E.** (1825–75) Maj. Gen. CSA; Army of Northern Virginia (brigade cdr.) at Peninsula campaign; Army of Northern Virginia (div. cdr.) at battles of Fredericksburg and Gettysburg; Dept. of Virginia and North Carolina (cdr., Sept. 1863–May 1864) at battle of Drewry's Bluff; Army of Northern Virginia (div. cdr.) at battle of Cold Harbor and Petersburg and Appomattox campaigns.

**Pinkerton, Allan** (1819–84) Union spymaster and counterespionage agent; Army of the Potomac (chief detective, Aug. 1861–Nov. 1862).

**Pleasonton, Alfred** (1824–97) Maj. Gen. USA; Peninsula campaign; Army of the Potomac (cav. div. cdr.) at battles of Antietam, Fredericksburg, and Chancellorsville; Army of the Potomac (cav. corps cdr.) at battle of Gettysburg.

**Polk, Leonidas** (1806–64) Lt. Gen. CSA; Western Dept. (cdr., July–Sept. 1861) at battle of Belmont; Army of Mississippi (corps cdr.) at battle of Shiloh; Army of Mississippi (cdr.) at battle of Perryville; Army of Tennessee (corps cdr.) at battle of Murfreesboro; Army of Tennessee (right wing cdr.) at battle of Chickamauga; Army of Tennessee (corps cdr.) at Atlanta campaign; killed at battle of Pine Mountain, June 14, 1864.

**Pope, John** (1822–92) Maj. Gen. USA; Army of the Mississippi (cdr., Feb.–June 1862) at battles of New Madrid and Island No. 10; Army of Virginia (cdr.) at second battle of Bull Run; Dept. of the Northwest (cdr., Sept.–Nov. 1862 and Feb. 1863–Feb. 1865).

**Porter, David Dixon** (1813–91) Rear Adm. USN; at capture of New Orleans; Mississippi Squadron (cdr., Oct. 1862–July 1863) at battle of Fort Hindman, Vicksburg; Lower Mississippi River fleet (cdr., Aug. 1863–Oct. 1864) at Red River campaign; North Atlantic Blockading Squadron (cdr., Oct. 1864–April 1865) at battle of Fort Fisher.

**Porter, Fitz–John** (1822–1901) Maj. Gen. USA; Army of the Potomac (div. cdr.) at battle of Yorktown; Army of the Potomac (corps cdr.) at Peninsula campaign, second battle of Bull Run, and battle of Antietam; relieved of command, Nov. 1862, and court-martialed for conduct unbecoming at second battle of Bull Run (exonerated, 1886).

**Powell, Lewis** (a.k.a. Lewis Paine) (1845–65) Booth conspirator who attempted assassination of Secretary of State Seward, April 14, 1865; hanged, July 7, 1865.

**Price, Sterling** (1809–67) Maj. Gen. CSA; Missouri State Guard (cdr.) at battles of Wilson's Creek, Lexington, and Pea Ridge; Army of the West (cdr.) at battle of Iuka; Army of West Tennessee (corps cdr.) at battle of Corinth; leader of Missouri Raid, Sept.–Oct. 1864.

**Quantrill, William C.** (1837–65) Cpt. CSA; at battle of Wilson's Creek; guerrilla leader of raids against Independence, Missouri, Lawrence, Kansas, and Baxter Springs, Kansas; shot in Kentucky, May 10, 1865; died June 6, 1865.

**Reynolds, John F.** (1820–63) Maj. Gen. USA; Army of the Potomac (brigade cdr.) at Peninsula campaign; Army of the Potomac (div. cdr.) at second battle of Bull Run; Army of the Potomac (corps cdr.) at battles of Fredericksburg, Chancellorsville, and Gettysburg, where he was killed, July 1, 1863.

**Rosecrans, William S.** (1819–98) Maj. Gen. USA; at Rich Mountain; Army of Occupation and Dept. of West Virginia, July 1861–March 1862; Army of the Mississippi (cdr.) at battles of Iuka and Corinth; Army of the Cumberland (cdr.) at battles of Murfreesboro and Chickamauga; relieved Oct. 1863 for conduct at battle of Chickamauga.

**Schofield, John** (1831–1906) Maj. Gen. USA; at battle of Wilson's Creek; Missouri district and dept. cdr., Nov. 1861–Jan. 1864; Army of the Ohio (cdr.) at battles of Atlanta, Franklin, and Nashville, and in the Carolinas.

**Schurz, Carl** (1829–1906) Maj. Gen. USA; German-born U.S. minister to Spain, 1861–62; Army of Virginia (div. cdr.) at second battle of Bull Run; Army of the Potomac (div. cdr.) at battle of Chancellorsville; Army of the Cumberland (div. cdr.) at Chattanooga campaign.

**Scott, Winfield** (1786–1866) Lt. Gen. USA, General-in-chief, USA, 1841–61; proposed "Anaconda" blockade; retired, 1861.

**Seddon, James A.** (1815–80) Confederate secretary of war, Nov. 1862–Feb. 1865.

**Semmes, Raphael** (1809–77) Rear Adm. CSN; commanded Confederate commerce raiders Sumter, June 1861–Jan. 1862, and Alabama, Aug. 1862–June 1864. After losing battle with USS *Kearsarge*, June 19, 1864, commanded James River squadron.

**Seward, William H.** (1801–72) U.S. secretary of state, 1861–69; wounded in assassination attempt, April 14, 1865.

**Sheridan, Philip H.** (1831–88) Maj. Gen. USA; Army of the Ohio (div. cdr.) at battle of Perryville; Army of the Cumberland (div. cdr.) at battles of Murfreesboro and Chickamauga and Chattanooga campaign; Army of the Potomac (cav. corps cdr.) at battles of the Wilderness and Spotsylvania, Richmond Raid, battle of Cold Harbor, and Appomattox campaign; Army of the Shenandoah (cdr.), Aug. 1864–March 1865.

**Sherman, William Tecumseh** (1820–91) Maj. Gen. USA; brigade cdr. at first battle of Bull Run; Dept. of the Cumberland (cdr., Oct.–Nov. 1861); Army of the Tennessee (div. cdr.) at battle of Shiloh; Army of the Tennessee (corps cdr.) at battles of Chickasaw Bluffs and Fort Hindman and Vicksburg campaign; Army of the Tennessee (cdr., Oct. 1863–March 1864) at battles of Chattanooga and Meridian; Military Div. of the Mississippi (cdr., March 1864–April 1865) at Atlanta campaign, Sherman's March to the Sea, and in the Carolinas.

**Sickles, Daniel E.** (1819–1914) Maj. Gen. USA; Army of the Potomac (brigade cdr.) at Peninsula campaign; Army of the Potomac (div. cdr.) at battle of Fredericksburg; Army of the Potomac (corps cdr.) at battles of Chancellorsville and Gettysburg.

**Sigel, Franz** (1824–1902) Maj. Gen. USA; German-born organizer of German-American troops and war support; at battle of Wilson's Creek; div. cdr. at battle of Pea Ridge; Army of Virginia (corps cdr.) at second battle of Bull Run; Army of the Potomac (corps cdr., Sept. 1862–Feb. 1863); Dept. of West Virginia (cdr., March–May 1864) at battle of New Market; relieved of command, July 1864.

**Slidell, John** (1793–1871) Confederate commissioner to France, Aug. 1861; captured in *Trent* affair, Nov. 1861.

**Smith, Edmund Kirby** (1824–93) Gen. CSA; brigade cdr. at first battle of Bull Run; Dept. of East Tennessee (cdr.) during invasion of Kentucky; Trans–Mississippi Dept. (cdr., March 1863–May 1865) at Red River campaign; commanded last Confederate operational unit to surrender, May 26, 1865.

**Stanton, Edwin McMasters** (1814–69) U.S. attorney general, Dec. 1860–March 1861; U.S. secretary of war, Jan. 1862–May 1868.

**Stephens, Alexander H.** (1812–83) Vice president of the Confederacy.

**Stoneman, George** (1822–94) Maj. Gen. USA; Army of the Potomac (cav. div. cdr.) at Peninsula campaign; Army of the Potomac (corps cdr.) at battle of Fredericksburg; Army of the Potomac (cav. corps cdr.) at battle of Chancellorsville; Cav. bureau chief, July 1863–Jan. 1864; Army of the Ohio (cav. div. cdr.) at Atlanta campaign; Dept. of the Ohio (cdr., Nov. 1864–Jan. 1865); District of East Tennessee (cdr., March–April 1865).

**Stuart, J. E. B.** (1833–64) Maj. Gen. CSA; at first battle of Bull Run; Army of Northern Virginia (cav. cdr.) at Peninsula campaign (led first "ride around" Army of the Potomac); second battle of Bull Run; battles of Antietam (led second "ride around" Army of the Potomac), Fredericksburg, and Chancellorsville; held temporary command of Jackson's corps at battle of Brandy Station, in Gettysburg Raid, and at battles of the Wilderness,

Spotsylvania, and Yellow Tavern, where he was mortally wounded, May 11, 1864; died May 12, 1864.

**Sumner, Edwin V.** (1797–1863) Maj. Gen. USA; Army of the Potomac (corps cdr.) at Peninsula campaign and battle of Antietam; Army of the Potomac (Right Grand Div. cdr.) at battle of Fredericksburg.

**Thomas, George H.** ("Rock of Chickamauga") (1816–70), Maj. Gen. USA; Army of the Ohio (div. cdr.) at battle of Mill Springs; Army of the Ohio (second in command) at battle of Perryville; Army of the Cumberland (cdr. of the center) at battle of Murfreesboro; Army of the Cumberland (corps cdr.) at battle of Chickamauga; Army of the Cumberland (cdr.) at Chattanooga and Atlanta campaigns and battles of Franklin and Nashville.

**Toombs, Robert** (1810–85) Brig. Gen. CSA; Confederate secretary of state, Feb.–July 1861; Army of Northern Virginia (brigade cdr.) at Peninsula campaign, second battle of Bull Run, battle of Antietam.

**Vallandigham, Clement L.** (1820–71) U.S. congressman from Ohio, 1858–63; Copperhead leader; banished to the South on May 1863, he ran in absentia and unsuccessfully for Ohio governorship, Oct. 1863; returned to the North, wrote peace platform at Democratic Party National Convention, Aug. 1864.

**Van Dorn, Earl** (1820–63) Maj. Gen. CSA; Army of the West (cdr.) at battle of Pea Ridge; Army of West Tennessee (cdr.) at battles of Corinth and Holly Springs; murdered by a civilian, May 7, 1863.

**Wallace, Lew** (1827–1905) Maj. Gen. USA; Div. cdr. at battle of Fort Donelson; Army of the Tennessee (div. cdr.) at battle of Shiloh; led defense of Monocacy.

**Watie, Stand (Isaac S. Watie)** (1806–71) Brig. Gen. CSA; First Cherokee Mounted Rifles (cdr.); leader of Cherokee Nation; last Confederate general to surrender, June 23, 1865.

**Welles, Gideon** ("Old Neptune") (1802–78) U.S. secretary of the navy, March 1861–March 1869.

**Wheeler, Joseph** (1836–1906) Lt. Gen. CSA; Shiloh; Army of Mississippi (cav. brigade cdr.) at battle of Perryville; Army of Tennessee (cav. brigade cdr.) at battle of Murfreesboro; Army of Tennessee (cav. corps cdr.) at battles of Chickamauga and Knoxville, and Atlanta campaign, Sherman's March to the Sea, and in the Carolinas.

**Wilkes, Charles** (1798–1877) Cdre. USN; USS *San Jacinto* captain who apprehended Confederate commissioners James M. Mason and John Slidell from British vessel *Trent*, Nov. 1861.

**Wirz, Henry** (1823–65) Maj. CSA; Andersonville Prison commandant, Jan. 1864–April 1865; convicted of war crimes, he was the only Confederate executed (Nov. 10, 1865) for actions committed during the war.

# AUTHOR'S NOTE

**B**IBLIOGRAPHERS CALCULATE THAT MORE THAN 65,000 BOOKS HAVE BEEN PUBLISHED IN ENGLISH on the Civil War since 1865. You'd think we'd have it nailed by now. But I don't think we have, and that's why I've written this book.

Back in 1991, Charles P. Roland titled his history of the Civil War *An American Iliad*, and while he surely meant this to convey the epic nature of the war, the allusion implies something of even greater significance. Like the subject of Homer's *Iliad*, much of our Civil War is shrouded in legend and mythology, some of it hallowed by popular tradition, some even fossilized by academic historians. I intend *The Real History of the Civil War* to sweep aside at least some of the halos as well as the cobwebs that have accumulated over a century and a half. My purpose, however, is not to present some new "revisionist view" of the war, but a clear view of it in the form of a fresh introduction intended not so much for historians and confirmed Civil War buffs, but for the curious general reader who is looking for the right start, an intellectual leg up into this inexhaustibly fascinating subject.

Yet it is a mistake to take for granted that clarity is a sovereign virtue in and of itself. Of all the distortions created by viewing the Civil War through the lens of mythology, the most egregious are interpretations that fail to convey what all war is above all: chaos. I want you to understand the issues—and there were many—that orbited about the Civil War at its origin, during its course, and after its end, but I want above all to convey to you the experience of this war, which was bigger, more destructive, more heartbreaking, more confusing, more idealistic, and more cravenly base than anything else that Americans have confronted before or since. It was the militarization of the most unmilitary people on earth. It was a struggle over the most ancient of issues—legal rights, territorial rights, human rights—yet it was fought with weapons of unprecedented modernity, the products of a new industrial society. It was both a nearly fatal challenge to the values on which the United States—the place Lincoln called the "last best hope of earth"—was founded and a bloody vindication of those values. It was a family fight, a tribal fight, and an ideological fight. All of these are the elements of the real Civil War, and it is to these—not some theory of causation or debate over outcomes—that I most vividly want to introduce you.

My approach leaves me few axes to grind. I do offer opinions, based on a consensus of military historians, concerning the relative skill of different commanders (a military history needs to do that), and I make no bones about the role the slavery issue played as a cause for war. Historians and other enthusiasts of the "Lost Cause" school (you'll encounter it in Chapter 21) have long argued that the Civil War had nothing, really, to do with slavery. The truth is that were it not for the institution of slavery in the United States, there would have been no war between the states, and librarians would have 65,000 fewer volumes to contend with.

Now that I have revealed my prejudices, I invite you to read *The Real History of the Civil War.*

As always, I owe a great debt to my editors, Barbara Berger and Joe Rhatigan, and to Michael Fragnito, Sterling's editorial director.

—Alan Axelrod
Atlanta, Georgia

## PART ONE

# TITLE PAGE TO A GREAT TRAGIC VOLUME

# CHAPTER 1

## "THEY ARE PREPARING
## FOR WAR"

### *Backstory in Black and White*

AT FORTY, WHEN MOST MEN OF SUBSTANCE ARE WELL SETTLED INTO comfortable lives, William Tecumseh Sherman was just beginning to enjoy a hint of financial stability. It was Christmas Eve 1860, and he, first superintendent of the brand-new Louisiana State Seminary of Learning & Military Academy in Pineville, Louisiana, was enjoying a leisurely dinner with the institution's professor of classics. An Ohioan by birth and upbringing, Sherman liked the South, he liked the Southern climate, he liked his Southern job, and, most of all, he liked the Southern people. But the last one was about to change. That very day, the state of South Carolina proclaimed its secession from the United States of America. The news of it broke into the superintendent's dinner.

"This country will be drenched in blood," Sherman warned his dinner companion, "and God only knows how it will end. It is all folly, madness, a crime against civilization! You people"—and by this he meant the *Southern* people—"speak so lightly of war; you don't know what you're talking about. War is a terrible thing!"

## Civilian Nation

Sherman knew something of war, though less than one might expect. He had been born into a prominent family in 1820, his father an attorney who had been sitting on the Supreme Court of Ohio when he died suddenly in 1829. His widow was left with their eleven children, including nine-year-old "Cump" (as the family called William Tecumseh), and the bitter realization that her husband had hardly been as prosperous as she believed. As it turned out, there was no inheritance to speak of, and Cump was put in the care of Thomas Ewing, a neighbor who was a rising star in the Whig Party. The misfortune of his father's death and mother's financial plight became Cump's salvation. In 1830, Ewing was elected to the U.S. Senate, from which office in 1836, he appointed sixteen-year-old Sherman to West Point. Four years later, the young cadet graduated near the top of the class of 1840 and had what he took to be the great good luck of immediately falling into a war, without which a military career in the U.S. Army was a dead end. It was, however, a war against the Seminoles, who, like their neighbors the Cherokee, resisted the federally ordered "removal" from their Florida and Georgia homelands to Indian Territory in the arid West. The work of finding their hiding places in the Florida swampland, rousting them, and then fighting them was bloody, but it was also dirty and distasteful to most Americans and therefore inglorious—certainly no way for a freshly minted second lieutenant to make a name for himself. But hard on the heels of the Seminole War came the U.S.-Mexican War of 1846–48. For most of the generation of professional soldiers who would find themselves in the Union or Confederate army, Mexico was a training ground for the Civil War, their first experience of real combat.

*"This country will be drenched in blood," William Tecumseh Sherman warned when word of South Carolina's secession reached him. "It is all folly, madness, a crime against civilization!" He would emerge as one of the Union's fiercest generals.*

**Details, Details**
**Civil War Survivor**

Despite its quaint, antique-sounding name, the Louisiana State Seminary of Learning & Military Academy, authorized by the Louisiana General Assembly in 1853 but not opened until January 2, 1860, survived the Civil War and flourishes to this day. A year after moving from Pineville to the state capital, Baton Rouge, in 1869, it was renamed Louisiana State University, but students and alumni still call it "The Ole War Skule" and point to a pair of cannons mounted in front of the Military Science Building. They were a post–Civil War gift from William Tecumseh Sherman and had been used by Confederate general P. G. T. Beauregard's forces in Charleston to fire on Fort Sumter, thereby starting the war.

**Previous Spread:** Frank Leslie's Illustrated Newspaper *published this wood engraving, captioned "The Harper's Ferry insurrection—The U.S. Marines storming the engine house—Insurgents firing through the holes in the doors," on October 29, 1859.*

## Civil War Warm-Up

The Civil War of 1861–65 was not the first American conflict that threatened to tear the nation apart. The War of 1812 (1812–15) was so unpopular in New England that several states seriously considered secession from the Union. The U.S.-Mexican War (1846–48) provoked similar dissension, New Englanders in particular objecting to an "immoral" war fought for the purpose of seizing Mexican territory. Sherman and Ulysses S. Grant were among the host of young officers destined to become Civil War generals either for the Union or the Confederacy. Gettysburg victor George Meade, Army of the Potomac commander George McClellan, and the Confederacy's Stonewall Jackson and Robert E. Lee all saw action in the Mexican War, without which neither side would have fielded officers who had experienced army-on-army combat. One of the standout heroes of that conflict was Jefferson Davis, who would become the first and only president of the Confederate States of America.

For Sherman, however, apparent good luck turned bad, as he was posted well to the rear of the battle lines, in California, where he was assigned as an administrative officer. He saw no combat at all in the war, and so, when he told his dinner companion that Christmas Eve of 1860 that war was a terrible thing, it was an assessment based more on assumption than observation.

Absent the glory of a combat record in a triumphant conflict, Sherman knew that his prospects for continued promotion (he had made captain) in the peacetime army were slim to none, and so, in 1853, he resigned his commission to join a St. Louis banking firm at its San Francisco branch. The national financial panic of 1857 knocked the props from under that enterprise and sent Sherman scrambling for other ways to make a living.

He failed at them all. In this, his experience was eerily similar to that of the man to whom his Civil War career would be closely bound, Ulysses S. Grant. Grant graduated from West Point three years after Sherman and, like his upperclassman colleague, was sent to the Mexican War not as a combat officer, but as part of the quartermaster corps. Although Grant was, in effect, a mere supply clerk, he managed to get closer to the action than Sherman did and even earned two brevets for gallantry. These did him little good in the peacetime army, however, and, with a new family to support, he resigned his commission in 1854, turned to farming, failed, became a professional bill collector in St. Louis, failed, and finally humbled himself before his father to cadge a job as a clerk in the family's Galena, Illinois, leather goods business. That's where he was when the Civil War found him.

"A military life had no charms for me, and I had not the faintest idea of staying in the army even if I should be graduated [from West Point], which I did not expect. . . . I did not take hold of my studies with avidity, in fact I rarely ever read over a lesson the second time during my entire cadetship. . . . Much of the time, I am sorry to say, was devoted to novels."

*Ulysses S. Grant*, Personal Memoirs, *1885*

That two of the central figures in the deadliest and most consequential war the United States has ever fought failed miserably as civilians is no coincidence. They were, it turned out, born warriors, but they shared the misfortune of having been born into a country that had little use for warriors—at least as long as there was no war on. In 1775, Americans had begun a revolution (in part) against the British government's imposition of a standing army among them and would, for generations to come, look upon the regular army with distrust and scorn. American soldiers fought, and when the fighting was done, they were all but discarded. Some of them—really the best of them—had a hard time out of uniform.

## ODDS AGAINST THE SOUTH

AFTER THE COLLAPSE OF THE BANK, Sherman contacted a pair of army buddies, Braxton Bragg and P. G. T. Beauregard (both Mexican War veterans destined to serve the Confederacy as generals), who helped him secure the position of superintendent at the Louisiana Seminary of Learning & Military Academy. And now, with the secession of South Carolina, Sherman knew he would have to leave that job as well. As if it might somehow head off the coming war, he tried to persuade his Christmas Eve dinner guest that the South didn't have a chance. "War is a terrible thing!" he said:

> Besides, where are your men and appliances of war . . . ? The North can make a steam engine, locomotive or railway car; hardly a yard of cloth or a pair of shoes can you make. You are rushing into war with one of the most powerful, ingeniously mechanical and determined people on earth— right at your doors. You are bound to fail. Only in your spirit and determination are you prepared for war. In all else you are totally unprepared, with a bad cause to start with. At first you will make headway, but as your limited resources begin to fail, shut out from the markets of Europe as you will be, your cause will begin to wane. If your people will but stop and think, they must see that in the end you will surely fail.

The South would prove itself surprisingly capable of fighting a war through years of combat, yet Sherman's assessment accurately reflected the state of things in December 1860. South Carolina would be

*No one at the outbreak of the Civil War would have predicted that Ulysses S. Grant would become the general who led the Union to ultimate victory. After compiling a mediocre academic record at West Point, he fought well in the U.S.-Mexican War of 1846–48, only to fail dismally in civilian life after that war. He was working as a lowly clerk in his family's leather goods business in their hometown of Galena, Illinois, when the Civil War began.*

*Life in the industrial North—a Pennsylvania factory, as painted c. 1857 by watercolorist James Fuller Queen.*

joined by ten other states, which, together, would style themselves the Confederate States of America. Collectively, they had a population of twelve million, one-third of which—four million people—were slaves. On the other side, the twenty-three "loyal states" that constituted the Union (more would be added before the war ended) contained twenty-two million men, women, and children, all of them free. It was a stretch to claim the South had no industrial capacity. Actually, the seceded states had about twenty thousand factories, most of them quite small, together employing 100,000 industrial workers. It was true, though, that the North had five times the industrial infrastructure, more than 100,000 manufactories, and an industrial workforce fifty times larger than that of the South. About a million Northerners made their living making things in factories. Equally important, the North possessed a rail network sufficient to transport both goods and people—as well as munitions and soldiers. Twenty thousand miles of track networked the Union, whereas the Confederacy had less than half this mileage, the utility of which was greatly compromised by a bewildering array of gauges (widths between the rails), which meant that a trip of any distance was repeatedly interrupted and delayed by unloading freight and passengers from a train suited to one gauge and loading them onto another to continue their journey on tracks of a different gauge.

Finally, like most modern human undertakings, war at some point comes down to money. Banks in the Union held most of it—81 percent of the nation's deposits, together with some $56 million in gold bullion. This made for a nearly unlimited line of international credit, whereas the perpetually cash- and gold-starved South depended for sustenance and survival on its ability to export cotton, as well as rice and indigo, to Europe. Disrupt this trade, and Southern credit would dry up almost instantly, rendering the Confederacy incapable of doing much of anything. Without credit, there was no credibility; no foreign power would recognize the sovereign legitimacy of eleven threadbare states.

There is no record of how Sherman's dinner companion responded to the superintendent's lecture, but to Sherman himself the situation seemed clear beyond dispute. For the South to make war against the North was the act of madmen, as deluded as they were doomed. And yet that was precisely the great danger in this crisis. Madmen are by definition immune to rational argument, and their delusions may give them strength beyond their apparent means.

Sherman did not resign his superintendency until January 18, 1861, and it took another four weeks for him to settle necessary administrative affairs there. In mid-March, his brother John, now a U.S. senator, advised him to call on Abraham Lincoln, who was sworn in as the broken nation's sixteenth president on March 4, and offer his services to the army of the Union.

*Life in the agricultural South—picking cotton on a Georgia plantation, as depicted in a wood engraving published in 1858 in* Ballou's Pictorial, *a popular magazine of the time.*

## THE CAPITAL DROWSES

TO SHERMAN'S EYES, THE NATION'S CAPITAL did not look like a city on the verge of war. If the secession states were manifestly ill-equipped for sustained military action, Washington, D.C., appeared utterly incapable of military action of any kind. It had always been a sleepy little city, muddy in rain and dusty in dry weather, a town more Southern than Northern in appearance and manner. If the slaveholding states of Virginia and Maryland decided to join the secession (as of March 1861, Virginia seemed almost sure to slip away, whereas Maryland was less certain), the Southern enemy would be at its very borders. The city's defenses consisted of a hundred regular army troops, many of them more comfortable behind a desk than a musket, and three, perhaps four, hundred marines, who were quartered in the old barracks at the corner of Eighth and I streets. There were some private militia companies throughout the town, but these were more social than martial in character. In his postwar *Memoirs,* Sherman sketchily recalled his meeting with Lincoln. His brother, Senator John Sherman, presented him to the president, explaining that he had just resigned from a post in the South. "Ah," Lincoln exclaimed affably, "how are they getting along down there?"

Taken aback by the commander-in-chief's light and bantering tone, Sherman responded acerbically: "They think they are getting along swimmingly." Then he stated a fact he hoped would wake Lincoln up: "They are preparing for war." "Oh, well," the president sighed, "I guess we'll manage to keep house." Sherman (as he wrote in his *Memoirs*) was utterly "silenced" by this remark. He "said no more" to the president and left with his brother as quickly as courtesy permitted. No sooner were they safely out the White House door than Cump exploded. With a curse 'on all politicians, he leveled his eyes on John: "You have got things in a hell of a fix and you may get them out as best you can." All thought of offering his military services, let alone humbly *asking* for a command, dissolved in an instant.

William T. Sherman left Washington for St. Louis to accept an offer to manage a streetcar company there. To John he soon wrote that Lincoln and the rest of the Republican government were guilty of "shameful neglect & pusillanimity." Instead of scrambling to attract those West Point men who had not yet joined the Southern cause—as much of the West Point–trained officer corps had—they were recruiting political hacks inexperienced in military matters. "Had Lincoln intimated to me any word of encouragement, I would have waited" in Washington, Sherman told his brother. But Lincoln hadn't; the situation was all a great muddle, and Sherman resolved to wash his hands of it. When Postmaster General Montgomery Blair transmitted to him on April 8 an invitation to become chief clerk of the War Department, he wrote back to thank him "for the compliment" and to assure him "that I wish the Administration all success in its almost impossible task of governing this distracted and anarchical people." If there was anything less than brutally frank in this

*"Washington City," as Washington, D.C., was familiarly known, was capital of the Union during the Civil War. It precariously bordered the principal state of the Confederacy, Virginia, and a slaveholding Union state, Maryland, most of whose citizens sympathized with the South. This photograph, published on June 27, 1861, looks northwest over the city from the roof of the Capitol.*

blunt response, it was the inclusion of the word "almost." Sherman took it all very personally. He shouldn't have. He was just one man caught up in the great paradox of the national character. The United States had been born in violence, and Americans frequently showed themselves capable of considerable violence, most recently against the Mexicans and, as always, against the Indians. Nevertheless, Americans were decidedly not a martial people. They did not like armies, they did not raise armies, and they did not maintain armies. Neither the South nor the North was prepared to fight a war, yet the United States had been moving toward war—sometimes drifting in its direction, sometimes hurtling toward it—since September 17, 1787, when the Constitutional Convention delivered the final draft of the new Constitution to Congress without including a definitive resolution of the profound and explosive issue of slavery. The document sent a mixed message on slavery, leaving it to the legal discretion of each state, yet also protecting it where it existed, even as it allowed for federal legislation ending the slave trade (the importation of slaves), provided it was not enacted before 1808. This last provision seemed to imply that the eventual end of slavery itself was desirable. Remarkably, the framers of the Constitution juggled all this without once actually using the words *slave* or *slavery*.

Virginian George Mason, a delegate to the Constitutional Convention, warned that the failure to resolve the slavery issue would "bring the judgment of Heaven" on the country. If that is what a war that claimed the lives of 620,000 soldiers was, it nevertheless took three-quarters of a century to descend upon the nation.

"The young bloods of the South: sons of planters, lawyers about towns, good billiard-players and sportsmen, men who never did work and never will. War suits them, and the rascals are brave, fine riders, bold to rashness, and dangerous subjects in every sense. . . . These men must all be killed or employed by us before we can hope for peace."

*William Tecumseh Sherman, letter to*
*Major General Henry W. Halleck, September 17, 1863*

# HAD COMMON SENSE PREVAILED

As we are about to see in the remainder of this chapter and through the next, the United States had been in the process of breaking apart since almost the day the nation came into being. The issue was slavery, and the failure to resolve it always loomed as an invitation to war.

Yet even after all the compromises had failed and, as we will see in Chapter 2, the Supreme Court's decision against Dred Scott had taken the matter far beyond any hope of additional compromise, there remains the fact that neither the South nor the North was prepared for war. What is more, a majority of Southerners and Northerners understood this, and, except for the South's radical "fire-eaters" and the North's radical abolitionists, the majority in both slave states and free wanted no war. Few in 1861 could have imagined the scope and enormity of the conflict they were beginning. (Sherman *did* imagine it, though, and talked at the outset of the war about the involvement of hundreds of thousands of men. All who heard him assumed he was in the throes of a nervous breakdown and total mental collapse.) Yet anyone with common sense could have seen that an antimilitaristic, resolutely civilian nation like the United States had no business taking up arms. In the spring of 1861, common sense alone should have been sufficient to evaluate the tiny army

of the North and the nonexistent army of the South and motivate a decision not to fight. But it did not happen that way. Firstly, Americans were accustomed to fighting wars for which they were unprepared. At the start of the American Revolution, a handful of local militiamen and a few merchant captains made bold to wage war against the country that possessed the biggest army and greatest navy in the world. In the War of 1812, America's miniscule, poorly equipped, and indifferently trained regular army propped itself up with a hastily assembled hodgepodge of militiamen to fight British veterans of the Napoleonic Wars, which were then rapidly winding down. Even in the Mexican War, U.S. forces were always outnumbered and faced an army that, on paper at least, looked formidable indeed.

And secondly, even as they took up arms against one another—"brother against brother," as the cliché goes—they found it hard to believe that they were actually at war. The realization came as the casualties mounted, but by then, there was no turning back.

## SLAVE NATION

THE VERY YEAR THAT THE CONSTITUTION was drafted without resolving the slavery issue, Congress enacted the Northwest Ordinance of 1787, which (among other provisions) explicitly barred slavery from the Northwest Territory, the vast tract of the continent east of the Mississippi River and between the Ohio River and the Great Lakes. Those who opposed slavery interpreted the Northwest Ordinance, in conjunction with the constitutional hint of an eventual end to the slave trade, as an expression of a federal will to end slavery altogether. In fact, even among those who supported slavery, there was by the close of the eighteenth century a growing sense that the institution would eventually die a sort of natural death. The end of the American Revolution had brought a steady influx of European immigrants, most of whom offered cheap agricultural labor and were an increasingly viable alternative to the work of slaves. In any case, the market for Southern crops produced by slave labor—tobacco, rice, and indigo—was mature and at the limit of its growth. This meant, in turn, that the need for slaves was finite and, on balance, shrinking.

*Theodore R. Davis (1840–94) was a popular Civil War artist whose work regularly appeared in* Harper's Weekly*, which published this wood engraving of "A Slave Auction at the South" on July 13, 1861.*

Some plantations did raise another crop—black-seed, long-staple cotton—but its cultivation was strictly limited to a narrow strip along the southern Atlantic coast. The vast interior of the region could not support this variety of the plant. Although it was possible to grow green-seed, short-staple cotton in the lower South, the profitability of this crop was virtually nil. Before cotton can be exported for weaving, its fiber must be separated from the seeds that cling to it. With black-seed cotton, this can be accomplished merely by running the bolls through a pair of rollers. The only way to clean the more plentiful green-seed variety, however, was to pick the seeds from the fiber by hand, one cotton boll at a time. The work was not only mind-numbing and painful, it was so time consuming that it priced the product out of the market even with slave labor. Cotton cultivation, therefore, did not appear likely to perpetuate the demand for slaves.

That all changed in 1792 when Massachusetts-born and Yale-educated Eli Whitney pursued the offer of a teaching job in Georgia only to discover, once he had arrived, that the job had mysteriously vanished. Marooned, he was befriended by the proprietor of Mulberry Grove plantation, Catherine Lidfield Greene, who provided Whitney with a roof and introduced him to the manager of her property, Phineas Miller. To Whitney, Miller mused about the Southern fortunes to be made if only green-seed, short-staple cotton could be cheaply cleaned for cost-effective export. Across the Atlantic, the English were building a great textile industry, and their newfangled automated looms were starved for raw cotton.

*Invented at the close of the eighteenth century by Eli Whitney—a Connecticut Yankee—the cotton gin efficiently separated cotton fiber from cotton seeds. This process made the mass production of short-staple cotton commercially feasible, giving the South its dominant economic driver and reviving the flagging demand for plantation slave labor. William L. Sheppard's illustration "The First Cotton Gin" was published in* Harper's Weekly *on December 18, 1869, and depicts slaves using the machine.*

Whitney turned Miller's musing into the reality of a four-part machine as simple as it was ingenious. It was fitted with a hopper that fed cotton onto a revolving cylinder studded with hundreds of wire hooks set in close rows that meshed with fine grooves cut into a stationary piece of the machine. The hooks teased the fiber away from the seeds, which slid away along the grooves of the stationary component. A cylindrical set of bristles, which meshed with the hook-studded cylinder, cleaned the cotton fiber from the hooks and, by means of centrifugal force, sent it flying into a collector. In a September 11, 1793, letter to his father, Eli Whitney wrote:

There were a number of very respectable Gentlemen at Mrs. Greene's who all agreed that if a machine could be invented which could clean the cotton with expedition, it would be a great thing both to the Country and to the inventor. . . . I made one . . . which required the labor of one man to turn it and with which one man will clean ten times as much cotton as he can in any other way before known, and also cleanse it much better than in the usual mode.

Eli Whitney's cotton gin, patented in 1794, suddenly made the green-seed cotton of the lower South so profitable that, through the first half of the nineteenth century, Southern cotton exports exceeded the combined value of all other American exports, accounting for 60 percent of the national export total. Plantations were soon entirely given over to cotton, as was the entire Southern economy. England's mills proved insatiable, as did the renewed demand for slaves.

## THE WAY OF SLAVERY, THE PATH TO WAR

RAISE THE SUBJECT OF WHAT TRIGGERED the American Revolution and someone is sure to proclaim in a tone of cynical authority that, say what you will about life, liberty, and the pursuit of happiness, the *real* cause of the revolution was "economics"—rich colonial merchants wanted to be even richer American merchants. Now, ask the question, *What caused the Civil War?* and you are bound to hear from someone—speaking in that same all-knowing tone—that the war really had nothing to do with slavery and everything to do with (what else?) "economics."

The truth is that, just as life, liberty, and the pursuit of happiness were intimately bound up with economics in 1775 and 1776, so slavery was as at least as much an economic issue as it was a moral one. As South Carolina senator James H. Hammond warned his Northern colleagues in a speech on March 4, 1858, "You dare not make war upon cotton! No power on earth dares make war upon it. Cotton is king." And the kingdom stood on the backs of slaves.

As more than a million black hands cranked the gins, the Southern focus radically narrowed to cotton and all that served its production. To Thomas Jefferson and most other Americans, the Louisiana Purchase of 1803 was a means of avoiding war with Spain, or France, or both; of protecting and promoting western trade; of staking a claim on the continent even to the very shores of the Pacific; and of providing a space to which the Indians living east of the Mississippi River might be peacefully relocated. Southerners, however, saw in the Louisiana Purchase just one thing: the mother of all cotton fields. That, of course, would mean more slaves, many more slaves. Opponents of slavery—by now they were called abolitionists— cited the Northwest Ordinance as a legal precedent for a federal bar on slavery in all new territories. This unleashed by way of response a legal barrage from Southern lawyers and legislators. They conceded that the Constitution did allow for the eventual end to the slave trade, but it not only avoided any federal restrictions on slavery itself, it certified the legality of slavery with its Three-Fifths Compromise (by which slaves were to be counted as three-fifths of a person for the purpose of apportioning congressional representation in the House), its fugitive slave clause (Section 2, Clause 3: "No person held to service or labor in one state, under the laws thereof, escaping into another, shall, in consequence of any law or regulation therein, be discharged from such service or labor, but shall be delivered up on claim of the party to whom such service or labor may be due"), and, by obvious application, the Fifth Amendment, which forbade deprivation of "life, liberty, *or property*, without due process of law [emphasis added]."

**DETAILS, DETAILS**
**What's in a Word?**
The term "cotton gin" may seem more appropriate to describe a mythical alcoholic beverage than a machine that created an industry and transformed a nation, but the origin of the term is easily traced. At the end of the eighteenth century, just about any mechanical device was called an "engine." Ordinary folk— the people who actually used such an engine— typically shortened this to *gin*.

But the argument Southern legal minds believed made slavery absolutely unassailable was the constitutional provision that gave to the individual states all powers and authority the Constitution itself did not explicitly reserve for the federal government. Because the Constitution does not include the regulation of slavery as a federal power, they argued, it must therefore be a matter subject to the laws of the individual states. Without question, states opposed to slavery can exclude it from within their own borders, but those states that favor the institution have the right to regulate and protect it within their borders. Forever.

## A TORTURED COMPROMISE

THE LOUISIANA PURCHASE hardened the positions of the nation's proslavery and antislavery factions, creating the conditions for a major crisis in 1818–19, when the territory of Missouri applied to Congress for admission to the Union as a slaveholding state.

Since the ratification of the Constitution, the delicate balance between slave states and free states had been precariously maintained. Because representation in the House is proportional to population, the free states of the North enjoyed a majority of representatives—though not all of them were willing to actively oppose slavery. However, representation in the Senate was equal, which meant that senators from slave states could

*Samuel Lewis's "Louisiana" appeared in* A New and Elegant General Atlas *by Aaron Arrowsmith, published in 1804, and is the first published map of the Louisiana Purchase territory.*

block antislavery legislation. If the admission of a new slave state gave this Senate faction a majority, its power to block legislation would be enhanced, and the majority might even be able to pass laws favorable to the protection or expansion of slavery. On the other hand, if a new free state was admitted, then the antislavery forces would likely be able to control majorities in both the House and the Senate. In 1819, the Senate consisted of twenty-two Northern senators and twenty-two Southern. Admitting Missouri threatened to tip the balance toward the proslavery side. Congressman James Tallmadge of New York proposed amending the statehood bill so as to end slavery in the state within a generation by prohibiting "the further introduction of slavery" into Missouri after it was admitted to the Union and further stipulating that "all children born within the said State, after the admission thereof into the Union, shall be free at the age of twenty-five years." The House passed the Tallmadge Amendment in February 1819, shortly after it was proposed, but the Senate rejected it and adjourned, leaving Missouri statehood in limbo until the Senate reconvened later in the year and began a bitter debate. Northern Senators held that Congress had the right to ban slavery in new states, whereas Southerners asserted that each new state had the same inherent rights as the original thirteen. Among these was the right to decide the issue of slavery within its own borders.

Debate yielded to a clumsy, clearly fragile compromise on February 16, 1820. It was agreed that Missouri would be admitted as a slave state, but, at the same time, Maine—split off from Massachusetts, of which it had been a part—would enter as a free state. This would maintain the balance between "free" and "slave" senators. The "Missouri Compromise" (not a single bill, but a set of related legislation) also provided for a line to be drawn across the Louisiana Territory at 36°30' north latitude. Slavery would be forever barred north of this line, except in the state of Missouri itself.

The Missouri Compromise was intended, first and foremost, to end the crisis created by the impending statehood of Missouri, but the so-called compromise line was a nod toward the future, a stab at resolving the question of slavery or its exclusion in the territories. Yet few sincerely believed that the Missouri Compromise would permanently settle the crisis slavery had created. The most anyone hoped for was to avert—or at least slow the drift toward—civil war.

**NUMBERS**
**Population Explosion**
In 1790, the first-ever U.S. census counted 697,897 slaves. Despite the constitutional ban on slave importation, which went into effect in 1808, the census of 1810 counted 1,191,354 slaves, and in 1860, the very eve of the Civil War, census rolls carried nearly four million slaves.

**TAKEAWAY**
Neither Northerners nor Southerners wanted a war or were prepared to fight one in 1861, yet the failure of the framers of the Constitution to resolve the issue of slavery made the dissolution of the Union virtually inevitable, and if the federal government chose to resist that dissolution, it made war inevitable as well. The spiral toward the Civil War began three-quarters of a century before the first shot was fired.

# CHAPTER 2

## "FIRE BELL IN THE NIGHT"

### The People March beyond Compromise

THE MISSOURI COMPROMISE SUCCEEDED IN BRINGING A SENSE OF RELIEF to some, especially those who feared the immediate dissolution of the Union and the outbreak of war. But for two men who had been instrumental in creating the United States, it brought nothing but dread. "Like a fire bell in the night," the seventy-seven-year-old Thomas Jefferson wrote, the compromise "awakened and filled me with terror." John Adams, eighty-five at the time, read it as the "title page to a great tragic volume."

Despite such forebodings—and Jefferson and Adams were not alone in feeling them—the Missouri Compromise endured for three decades, only to fall apart all at once when the gold rush of 1849 drew more than eighty thousand wide-eyed seekers of fortune to California, newly wrested by war from Mexico. The human flood instantly brought its population to a level that demanded statehood. Under the terms of the Missouri Compromise, California would be admitted as a free state, and this "intolerable" event, South Carolinian and Secretary of War John C. Calhoun warned, would almost certainly propel the nation into civil war.

## THE NULLIFICATION CRISIS

CALHOUN—WHOSE DISTINGUISHED TITLES included U.S. representative from South Carolina, senator, President James Monroe's secretary of war, vice president under both John Quincy Adams and Andrew Jackson, and secretary of state in the cabinet of James Buchanan—had issued an identical warning years earlier in connection with a matter only indirectly related to the Missouri Compromise.

In 1828, a Congress dominated by the increasingly industrial North had passed a new tariff law that levied a stiff duty on manufactured goods imported from abroad. The law was intended to foster and protect what was still a fledgling American industrial base by ensuring that consumers would find domestically manufactured goods more attractively priced than the heavily taxed imports. Southern lawmakers decried the new legislation as the "Tariff of Abominations," because it threatened the very livelihood of their region. Unlike the industrializing North, the economy of the agricultural South relied on export trade in such commodities as rice, indigo, and cotton. Of these, as we saw in Chapter 1, "cotton was king," and most of it was shipped to England, whose burgeoning mills turned it into cloth and clothing, a good bit of which was exported to the United States. The 1828 tariff, however, threatened to drive the price of imported cloth and clothing beyond the reach of most Americans, and this, in turn, would force the English as well as the South's other European customers to drastically cut their Southern cotton imports.

*John C. Calhoun was the chief Southern theorist of nullification and states' rights—doctrines espousing ultimate supremacy of the states over the federal government. This copy of an original daguerreotype portrait dates to about 1850.*

Vice President Calhoun denounced the Tariff of Abominations as discriminatory against the South and therefore unconstitutional. He quickly drew up and published the "South Carolina Exposition and Protest," which held that any state had the right to unilaterally deem unconstitutional any act of the federal government and pronounce it "null and void." Calhoun could point to a very compelling precedent for this "nullification" theory. At the end of the eighteenth century, none other than James Madison and Thomas Jefferson had introduced the concept in the Virginia and Kentucky resolutions of 1798 and 1799, which Madison and Jefferson, respectively, drafted on behalf of the two states as a response to the Alien and Sedition Acts passed during the administration of President John Adams. The resolutions declared the acts to be violations of the Constitution's Bill of Rights and therefore null and void in Virginia and Kentucky.

# UNNATURAL ACTS

Democracy is incompatible with fear. More than a few times, Americans, under stress, sought to trade liberty for security, ceding to the government the authority to conduct warrantless wiretaps in the "Patriot Act" that followed the terrorist attacks of September 11, 2001, taking the reckless, ruinous Red-baiting of Senator Joseph McCarthy as gospel in the early 1950s, clamoring for the forced removal and "internment" of American citizens of Japanese descent during World War II, and passing, during the summer of 1798, the infamous Alien and Sedition Acts.

These included a Naturalization Act, which raised the prerequisite for American citizenship from five to fourteen years of continuous U.S. residence; the Alien Act, giving the president sovereign authority to deport, without trial, any alien he and he alone deemed dangerous; and the Alien Enemies Act, which gave the president the extraordinary wartime power to summarily imprison or deport subjects of any enemy power. The Sedition Act, the most egregious law in this set of legislation, criminalized all public assembly convened "with intent to oppose any measure of the government" and outlawed publishing or even saying—verbally—anything pertaining to the federal government deemed to be of a nature "false, scandalous, and malicious." Jefferson and Madison led the charge against these measures, targeting in particular the Sedition Act, which, in any case, expired in 1801, during Jefferson's first presidential term, and was never renewed.

The idea that any state could choose to obey or ignore federal authority would have been deeply controversial at any time, but in the poisonous climate of the slavery dispute and with regional relations so precarious, nullification was downright explosive. If a state could "nullify" a federal tariff law, it could also nullify on purportedly constitutional grounds any federal attempt to control, let alone abolish, slavery. What's more, if a state could nullify a federal law, what meaning did the federal union—the United States—have? For nullification implied the independence and autonomy of each state. Nullification enabled secession and, with it, the dissolution of the nation. Even worse, if a state's defiance of federal authority should move the national government to enforce compliance by armed means, the result would almost certainly be civil war.

Just when such a showdown seemed inevitable, the crisis came to an anticlimax in November 1828 with the defeat of incumbent president John Quincy Adams, a New Englander, by Andrew Jackson, a Southerner who promised tariff reform. Once Jackson was in office, however, the scope of tariff reform he had pledged was so narrow that when the Tariff of 1832 was signed into law on July 14, agitated South Carolinians gathered in convention and, on November 24, passed an Ordinance of Nullification, which forbade the collection of tariff duties within state borders.

> "This right of interposition . . . be it called what it may—State-right, veto, nullification, or by any other name—I conceive to be the fundamental principle of our system, resting on facts as historically certain as our revolution itself. . . . Stripped of all its covering, the naked question is, whether ours is a federal or a consolidated government; a constitutional or an absolute one; a government resting ultimately on the solid basis of the sovereignty of the States, or on the unrestrained will of the majority."

*Senator John C. Calhoun, July 26, 1831*

*John C. Calhoun was stunned when President Andrew Jackson, a fellow son of the South, answered nullification and states' rights with a threat to use the army to enforce federal law in South Carolina. This portrait of Jackson was painted during his presidency (1829–37), but was engraved some thirty years later, on the eve of the Civil War.*

The champions of nullification believed that passage of the ordinance would compel Jackson, a Carolina native, to lock arms with his fellow Southerners. The president, however, did no such thing. Instead, on December 10, he issued a proclamation that affirmed the constitutionality of the tariff, denied the authority of any state to interfere with the execution of federal law, and vowed to use the U.S. Army to enforce the collection of duties. Jackson put iron in his proclamation by persuading Congress to pass a Force Act, giving him standing authority to call out federal troops.

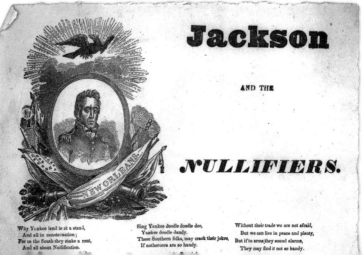

*Politics in the "Age of Jackson" often called for a catchy tune. This ballad of "Jackson and the Nullifiers"—federal authority versus the South's assertion of states' rights— was published in broadside form and intended to be sung to the tune of "Yankee Doodle."*

## ALTERNATE TAKE

### Civil War in 1832?

What if the nullification crisis of 1832 had actually resulted in military intervention by the Jackson administration? Would this have provoked full-scale civil war? Perhaps. But if it had, the Civil War of 1832 would have been very different from that which broke out in 1861. The main issue would have been economic, with slavery a mere side show. Calhoun might have amplified this into an ideological struggle against tyranny, but would it have sustained a major war? Remember, those who fought for the Confederacy in 1861–65 believed they were not only taking a stand against Northern tyranny and struggling for economic survival, but also defending a way of life. Slavery was the issue that, more than any other, both provoked and sustained the fighting.

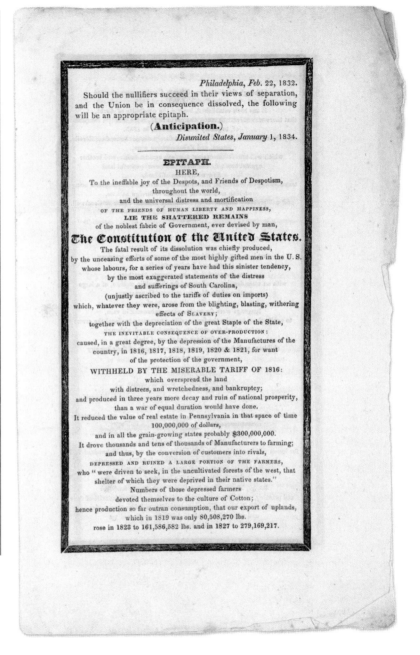

*Philadelphia, Feb.* 22, 1832.
Should the nullifiers succeed in their views of separation, and the Union be in consequence dissolved, the following will be an appropriate epitaph.

**(Anticipation.)**
*Disunited States, January* 1, 1834.

**EPITAPH.**
HERE,
To the ineffable joy of the Despots, and Friends of Despotism, throughout the world, and the universal distress and mortification
OF THE FRIENDS OF HUMAN LIBERTY AND HAPPINESS,
**LIE THE SHATTERED REMAINS**
of the noblest fabric of Government, ever devised by man,
**The Constitution of the United States.**
The fatal result of its dissolution was chiefly produced, by the unceasing efforts of some of the most highly gifted men in the U.S. whose labours, for a series of years have had this sinister tendency, by the most exaggerated statements of the distress and sufferings of South Carolina, (unjustly ascribed to the tariffs of duties on imports) which, whatever they were, arose from the blighting, blasting, withering effects of SLAVERY; together with the depreciation of the great Staple of the State, THE INEVITABLE CONSEQUENCE OF OVER-PRODUCTION: caused, in a great degree, by the depression of the Manufactures of the country, in 1816, 1817, 1818, 1819, 1820 & 1821, for want of the protection of the government,
WITHHELD BY THE MISERABLE TARIFF OF 1816: which overspread the land with distress, and wretchedness, and bankruptcy; and produced in three years more decay and ruin of national prosperity, than a war of equal duration would have done. It reduced the value of real estate in Pennsylvania in that space of time 100,000,000 of dollars, and in all the grain-growing states probably $300,000,000. It drove thousands and tens of thousands of Manufacturers to farming; and thus, by the conversion of customers into rivals, DEPRESSED AND RUINED A LARGE PORTION OF THE FARMERS, who " were driven to seek, in the uncultivated forests of the west, that shelter of which they were deprived in their native states." Numbers of those depressed farmers devoted themselves to the culture of Cotton; hence production so far outran consumption, that our export of uplands, which in 1819 was only 80,508,270 lbs. rose in 1823 to 161,586,582 lbs. and in 1827 to 279,169,217.

*Most Northerners believed that yielding to South Carolina's assertion of the supremacy of states' rights over federal law would mean the death of the Union. A Philadelphia editor therefore composed and published a fitting "Epitaph."*

Just as a civil war loomed, Congress enacted a more moderate tariff in 1833. The South Carolina legislature passed a wholly symbolic resolution nullifying the Force Act even as it voted to accept the compromise tariff of 1833.

Once again, civil war was averted or, at least, put off, but the *theory* of nullification—with its ultimate implication of secession—was still very much alive, and it loomed darkly in 1849 over the issue of California statehood.

## MOVE AND COUNTERMOVE

NULLIFICATION, SECESSION, and the other issues that always dogged the prospect of admitting a new state resurfaced in 1846, the first year of the war with Mexico. Seeking a way to cut that war short, Congress debated in 1846 a $2 million appropriation to pay Mexico for what the proposed legislation blandly labeled "territorial adjustments." Pennsylvania congressman David Wilmot, an ardent abolitionist, effectively hijacked the appropriation bill by attaching an amendment to it, the so-called Wilmot Proviso, which banned the introduction of slavery into any territory the United States acquired in consequence of the Mexican War.

To John C. Calhoun, now a U.S. senator and chairman of the powerful Finance Committee, the Wilmot Proviso was a gauntlet thrown down at his feet. Instead of merely objecting to it, he proposed four Senate resolutions in response. The gist of these was:

1. All territories, including those acquired as a result of the war, were to be treated not as federal property but as the joint property of the states.
2. Congress is not properly an organ of the federal government so much as it is an "agent" acting on behalf of the states and, as such, it can make no law that favors one state over another or that deprives any state of its rights with regard to so-called federal territory, which was really (according to Calhoun) territory the states held jointly.
3. The passage of any national law relating to slavery violates the Constitution (which does not reserve slavery matters to federal jurisdiction) and the doctrine of states' rights.
4. The Constitution stipulates but a single requirement of state governments—that they must be republican in form and principle; outside of this, the people of each state have the right to establish whatever kind of state government they wish.

*William Lloyd Garrison, founder and editor of the* Liberator, *was also a cofounder of the American Anti-Slavery Society and the most closely followed figure among the Northern abolitionists.*

The senator did not offer these resolutions as statements of theory. He sternly warned his colleagues that failure to act upon them would unbalance the federal representation of the North and the South. The South would never let the North tyrannize over it. Failure to adopt the resolutions would inevitably bring civil war.

Congress rarely moves swiftly, even in the face of ultimatum. The year 1846 turned out to be only the first of three years consumed in a debate on the Missouri Compromise, which, lawmakers hoped, they could saw, and nail, and patch into something capable of continuing to hold back the flood that threatened to engulf the Union.

It seemed well-nigh hopeless. If Calhoun and his followers were strident, unwilling to abandon slavery, nullification, states' rights, and all that these implied, so, too, were the swelling ranks of the abolitionists. By no means was the population of the North uniform in its opposition to slavery, but the loudest, clearest, and most eloquent Northern voices were those of people like William Lloyd Garrison, the white proprietor of the *Liberator*, the nation's most radical and widely read abolitionist journal, and Frederick Douglass, a former slave, whose eloquence, born of bitter personal experience, moved people and politicians alike. For them, no compromise was acceptable. They would settle for nothing less than the abolition of slavery throughout the United States. Still, the American majority, North and South, was reluctant to go to war, so Senator Lewis Cass of Michigan, looking for an alternative to stalemate on the one hand and a fight on the other, took a new tack. He proposed what he called "popular sovereignty," a policy by which new territories would be organized without mention of slavery at all. Only when the territory drew up its constitution and applied for statehood would the people actually living within the territory vote their proposed state slave or free. Neither the federal government nor territorial leaders would have anything to say in the matter.

*An escaped slave, the self-educated Frederick Douglass was a passionate and eloquent spokesman for abolition. For many white Americans, his 1845 autobiography,* Narrative of the Life of Frederick Douglass, An American Slave, *put a human face on the horrors of slavery.*

*Lewis Cass of Michigan was the Senate's leading proponent of the doctrine of popular sovereignty, which proposed to resolve the issue of extending slavery into federal territories by allowing the citizens living in those territories to decide whether or not they would permit slavery there.*

# THE SOUTH'S "CAST" TYPE IRON MAN"

Through a political career that reached deep into two of three branches of American government—he never served in the judiciary—John Caldwell Calhoun defended slavery as a natural, inevitable, and laudable institution, and constructed such a formidable ideological bastion from which he conducted the defense that he was known as the mind of the South.

Calhoun's political career presents a genuine evolution. Elected to Congress in 1810, he was a War Hawk who helped ignite the War of 1812. This attitude was very much a part of his intense nationalism, which also led him to support the national bank and high tariffs to protect fledgling American industry—two positions that he vehemently repudiated during his mature career. Indeed, his political journey took him from nationalism to regionalism as he supported the interests of the South generally and the effective supremacy of individual states over the federal government.

It was largely thanks to Calhoun that slavery was linked to the concept of states' rights. He argued that, by avoiding all reference to slavery—except to protect it as a property right and to allow for ending the importation of slaves—the Constitution yielded to the states all authority on the issue. Thus, whereas abolitionists saw Southern slavery as an evil curb on liberty, Calhoun pictured it as the very essence of liberty, the right of states to govern without interference in all areas not explicitly assigned by the Constitution to national authority. From this foundation of states' rights, Calhoun presented the concept of nullification, whereby any state could nullify any federal law it deemed a violation of the Constitution, which in turn implied that the United States was not so much one nation as a confederation of individual states. This being the case, secession was neither illegal nor necessarily a desperate last resort, but was the right of every state. More than any other single figure in the South, John C. Calhoun offered the intellectual rationale for secession and the creation of the *Confederate* States of America, which, perforce, was also (from the Southern perspective) the rationale for the Civil War.

## ANOTHER COMPROMISE

POPULAR SOVEREIGNTY WAS LESS OFFENSIVE to the proslavery faction than federal intervention and also less offensive to the antislavery faction than the federal government's actively protecting slavery within a geographical region. However, popular sovereignty truly satisfied neither side. For Southerners in particular, there was the immediate problem of California. Acquired from Mexico in 1848, its population exploded during the gold rush the following year, so it was to be admitted to the Union without passing through an interim territorial status. Under the Missouri Compromise, California had to be admitted as a free state. In search of a way to appease the South, Senators Henry Clay of Kentucky and Daniel Webster of Massachusetts proposed the

# GOLD!

If there is any episode in American history one would expect to have been mythologized and exaggerated out of all proportion to reality, it is the California gold rush of 1849. Yet the fact is that most everything that's been said about it is substantially true—though it didn't happen as soon as James Wilson Marshall discovered gold in his boss's mill race, and there is no evidence that the man shouted "Eureka!" when he found it.

Marshall worked on the central California ranch of Johann Augustus Sutter, who had come to the American Southwest in flight from the curse of bankruptcy that clung to him in his native Germany. Twice he tried his hand at the Santa Fe trade, and two more times he went bust. This prompted him to flee once more, this time to California, which back in 1838 was still Mexican. He built a sprawling ranch in the Central Valley, and it was there on January 24, 1848, that Marshall, inspecting the "race" (or sluice) of a new mill, spied the gold. Sutter had good reason to believe he had come to the proverbial turning in his long, sad road—but, in fact, Marshall's discovery caused all of Sutter's ranch hands to desert him and go prospecting. This precipitated the collapse of his ranching enterprise, and, when he tried to make up his losses with gold, a court found that his claims to the land on which his mill sat were null and void. He lost the land, went broke again, and lingered in a life of bankrupt want until 1880.

It took a year or more for word of the gold strike to spread beyond the Central Valley, but when it did in 1849, working men in every part of the country dropped their tools where they stood and headed west. Quite a few of the early arrivals found gold, but very few found enough to pay for their journey and prospecting labor, let alone enough to get rich. The real money was in financing the prospectors and selling groceries, hardware, and other goods and accommodations to them. This was how the likes of Leland Stanford, Collis P. Huntington, Mark Hopkins, and Charles Crocker became the wealthiest men in California, rich enough to build the western half of the nation's first transcontinental railroad.

*The 1848 discovery of gold in California drew a flood of prospectors the following year and instantly brought the population of the territory, freshly wrested from Mexico, to a level that qualified it for statehood—along with congressional representation, presumably as a free state. The hamlet of Butte City, depicted here in an 1854 watercolor by George Henry Burgess (1831–1905), was typical of California's many newly minted mining towns.*

admission of California as a free state, with the stipulation that all other territories acquired as a result of the Mexican War would be subject to popular sovereignty. Chances were that this would ultimately result in a balance of free and slave states, but whatever happened would be the will of the people rather than the work of the federal government. Southerners, therefore, could not accuse the North-dominated Congress of unconstitutional tyranny. Because abolitionists did not want the federal government to relinquish its authority to curb the expansion of slavery, Clay and Webster looked for a way to appease them. They therefore included in the proposed compromise a bill to shut down the slave market that had long operated in the District of Columbia, seat of the American democracy. This pro-abolition provision was balanced by a nod to the South in the form of a new, ironclad fugitive slave law, which explicitly forbade anyone to give refuge to escaped slaves, under stiff federal penalties.

## "BLEEDING KANSAS"

WHILE THE COMPROMISE OF 1850 staved off a national war, its fugitive slave provision enflamed the abolitionists. Ardent states' rights champions, on the other hand, feared that popular sovereignty was merely another ploy to shift the congressional balance to the North. Ignoring this, Congress extended popular sovereignty and retained the Fugitive Slave Law in 1854 when the territories of Nebraska and Kansas applied for statehood. Repealing the Missouri Compromise, legislators passed the Kansas-Nebraska Act, which erased the boundary between slave and free territory established in 1820 and applied popular sovereignty to all new territories— not just those acquired as a result of the war with Mexico. In effect, the federal government washed its hands

FORCING SLAVERY DOWN THE THROAT OF A FREESOILER

*Nineteenth-century American political cartoons were often brutal. This 1856 piece by John L. Magee, a response to the Kansas-Nebraska Act, depicts Democrats James Buchanan (a presidential nominee), Senator Lewis Cass, Senator Stephen A. Douglas, and incumbent President Franklin Pierce forcing slavery (in the form of a slave) down the throat of a Free Soiler who is literally bound to the Democratic platform. The platform is marked "Kansas," "Cuba," and "Central America"—implying Democratic ambitions for spreading slavery to targets of eventual U.S. annexation—and the background depicts scenes of "Bleeding Kansas": burning, pillaging, and lynching.*

## NUMBERS

### How Bloody Was Bleeding Kansas?

The nation was horrified by stories from "Bleeding Kansas," and most historians have assumed that what happened there between roughly 1854 and 1861 was a full-scale guerrilla war. In an article published by the Kansas Historical Society in 1995, Dale E. Watts presented the results of his study of the records of the period and found evidence of no more than 157 "violent deaths during the territorial period," of which only 56 could be "attributed with some confidence to the political conflict or the slavery issue." Of the 101 remaining fatalities 52 seem to have been the result of ordinary brawls, and in 16 instances there is simply no way to determine the cause. Professor Watts allows that perhaps an additional 25 of the 101 remainder might have resulted from disputes over slavery. The population of Lawrence and vicinity was just under 8,000 in 1856.

of all decisions when it came to the future of slavery. It left to the people—not as a nation, but as the occupants of particular states—the power to lay down the law with regard to slavery versus freedom.

Like most attempts to evade responsibility, the Kansas-Nebraska Act only made a bad situation worse. No one doubted the outcome in Nebraska. Popular sovereignty brought it in as a free state. Kansas, however, seemed up for grabs, and while the territory prepared to vote itself into statehood, proslavery Missourians and antislavery Iowans rushed across the territorial line in an effort to tilt the popular sovereignty majority one way or the other. In the end, the incoming Missourians outnumbered the Iowans and were thereby able to install a proslavery territorial legislature. No sooner had they done this, however, than most of them returned to their permanent homes in Missouri. The Iowa newcomers, in contrast, remained in Kansas, and the territory erupted into its own civil war between the factions.

Unlike the national Civil War to come, the Kansas conflict was not fought between uniformed armies, but between civilian mobs. Onlookers called it "Bleeding Kansas." What happened in the spring of 1856 was typical. On May 21, a band of about one thousand so-called border ruffians—militant proslavery men—invaded and occupied Lawrence, a stronghold of the Kansas antislavery faction. They brandished two flags, one bearing the phrase *Southern Rights* emblazoned on a blood-red field, the other, Old Glory. The ruffians smashed up two newspaper printing offices and then stormed the Free State Hotel, which they succeeded in burning to the ground after several failed attempts. This act of arson was followed by indiscriminate looting and the burning of one residence. Remarkably, the spree resulted in only one death—that of a proslavery man, who was buried in the collapse of part of the Free State.

### Who are the Ruffians, Murderers, and Robbers in Kansas?

The Democratic party have contended from the beginning of the Kansas troubles, that the free state men, as they call themselves, are equally guilty with the pro-slavery men in committing outrages in the territory of Kansas. The Fremonters have always denied this, and charged all these outrages upon the proslavery men. Now let us see which is right. Dr. Calvin Cutter ought to be

But you will inquire of the wars—of the horrid war. Well I have seen some of it—have heard some whistling of bullets—have heard the booming of the loud mouthed cannon—have seen the dead and wounded on the battle field—have dressed the wounds of the bleeding and dying on the field, and performed amputation in the hospital. These are some of the necessary acts of active campaign war. *Our loss compared with our success has been comparatively small.* We know that the ruffians have lost SIX where we have lost *one. Our men have gained every battle but one,* namely, that of Ossawatamie. In that we were obliged to flee —but not until *we killed more of the rascals than the number of men we had engaged, while we wounded twice as many more,* so that the killed and wounded of the enemy numbered three times our entire force engaged. This was doing well by the villians. At Bull Creek, three days after, we routed in dismay their entire body and drove them into the Missouri.

In Bleeding Kansas, no act of violence could long remain an isolated incident. At precisely this time, John Brown found himself the leader of an armed band that had taken to calling itself the "Free Soil Militia." It was not a position he had sought so much as he had been drawn to it. John Brown was born in Connecticut in 1800 but grew up in Ohio, where his father opened a tannery and where John matured into an intensely religious young man with aspirations to become a Congregationalist minister. Dogged by a shortage of cash and excruciating chronic inflammation of the eyes, Brown instead took up his father's tanning trade and then made a stab at farming. Illness contributed to the failure of both enterprises, and, over the next several years, Brown borrowed what he could in an effort to find some business with which to dig himself out of the debt that only grew with each new loan he took.

His life of drift and failure, mechanical and dull, suddenly took fire on news of the death of Elijah P. Lovejoy, a Presbyterian minister and vehement abolitionist who was killed by an Alton, Illinois, mob in 1837. "Here, before God," Brown publicly proclaimed, "in the presence of these witnesses, from this time, I consecrate my life to the destruction of slavery!"

But his slide into financial ruin continued unabated. A federal court declared him bankrupt in 1843, and, in the space of a few days during that year, four of his eleven children succumbed to dysentery. After this, Brown's fortunes revived somewhat as he discovered in himself a talent for raising sheep, but the collapse of yet another business venture sent him packing in 1848 to North Elba, New York, in the Adirondacks. Here the prosperous abolitionist Gerrit Smith was granting land to poor black men, and Brown decided to move and settle his family among them. Early in 1856, he received urgent word from his four adult sons, who had moved to Kansas, that they and their families were in grave danger from marauding proslavery mobs. Roused, John Brown joined his sons, and, in company with a pair of Free Soil militiamen, he led them on the night of May 24 of that year in a lightning raid on proslavery settlers along the Pottawatomie River.

What distinguished Brown and his men from a mere murderous mob—at least in their own eyes—was their noble cause and their choice of distinctly martial weapons: cavalry sabers. These they used to hack to death five unarmed settlers, after which they rode back to the town of Lawrence, where John Brown proudly proclaimed his responsibility for having avenged the "sack of Lawrence."

*Before the radical abolitionist John Brown entered history with his 1859 raid on the federal arsenal at Harpers Ferry, Virginia (now West Virginia), in an attempt to stir the Southern slaves to mass rebellion, he made himself famous—or infamous—in 1856 for leading (or possibly just authorizing) a bloody attack in which five proslavery Kansas settlers were hacked to death with broadswords.*

FAR LEFT: *American newspapers of the mid-1850s were filled with horrific accounts of "ruffians, murderers, and robbers" waging guerrilla war in "Bleeding Kansas."*

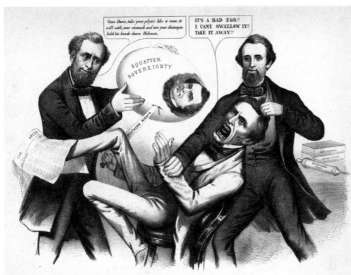

A BAD EGG FOR A SOUTHERN STOMACH.

*When popular sovereignty (aka "squatter sovereignty") turned against slavery in Kansas, Southerners like future Confederate president Jefferson Davis saw a grave threat to Southern rights. This political cartoon shows Davis being forced to swallow the popular sovereignty contained in the Compromise of 1850, controversially sponsored by Illinois senator Stephen A. Douglas—whose likeness serves here as the yolk of the unpalatable egg.*

## A LAWSUIT OF SUPREME CONSEQUENCE

AMERICA—INDEED, THE WORLD—would hear more of John Brown, and Kansas would continue to bleed right into the Civil War itself. While guerrilla violence raged in the territory, the competing factions each asserted their legitimacy to govern. In 1855, the so-called Topeka Constitution purported to create a free state but was countered in 1857 by a constitutional convention convened at Lecompton, which claimed to establish a slave state. The Free Soil citizens boycotted the ratification vote, but President James Buchanan—of whom we will soon hear more—urged both Kansans and the U.S. Congress to accept the Lecompton Constitution and admit Kansas to the Union as a slave state. The Senate and House, however, ordered another vote, which, this time, was boycotted by the proslavery faction, thereby killing the Lecompton Constitution. By mid-1859, a new document, the Wyandotte Constitution, had been completed, reflecting the sentiments of the territory's permanent abolitionist majority. Approved two to one by the electorate, it became the constitution of the free state of Kansas when it entered the Union on January 29, 1861.

In the meantime, another battle, bloodless but no less bitter, was fought in the Supreme Court, which heard the case of Dred Scott, a man legally designated a fugitive slave. He had been the property of Dr.

John Emerson of St. Louis, a U.S. Army surgeon, who, when he was transferred to Illinois and then to Wisconsin Territory, had taken Scott with him. After Emerson's death in 1846, Scott returned to St. Louis and (using lawyers hired by an abolitionist group) sued the doctor's widow for his freedom, arguing that he was now a citizen of Missouri. He had been a resident of Illinois, where slavery had been banned by the Northwest Ordinance, and also of Wisconsin Territory, where the provisions of the Missouri Compromise (in effect during his residence there) had made slavery illegal, and thus, he argued, he had been emancipated. The Missouri court in which Scott brought suit decided against him, which prompted an appeal to the Supreme Court.

In an agony of anticipation, the nation awaited the high court's verdict. James Buchanan, elected as the anxious nation's fifteenth president in 1856, even mentioned the impending decision in his inaugural address, delivered on March 4, 1857. He brought up the crisis created by the fate of the extension of slavery into the territories only to brush it aside, incredibly enough, as "happily, a matter of but little practical importance." Why? The Supreme Court was about to deliver an opinion, he said, that would settle the issue "speedily and finally," and the new president promised his hearers that he would "in common with all good citizens . . . cheerfully submit" to the court's decision—adding "whatever [it] might be."

*Whatever it might be?* On the very threshold of his presidency, Buchanan blithely bowed to the authority of the Supreme Court—as if a legal ruling could actually settle a matter that had been festering since the end of the eighteenth century. Those listening assumed the president was in as much suspense as they regarding just what that ruling would be. But the fact was that Chief Justice Roger B. Taney was an alumnus of Dickinson College, Buchanan's alma mater, and a good friend to boot. He was seen whispering in the president-elect's ear just before Buchanan mounted the rostrum. Was he telling him that the court was about to decide the Dred Scott case just the way Buchanan had wanted it decided? Taney was a Virginian. It was expected that he would vote against Scott. But, unknown at the time, the president-elect had buttonholed Associate Supreme Court Justice Robert Cooper Grier, a fellow Pennsylvanian, and talked him into voting with the Southern majority. This, together with Taney's presumed whisper, was an improper, probably unconstitutional violation of the separation

*The March 6, 1857, decision of the U.S. Supreme Court upholding a lower court's decision against Dred Scott's landmark suit for freedom ended all possibility of peaceful compromise on the question of slavery in the United States. Scott is pictured here at the time of the decision.*

*Roger B. Taney, chief justice of the U.S. Supreme Court, wrote the fateful decision in the case of Dred Scott.*

of powers. But Buchanan was desperate to make the slavery issue and the possibility of civil war go away by the time he took office.

It didn't turn out that way.

Just two days after Buchanan's inauguration, Taney issued the majority opinion he had written in the matter of Dred Scott. Because Scott was a "Negro" and a slave, the opinion held, he was not a citizen and therefore had no legal standing. He could bring suit against no one. With this, the Dred Scott appeal was dismissed—but the chief justice wanted to do far more than settle the case of an individual slave. In tortured prose, Taney went on to hold the Missouri Compromise unconstitutional. Although Congress had already repealed the compromise, Scott's attorneys asserted that it *had been* the law of the land when their client was transported to free territory. Taney met this assertion by finding that the Missouri Compromise violated the Fifth Amendment, which barred the government from depriving persons of "life, liberty, or property" without due process of law. Congress, Taney's decision decreed, never legally had the power to exclude slavery from the territories or anywhere else.

James Buchanan occupies a place at the very bottom of most historians' rankings of the American presidents. Even as he addressed the nation after taking the oath of office, he sought to make the issue of the extension of slavery a matter of settled law by relinquishing both his executive authority and the legislative power of Congress to the opinion of the Supreme Court. But instead of quietly ending the slavery debate, the Dred Scott decision effectively made the Civil War inevitable.

*James Buchanan, fifteenth president of the United States, entered office blithely confident that the Supreme Court's decision in the Dred Scott case would settle the slavery issue "speedily and finally."*

"The right of property in a slave is distinctly and expressly affirmed in the Constitution. . . . It is the opinion of the court that the Act of Congress [the Missouri Compromise] which prohibited a citizen from holding and owning property of this kind in the territory of the United States north of the line therein mentioned, is not warranted by the Constitution, and is therefore void."

*Chief Justice Roger B. Taney,*
*decision in the Dred Scott case,*
*March 6, 1857*

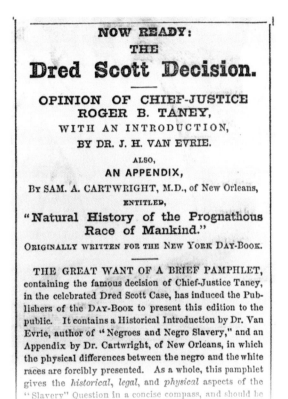

Firstly, not only hardcore abolitionists but many people of conscience were appalled by a decision that used the Bill of Rights to *keep* a human being in chains. Secondly, all those who opposed the extension of slavery were outraged by a ruling that, in a single stroke, trumped any congressional legislation or even popular sovereignty. Thirdly, because Taney's opinion had reduced slavery to an issue of property, which was protected by the Fifth Amendment, it obliged every official of every state to protect the ownership of slaves; it thereby put slavery beyond the possibility of any more compromises. The only way to end slavery would be with a constitutional amendment. By design, the Constitution is not easy to amend. Not only a simple majority, but two-thirds of both houses of Congress would have to approve an amendment, which then had to be ratified by three-fourths of the state legislatures or by special ratifying conventions in three-fourths of the states. Obviously, the Southern states would never ratify an antislavery amendment, which, in fact, would never even get out of the Senate. If the abolitionists, a growing faction in the North, wanted to outlaw slavery, the South would have to be made to yield, and that meant only one thing: war.

*Breathlessly awaited by the nation, the Dred Scott Decision was published commercially and offered for sale.*

# ONE MAN AND GOD

IN MID-NINETEENTH-CENTURY AMERICA, it was not terribly unusual to find very old men and women who had lived through the American Revolution and somewhat younger people whose fathers had actually fought in it. The idea of defying immoral laws, even violently, was hardly foreign to those who were appalled by the Dred Scott decision. Among these men was one who had already proved himself capable of shedding blood for the sake of what he deemed justice. Shortly after Taney handed down his decision, John Brown moved from Bleeding Kansas to Boston, the very heart of the radical abolitionist movement. He quickly attracted the backing of six high-profile abolitionist activists: Samuel Gridley Howe, Thomas Wentworth Higginson, Theodore Parker, Franklin Sanborn, George L. Stearns, and Gerrit Smith (on whose Adirondack land Brown had lived). They agreed to finance Brown's scheme to storm the federal arsenal at Harpers Ferry, Virginia (today West Virginia), liberate its cache of guns and ammunition, and distribute these to local slaves, who would form the nucleus of a mass uprising. Once this was under way, Brown was confident that white men of conscience from all over the United States would join in, overwhelm the slaveholders, and force abolition on the South. If the odds seemed staggeringly stacked against him, Brown shrugged them off. "One man and God can overturn the universe," he declared.

On October 16, 1859, Brown led a raiding party of sixteen white men and five black men in a nighttime raid on the arsenal and armory nestled in the elbow of land at the joining of the Shenandoah and Potomac rivers. Largely unguarded, the armory was quickly taken, as was the nearby Hall's Rifle Works. Brown knew that it was one thing to overrun these prizes and another to hold on to them, so he took about sixty citizens of the town of Harpers Ferry hostage, among them the great-grand-nephew of George Washington. Hunkered down in the arsenal, Brown sent two of his black raiders to raise

*John Brown, his men, and their hostages holed up in the Engine House (where fire equipment was stored) of the Harpers Ferry arsenal complex. This wood engraving, published in* Frank Leslie's Illustrated Newspaper *on November 5, 1859, depicts the moments just before a contingent of U.S. Marines and local militia stormed the stronghold.*

# BIRTH OF AN ANTHEM

In 1861, the abolitionist poet Julia Ward Howe watched a review of Union troops in Washington, D.C., and heard them sing a marching song set to the tune of a campfire spiritual that had been written in 1855 by William Steffe. While the tune was stirring, the words, penned by a Vermont-born member of the Massachusetts Infantry, Thomas Bishop, were harsh, even ugly:

> John Brown's body lies a-mouldering in
>     the grave;
> John Brown's body lies a-mouldering in
>     the grave;
> John Brown's body lies a-mouldering in
>     the grave;
> His soul is marching on!

A friend of Howe's, the Reverend James Freeman Clarke, challenged her to put more appropriate words to the fine tune, and in the February 1862 issue of *Atlantic Monthly* she published the verses titled "The Battle Hymn of the Republic." The first verse went like this—

> Mine eyes have seen the glory of
>     the coming of the Lord:
> He is trampling out the vintage where
>     the grapes of wrath
>     are stored;
> He hath loosed the fateful lightning of
>     His terrible swift
>     sword:
> His truth is marching on.

—and was quickly and widely adopted by the soldiers of the Union army as their unofficial marching song. For many Northerners, it became an anthem that ennobled their cause, and it remains one of America's best-known songs.

*Before the abolitionist poet Julia Ward Howe wrote the lyrics to "The Battle Hymn of the Republic" in 1861 (published 1862), the campfire spiritual tune (composed in 1855) carried lyrics commemorating John Brown, whose body "lies a-mouldering in the grave," but whose "soul's marching on."*

INDIANA

C. Magnus 12 Frankfort St N Y

## JOHN BROWN SONG.

John Brown's body lies a mouldering in the grave,
John Brown's body lies a mouldering in the grave,
John Brown's body lies a mouldering in the grave.
His soul's marching on !

**Chorus.**

Glory Hally, Hallelujah ! Glory Hally, Hallelujah ! Glory
    Hally, Hallelujah !
    His soul's marching on !

He's gone to be a soldier in the army of our Lord,
He's gone to be a soldier in the army of our Lord,
He's gone to be a soldier in the army of our Lord.
    His soul's marching on !

Chorus : Glory Hally, Hallelujah ! Glory Hally, Hallelujah !
    Glory Hally, Hallelujah !
    His soul's marching on !

a Paul Revere–style alarm among the local slaves, confident that, very soon, an army of thousands would join him.

Nothing of the kind came to pass, however, and well before daybreak, residents of Harpers Ferry surrounded the arsenal and opened fire. The very first "enemy" Brown's men managed to kill was a free black townsman.

Brown, his followers, and his hostages lay under siege through the morning and afternoon of October 17. After two of the leader's sons were killed, the surviving raiders dragged their hostages to a firehouse adjacent to the armory and holed up there. By this time, the residents' siege party had been joined by a company of marines—the only federal troops nearby—temporarily under army commanders, Lieutenant Colonel Robert E. Lee and Lieutenant James Ewell Brown "Jeb" Stuart. As if it weren't incongruous enough for marines to be led by army officers, Lee also hadn't even had time to change out of the civilian clothes he had been wearing when he was ordered to Harpers Ferry.

Amid the clamor of the townsfolk to free their fellow citizens and to head off a slave rebellion, the calm, even majestic Lee, his prematurely gray hair and beard giving him the appearance of a cross between scholar and soldier, refused to be goaded into hasty action. To attack immediately, in the failing light of the end of day, would risk killing a lot of hostages. He resolved therefore to let the night pass and, first thing on the morning of the eighteenth, sent the intrepid Jeb Stuart with a flag of truce to call on Brown and demand his surrender.

The waiting, the white flag, the call to surrender—all had been calm and methodical, an approach to be expected of the brilliant Lee, a West Point–trained military engineer. But Lee knew that battles aren't won by doing what is expected. Before he sent Stuart to parley, he told him to wave his hat if Brown refused to surrender.

When the lieutenant emerged from the firehouse holding his broad-brimmed cavalry hat by its crown then waving it in a wide arc above his head, Lee unleashed his forces. The battle that followed consumed three minutes. The marines targeted the firehouse door, smashed it like so much matchwood, and poured in. Immediately dispatching two of the raiders with their bayonets, the marines did what they could to save the hostages. Four of

"Harper's Ferry Insurrection—Burying the Dead Insurgents," published in Frank Leslie's Illustrated Newspaper, November 5, 1859. By the middle of the next decade, there would be some 625,000 more bodies to bury, Northern and Southern.

them fell in the melee, however, including the town mayor. One marine was also killed. As for Brown and his men, only four escaped death, including Brown himself, deeply gashed by a marine saber.

> "I John Brown am now quite certain
> that the crimes of this guilty land: will never
> be purged away; but with Blood."

*John Brown, written on the day of his execution,*
*December 2, 1859*

Not surprisingly, in the aftermath of Harpers Ferry, President Buchanan was content to let the state of Virginia deal with Brown and the other survivors. They were duly charged with treason against Virginia as well as murder and conspiracy to foment "servile insurrection," tried within ten days of their capture, and sentenced to hang. Hangings were commonly public spectacles in those days, and the state authorities believed that the execution of those who dared to turn the slaves against their masters would be especially edifying. Perhaps this was on the mind of one Virginia Military Institute professor, Thomas Jackson, a Mexican War veteran, who, acting on the orders of Virginia governor Henry A. Wise, led a cadre of callow VMI cadets to the execution site to help maintain order, since Virginia at this time had no standing army. But the execution had precisely the opposite effect the executioners had intended. Unrepentant to the end, Brown recited to judge and jury the words of Jesus Christ: "Remember them that are in bonds, as bound with them." He continued, quietly and with great dignity: "Now, if it is deemed necessary that I should forfeit my life for the furtherance of the ends of justice, and mingle my blood further with the blood of my children and with the blood of millions in this slave country whose rights are disregarded by wicked, cruel, and unjust enactments—I submit; so let it be done." In killing John Brown, Virginia had given the abolitionist movement something it desperately needed—a martyr—and Professor Thomas Jackson would soon enough find himself transformed into General Stonewall Jackson, like so many others suddenly thrust into command of new-made soldiers on fields of battle as bloody as anything the hanged man had foretold.

## TAKEAWAY

One after another, desperate efforts to compromise on the issue of slavery gave way; they were altogether smashed by the Supreme Court's stunning decision in the 1857 Dred Scott case and the bold assault on the federal arsenal at Harpers Ferry by fiery abolitionist John Brown in 1859. Looming over the United States since the very day that its people had accepted a Constitution that failed to resolve the issue of slavery, civil war had become inevitable.

# CHAPTER 3

## "THE ESSENCE OF ANARCHY"

### A House Divided Falls

AMERICANS FORGIVE THEIR LEADERS FOR MANY THINGS, BUT PASSING THE the buck is not one of them. Abolitionists of all degrees of intensity—from those who applauded John Brown to those who still believed in pursuing some "legal" means of ending slavery—condemned Whig backers of the Kansas-Nebraska Act for having turned away from a momentous decision of right and wrong. Voters took their vengeance on the Whig Party, which fell apart after 1854. Some adherents crossed over to the Democrats, but others, who opposed slavery, splintered into a heap of tiny abolitionist parties—including the Liberty Party, Conscience Whigs, Free Soilers, the Anti-Nebraska Democratic Party, and more, whose names even historians scarcely remember.

### BIRTH OF A PRINCIPLED PARTY

THE HAMLET OF RIPON IN CENTRAL WISCONSIN was far from the East Coast sources of political power, and the little white schoolhouse of Ripon, with its single clapboard-clad room, was a far cry from the urban auditoriums in which political parties typically convened. It was here, however, on February 28, 1854, that some thirty men, outraged by the Kansas-Nebraska Act, assembled to create a new party designed to attract, organize, and unify abolition's scattered champions. Whereas the Whig position had been diluted by conservatives and moderates who wanted nothing more than the revival of the Missouri Compromise or some other federal action to curb the extension of slavery, the men who convened at Ripon believed the time for compromises was over. The only worthwhile goal now was to end all slavery in the United States.

It is unclear whether the Ripon group agreed on the name by which the party would be known— the Republicans—or whether the name was invented during the party's first convention, held on July 6, 1854, in Jackson, Michigan, but when the Ripon men left the schoolhouse, they fanned out through the Northern states on a vigorous campaign of organization. Within two years, the Republican Party had secured impressive footholds in the Midwest as well as the Northeast and fielded its first national candidates. Among these was presidential contender John C. Frémont, celebrated as the "Pathfinder" because of the Western exploration and surveying expeditions he had led and also famous for his leading role in the Bear Flag Revolt, the 1846 uprising that shook California loose from Mexico. Frémont served briefly as military governor of California during the war with Mexico and, in 1850, became one of the new state's first two U.S. senators. A radical abolitionist of proven daring and patriotism, Frémont seemed to the new party an ideal choice as its first presidential candidate. Four years later, in a three-way race with Democrat James Buchanan and Millard Fillmore (candidate of the anti-Catholic, anti-immigrant, pro-temperance "Know Nothing" Party), Frémont came in an impressive second behind Buchanan, carrying eleven states to the Democrat's nineteen. Moreover, the new party captured more than a hundred congressional seats, making it an emerging force to contend with.

*This woodcut of John C. Frémont, who was nicknamed the "Pathfinder," was used in his unsuccessful 1856 bid for the White House as the first presidential candidate of the newly created Republican Party.*

Frémont received fewer than six hundred votes from the slave states. That was to be expected, but his showing among free-state voters was sufficiently impressive to suggest that a Republican candidate might soon win the White House, even without a single Southern vote. The prospects for 1860 looked hopeful.

*In this campaign portrait, John C. Frémont trades in his frontier buckskins for an East Coast frock coat and cravat.*

## NUMBERS

### Maiden Voyage

In the 1856 run for the White House, the Republican Party's first-ever candidate, John C. Frémont, polled 1,342,345 popular votes (31.1 percent), claimed 114 electoral votes, and carried eleven states. "Know Nothing" contender Millard Fillmore garnered 873,053 popular votes (21.6 percent) and just 8 electoral votes, taking only a single state. The winner, Democrat James Buchanan, captured 1,836,072 popular votes (45.3 percent) and 174 electoral, taking nineteen states. From the slave states, Frémont received a meager 600 votes.

# PRAIRIE LAWYER

IN AN AGE WHEN THE AVERAGE HEIGHT of a man was about midway between five and six feet, Abraham Lincoln, at a fraction under six-foot-four, was a gangly giant. To some, he seemed a roughhewn frontiersman, whereas others found his frame grotesque, even laughable. They called him the "original gorilla." In truth, neither impression did him justice. He was a son of the backcountry, born on February 12, 1809, in a Hardin County, Kentucky, log cabin. By the election of 1860, such a humble birth dwelling was already an American icon of the "common man" candidate William Henry "Tippecanoe" Harrison, who laid claim to a log cabin birth in his so-called Log Cabin and Hard Cider presidential campaign of 1840. The difference was that Lincoln really had been born in a cabin, really was raised in hardscrabble frontier poverty, really did work his family's subsistence farm, built real muscles splitting log rails for fences, and really did teach himself almost everything he knew (including enough law to gain admission to the Illinois bar). Harrison? He had been born and raised in prosperity and comfort on a stately Virginia plantation. This said, Lincoln, the self-taught lawyer, was no rustic barrister. His family had moved from Kentucky to Indiana in 1816 and then settled in Illinois by 1830. He began his law practice in Springfield, the state capital, in 1837 and quickly earned a reputation as a formidable litigator who made a handsome living representing the likes of the Alton & Sangamon Railroad, successfully litigating against any number of big-city law firms.

Abraham Lincoln was certainly no gorilla, nor the simple frontiersmen his admirers and his political handlers portrayed him to be. He was a canny lawyer, whose interests included making money at his profession, reading Shakespeare, and devouring the Bible—partly, doubtless, as a source of spiritual enlightenment but mostly as a source on which he built his colloquial eloquence. He gained election to the U.S. House of Representatives in 1847, served out his term, and then returned to Springfield and the law, confessing to friends that he "was losing interest in politics."

The truth was that Abe Lincoln's more serious problem was keeping himself from losing interest in life itself. Lively, sociable, and a lover of a good joke, Lincoln was also given to periods of profound depression. Robert L. Wilson, one of his early colleagues in the Illinois General Assembly to which Lincoln was first elected in 1832, recalled a conversation in which Lincoln "told me that although he appeared to enjoy life rapturously, still he was the victim of terrible melancholy. He sought company, and indulged in fun and hilarity without restraint, or stint as to time. Still when by himself, he told me that he was so overcome with mental depression, that he never dare carry a knife in his pocket. As long as I was intimately acquainted with him . . . he never carried a pocket knife." His law partner William Herndon remarked that "his melancholy dripped from him as he walked."

Fortunately, just as his fits of melancholy were never permanent, so, too, his interest in politics revived—stirred into new life by the Kansas-Nebraska Act. Personally, he found slavery repugnant ("as I would not be a slave," he famously said, "so I would not be a master"), but he was no radical and would not even have described himself as an abolitionist. Yet he could not accept the doctrine of popular sovereignty as enshrined in the 1854 legislation, which he believed would extend slavery into the territories and thereby ensure its perpetuation. As a lawyer, Lincoln was convinced that, like it or not, the Constitution protected slavery in states where it already existed, but as a careful reader of the law, he was also persuaded that the Founding Fathers had intended to set slavery on a course to extinction when they enacted the Northwest Ordinance of 1787, which explicitly barred slavery from the Northwest Territory. So he ran as a Whig for the U.S. Senate in 1855, lost, and, the following year, joined the Republicans.

In 1858, Lincoln's new party nominated him for another Senate run, this time against the formidable Illinois incumbent, Democrat Stephen A. Douglas. Accepting the nomination on June 16, 1858, Lincoln delivered a forceful speech against what he described as a conspiracy among Douglas, Chief Justice Roger B. Taney, and Democratic presidents Franklin Pierce and James Buchanan to nationalize slavery. He could not stand for that, he said, and he went on to declare that successful compromise on slavery was impossible because the United States could not endure half slave and half free. Paraphrasing the Bible, he observed: "A house divided against itself cannot stand."

*In 1860,* candidate *Abraham Lincoln had yet to cultivate the beard of* President *Abraham Lincoln. This engraving was made after a painting by the noted American artist Thomas Hicks.*

The speech gained him a national audience, which was enlarged by a series of debates with Douglas. Both men performed brilliantly, and, in many ways, their positions on slavery were not all that different. Neither Lincoln nor Douglas wanted slavery extended into the territories, but Douglas nevertheless continued to insist that, to preserve the Union, continued compromise had to be found, and he believed that the best available compromise was the course of popular sovereignty embodied in the Kansas-Nebraska Act. Lincoln disagreed, and although he lost the race to his Democratic opponent, he won wide recognition as a principled moderate, a political voice for those who craved an alternative to both morally

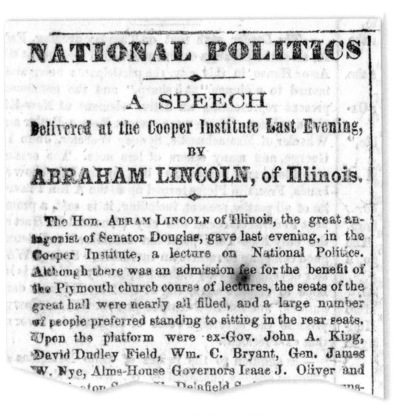

*The speech Lincoln made at New York's Cooper Union Institute on February 27, 1860, defined his position on slavery. While he believed that, without amendment, the Constitution protected slavery, he affirmed his equally strong belief that the federal government did have the authority to bar the expansion of slavery into the federal territories, and he further asserted his belief that the Founding Fathers had shared this position. Some historians believe that this speech sent Lincoln to the White House.*

bankrupt compromise and "fanatical" abolitionism bent on ending slavery even if it cost the nation. To a majority of Republican Party leaders, Lincoln seemed to speak the enlightened "mainstream" Northern mind, and so they nominated him as their presidential candidate in 1860.

> "'A house divided against itself cannot stand.'
> I believe this government cannot endure
> permanently half slave and half free. I do not expect
> the Union to be dissolved—I do not expect the house
> to fall—but I do expect it will cease to be divided.
> It will become all one thing, or all the other."
>
> *Abraham Lincoln, speech, June 16, 1858*

*Lincoln came to national prominence as a result of his debates with Senator Stephen A. Douglas of Illinois during his 1858 run for the Senate. Lincoln performed brilliantly in the debates, but Douglas defeated him for the Senate nevertheless. He in turn would be defeated by Lincoln for the presidency in 1860. This photograph of Douglas was published in 1859.*

## Ultimatum

Lincoln may have seemed "moderate" to his fellow Republicans, but to Southerners, no Republican was moderate, and Democratic leaders in the slave states warned that if any Republican were elected president in 1860, the South would leave the Union. Like others who all along tried to reduce Lincoln to a stereotype—log cabin frontiersman, original gorilla—proslavery Southerners labeled him "Black Lincoln" and warned their compatriots that, if elected, he would free the slaves; make *them* the masters; and destroy the South, its economy, and its way of life.

Had the North rallied around Abraham Lincoln, no Democratic candidate could have defeated him. Had the Democrats, North and South, entered the election as a unified party, Lincoln would almost certainly have lost. But the country was not so neatly divided geographically on the slavery issue, and the Democratic Party was hardly united. Many Northerners, unwilling to risk the dissolution of the Union, supported Douglas, who had alienated Southern Democrats by splitting with President Buchanan and denouncing the proslavery Lecompton Constitution that had initially been adopted by Kansas. When the party's Northern majority nominated Douglas, Southerners broke away to form the Southern Democratic Party, which nominated John C. Breckinridge. Yet another splinter faction, the Constitutional Union

*Lincoln's first name suffers abbreviation in this campaign banner from 1860.*

## NUMBERS

### Plurality President

Abraham Lincoln won a clear majority of electoral ballots, but his popular vote victory was a mere plurality. He received 1,865,908 votes versus the 2,815,617 cast for his three opponents. A minority of Americans put Lincoln in the White House, and, in the South, Lincoln was not even on the ballot.

Party, fielded its own candidate. Thus broken, the rival Democrats divided 123 electoral votes among themselves, whereas 180 went to Lincoln, by no means the unanimous candidate of the North, but the unanimous candidate of a unified Republican Party.

On December 20, 1860, South Carolina became the first slave state to act on the Southern ultimatum to the North. In direct response to the election of Black Lincoln, a state convention voted to secede from the Union.

The secession resolution declaimed:

> We affirm that these ends for which this Government was instituted have been defeated, and the Government itself has been made destructive of them by the action of the non-slaveholding States. Those States have assumed the right of deciding upon the propriety of our domestic institutions; and have denied the rights of property established in fifteen of the States and recognized by the Constitution; they have denounced as sinful the institution of slavery; they have permitted open establishment among them of societies, whose avowed object is to disturb the peace and to eloign the property of the citizens of other States. They have encouraged and assisted thousands of our slaves to leave their homes; and those who remain, have been incited by emissaries, books and pictures to servile insurrection.

*The 1860 general election was a fractious affair among multiple candidates, who are depicted in this political cartoon as tearing the nation apart: Lincoln and Douglas fight over the West; Breckinridge grabs the South; and Senator John Bell of Tennessee struggles to keep the moribund Whig Party alive by pasting together the tattered Northeast.*

Published in London and Edinburgh in 1857, this map shows "the area and extent of the free & slave-holding states, and the territories of the Union: also the boundary of the seceding states."

## WASHINGTON ADRIFT

IF THE SOUTH DEEMED ITSELF to have been driven out of the Union by the election of Lincoln, few in the North, even those who voted for him, were enthusiastic about their new president. But there was at least one man who was pleased with the election—though he would have been delighted with any victor. That man was James Buchanan, fifteenth president of the United States, who was thrilled just to be leaving the White House. History books generally note two things about Buchanan: First, that he was the nation's only bachelor president, and, second, that he was apparently unburdened by high moral character, lofty principles, or the will to lead. The secession crisis that loomed and then began during his administration paralyzed him rather than moved him to act.

## DETAILS DETAILS

### Secession's Roll Call

South Carolina seceded from the Union on December 20, 1860, followed by Mississippi on January 9, 1861; Florida, January 10; Alabama, January 11; and Georgia on January 19. Louisiana seceded on January 26, and Texas on February 23. The Texas Declaration of Secession accused "all the non-slaveholding States" of having violated "that good faith and comity which should exist between entirely distinct nations" by forming "themselves into a great sectional party, now strong enough in numbers to control the affairs of each of those States, based upon an unnatural feeling of hostility to these Southern States and their beneficent and patriarchal system of African slavery, proclaiming the debasing doctrine of equality of all men, irrespective of race or color—a doctrine at war with nature, in opposition to the experience of mankind, and in violation of the plainest revelations of Divine Law."

Arkansas seceded on May 6, North Carolina on May 20; Virginia ratified its April 17 secession on May 23; and Tennessee voters ratified the state's May 7 declaration on June 8.

Like Lincoln, Buchanan was born in a log cabin—this one in Pennsylvania—but he had a longer legislative career, serving in the House of Representatives for ten years and then in the Senate for another decade. Under President Andrew Jackson, he was U.S. minister to Russia; under President James Polk, secretary of state; and in the administration of Franklin Pierce, the fourteenth president of the United States, he was minister plenipotentiary to the Court of St. James's—ambassador to Great Britain. That last appointment was a principal reason for his election to the presidency. Because he was away in England during the Kansas-Nebraska debate, he emerged unscathed from the crisis, having been identified neither as an opponent nor an advocate of the extension of slavery. Indeed, Buchanan was a specimen of that pre–Civil War political animal known as the "doughface," a Northerner with vaguely Southern sympathies. Although he personally found slavery repugnant, he proposed to do absolutely nothing to oppose it.

> "Mr. Buchanan is an able man,
> but is in small matters without judgment
> and sometimes acts like an old maid."
>
> *President James K. Polk,*
> *diary entry, February 27, 1849*

As a presidential candidate, Buchanan offered neutrality. Once in office, however, his tendency was consistently to knuckle under to proslavery interests. If he had any plan for preserving the Union, it was to appease the South by acting to discourage and suppress Northern abolitionist "agitation" and to ensure that the Fugitive Slave Act that was part of the Compromise of 1850 was always vigorously enforced. As mentioned in Chapter 2, he sought to stanch the bleeding of Bleeding Kansas by prevailing upon all Kansans to accept the proslavery Lecompton Constitution—regardless of its manifest illegitimacy. Beyond such gestures of appeasement, Buchanan did nothing to arrest the movement toward the dissolution of the Union, and once Lincoln was elected, he waited out the clock, denouncing the secession of the first seven "Confederate" states, but impotently pleading that he had no constitutional authority to prevent their leaving. It was not until ratification of the Twentieth Amendment in 1933 that Inauguration Day was moved to January 20 from March 4; four long months separated the election of Lincoln from his first day in office. During this interval, Buchanan fretted but failed to act, and the president-elect, apparently unwilling to weigh in before he had any statutory authority, observed a silence as strict as it was stubborn. The result may be summed up in a single word: *drift*.

## Forlorn Hope

THE CIVIL WAR IS TYPICALLY DESCRIBED as a struggle between the North and the South—and so it was—yet it was never quite so geographically clear-cut. The North had its Southern sympathizers, chief among them doughfaces, such as Buchanan, who tried to appease both sides, and (as we will see) "copperheads," Northerners who more or less actively supported the South. Likewise, the South had its loyalists, who had never wanted to leave the Union. There were also a set of slave states that chose not to secede. One of these so-called border states was Kentucky, birthplace of both president-elect Lincoln and soon-to-be Confederate president Jefferson Davis. It was also the home state of none other than Senator Henry Clay, the "Great Compromiser," who had championed the Missouri Compromise back in 1820, had drawn up the compromise tariff of 1834 that ended the Nullification Crisis, and was a prime mover of the Compromise of 1850. Although Kentucky resolved to cling to the Union, it also declared itself neutral once war broke out. The senior senator from the state, John J. Crittenden—one of whose sons would join the Union army, the other the Confederate army—took up the tradition of compromise and sought to hold the Union together, even as secession began, by proposing in December 1860 no fewer than six constitutional amendments collectively known as the Crittenden Compromise. The thrust of the amendments was this:

- To resurrect and render constitutional the defunct and discredited Missouri Compromise of 1820
- To extend the original "Compromise Line" dividing slave states from free all the way to the Pacific
- To enshrine the Fugitive Slave Law in a constitutional amendment and provide for its stringent permanent enforcement

## DETAILS, DETAILS
### On the Fence
Delaware, Maryland, Missouri, and Kentucky were all slave states that declined to secede from the Union. The westernmost counties of Virginia also chose to remain loyal after the rest of the state seceded, and, on June 20, 1863, this region was admitted to the Union as the new state of West Virginia, even though, like the other so-called border states, it allowed slavery. (Though in truth, the region was so poor that few citizens owned slaves.) Throughout the war, the border states were treated most gingerly by Abraham Lincoln, who was acutely wary of alienating them and driving them into the Confederate camp.

- To provide an indemnity for owners of fugitive slaves whose returns were successfully blocked by anyone—presumably Northern abolitionists
- To extend popular sovereignty to all the territories, even those north of the revived Missouri Compromise line
- To constitutionally protect slavery in the District of Columbia, so that neither Congress nor the president could limit or abolish it

Predictably, the outgoing fifteenth president neither endorsed nor condemned the Crittenden Compromise. The incoming president-elect likewise made no public pronouncements on the proposal but did privately direct a Republican colleague to "entertain no proposition for a compromise in regard to the extension of slavery." When word of this leaked, the Crittenden Compromise was doomed.

*Senator John J. Crittenden, from the deeply divided state of Kentucky, proposed in December 1860 a package of six constitutional amendments intended to put a stop to secession. This last-ditch effort to avert civil war failed to gain traction either in Congress or the White House.*

## ADVANCE AND RETREAT

As BUCHANAN BIT HIS NAILS and bided his time, Major Robert Anderson, commandant of a U.S. Army garrison at Fort Moultrie, on Sullivan's Island, South Carolina, decided that the time had come to move his men to a stronger, more readily defended position, especially since Moultrie had yet to be furnished with artillery. On the night after

*"A Cure for Republican Lock-jaw," an 1861 political cartoon, depicts a doomed attempt to force the bitter pill of the Crittenden Compromise down the throat of a Republican Party unwilling to compromise on the extension of slavery.*

A CURE FOR REPUBLICAN LOCK-JAW

Frank Leslie's Illustrated Newspaper *captured Major Robert Anderson assuming command at Fort Sumter on December 27, 1860. He presides over the raising of the very flag he would see lowered on April 13, 1861.*

Christmas—six days after South Carolina proclaimed its secession—he led his command from Fort Moultrie to nearby Fort Sumter in Charleston Harbor. Observing this movement, South Carolina issued a formal protest to President Buchanan as if it were one sovereign nation communicating with another. The South Carolinians demanded the immediate surrender of both forts.

The effrontery was sufficiently insulting to rouse even Buchanan to act. He refused to surrender Fort Sumter (he could do nothing about Fort Moultrie, since it had been evacuated) and ordered that it be resupplied and reinforced. Yet he could not bring himself to take the decisive, albeit provocative, step of sending the supplies and men via a U.S. Navy warship. Instead, he hired an unarmed merchant steamer, the *Star of the West*, hoping it would slip by the cannons the "rebels" had moved into Fort Moultrie.

It did not.

As the *Star of the West* steamed within range, Moultrie's guns opened fire, and the skipper got the message. He ordered the steamship to turn hard about, sending the *Star* back where it came from. The nation's

*Major Robert Anderson was depicted as "The Hero of Fort Sumter" in this 1861 print popular in the North.*

*A reluctant President James Buchanan dispatched the sidewheel steamer* Star of the West *with supplies for besieged Fort Sumter. After drawing fire from Charleston shore batteries, the ship abruptly turned back without unloading its cargo.*

commander-in-chief made no further attempt to aid Fort Sumter, but neither did he order Anderson and his men to evacuate it. He only hoped that whatever happened next would happen to President Abraham Lincoln and not to himself.

## LINCOLN'S LONG JOURNEY

IN THE BEST OF TIMES, February on the Illinois prairie is bleak, and these were far from the best of times. A half-frozen drizzle pelted the locomotive idling with its single coach at the Springfield Great Western Depot. The engineer blew the all-aboard at precisely eight on the morning of the eleventh, and the president-elect mounted the steps of the car and then walked out to its canopied observation platform. A crowd had gathered to see him off. He had won the election of 1860, but there was no cheering. "My friends," Abraham Lincoln began—

> No one not in my situation can appreciate my feeling of sadness at this parting. To this place and the kindness of these people I owe everything. Here I have lived for a quarter of a century, and have passed from a young to an old man. Here my children have been born, and one is buried. I now leave, not knowing when, or whether ever, I may return, with a task before me greater than that which rested upon Washington. Without the assistance of that Divine Being who ever attended him, I cannot succeed. With that assistance I cannot fail. Trusting in Him who can go with me and remain with you and be everywhere for good, let us confidently hope that all will yet be well. To His care commending you, as I hope in your prayers you will commend me, I bid you an affectionate farewell.

Abraham Lincoln would turn fifty-two en route to Washington City (as the capital was then commonly known), younger than any of the fifteen chief executives who had come before him. It would be a slow journey with many stops—Indianapolis, Cincinnati, Columbus, Pittsburgh, Cleveland, Erie, Buffalo, Albany, New York City, Trenton, Newark, Philadelphia, Harrisburg—and at Baltimore, the president-elect would not only stop, but change trains. A horse-drawn carriage would take him from the Calvert Street Station to Camden Station, where he would board the train to Washington and his inauguration.

That change of trains deeply worried Allan J. Pinkerton, the already famous private detective whom the president of the Philadelphia, Wilmington and Baltimore Railroad had personally hired to accompany Lincoln. This after his line's master mechanic reported to him that the "son of a distinguished citizen of Maryland" was boasting of an oath he and others had taken to assassinate the president-elect before he reached Washington. Pinkerton planted his most reliable "operatives" to infiltrate Baltimore's extensive network of proslavery zealots, and he was soon flooded with tips. The assassination plot was very real, and it was being plotted as the prelude to an invasion of the nation's capital intended to demoralize the North so that it would give up any idea of imposing its will upon the South. Lincoln was to be shot at Calvert Street Station as soon as he left his train.

Kate Warne, one of Pinkerton's "female operatives," met Lincoln's train when it stopped in New York. She conveyed everything she and Pinkerton knew of the plot to Norman Judd, a member of the inaugural party. Judd shared the information with the president-elect as the train rolled into Philadelphia on February 21. Pinkerton advised abbreviating the rest of the announced itinerary and proceeding, nonstop, directly to Washington, but Lincoln protested that he had "promised to raise the flag

## GREAT WESTERN RAILROAD.
## TIME CARD
### For a Special Train, Monday, Feb. 11, 1861,
### WITH
### His Excellency, Abraham Lincoln, President Elect.

| | | |
|---|---|---|
| Leave SPRINGFIELD, | 8.00 A. M. | |
| " JAMESTOWN, | 8.15 | " |
| " DAWSON, | 8.24 | " |
| " MECHANICSBURG, | 8.30 | " |
| " LANESVILLE, | 8.37 | " |
| " ILLIOPOLIS, | 8.49 | " |
| " NIANTIC, | 8.58 | " |
| " SUMMIT, | 9.07 | " |
| Arrive at DECATUR, | 9.24 | " |
| Leave DECATUR, | 9.29 | " |
| " OAKLEY, | 9.45 | " |
| " CERRO GORDO, | 9.54 | " |
| " BEMENT, | 10.13 | " |
| " SADORUS, | 10.40 | " |
| Arrive at TOLONO, | 10.50 | " |
| Leave " | 10.55 | " |
| " PHILO, | 11.07 | " |
| " SIDNEY, | 11.17 | " |
| " HOMER, | 11.30 | " |
| " SALINA, | 11.45 | " |
| " CATLIN, | 11.59 | " |
| " BRYANT, | 12.07 P. M. | |
| " DANVILLE, | 12.12 | " |
| Arrive at STATE LINE, | 12.30 P. M. | |

This train will be entitled to the road, *and all other trains must be kept out of the way.*

Trains to be passed and met must be on the side track at least 10 minutes before this train is due.

Agents at all stations between Springfield and State Line must be on duty when this train passes, and examine the switches and know that *all is right before it passes.*

Operators at Telegraph Stations between Springfield and State Line must remain on duty until this train passes, and immediately report its time to Chas. H. Speed, Springfield.

All Foremen and men under their direction must be on the track and know positively that the track is in order.

It is very important that this train should pass over the road in safety, and all employees are expected to render all assistance in their power.

*Red is the signal for danger,* but any signal apparently intended to indicate alarm or danger must be regarded, the train stopped, and the meaning of it ascertained.

Carefulness is particularly enjoined.

F. W. BOWEN, Supt.

*This time card is a record of the first leg of Lincoln's long inaugural journey— "Great Western Railroad. Time card For a Special Train, Monday, Feb. 11, 1861, with His Excellency, Abraham Lincoln, President Elect."*

*Allan J. Pinkerton was already the nation's most famous private investigator when he was hired to protect Abraham Lincoln, en route to his inauguration in Washington, D.C., from would-be assassins.*

over Independence Hall to-morrow morning, and to visit the legislature at Harrisburg in the afternoon." Let him keep these promises, Lincoln said, and then he would entrust himself entirely to Pinkerton's care. The detective agreed. Following the Harrisburg ceremonies, Lincoln would return to Philadelphia and then board a Baltimore-bound train—not the scheduled special train from Harrisburg, but the regular eleven o'clock from Philadelphia. Anxious to prevent anyone from alerting Baltimore to the change in plans, Pinkerton arranged for all telegraph traffic between Harrisburg and Baltimore to be intercepted and delivered to him before it was passed on.

Pinkerton may have formulated one more piece of deception. Lincoln finished an early dinner in the dining room of a Harrisburg hotel and then changed out of his dinner clothes and into a traveling suit. According to the *New York Times'* Joseph Howard Jr. (whose reporting a number of recent historians have questioned), Lincoln, following Pinkerton's instructions, carried a shawl upon one arm, as if he were an invalid, and had a soft felt "Scotch cap" tucked into his coat pocket. The train arrived in Philadelphia shortly after ten, and Pinkerton escorted him by coach to another depot. Kate Warne was waiting for him there, having hired the entire rear half of a Baltimore-bound sleeping car to accommodate "her invalid brother." She greeted the president-elect boisterously as her brother and then helped him into the sleeping car.

## Whistling Dixie

Lincoln's inaugural journey had been intended as a celebration of the continuity of government, every stop in each city a public event. Following Pinkerton's advice, however, the itinerary had been abridged; instead of steaming into the Baltimore sunshine to the sound of brass bands, the president-elect slipped into the Calvert Street Station at 3:30 a.m. He did not even descend from his sleeping car. Uncoupled from the locomotive, it was drawn by horses over the streetcar tracks to the Camden Street Station. Here, for the first time, Pinkerton's carefully laid plans stumbled as the Washington train was delayed. Gathered in the stationary sleeper, everyone was on edge, except for the president-elect, who lay at ease in his berth, quietly swapping jokes.

Despite the ungodly hour, there was already a hum of activity in and around the depot—or rather a whistling. The tunes were varied,

# "WE NEVER SLEEP"

Allan J. Pinkerton, the original "private eye"—that ubiquitous icon of American popular literature, film, and television—was born in Glasgow, Scotland, in 1819, grew up poor, made a meager living as a cooper (barrel maker), and then emigrated to the United States in 1842 when he was twenty-three. Settling on the banks of the Fox River near Chicago, he was cutting barrel wood on an island in the river when he stumbled upon the hideout of a band of counterfeiters.

Perhaps bored with barrel making, Pinkerton organized a group of fellow citizens for a raid on the malefactors; instantly made a name for himself; and was soon being hired for various odd jobs of detection, such as rounding up local horse thieves. His rapidly growing reputation earned him in 1849 an appointment as the first detective hired by the Chicago Police Department, and in the 1850s, he went private, partnering with a Chicago attorney to found the North-Western Police Agency, which became the Pinkerton National Detective Agency. The firm's trademark was a single wide-open eye above the legend, *We never sleep*.

The Pinkerton firm did do its share of gumshoe work—and it did develop the classic private-eye techniques of "shadowing" (stealthy surveillance) and undercover infiltration—but it was mainly a private security force serving the nation's expanding railroads. Although the detective's work protecting Lincoln during his inaugural train journey was efficient and successful, his subsequent service during the Civil War as a spymaster yielded more

*During the early part of the Civil War, Allan J. Pinkerton (left) served as the unofficial head of an unofficial "secret service," responsible for some aspects of presidential security and for some aspects of military intelligence. Major General John A. McClernand is on the right, and President Lincoln, of course, is in the middle. The photograph was taken during Lincoln's visit to Antietam, Maryland, a few weeks after the fateful battle there.*

bad intelligence than useful information. After the war, Pinkerton's men typically served as private police—often barely a step up from strong-arm thugs—protecting railroads from robbery and brutally breaking labor strikes at the behest of American heavy industry.

but the most insistent among them was "Dixie." A minstrel show ditty composed in 1859 by the popular song and dance man Daniel Decatur Emmett, an Ohioan by birth and upbringing, it was embraced throughout the South, which adopted it as its unofficial anthem. Lincoln recognized the tune. It was one he particularly liked. "No doubt," he remarked drily to those seated by his berth, "there will be a great time in Dixie by and by."

> "In Dixie Land I'll took [sic] my stand,
> To lib an' die in Dixie!"

*Daniel Decatur Emmett, "Dixie," composed April 1859*

## Washington City

Two hours behind schedule, the Washington-bound train arrived, and the inaugural party rolled into the capital shortly after six. According to reporter Howard, Lincoln wrapped his shoulders in the shawl he had been given, placed the cap on his head, and descended to the platform and was hurriedly bundled into a carriage, which deposited him at the Willard Hotel, on Fourteenth and E streets. This would be his family's home until Inauguration Day.

For his part, Allan Pinkerton was relieved to have delivered the president safely to the capital, and he was pleased that nobody had recognized the tall, gangly figure. Again, Howard reported that the president-elect was disguised in shawl and cap, but there are no other eyewitness accounts confirming this, and many historians now believe that the "news" story was the reporter's fabrication. Fact or fiction, the story prompted detractors to spread the word that Abe Lincoln—the mighty "Rail Splitter," the vaunted "Savior of the Union"—had sneaked into the nation's capital cloaked in the get-up of an ailing grandma. The hotel in which he lodged was always busy, but just now it was even busier than usual, hosting what had been billed as a "Peace Convention" sponsored by the state of Virginia and commencing on February 4. Attended by representatives from twenty-one states, including the Southern states that had not yet seceded, it was well intentioned but had a feeble, geriatric air about it. Most of the 131 delegates in attendance were well past their prime, and the chairman, former president John Tyler, showed every one of his seventy-one years. Nevertheless, the convention managed to churn out a small package of proposals, which were duly delivered to Congress on March 1, and which Congress duly ignored. On the very next day, Crittenden's Compromise, lacking support from both the outgoing and incoming chief executives, failed to emerge from the Senate.

It was the last legislative attempt to head off a war, and the very next piece of legislation Congress enacted seemed deliberately designed to provoke one.

On March 2, just two days before the inauguration, the Morrill Tariff Act, brainchild of Vermont representative Justin S. Morrill, one of the founders of the Republican Party, was passed. Like the Tariff of Abominations (Chapter 2) that had precipitated the Nullification Crisis nearly three decades earlier, the Morrill Tariff sought to protect and promote domestic manufactures by levying exorbitant duties on certain imported goods. The Morrill duties were much heavier than those of the tariff that had nearly brought civil war under President Jackson, and the South, feeling grievously injured by the North, now counted itself even more insulted.

> "A Union that can only be maintained by swords and bayonets, and in which strife and civil war are to take the place of brotherly love and kindness, has no charm for me."
>
> *Robert E. Lee, letter to his son, January 23, 1861*

## THE ESSENCE OF ANARCHY

AS HAD BECOME THE CORDIAL CUSTOM in American executive politics, President James Buchanan rode up to the Willard Hotel on the morning of March 4, 1861, to escort the president-elect to his inauguration. The two men rode to the Capitol ceremony seated side by side in a carriage open to the chill air of a lingering winter. Buchanan turned to his companion. "If you are as happy, my dear sir, on entering the house [the Executive Mansion] as I am in leaving it and returning home," he said, "you are the happiest man in this country."

The few surviving daguerreotypes of the inauguration on the Capitol's east portico are both elegiac and foreboding. The Capitol, still under construction in 1861, looms unfinished behind the dignitaries assembled on the inaugural rostrum. As yet domeless, the building presides over the scene like a decapitated titan. Among those awaiting the completion of the dome and visible in at least one photograph is an allegorical sculpture of *Freedom* intended to grace the summit of the Capitol. A bronze maiden arrayed in ancient Roman drapery, laurel wreath in one hand, sword in the other, she lies in the grass before the headless building, stiff in her prostration.

THE INAUGURAL PROCESSION AT WASHINGTON PASSING THE GATE OF THE CAPITOL GROUNDS.—From a Sketch by our Special Artist.—[See Page 181.]

*President Buchanan accompanies President-elect Lincoln to the Capitol for the inauguration. "If you are as happy, my dear sir, on entering the house [the Executive Mansion] as I am in leaving it and returning home," he remarked to Lincoln, "you are the happiest man in this country."*

The president-elect mounted the rostrum and spoke his first substantive political words since his election.

"I have no purpose, directly or indirectly, to interfere with the institution of slavery in the states where it exists. I believe I have no lawful right to do so." They were words that doubtless disappointed the Northern abolitionists, but that were meant to be heard deep into the South. Had he stopped here, he could have been James Buchanan speaking on the issue of slavery. But he did not stop. He offered next the straightforward logical proposition that "no government proper ever had a provision in its organic law for its own termination. . . . No state upon its own mere motion can lawfully get out of the Union," and he announced his intention to use the "power confided in me . . . to hold, occupy and possess the property and places belonging to the government, and to collect the duties and imposts"—that is, to resist secession and any other defiance of federal authority.

What Lincoln went on to say was so different in spirit and content from what Buchanan had offered four years earlier that the two men might have been of different species rather than merely of different political parties. Lincoln asked, "Shall fugitives from labor be surrendered by national or State authority?" He answered, "The Constitution does not expressly say." He asked, "Must Congress protect slavery in the Territories?" He answered, "The Constitution does not expressly say." And thus he laid before his fellow citizens the terrible dilemma that was neither Northern nor Southern but common to the country. "From questions of this class spring all our constitutional controversies, and we divide upon them into majorities and minorities. If the minority will not acquiesce, the majority must, or the government must cease. There is no other alternative; for continuing the government is acquiescence of one side or the other." Anticipating the answer of the South—secession—he continued: "If a minority in such case will secede rather than acquiesce, they make a precedent which in turn will divide and ruin them; for a minority of their own will secede from them whenever a majority refuses to be controlled by such a minority. . . . Plainly, the central idea of secession is the essence of anarchy."

As Lincoln saw it, a "majority held in restraint by constitutional checks and limitations, and always changing easily with deliberate changes of popular opinions and sentiments" was, for a "free people," the only alternative to anarchy. To reject it was to "fly to anarchy or to despotism." As for "unanimity," it was too much to hope for in government, the president-elect explained. It was "impossible." Yet to assert "the rule of a minority, as a permanent arrangement, is wholly inadmissible," so that "rejecting the majority principle, anarchy or despotism in some form is all that is left."

The logic of Lincoln's position was airtight and self-evident. It did not lead him to offer a threat, but only to carry the logic to its logical conclusion: "In your hands, my dissatisfied fellow countrymen, and not in mine, is the momentous issue of civil war. The government will not assail you. You can have no conflict without being yourselves the aggressors. You have no oath registered in heaven to destroy the government, while I shall have the most solemn one to 'preserve, protect and defend it.'"

Logically, it was the perfect peroration on which to conclude his inaugural address in this time of crisis and dissolution. But Abraham Lincoln knew that humanity does not decide, does not act, does not live by logic alone. "I am loath to close," he continued, and then he closed on a note of lyric emotion that still leaves one breathless in the reading of it:

> We are not enemies, but friends. We must not be enemies. Though passion may have strained, it must not break our bonds of affection. The mystic chords of memory, stretching from every battlefield and patriot grave to every living heart and hearthstone all over this broad land, will yet swell the chorus of the Union when again touched, as surely they will be, by the better angels of our nature.

Abraham Lincoln fell silent, turned to face the wizened form of Chief Justice Roger Taney, in whose palsied grasp the proffered Bible trembled. The president-elect laid his strong palm upon its cover, raised his other long-fingered hand, and spoke the constitutional oath.

**TAKEAWAY**

The failure of the Whig Party to take a strong stand against slavery led to its collapse and the subsequent rise of the Republican Party, which found in Abraham Lincoln a principled moderate alternative to either the perpetuation of slavery or the "fanatical" abolition of slavery. By the time of his election, however, after years of drift culminating in the feeble administration of President James Buchanan, the South was beyond compromise, and the nation hurtled toward the Civil War.

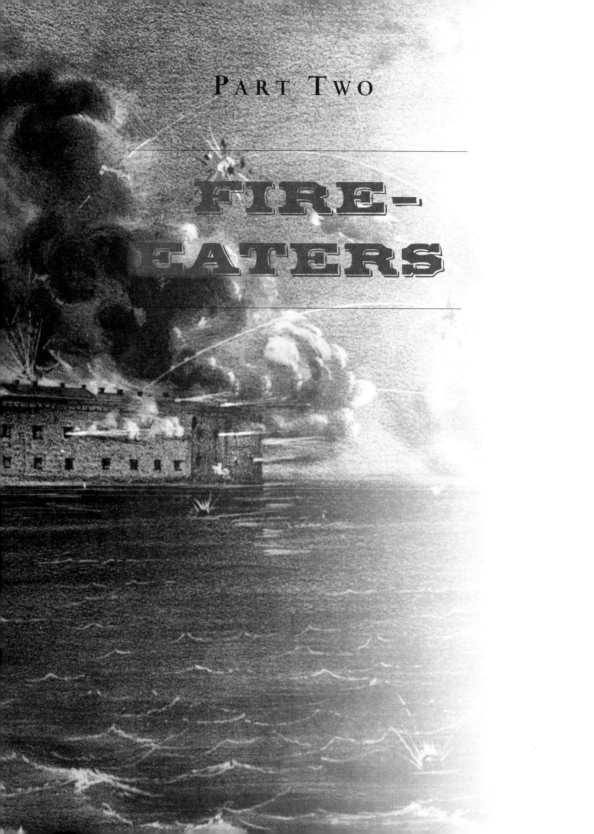

# PART TWO

# FIRE-EATERS

# CHAPTER 4

## "STRIKE A BLOW!"

### *Sumter Falls, Battle Rises*

 Y THE TIME ABRAHAM LINCOLN WAS INAUGURATED AS THE SIXTEENTH president of the United States on March 4, 1861, Jefferson Davis had already served as president of the Confederate States of America for two weeks. He was sworn in on February 18 after the delegates to the Confederate consti-tutional convention in Montgomery, Alabama, unanimously elected him on February 9, the day after they adopted a provisional constitution. While the Washington government drifted, that of the Confederacy willed itself into existence with headlong speed.

*Jefferson Davis was inaugurated as the first president of the Confederate States of America on the steps of the Alabama State Capitol in Montgomery on February 18, 1861.*

# The Executives

The two presidents were sons of the same "border state," Kentucky, a slave state culturally more Southern than Northern, but one that remained loyal to the Union, albeit a self-proclaimed neutral in the emerging war. Had Lincoln remained a Kentuckian, he might well have become a Confederate, and had Davis also lived more of his life in that state, he might have become a Union man. Who can tell? Like the other border states, Kentucky was populated by people whose sympathies were strong for one side or the other, as well as by those who felt little allegiance to either.

But Lincoln's family moved north when he was a child, first to Indiana and then to Illinois. One thing never changed, however: Thomas Lincoln, the boy's father, remained an impecunious, hardscrabble backwoodsman. Davis was also born in a log cabin, but when the boy was only two years old, his father resettled the family in Woodville, Mississippi, on a three-hundred-acre plantation he called Rosemont, and Jefferson Davis grew up in the simple elegance of the Federal-style home that still stands where it was built in 1810. The plantation—slaves and all, naturally—made Davis's father a man of substance. He sent his son at age seven to a Dominican boys' school back in Kentucky and then enrolled him, at thirteen, in Transylvania College, Lexington. From there, Jefferson Davis went to West Point, graduating with the class of 1828.

Davis resigned his commission in 1835 to become a planter near Vicksburg, Mississippi. His beautiful young bride, Sarah Knox Taylor, was the daughter of his former commanding officer, the future president Zachary Taylor. Scarcely three months after the newlyweds moved into their new plantation house, Sarah was stricken with malaria and died. The light of his life extinguished, Jefferson Davis withdrew into the daily running of the plantation, managing it personally and enlarging it by adding land as well as more slaves. After work, in the long, lonely evenings, he immersed himself in the study of general and constitutional law leavened with a dose of abstruse philosophy. His

*This handsome portrait of Jefferson Davis was made shortly before the Civil War, probably between 1858 and 1860, when he was a U.S. senator from Mississippi.*

*This rare photograph of Thomas Lincoln (1778–1851), the president's father, was presumably made very near the end of his life.*

**Previous Spread:**
*The nation's premier producer of lithographs, Currier & Ives, most likely published "Bombardment of Fort Sumter, Charleston Harbor, 12th & 13th of April, 1861" soon after the event.*

Like Lincoln, Jefferson Davis was born in a log cabin, but his father soon made good, and young Davis grew up in the handsome plantation house, in Woodville, Mississippi, pictured here.

"Slave Quarters of Jefferson Davis Plantation": "Brierfield," Jefferson's home, was located near Vicksburg, Mississippi. As with so many other prosperous Southerners, slave-holding was a way of life for the future Confederate president. Taken shortly after the Civil War, the photograph was (according to its inscription) "Sent home by Elizabeth Findley Missionary to the freedmen."

life of isolation ended in 1845 when he was elected to the U.S. House of Representatives and remarried. A year later, the outbreak of the U.S.-Mexican War prompted him to resign his seat and enroll as colonel of the 1st Mississippi Regiment of Volunteers, which put him once again under the command of Zachary Taylor.

In a speech on the floor of Congress, July 27, 1848, Lincoln poked fun at his own brief military career. "By the way, Mr. Speaker, did you know I am a military hero?" he asked rhetorically. "Yes, sir; in the days of the Black Hawk war I fought, bled, and came away. . . . I had a good many bloody struggles with the mosquitoes, and although I never fainted from the loss of blood, I can truly say I was often very hungry." Davis, however, really was a military hero. In the battle of Buena Vista (February 22–23, 1847), he led his Mississippians in what was described as an "inspired V-formation" attack against a vastly superior Mexican force commanded under no less than General Antonio López de Santa Anna. This remarkable action helped turn a probable U.S. defeat into a magnificent victory. The deed cost Davis dearly, however. He was so severely wounded in the foot that he had to be invalided out of the war and hobbled for painful months on crutches. Still, he was hailed as the hero of Buena Vista, and, never one to admit the affliction of humility, he spent his convalescence accustoming himself to the conviction that he was not just a hero, but a military genius.

Davis rode his war record to a new political career. In August 1847, Mississippi's governor appointed him to serve out the remainder of the Senate term of Jesse Speight, who had died in office, and his fellow senators made him chairman of the Committee on Military Affairs. With the expiration of Speight's term, Davis was elected to the same seat, but resigned within a year to make a run for governor of Mississippi as an opponent of the Compromise of 1850. Defeated by fewer than a thousand votes, he plunged into the cause of states' rights and became a vigorous campaigner on behalf of Democratic presidential candidate Franklin Pierce, who, after winning the election, named him secretary of war. Feeling that he now had an ample and appropriate field for the exercise of his military genius, Davis delivered to Congress unprecedented and extraordinarily detailed reports urging the reform of the U.S. military, and he also championed western exploration and survey for the purpose of determining the best route for a transcontinental railroad.

With the end of the Pierce presidency, so ended Davis's tenure as secretary of war. He ran for the Senate, which he reentered in 1857, but a debilitating affliction of the left eye nearly resulted in its loss and kept him out of much of the turbulent Senate debate of the period. He made it clear, however, that, while loyal to his state and region, he was no secessionist, and in 1858, he delivered two memorable antisecession speeches before returning to active service in the Senate: one near Boston on July 4, 1858, and another in that city's Faneuil Hall on October 11.

*Whereas Abraham Lincoln's antebellum military experience was limited to a brief stint as an Illinois militia captain, Jefferson Davis was a West Point–educated officer who performed heroically at the battle of Buena Vista (February 22–23, 1847) in the U.S.-Mexican War, 1846–48. He went on to serve as secretary of war under President Franklin Pierce from 1853 to 1857.*

# CAPTAIN ABE LINCOLN

Abraham Lincoln never laid claim to military heroism, and his military experience was typical of many men of his era, especially in the frontier region. He had been a short-term militia volunteer. In July 1831, he was working at New Salem for a failing business and decided to join the fight against the "rebellious" Sauk and Fox chief Black Hawk, not so much out of a sense of duty perhaps, but to see a little more of the world and to earn some money.

He was well acquainted with most of the other local volunteers, who assembled at the farm of Dallis (or Dallas) Scott on April 21, 1832, to be sworn into service. Presumably, Lincoln's charisma and perceived leadership ability moved the other militiamen to elect him as their captain; however, in the 1870s, amateur historian J. F. Snyder (who later became president of the Illinois State Historical Society) interviewed a number of men who had served in Lincoln's militia company and reported that the interviewees "never spoke of malice of Lincoln but always in a spirit of ridicule."

*Captain Lincoln–1832, a sculpture by Leonard Crunelle, was unveiled in Dixon, Illinois, on September 24, 1930. Lincoln, who wryly pointed out that the only blood he spilled during his militia service in the Black Hawk War was lost to mosquitoes, would doubtless have enjoyed a characteristically self-deprecating laugh at that unveiling.*

They characterized him as "indolent and vulgar . . . a joke, an absurdity, and had serious doubts about his courage. Any old woman, they said, would have made a more credible commander than he did."

Lincoln himself was proud of having been elected captain, as he made clear in a letter of December 20, 1859, to his friend J. W. Fell:

I was raised to farm work, which I continued till I was twenty-two. At twenty-one I came to Illinois, Macon County. Then I got to New Salem, at that time in Sangamon, now in Menard County, where I remained a year as a sort of clerk in a store.

Then came the Black Hawk War; and I was elected a captain of volunteers, a success which gave me more pleasure than any I have had since.

Despite the meager extent of his military experience, Lincoln would prove to be a quick study during the Civil War, with a keen grasp of strategy and logistics that earned him the respect of most of the army's commanders.

Much as Lincoln's views on slavery and its abolition were complex—Lincoln personally hated slavery but believed the Constitution bound the government to protect it—so Davis's views on secession were circumscribed by his understanding of practical reality. He was a believer and champion of states' rights, who held that each state was sovereign and that the United States was a "confederation" of the sovereign states rather than a union under a sovereign nation. Yet he was convinced that the North would never allow the Southern states to secede peacefully, and that put the South, which lacked an army, a navy, and the resources to build both, in a very weak position. If the North wanted war, he was sure the South would lose. So he counseled compromise and reconciliation, and he continued to do so even after the election of Abraham Lincoln in November 1860 and the secession of South Carolina the next month. Still, he was convinced that the election of Lincoln meant just one thing. The "Northern" government would use every means of coercion at its command to force the Southern states into renouncing slavery, and that, in short order, would mean the end of the Southern economy and the Southern way of life.

## "I Am Sure I Feel No Hostility to You"

On January 21, 1861, less than two weeks after Mississippi's secession, Jefferson Davis gave his farewell speech to the Senate, explaining that, in leaving the Union, he and his fellow Mississippians

recur to the principles upon which our Government was founded; and when you deny them, and when you deny to us the right to withdraw from a Government which thus perverted threatens to be destructive of our rights, we but tread in the path of our fathers when we proclaim our independence, and take the hazard. This is done not in hostility to others, not to injure any section of the country, not even for our own pecuniary benefit; but from the high and solemn motive of defending and protecting the rights we inherited, and which it is our sacred duty to transmit unshorn to our children. . . . I am sure I feel no hostility to you, Senators from the North. I am sure there is not one of you, whatever sharp discussion there may have been between us, to whom

# WHAT'S IN A NAME?

The name of the purported nation created by the Southern states, the *Confederate States of America*, was a reflection of the political theory that drove the secession. Most Northerners believed that the *United* States was a national union of states that enjoyed considerable autonomy in internal and local matters but that were collectively subordinate to the central federal government.

In effect, the American people were citizens of the United States and, secondarily, of their home state. In the South, John C. Calhoun and others promoted the political theory of states' rights, arguing that the states were "confederated" not so much as a single nation but as an *alliance* of states. Central authority was highly circumscribed, much as it had been when the United States was loosely governed under the Articles of Confederation (1781–1788), and each state was significantly autonomous. In a confederation, people were primarily citizens of their home state and only secondarily citizens of their nation. Indeed, this attitude was pervasive in the South—Robert E. Lee, when he resigned his U.S. Army commission to join the Confederate forces, was typical in referring to Virginia as "his country"—and certainly familiar, if less compelling, in the North. Only after the Civil War did it become thoroughly customary to identify oneself as "an American" rather than as "a Virginian," "an Ohioan," and so on.

> I cannot now say, in the presence of my God, I wish you well; and such, I am sure, is the feeling of the people whom I represent towards those whom you represent. I therefore feel that I but express their desire when I say I hope, and they hope, for peaceful relations with you, though we must part.

Commissioned by the state of Mississippi to lead its army, Davis was almost immediately tapped by the Confederate convention in Montgomery, Alabama, to serve as provisional president of the Confederacy itself. He accepted, but even then continued to push for peace. Not long after he was inaugurated, he dispatched a "peace commission" to Washington, D.C. President Lincoln believed that granting the commission an official audience would be tantamount to recognizing the Confederacy's claim to sovereign legitimacy. He therefore turned the commissioners away without hearing their proposals. Thus, early in April, when President Lincoln did what President Buchanan had refused to do—send armed naval vessels to reinforce and resupply Fort Sumter—Jefferson Davis reluctantly ordered bombardment of the fort and thus the commencement of war.

Davis, of course, knew that the South was hardly prepared to fight a major war, a long war, against the North. In April 1861, the North commanded a regular army of just over 16,000 men—but it was 16,000 more men than the Army of the Confederate States of America had. In fact, although that army was established by the Confederate Provisional Congress on March 6, 1861, it never came into much more than a paper existence. The Confederacy actually fought with volunteers of the Provisional Army of the Confederate States of America, which had been established by acts of February 28 and March 6. When more men were needed, the Confederate Provisional Congress passed a conscription act on April 16, 1862, fully a year before the Union began drafting men into service. To preserve the fiction of states' rights, however, the Confederate conscripts were drafted through the individual states rather than directly by Confederate authority—yet it was the central government that imposed quotas on the states. As for a navy, the Union had one, and Confederacy did not—though defections would soon give it the nucleus of a navy. At the outbreak of the war, the South did have the services of 313 of the most experienced officers of the U.S. Army, who resigned their commissions to fight not for the Confederacy, but in (as they saw it) the defense of their home states.

## NUMBERS
### Anchors Aweigh

In 1861, the U.S. Navy consisted of 1,457 officers and 7,600 men who were widely broadcast in "stations" all over the world. Some ninety vessels were listed on the navy's rolls, but fewer than half this number were in a seaworthy condition. At the start of the war, 16 captains, 34 commanders, 76 lieutenants, and 111 regular and acting midshipmen defected to the Confederate service. The Gosport Navy Yard, in Virginia, was evacuated on April 20–21, 1861, thereby delivering eleven warships and some three thousand items of ordnance to the South.

*Fearing that Confederate forces were about to seize the Gosport Navy Yard in Norfolk, Virginia, commandant Charles S. McCauley ordered it burned on the night of April 20, 1861, along with the ships in it, including the USS Pennsylvania, a 140-gun ship-of-the-line.*

*The opposing armies of the Civil War are often called "the Blue and the Gray," but the fact is that individual regiments on both sides wore a variety of uniforms in a range of colors, some Union troops clad in gray and some Confederates—like these members of the Flying Artillery, a South Carolina militia organization in the spring of 1861—wearing blue uniforms virtually indistinguishable from the standard federal issue of the U.S. Army.*

President Davis was confident that many Southerners would rally to the brand-new flag, but he believed that only by winning a number of quick victories, preferably close to Washington, would the Confederacy have a chance of so demoralizing the North that it would lose its will to fight, which did not seem very strong in the first place. Davis was well aware that many Northerners agreed with *New York Tribune* publisher Horace Greeley, who, in an editorial, advised President Lincoln to release the Southern states—to "let the erring sisters go." If Davis put up a sharp fight in a short time, Lincoln might have no choice but to take the newspaperman's advice.

> ### "Say to the seceded States, 'Wayward sisters, depart in peace!'"
>
> *Winfield Scott, U.S. Army general in chief, to incoming secretary of state, William H. Seward, March 3, 1861*

If the war lasted any considerable length of time, the prospects for the Confederacy were grim. As William T. Sherman had pointed out to his Louisiana dinner guest, the North had most of the nation's population, heavy industry, and money, and it commanded virtually all of the nation's international credit. Demographically and mathematically, the Southern cause was a lost cause—provided that the North fought on.

## PUPIL AND TEACHER

IT SAYS MUCH ABOUT THE LOW PLACE military matters occupied in the American agenda throughout most of the first half of the nineteenth century that the building of Fort Sumter, on an artificial island of New England granite transported to Charleston Harbor, began in 1829 and was still far from finished on the day after Christmas 1860. That was the day that Major Robert Anderson and his garrison of two U.S. Army artillery batteries—sixty-eight soldiers, nine officers, and eight bandsmen, along with a handful of civilian workers—moved into it from nearby Fort Moultrie. South Carolina had seceded six days earlier and quickly occupied or confiscated all federal property, especially forts and arms. President Buchanan indignantly refused to order the surrender of Fort Sumter, but he did little enough to give Major Anderson any means of holding the fort. Thus the installation lay effectively under rebel siege through the balance of Buchanan's term and the first several weeks of Lincoln's. At last, on April 11, 1861, P. G. T. Beauregard, in command of the artillery forces as yet silently arrayed against Fort Sumter, put Colonel James Chesnut, a prominent South Carolina politician, and another man in a rowboat and sent them into Charleston Harbor under a flag of truce. Beauregard looked every inch the Southern officer, to modern eyes a Confederate fresh out of a Hollywood casting office: prominent arched eyebrows, a generous mustache just verging on handlebars, and a hint of beard sharply trimmed in the "imperial fashion" popular with military men who emulated the example of France's Napoleon III. He would have been easy to dismiss as a martial peacock, but Beauregard was in fact a fine military engineer and a highly competent artillerist. His instructor in the latter science had been his West Point mentor: Major Robert Anderson.

Beauregard deployed his guns in batteries at Morris, James, and Sullivan's Islands, Mount Pleasant, and Forts Moultrie and Johnson.

*Battlefront artist Alfred R. Waud sketched "Negroes mounting Cannon in the works for the attack on Ft. Sumter 1861—Morris Island." Presumably, the "Negroes" doing the heavy lifting were all slaves laboring to defend the way of life that kept them enslaved.*

# FIGHTING MEN

The great myth of the Civil War fighting man is that he was, more often than not, a rugged frontiersmen, a cowboy, and a maverick, resistant to discipline but eager for a fight and highly capable of fighting. But in both armies, the reality was far different. The forces reflected the make-up of the general population.

On both sides, the typical soldier was an unmarried, white, Protestant farmer, laborer, factory worker, or clerk aged eighteen to twenty-nine. (There were exceptions: one Curtis King enlisted in the 37th Iowa at age eighty, whereas Edward Black joined as a drummer boy in the 21st Indiana Regiment at age nine.) Most troops on both sides were native born, though one out of four Northern soldiers was a first- or second-generation immigrant, usually German or Irish. Three brigades of Cherokees, Choctaws, Chickasaws, and Seminoles fought for the Confederacy, while one brigade of Creeks enlisted in the Union army. By the end of the war, 10 percent of the U.S. Army was African-American, and every black soldier was a volunteer. Hard up for manpower, the Confederate Congress proposed creating the Confederate States Colored Troops and set a goal of inducting 300,000 "negroes." The war ended before this came to pass.

Before they became soldiers, most of the men of both armies had lived in houses and tenements, slept on beds with mattresses—some stuffed with straw or corncobs, but most with feathers—and bought rather than killed the food they put on their tables. Few had ever handled firearms, and while they were drilled and marched when they mustered in, they did very little shooting, what with the high cost of lead and powder. Not surprisingly, therefore, they performed abysmally on the field of battle. That so many soldiers were killed in the war was not the result of good marksmanship but of so many soldiers pulling so many triggers so many times.

*Civil War photographs of African Americans, especially African American soldiers, are rare. William Morris Smith made this one, c. 1863, depicting twenty-seven members of Company E, 4th U.S. Colored Infantry, at Fort Lincoln, Washington, D.C.*

All drew a bead against Fort Sumter. The men in the rowboat bore Beauregard's personal note to Anderson, calling for (demanding is too strong a word) his surrender and promising that all "proper facilities will be afforded for the removal of yourself and command, together with company arms and property, and all private property, to any post in the United States which you may elect. The flag which you have upheld so long and with so much fortitude, under the most trying circumstances, may be saluted by you on taking it down."

As regards chivalry, Robert Anderson would have expected no less from the dashing Louisianan he had first encountered at the military academy. In fact, Anderson admired the South and Southerners: He was born in the border state of Kentucky and married a woman from a fine Georgia family. But while he sympathized with the South, his duty, as he saw it, lay with the North, and he asked for the messengers' indulgence as he composed a reply to his former pupil. He explained that the demand was one "with which I regret that my sense of honor, and of my obligations to my government, prevent my compliance." As he handed over the reply, he confided to the envoys: "Gentlemen, if you do not batter the fort to pieces about us, we shall be starved out in a few days"—a far cry from John Paul Jones's defiant, "I have not yet begun to fight."

*Major Robert Anderson, U.S. Army, had the dubious honor of defending Fort Sumter against Confederate cannon. Years earlier, at West Point, he had instructed P. G. T. Beauregard in the art and science of artillery.*

Just before one o'clock on the morning of April 12, 1861, Chesnut, with three other men, again rowed to the fort to advise Major Anderson that General Beauregard would hold his fire on condition that Anderson provide a firm date and time for his withdrawal from Fort Sumter. Anderson retired for what he said was a conference with his officers and did not reemerge until 3:10 a.m. He handed Chesnut his reply. He would evacuate by April 15—unless he received orders to the contrary from "my government." Chesnut, on whom Beauregard had conferred plenipotentiary authority, told

*Pierre Gustave Toutant Beauregard, Confederate commander of the assault on Fort Sumter, was every inch the Southern military officer.*

Anderson that his conditions were unacceptable. On the spot, Chesnut scrawled a declaration warning Anderson that the bombardment of Fort Sumter would commence in one hour. With this, he rowed away. Anderson and his men prepared to be blown to bits.

## Opening Shots

As Beauregard was punctilious about the terms offered Major Anderson, so he was acutely conscious of protocol when he ordered the firing of the first shot of the Civil War. That honor was offered to Roger Pryor, one of the South's "fire eaters," as the most ardent secessionists were called. Having resigned from Congress on March 3, 1861, to join the Confederate colors, he called on South Carolinians to "Strike a blow!" against Fort Sumter. Now, however, he turned away Beauregard's offer, pleading that he "could not fire the first gun of the war."

It was 4:30 on the morning of April 12, 1861, and by the terms Chesnut had handed Major Anderson, the time had come for *someone* to commence firing. According to traditional accounts, General Beauregard offered the lanyard to Edmund Ruffin, the sixty-seven-year-old editor of a backwoods Virginia newspaper and one of the most strident defenders of slavery and the Southern way of life. His white hair worn long and wild in the frontier manner, his

*A Currier & Ives depiction of the interior of Fort Sumter during the assault. The popular printmaker barely hints at the chaotic terror the defenders endured during the two-day bombardment.*

## EYEWITNESS

William Howard Russell, correspondent for the *Times* of London, reported on the atmosphere in Charleston on April 12, 1861:

*The streets of Charleston present some such aspect as those of Paris in the last revolution [of 1848]. Crowds of armed men singing and promenading the streets. The battle blood running through their veins—that hot oxygen which is called 'the flush of victory' on the cheek; restaurants full, reveling in bar rooms, club-rooms crowded, orgies and carousings in tavern or private house.... Sumter has set them distraught; never was such a victory.... It is a bloodless Waterloo.*

eyes wide and fiery, Ruffin, it is said, entertained none of Pryor's scruples and eagerly let his cannon speak. The only problem with this account is that the source, Edmund Ruffin himself, made it all up. It is now universally agreed that a Lieutenant Henry Farley, commanding a two-mortar battery on James Island, fired precisely at 4:30. This was the first shot of the war.

It was a very long day, during which the bombardment was unceasing and continued all that Friday and into Saturday, April 13, when Major Anderson, having decided that enduring a two-day bombardment without hope of reinforcement or relief was sufficient to satisfy both duty and honor, lowered the Stars and Stripes. At this, the Confederate guns fell silent. Fort Sumter had taken hits from some four thousand rounds—which, astoundingly, had failed to hurt a single soldier of the garrison.

## CAPITAL OF FEAR

As WILLIAM TECUMSEH SHERMAN DISCOVERED when he called on the president (Chapter 1) before the attack on Fort Sumter, Washington was garrisoned by a few regular army troops—mostly military clerks rather than combat soldiers—and by the marines headquartered at the USMC barracks on Eighth and "Eye" Streets. A small number of volunteer

*The Civil War pitted "brother against brother"—sometimes literally. Two sons of John J. Crittenden fought in the war that the Kentucky senator had hoped to avert with the ill-fated compromise named after him. George Bibb Crittenden (left) was a Confederate major general, while his brother, Thomas L. Crittenden (right), held the same rank in the Union army.*

**POP CULTURE**

### "Brother against Brother"

The phrase "brother against brother" quickly became—and remains—a convenient label for the nature of the Civil War. Of course, most of the combatants were unrelated, but there were notable instances of actual brothers who found themselves on opposite sides, as was the case with Senator John J. Crittenden's sons, George B. and Thomas Leonidas Crittenden, both brigadier generals, the former for the Confederacy, the latter for the Union. Perhaps even more meaningful were the many instances of brothers in arms—including many veterans of the U.S.-Mexican War—who found themselves transformed into enemies, as was the case with Grant and Lee as well as with Anderson and Beauregard.

militia units were also available around town. They functioned more as social clubs than as effective military organizations. The only action the grandly named Potomac Light Infantry took when its members mustered in April was to vote to disband "until peace was restored." After this vote, the now-former militiamen retreated to a local saloon, where one of their number proposed a toast: "The P.L.I., invincible in peace, invisible in war!"

Whereas the Potomac Light Infantry decamped, other citizen militias rushed themselves into creation, among them the Silver Grays' Home Guard, which consisted entirely of veterans of the War of 1812. If that seemed desperate, it is well to bear in mind that the U.S. Army's highest-ranking commander, its general-in-chief, was Winfield Scott, a hero of the War of 1812 and the most daring and successful commander in the U.S.-Mexican War. He was now a grandiosely rotund figure of seventy-five and so fond of ornate uniforms that he was universally known as "Old Fuss and Feathers."

After Fort Sumter fell, President Lincoln called in two military units to defend the capital, the New York 7th Militia, and the 6th Massachusetts Regiment. As the Massachusetts troops changed trains in Baltimore, marching from one station to another, their ranks were swarmed by an angry mob armed with bricks and stones. These missiles proved deadly enough, and

*From the ship that carried him and his command back to the North, Major Robert Anderson telegraphed Secretary of War Simon Cameron that, "having defended Fort Sumter for thirty-four hours until the quarters were entirely burned," he had "accepted terms of evacuation offered by General Beauregard" and marched out of the fort "with colors flying and drums beating."*

# FIRST CASUALTIES

The shooting stopped when the American flag was lowered. No one had been killed or even injured. But there *would* be casualties before the surrender of Fort Sumter was formalized.

The first was bizarre, the second tragic. The "fire eater" Roger Pryor, who demurred when it was time to fire the first shot of the war he had urged on his fellow Southerners, was among the very first to enter into what was left of Fort Sumter. General Beauregard had asked him to preside over the nitty-gritty of Anderson's surrender. While seated on a chair in Fort Sumter's empty infirmary, waiting for a clerk to write out a fair copy of the terms he had dictated, Pryor, whether parched from the exhilaration of victory or merely the effort the dictation had cost him, laid his hands on the closest bottle. He slammed the contents down his throat—and only afterward thought to read the label. Discovering that he had just poisoned himself with "Iodine of Potassium," he yelled for help, and the fort's surgeon promptly pumped his stomach, saving his life.

The next day, the ever proper Beauregard kept his word to Major Anderson, giving him permission to fire a fifty-gun salute to his fallen colors. In the process, a bright ember landed on a powder keg, igniting a blast that injured five and killed one, Union private Daniel Hough, the first soldier to die in the Civil War.

four bluecoats were killed. The Massachusetts men fired on their attackers, killing a dozen Baltimoreans and wounding more before resuming their journey to Washington.

When a self-righteous citizens' committee called on President Lincoln to protest what they deemed the "pollution" of Maryland soil by an invading army, Lincoln replied as calmly as he could: "Our men are not moles, and cannot dig under the earth. They are not birds, and cannot fly through the air. There is no way but to march across, and that they must do."

The president's words only enflamed the mob all the more. Riots broke out in Baltimore on April 20. Mobs tore up railroad tracks and blew up bridges, blocking most railroad and carriage traffic, and they seized the telegraph office. Washington, some forty miles to the south, was effectively cut off from the rest of the North. Those Washingtonians who did not flee on foot or by carriage hunkered down behind the boarded windows of their businesses and dwellings. The sight of workers swarming over the Treasury Building to install iron bars on every opening to the outside was hardly reassuring. The hot rumor was that the building was also being mined with explosive charges, just in case the rebels overran it. And a rebel invasion was expected any day.

Frank Leslie's Illustrated Newspaper *carried this wood engraving of Union troops of the 6th Massachusetts Regiment firing on Baltimore rioters who attempted to halt their march to the defense of Washington, D.C., on April 19, 1861. A slave-holding "border state," Maryland remained nominally loyal to the Union, but most of its citizens favored the Confederacy.*

"Avenge the patriotic gore
That flecked the streets of Baltimore,
And be the battle queen of yore,
Maryland! My Maryland!"

*James R. Randall, "Maryland, My Maryland!";
anthem composed in 1861 after Union troops fired
on a Baltimore crowd on April 20, 1861*

Lincoln ordered General Benjamin F. Butler to march into Baltimore in strength, occupy the city, and impose martial law. He ordered Butler to jail anyone he considered dangerous, and in perhaps the most controversial act of his presidency, Lincoln suspended habeas corpus, the constitutional protection from imprisonment without due process of law. Even some Republicans accused him of exercising a tyrant's power.

As for Butler, he had not been a Lincoln man. As a Massachusetts Democrat, he had championed the nomination of Jefferson Davis as his party's presidential candidate in 1860. Once the war broke out, however, he became an outspoken, even rabid Unionist, and he now sent his troops through the city to round up everyone who so much as looked angry. Butler's many arrests included nine members of the state legislature, Mayor George William Brown, and Baltimore's police chief.

Invasion by a Confederate army or a Confederate mob was not the only danger the capital faced. Allan J. Pinkerton, who had been hired to run a quasi-official intelligence service, spoke of a "secret enemy . . . conveying beyond the lines the coveted information of every movement made or contemplated." This enemy included "Men who formerly occupied places of dignity, power and trust" as well as "Aristocratic ladies, who had previously opened the doors of their luxurious residences to those high in office and who had hospitably entertained the dignitaries of the land."

Saboteurs abounded. Franklin Buchanan of Maryland resigned as commander of the Washington Navy Yard, he said, because his sympathies lay with the Confederacy, and although he ostentatiously implored his men to do their duty and remain loyal to the government they served, inspectors discovered that large numbers of bombshells built at the yard were filled not with explosive black powder, but sand and sawdust.

*Union major general Benjamin F. Butler enforced ruthless martial law on a rebellious Baltimore. His arrests included nine members of the Maryland legislature, the mayor of Baltimore, the city's police chief, and hordes of ordinary citizens.*

"You might as well attempt to put out the flames of a burning house with a squirt-gun. I think this is to be a long war—very long— much longer than any politician thinks."

*William Tecumseh Sherman,*
*after the fall of Fort Sumter, 1861*

*This contemporary political cartoon was published by acclaimed Civil War photographer Mathew Brady (it was sold as a carte de visite card in his New York or Washington gallery). The conflict is characterized as "A Family Quarrel" between the federal government (Uncle Sam) and the seceded states of the South (the woman shaking her fist). Taking advantage of the distracted disputants is a slave who merrily sneaks off to freedom.*

A FAMILY QUARREL.

## MEN OF DESTINY

IF LINCOLN AND ALL WASHINGTON seemed uncertain, even dazed at the outbreak of war, Jefferson Davis, presiding over a government that hardly yet existed and with an army just coming into being, looked by comparison strong and decisive. As a former military officer, Davis certainly knew how to give orders, but his commanding appearance and approach were not truly suited to the situation of the Confederacy. Lincoln had nailed it in his inaugural address: A government founded on the principle of dissolution of government invites its own dissolution.

Davis's task was exceedingly complicated because he was charged with carrying out a political paradox, a *revolution* intended to *preserve* the status quo. Rebellion is, by definition, change. What Davis was supposed to lead was a rebellion in resistance to change. As if this weren't a sufficiently daunting logical, administrative, and emotional conundrum, Davis's need to conjure up an instant government presented an even more Herculean task; for not only did the government need to come into existence immediately, it had to wield central authority sufficient to fight a war, yet to do so without coming into conflict with the doctrine at the core of the South's rebellion: states' rights. The very name of the new nation, *Confederate* States, was a denial of central authority—really a denial of nationhood itself.

# CONFEDERATE MATA HARI

Born Maria Rosatta O'Neale in Port Tobacco, Maryland, in 1813 or 1814, and orphaned young, the girl destined to become the most celebrated early spy for the Confederacy was raised by an aunt in Washington. She grew into a raven-haired beauty—they called her the "Wild Rose"—became intellectually and perhaps romantically involved with John C. Calhoun, and married Dr. Robert Greenhow, a U.S. State Department official, who frequently shared confidential documents with his intensely curious wife.

Dr. Greenhow died shortly before the Civil War broke out, and Rose began entertaining a succession of highly placed government officials, including President James Buchanan. Through at least some of these connections, she obtained secret information, which she passed on via couriers to General P. G. T. Beauregard. Her most important intelligence was a detailed summary of Union general Irvin McDowell's plans for the first battle of Bull Run on July 21, 1861, which was a humiliating defeat for the U.S. Army.

Outspoken in her pro-Southern views, Rose Greenhow was widely suspected of espionage and even christened the "Rebel Rose." After the Bull Run disaster, Allan J. Pinkerton, Washington's master of counterintelligence, placed her under surveillance (most of which consisted of his peeking through her windows) and arrested her on August 23, 1861. She and her eight-year-old daughter, "Little Rose," were consigned to Washington's Old Capitol Prison, but paroled on May 31, 1862, to Richmond, Virginia, on condition that she never return to the North. Jefferson Davis personally welcomed her homecoming and recruited her as a courier to Europe. She served as a liaison with Confederate sympathizers in France and England during 1863 and 1864 and was received by Napoleon III as well as Queen Victoria. In the fall of 1864, she embarked for the Confederate States on the *Condor*, a British blockade runner, carrying dispatches and some $2,000 in gold—royalties from her quickly composed and instantly popular memoirs, which she intended to donate to the impecunious Confederate treasury. On October 1, pursued by a Union gunboat, her vessel ran aground near Wilmington, North Carolina. Hoping to escape capture, Greenhow took to a rowboat, which capsized in the turbulent waters at the mouth of the Cape Fear River. Weighed down by her gold, she drowned.

*Rose O'Neale Greenhow, a high-profile Washington spy for the Confederacy, was intimate with some of the capital's most powerful men. She and her daughter, known as "Little Rose," were confined to the Old Capitol Prison, in whose yard the pair posed for this portrait.*

The one advantage the Confederacy possessed was that it did not have to create its government entirely from scratch. Most of the constitution it adopted on March 11, 1861, was simply lifted from that of the United States—although the clauses protecting slavery were made more explicit. But, given the constraints of time, resources, and ideology Davis faced, it is not surprising that the administration he hastily cobbled together was mostly inept. His cabinet was overwhelmingly mediocre, consisting largely of undistinguished men unequal to the demands of war. Just one member, the brilliant and energetic Judah P. Benjamin, former senator from Louisiana, showed a genuine aptitude for the craft of governance. He served successively as attorney general, then—briefly—as secretary of war, and, finally, as secretary of state. At the middle job in his Confederate résumé, Benjamin failed—as did the other five men who attempted to head the War Department. It was hard enough trying to fight a war with few and ever-dwindling resources, but the war secretaries were also obliged to fight Davis. The president was a chronic micromanager who demonstrated little confidence in any of his cabinet officers and, because his experience at the battle of Buena Vista more than a decade earlier had convinced him that he was a military genius, the cabinet officers he trusted least were his hapless secretaries of war.

*Jefferson Davis and his first Cabinet (left to right): Secretary of the Navy Stephen Mallory, Attorney General Judah P. Benjamin, Secretary of War LeRoy Pope Walker, President Davis, military adviser Robert E. Lee (not a Cabinet member), Postmaster General John H. Reagan, Secretary of the Treasury Christopher Memminger, Vice President Alexander Stephens, and Secretary of State Robert Toombs.*

*Lincoln and his first Cabinet (left to right): Postmaster General Montgomery Blair (in back), Secretary of the Interior Caleb Blood Smith, Secretary of the Treasury Salmon P. Chase, President Lincoln, Secretary of State William H. Seward, Secretary of War Simon Cameron, Attorney General Edward Bates, and Secretary of the Navy Gideon Welles.*

In personality as well as approach to governing, Abraham Lincoln was very different from Jefferson Davis. Whereas Davis was inflexible, Lincoln was naturally moderate, and whereas Davis failed to forge an effective cabinet, Lincoln built a remarkable one, which, as the historian Doris Kearns Goodwin explained in her popular book *Team of Rivals,* included a number of men who had opposed or at least differed sharply with Lincoln. Faced with a crisis of intense dissent, the new president decided to incorporate dissent into the innermost workings of the executive branch. It proved to be a stroke of genius.

Edwin M. Stanton was one of these who mocked Lincoln as the evolutionary "missing link," publicly referring to him as the "original gorilla." Yet when his first choice for secretary of war, Simon Cameron, proved corrupt in the office, Lincoln asked Stanton to replace him in January 1862. With considerable reluctance, Stanton accepted the appointment. In this man, Lincoln saw the combination of boundless ambition and will to power that made him dangerous as a political rival, but invaluable as the minister charged with managing a desperate military struggle. The new president's choice for another key post, secretary of state, was William H. Seward, who had lost the Republican nomination to Lincoln in 1860 and was unremittingly bitter about it. He sincerely believed that he was far more qualified to lead the nation than a backwoods lawyer like Lincoln, and even

## TAKEAWAY

Neither the North nor the South was prepared for war, but, led by the militaristic Jefferson Davis, the Confederacy manifested more unity of purpose and sheer war will than the North and its government, which was left in a state of dazed panic after the fall of Fort Sumter. Nevertheless, the government Lincoln set about building would bear the stamp of the president's political savvy and deeply democratic character, whereas the Confederate administration was marked by a general mediocrity tyrannized over by the inflexible and unimaginative Davis.

when he agreed to accept the appointment to secretary of state, he did so with the intention of hijacking the presidency, confident that he could use his position to pull Lincoln's strings, prompting him to govern according to his far superior lights. Fully aware of Seward's attitude, Lincoln also believed that he was the man most eminently qualified for the most powerful cabinet post. Lincoln repeatedly out-maneuvered Seward even as he empowered him, and, incrementally, Seward grew to respect the president. Eventually, he even willingly subordinated himself to Lincoln.

In April 1861, there was no denying the immediate peril to the seat of American government or the more profound and further-reaching danger posed by the threat to the union that had been the United States. Should that gravely menaced nation now perish, it would be the death of what Lincoln later called "the last best hope of earth." The stakes in this Civil War could not have been higher.

Five hundred years before Christ, the Greek philosopher Heraclitus observed that "character is destiny." For all the threat the outbreak of war presented—for all the loss and pain it promised, for all the evident confusion in the North, the unpreparedness, the paucity of war will, and the absence of anything approaching unanimity of purpose and goal—the ancient wisdom favored the character of Abraham Lincoln over that of Jefferson Davis and thus the destiny of the Union over that of the Confederacy. Not that any of this was apparent to those engulfed in the struggle—an epic of agony, doubt, and despair destined to last four bloody years.

*Artist Arthur Lumley sketched this "Reception of the officers of the Army by Secretary of War Stanton." Nominated to replace the notoriously corrupt Simon Cameron on January 13, 1862, Stanton met with top Union army officers on January 20. A harsh critic of Lincoln, Stanton nevertheless served him faithfully and proved to be a ruthlessly efficient secretary of war.*

# CHAPTER 5

## AN ANACONDA
## AND THE FURIES

### *The Stumbling March to Bull Run*

---

SOUTH VERSUS NORTH. WHAT COULD BE SIMPLER? BY JUNE 8, 1861, WHEN Tennessee left the Union, eleven Confederate states were fighting for independence from the twenty-four states that had remained loyal to the Union. (The addition of West Virginia would make twenty-five on June 20, 1863.) On paper, the outcome seemed not only clear, but inevitable. The North, with its far greater population, established (if modest) military, and vigorous industrial and agricultural economy was destined to prevail.

But wars are not fought on paper. For all its advantages, the North entered the war without a clear and unified aim. Lincoln and other moderates wanted to do no more than restore and preserve the Union, whereas committed abolitionists wanted the objective to be no less than the liberation of the slaves. Many others in the North wanted to restore the Union, but had no desire to fight for the abolition of slavery. In the mid-nineteenth century, most whites, probably the majority in America as well as Europe, believed that the black race was inherently inferior. Among even those who did not approve of the enslavement of Africans, few thought they should be elevated to equal status with whites. A good many white American men, especially newly arrived immigrants, went further. They feared that abolition would flood the Northern labor market with freed slaves, who would work more cheaply than they and therefore push them out of their jobs. Finally, a sizable number of Northerners simply did not care. If the South wanted slaves, let it have slaves. If the South wanted to secede, let it.

## HEARTS, MINDS, AND MEANS

LINCOLN KNEW THAT HIS MAIN PROBLEM in fighting the war was not getting weapons and men—the North could make the weapons, and it had the men—but persuading those men to fight and to keep fighting all the way to absolute victory, which he defined as the unconditional restoration of the Union. If he failed in persuading them, the South, meager though its resources were, would prevail, and the Union would be broken.

Lincoln decided that his best chance of raising and sustaining the North's will to fight was to focus the struggle simply and directly on suppressing the rebellion in order to restore the Union. The abolitionists would not embrace this comparatively modest objective, but they did not constitute the majority of Northerners. Lincoln did not believe that most Northern men would be willing to fight a war

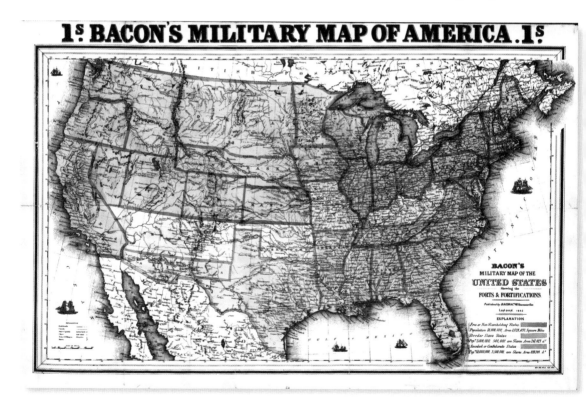

*The London mapmaker Bacon and Company published its "Military Map of the United States Shewing [sic] the Forts & Fortifications" in 1862. "Free or non-slaveholding states" are in green, "border slave states" yellow, and "seceded or Confederate states" pink.*

to end slavery, whereas the abolitionists would at least be somewhat mollified that the free states were fighting against the slave states, regardless of the objective. Finally, not all of the loyal states were free. The "border states"—those slave states that had not seceded—posed a problem. If Lincoln suddenly attempted to rally the North to fight a crusade for abolition, those states would almost certainly fly into Southern arms and join the secession.

Having defined a war aim—to restore the Union—Lincoln still had to figure out a way of attaining this goal. He turned to the U.S. Army's ranking officer, Major General Winfield Scott, by far the most experienced military man on the North American continent, hero of the War of 1812 and the U.S.-Mexican War. In the latter conflict, he had exhibited boldness and daring as well as tactical mastery and something at least approaching strategic genius. His spectacular invasion at Veracruz, the first amphibious operation in U.S. Army history, put him in position to march inland, capture Mexico City, and bring the war to a triumphant conclusion.

But the battle of Mexico City was in 1847, when Scott was already sixty-one years old. At the outbreak of the Civil War, he was seventy-five and enormously fat. Age and girth combined with severe gout to disenable him from doing much walking, let alone riding a horse. He did not see a single battle in the war.

Nevertheless, he did have a plan to offer his president. Scott balanced the great economic, population, and industrial advantages of the North against the South's deficiencies in these same areas. He also recognized that the North's miniscule regular army and its hodgepodge of indifferently trained, poorly equipped, and largely undisciplined state and local militia units were hardly adequate to mount a major offensive into the South. It was true that the Confederate army was just getting organized, but it would have one nearly incalculable advantage. It would be fighting a war in defense of its "homeland," and it would be doing so at home and close to sources of supply. Although the population of the Southern states was much smaller than that of the Northern states, Dixie was still a very large geographical area. It would take a large army to stamp out rebellion throughout the region. Time, Scott recognized, had to be enlisted as an ally. Given time, the North could build an army sufficient to invade and control the South. He therefore advocated delaying any major offensive against the Confederacy

# OLD FUSS AND FEATHERS

Few Americans remember Winfield Scott today, and among those who do, his given name either summons up the sobriquet by which he was known at the outbreak of the Civil War, "Old Fuss and Feathers," or the other nickname by which he was more privately mocked, "Old Fat and Feeble."

*Winfield Scott, general-in-chief of the United States Army, is shown here early in the war—though near the end of his career.*

Photographs of the era indeed depict a fat old man stuffed into a double-breasted uniform frock coat, his multiple chins oozing over his wing collar. But the daguerreotype image, while true to life, is grossly unfair: By 1861, he weighed over three hundred pounds and was certainly over-fond of fancy uniforms, but he was also one of the most remarkable soldiers to have served any nation.

His half-century of service began when he was commissioned a captain of artillery in 1808. Never a yes-man, he suffered a year's suspension after a court martial found him guilty of insubordination because he dared criticize his commanding general, the exuberantly corrupt James Wilkinson. Scott entered the War of 1812 a lieutenant colonel and emerged with the brevet rank of brigadier general; he had achieved in the battle of Chippewa one of the few American victories of the war and nearly lost his life at Lundy's Lane, where the fiercest combat of the war had taken place.

Scott had the unenviable duty of executing the "Cherokee removal" mandated by the Indian Removal Act of 1830, and in 1839 revealed himself to be an adept diplomat in bringing a peaceful resolution to a border dispute between Canadian New Brunswick and Maine in the Aroostook War. This resulted in his promotion to major general in 1841, at the time the highest rank in the U.S. Army, and the post of general-in-chief. In the U.S.-Mexican War of 1846–48, Scott's amphibious invasion of Mexico was so innovative and daring that Arthur Wellesley,

Duke of Wellington and vanquisher of Napoleon at Waterloo, predicted that his "reckless" action would result in disaster. But Scott raced inland to Mexico City, overran it, and forced a victorious conclusion to the war. Quick to admit that he had been wrong, Wellington pronounced Scott "the greatest living general."

In 1852, the Whig Party nominated Scott as its presidential candidate. A Virginian, he nevertheless opposed slavery, thereby losing the support of Southern voters. Yet, as a Whig, he was associated with a party that refused to oppose slavery, and so he lost support in the North. Although defeated, he remained a national hero and was recognized by Congress with a brevet promotion to lieutenant general, only the second U.S. officer to hold that rank. The first had been George Washington.

Unlike Robert E. Lee and several other Virginians, Scott remained loyal to the Union and the United States Army at the outbreak of the Civil War. His war strategy of blockade and incremental invasion, scorned as "Scott's Anaconda," would in fact prove highly effective in the long run. Under both political and military pressure, however, he resigned as general-in-chief on November 1, 1861, and died five years later, on May 29, 1866, having lived to see Union victory in his final war.

until sufficient forces had been built up. The only major operation he recommended in the short term was a massive maritime blockade of the South. While the North built its forces, the blockade would choke the South, starving it both literally and economically. It would be able neither to export cotton and other trade goods nor to import foodstuffs and European-manufactured arms and ammunition. By the time the armies of the North were prepared to invade, the South would be staggered by hunger and want.

The old general's plan called for a double-barreled blockade. He proposed cutting off the region's ports in the Atlantic and the Gulf of Mexico while simultaneously sending an army of sixty thousand "rough-vigor fellows" along with a flotilla of naval gunboats down the Mississippi River to capture New Orleans, the single most strategic port in the South, with access to the Gulf (and therefore the Atlantic) as well as to the interior via the Mississippi. These simultaneous operations were intended to strangle the Confederacy economically while also cutting it in half geographically—if you captured control of the Mississippi, the Confederate states of the east would be isolated from those of the west. As attrition set in and the Union army continued to build, any number of offensive operations could be planned and executed upon an all-but-prostrate enemy.

On paper, Scott's plan was brilliant. In its execution, however, there were two problems. First, the Confederacy controlled a coastline replete with gulfs and inlets, making it some thirty-five hundred miles long. No fewer than ten substantial ports dotted this expanse. The U.S. Navy would need hundreds, perhaps thousands, of ships to adequately blockade such a coast. As of spring 1861, the Union's navy consisted of forty-two seaworthy vessels of war. Any blockade would be more sieve than barrier.

Ever the realist, Lincoln understood the logistical and tactical inadequacies of Scott's plan. But it was a plan, which was more than anyone else had offered him, and he approved it.

That raised the second problem.

Nobody but Winfield Scott and Abraham Lincoln believed in the plan. The press on both sides mocked it as "Scott's Anaconda," and political cartoonists pictured it as a great constrictor—its head comically portrayed as that of the president or the general—coiling

**REALITY CHECK**
**Scott the Realist**
Scott knew that the North had a vast pool of manpower on which to draw, but his experience in war after war had repeatedly revealed to him the yawning gulf separating untrained if well-meaning civilian soldiers from professional men at arms. He had great confidence in the regular U.S. Army, small though it was, but very little faith in short-term volunteers and militiamen, whom he had seen perform badly in both the War of 1812 and the U.S.-Mexican War. His "Anaconda" was intended to buy time to enlarge the regular army, not just to rally a mob of volunteers. Unfortunately, the public and politicians continued to believe that—given a gun and a cause—anyone could fight and fight effectively. Although it was put into effect and sustained throughout the war, the Anaconda never gained wholehearted popular or political acceptance.

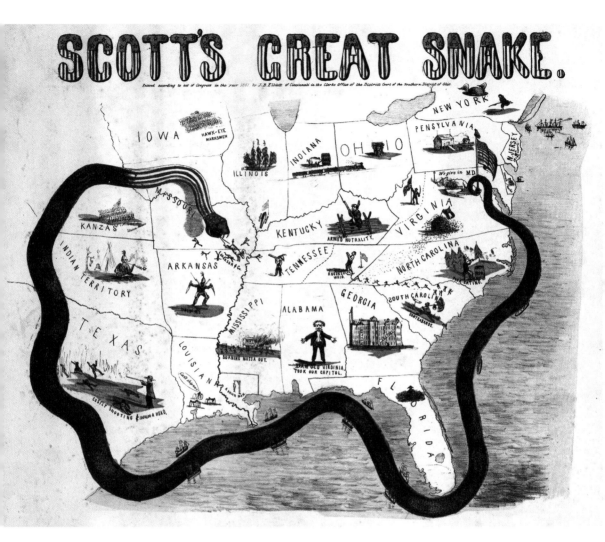

*Much derided in both the Northern and Southern press, "Scott's Anaconda"— the Union general-in-chief's ambitious war strategy for strangling the Confederacy with a blockade—was nevertheless quite effective in the long run. This cartoon map was published in 1861 by J. B. Elliott of Cincinnati.*

around Dixie's coast. Editorials called it impractical (which, until the Union built more ships, it was), but that was not the chief objection. Throwing up a blockade was no way to win a war, editors complained. It lacked "dash," and it was void of "honor" and "glory." Wars are properly won not by strangulation, they argued, but by the slash of sword, the thrust of bayonet, the explosion of shell, and the impact of bullet. They are won on land by means of bold combat, close up, hand to hand. Only act with courage and daring, the Northern papers bellowed, and the "rebels" could be vanquished on their home soil in a matter of months, if not weeks.

"Now, therefore, I, Abraham Lincoln, President of the United States, . . . have . . . deemed it advisable to set on foot a blockade of the ports within the States aforesaid, in pursuance of the laws of the United States. . . . For this purpose a competent force will be posted so as to prevent entrance and exit of vessels from the ports aforesaid."

*From President Lincoln's Proclamation of Blockade against Southern Ports, April 19, 1861*

### Humiliation

Critics notwithstanding, the "Anaconda" was launched. Union navy and army commanders decided to concentrate first on gaining control of the waterways leading most directly into Virginia. At the same time, Confederate planners had blockading ambitions of their own. Using artillery abandoned by the U.S. Army, they set up shore batteries to cut off the Chesapeake Bay and Potomac River approaches to Washington. The first Union offensive actions of the war were naval, as Union gunboats attacked the shore batteries at Sewells Point, near Norfolk, Virginia, during May 18–19, 1861, and at Aquia Creek from May 29 to June 1. The batteries returned fire, but the engagements were indecisive.

Union ground forces finally entered the fray on June 10 at Big Bethel, in Hampton and York counties, Virginia, hoping to root out Confederates near Union-held Fort Monroe. The green Union troops performed poorly, however, and the gray uniforms some volunteer units wore created endless confusion. The shooting lasted perhaps an hour, during which eighteen

*Another cartoon view of General Scott's blockade—this one based on his own succinct explanation of his strategy: "When I wish to catch rats, I first stop their holes."*

" When I wish to catch rats, I first stop their holes."
*Gen'l Scott*

*Civil War battlefront artist Alfred R. Waud was seemingly every-where during the conflict. Here is his drawing of the attack of the USS* Pawnee *and USS* Freeborn *against Confederate batteries at Aquia Creek, Virginia. Waud's quickly executed work was intended to be engraved for reproduction in illustrated newspapers. Accordingly, he limited himself to a few high-impact media—in this case, pencil and black ink wash, plus "Chinese white" (zinc oxide) for the smoke effects.*

Union soldiers were killed, fifty-three wounded, and five went missing out of the twenty-five hundred engaged. Confederate losses were one killed and seven wounded out of twelve hundred men. The Northern public had expected that the rebels would be taught a lesson at Big Bethel. Disappointment lay heavily over the North.

After the humiliation of Big Bethel, Union gunboats returned to the task of patrolling Chesapeake Bay in an effort to keep it clear for passage in and out of the capital. Despite this, Confederate artillery continued to menace shipping into and out of Washington.

## Rebel Diplomacy

While the South did more than hold its own on the Chesapeake and at Big Bethel, the Davis government did not grow complacent. Davis and his advisers—especially the sagacious Judah Benjamin—understood what many up North failed to understand: that, given sufficient time, "Scott's Anaconda" would eventually have enough ships to create an effective blockade. The South would feel the pinch, and, by and by, that pinch would escalate into a full-out stranglehold. If the North's will to fight could not be broken and broken quickly, the South would need to find the means of obtaining for itself everything it formerly obtained from the North. Its survival, let alone its prospects for victory, depended on this.

With limited manufacturing capacity—though such facilities as Richmond's long-established Tredegar Ironworks would expand impressively during the war—the Confederacy would have to rely heavily on importation. Most arms, ammunition, and warships would have to be purchased in Europe, sailed across an increasingly well-patrolled Atlantic, and then, by stealth, run through an ever-thickening Union blockade. And that blockade worked both ways, impeding exports as well as imports. International trade required gold, and getting gold required selling cotton and other raw materials to European markets. Getting these commodities through the coils of the Anaconda would become more and more difficult.

The only alternative to a steady stream of incoming gold was foreign credit. At the outbreak of the war, this was practically nil. The Davis government realized that it needed European allies or, at the very least, recognition as a sovereign nation by European trading partners and potential creditors.

During the American Revolution, the United States had sought international allies by promoting the ideological value of its cause as a fight for liberty and justice on behalf of all mankind and by offering foreign powers, primarily France and Spain, an alliance against Great Britain. The Confederacy could not successfully market its ideology. By the 1860s, the United States was the only major Western power that still practiced slavery. Even czarist Russia ended serfdom in 1861. As for an alliance against the United States, no one in Europe earnestly wanted one. What, then, did Davis and his government have to offer potential allies?

France and England relied heavily on the South as a trading partner—so heavily that the region, ever since Eli Whitney perfected the cotton gin, relied almost entirely on the export of "King Cotton" as the basis of its economy. This focus became so narrow that prosperous Southern planters pushed out of their minds the consciousness that the English and the French also traded with the North. Indeed, while cotton was king in the South, the grain produced on America's vast plains in the West and Midwest was coming to displace cotton as the major U.S. export to Europe.

*Former Louisiana senator Judah P. Benjamin was by far the ablest member of the Confederate Cabinet, serving variously as attorney general, secretary of war, and secretary of state.*

*The Davis government scrambled desperately to establish diplomatic relations with Great Britain and France, both of which valued trade with the South but balked at openly allying themselves with a faction fighting to uphold slavery. This Northern cartoon depicts President Davis's overtures in a wholly ficti-tious meeting with France's Napoleon III and England's Victoria. The French emperor refuses his offer of bonds and cotton: "Not any, we thank you, Mr. Davis." Queen Victoria looks on, holding aloft what is undoubt-edly her own neutrality proclama-tion of May 13, 1861.*

"NOT ANY. WE THANK YOU MR DAVIS.

**ALTERNATE TAKE**

## Should Lincoln Have Called It a Crusade?

As we will see in Chapter 11, President Lincoln did not link the slavery issue to the Civil War until the fall of 1862, when he issued the Preliminary Emancipation Proclamation. *Should* he have done so sooner, in effect labeling the war a crusade against slavery? Had he done this, it is unlikely that any European power would have supported the Confederacy in any way. Neither France nor England wanted to be seen as enabling and endorsing slavery. Yet had the president linked the war to abolition from the outset, he would likely have alienated the slaveholding border states as well as the majority of Northerners who were *not* abolitionists. While Lincoln's explicit focus on restoring the Union without reference to slavery gave Confederate diplomats a narrow window through which to approach the English and French governments, it also ensured that the Northern support for the war would not be sacrificed to principle, no matter how noble.

Still, Southern trade was important—and its importance was augmented by the nature of government in France and England. Both countries were monarchies in a Europe that, as recently as 1848, had been convulsed by multiple seizures of republican revolution. Instead of prejudicing these governments against a rebellion in North America, the secession of the South, which portrayed itself as a conservative "empire" presided over by a largely hereditary landed aristocracy, seemed like a blow against the radicalizing forces of the North's industrial democracy in which anyone with money could rise to power. Both culturally and ideologically, the South was far more congenial to European monarchy than the North was. Furthermore, the spectacle of the dissolution of the world's only true democracy would be proof to that world that democracy was destined to fail, whereas monarchical governments had stood the test of time and would continue to endure. Thus, Jefferson Davis appointed James M. Mason of Virginia minister to England and Louisiana's John Slidell minister to France and sent both to Europe in search of alliance.

### The *Trent* Affair

Early in October 1861, Mason and Slidell sailed undetected out of Charleston on a rebel blockade runner—a commercial ship whose skipper plied the high-stakes trade of evading the Anaconda—and made port at Havana, Cuba. The diplomats boarded the British mail packet *Trent* bound for England, apparently home free. The ministers were traveling undetected; besides, Great Britain was officially neutral in the Civil War. Aboard the *Trent,* they were untouchable—or so it would seem.

By sheer chance, the screw frigate (hybrid sail and steam vessel) USS *San Jacinto,* having been recalled to the United States from its prewar station along the African coast, made a stopover in Havana trolling for intelligence relating to Confederate commerce raiders (see Chapter 20). Like the fisherman who casts his net for small fry and finds big game instead, Captain Charles Wilkes, the *San Jacinto*'s skipper, learned that Mason and Slidell had just steamed out of port. Giving the order to weigh anchor, he laid on all available steam, and set out for the Bahamas Channel, where he knew he would meet up with the *Trent.* Sighting the packet on November 8, he let fly two warning shots across her bow.

# THE BLUE AND THE GRAY

**W**hen we aren't thinking of the Civil War as a straightforward contest between the North and the South, we tend to picture it as a fight between "the Blue and the Gray." Although it is true that the standard-issue regular U.S. Army uniform was blue—a dark blue coat with trousers of a lighter blue—and the Provisional Confederate Army generally wore gray uniforms of roughly the same design, the many state and local volunteer units on both sides wore a variety of uniforms in a variety of colors. In the case of the Confederacy, some units had no standard uniforms at all. Early in the war, many Union volunteer regiments wore gray uniforms, and at Big Bethel (among other early battles), this resulted in what today would be called "friendly fire" casualties, as blue-clad Union soldiers mistakenly fired on their gray-clad comrades.

*This infantry frock coat was standard for company-grade officers (captain and lower) in the U.S. Army. Troops hated the bold eagle medallion on the cross belt. Handsome though it was, it gave Confederate riflemen a fine, shiny target to aim at.*

*Torn from Alfred R. Waud's sketchbook: The advance of Union troops against Big Bethel, Virginia, June 10, 1861. The influence of the French military in U.S. Civil War uniforms is especially evident in the officer's cap. Most American military headgear of the period was modeled after the French kepi, but the addition of the over-neck cloth recalls most specifically the French Foreign Legion style.*

*Harper's Weekly, a Northern illustrated paper, mocked the very notion that the Confederate envoys Mason and Slidell should be dignified by the title of "diplomat." In this November 1861 cartoon, they are depicted instead as "well-known Rogues . . . about to Pawn some of their late Employer's Property at Messrs. Bull, Crapaud & Co.'s Shop." "Policeman" Wilkes "nabbed them in the nick of time." ("Bull" recalls John Bull, a familiar personification of Britain, while the French-sounding "Crapaud," suggests France. The two names together are a blunt editorial comment on the entire Mason-Slidell mission.)*

This forced the *Trent's* skipper to heave to, bringing the vessel to a near standstill. Putting his speaking trumpet to his mouth, the skipper bellowed over the rail: "What do you mean by heaving my vessel to in this way?"

Wilkes responded by sending Lieutenant D. MacNeill Fairfax in the lead boat of a two-boat boarding party. At their approach, Slidell approached the rail and confronted Fairfax as he climbed aboard. Mason was close behind. Fairfax placed both men under arrest and took them back to the *San Jacinto*, which steamed away and deposited the two Confederates at Fort Warren in Boston Harbor.

The popular press in the North took fire at Wilkes's bold action. Congress hastened to pass a resolution of thanks, but the British government, already sympathetic to the Confederate cause, sent eleven thousand troops to Canada, placed the Royal Navy on high alert, and demanded an apology from the U.S. government as well as the release of the prisoners.

Secretary of State William Seward was hardly eager to apologize and advised the president to let the situation stand. It was not that the British government's high dudgeon provoked him, but that he believed a war with Great Britain might just end the war at home; the South might join the North against the threat posed by an enemy they once had in common, Seward argued. It was, on the face of it, a wild interpretation of the incident. President Lincoln understood that, if anything, the Davis administration welcomed a British attack on the North. Rather than scold his secretary of state, however, he said simply, "One war at a time." Brought to his senses, Seward conceded that courting conflict with the British was undoubtedly a dangerous gambit and immediately wrote an order for the release of Mason and Slidell. On December 26, 1861, he presented to Lord Richard Lyons, British minister to the United States, an official note defending the boarding of the *Trent* and the seizure of Mason and Slidell but claiming that Wilkes had acted without the approval of his government before taking prisoner the "contraband of war."

As the United States and Great Britain mutually backed away from armed conflict, Davis realized that a great opportunity had slipped through his grasp. Nevertheless, most Britons and the British government continued to show favoritism to the Confederacy. British law was unambiguous: The empire was supposed to conduct itself strictly as a neutral in this civil conflict. But Prime Minister Henry John Temple (Lord Palmerston) and Parliament consistently winked at the increased production in British munitions works and shipyards, which were making handsome profits by surreptitiously supplying the Confederacy. Worse, on May 13, 1861, Queen Victoria herself conferred on the Confederacy the first (and only) international recognition it would gain, treating it as a "belligerent" entity—the term applied to sovereign nations at war with other sovereign nations.

## Lyon Roars

The *Trent* affair had loomed as a major crisis only to fizzle out in a diplomatic note from Seward and its acknowledgment by the Palmerston government. At about the same time, two more crises simmered much closer to home. Among the border states, the continued loyalty of Kentucky and Missouri was most in doubt. Kentucky's governor favored secession, but the state legislature was solidly pro-Union. The two positions effectively cancelled one another out, resulting in a declaration of neutrality that neither Lincoln nor Davis wanted to test. Unofficially, both sides recruited troops in the state, but both Washington and Richmond (the Confederate capital had moved from Montgomery, Alabama, to the Virginia state capital shortly after the fall of Fort Sumter) officially kept hands-off.

Missouri's status was not to be resolved so peacefully. As was the case with Kentucky, Missouri's governor, Claiborne F. Jackson, wanted to take his state into the Confederacy, whereas a majority of the legislature (a slimmer majority than in Kentucky) favored remaining loyal. Jackson saw the fall of Fort Sumter as a signal to seize the federal arsenal at St. Louis, the legislature be damned. Captain Nathaniel S. Lyon, in command of a single company of the 2nd U.S. Infantry Regiment (about a hundred men) took it upon himself to garrison the arsenal. At this, troops loyal to Governor Jackson established Camp Jackson on the outskirts of St. Louis and awaited developments.

*Harper's Weekly (June 1, 1861) depicted the attack on the "Wide Awake" pro-Union volunteers by a prosecession mob in St. Louis on May 10, 1861. The volunteers responded by firing on the prosecession civilians, killing twenty-eight and wounding some seventy-five.*

Lyon did more than bide his time. On the eve of war, he had been a member of the St. Louis "Wide Awakes," an unofficial militia organized in defense of the Union. Without legal authority, let alone orders, Lyon summoned the Wide Awakes to the arsenal by night and surreptitiously distributed arms and ammunition to them. This done, he secretly transferred most of the arsenal's remaining weapons to the safety of Illinois, then, on May 10, sent the combined forces of his infantry company and Wide Awake volunteers to take Camp Jackson. Jackson's men surrendered without a fight, and Lyon marched his prisoners through St. Louis, intending to hold them in the mostly empty arsenal. Predictably, the impromptu parade incited a pro-secession riot in the city, to which Lyon's men responded by firing into the rioters, killing twenty-eight and wounding as many as seventy-five.

Brigadier General William S. Harney, in command of the Union's "Army of the West"—its grandiose name belied by its puny size—had tried to keep a lid on Missouri by maintaining something between a stalemate and a truce with Jackson's forces. At this point, neither Harney nor Jackson believed he had enough popular support or armed men to compel Missouri to embrace one side or the other, and neither man wanted to act in such a way that would alienate the people of the state. But Lyon's action forced the issue, and U.S. Army high command, propelled by its momentum, summarily replaced Harney with Lyon, who jumped from captain to brigadier general and was given command of the Army of the West on July 2.

"I look upon secession as anarchy. If I owned
the four millions of slaves at the South,
I would sacrifice all to the Union; but how
can I draw my sword upon Virginia?"

*Robert E. Lee, April 1861*

## Neosho and Wilson's Creek

The Lyon momentum carried more than the U.S. Army. Governor Jackson defied the state legislature by unilaterally proclaiming a Confederate state government at the town of Neosho. In defense of this, a ragged collection of Confederate sympathizers clashed with Union troops under Brigadier General Franz Sigel at the nearby town of Carthage, on July 5, 1861. Outnumbered, Sigel prudently withdrew. Lyon more than compensated for Sigel's prudence by impetuously leading his 5,600 men against 10,175 Confederates under Brigadier General Benjamin McCulloch at Wilson's Creek, just south of Springfield, on the morning of August 10.

The intensity of the fighting stunned both sides—though it was no more than a bitter foretaste of the torrents of blood to come. Lyon fought conspicuously in the vanguard of his men, and he paid the price for it. Wounded once and then again, he kept fighting. His men saw their wounded commander turn, saber held aloft in a rallying gesture. At that

*The Chicago firm of Kurz & Allison, second only to Currier & Ives as a producer of popular prints, published this depiction of the August 10, 1861, battle of Wilson's Creek c. 1893.*

moment, a volley of three more shots hit him in a succession so rapid as to be virtually simultaneous. Lead tore through his leg, lead shattered his skull, and lead exploded in his chest. Sword upraised, he spun one way, then the other, then off his feet and into the red Missouri clay.

With his fall, the Army of the West retreated, beaten. Yet, arguably, Lyon's death had not been in vain. The Confederates would remain in control of southwestern Missouri for some time, but the state did not secede and never would—though it was chronically torn throughout the war by a species of violent criminality that military commanders on both sides dignified by the phrase *guerrilla warfare.*

## VIRGINIA SECESSIONS

VIRGINIA WAS IN THE FINAL WAVE of Southern secession states, clinging to the Union until May 23. The hard-pressed, hardscrabble subsistence farmers of the state's ruggedly mountainous western counties did not so much love the Union as they resented the wealthy planters who lived on Virginia's Tidewater (coastal region) and controlled the government. *They* could leave the United States, but the mountaineers were not going with them. The western counties broke with the rest of the state.

The western backcountry of Virginia provided the stage on which the man who promised to be the star of the Union forces made his debut. George Brinton McClellan was born in 1826 to a prominent Philadelphia family (his father, a pioneering ophthalmological surgeon, founded Jefferson Medical College in the city) and graduated from West Point second in the class of 1846. From the military academy, he marched to battle in the U.S.-Mexican War and compiled an enviable record, breveted—promoted for bravery—no fewer than three times. Despite his performance and the acclaim it garnered, McClellan found himself in the same position as those other Mexican War veterans, Sherman and Grant. He was mired in a peacetime army that offered little opportunity for meaningful advancement. In 1857, McClellan resigned his commission to become vice president of the Illinois Central Railroad. In this job he met Abraham Lincoln, at the time a leading lawyer for the ICRR.

Appointed major general of the Ohio volunteers at the start of the Civil War, McClellan was rapidly promoted, quickly becoming major general in the regular army and assigned to lead the U.S. Army's

Department of the Ohio. On the night of June 3, 1861, he commanded a stealthy assault on a camp of sleeping Confederates near the village of Philippi. His rout of perhaps fifteen hundred rebels was, to be sure, a minor victory, but in these early days of the war, when the Union army seemed utterly incapable of gaining any traction, the modest triumph shone brilliantly. It helped, too, that McClellan was still youthful at thirty-five and that he was comely in an appropriately martial way, affecting the mustache and abbreviated chin whiskers known as "the Imperial." True, he was a short man—his men affectionately called him "Little Mac"—but that was just fine with the Northern press, who dubbed him the "Young Napoleon," not in acknowledgment of the tonsorial style of Napoleon III, but in the hope—and hope it was—that McClellan would prove to have more in common with the victor of Marengo and Austerlitz than short stature.

## Manassas

Except for the fall of Fort Sumter, the war was being fought, it seemed, on the nation's fringes—the backwaters of Missouri and the backcountry of Virginia. McClellan's success at Philippi was all well and good, but the Northern press, with Horace Greeley and his *New York Daily Tribune* in the vanguard, was clamoring for the Union army to strike a blow that would not only avenge Fort Sumter but teach the rebels a very hard lesson.

*Trim, handsome, and adorned with the "Imperial" (the moustache and abbreviated goatee combination in emulation of Napoleon III), Major General George B. McClellan looked every inch of what the Northern press would soon dub him: "the Young Napoleon." This photograph was mass produced by the firm of Mathew Brady in 1861.*

The job of striking that blow fell to Brigadier General Irvin McDowell, commanding what was then called the Army of Northeastern Virginia. Educated in France and at West Point—graduating in the class of 1836 alongside P. G. T. Beauregard—McDowell was well trained and had even seen action in the U.S.-Mexican War, though not as a commander of troops in combat. His upward progress through the officer ranks was accelerated not by dint of demonstrated military prowess so much as

*Union brigadier general Irvin McDowell graduated in the same 1836 West Point class as Confederate general P. G. T. Beauregard, who dealt him a stunning defeat at the first battle of Bull Run on July 21, 1861.*

his friendship with Salmon P. Chase, Lincoln's powerful secretary of the treasury. On both sides—but in the Union army more than that of the Confederacy—so-called political generals held commands gained through the clout of social and political connections rather than earned by professional military merit. As a West Pointer, McDowell was significantly superior to the average political general, but the fact is that he had been carried to his command on the shoulders of Chase and not on his own record.

To his credit, he did have the pulse of his men and knew full well that his summer soldiers, freshly enlisted as if for a lark, were hardly ready for combat. Yet even a more battlefield-savvy commander than McDowell would have found it difficult, perhaps impossible, to resist the pressure of politicians, who in turn could not resist the pressure of their constituents, to strike a blow sufficiently decisive to end the rebellion once and for all. To most Northern civilians, this really did not seem to be asking for too much.

McDowell decided to launch an offensive against the Confederate forces massed in northern Virginia, a stone's throw from Washington. As if determined to display his West Point book learning, he drew up a highly polished plan of attack, the complexities of which were far better suited to the classroom than to execution by his untutored troops and their scarcely better-prepared commanders. Nevertheless, it all looked very good on paper, and by the third week in July 1861, he had assembled 28,452 blue-coated men in Alexandria, Virginia. It was the largest single field army ever to muster on the North American continent to that time.

His plan was to march against a Confederate force of some twenty thousand men under P. G. T. Beauregard who were deployed at Bull Run Creek near Manassas Junction, a crossroads that controlled access to Richmond, the Confederate capital: Overwhelm this force, sweep it aside, and then advance against Richmond. Such was the plan, and, with luck, the war would be over in a matter of weeks or even days.

It was not a wild fantasy. Although he lacked experience as a combat commander, McDowell knew that he was better prepared than most other officers on either side. And if his troops were callow—well, so were Beauregard's rebels. Even President Lincoln sought to put iron in his general's spine by reassuring him: "You are green, it is true, but they are green also; you are all green alike." Nor was McDowell blindly confident of success. He could read a map, and what his map told him was that while he enjoyed a significant numerical advantage over Beauregard, out near Harpers Ferry another nine thousand Confederate troops were assembled under Joseph Johnston. They, however, were outnumbered by the Union force opposing them, sixteen thousand men commanded by Brigadier General Robert Patterson. Knowing full well that the odds could shift drastically against the Union if Johnston somehow got his men past Patterson to reinforce Beauregard, McDowell warned Patterson to tie Johnston down by keeping him occupied.

## Blackberrying

McDowell led his big army out of Alexandria on July 16. Almost immediately it became clear to the commanding general and his officers that the men under their command were scarcely an army at all. The march of so many troops was slow and halting and the mid-summer day awfully warm. Overheated or just plain bored, troops repeatedly broke ranks. Some stretched out alongside inviting runs of water. Others, laughing, knotted into groups and went off to pick blackberries together.

For some, the blackberrying ended abruptly on July 18, when Brigadier General Daniel Tyler's division, passing the Confederate right (southeast) flank, was attacked at Blackburn's Ford over Bull Run. Tyler's division, which greatly outnumbered the attackers, fought back, but could not seem to push back hard enough. The Confederates held their ground, and it was Tyler who was forced to withdraw. Irvin McDowell may not have been a general of legendary renown, but he was a gastronome of prodigious reputation, known to devour a multicourse meal and chase it with an entire watermelon for dessert, characteristically pronouncing the repast "monstrous fine." Now, however, he felt a gripping nausea in the pit of his cast-iron stomach. In his first brush with the enemy, he had suffered defeat. He called in his field commanders and quickly laid out a new plan of attack, this one targeting the Confederate left (northwest) flank.

It was not a bad plan—fail on one side, get a fresh start on the other. It did require, however, a great deal of shifting of troops, and this cost McDowell time—time that Johnston, out in the Shenandoah Valley, exploited brilliantly to elude Patterson and strike out in a forced march to reinforce Beauregard.

## FIRST BULL RUN, JULY 21, 1861

BY JULY 21, THE ODDS, so favorable to the Union at the outset, had slipped and slipped badly. McDowell no longer outnumbered Beauregard, who, reinforced, had more than 32,000 men against McDowell's 28,452 effectives. Doubtless, the hordes of fashionably dressed Washingtonians who rode down to Centreville, Virginia, barely twenty miles from the capital, were unaware of this. Their only object was to pass an afternoon watching their army defeat the rebels while they, ensconced in carriages stocked with commodious picnic hampers and chilled bottles of champagne, shared the view through an assortment of telescopes, binoculars, and even opera glasses.

*Kurz & Allison issued this highly romanticized version of the first battle of Bull Run for a collection of Civil War prints published in 1889 or 1890. The men in scarlet trousers are Zouaves, members of regiments who wore uniforms emulating colorful French colonial troops.*

At first, the picnickers had plenty to cheer about. Even reinforced, Beauregard's Confederates seemed no match for McDowell's bluecoats. On first contact, the Union boys uprooted the rebels from their defensive perches and firing holes. They even began to turn—force back—the entire Confederate left flank. Lincoln must have been right after all. They *were* green!

Actually, it was not so much that the soldiers on both sides were green as that the top commanders on both sides, McDowell as well as Beauregard, failed to make allowances for the inexperience of their men. Like McDowell, Beauregard had created a battle plan that was too complicated for marginally trained troops to execute effectively. The similarities of soldiers and commanders on both sides tended to cancel each other out. Still, even with the modest numerical advantage the Confederates enjoyed, it seemed certain now that Beauregard would suffer a bad defeat. His men, confused, tired, and unable to translate their orders into meaningful actions, began to crumble, to break, to run—*skedaddle* was the verb the soldiers used.

That was when Brigadier General Thomas J. Jackson, West Point class of 1846, twice brevetted in the Mexican War, most recently a professor at the Virginia Military Institute, rode up, leading his Virginia brigade. Amid the din of fleeing men, Brigadier General Barnard Bee recognized Jackson instantly. It was hard not to. He was from one of those western Virginia counties that had broken with the rest of the state, a stark sculpture of a man whose black beard, high forehead, and aquiline nose would have given him the appearance of an Appalachian backwoodsman if it hadn't been for the unearthly blue of his eyes—"Old Blue Light," his men liked to call him. Those were the eyes of an Old Testament prophet, a prophet with saber in hand.

Bee would be out of the fighting soon. He would be wounded, linger long enough to learn of his side's victory, and then die early the next day. But right now, seeing Jackson, he rode up to him. "General, they are driving us!" he complained. "Then, Sir, we will give them the bayonet," Jackson replied with perfect calm.

It is said that Bee now turned back in the direction of his own troops and shouted out

*Stonewall Jackson at the first battle of Bull Run—as envisioned by an anonymous early twentieth-century illustrator.*

to them: "There's Jackson standing like a stone wall!" motioning toward him with his saber. Then inscribing with its point a large circle in the air above his head, he shouted: "Rally behind the Virginians!"

When battles begin to go bad, they almost always end badly. But not this time.

Bee's exhortation, combined with Jackson's arrival—he would be called "Stonewall" from this day forward—shot both discipline and spirit through the faltering Confederates. For the rest of that long, hot afternoon, the battle, which had so far tilted in favor of the Union men, now wavered, first one way, and then the other. At about three in the afternoon, the men of the 33rd Virginia overran two Union artillery positions that had been strategically planted to enfilade the Confederate line, to fire against its flank. As chance would have it, these particular Confederate troops were outfitted in blue uniforms. Thinking they were approaching comrades, the Union defenders of the artillery posi-

*General Thomas J. Jackson earned his celebrated sobriquet, "Stonewall," at the first battle of Bull Run. This image was originally published early in the twentieth century.*

## EYEWITNESS

Times of London correspondent William Howard Russell posted this report from the first battle of Bull Run:

*I perceived several wagons coming from the direction of the battlefield, the drivers of which were endeavouring to force their horses past the ammunition carts going in the contrary direction. . . . [They] cried out with the most vehement gestures, "Turn back! Turn back! We are whipped!"*

**TAKEAWAY**

The Union's superannuated general-in-chief, Winfield Scott, understood that it would take time to build and train an army sufficient to end the rebellion of the South and proposed a naval blockade of the Confederacy as a means of buying that time. Northern politicians and public alike, however, were impatient, derided the blockade they called "Scott's Anaconda," and insisted on a bold Union offensive. The result, the first battle of Bull Run, ended in a stunning and demoralizing Union defeat, which boded ominously for the course of the war.

tion held their fire. It was a fatal error. The taking of these two guns was like the moment in which a hairline crack in a dam suddenly splits, and then explodes in a torrent.

McDowell rushed to fill the gap, and he did so with such efficiency that the Union troops at the point of the Confederate breakthrough outnumbered the enemy better than two to one. But those outnumbered men were led by Stonewall Jackson, who calmly exhorted them to hold their fire until they were within fifty yards. Once they were at that range, they were to open fire "and give them the bayonet! And when you charge, yell like furies!"

The first tactical command was at least as old as the battle of Bunker Hill, when Colonel William Prescott issued to his Yankees the famous order to hold fire "until you see the whites of their eyes." The second, however, was apparently an inspiration uniquely Jackson's. *Yell like furies.* It was the first use of the war's first secret weapon: the "rebel yell." Accounts vary as to just what this was, but all agree that it was high in pitch, otherworldly, and utterly terrifying.

Musket fire, bayonet point, the keening cry of the rebels—all combined to break the Union lines, everywhere and all at once, sending the soldiers of the United States flying back along the very roads from whose margins they had so recently gleaned handfuls of blackberries. Panting, choked with fear and dust, the Union army shouldered past the picnickers, who forsook their baskets and bottles as they joined their army in its flight.

## PART THREE

# HELL BEFORE NIGHT

# CHAPTER 6

## THREE GENERALS

*McClellan, Grant, and Halleck*

F ROM HIS VICTORY OVER A SLEEPING CONFEDERATE CAMP AT PHILIPPI in what would become West Virginia, George B. McClellan marched south into Randolph County and reached Rich Mountain on July 9, 1861. At the same time, a Union brigade under his subordinate Brigadier General Thomas A. Morris fought Confederates commanded by Brigadier General Robert S. Garnett at nearby Laurel Hill, and, on July 11, another of McClellan's commanders, Brigadier General William S. Rosecrans, attacked Lieutenant Colonel John Pegram's Confederates at Rich Mountain, approaching from the rear and splitting the enemy in two. Half of the force managed to evade Rosecrans, but Pegram himself and the other half surrendered to him on July 13. News of this defeat prompted Garnett to withdraw from Laurel Hill, only to be cornered on July 13 at Corrick's Ford, where he was killed in combat.

Collectively known as the battle of Rich Mountain, these skirmishes amounted to a victory even smaller than that at Philippi. The Union suffered 46 killed or wounded and the Confederates 170 killed or wounded and perhaps as many as 554 captured (some sources suggest far fewer Confederate casualties), however Garnett was the first general killed in the war. But when word of the victory reached Washington, all eyes and hopes turned to McClellan, and on July 22, the day after Irvin McDowell's defeat at Bull Run, the victor of Philippi and Rich Mountain was summoned to the capital. Carried in a special train, he was met at Wheeling and was cheered in Pittsburgh and Philadelphia, as well as all the stops in between. A jubilant throng pressed upon him at the Washington station on July 26, and he was swiftly bundled off to the White House, where President Lincoln greeted him and announced his appointment—on the spot—as commander of the Military Division of the Potomac. At the time, the division was responsible principally for the defense of the capital, but by late August other units were added to it, and McClellan gave the new

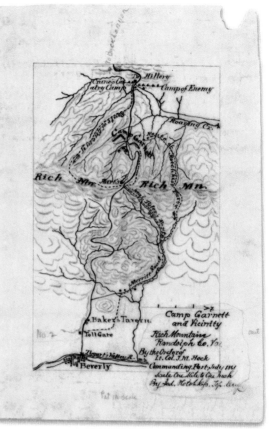

unit the resplendent name of the Army of the Potomac, as befit the biggest military formation ever raised on the continent to that date. "I find myself in a new and strange position here," he gushed in a letter to his wife. "Presdt, Cabinet, Genl Scott & all deferring to me—by some strange operation of magic I seem to have become the power of the land."

He was right. Bull Run had made everyone, from the president on down, desperate. The trouble was that McClellan was more absorbed in the adulation born of desperation than he was in the mission that confronted him. "I almost think that were I to win some small success now I could become Dictator or anything else that might please me," he wrote to his wife. Perhaps he was right about this, too. But if "some small success" was all that was needed to make him dictator, it was hardly all that was needed to bring a quick and victorious end to the Civil War. McClellan, vainglorious, was setting his sights much too low.

*Mapmaking was a subject taught at West Point— although this map of a Union encampment at Rich Mountain is by a civilian "topographical engineer" named Jed Hotchkiss.*

**PREVIOUS SPREAD:**
*Currier & Ives produced a colorful depiction of the bombardment and capture of the Confederate Fort Henry by U.S. Navy gunboats under the command of Flag Officer Andrew H. Foute on February 6, 1862.*

"I will hold McClellan's horse if he
will only bring us success."

*President Abraham Lincoln,*
*to his secretary John Hay, November 13, 1861*

## INSTALLATION OF THE YOUNG NAPOLEON

MCCLELLAN DID NOT LEAD HIS NEW ARMY immediately into battle, but
spent the rest of the summer and early autumn of 1861 building it,
organizing it, and training it. He set about transforming Washington
into a fortress, ringing it with forty-eight strong points and a number
of full-fledged forts. The defenses bristled with nearly five hundred cannons. This done, he appealed to General Winfield Scott to lay aside the
Anaconda, the strategy of slow strangulation and build-up, and instead
throw everything into making the Army of the Potomac even larger
than it already was. He asked for a force of 273,000 men and some six
hundred guns. The press was calling him the "Young Napoleon," and
perhaps he took it to heart; what he proposed was to march this massive
army into Virginia and force the Confederates to a stand, a grand battle
of Napoleonic proportions that would crush the army of the secession
in a single blow. This, he argued, would do little harm to the civilian
population of the South but would end the rebellion by neutralizing
the enemy army. He took Lincoln at his word: He did not want to free
the slaves, but only to restore the Union.

Neither Scott nor the president gave McClellan what he wanted, but
he nevertheless continued to drill and hone the Army of the Potomac.
Unlike most generals of the period, McClellan did not hold himself aloof
from his men. On the contrary, he visited the camps frequently. He spoke
directly to "Billy Yank," the common soldier. In this way, he not only
created a disciplined and soldierly army, he forged a fighting force of the
highest morale. It was a splendid achievement, especially coming, as it
did, hard on the heels of the Bull Run humiliation.

Yet McClellan remained obsessed with Napoleonic numbers. He
believed that he could not mount an effective offensive until he had an
army approaching 300,000, and he believed this because he was confident that the Confederates were organizing a comparably massive force

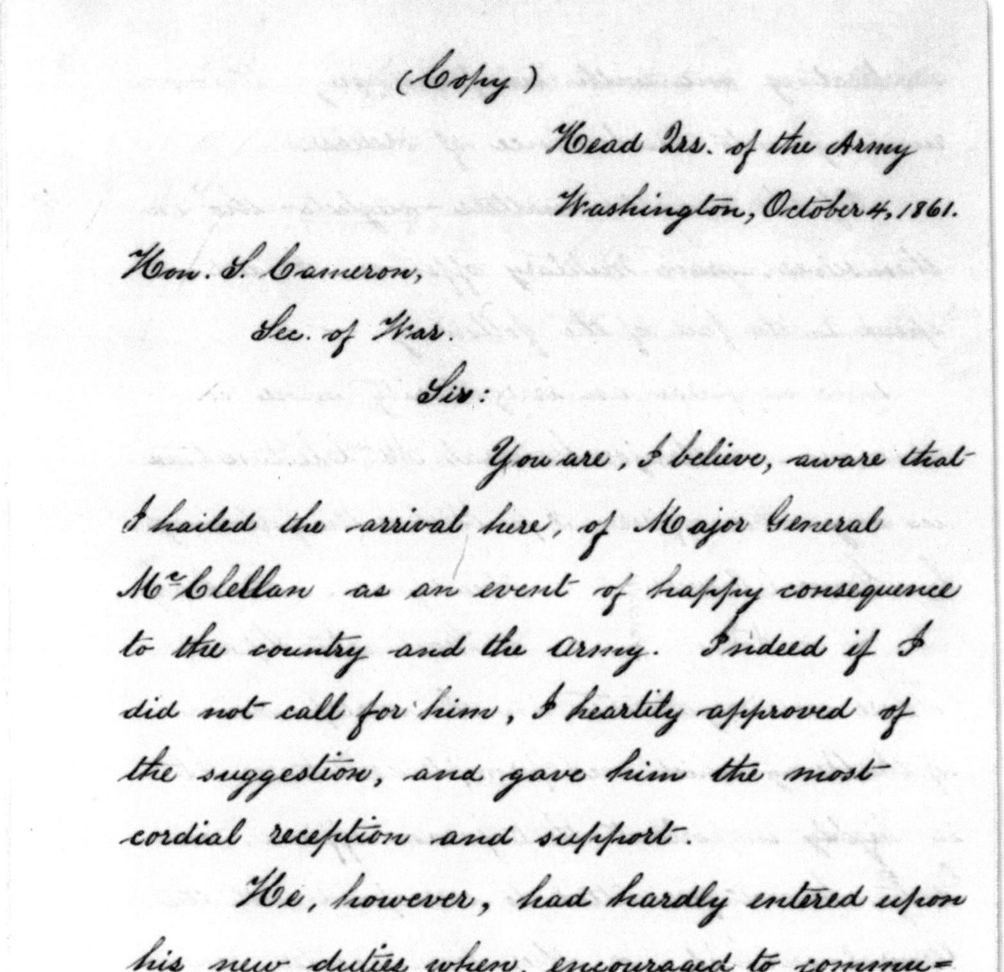

(Copy)

Head Qrs. of the Army
Washington, October 4, 1861.

Hon. S. Cameron,
     Sec. of War.

        Sir:

          You are, I believe, aware that I hailed the arrival here, of Major General McClellan as an event of happy consequence to the country and the Army. Indeed if I did not call for him, I heartily approved of the suggestion, and gave him the most cordial reception and support.

          He, however, had hardly entered upon his new duties when, encouraged to communicate directly with the President and certain members of the Cabinet, he, in a few days, forgot that he had any intermediate commander, and has now long prided himself
in

*Hyper-cautious on the field of battle, Major General George B. McClellan was recklessly arrogant when it came to his relations with other officers—especially those senior to him. General-in-chief Winfield Scott was sufficiently provoked to write Secretary of War Simon Cameron a letter of complaint about the "impertinence" of the man the newspapers were calling the "Young Napoleon."*

*These "Napoleons," the standard field artillery of the U.S. Army, line a Washington street, ready for quick transport either to the nearest front or to the defense of the capital itself.*

against him—a hundred thousand or more. This estimate was largely the product of his chronically fevered imagination, perhaps the projection upon the Confederates of his own ambitions. He threw the capital into a panic by declaring a state of emergency in August, and during this period, his estimate of enemy strength grew daily. By the middle of the month, he was certain that at least 150,000 rebels menaced the capital.

## From Squabble to Shock

McClellan got on famously with his subordinates, especially the common soldiers, but he could not abide commanders above him. Privately, he condemned Winfield Scott as either "a traitor, or an incompetent" and complained of perpetually having to "fight my way against him." For his part, aware that he and the Army of the Potomac commander were as oil and water, Scott did what he had never before done in his military career: He surrendered, tendering his resignation to President Lincoln. At first, the president refused to accept it. Then, in the overheated climate of the capital, rumors took flame. It was said (though never by McClellan himself) that McClellan would resign if Scott did not step down first. The prospect of losing the "Young Napoleon" was bad enough, but soon whispers began that, if Old Fuss and Feathers remained general-in-chief, McClellan would lead a military coup for the good of the country. Amid the buzz of speculation, Lincoln called an emergency Cabinet meeting on

October 18, and it was decided to accept Scott's resignation for "reasons of health." It was not entirely a lie. Old, obese, gouty, and rheumatic, Scott had a very hard time getting around. With Scott out of the way, McClellan was jumped from commanding general of the Army of the Potomac to general-in-chief of the entire Union army.

> "I went to the White House shortly
> after tea where I found 'the original gorilla,' about
> as intelligent as ever. What a specimen to be at the
> head of our affairs now!"

*George B. McClellan, letter to his wife, November 17, 1861
(McClellan picked up the phrase "original gorilla"
from Edwin Stanton, Lincoln's secretary of war.)*

# IF McCLELLAN HAD HAD HIS WAY

George McClellan's request for a single army of nearly 300,000 men was impractical at best for at least two reasons. First, it would have taken a long time to assemble and train, time that the Confederates already in the field would have used to make gains wherever they could, winning victories that would likely have sapped the North's will to continue the war.

econd, both the U.S. and Confederate armies lacked a key element of the command structure of modern armies: an extensive staff level. Staff officers occupy the organizational level between the highest command and the commanders in the field. They ensure that orders are properly transmitted and—more importantly—are properly executed. They monitor and coordinate the implementation of the strategy and tactics dictated from the top commanders. Absent a full staff level, communication and coordination becomes extremely difficult, especially with a large force. Even a "Young Napoleon" would have found a 300,000-man army unwieldy, perhaps even beyond the possibility of effective command.

What if McClellan could have accomplished what he said he wanted to—deliver a single massive blow against the Confederate army in Virginia? He believed the war would end with the destruction of the enemy army and not the devastation of the "enemy" population. Perhaps. But not likely. A severe blow so early in the war would have badly crippled the Confederate army, but it would probably have transformed the Civil War from a war between organized military formations into a guerrilla war, in which determined Confederate bands would have fought an insurgent action, perhaps for many, many years, and without a definitive conclusion. Defeating the Southern military without defeating the South itself would almost certainly have left the nation divided.

## Overestimator

George B. McClellan was a competent commander with a fatal flaw: He was a compulsive overestimator of his enemy's numbers. During 1861–62, the strength of Confederate forces arrayed against the Army of the Potomac varied from 35,000 to 60,000 men. McClellan commanded between 122,000 and 190,000 troops during this period, at minimum possessing better than a two-to-one advantage at any one time; he often enjoyed even better odds. Historians typically blame Allan J. Pinkerton, whom McClellan used as his chief intelligence officer, for delivering the gross misestimates of rebel strength. However, the Army of the Potomac commander overestimated the enemy on his own, even *before* Pinkerton entered McClellan's service. Pinkerton was merely an enabler of McClellan's fears. In any case, the result was strategic paralysis, which certainly prolonged the war.

*General McClellan hired private detective Allan Pinkerton to lead the "Secret Service Department" of his Army of the Potomac. America's original private eye, Pinkerton was wholly inexperienced in military intelligence, and his operatives almost always grossly overestimated the strength of enemy forces, thereby exacerbating McClellan's well-nigh pathological tendency to avoid bold commitment to aggressive battle. Pinkerton stands between the tent rope and tent pole just to the right of center. His brother William, also in civilian dress, stands beside him.*

What would he do with this new authority? Far less than anyone expected.

On October 19, the day after the Cabinet accepted Scott's resignation, McClellan sent a division under Brigadier General George A. McCall to Dranesville, Virginia, for the purpose of probing Confederate movements in that area and also in the vicinity of Leesburg. No sooner was this done than McClellan ordered McCall back to the division's main camp at Langley, Virginia, a few miles from the capital. McCall, however, lingered just long enough to map roads in the area. In the meantime, McClellan dispatched Brigadier General Charles Stone on another tentative mission, ordering him to stage "a slight demonstration" intended to provoke a Confederate response. Picking up on McClellan's caution, Stone moved a small force across the Potomac at Edwards Ferry, and, eliciting no Confederate reaction, quickly pulled this unit back, but ordered the commander of the 15th Massachusetts Infantry to send a twenty-man night patrol to reconnoiter the enemy position. In the darkness, the patrol's leader, a callow captain named Chase Philbrick, mistook a stand of trees for Confederate tents. Fearing that he and his few men would be discovered, he hightailed it back to regimental headquarters with his report. This prompted General Stone to order an attack on the "camp" with three hundred men at first light on October 21.

Daylight quickly revealed Philbrick's error, but, having crossed the river with his raiding party, Colonel Charles Devens decided to wait for instructions from General Stone before he turned back. Stone responded by sending the rest of 15th Massachusetts (another 350 men) to join the raiding party, and the combined force of 750 men was ordered to march toward Leesburg for a reconnaissance there. In the meantime, Edward Dickinson Baker, a U.S. senator and a Union colonel, arrived in Stone's camp. Stone welcomed him and promptly dispatched him to find out just what Devens was doing. Stone gave him authority either to withdraw the troops from Virginia altogether or to send in more.

En route to Devens's position, Baker learned that a small skirmish had taken place. Eager for action, Baker used the carte blanche Stone had given him to order as many troops as could be quickly rounded up to cross the Potomac. It was one thing to issue such an impulsive order and quite another to execute it, especially in the absence of a sufficient number of boats to make the crossing en masse. As the soldiers trickled across a few at a time, the fighting began to heat up on the Confederate side of the river, at a place called Ball's Bluff. It was a wild, thickly wooded, steep-sided hill some thirty miles up the river from Washington. Baker marched to the sound of the guns—and paid with his life. He was the only U.S. senator killed in action before or since.

The battle that had begun so hesitantly now exploded. Most of Devens's men, about 650, were bottled up atop the steep bluff. The same paucity of boats that had reduced reinforcements to a trickle now created chaos as Union troops attempted to retreat back across the Potomac. Essentially trapped on Ball's Bluff and between it and the river, the Union forces were fully exposed when the 17th Mississippi Regiment arrived on the scene. The Confederates charged up the bluff, driving the bluecoats down its precipitous slope and into the river. Fleeing the rebels' bayonets, the men ran, jumping down from

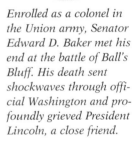

*Enrolled as a colonel in the Union army, Senator Edward D. Baker met his end at the battle of Ball's Bluff. His death sent shockwaves through official Washington and profoundly grieved President Lincoln, a close friend.*

*By later Civil War standards, the battle of Ball's Bluff was relatively minor, but the Union's defeat here was humiliating and did not bode well for the Union cause. This depiction of the "retreat of the Federalists after the fight at Ball's Bluff" was published in the* Illustrated London News *on November 23, 1861.*

the cliff and landing one atop another, some skewering themselves on the bayonets of those who had leaped first. Panic-stricken troops piled into the few available boats, capsizing most of them.

That is when the bodies began to pass downriver, where Washing-tonians could see them float in a lazy current tinged now with Union blood.

Compared to the battles that had yet to be fought, the Union casualties, though gory, were actually modest—between nine hundred to more than a thousand killed, wounded, or captured—but the psychological effect on the Washington government was catastrophic. Senator Baker had been a close personal friend of the president, and his death hit Lincoln hard. Worse, some members of Congress believed he had actually been assassinated as part of a treasonous conspiracy to undermine the Union. Without ambiguity, the Constitution names the president of the United States as commander-in-chief of the armed forces. Driven by the conspiracy theory, Congress ignored the Constitution and created a Joint Committee on the Conduct of the War, which spent the rest of the Civil War looking over Lincoln's shoulder and even second-guessing senior commanders in the field. Coming after two significant Union defeats—Bull Run and Wilson's Creek—the ugly outcome of Ball's Bluff effectively moved Congress to compound the difficulty of fighting the war.

One of the first acts of the new committee was to haul General Stone into the Capitol to explain what had happened at Ball's Bluff. When the committee members didn't like what he told them—he attributed the debacle largely to the bumbling inexperience of senator-cum-colonel Baker—they ordered his arrest and imprisonment on suspicion (he was never charged) of treason. This treatment was both unprecedented and unrepeated in U.S. history. A profound injustice against Stone, it was a great boon to George B. McClellan. After all, the American public needed but one scapegoat, and the Young Napoleon therefore emerged from Ball's Bluff—small as it was, his biggest battle yet—unscathed.

# SCAPEGOAT

Born in 1824 in Greenfield, Massachusetts, Brigadier General Charles P. Stone graduated from West Point near the top of the class of 1845, fought gallantly in the U.S.-Mexican War, and, in the Civil War, as a result of the Ball's Bluff fiasco, was called to testify before the newly created Congressional Joint Committee on the Conduct of the War.

When he dared to criticize the incompetent tactical leadership of Colonel— and Senator—Edward Baker (whose bravery he nonetheless praised), he was arrested on suspicion of treason. Imprisoned and held in solitary confinement for 189 days without formal charges or a hearing, he was released with neither explanation nor apology. Although he was returned to duty, he would receive no important assignment for the rest of the war. He resigned his commission at the end of the war, worked as a mining engineer from 1865 to 1869, and then embarked on a career as a mercenary, accepting appointment as the chief of the General Staff of the army of the Khedive of Egypt. He did not leave this service until 1883, when he retired a wealthy man with the colorful title of "pasha." He returned to the United States and engineering and, as if to reassert his patriotic loyalty, served as chief engineer for the construction of the base for the Statue of Liberty. Stone died in 1887.

*Brigadier General Charles P. Stone, a stellar West Point graduate in 1845 and a minor hero of the U.S.-Mexican War, criticized the tactical leadership of Colonel Edward Baker, the popular senator killed at Ball's Bluff. For daring to speak his mind, Stone was scapegoated—held in solitary confinement without trial for 189 days on "suspicion" of treason.*

## THE TANNER'S SON

DESPITE BALL'S BLUFF and the other disappointments, horrors, and humiliations, the people and politicians of the Union continued to look both hopefully and admiringly to George B. McClellan and to the unfolding war's eastern theater. They took little enough notice of action in the western theater (involving the region west of the Appalachians) and practically no one said anything at all about a brigadier general out there, Ulysses S. Grant.

Little wonder. He was not particularly impressive. In fact, there seemed to be remarkably little substance to the man. Whereas McClellan was the son of a prominent Philadelphia family, Grant was born in 1822 to a tanner in the Ohio hamlet of Point Pleasant. He came to adulthood not

*The noted American artist and illustrator Will Sartain created this group portrait of Ulysses S. Grant and his family, which was published as a mezzotint around 1867.*

*The Civil War occasioned the appointment of many generals on both sides. A few were brilliant. Many were earnest, patriotic, and remarkably brave. A considerable number were simply incompetent. Near the head of this latter class was the pompous Tennessean Gideon J. Pillow of the Confederate States Army.*

even owning his own name. For in 1839, seventeen-year-old Hiram Ulysses Grant—such was his birth name—was enrolled at West Point, having been nominated by a local congressman who knew so little of him that he forwarded to the academy the name "Ulysses S. Grant of Ohio." Perhaps because he liked the initials "U.S.," perhaps because he did not want the initials "HUG" stitched into his clothing as a laundry mark (the other cadets would have had a laugh over that!), or perhaps because he didn't much care, Grant took the mistaken name as his own—and didn't even bother to make up a full name to attach to the middle initial the congressman had given him. (The "Simpson" would come later.)

His academy record was mediocre—he graduated in 1843, twenty-first in a class of thirty-nine—and, at the outbreak of the U.S.-Mexican War, he was relegated to service in a regimental quartermaster corps. Like William Tecumseh Sherman, he was a supply clerk. Unlike Sherman, he did manage to see action, but, like him and so many other young officers, he found career prospects after the war in the peacetime army grim. Grant resigned his commission in 1854, and, as mentioned in Chapter 1, proceeded to fail at every civilian occupation he attempted, from farmer to bill collector. After the fall of Fort Sumter, Grant, who was supporting himself and his family with a clerkship in his father's Galena, Illinois, tannery, helped raise and train a volunteer regiment in Illinois. In August 1861, President Lincoln commissioned him a brigadier general of volunteers, and at the end of the month, Major General John C. Frémont, presiding over the western theater at the time, named him to command the turbulent District of Southeastern Missouri.

In November 1861, Grant loaded some three thousand troops into boats at Cairo, Illinois, the tip of the state, where the Mississippi meets the Ohio, and crossed the Mississippi into Missouri, landing at Belmont. Here he engaged and defeated a Confederate force under General Gideon Pillow. A vainglorious Tennessee politician who, during the U.S.-Mexican War, had sent a pseudonymous letter to the *New Orleans Delta* newspaper claiming credit for victories actually won by Winfield Scott, Pillow was a congenitally incompetent commander, so beating him was no signal accomplishment. Nevertheless, Grant was pleased, and he turned his troops loose on the abandoned Confederate camp, bidding them take and enjoy whatever they could find.

All military formations live or die by discipline. By giving his men permission to behave like a mob, Grant had committed a grave error, and Pillow was there to make the most of it. Seeing Grant's wild men swarming over the camp, he unleashed a surprise artillery bombardment, creating frenzied confusion that he further exploited by assembling ten thousand troops below Belmont ready to sever Grant from his river transports.

Grant had put himself and his command in a tactical cul de sac. It was a mistake. It was stupid. It might have been cataclysmic. But Grant refused to brood or panic. When one of his officers, with a face full of doom, blubbered the obvious—*we are surrounded*—Grant replied with perfectly matter-of-fact equanimity: "Well, we must cut our way out as we cut our way in."

"I learned later . . . that [the battle of] Belmont had caused more mourning than almost any other battle up to that time. The National [that is, Union] troops acquired a confidence in themselves at Belmont that did not desert them through the war."

*Ulysses S. Grant,* Personal Memoirs, *1885*

A retreat is seldom praised as a victory, and so the battle of Belmont, November 7, 1861, should be counted a Union defeat, but retreating is actually the most difficult and hazardous movement a military force can make. For one army to turn its back or expose its flank to another invites disaster. In withdrawing from the camp so recently captured, Grant reasserted discipline and was able to make an effective fighting retreat, cutting his way out, as he said, while preserving his command intact. In the end, the Confederates held the field, but had lost 641 (killed, wounded, or missing) out of some 5,000 engaged, whereas Grant suffered 607 casualties out of 3,114 men.

## REALITY CHECK
### And the Winner Was . . . ?

Most Civil War historians consider the outcome of the battle of Belmont (November 7, 1861) to have been inconclusive, a draw; however, by the standards of the time, it was a Confederate victory inasmuch as Grant was forced from the field. This said, it was a costly victory for Southern forces, which incurred 641 casualties (105 killed, 419 wounded, 117 missing or captured) out of about 5,000 men engaged versus 607 (120 killed, 383 wounded, 104 missing or captured) out of Grant's engaged complement of 3,114 men.

## Under Old Brains

For Grant, it was a bad beginning. But he and most of his men would live to fight another day. And maybe it was just as well that the mass of Americans, both Northerners and Southerners, hardly noticed Grant's failure—they were too busy watching McClellan.

East of the Appalachians, the Civil War took on an aura of Napoleonic grandeur, whereas to the west, it was, in its first year, an affair of far fewer numbers, more workmanlike maneuvers, and slaughter on a more modest scale. The western theater was the war's backwater, and the U.S. Army had put it under the command of an officer whose abilities were known to be limited. Nobody questioned the courage of John Charles Frémont, an intrepid Western explorer popularly known as "The Pathfinder." Besides, he was the son-in-law of the late Thomas Hart Benton, a powerful senator from Missouri, and he remained very well connected. Frémont, the military believed, was good enough, *just* good enough, for a backwater war.

To his credit, Frémont did fully appreciate the strategic, tactical, and logistical importance of the three great rivers that watered the western theater—the Mississippi, Tennessee, and Cumberland—and he devoted much time and effort to hurriedly building a fleet of gunboats. Not that they were all that hard to build. Ugly, squat, and drawing very little water, they were not much more than floating platforms for artillery. Slow to move and difficult to maneuver, they were sometimes clad in iron plates to minimize the damage inflicted by enemy fire.

*Behold the Union gunboat: squat, ugly, hard to kill, and perfectly suited to river warfare. Pictured is the USS* Cincinnati, *"the gunboat that fired the first shot at Fort Henry."*

In September 1861, after General Polk invaded Kentucky and installed an occupation force at Columbus, a town perched commandingly on a bluff above the Mississippi, the state abandoned its claim to neutrality, now declaring itself wholeheartedly for the Union. Encouraged by this, Grant responded to the Confederate occupation of Columbus by occupying Paducah, Kentucky, from which the mouths of both the Tennessee and Cumberland Rivers could be strategically defended.

Much as the U.S. Congress insinuated itself into Union military affairs with almost invariably poor results, so President Jefferson Davis put his hand in Confederate military field operations, also typically to the detriment of sound strategy and tactics. Today, he would be condemned as a micromanager. Nevertheless, in the fall of 1861, Davis saw what the Union high command failed to see—that control of the western rivers would be critical to the outcome of the war. Whereas the Union put the western theater in the hands of a third-rate commander, Davis tapped Albert Sidney Johnston, a West Pointer who had fought in the Texas War of Independence in 1836 and the U.S.-Mexican War ten years later, to take charge of the western theater for the Confederacy. At the time, he was considered the best all-round commander in the entire Confederate army.

Like Davis, Johnston appreciated the critical importance of the rivers. He sought to dominate the Mississippi by reinforcing Columbus, and he hastily erected fortified strong points along the Cumberland and Tennessee Rivers. On the Tennessee, he had built one full-fledged fort, Fort Henry, and on the Cumberland another, Fort Donelson. As the rivers were being fortified by both sides, Union high command rethought its choice of theater commander and in November 1861 replaced Frémont with

*Jefferson Davis was a great admirer of Albert Sidney Johnston, a West Point graduate and veteran of the Texas War of Independence of 1836 as well as the U.S.-Mexican War of 1846–48. Ulysses S. Grant judged him a "man of high character and ability" but did not find him a particularly formidable adversary. His actions, Grant wrote, were "vacillating and undecided."*

**DETAILS, DETAILS**
**Gunboat Ugly**
The Union navy of the Civil War consisted mostly of gunboats—squat, ugly vessels designed for riverborne warfare. Typical was the 233-ton USS *Peosta*, about 151 feet stem to stern with a beam (width) of 34 feet 3 inches. She drew just six feet of water when fully loaded—ideal for shallows—and could crawl along at five knots. Armament included three 30-pounder Parrott rifles (rifled cannons that fired 30-pound projectiles), three 32-pounders (smoothbores), six 24-pounder howitzers (cannons designed to fire at a high trajectory against shore fortifications), and a pair of 12-pounder smoothbores. USS *Peosta* started life as a wooden sidewheel commercial steamer, which the navy bought in Dubuque, Iowa, in June 1863 for $22,000, and converted for combat by reinforcing above-water superstructure with sloping wooden sides. Some gunboats added to these sloping sides tin or iron cladding and were therefore called ironclads. This technology would evolve into the all-metal construction of the *Monitor* class of warship (see Chapter 7).

*Major General Henry Wager Halleck as depicted by Currier & Ives in 1862. Halleck is derided by most modern historians, and he was, in fact, an undistinguished combat commander. As a bureaucratic organizer and expediter, however, Halleck was unexcelled. He served admirably, late in the war, as the first chief of staff of the U.S. Army.*

Major General Henry Wager Halleck. The author of the first important military textbook written in the United States, *Elements of Military Art and Science*, published in 1846, Halleck was more comfortable as a theorist than as a field commander—a fact commemorated in the nickname given to him, first in affection, but soon in contempt. He was called "Old Brains."

Old Brains was probably an improvement over Frémont, but the Union lost any advantage his assignment might have created by deciding to split the western command. Halleck was assigned the region west of the Cumberland River, and Brigadier General Don Carlos Buell was given command east of the river.

Splitting command in the theater was a bad idea. Halleck was a thinker, and Buell, who had been a veritable tiger in the days of the U.S.-Mexican War, had mellowed in judgment, becoming slow and deliberative. Thus, temperamentally, Halleck and Buell were not all that different from one another; neither man was given to bold, aggressive action. This was a serious defect of command because, together, Halleck and Buell presided over a combined force significantly larger than that of Johnston. This being the case, a maximum of aggression was called for. Neither of these commanders was prepared to deliver it.

Nor was conservatism their only liability. Despite the similarity of attitude—perhaps because of it—Halleck and Buell most cordially hated one another. They repeatedly failed to collaborate. Often, they avoided so much as speaking to one another, thereby rarely succeeding in coordinating plans and operations. It was as if the Union had thrown away its advantage in numbers by purposely dividing its army in the West.

*Early in the war, Brigadier General Don Carlos Buell shared command with Halleck in the Tennessee-Kentucky area. The two generals hated one another, refusing to coordinate their forces. Together, they threw away an opportunity for early victory in their theater of operations.*

## "Unconditional Surrender"

Whatever else they may be, the fortunes of war are rarely just. Despite the defects in Union command, the first assault against Johnston's army succeeded splendidly, as Union general George H. Thomas defeated George B. Crittenden's Confederates at the battle of Mill Springs, Kentucky, on January 19, 1862.

Grant then proposed to Halleck a plan for capturing the two major Confederate forts on the Tennessee and Cumberland Rivers. Old Brains was not inclined to approve the plan. For one thing, it struck him as too ambitiously aggressive, and, for another—this was even more important to him—Grant was overly fond of drink. Or at least Halleck believed the rumors of Grant's drunkenness. But Lincoln did to Halleck in the West what he was doing to McClellan in the East. He piled on the pressure to attack, and, finally, it seemed easier to Halleck to allow Grant to fight the rebels instead of being forced himself to fight the president. So he set Grant at the head of fifteen thousand men. Supported by a gunboat squadron under naval Flag Officer Andrew Foote, Grant's troops moved against Fort Henry on the Tennessee. The fort succumbed to a combined land and river assault on February 6.

What happened next showed what Grant was made of. He did not linger following his victory, but immediately turned his columns eastward and marched them from the Tennessee to the Cumberland River. Once again coordinating with Foote's gunboats, Grant positioned himself to attack Fort Donelson. For his part, however, General Johnston was determined not to allow a repetition of the fall of Fort Henry. Anticipating Grant's next move, he withdrew fifteen thousand troops from Bowling Green, Kentucky, and used them to reinforce Fort Donelson, which held out against Grant for three brutal days.

The Napoleonic model to which all instructors at West Point adhered—and to which virtually all officers, Union and Confederate, aspired—called above all for "dash": daring, bold, swift, sharp, sweeping actions. Ulysses Grant was willing to go against the Napoleonic grain. He was willing to plod, to hammer, to kill, and to be killed in return until his objective was achieved. As he saw it, war was less a matter of dash than of hard and painful labor. Instead of pulling back from the reinforced fort, he held his ground until artillery reinforcements arrived and he could pound Fort Donelson and its adjacent positions with massed cannon.

### REALITY CHECK
### A "Butcher" with Brains

As we will see later (Chapter 17), Grant's willingness to inflict as well as absorb heavy casualties eventually earned him the epithet "Butcher Grant." Some military historians still criticize his judgment in persisting in the assault on Fort Donelson after Johnston reinforced it. But Grant's decision was the product neither of obstinacy nor foolhardiness. Sure, Grant was aggressive, but he was also a sagacious tactician. As he explained in his memoirs: "I had known General Pillow in Mexico, and judged that with any force, no matter how small, I could march up to within gunshot of any intrenchments he was given to hold. I said this to the officers of my staff at the time. I knew that Floyd was in command [of Fort Donelson], but he was no soldier, and I judged that he would yield to Pillow's pretensions." Grant knew his enemies, for they had once been his colleagues and comrades—and he acted accordingly.

*Union general George H. Thomas bested Confederate George B. Crittenden at the battle of Mill Springs, Kentucky, on January 19, 1862. Relatively minor though it was, the engagement merited a handsome chromolithograph from Currier & Ives.*

Under Grant's unremitting assault, the four top Confederate commanders withdrew to a little inn at Dover, the hamlet just outside of Fort Donelson. Although they were just four muddy men huddled in a barroom, they dubbed their gathering a "counsel of war." Its subject was straightforward—surrender—but none of the senior Confederates in the field, neither General John Buchanan Floyd nor General Pillow, was willing to be the one to tender the capitulation. Floyd, who had actual command of the fort and its garrison, deftly sought to pass the burden to Pillow.

"I turn command over, sir," he declared to Pillow. Undaunted and scarcely pausing for breath, Pillow, accepting it, turned to General Simon Bolivar Buckner. "I pass it," he said. "I assume it," Buckner responded. Watching and listening to this martial minuet, General Nathan Bedford Forrest—a tough, profane, self-taught, self-made blacksmith's son—spat out, "I did not come here for the purpose of surrendering my command," turned on his heel, left the inn, mounted his waiting horse, rode back to his headquarters, and, acting on his own authority, assembled his command, which he led off the field. They would fight another day. In the meantime, having tossed the hot potato of surrender to Buckner, Floyd and Pillow decamped. Both evaded Union capture, but Jefferson Davis found their absence of fighting spirit intolerable. Without bothering to convene a court martial, the Confederate president relieved Floyd of command. Pillow he only suspended—but forever afterward withheld from him any major command.

It fell, then, to Buckner to send the customarily chivalrous note to Grant proposing that each general appoint "commissioners to agree upon terms of capitulation of the forces and fort [some sources say "post"] under my command."

But Grant was having none of it. He sat down and wrote a note of his own: "No terms except an unconditional and immediate surrender can be accepted. I propose to move immediately upon your works." When this reply found its way to the newspapers, Grant learned that he had acquired yet *another* name: "Unconditional Surrender" Grant.

## A WINNING GENERAL GOES UNAPPRECIATED

UP TO THIS POINT, THE NORTHERN PUBLIC, grasping at straws, had inflated the significance of every Union victory, few and minor as they mostly were. Now, in taking the forts on the Tennessee and the Cumberland, the Union army and navy really had won important triumphs. Having lost control of the major arteries in the region, Johnston had no choice but to evacuate Nashville—and to do so post-haste, which meant abandoning supplies the Confederacy could hardly afford to relinquish. Moreover, with Forts Henry and Donelson gone, the well-fortified Confederate position at Columbus was fully exposed and therefore had to be abandoned as well.

Thus by the second month of 1862, the Union had a general in the East, George B. McClellan, who had made a reputation out of all proportion to his achievements, and a general in the West, whose major victories were just beginning to attract notice. Where McClellan was polished but pathologically cautious, Grant was crude in manner but skillfully aggressive in command. President Lincoln, as we will see in Chapter 9, was, at this point, losing patience with his "Young Napoleon." After the battle of Belmont, Grant's commanding officer, "Old Brains" Halleck, eager to make its ambiguous outcome appear to be an outright victory, had obtained promotion for Grant from

**POP CULTURE**

**Binge Drinker**

Mention the name of Ulysses S. Grant to a random collection of people, and it is virtually certain that at least one of them will say something like, "He was an alcoholic, you know." Someone else will respond that this was just a rumor created by generals and politicians who were jealous of him. The truth probably lies somewhere between these two positions. Grant did sometimes drink on duty—so did other officers—and he may sometimes have been fully and floridly drunk. We do know that he was by no means a daily drinker, but it does seem he indulged in occasional binges. When some suggested to Lincoln that Grant was a drunkard and should be relieved of command, the president famously replied, "If it [liquor] makes fighting men like Grant, then find out what he drinks, and send my other commanders a case!"

brigadier general to major general of volunteers, along with other brigadiers under his command; however, after Grant dared to pay a call on Halleck's rival, Don Carlos Buell, in Nashville, Halleck relieved Grant of command on suspicion of alcoholism. Although he soon returned Grant to command, he never pointed to him with the pride he surely deserved. Had he done so, perhaps Lincoln would have found right then and there what he spent the next two blood-soaked and heartbreaking years groping after: a winning general.

## UNCONQUERABLE CAUTION

TRANSFERRED FROM VIRGINIA to serve as General Johnston's right hand in Tennessee, P. G. T. Beauregard found his first assignment most distasteful. It was to lead the evacuation of the Columbus garrison, marching the men out of the town and to the south, where they were to link up with the main body of Johnston's troops at Corinth, Mississippi, the major rail junction in the vicinity. Johnston's intention was to build a force of some fifty thousand men to make a credible stand against the Union. Obviously, the winning move for the Union army at this point would have been to meet the combined forces of Johnston and Beauregard with overwhelming force. It was a mission well within the realm of possibility. If, together, Johnston and Beauregard could mass fifty thousand men, Halleck and Buell could easily send seventy thousand troops against this force.

While Grant prodded Old Brains to do just this, pleading with him to pursue the retreating rebels with *everything* available, Halleck responded by pondering and plodding, and Buell, for his part, moved no faster. In war, the only possession more valuable than geographical position is time. Halleck and Buell gave Beauregard and Johnston all the time they needed to unite, regroup, and take up a strong position at Corinth.

For every Grant, the Union army seemed to have ten McClellans, ten Hallecks, and ten Buells: well-meaning, well-trained professional soldiers, who lacked only the fire in the belly that makes all the difference between a bold commander and a timid one. As there would be a terrible price to pay for McClellan's unconquerable caution, so the hesitations of Halleck and Buell would bring a dreadful reckoning, but neither Halleck nor Buell would pay. It would be left to Grant and his men, as well as the gray enemy they faced, to settle their open account with unprecedented savagery, at a place called Shiloh.

# CHAPTER 7

## IRON AGE

*Civil War and Industrial Revolution*

NO STUDENT ESCAPES AN AMERICAN CLASSROOM WITHOUT HEARING a whole lot about the "Industrial Revolution," the first of which began in England toward the end of the eighteenth century and made itself felt in America through a handful of inventions, among them Eli Whitney's cotton gin—patented in 1794—before accelerating during 1820 to 1870, engulfing most of the Western hemisphere and nowhere more than the United States. As we already know (see Chapter 2), the South, whose economy relied on "King Cotton"—largely because of that cotton gin—resisted America's participation in the subsequent portion of the Industrial Revolution by vehemently opposing protectionist tariffs. Yet ironically, it was this very phase of technological evolution that created an English Midlands landscape of textile mills and drove Europe's demand for Southern cotton. The Southern antitariff protest was loud and vehement, and it threatened civil war more than three decades before the events of 1860–61 at Fort Sumter, but it could not arrest the industrialization of the United States, which took place mostly (though not exclusively) in the North.

It was a revolution made of raw iron and run on iron rails. During the four years of the Civil War, much of that metal went into firearms, cannons, and ships. The soldiers of the Civil War were anything but born warriors. Many, probably most, of them were newcomers to the use of firearms and, quite literally, couldn't shoot straight. But into the hands of this generation, a new Iron Age delivered warfare's first weapons of mass destruction, and so the Civil War savaged America.

*Taken in April 1865 at Broadway Landing on the Appomattox River in Virginia, this photograph vividly demonstrates the prodigious capacity of Northern industry to turn out arms. What it does not explain is whether the ordnance shown here has been returned from the field for shipment back north or whether it is newly arrived, destined never to be used in a war just concluded.*

## OF RIFLE-MUSKETS AND MINIÉ BALLS

DURING THE U.S.-MEXICAN WAR of 1846–48, the U.S. Army standard-issue long arm was the .69-caliber smoothbore flintlock musket. Its technology predated the American Revolution, although the model most widely used early in the Civil War had been introduced in 1822. The weapon had an effective range of about one hundred yards, after which the lead ball it shot would lose momentum and, even more important, accuracy. During the first year of the Civil War, most soldiers on both sides still used this and similar weapons, but, during the war, the smoothbores were replaced by rifle-muskets—most of them manufactured in the United States by the Springfield (Massachusetts) Arsenal and in England by Enfield. These weapons tripled the effective range of the old smoothbore flintlock from one hundred to three hundred yards. The reason was the rifling—the spiral grooves machined into the interior of the barrel—imparted a spin to the projectile, giving it greater muzzle velocity and far greater accuracy.

Mass producing any reliable firearm requires advanced manufacturing techniques and facilities, and turning out a rifled firearm calls for tools capable of machining an accurate spiral groove inside a weapon's barrel. In the already highly industrialized North, this was no problem, but in the South, sophisticated arms manufacturers were few and far between. The Springfield Arsenal produced 800,000 .58 caliber rifle-muskets between 1861 and 1863 (Northern private contractors supplied an additional 600,000 during this period), whereas the principal Southern factory, in Richmond, turned out 322,231 long arms of all kinds between 1861 and 1865. The South looked to British

Eli Whitney is best remembered as the inventor
of the cotton gin. He made his greatest fortune, however,
as a mass producer of firearms, such as this .69-caliber 1812 Contract
Flintlock Musket—manufactured, as the name implies, under U.S. Army
contract for the War of 1812. This musket was obsolescent by the time of
the U.S.-Mexican War and obsolete by the Civil War, yet some army and
militia units nevertheless used it in both conflicts.

The minié ball made firing
from rifled shoulder arms
practical. From left to right
are a .557 Enfiled minié
bullet, a pair of Burton
Pattern minié bullets for
the .58-caliber Springfield, a
"Clean Out Bullet" (loaded
to clean out the "fouling,"
or residue, deposited in a
rifle barrel by black powder;
this one is missing its zinc
base), and a .69 caliber
minié bullet modified for
use in the Model 1843
Springfield Musket.

The .58-caliber Model 1855 Springfield Rifle-Musket was a reasonably
modern weapon at the time of the Civil War, employing the more reliable
percussion priming system rather than the outdated flintlock. Regardless,
as a single-shot muzzleloader in an era in which breech-loaded repeating
rifles were available, it betrays the technological conservatism of both the
Union and Confederate armies in the Civil War. Many officers believed
that breech-loading repeating rifles were less reliable than cumbersome
single-shot muzzleloaders because they were more mechanically complex.
High command also believed the new weapons encouraged soldiers to
waste expensive ammunition rather than try to make each shot count.

suppliers, like Enfield, to make up the shortfall. This required British
firms to violate Her Majesty's poorly enforced neutrality laws—a
source of continual friction between the United States and Great
Britain—and it required Southern mariners to risk their ships and
lives running the Anaconda blockade of Confederate ports.

Before you can make a rifled firearm, you need ammunition that can
be fired from it. In the Civil War, this was the minié ball. It was a remarkable, ingenious, and revolutionary piece of ammunition, but it was not,
despite its name, a ball. Invented by the Frenchman Claude-Etienne Minié
in 1848, it was a bullet in shape, with a pointed front end, greased grooves
(called rings) scored into the trailing end, and a concave base. Now, here's
where the ingenuity comes in: The minié ball was smaller in diameter
than the barrel of the rifle-musket, which made muzzle loading a snap;
the soldier did not have to struggle to ram a ball into the barrel. When the
weapon was fired, the gases created by the burning gunpowder would fill
the concavity in the bullet's base, expanding the soft lead even as those

*The Spencer repeating carbines these two Union cavalrymen display in this tintype photograph are more modern weapons than most Civil War warriors took into battle. Breech-loaded with short barrels, repeating carbines were made to be fired from the saddle. The troopers' Colt Army revolvers and Model 1860 sabers are also cavalry weapons.*

same explosively expanding gases propelled the bullet through the barrel. The ridges of the expanded bullet would engage the barrel's spiral rifling as the projectile traveled through it, causing the minié ball to spin as it emerged from the muzzle.

Although the armies on both sides eagerly embraced the rifle-musket, they were far more reluctant about adopting another innovation of potentially equal importance. The rifle-muskets used by Union and Confederate infantrymen were muzzleloaders. This meant that the bullet had to be inserted into the muzzle (front) end of the barrel and rammed down using the ramrod that was stored below the barrel. Each minié ball was packaged with a paper cartridge, which contained the black powder that propelled the bullet. Some varieties placed the bullet within the cartridge, whereas others affixed the cartridge to the base of the minié ball, leaving the actual bullet exposed.

Unifying the cartridge and the bullet was a vast improvement over the earlier muzzle-loading smoothbore, in which the soldier had to first ram down a black powder cartridge and then ram down the ball after it, but even with the rifle-musket and minié ball, muzzle loading was arduous and time consuming, and it typically exposed the soldier to enemy fire.

There was an alternative: the breechloader, which was designed to accept ammunition through the rear (breech) of the barrel. Loading was therefore faster and far less cumbersome, meaning that the shooter could get off more shots more quickly without having to put himself in positions that made him an easy target. If loading and reloading a muzzleloader was difficult for a foot soldier, it was nearly impossible for a cavalryman perched on his horse. For this reason, the cavalry on both sides readily adopted breechloaders, such as the Spencer carbine (a carbine has a shorter barrel than a rifle-musket and is therefore easier to manage on horseback), but the high command of the Confederacy and the Union alike shunned breechloaders for infantry use precisely

The U.S. Rifle Model 1841 is an example of a popular type of older firearm that was often refurbished and modernized for use in the Civil War. As originally manufactured, the weapon was not equipped with an adjustable sight or a bayonet socket; both were added to those the Union reconditioned for use in 1861–65.

**NUMBERS**

**Death's Workhorse**
Rifle-muskets manufactured by Springfield and Enfield were responsible for more than 85 percent of Civil War casualties on both sides.

because they could fire rapidly. Ammunition was difficult and expensive to manufacture, and commanders wanted their men to make each shot count. In effect, they traded lives for ammunition.

If the two armies were reluctant to trade muzzleloaders for breechloaders, they were even more reluctant to deploy in large numbers the recently invented Henry repeating rifle. The rifle-musket was a single-shot weapon, and the Spencer carbine had a tube magazine that held seven shots. The seven-shot Spencer was an improvement over single-shot weapons, but, even at that, its reloading action was slow. In contrast, the Henry repeating rifle carried one round of .44 caliber ammunition in the chamber and fifteen more rounds in an improved tube magazine, which more rapidly fed the ammunition into firing position with each shot. Thus a soldier could shoot not one, not seven, but sixteen times before reloading. The objection to the widespread use of this weapon was twofold. First, there was the matter of "wasting" valuable ammunition. Second, was the reliability of the Henry's repeating mechanism. Single-shot weapons had the virtue of mechanical simplicity. There was little to go wrong. Complex repeating weapons such as the Henry rifle often jammed, however, especially when they got dirty (and they always got dirty) or when soldiers failed to clean them properly (and they typically failed to clean them at all).

## BIG GUNS

"GOD FIGHTS ON THE SIDE with the best artillery," Napoleon Bonaparte cynically remarked, and the most widely used field artillery piece of the Civil War, officially designated by the U.S. Army as "Twelve-Pounder Field Gun, Model 1857," was universally dubbed a "Napoleon." This, however, was not a bow to Bonaparte but to Louis Napoleon—Emperor Napoleon III—who had commissioned the weapon's development for the French

The handsome brass 12-pounder "Napoleon" was the classic "light" field cannon of the Civil War. The drawing was made by Edwin Forbes and is dated August 27, 1863.

army. Nevertheless, virtually every Civil War commander would have seconded the first Napoleon's bon mot. As important as artillery was during the Napoleonic Wars of the first fifteen years of the nineteenth century, it was even more crucial—and far more destructive—during 1861 to 1865.

Technology made it so. The best Napoleons had smoothbore brass barrels, although the Confederates sometimes made do with iron-barreled twelve-pounders turned out by the Tredegar Iron Works in Richmond. Less prone to bursting or exploding than iron, a brass barrel allowed the artillerist to pack more powder into the cannon and thereby achieve a higher muzzle velocity for greater range and greater destructiveness.

Just as a rifle-musket was more accurate and more powerful than a smoothbore musket, so a rifled cannon had the same advantages over smoothbores. Rifling a brass cannon is extremely difficult and expensive; but although it is far easier to rifle a cast-iron cannon, such a weapon is far more likely to explode—with catastrophic consequences. A Union man, Robert P. Parrott, came up with a practical solution in the so-called Parrott rifle, which featured a cast-iron barrel whose breach was reinforced with a wrought-iron band (though harder to manufacture, wrought iron is stronger than cast iron). This made the Parrott rifle look rather like a giant bottle, its fat breech end tapering to a slender muzzle. Parrott rifles still exploded from time to time, but, when they worked, they delivered a long-range and accurate shot. A bit later in the war, the ordnance rifle was introduced into the Union arsenal. One hundred pounds lighter than the Parrott, it was more maneuverable in the field, and although its range was shorter—1,835 yards versus the Parrott's more than 2,000 yards—it almost never blew up.

*Called the "Swamp Angel," this 16,500-pound Parrott rifle fired a projectile eight inches in diameter and was used in August 1863 to shell the city of Charleston from an emplacement at Morris Island, South Carolina.*

## HEAVY ARTILLERY

NAPOLEONS, PARROTT RIFLES, and ordnance rifles were all *field artillery*, meaning that they were portable, readily transported to and from the place of battle and just as readily moved about the battlefield during the fight. Both the Union and Confederate armies also deployed *heavy artillery*, which was used for coastal and fortress defense and for long-term siege operations.

The most widely used heavy artillery pieces were called columbiads, which fired shells ranging

from eight inches in diameter to fifteen. The Model 1844 could lob a ten-inch shell eighteen hundred yards, whereas the Model 1861 Rodman was capable of propelling a massive fifteen-inch shell nearly five thousand yards—more than two and a half miles. Captain Thomas J. Rodman, the U.S. Army ordnance engineer who invented it, developed a manufacturing method by which the iron barrel of the cannon was cooled after casting by running a stream of water through it, thereby reducing its temperature from the inside out, which crystallized the metal in a way that gave it more strength than conventionally cooled cast iron. Rodman also designed a bottle shape, similar to the Parrott rifle, which further enhanced the integrity of the weapon.

*Although used in some field guns, the Parrott design was best applied to large artillery fired from fixed fortifications, such as the guns of Company C, 1st Connecticut Heavy Artillery, at Fort Brady, Virginia.*

Northern foundries produced a few truly monstrous guns, including the so-called Swamp Angel, which bombarded Charleston, South Carolina, with eight-inch shells propelled by two hundred pounds of black powder to a range approaching eight thousand yards. But the most gargantuan of all were the seacoast mortars. Short and squat with enormously thick barrels, these were used to lob heavy cannonballs and other types of ammunition against fortifications and other fixed objectives at high trajectories. As the name suggests, they were developed for coastal defense, but during the war, they were more often used in sieges. The most famous of these weapons was the Union's "Dictator," which

*This photograph of ruins in majestic Charleston, South Carolina, calls to mind similar images of European cities in World War II. The destruction here, however, was not made by massive air raids, but by intense bombardment from the Union's heavy artillery, including the mammoth "Swamp Angel" Parrott rifle.*

# THE ULTIMATE WEAPON THAT WASN'T

People trying to sell a new weapon rarely tout their merchandise as a lifesaver, but U.S. inventor Dr. Richard J. Gatling promoted his Gatling gun (invented in 1861 and patented the following year) as just that. It would enable wars to be fought with fewer men, thereby reducing the number of deaths.

Typically regarded as a distant precursor of the modern machine gun, the Gatling gun used a hand crank to turn its six barrels around a central shaft, each of which fired in turn. The faster the gunner cranked, the more rapid the rate of fire. As originally designed, ammunition consisted of a steel cylinder charged with black powder and primed with a percussion cap. Shells were fed into a hopper on top of the gun and descended by gravity into the breech. Each barrel fired once per revolution, and a new shell would drop into the breech as the barrel was cranked into position beneath the hopper. The cranking action also cocked and fired each barrel in turn. Eventually, Gatling created a weapon capable of firing 400 rounds per load at a theoretical rate of 1,200 rounds per minute. In reality, nobody could crank the gun that fast, and, in any case, the barrels would have become too hot at this rate.

In theory, the Gatling gun might have been a war-winning weapon, but neither the Confederate army nor the U.S. Army seized on it.

Both sides considered it too unreliable, which, in its earliest versions, it almost certainly was.

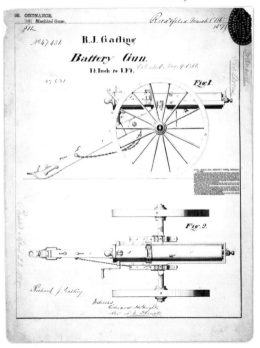

*Gatling prepared this drawing of a relatively late version of his rapid-fire gun for an 1865 U.S. patent application.*

*Trained as a physician, Dr. Richard Jordan Gatling never practiced, but took up inventing instead. His most famous breakthrough was the Gatling gun, a precursor of the machine gun that used multiple revolving barrels to produce rapid fire. Invented in 1861 and patented in 1862, the Gatling gun failed to impress technologically conservative army leaders and was not used on either side in the Civil War.*

weighed 17,000 pounds and fired thirteen-inch, 200-pound cannonballs more than a mile. The Dictator, and other mortars like it, were transported by rail and fired from the rail car that carried them.

## THE IRON AGE NAVY

BY LATE 1861 AND EARLY 1862, Winfield Scott's much-derided Anaconda naval blockade was intercepting fewer than one in ten blockade runners. The Confederate government understood, however, that as the Union built more ships and put them on the line, the rate of interdiction would become much higher. (In fact, by the end of the war, the Union navy intercepted one of every three blockade runners.) Modest as the North's navy was, the Confederacy's was far smaller. How could its commanders hope to make even a dent in the Anaconda blockade?

Perhaps there was a way. The U.S. Navy's Gosport Navy Yard, located on the south shore of Hampton Roads, Virginia, had been evacuated at the start of the war—so hurriedly that there was neither the time nor the personnel to sail all the ships back to Northern ports. Determined to keep the frigate USS *Merrimack* out of Confederate hands, Union sailors burned her to the waterline then scuttled her before they left. The waters of the yard's harbor were shallow, and refloating the *Merrimack* was not particularly difficult; however, with the blockade tight across Hampton Roads, the Confederates were hardly in a position to sail their prize anywhere—unless they could devise some way to punch through the blockading fleet.

Founded in 1833, Richmond's Tredegar Iron Works was, by the time of the Civil War, as impressive an iron foundry as any to be found up north. Using slave labor, it rushed cannons and other weapons through production. Early in 1862, it was ordered to turn out a large number of flat iron plates, which Confederate engineers used to clad what little of the refloated and highly modified *Merrimack* protruded above the waterline. The cladding was laid on in a sloping silhouette, designed to repel cannonballs, and was punctuated by ports through which cannons protruded. Rechristened the CSS *Virginia*, it was the Confederacy's first ironclad warship.

On March 8, 1862, Franklin Buchanan, the same man who at the outbreak of the war had resigned as commandant of the Brooklyn Navy Yard to defect to the Confederacy, sailed the *Virginia* into Hampton Roads to confront the wooden-hulled ships of the Union blockading fleet. The sailors

## NUMBERS

### The Arithmetic of Blockade Running

While the war had a disastrous impact on most Southern enterprises, blockade running became a growth industry. All a mariner needed was a shallow-draft ship and an abundance of guts. It has been estimated that sea captains made some thirteen hundred attempts to break through the blockade, of which around a thousand were successful. Put another way, the average blockade runner made four one-way or two two-way voyages before either wrecking on the treacherous shallows near the obscure landing places in use or being intercepted and captured by the U.S. Navy. The navy captured 1,149 Confederate ships and destroyed 351 more. Of those captured, 136 were blockade runners; of those destroyed, 85 were blockade runners.

Was it worth the risk? A ship's captain earned $150 for a routine trip to the British Caribbean; the same trip, including running the blockade, netted $5,000.

*The ironclad CSS Virginia (ex-USS Merrimack) attacks the wood-and-sail USS* Cumberland *on March 8, 1862, prior to the battle of Hampton Roads between Virginia and USS* Monitor. *This illustration was created in the early twentieth century.*

of that fleet hardly knew what to make of the approaching vessel. She looked, one of them later remarked, "like the roof of a very big barn belching . . . smoke." To another, she appeared to be "a huge half-submerged crocodile." As she drew closer, her guns became visible, poking through the narrow ports in her sloping ironclad sides. Also visible was the massive iron ram mounted on her prow.

The skippers of the Union warships ordered their guns to speak, as did the commanding officer of the nearby Union shore batteries. The result was a violent fusillade, but through the smoke, the pilot aboard USS *Cumberland* saw with horror and amazement that none of the cannonballs had penetrated the Confederate ironclad, but instead had bounced "upon her mailed sides like India-rubber."

And now it was time for the CSS *Virginia* to reply. She opened up on the Cumberland. Five marines aboard the Union vessel were killed instantly in the storm of shrapnel and splinters that accompanied the first barrage. When *Cumberland*'s guns fell silent, the ironclad bellowed, making all the steam she could, and bore down on the stricken ship. On she came, driving her iron ram through *Cumberland*'s hull, the stout timbers breaking apart like so much matchwood. The gash in her side reached well below the waterline, and the *Cumberland* took on water, sucking it through her gaping wound. It heeled over, but, fortunately, settled into the sandy shallow just beyond the Roads before she could capsize. Her masts, mostly undamaged, remained above the waves, the Stars and Stripes flapping in a steady breeze, and her sailors clinging to yardarms, ratlines, and ropes.

While this fight had been going on, the ships near the *Cumberland* maneuvered in search of new positions from which to train fire on the ironclad. In the process, USS *Congress* ran aground in the treacherous shallows and, helpless now, awaited her fate.

It was not long in coming.

Steaming up close, CSS *Virginia* fired a broadside, and the *Congress* burst into flame and struck its colors. Buchanan sent a rescue party from another Confederate ship. Misinterpreting this gesture of chivalry as an act of cold conquest, the Union shore batteries opened up on the rescuers. Enraged at this, Buchanan seized a rifle and personally tried to pick off the Union artillerists. An angry man aiming a rifle makes a fine target, and Buchanan soon took a bullet in the leg. He summoned Lieutenant Catesby ap R. Jones to assume command while he was carried below decks. The lieutenant fought on, forcing aground the USS *Minnesota* and two smaller Union frigates. With the approach of sunset, he judged his day's work done and decided to return to port. There would be plenty of time to finish off these ships tomorrow.

There was also plenty of time for telegraphed accounts of the stunning battle to reach Washington and ignite rumors that the rebel ironclad, indestructible as it was, would steam straight up the Potomac, heave to within sight of the Capitol and the White House, and then bombard them mercilessly. Perhaps the entire city would be put to the torch. President Lincoln summoned his Cabinet for an emergency meeting. The assembled executive branch of the United States of America could think of nothing better to do than pray.

*Fort Monroe and the Gosport Navy Yard were seized by the Confederates after the secession of Virginia at the beginning of the war. This map shows forts Monroe, Calhoun, Nelson, and Norfolk in addition to Confederate artillery batteries on Sewall's Point—all defending the entrance to Chesapeake Bay, Norfolk, and the navy yard.*

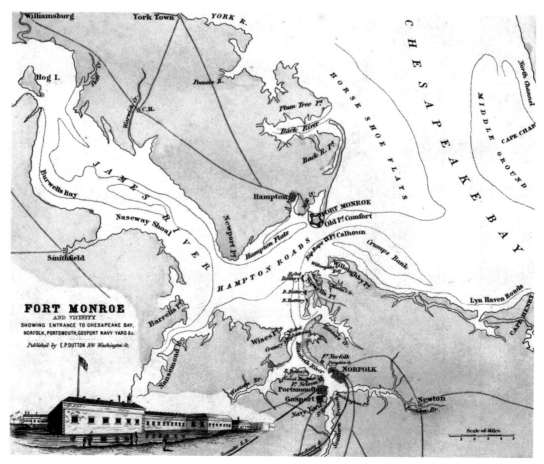

## Iron against Iron

The attack of CSS *Virginia* had not come as a total surprise. Months earlier, Union spies reported that the Confederates were hard at work raising the *Merrimack* with the intention of converting her into an ironclad. In October 1861, the U.S. Congress authorized letting a contract to John Ericsson, a Swedish-born New Yorker who had already tried (unsuccessfully) to sell a design for an ironclad battleship to France's Napoleon III, to build an iron ship capable of killing another iron ship. The really difficult part? The contract gave him just one hundred days from design to launch.

He did not make it by the hundredth day, but when intelligence reached him that CSS *Virginia* was nearing completion, he threw himself into a frenzy of round-the-clock work and managed to put the USS *Monitor* into the water on March 6. There would be no time for basic testing, let alone a formal "shakedown" (troubleshooting) cruise. The ship went directly to war.

She was far from being a majestic sight. Some who saw her called her a "tin can on a shingle." Others described the *Monitor* as a "cheesebox on a raft." Disparaging as these appraisals were, they were accurately evocative. Ericsson's ship was built of iron—not iron cladding over wood, but sheet iron. She was black, dull, and flat as a raft. But atop her deck was the "can" or the "cheesebox"—this warship's most revolutionary feature: a revolving armored turret equipped with two 11-inch guns. Like the opponent she was about to face, the *Monitor* was unwieldy. She sailed slowly and maneuvered poorly. Worst of all, she rode so low in the water that even a moderate swell could swamp her. However, while the fixed broadside guns of the *Virginia* had to be aimed by steering the whole ship, the revolving turret of the *Monitor* allowed her to place a shot anywhere within 360 degrees without so much as a turn of the helm.

In a nick-of-time entrance worthy of nineteenth-century melodrama, the USS *Monitor*, commanded by Lieutenant John L. Worden, arrived in Hampton Roads on the morning of March 9. Seeing the

*Perhaps the most radical innovation aboard USS* Monitor *was its 360-degree revolving turret, shown here. Not only did it afford gun crews armored protection, it allowed rapid redirection of fire without the time-consuming necessity of maneuvering the entire vessel. As much as steam power and iron construction, the revolving turret outlined the future of naval warfare well into the next century.*

predicament of the grounded *Minnesota*, Worden maneuvered into a covering position and awaited the appearance of CSS *Virginia*.

The Confederate ironclad steamed up at nine in the morning and immediately opened fire on the *Monitor*. From that moment on and for the next three hours, the two iron ships hurled iron against each another. Smaller than the *Virginia*, the *Monitor*, lumbering though she was, consistently outmaneuvered her adversary. Yet *Virginia* continually returned as good as she got. The hulls of both vessels withstood the exchange, but the ceaseless and merciless impact of iron against iron fell like the blows of an inexhaustible boxer on each and every man aboard both ships. First it was eardrums that burst. Then it was the very soles of the crewmen's feet. Pounded by shockwave upon shockwave, they bled, it seemed, right through unbroken skin, so that every step was taken in the blood that filled their shoes. This was not a fight between human beings, but of one machine against another. The men were caught between, as if in the indifferent teeth of clashing gears.

*This stereograph shows John L. Worden, the intrepid commander of USS* Monitor *in its epoch-making duel with* CSS Virginia.

Lieutenant Worden commanded the inhuman duel from the *Monitor*'s iron pilot house. Gingerly, from time to time, he pressed his face against one of the narrow observation slits cut into the iron wall. About noon, as he peered out, like a medieval knight squinting through the slit of his heavy helmet's visor, a shell burst against the outside wall of the pilot house. Worden fell back in agony, blinded—temporarily, as it turned out, but sightless for the duration of the battle.

At first, no one noticed, and the *Monitor* drifted out of control. Seeing this, Jones, skippering the *Virginia*, concluded that the enemy had had enough and was withdrawing from the fight.

It was a relief, for the *Virginia* was badly damaged. The incessant pounding had opened up seams below her waterline, and the low-riding vessel was rapidly taking on water. Powder was running low, too, and the crew had given all they had to give. CSS *Virginia* sheered away, and sailed for home. (She would, in fact, never fight again. The ironclad ran aground on May 11, 1862, and, unable to free her, her crew put her to the torch.)

*Currier & Ives published "Terrific combat between 'Monitor' 2 guns & 'Merrimac' 11 guns in Hampton Roads March 9th, 1862" shortly after the battle took place. The lithograph is hand-colored.*

## DETAILS, DETAILS

### First of the Breed

Like the CSS *Virginia*, the *Monitor* was not destined for a long life. Barely seaworthy to begin with, she foundered in rough seas off Cape Hatteras, North Carolina, on December 31, 1862, taking sixteen sailors with her to the bottom. Brief as her own existence was, she gave birth to the modern battleship, transforming naval warfare forever.

## EYEWITNESS

Lieutenant Samuel Dana Greene wrote this harrowing account of his experience on assuming command of USS *Monitor* at the battle of Hampton Roads, March 9, 1862:

*[Worden, skipper of USS* Monitor*] was a ghastly sight, with his eyes closed and the blood apparently rushing from every pore in the upper part of his face. He told me that he was seriously wounded, and directed me to take command. . . . The steering gear was still intact, and the pilot-house was not totally destroyed, as had been feared. In the confusion of the moment resulting from so serious an injury to the commanding officer, the* Monitor *had been moving without direction. During this time the* Merrimac *[sic], which was leaking badly, had started in the direction of the Elizabeth River; and . . . , on taking my station in the pilot-house and turning the vessel's head in the direction of the* Merrimac *[sic], I saw that she was already in retreat. A few shots were fired at the retiring vessel, and she continued on to Norfolk. . . . The fight was over.*

The USS *Monitor* could not claim a clear victory. To all appearances, she had been the first to break off the fight, prompting *Virginia* to do the same. That meant the contest was at best a draw. And yet the fact was that the *Monitor* had rescued the helpless *Minnesota* and had foiled the Confederates in their bid to break the blockade. If there was any clear loser in this battle, it was all the old navies of the world—the navies built of wood and driven by sail. They died, all of them, at Hampton Roads that day . . . casualties of the Civil War.

## FLESH AND IRON

ARMIES AND NAVIES BREAK THINGS and kill people. That is what they do, and the army and navy that have the weapons capable of breaking the most and killing the most live to break and kill even more another day. The rifle-musket and the minié ball, the panoply of artillery, the emergence of iron ships—all of these upped the ante of devastation. But the real horror was that iron was not merely hurled against iron. It was also blasted against bone, brain, muscle, and flesh, and whereas the industrial technology of weaponry would make great strides in the Civil War, the science of repairing what those weapons destroyed lagged far behind.

War in the new Iron Age created wounds even the most experienced military surgeons had never imagined, let alone actually seen

# LETHAL MENU

Many Civil War artillery weapons fired much more than the simple solid cannonball. In addition to this "solid shot" (as it was called), armies used three additional ammunition types, and navies added another two.

**S**hells were hollowed-out versions of solid shot, into which gunpowder was tightly packed. Whereas solid shot did its damage merely by force of impact, shells were fused and designed to explode in flight, sending jagged iron fragments—shrapnel—in all directions. Shells, which came in a dazzling variety of shapes, were antipersonnel weapons, intended to kill or injure as many men within the blast radius of the ammunition as possible.

*Case shot* was another form of antipersonnel ammunition. The thin-walled projectile was filled with lead or iron balls packed tightly in a compound of sulfur or in asphalt. The case

shot included a small fused "bursting charge" of gunpowder, which exploded in flight, scattering the balls. Case shot transformed a cannon into a giant shotgun.

*Canister shot* consisted of lead or iron balls packed in sawdust inside a tin or tinned iron cylinder. The cylinder was nailed to a wooden plug on one end and crimped over an iron plate on the other. When the cannon was fired, the thin canister disintegrated as it emerged from the muzzle, spraying the balls over a wide area.

Civil War–era ships often fired *grapeshot,* which sandwiched nine to twenty-seven iron balls in layers between a series of iron plates that were held together by a bolt. The gunner would load the grapeshot into the cannon, remove the nut from the end of the bolt, and fire. The scattering balls killed sailors on the enemy ship and wreaked havoc with masts, spars, and rigging.

*Chain shot,* another naval weapon, consisted of two cannonballs linked by a single short chain. Fired together, the balls would spin like a hurled bolo, destroying the rigging of the enemy ship.

*Heavy, large-caliber Confederate cannonballs are stacked unused at the arsenal in Richmond, Virginia, after the fall of the South's capital city in 1865. The image is by the great Union combat photographer Alexander Gardner.*

*Photographer James F. Gibson captured the scene at an improvised Union field hospital at Savage's Station, Virginia, during McClellan's ill-fated 1862 Peninsula Campaign. This photograph was later hand colored.*

*Dorothea Lynde Dix led the newly created nursing corps of the United States Army. A formidably authoritarian leader, she was dubbed "Dragon Dix" Dix by the male as well as female personnel she supervised.*

or attempted to treat. If a soldier was hit in the gut or the head and had the misfortune to cling to life for a while, there was really nothing to be done for him beyond attempting to palliate the pain, usually with whiskey or brandy. Wounds in the extremities were treated with a single sovereign remedy: immediate amputation, usually in a tent hospital, behind which the discarded severed limbs accumulated like cordwood.

If the wounded man was lucky, he would find himself in a hospital stocked with chloroform, the only anesthetic (other than liquor) available at the time. But while anesthesia was at least in its infancy in the 1860s, antisepsis—the practice of sterile treatment and the attempt to avoid infection by killing bacteria—was unknown to medicine. It wasn't until 1865, the final year of the Civil War, that the English physician Joseph Lister would read about the discoveries of the French chemist and pioneering microbiologist Louis Pasteur and introduce to a highly skeptical medical community the uncanny notion that deadly infection in even the biggest and strongest of men was caused by organisms much too small to be seen without a microscope. Civil War surgeons were often remarkably skillful, their amputations swift and executed so as to do a minimum of damage to surviving tissue. But they rarely so much as washed their hands between surgeries, wounds were cleaned superficially at best, and dressings were always contaminated. Many a patient survived the operation only to die days or hours later from infection.

If it took bravery to fight the war, in some ways it required even more bravery to treat the war's victims. In this, the work of women was most notable. Dorothea Lynde Dix, already famous before the war as a tireless crusader for the humane treatment of prison inmates and the mentally ill, volunteered to lead the brand-new nursing corps of the U.S. Army. While the army had long employed untrained male nurses, Dix recruited women, who, she believed, could be quickly schooled to deliver a higher level of compassionate care. She herself was tough as nails. The men with whom she worked, from generals down to privates, called her "Dragon Dix," and it was probably because of her formidable demeanor that she never earned the fame and the affection lavished on Clara Barton, celebrated as the "Angel of the Battlefield."

*An unassuming government clerk, Clara Barton single-handedly organized the distribution of supplies, fresh food, and basic comforts to wounded Union soldiers—work for which she became known as the "Angel of the Battlefield." She went on after the war to found the American Red Cross.*

"I would fain be allowed to go and administer comfort to our brave men, who peril life and limb in defense of the priceless boon the fathers so dearly won. . . . I ask neither pay nor praise, simply a soldier's fare and the sanction of your Excellency to go and do with my might, what ever my hands find to do."

Clara Barton, letter to
Massachusetts governor
John A. Andrew, March 20, 1862

### TAKEAWAY

The weapons of the Civil War were products of a phase of the Industrial Revolution that advanced the technology of destruction to an unprecedented level of efficiency and cruelty. The rifle-musket, minié ball, advances in artillery design, and the emergence of the iron battleship with revolving turret laid the foundation for modern warfare.

Barton was born in Massachusetts in 1821, the daughter of abolitionist activists. She taught school for eighteen years, and then took a job as a clerk in the otherwise all-male world of the U.S. Patent Office in Washington, D.C. When the Civil War began, she single-handedly organized an agency to secure and distribute supplies to wounded soldiers in military hospitals as well as in the field. Much of this work she did personally, driving a supply wagon and then taking time to visit the wounded, to hold a hand, to say a kind word. She could do no more than this to help those torn by the technology of modern combat, but she and others like her did what they could. Into a terrible war made more terrible by ingenious engines of sheer cruelty, they brought a measure of humanity. Years afterward, Clara Barton, having seen modern warfare up close, would bring to the United States a movement that had first come into being in Europe, during yet another bloody conflict, the Franco-Prussian War of 1870. It was called the Red Cross.

*The Armory Square Hospital, Washington, D.C., was a model medical facility hardly typical of the overcrowded and generally appalling conditions that prevailed in Civil War hospitals in the North as well as the South.*

# CHAPTER 8

## "EVERY PROMISE OF A FINE DAY"

### A Commitment in Blood

THE EUROPEANS WHO BEGAN SETTLING (OR INVADING, THE WORD CHOICE is a function of perspective) what they called the New World brought from the Old World much that was good and much that was bad, but most of all, much that was familiar. To places that bore what were to them the uncouth names bestowed by "savages" or places that had no names at all, they gave the names they already knew. Among these was Shiloh, a little Methodist log chapel built in the 1850s, whose name was bestowed upon the patch of woods surrounding it in middle Tennessee, two or three miles west of the Tennessee River. It was a very good name for church ground, as it was borrowed from the Old Testament Book of Joshua, which speaks of Shiloh as a place where a sanctuary sheltered the Ark of the Covenant. "Place of Peace" is the usual translation of the Hebrew *shiloh*, which makes it a bitterly ironic name for a battle that killed or injured nearly twenty-four thousand young men in little more than twelve hours. The original chapel itself was destroyed soon after the battle.

Far more bitter than that irony was the harsh awakening Shiloh brought to the broken nation. "Up to the battle of Shiloh," Ulysses Grant wrote near the end of his life,

> I, as well as thousands of other citizens, believed the rebellion against the Government would collapse suddenly and soon, if a decisive victory could be gained over any of its armies. [The capture of Confederate Forts] Donelson and Henry were such victories. An army of more than 21,000 men was captured or destroyed. Bowling Green, Columbus and Hickman, Kentucky, fell in consequence, and Clarksville and Nashville, Tennessee, the last two with an immense amount of stores, also fell into our hands. The Tennessee and Cumberland rivers, from their mouths to the head of navigation, were secured.

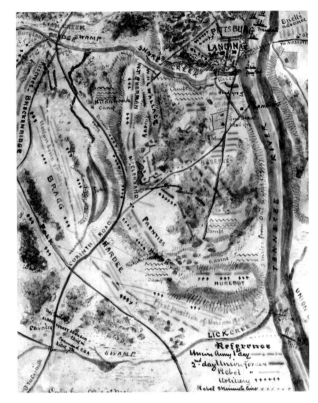

*Robert Knox Sneden, a landscape painter by profession, was employed by the Union army as a mapmaker. This is his official map of the battle of Shiloh.*

But as Grant well knew, his commanding officers, Henry Wager Halleck and Don Carlos Buell, had refused to allow him to pursue the retreating Confederate forces, which, in consequence, "not only attempted to hold a line farther south, from Memphis to Chattanooga, Knoxville and to the Atlantic, but assumed the offensive." In fact, Grant wrote, they "made such a gallant effort to regain what had been lost . . . [that] I gave up all idea of saving the Union except by complete conquest."

## "To Consume Everything"

Shiloh would be the Civil War's first turning point, not because of a victory gained by one side or a defeat inflicted on the other, but by what both sides sacrificed and proved themselves willing to continue to sacrifice. The contest was a commitment in blood unprecedented on the North American continent. Before the battle

*Best known as the Welsh journalist who trekked through Africa in search of the missing missionary Dr. David Livingstone from 1871–72, a very young Henry Morton Stanley served with a Confederate unit at the battle of Shiloh and left a vivid record of the experience. This photograph is from Stanley's 1885 book,* The Congo and the Founding of Its Free State: A Story of Work and Exploration.

of Shiloh, Grant observed, "it had been the policy of our army, certainly of that portion commanded by me, to protect the property of the citizens whose territory was invaded, without regard to their sentiments, whether Union or Secession." After Shiloh, "I regarded it as humane to both sides to protect the persons of those found at their homes, but to consume everything that could be used to support or supply armies."

What horror could have created such a change of policy, transforming a military operation to suppress an insurrection into total war?

If objectivity in an account of battle is hard to come by, an objective account by an actual participant in combat seems too much to ask for, but Shiloh had at least one uniquely objective participant. John Rowlands was born in 1841 in Denbigh, Wales, apparently (for there is some dispute over this) the bastard son of a nineteen-year-old mother and her alcoholic lover. Raised by a grandfather who died when he was five, Rowlands endured the Dickensian horrors of a Victorian workhouse until he was fifteen. He acquired sufficient education to earn his bread teaching elementary school, and then, in 1859, at the age of eighteen, he took sail for the United States. He landed in New Orleans, wandered the city's quays and levees for a time and happened upon a merchant trader named Stanley who was sitting outside his store. Rowlands approached him and asked for a job. At least he meant to ask for a job, but being a Welsh lad he framed his inquiry in the Victorian British idiom: "Do you want a boy, sir?" As it happened, Stanley, childless, did want a boy, a son, and he took John Rowlands into his home.

Although Stanley never formally adopted him, the boy took his name and called himself Henry Morton Stanley. Years later, he would make himself known to the world as an intrepid journalist-traveler and would be commissioned by James Gordon Bennett, publisher of the *New York Herald*, to search Africa for the famed Scots missionary David Livingstone, who had not been heard from for years. After months of trekking the bush, Stanley would find his man and greet him (so Stanley himself reported) with a phrase that has reverberated since it was first published in Bennett's paper: "Dr. Livingstone, I presume?"

But, years before this, young Stanley, adoptive citizen of New Orleans, encountered the American Civil War, joined (like so many other Southern boys) the Confederate army, and found himself at the place called Shiloh.

# VOM KRIEGE

Carl Philipp Gottlieb von Clausewitz (1780–1831) was named director of the Prussian *Kriegsakademie* (War College) in 1818 and was Europe's foremost military theorist. As chief of staff of the Prussian army in 1830, he led a force to the Polish border in anticipation of a war and died there the following year of cholera. In 1832, his widow published the incomplete manuscript of a book he had long been working on, *Vom Kriege (On War)*.

The single most influential work of military science ever written, *On War* has given soldiers and historians alike such concepts as "the fog of war" (the inevitability of confusion in battle, with profound tactical and strategic consequences), "the friction of war" (the gulf between plans and their execution), and, most of all, the idea of "total war" (warfare directed not just against an enemy army, but against an entire enemy population). The latter concept, a hallmark of the two world wars of the twentieth century, has become so pervasive that many historians and casual

*Carl von Clausewitz, as he was honored on a 1981 West German postage stamp.*

history buffs alike have seen the hand of Clausewitz behind the strategies of Grant ("complete conquest") and of William Tecumseh Sherman (his "March to the Sea," Chapter 18). After Shiloh, there is no question that the Civil War became "total war" in a way that Clausewitz would have thoroughly understood, but the writings of Clausewitz had nothing to do with it. Astoundingly enough, *On War* had no place in the West Point curriculum before the twentieth century.

In his posthumous autobiography, published in 1909, Henry Morton Stanley made vividly clear just why nothing short of what Grant called "complete conquest" would ever end the Civil War. Decisively defeated at Forts Henry and Donelson, the Confederate army that reassembled around Corinth, Mississippi, by no means acknowledged itself a *beaten* army. It certainly looked like one, as Stanley recalled, its ragtag boy soldiers unrested and underfed. To its commanders, however, this hardly seemed to matter. "Generals Johnston and Beauregard," Stanley explained, "proposed to hurl into the Tennessee River an army of nearly 50,000 rested and well-fed [Union] troops, by means of 40,000 [Confederate] soldiers, who, for two days, had subsisted on sodden biscuit and raw bacon, who had been exposed for two nights to rain and dew, and had marched twenty-three miles!" An army led by such generals— and, what is more, peopled by tired, hungry, battle-battered boys willing to obey them—would not be stopped except by "complete conquest."

## A LAPSE OF ATTENTION

GENERAL GRANT'S ARMY of the Tennessee consisted of 48,894 soldiers divided not into corps but into six divisions. Grant encamped five of these divisions (about 42,000 men total) at Pittsburg Landing, Tennessee, on the west bank of the Tennessee River, which was a short distance northeast of the Confederate position at Corinth, Mississippi. The sixth division, under Major General Lew Wallace (who would earn his greatest fame after the Civil War from his best-selling novel of early Christianity, *Ben-Hur*) was deployed five miles downstream along the Tennessee, at Crump's Landing. This was done to ensure that the Confederates could not establish artillery along the river and also to be in position to seize the railway tracks at the nearby Bethel Station once a major battle began.

Ulysses Grant habitually planned his battles and campaigns with great intensity of focus, yet therein lay his one significant flaw as a general. For his focus was invariably on *his* plans and not on those of his adversaries. Because he had served in the pre–Civil War army with many of the generals he now confronted as enemies, Grant often had considerable

# ARMIES OF ARMIES

Both the U.S. Army and the Confederate army were organized according to the same federal military manuals. Each force was divided into armies, the largest units of organization. Beginning with the Army of the Potomac, Union armies were named after the major river in their region (Army of the Tennessee, Army of the James, etc.), whereas Confederate armies were named after states (Army of Northern Virginia, Army of Tennessee, Army of Missouri, etc.).

Throughout the war, various militias and volunteer regiments were incorporated into these armies on both sides. In theory (but not always in practice), an *army* was subdivided into *corps*: the Army of the Potomac in 1863 had seven infantry corps and a cavalry corps, whereas the typical Confederate army had three infantry corps, which (at least on paper) were usually much bigger than Union corps. Each corps typically included three infantry *divisions* and an artillery *brigade* (in the Union army) or an artillery *battalion* (in the Confederate army). Each division was composed of two to four *infantry*

*brigades*, and each brigade was divided into four to six *regiments*. These regiments were the primary unit used by commanders in battle.

Led by a colonel, a regiment normally consisted of more than a thousand officers and men, but, in actual combat, numbers were often lower. Each regiment was divided into ten *companies* of one hundred men each at full strength, and each company (commanded by a captain) was divided into two equal *platoons* (each commanded by a lieutenant). These, in turn, were divided into *squads* (led by a sergeant or corporal).

insight into the character and inclinations of opposing commanders; and yet he rarely extended this insight into fully anticipating the enemy's intentions. He did not design strategy and tactics to meet and defeat what he supposed would be the strategy and tactics of his adversary, but instead created what he believed was the plan best suited to allow him to attack. His intention was always

to initiate action, not to respond to action initiated by the enemy. This led him to deploy his troops in an encampment that military men call a *bivouac*—an arrangement temporary and exposed, without defensive trenches, artillery emplacements, and the like. After the battle, many would criticize this as negligence, but, actually, it was by design. Grant did not want to establish a defensive position because he did not want to prepare his troops for a defensive campaign. His intention was "complete conquest," which is achieved by attacking, not defending. The "troops with me, officers and men, needed discipline and drill more than they did experience with the pick, shovel and axe," Grant wrote years later. Honing his forces for the attack, he "concluded that drill and discipline were worth more to our men than fortifications."

What Grant never explained, however, was why he had chosen not to deploy guards ("pickets," as they were called) remote from the encampment or to use cavalry patrols as prescribed by mid-nineteenth-century U.S. military doctrine, as reconnaissance teams to provide early warning of attack. Perhaps it was because he was distracted by the intense pain of a badly sprained ankle, or maybe because he did not yet fully understand what Stanley was just then experiencing: the willingness of the Confederate commanders to attack superior numbers with inferior numbers and, moreover, to do so with an army of battle-weary, underfed boys.

Did Grant know the meaning of the Hebrew *shiloh*? He certainly seemed to have expected that it would be a "place of peace," at least until *he* chose to attack.

*Like his older brother Alfred R. Waud, William Waud worked as an artist-correspondent during the Civil War. This evocative water-color wash titled "Night Signalling" shows Union signalmen using torches to signal across the James River during Grant's Overland campaign in October 1864. Rapid communication and coordination of forces in the field was always difficult. The illustration was published in* Harper's Weekly *on November 12, 1864.*

**REALITY CHECK**

## The Friction of War

What Stanley called a "misunderstanding" was the rule rather than the exception in nineteenth-century combat. Even in an era of telegraphy and well-developed semaphore-style signaling with flags (called "wig-wag signaling"), coordinated communication with large numbers of troops, especially in the absence of a well-developed staff-officer cadre, was highly imperfect. What Carl von Clausewitz called the "friction of war" was not merely an annoyance, but a major, even dominant, factor in virtually every campaign, battle, and operation. Plans were made, and orders issued accordingly, but myriad obstacles and stumbling blocks intervened between order and execution. Above all, armies rarely moved as quickly as their commanders anticipated they would, and the general who failed to appreciate this product of "friction" was rarely victorious.

# PICKING VIOLETS

"ON APRIL 2, 1862, we received orders to prepare three days' cooked rations," Henry Morton Stanley recalled. "Through some misunderstanding," however, his regiment, "the 6th Arkansas Regiment of Hindman's brigade, Hardee's corps," did not get under way until two days later. The men left their knapsacks and tents behind, and after "two days of marching, and two nights of bivouacking and living on cold rations, our spirits were not so buoyant at dawn of Sunday, the 6th April, as they ought to have been for the serious task before us. Many wished, like myself, that we had not been required to undergo this discomfort before being precipitated into the midst of a great battle."

Stanley rose with his regiment at four o'clock in the morning, wolfed down a bad breakfast, and then "formed into line. We stood in rank for half an hour or so, while the military dispositions were being completed along the three-mile front." The brigade, of which his regiment was a part, was at the very center of the attack.

> Day broke with every promise of a fine day. Next to me, on my right, was a boy of seventeen, Henry Parker. I remember it because, while we stood-at-ease, he drew my attention to some violets at his feet, and said, "It would be a good idea to put a few into my cap. Perhaps the Yanks won't shoot me if they see me wearing such flowers, for they are a sign of peace." "Capital," said I, "I will do the same." We plucked a bunch, and arranged the violets in our caps. The men in the ranks laughed at our proceedings, and had not the enemy been so near, their merry mood might have been communicated to the army.

The men of Stanley's regiment, the Dixie Greys, loaded their muskets and prepared their cartridge pouches. "Our weapons were the obsolete [smoothbore] flintlocks, and the ammunition was rolled in cartridge-paper, which contained powder, a round ball, and three buckshot. When we loaded we had to tear the paper with our teeth, empty a little powder into the pan, lock it, empty the rest of the powder into the barrel, press paper and ball into the muzzle, and ram home." Soon, the regiment "swayed forward in line, with shouldered arms. Newton Story, big, broad, and straight, bore our company-banner of gay silk, at which the ladies of our neighbourhood had laboured."

Some men marching to battle are numbed by fear, while, in others, the prospect of imminent combat makes the senses more acute. Henry Stanley was one of the latter. "As we tramped solemnly and silently through the thin forest, and over its grass, still in its withered and wintry hue, I noticed that the sun was not far from appearing, that our regiment was keeping its formation admirably, that the woods would have been a grand place for a picnic. . . ."

*This "Scene at Pittsburg Landing, Tennessee River, Sunday Afternoon, 6th April 1862" was published in* Frank Leslie's Illustrated Newspaper *on May 8, 1862.*

Before they had advanced "five hundred paces, our serenity was disturbed by some desultory firing in front. It was then a quarter-past five." L. G. Smith, captain of Stanley's company, spoke softly: "Stand by, gentlemen." At this, the steps of the Dixie Greys "became unconsciously brisker, and alertness was noticeable in everybody. The firing continued at intervals, deliberate and scattered, as at target-practice. We drew nearer to the firing, and soon a sharper rattling of musketry was heard. 'That is the enemy waking up,' we said. Within a few minutes, there was another explosive burst of musketry, the air was pierced by many missiles, which hummed and pinged sharply by our ears, pattered through the tree-tops, and brought twigs and leaves down on us. 'Those are bullets,' [Stanley's comrade] Henry whispered with awe."

Against the bullets' very flight, Stanley and the others advanced, like travelers through a hailstorm, heads lowered. The hail of lead grew thicker with each step. "At two hundred yards further, a dreadful roar of musketry broke out from a regiment adjoining ours. It was followed by another further off, and the sound had scarcely died away when regiment after regiment blazed away and made a continuous roll of sound. 'We are in for it now,' said Henry; but as yet we had seen nothing, though our ears were tingling under the animated volleys."

To those on the receiving end of the attack, Grant's encampment, none of the hunger, weariness, and fear that Stanley described was evident. None of the Union soldiers could have imagined that two of their attackers had paused in their callow innocence to decorate their caps with violet talismans. All that the men of the Union bivouac saw and felt was the ferocity of the attack, its utter unexpectedness making it all the fiercer. From the Union perspective, the Confederates, arrayed in four divisions from west to east—under William J. Hardee, Leonidas Polk, Braxton Bragg, and John C. Breckinridge—plunged through the woods and exploded everywhere upon their drowsy encampment.

### "One Tremendous Ruin"

Panic shot through the vicinity of Shiloh as thickly and as violently as Confederate bullets. For the rest of the morning, it would be mostly a Union rout—humiliating . . . demoralizing . . . many of the bluecoats seeking places to hide rather than positions from which they might make a stand.

To Stanley, it hardly seemed so one-sidedly simple. "Forward, gentlemen, make ready!" Captain Smith urged his company, which, in response, surged ahead, "for the first time marring the alignment. We trampled recklessly over the grass and young sprouts. Beams of sunlight stole athwart our course." Soon they overtook their own skirmishers—the vanguard sent in advance of the main body of troops. After passing beyond them, someone sighted the enemy: "There they are!" No sooner was this uttered, "than we cracked into them with levelled muskets. 'Aim low, men!' commanded Captain Smith."

In all mass combat, but especially in the age before the invention of so-called smokeless powder, no soldier *in* the battle *sees* the battle. All he witnesses, really, is the effect of battle on himself. In Stanley's case, this induced him to look "around to see the effect on others." Were others as overwhelmed as he by the impression of universal destruction? Stanley couldn't tell, but he was nevertheless "glad to notice that each was possessed with his own thoughts. All were pale, solemn, and absorbed." Although it was impossible for him to discover just what they were thinking, "by transmission of sympathy, I felt that they would gladly prefer to be elsewhere," yet, inexpli-

## EYEWITNESS

Welsh-born Henry Morton Stanley was twenty-one when he fought for the Confederacy at Shiloh. He recalled the experience years later in an autobiography published after his death.

*I tried hard to see some living thing to shoot at, for it appeared absurd to be blazing away at shadows. But, still advancing, firing as we moved, I, at last, saw a row of little globes of pearly smoke streaked with crimson, breaking-out, with spurtive quickness, from a long line of bluey figures in front; and, simultaneously, there broke upon our ears an appalling crash of sound, the series of fusillades following one another with startling suddenness, which suggested to my somewhat moidered sense a mountain upheaved, with huge rocks tumbling and thundering down a slope, and the echoes rumbling and receding through space. Again and again, these loud and quick explosions were repeated, seemingly with increased violence, until they rose to the highest pitch of fury, and in unbroken continuity. All the world seemed involved in one tremendous ruin!*

cably, "at no time were we more instinctively inclined to obey the voice of command. We had no individuality at this moment, but all motions and thoughts were surrendered to the unseen influence which directed our movements." Stanley and his comrades ". . . plied our arms, loaded, and fired, with such nervous haste as though it depended on each of us how soon this fiendish uproar would be hushed. My nerves tingled, my pulses beat double-quick, my heart throbbed loudly, and almost painfully; but, amid all the excitement, my thoughts, swift as the flash of lightning, took all sound, and sight, and self, into their purview. I listened to the battle raging far away on the flanks, to the thunder in front, to the various sounds made by the leaden storm."

*The American chromolithograph firm of L. Prang & Co. published this depiction of the battle of Shiloh in 1888, more than a quarter-century after it had been fought.*

At last it was apparent to Stanley that the enemy was falling back. His every thought now focused on the movements of the bluecoats. "To every forward step, they took a backward move, loading and firing as they slowly withdrew. Twenty thousand muskets were being fired at this stage, but, though accuracy of aim was impossible, owing to our labouring hearts, and the jarring and excitement, many bullets found their destined billets on both sides."

In combat of this era, when loading, firing, and reloading a musket was a time-consuming labor, there would come a phase in the battle when officers judged that their men were within thrusting range of the retreating enemy. At that moment the order would be given to, *Fix bayonets!* Stanley recalled thrilling to the very tone of that command.

> There was a simultaneous bound forward, each soul doing his best for the emergency. The Federals appeared inclined to await us; but, at this juncture, our men raised a yell, thousands responded to it, and burst out into the wildest yelling it has ever been my lot to hear. It drove all sanity and order from among us. It served the double purpose of relieving pent-up feelings, and transmitting encouragement along the attacking line. I rejoiced in the shouting like the rest. It reminded me that there were about four hundred companies like the Dixie Greys, who shared our feelings. Most of us, engrossed with the musket-work, had

forgotten the fact; but the wave after wave of human voices, louder than all other battle-sounds together, penetrated to every sense, and stimulated our energies to the utmost.

"'They fly!' was echoed from lip to lip." The cry quickened the Confederate advance. "It deluged us with rapture, and transfigured each Southerner into an exulting victor. At such a moment, nothing could have halted us. Those savage yells, and the sight of thousands of racing figures coming towards them, discomfited the blue-coats; and when we arrived upon the place where they had stood, they had vanished."

Stanley marveled at the "sight of their beautiful array of tents, before which they had made their stand, after being roused from their Sunday-morning sleep. . . . The half-dressed dead and wounded showed what a surprise our attack had been. . . . Signs of a hasty rouse to the battle were abundant. Military equipments, uniform-coats, half-packed knapsacks, bedding, of a new and superior quality, littered the company streets." However, Stanley also saw that "a series of other camps lay behind the first array of tents" and that the resistance of the first array, however fleeting, had "enabled the brigades in rear of the advance camp to recover from the shock of the surprise."

There were still wide gaps between the Union divisions, through which the attackers pushed; however, the blue lines began to coalesce, and by the afternoon, the initial rout had been stemmed, and the federal soldiers were establishing a credible battle line in a dense thicket between the Tennessee River to the east and Owl Creek to the west. The Confederates would dub it the Hornet's Nest.

### The Hornet's Sting

The commander most responsible for having arrested the Union rout was William Tecumseh Sherman, whose troops, formed on either side of Shiloh Chapel, on the westernmost sector of the battle, had absorbed the first major impact of the attack. They had cut, and, shamelessly, they had run—but Sherman, unshaken, personally set about rallying his dispirited troops. Grant marveled at how he inspired confidence in all ranks, enabling both officers and men "to render services on that bloody battlefield worthy of the best of veterans."

Grant had been an admirer of Sherman ever since Sherman had been transferred to his Army of the Tennessee in February 1862. At the time, Grant was practically alone in his admiration. In the gloomy wake of the first battle of Bull Run, Sherman was assigned as commanding general of the Department of the Cumberland in Kentucky, where he was relentless in his criticism of what he deemed the Union high command's unrealistically optimistic strategic policy. To his superiors, to the popular press, to anyone who would listen, he tried to explain that this war was no mere rebellion, but a martial cataclysm of unprecedented magnitude. Hundreds of thousands of men would be required to defeat the Confederacy, he said. For this, he was accused of mental disability and even outright insanity. Now Shiloh showed that he had been right all along, and the combat, inhuman in its intensity, immense in its scale, also revealed him as one the Union's most determined, clear-sighted, and ruthless warriors.

# SCAPEGOAT HERO

Benjamin Mayberry Prentiss (1819–1901) was born in Belleville, Virginia, but came of age in Missouri and Illinois. Making his living as a rope maker and auctioneer, he fathered a family of a dozen children by two wives, ran unsuccessfully for Congress on the eve of the Civil War, and then rose to command a division in the Army of the Tennessee.

His division was mauled in the opening hours of Shiloh, but he managed to re-form its survivors at the Hornet's Nest, where the resistance he led slowed the Confederate advance, buying time for the arrival of Lew Wallace's division and units of Major General Don Carlos Buell's Army of the Ohio.

Prentiss's stand was costly, and he was captured at the Hornet's Nest along with twenty-two hundred other Union soldiers. The press targeted him as a scapegoat, disseminating as fact the wild rumor that he and his command had been captured in their beds. Grant, who personally disliked Prentiss, refused to hail him as a hero, observing in his *Personal Memoirs* that his stand had exposed him to defeat and capture. Yet Grant also refused to let the press dishonor the man, writing that the story about his having been taken in his sleep was "without any foundation whatever" and observing simply that, had it been true, "there would not have been an all-day struggle, with the loss of thousands killed and wounded on the Confederate side."

Prentiss was soon released in a prisoner exchange, but, though promoted from brigadier to major general, he fought in only one more battle, at Helena, Arkansas, on July 4, 1863, winning a victory that was lost in the shadow of Gettysburg. After the war, Prentiss practiced law and then served as postmaster in the administrations of Presidents Benjamin Harrison and William McKinley.

*Brigadier General Benjamin M. Prentiss made a gallant, stubborn, and ultimately controversial stand at Shiloh's Hornet's Nest.*

## NUMBERS

### Shiloh's Toll

Of 66,812 Union troops engaged, 1,754 were killed, 8,408 wounded, and 2,885 captured or missing. Of 44,699 Confederate troops engaged, 1,728 were killed, 8,012 were wounded, and 959 were captured or missing; an additional 3,500 would be captured when General Pope cut off the Confederate retreat after the battle.

There were others in blue who also stood with skill and heroism against the gray tide that threatened to overwhelm the Army of the Tennessee. It was around Brigadier General Benjamin M. Prentiss's extraordinary resistance on a wooded eminence at the center of the Union's beleaguered position that the Hornet's Nest coalesced.

After passing through the first abandoned Union camp, Stanley assumed that "the battle was well-nigh over," only to realize that "it was only a brief prologue of the long and exhaustive series of struggles which took place that day." As his regiment continued their advance, they saw "the tops of another mass of white tents, and, almost at the same time, were met by a furious storm of bullets, poured on us from a long line of blue-coats, whose attitude of assurance proved to us that we should have tough work here."

Tough indeed. With "terrific suddenness . . . the world seemed bursting into fragments. Cannon and musket, shell and bullet, lent their several intensities to the distracting uproar. . . . I likened the cannon, with their deep bass, to the roaring of a great herd of lions; the ripping, cracking musketry, to the incessant yapping of terriers; the windy whisk of shells, and zipping of minie bullets, to the swoop of eagles, and the buzz of angry wasps. All the opposing armies of Grey and Blue fiercely blazed at each other."

The order came to "Lie down, men, and continue your firing!"

Stanley found a "prostrate tree, about fifteen inches in diameter, with a narrow strip of light between it and the ground. Behind this shelter a dozen of us flung ourselves. The security it appeared to offer restored me to my individuality. We could fight, and think, and observe, better than out in the open." Yet the "sharp rending explosions and hurtling fragments" of incoming cannonballs, canister shot, and small-arms fire tearing through the woods made everyone "shrink and cower, despite our utmost efforts to be cool and collected. I marvelled, as I heard the unintermitting patter, snip, thud, and hum of the bullets, how anyone could live under this raining death."

In response to a command to move forward, Stanley bent his body "for the onset," only to hear at that moment a boy's voice cry out: "Oh, stop, *please* stop a bit, I have been hurt, and can't move!" It was Henry Parker, standing on one leg, his other foot smashed. There was no time to help him.

At about two thirty that Sunday afternoon, General Albert Sidney Johnston took a minié ball in his leg. Charged with adrenaline and a sense of duty, he ignored it—or tried to—but soon he was having a hard time remaining upright in the saddle. Seeing this, an aide rode up to him. "General, are you hurt?" he asked. "Yes, and I fear seriously."

The general's right boot, a tall cavalry boot that reached above his knee, had filled to overflowing with blood. The bullet had torn through the femoral artery. No sooner had the words assessing the gravity of his situation left his lips than Albert Sidney Johnston bled to death. That night, with the battle having sputtered into sporadic exchanges of fire, General P. G. T. Beauregard telegraphed President Jefferson Davis the hard news that the general widely considered by his fellow commanders to be the most brilliant and able officer of the Confederacy had been killed. The blow was softened, however, by the added news that victory was assured at Shiloh.

*Today, most historians count the battle of Shiloh either as a draw or a very slim Union victory. The Southern composer of this piece, however, had no doubt that it had been a Confederate triumph.*

### "Something Appalling at the Last Moment"

Beauregard's report of imminent victory was plausible enough. At many places along the line of attack, the Confederates continued to advance. Stanley's own company succeeded in taking the second line of Union camps and advanced beyond them. But then something struck Stanley's belt buckle with such force that he tumbled headlong to the ground and lost consciousness. When he came to, he found himself alone.

Within "half an hour, feeling renovated, I struck north in the direction which my regiment had taken, over a ground strewn with bodies and the debris of war." Those "ghastly relics," he wrote, "appalled every sense." Beside the body of a sergeant was that of "a young Lieutenant, who, judging by the new gloss on his uniform, must have been some father's darling. A clean bullet-hole through the centre of his forehead had instantly ended his career." Further on "were some twenty bodies, lying in various postures, each by its own pool of viscous blood, which emitted a peculiar scent, which was new to me, but which I have since learned is inseparable from a battle-field. Beyond these, a still larger group lay, body overlying body, knees crooked, arms erect, or wide-stretched and rigid, according as the last spasm overtook them. The company opposed to them must have shot straight. . . . I can never forget the impression those wide-open dead eyes made on

*The insufferable John Pope was among the least popular officers in the Union army, yet it was he who proposed the brilliant bypass of the Confederate fortification of Island No. 10, which led to the Union gaining control of a large stretch of the strategically vital Mississippi River.*

## POP CULTURE

### Ass from Elbow

The pompous General Pope was fond of issuing messages signed "Headquarters in the Saddle." This elicited jokes from fellow officers—some even said they were repeated by President Lincoln himself—to the effect that this explained Pope's deficiencies as a commander: "The general has his headquarters where his hindquarters ought to be."

me. Each seemed to be starting out of its socket, with a look similar to the fixed wondering gaze of an infant, as though the dying had viewed something appalling at the last moment."

By late afternoon, Stanley had caught up with his regiment, but by that time, Union gunboats on the Tennessee had begun firing against them, hurling "their enormous projectiles far beyond us; but, though they made great havoc among the trees, and created terror, they did comparatively little damage to those in close touch with the enemy." Nevertheless, by about four o'clock, even "the pluckiest of the men lacked the spontaneity and springing ardour which had distinguished them earlier in the day. Several of our company lagged wearily behind, and the remainder showed, by their drawn faces, the effects of their efforts. . . . As for myself, I had only one wish, and that was for repose."

Stanley survived that Sunday, April 6, to sleep the sleep of utter exhaustion that night. He awoke not only refreshed but, in common with the others around him—and, for that matter, with General Beauregard himself—holding the belief that his side had won a great victory. Yet when he "fell in" (reported for duty) with the other Dixie Greys later that morning, only about fifty were present. There were soldiers from other regiments assembled alongside the Greys, "but, even to my inexperienced eyes, the troops were in ill-condition for repeating the efforts of Sunday." Henry Morton Stanley was captured later that day. Taken prisoner, he soon deserted the Confederate army to join the Union navy, which he also promptly deserted, slipping away, to make his separate peace with both sides in the Civil War.

As for Shiloh, some historians consider it a draw, others a narrow Union victory. Tactically, it was that close. Strategically, however, it was clearly a Southern defeat; for the Confederacy never regained the initiative in the western theater.

Back in March, Union Brigadier General John Pope's 25,000-man Army of the Mississippi had begun chipping away at the Confederate defenses along the Mississippi River. The most formidable of these was called Island No. 10, at the "Kentucky Bend" of the river, where Tennessee meets Kentucky. The Confederates had placed fifty guns here where the island fortress was positioned at a double hairpin turn that not even an ironclad could negotiate speedily enough to avoid annihilation. If an ironclad was doomed, how could troop transports get by?

A braggart unpopular with his fellow officers (who considered him marginally competent at best), Pope nevertheless devised a brilliant solution to the problem posed by Island No. 10. He ordered his engineers to cut a shallow canal joining the Mississippi River to Wilson's Bayou in Kentucky. This stream rejoined the Mississippi *below* Island No. 10. By April 7, the second day of Shiloh, the canal was ready, and Pope's troop transports used it to bypass the Confederate defenses altogether. By this brilliant stroke, Pope cut off the Confederate line of retreat from Shiloh at Tiptonville, Tennessee, which resulted in the capture of thirty-five hundred men. And by neutralizing the Mississippi defenses, this opened the great river all the way to Fort Pillow, a Confederate stronghold that would fall in June, ensuring the end of Confederate control over the Mississippi and thereby cutting the Confederacy in two, severing east from west.

The cost of Shiloh was nearly incomprehensible. At the time, it was the deadliest battle ever fought on the North American continent. It was a terrible distinction that would not long stand, but, at the time, Abraham Lincoln was inundated with demands that he relieve "Butcher" Grant from command. To these, he replied without a trace of sentiment: "I can't spare this man; he fights."

## TAKEAWAY

When it took place, the battle of Shiloh (April 6–7, 1862) was the biggest and deadliest battle ever fought in North America. It changed the course of the war, convincing commanders, politicians, and people on both sides that only a total victory—"complete conquest," General Grant called it—would end the conflict. Shiloh transformed the Civil War from a war of rebellion and its suppression to a total war between the North and the South.

*Published in* Century Magazine *in 1885, this map shows the line of the canal ("Timber Cut") General Pope's engineers excavated to bypass the Confederate artillery at Island No. 10.*

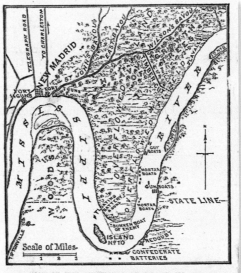

MAP OF THE MISSISSIPPI AT ISLAND NO. 10.
Showing (corrected) line of the channel cut by the Engineer Regiment.

## PART FOUR

# BROKEN GENERALS

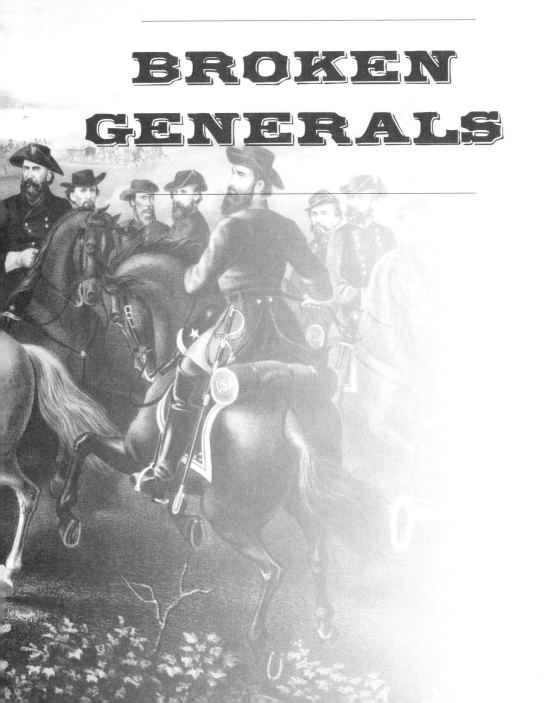

# CHAPTER 9

## PENINSULA AND VALLEY

*Opportunities Lost and Found*

T HE BLOODY BUSINESS OF WAR CREATES A GREAT DEMAND FOR GUNS, bullets, bayonets—and heroes. As the Civil War entered its second year, the North continued to look to its "Young Napoleon" to furnish that last commodity. When Lincoln made him general in chief of the U.S. Army, George B. McClellan assured him, "I can do it all," and then sat down to write to his wife: "Who would have thought, when we were married, that I should so soon be called upon to save my country?" He created a great military force in the Army of the Potomac, but, as the war entered its second year, that army, the largest ever raised on the continent, had astoundingly little to show for itself. In the meantime, to the west, Ulysses Grant was producing extraordinary results, seizing the Mississippi River itself from the Confederate grasp. All the public saw, however—when they bothered to look away from Virginia and the rest of the eastern theater—was the cost of it all. Shiloh was a nightmare, and Grant a butcher. McClellan remained the champion of the papers and the people.

Among secessionist Southerners, every general was a potential hero, but the standout among them all was Albert Sidney Johnston. While he was faulted for the failings of his subordinate commanders at Forts Henry and Donelson (Chapter 6), his reputation remained lofty as he entered the battle of Shiloh, which he came close to winning, even against a superior force (Chapter 8). His death in that battle left a vacuum, and a new hero was needed.

## GRANNY LEE AND TARDY GEORGE

IT IS EASY TO UNDERSTAND why the people and politicians of the North did not immediately seize on Ulysses S. Grant as their hero. Unsoldierly in appearance—he typically shunned the custom-tailored uniforms other generals wore (they cost as much as twelve-hundred 1860s dollars!) and wore the plain blue government-issue blouse of a private—a heavy drinker, and unafraid to commit and to lose men in battle, Grant was hardly an appealing figure. But in the retrospect of history, it is far more difficult to understand why Southerners took so long to recognize the martial greatness of Robert E. Lee, who is today among the most admired of all the Civil War generals.

### An Agonizing Decision

At the outbreak of the war, General in Chief Winfield Scott personally offered Lee a key command in the Union armies. And for good reason: His military record was long and distinguished. He was born in 1807 at Stratford Hall Plantation in Westmoreland County, Virginia, the son of no less a father than Major General Henry ("Light Horse Harry") Lee, a celebrated hero of the American Revolution. Robert enrolled at West Point in 1825 and was promoted to cadet sergeant by the end of his first year, a feat unprecedented at the academy. Not surprisingly, he graduated at the top of the class of 1829 in artillery and tactics and, through four years, had incurred not a single demerit.

The best and brightest West Point men were typically commissioned as officers in the Corps of Engineers, and Lee became a brilliant engineer, who designed fortifications and defensive works all over the eastern seaboard. In the U.S.-Mexican War (1846–48), he was a top aide to General Scott, earned renown for perilous personal reconnaissance missions, and was responsible for identifying routes of attack on Mexico City that the Mexicans, having deemed impassable, failed to defend.

*A skilled tactician and canny strategist, Robert E. Lee also possessed an abundance of what military professionals call "command presence," as this handsome engraving suggests.*

PREVIOUS SPREAD:
*Two years after he surrendered to Ulysses S. Grant at Appomattox, Robert E. Lee and twenty-one of his generals were celebrated in this lithograph by Augustus Tholey, a popular illustrator of historical subjects. Perhaps no figure, not Grant and not even Lincoln, emerged from the Civil War less tarnished and more universally venerated than the defeated commander of the Confederacy's Army of Northern Virginia.*

## REALITY CHECK

### "Virginia Is My Country"

Robert E. Lee's determination to defend his "native state" said much about the way Americans thought of themselves in the mid-nineteenth century. Most identified themselves first as citizens of their state—Lee often referred to Virginia as "my country"—and secondarily as citizens of the United States. Only after, and as a result of the Civil War, would it become commonplace for Americans to think of themselves as citizens of the national government first. In 1850, if an Englishman had asked Abraham Lincoln to say where he'd come from, Lincoln would have answered "Illinois." Had Lincoln survived the Civil War, he almost certainly would have replied to that same question, "I am an American."

In 1861, no U.S. Army officer was more widely admired than Robert E. Lee, but Scott's offer of high command cast him into a moral agony. Seven states had seceded by March 1861, when Lee accepted from Scott a promotion to colonel. He had already privately expressed contempt for the whole idea of secession and "Confederacy." This son of a Revolutionary War hero denounced it as a betrayal of the revolution itself, and when one of his subordinates asked him if he would fight for the Confederacy, Lee responded: "I shall never bear arms against the Union, but it may be necessary for me to carry a musket in the defense of my native state, Virginia, in which case I shall not prove recreant to my duty." At this time, Virginia had yet to secede, and when Jefferson Davis offered him an important command in the Confederate army, he declined. But after Lincoln formally called for volunteers to suppress the rebellion, Lee knew that Virginia would inevitably secede. On April 18, Scott offered him promotion to major general in the U.S. Army—at the time, the highest rank that army conferred. Two days later, Lee resigned his commission. His letter to General Scott is heartbreaking:

> Since my interview with you on the 18th Inst: I have felt that I ought not longer to retain my Commission in the Army. I therefore tender my resignation which I request you will recommend for acceptance. It would have been presented at once but for the struggle it has Cost me to separate myself from a Service to which I have devoted all the best years of my life, & all the ability I possessed. During the whole of that time, more than a quarter of a century, I have experienced nothing but kindness from my superiors, & the most Cordial friendship from my Comrades. To no one Genl have I been as much indebted as to yourself for kindness & Consideration & it has always been my ardent desire to merit your approbation. I shall carry with me, to the grave the most grateful recollections of your kind Consideration, & your name & fame will always be dear to me. Save in the defense of my native state shall I ever again draw my sword. Be pleased to accept my most earnest wishes for the Continuance of your happiness & prosperity & believe me

> Most truly yours
> R. E. Lee

On April 23, Lee accepted a command, not in the Confederate army, but of the *state* forces of Virginia. Jefferson Davis soon named Lee as his personal military adviser, a dubious honor, since Davis was loath to accept military advice from anyone. Worse, Lee's first command in the field was hardly auspicious. Operating in western Virginia— the part of the state that rebelled against secession and would later break away as the separate, loyal state of West Virginia—Lee was burdened not only by the hostility of the locals but by his own willful and insubordinate officers. As the war progressed, no

*This photograph of Stratford Hall, Lee's boyhood home in Westmoreland County, Virginia, was taken in the 1930s.*

officer on either side would enjoy greater loyalty than Robert E. Lee, but his leadership style relied more on his personal magnetism than it did on a firm command presence. Often, he framed his orders as mere requests, from one gentleman to another, and while this created a graceful and collegial climate among his subordinates and himself, it also had the potential for creating military disaster.

## Evacuating Lee

On September 12, 1861, Lee led an assault on lofty, rugged Cheat Mountain, in western Virginia. It was a key strategic position in the area because it controlled an important turnpike as well as a number of passes through the mountains. Union POWs captured in the red spruce forest on the mountain slope told Lee that the summit was held by a force of four thousand, far outnumbering him. In truth, just three hundred Union soldiers occupied Cheat's summit, but Lee, a gentleman, treated the prisoners as gentlemen, taking them at their word. He vacillated just long enough to lose the element of surprise. By the time he resolved to attack, he found himself facing very real Union reinforcements newly arrived. Lee sporadically sparred with the enemy over some forty-eight hours before withdrawing. It could have been a lot worse. Lee's losses were light, but, having been suckered, it was a dismal way to enter the war. While one Richmond paper labeled Lee—whose prematurely snowy hair and beard made him look older than his years—"Granny," another dubbed him "Evacuating Lee."

> "If General McClellan does not want to use the Army,
> I would like to *borrow* it for a time, provided I could
> see how it could be made to do something."
>
> *President Abraham Lincoln, expressing his exasperation*
> *with George B. McClellan's inaction, January 10, 1862*

### A Circuitous Plan

If Lee's star seemed unable to rise, McClellan's was at last beginning to
dim and descend. In the weeks and then months that followed his assurance to Lincoln that he could "do it all," he did practically nothing. On
January 27, 1862, President Lincoln took the initiative by issuing "General
War Order No. 1," which directed McClellan to begin an offensive against
the enemy no later than February 22. When McClellan failed to do this,
Lincoln, on March 11, relieved him as general in chief of the armies and
returned him to command of only the Army of the Potomac. He hoped
this "demotion"—the Army of the Potomac was still by far the largest
and most important of the Union armies—would kick McClellan into
decisive action, namely an advance from Washington to Richmond.
McClellan responded with a much more circuitous plan.

The logic of attacking Richmond directly was this: Menacing the
capital of the South would force the Confederate armies to come to
its defense, which meant that they would have to pull back and yield
territory to Union control. Moreover, in the process of withdrawing,
the armies would be vulnerable; turning your back on the enemy was
always dangerous. McClellan, however, wanted to avoid a direct overland march on Richmond and instead proposed to transport the entire
Army of the Potomac by ship, sailing down the Chesapeake Bay to
the James River for an amphibious landing south of General Joseph E.
Johnston's lines at Manassas, site of the Bull Run battle. (J. E. Johnston
was not related to the late Albert Sidney Johnston.) This would outflank Johnston's army, forcing it to pull back from the vicinity of
Washington. Thus McClellan would not only avoid the risk of a major
battle, but, with the pressure on Washington relieved, would receive
reinforcements released from garrison duty. Once the Army of the
Potomac had reached what McClellan deemed sufficient strength, the
advance could be directed against Richmond.

Executive Mansion,

Washington, January 27, 1862.

Presidents general
War Order No 1

Ordered that the 22nd day of February 1862, be the day for a general movement of the Land and Naval forces of the United States against the insurgent forces.

That especially—

The Army at & about, Fortress Monroe.
The Army of the Potomac.
The Army of Western Virginia
The Army near Munfordsville, Ky.
The Army and Flotilla at Cairo,
And a Naval force in the Gulf of Mexico, be ready for a movement on that day.

That all other forces, both Land and Naval, with their respective commanders, obey existing orders, for the time, and be ready to obey additional orders when duly given.

That the Heads of Departments, and especially the Secretaries of War and of the Navy,

*Lincoln drafted "General War Order No. 1" on January 27, 1862, in an effort to force the ever-reluctant George B. McClellan into aggressive action "against the insurgent forces."*

Under pressure from officers loyal to McClellan and against his better judgment, Lincoln agreed to the plan. There was, in any case, a certain logic to it—though it was the logic of a leisurely chess player, not a general in the field. For it failed to take into account the cost in time and effort required to mount a large-scale amphibious operation. By the time the Army of the Potomac even got under way, McClellan received intelligence that Johnston had left Manassas and marched farther south to the Rappahannock River, closer to Richmond.

This maneuver did two things. First, it made McClellan look supremely foolish. While he puttered, the enemy slipped away. Worse, when his men inspected the abandoned Confederate trenches at Manassas, they discovered that what they had thought were large numbers of cannon were nothing but logs painted dull black. "Quaker guns," a scornful Northern press called them, and one reporter observed that, ". . . our enemies, like the Chinese, have frightened us by the sound of

*Union troops occupy an abandoned Confederate fort at Centreville, Virginia, which had been "defended" (and quite successfully!) by little more than "Quaker guns."*

gongs and the wearing of devils' masks." Yet if the enemy pulled back, that did mean he was yielding territory. Wasn't this what McClellan had hoped to achieve by his landings?

It was, however, Johnston who gained the greater advantage. By pulling back, he drew McClellan closer to the Confederate forces consolidated around Richmond. Johnston was willing to use the South's capital as bait, forcing McClellan, far from his sources of supply and reinforcement, to a fight against the bulk of the Confederate army in its home territory. Clearly, McClellan would have been better off had he simply followed Lincoln's initial order and attacked Richmond directly and without delay. By doing this, the Army of the Potomac would have faced a far smaller force. The irony is that McClellan had postponed his advance into the Confederacy precisely because he believed that the Confederate army outnumbered him everywhere. In his halting advance southward, his natural tendency toward dramatically overestimating the size of the enemy (see Chapter 6) was exacerbated by the well-meaning but inept intelligence work of Allan J. Pinkerton's "operatives." Experienced as detectives, these men and women had no military training and therefore overestimated enemy numbers wildly. The figures Pinkerton handed McClellan were inflated by factors of two or three, perhaps even more.

## THE PENINSULA CAMPAIGN

FEARFUL OF BEING OVERWHELMED by superior numbers that didn't exist, "Tardy George" McClellan had delayed long enough to allow Johnston actually to build a bigger force closer to Richmond. It was still numerically inferior to the Army of the Potomac, but McClellan could not bring himself to believe this. Although his first attempt to sidestep and thereby outflank the enemy had failed, he decided to repeat the same tactic on an even larger scale. He would ferry his troops south to Fort Monroe, near Newport News and Hampton Roads, in the south-eastern corner of Virginia. As the first amphibious operation had been intended to take him south of the Confederate position, so the second would take him below the rebel capital itself. He would land, and then advance back toward the north, toward Richmond, traversing the peninsula separating the York from the James Rivers.

This idea of repeating an error but making it even bigger contained a whiff of logic just sufficient to make it appear strategically plausible. By attacking Richmond from the south, McClellan would give the capital's defenders nowhere to maneuver but toward the north. With luck, this might allow the Union army to envelop Richmond and, with it, the

# FROM THE CIVIL WAR TOP 40

By March 1862, Lincoln wasn't the only one impatient with McClellan. Around this time, many Americans were singing a new song titled "What Are You Waiting for, Tardy George?" by George H. Boker which went something like this:

hat are you waiting for, George,
     I pray?—
          To scour your cross-belts with
fresh pipe-clay?
To burnish your buttons, to brighten your guns;
Or wait you for May-day and warm spring suns?
Are you blowing your fingers because they are cold,
Or catching your breath ere you take a hold?
Is the mud knee-deep in valley and gorge
What are you waiting for, tardy George?

. . .

Now that you've marshaled your whole command,
Planned what you would, and changed what you
     planned;
Practiced with shot and practiced with shell,
Know to a hair where every one fell,
Made signs by day and signals by night;

Was it all done to keep out of a fight?
Is the whole matter too heavy a charge?
What are you waiting for, tardy George?

*The Civil War occasioned thousands of popular songs from amateur and professional composers on both sides, including the ruthless "Tardy George."*

SONGS FOR THE UNION.

TARDY GEORGE.

WHAT are you waiting for, George, I pray?
To scour your cross-belts with fresh pipe-clay?
To burnish your buttons, to brighten your guns;
Or wait you for May-day and warm spring suns?
Are you blowing your fingers because they are cold,
Or catching your breath ere you take a hold?

bulk of the Confederate army in Virginia. Besides, Napoleon had fought a famous "Peninsular War," so why shouldn't the Young Napoleon claim his own *Peninsula* campaign?

Certainly, it was Napoleonic in scale. The largest amphibious operation in American military history to that time, it gave McClellan what he most relished: something very big to plan. And plan it he did, beautifully and with great thoroughness. Yet what had he planned?

The problem—as Lincoln had seen—was really quite simple. Richmond was the Confederate capital. Take it, and the war would be over. Menace it, and it would be close to over. McClellan had a very big army. All he had to do was march it to Richmond and fight it out. Grant would have jumped at the chance and would have accepted the inevitably heavy losses as down payments on ultimate victory. McClellan, however, devised a means of complicating what was simple and calling the result by a grand Napoleonic name.

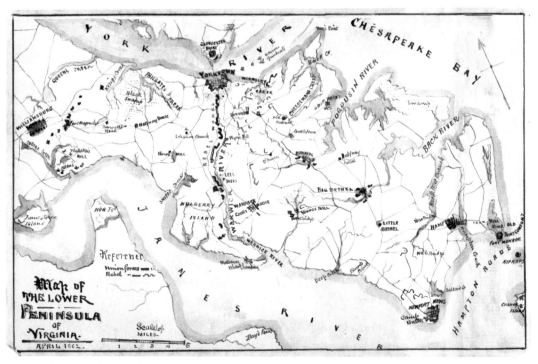

*Robert Knox Sneden, landscape artist and wartime mapmaker for the U.S. Army, drew this elaborate depiction of the lower peninsula of Virginia, showing the locations of both Confederate and Union forces, during McClellan's ill-fated Peninsula campaign.*

## Mud

The water-transport phase of the Peninsula campaign went remarkably well, but once the troops landed on April 4, 1862, on what passed for dry land, the difficulties multiplied. The men, more than 100,000 of them, disembarked in a heavy, relentless rain that churned the coastal mud flats of the Yorktown Peninsula into gumbo. As the Army of the Potomac began its miserable northerly slog, the part of Johnston's army that occupied the peninsula withdrew to well-prepared entrenchments at Yorktown.

*Yorktown.* The very name should have spurred McClellan to bold action. Here, after all, was where the culminating campaign of the American Revolution had been fought and won. Yet, once again persuaded that the numbers were against him, and complaining that he had been obliged to leave behind thirty thousand Army of the Potomac soldiers to garrison Washington, McClellan chose to lay siege to Yorktown rather than to overwhelm it in a single massive attack.

## Duped by a Prince

The more Lincoln goaded McClellan, the more ardently the general embraced Allan Pinkerton's latest intelligence, which "proved" that Yorktown was heavily defended by a force that substantially outnumbered the Army of the Potomac. The siege, McClellan responded to Lincoln, was necessary. To attempt to overrun the Confederate position without first softening it up with artillery would be suicidal.

The truth was that Johnston had repeated his customary tactic of strategic withdrawal. By the time McClellan began his siege, the Confederate general had withdrawn most of the Army of Northern Virginia yet closer to Richmond, leaving just fifteen thousand men in the Yorktown entrenchments under the command of General John Bankhead Magruder. Affectionately dubbed "Prince John" by his military colleagues, Magruder looked like a matinee idol and, in fact, enjoyed nothing more than mounting amateur theatricals. He exploited this avocation now to capitalize on McClellan's weakness. Magruder skillfully deployed his small force behind a network of wooden-walled trenches, some twelve miles of earthworks punctuated by many forts and other strong points. To give the illusion of having a far bigger army than he actually commanded, he marched his men back and forth, over and over, their continual movement suggesting the presence of multitudes. He hauled his modest complement of artillery

*Called "Prince John" because of his regal manner, Confederate general John Bankhead Magruder masterfully deceived McClellan at Yorktown, heaping delay upon delay.*

from one end of his entrenchments to the other in a remarkably successful effort to give the appearance of massive batteries, and whenever a bluecoat so much as showed his face along the Union siege lines, Magruder's batteries replied with a furious fusillade, which suggested a profusion of guns, ammunition, and the willingness to use them. These effects, combined with McClellan's predispositions and Pinkerton's abundant misinformation kept the Army of the Potomac meekly at bay. In this way, Magruder held off a force nearly six times greater than his.

Time, second in value only to manpower, was surrendered daily to the Confederacy. While Johnston continued to consolidate his forces around Richmond, Robert E. Lee, engineer that he was, took his soldiers' muskets from their hands and gave them picks and shovels instead. He used the time to expand the fortifications all around the Southern capital, adding layers of redundancy to them, so that the defenders could, if necessary, fall back from one line of trenches to another, pulling any attackers into a deadly field of fire. Each day of McClellan's futile siege made Richmond that much more formidable an objective.

*McClellan's Army of the Potomac bombarded the Yorktown fortification with massive barrages such as those from Battery 4, which mounted ten mortars, each weighing twenty thousand pounds. The thirteen-inch projectiles fell on mostly abandoned Confederate entrenchments.*

# OLD BLUE LIGHT

As McCLELLAN REVOLVED HIS PENINSULA CAMPAIGN over and over in his mind, Thomas J. Jackson—now widely known as "Stonewall," thanks to his performance at the first Bull Run (Chapter 5), but called by the officers and men closest to him "Old Blue Light," because of the intense azure clarity of his penetrating gaze—put his own campaign into action. Johnston, Lee, and other top Confederate commanders realized how anxious Abraham Lincoln was to defend Washington. They knew the president believed that if Washington were overrun or even successfully raided, Northern morale would collapse and, with it, the will to continue the war. The more the Confederates could menace Washington—or present even the appearance of menace—the more men Lincoln would use to defend it. The more men required to defend the capital, the fewer there would be to fight in the field. And *that* would do much to even the lopsided odds against the Confederacy.

Johnston and Lee dispatched Jackson to lead a sweep through Virginia's Shenandoah Valley, raiding, harassing, and generally trespassing in the vast backyard of the capital. The purpose of these demonstrations was to suggest that an invasion of Washington, not from the south but from the west, was afoot.

## Jackson's First Battles

The first battle of Jackson's Shenandoah campaign was fought on March 23, 1862, at Kernstown, near Winchester, Virginia. Jackson struck out boldly against what he took to be a four-regiment rear guard attached to Major General Nathaniel Prentice Banks's two divisions. Old Blue Light was stunned to discover that he was not facing a rear guard, but one entire division of some nine thousand men. Badly outnumbered, Jackson was soundly defeated and withdrew.

No general likes to lose a fight, but the tactical drubbing Jackson absorbed was leveraged into a strategic victory for the Confederacy. The Kernstown encounter convinced nervous Northern politicians that Washington was definitely in imminent danger of invasion. It was for this reason that Lincoln detached more than thirty thousand men from McClellan's Army of the Potomac to augment the capital's garrison. As we have seen, given McClellan's nature, the absence of these men effectively paralyzed him.

---

## NUMBERS

### How Big Was McClellan's Army?

As McClellan consistently overestimated the strength of the enemy, so he seems just as consistently to have underestimated his own strength. President Lincoln pointed this out in a letter to the general on April 9, 1862: "There is a curious mystery about the number of the troops now with you. When I telegraphed you on the 6th, saying you had over a hundred thousand with you, I had just obtained from the Secretary of War, a statement, taken as he said, from your own returns, making 108,000 then with you, and en route to you. You now say you will have but 85,000, when all en route to you shall have reached you. How can the discrepancy of 23,000 be accounted for?"

Today, historians believe that anywhere from 90,000 to 115,000 men of the Army of the Potomac participated in the Peninsula campaign.

*Artist Edwin Forbes sketched "The army of General [John C.] Frémont crossing the north fork of the Shenandoah [River] at Mt. Jackson—Pursuit of Stonewall Jackson" in the first Shenandoah campaign.*

Jackson did not fight the next battle of the Shenandoah campaign until May 8. Like Kernstown, it was far from a tactical triumph. Jackson forced the federals to retreat from McDowell, Virginia, but he sustained substantially more casualties. Authorities differ on the numbers, but the estimate is some 718 Confederate killed, wounded, captured, or missing against 590 for the Union.

On May 21, however, Stonewall finally put his genius as a cavalryman on full display. He sent a mounted detachment under the dashing Colonel Turner Ashby to lure General Banks into assuming that Jackson's entire force was moving west, toward Strasburg. In fact, while Banks was being successfully deceived, Jackson reaped a crop of reinforcements, and then, on May 22, advanced the bulk of his small Army of the Valley—now roughly seventeen thousand men—to Front Royal, Virginia, where 1,063 Union soldiers under Colonel John R. Kenly, one of Banks's commanders, were posted. Jackson's victory here on the following day was swift and complete. Nearly seven hundred of Kenly's soldiers surrendered for a loss to the Confederates of just thirty-six killed or wounded. Jackson also gathered up a pair of cannon and a cache of arms, along with other supplies. In mock gratitude, his men gave thanks to the Union general they now called "Commissary Banks."

"It is told that in 1862 Stonewall Jackson, leaning against a tree and staring down the Shenandoah Valley, was asked by one of his staff officers what he was doing. He is supposed to have replied, 'I'm trying to figure out what the Yankees are up to. If anyone in this army thinks he knows tell them to come up here and see me.'"

*Lieutenant General Victor H. Krulak,*
*in Marine Corps Gazette, November 1986*

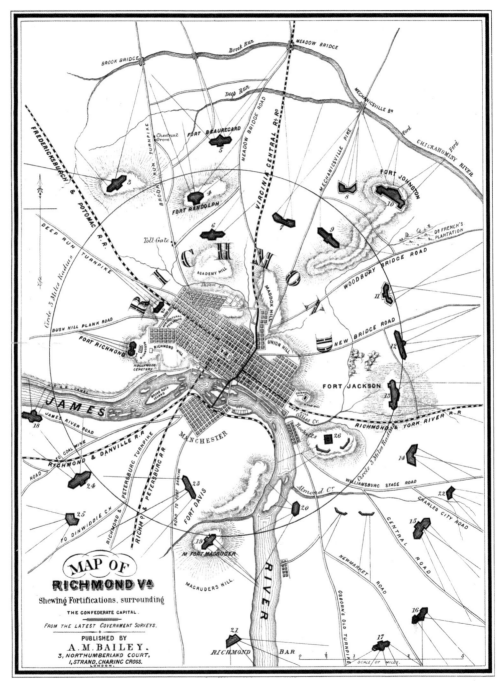

*A London lithographer published this map of Richmond, Virginia, complete with a description of its "Forts . . . with their armament." Britons followed the course of the American Civil War with keen interest.*

## THE SHENANDOAH CAMPAIGN CONTINUES

FRONT ROYAL WAS A TERRIBLE HUMILIATION for Banks and the Union army. Sheepishly, the Union general fell back on Winchester, Virginia. Foolishly, however, he violated a cardinal rule of battle tactics: Never divide your forces in the face of the enemy. In an effort to make it more difficult for Jackson to pursue his retreating forces, Banks did just that, and on May 24, Stonewall struck one of his columns at Middletown. The next day, he attacked the larger segment of Banks's divided forces, sending the general and his command in headlong retreat across the Potomac. Jackson gave chase, riding his men hard. After running Banks's command to ground at Harpers Ferry, Old Blue Light made it look as if he were about to cross the Potomac toward Washington—only to turn suddenly southward. It was the equivalent of a very rude hand gesture, flung into the faces of the American government and its army.

Major General John Charles Frémont, the same dashing but inept commander who had been replaced in the western theater by Henry Wager Halleck (Chapter 6), led 11,500 of the roughly 16,000 men of the so-called

*Forbes sketched this long view of "The battle of Cross Keys—Sunday June 7th 1862—Genl. Frémont and Genl. Jackson." Although outnumbered two to one, Stonewall Jackson's field commander, Richard S. Ewell, handily defeated Union general John C. Frémont's forces.*

Mountain Department in a raid against Major General Richard Ewell's Confederate bivouac at Cross Keys, Virginia, on June 8. Although he greatly outnumbered Ewell's 5,800-man force, Frémont's spirited attack lacked cohesion, and Ewell did not have a very difficult time beating it back.

On the same day, one of Frémont's subordinate commanders, Brigadier General James Shields, a tough and canny recent Irish immigrant, sent a detachment under Colonel Samuel S. Carroll in a raid against Jackson's position at Port Republic. Skillful and aggressive, the raiders very nearly captured none other than Stonewall himself before the general rallied an artillery and an infantry regiment to drive them off. Determined to retaliate, Jackson, on June 9, personally led an attack on Brigadier General Erastus Tyler's brigade, which had reinforced Carroll. Tyler's men made considerable headway against the attackers, but Jackson's troops fought with uncanny fury and closed in on Tyler's command for hand-to-hand combat. In a war fought mainly with the weapons of nineteenth-century industry, fighting at arm's length was a rarity. In this instance, however, it was a knock-down, drag-out brawl that enabled the Confederates to overrun and occupy a key Union artillery position. Through it all, Frémont and the main body of his Mountain Department, isolated on the opposite bank of the flood-swollen South Fork, could do nothing more than bear witness to the fight.

## JACKSON'S MASTERPIECE

JACKSON WAS THE BOLDEST OF BOLD COMMANDERS, but he knew just when he had gained all that he could, and so he also knew when it was time to break off the Shenandoah Valley campaign. The time was now, before the columns of Shields and Frémont could link up and turn against him.

Even the Union commanders, beaten and embarrassed, could not help but marvel at the sheer brilliance of what Stonewall Jackson had achieved. Through a series of lightning raids and stunning maneuvers back and forth over the lush valley, Jackson had leveraged his Army of the Valley—just seventeen thousand men—into a force that held at bay a total of fifty thousand Union soldiers, thirty thousand of whom would otherwise have been used in McClellan's faltering Peninsula campaign to attack Richmond. Jackson had seized and wielded with supreme virtuosity the one weapon that is truly ultimate in war: fear. It paralyzed—and for a long time—the biggest military force ever to fight in North America, and it saved, at least for the time being, the Confederate capital and the Confederate cause.

**TAKEAWAY**

The second year of the Civil War was ushered in for the Union by lost opportunities as Major General George B. McClellan, the vaunted "Young Napoleon," failed to commit his magnificent Army of the Potomac to a decisive campaign. In the meantime, Confederate commanders—especially Thomas J. "Stonewall" Jackson—leveraged their inferior numbers in brilliant actions (most notably Jackson's Shenandoah Valley campaign) that tied down and exhausted inordinate numbers of Union troops.

*Stonewall Jackson ordered the bridge near Mount Jackson burned in order to delay the Union forces pursuing him. This wood engraving, after a drawing by Edwin Forbes, was published in* Frank Leslie's Illustrated Newspaper *on July 5, 1862.*

# CHAPTER 10

# CRESCENT CITY AND
# POINTS WEST

## *Wider, Wilder Theaters*

THE PRESIDENT AND EVERYONE ELSE IN THE NORTH WHO LONGED FOR a quick end to the war were badly shaken by George McClellan's failures on the Virginia peninsula, but there was still hope. It lay to the west.

David Dixon Porter (1813–91) was the son of David Porter (1780–1843), a naval hero of the War of 1812. As bold on the water as McClellan was timid on land, David Dixon Porter drew up a secret plan to capture New Orleans. While the people of the North fretted over the elusive target that was Richmond, Porter understood that New Orleans, a far bigger city—the biggest city in the South—was a prize even more important. It stood at the mouth of the Mississippi, both an ocean port and a river port, strategically positioned for import, export, and internal transport deep into the Confederacy. It stood, too, as both the sentinel and doorkeeper between the Confederate states of the East and those of the West.

*David Dixon Porter, on the deck of the USS* Fulton. *This photograph was made between 1862 and 1865.*

# OBJECTIVE: NEW ORLEANS

PORTER NOMINATED DAVID GLASGOW FARRAGUT to lead the assault on the Crescent City. He knew him well. Farragut had served under David Dixon Porter's father, David Porter, aboard USS *Essex* during the War of 1812, and the elder Porter had thought so highly of Farragut that he gave the twelve-year-old midshipman command of a British ship that *Essex* had captured. He also informally adopted the boy, who traded his first name, *James*, for *David*, to honor the man who was both his captain and his adoptive father.

Although David Dixon Porter had chosen his own foster brother to command the assault on New Orleans, there was not a trace of nepotism about it. At sixty, Farragut was the most seasoned sailor in the United States Navy. Tall and slender in an era dominated by short men of ample girth, Farragut, in his seventh decade, was in better shape than most men half his age. His friends, family, and fellow sailors delighted in the ritual handspring he turned on every birthday, announcing, each time he recovered his feet, that he would retire from the service the moment that particular exercise gave him the slightest difficulty.

He pored over his foster brother's plans and marshaled a fleet of two steam frigates, seven screw sloops, nine gunboats, and twenty schooners, each of the latter refitted to carry a thirteen-inch mortar. These schooners would be responsible for delivering the principal bombardment against the forts defending New Orleans, and Farragut assigned command of them to none other than David Dixon Porter.

Farragut sailed his assault fleet across the Gulf of Mexico and into the mouth of the Mississippi. Beginning in mid-April 1862, he led a continuous bombardment of the two forts, Jackson and St. Philip, which stood sentry over the approach to the Crescent City. After a week of unrelenting mortar fire directed against them, Farragut judged that the forts had been neutralized, and, at two o'clock on the morning of April 24, he ordered his fleet to steam past them. With their shore batteries reduced to rubble, the Confederates improvised a defense by setting fire to unmanned rafts, which they launched into the river's slow current and against the invading fleet. Farragut, his skippers, and their crews strained every nerve and muscle to steer around the flaming platforms that streamed by them. The few armed

## DETAILS, DETAILS
### A Civil War Fleet

During the Civil War era, a *frigate* was a warship of thirty-two to fifty guns designed for speed and maneuverability. Those in Farragut's fleet were steam frigates, though their motive power was supplemented by sails. A *screw sloop* was smaller—and faster—than a frigate and was powered by a steam-driven propeller (screw). The *gunboats* in Farragut's fleet were small, shallow draft vessels suited for navigating coastal and inland waterways. His *schooners* were fore-and-aft-rigged sailing vessels modified to carry a single mortar.

*David Glasgow Farragut, in the uniform of a rear admiral, United States Navy.*

ships and boats the Confederate navy could muster also did their best to slow Farragut's progress, but his guns made short work of them.

Once past Forts Jackson and St. Philip, the flaming rafts, and the other ships, there were still more forts along the Mississippi's shore, but their commanders realized that, with the main defenses knocked out and the diminutive Confederate fleet destroyed, further resistance was futile. Cut off from support and reinforcement, the other forts surrendered to Farragut as his fleet chugged past them.

*Currier & Ives published this thrilling, if fanciful, print titled "Com. Farragut's fleet, passing the forts on the Mississippi, April 24th 1862" shortly after the battle. The focal point of the illustration is the U.S. frigate* Mississippi *destroying the rebel ram* Manassas.

## HOUR OF THE BEAST

THE NAVY TOOK NEW ORLEANS, and the army was sent in to occupy it. As a military man, Major General Benjamin Franklin Butler stood at the opposite end of the spectrum from Farragut. Whereas Farragut was lean, his features chiseled, his face clean shaven, Butler was great of girth, flaccid of face, and with an upper lip covered by a walrus-like moustache. He possessed slight military experience, as an officer in the Massachusetts militia, in contrast to Farragut, who had spent his life in arms at sea. Butler was a Democratic politician by trade, who had served in the Massachusetts House and Senate and who, as a delegate to the 1860 Democratic National Convention, had pushed for the nomination of Jefferson Davis and opposed Stephen A. Douglas. When Douglas won the nomination, Butler sided with the breakaway Southern branch of his party in supporting John C. Breckinridge for president. But when the Civil War came, Butler proclaimed himself a Union man, and his political connections, combined with his militia experience (such as it was), got him an appointment as a major general of volunteers. He was the epitome of the infamous breed of "political generals," installed in his rank not on the basis of proven martial prowess, but because of political position.

It was Butler who was given command of the troops tasked with taking possession of the fallen Confederate forts and of New Orleans itself. Possession of the Crescent City was a great Union triumph, but

Butler created less than a glorious record as the city's occupier. To give him his due, he had led the 8th Massachusetts Regiment and the 7th New York Infantry in the occupation of Baltimore at the start of the war and had thus experienced firsthand what it was like to preside over a hostile urban population. Although Butler was a skilled politician and an able negotiator, he had dealt harshly with the Baltimore rioters, and he meant in New Orleans to do the same, nipping any civil disobedience in the bud by imposing stringent martial law from day one. He seems, however, to have confused legitimate discipline with a tyrannical intolerance. One of his first public acts was to restore the Stars and Stripes to the flagpole atop the New Orleans mint. This provoked an angry mob to storm the building, scale its façade, and tear down the flag. When one of Butler's men subsequently arrested a citizen who displayed a shred of the flag as a boutonnière, Butler clapped him into jail and convened a drumhead court, which found the man guilty of treason and sentenced him to hang.

BUTLER HOLDING THE MOB IN CHECK AT NEW ORLEANS

To a more sensible leader tasked with policing a hostile population, the verdict and its sentence would have presented a golden opportunity to show clemency. The disciplinary point would have been made, but, tempered by brotherly mercy, would have spoken volumes about the Union's desire not merely to win the war but to heal the nation. Instead, Butler not only let the man hang, he made a grand spectacle of it by hanging him in a public proceeding directly in front of the mint.

It is never a good idea to give an unhappy people the martyr they crave. Yet, given their martyr, the men of New Orleans did nothing, and, in fact, the volume of unrest and protest dramatically subsided throughout the city. Except, that is, among the city's women.

*The distinguished American painter and illustrator Charles Stanley Reinhart created this highly idealized ink wash depiction of Union general Benjamin F. "Beast" Butler "holding the mob in check at New Orleans" for a series on the Civil War published in* Harper's Weekly *in 1896.*

## The Woman Order

The women seized every available opportunity to vent their indignation. They ostentatiously pinched and held their noses whenever a bluecoat happened by. They decorated their dresses and bonnets with Confederate military insignia. When they encountered Yankee soldiers walking toward them, they went out of their way to force the men off the "banquette" (sidewalk) and into the muck of the gutter.

Harper's Weekly *published this before-and-after depiction of the ladies of New Orleans as a commentary on General Butler's Woman Order. The transformation is pictured as a tongue-in-cheek miracle: ugly hags spitting in the face of a Union officer become attractive and respectful young women before whom the officer is delighted to tip his cap.*

The supreme indignity came one spring morning when a New Orleans grand dame (allegedly) peered out her upper-story window, drew a bead on no less a target than Flag Officer David Farragut, and, at precisely the right moment, discharged the contents of her chamber pot on his head. Butler fired back with what he called "General Order 28," dated May 15, 1862, but which became instantly infamous throughout the Confederacy (and even much of the North) as the "Woman Order":

> As the Officers and Soldiers of the United States have been subject to repeated insults from the women calling themselves ladies of New Orleans, in return for the most scrupulous non-interference and courtesy on our part, it is ordered that hereafter when any Female shall, by word, gesture, or movement, insult or show contempt for any officer of the United States, she shall be regarded and held liable to be treated as a woman of the town plying her avocation.

Butler knew that his Woman Order would touch a chivalrous Southern nerve. It was one thing to hang a man for tearing down a flag, but quite another to brand a Southern lady a whore. Of course, Butler went even further. He effectively invited his soldiers to reward any perceived insult with rape. Fortunately, the men of Butler's command had better sense than their commanding officer and restrained themselves; however, the people and the press—even in some Northern cities— condemned Benjamin Franklin Butler as "Beast" Butler. For his part, P. G. T. Beauregard, that most properly Southern of Southern officers, published a proclamation addressed to the "Men of the South!"

> Shall our mothers, our wives, our daughters and our sisters,
> be thus outraged by the ruffianly soldier of the North, to
> whom is given the right to treat, at their pleasure, the ladies
> of the South as common harlots? Arouse friends, and drive
> back from our soil, these infamous invaders of our homes
> and disturbers of our family ties.

Beast Butler's Woman Order and the Southern response to it show that the Civil War had become more than a political struggle, a fight for states' rights, or even a fight over slavery. Although it was certainly all of these things, it had become as well a war of scorn and hate, in which Southerners and Northerners were no longer human beings and fellow citizens, but beasts and whores.

## EYEWITNESS

Alexander Walker, a pro-Confederate New Orleans newspaperman, was among those arrested and sent to Ship Island prison after Butler took over New Orleans. He wrote a letter to Confederate president Jefferson Davis, September 13, 1862, complaining bitterly about Butler, his treatment of New Orleans women, and the prison conditions. The letter was published in contemporary newspapers, and is excerpted here:

*Several ladies of the highest social position have been imprisoned for the expression of sympathy with the Confederates and the wearing of ribbons of certain colors. Mrs. Dubois, an elderly lady long engaged in the business of teaching our children, was imprisoned on the charge of not being able to account for certain keys and books belonging to the schools, which were never in her possession. All the members of the Finance Committee of the City Council are imprisoned for authorizing the subscription of the city to the fund for its defense; and several hundred of our citizens who subscribed to this fund have been compelled to pay 25 percent of their subscription to Butler, under threat of imprisonment at hard labor. . . . And this is but a feeble and deficient presentment of the enormities and brutalities of this cowardly and brutal monster. . . . [General Butler] will permit no one to thwart his two great objects—to bid highest for the favor of the Northern mob and to accumulate a vast fortune by extortion and plunder. . . .*

*The prisons of New Orleans are crowded with citizens whose highest offense consists in the expressions of opinions and hopes of the success of the Confederate cause.*

## TRUE WEST

NEW ORLEANS WAS A GATEWAY and gatekeeper, giving passage to the South and also to the West. The casual student of the Civil War is sometimes confused by references to the war's "western theater." Usually, this meant the battles and campaigns conducted in Kentucky and Tennessee, as well as other parts of the Mississippi River valley. Yet there was also a far western theater, or a trans-Mississippi theater, the scene of combat in the region most of us think of as the true American West. Missouri, Arkansas, Kansas, Texas, New Mexico, and Arizona all saw Civil War combat.

It was a different kind of combat than what was fought in Virginia and other areas east of the Mississippi. No great armies contended with one another, there were no grand Napoleonic maneuvers, and no titanic battles for major cities. (There were no major cities.) Looked at in the short range, the trans-Mississippi Civil War achieved little that can be deemed decisively strategic, but regarded from the longer view, the war there was a struggle for the future. For the West was in the 1860s what it had been since the voyages of Christopher Columbus: a dream, a goal, an aspiration—in short, opportunity.

It is no accident that two major Western initiatives were advocated and enacted during the Lincoln administration, even in the depths of war.

### The Pacific Railway Act

The Pacific Railway Act of 1862 authorized and funded (with bonds and land grants) construction of a railroad spanning the continent. One of the great achievements of the Lincoln administration (though it was completed four years after the president's death and was overshadowed by the Civil War), the transcontinental railroad was a strategic military and political step designed to bind the West to the North, and, perhaps even more importantly, it was a profound expression of faith in the future of the United States; that is, it was an expression of the belief that the United States *had* a future.

*The Goliath, a locomotive of the Central Pacific Railroad, is pictured here at Wadsworth, near Big Bend of the Truckee River, in Nevada.*

# A WAR ON RAILS

The Civil War was the world's first war that relied heavily on rail transportation—for supplies, for troops, and for the evacuation of the sick and wounded. Railroads were even used to extend the reach of very heavy artillery. The Union mounted some of its coastal mortars, intended to be fired from fixed coastal installations, on specially reinforced flatcars, which served not only to carry the weapon where it was needed, but also functioned as the platform from which it was fired.

**U**nion high command and the Lincoln administration considered railroads of such great military importance that a Railways and Telegraph Act, passed on January 31, 1862, gave the president full authority to commandeer railways and telegraph lines. The next month, the War Department created the United States Military Railroads (USMRR), which managed the North's tracks and rolling stock and had direct and exclusive control over 419 locomotives, 6,330 cars, and 2,105 miles of track.

Railroads were important in the Confederate states, too, but the individual states refused to yield control to the central government, which greatly crippled military operations. Track, locomotives, cars—all were in short supply. The situation was made worse by the many different track gauges (width between rails) in use throughout the South, which meant that cargo and passengers had to

*Giant siege mortars like this Union monster were transported by railroad on specially reinforced flat cars, which also served as their firing platform. This one was used during the siege of Petersburg, Virginia, in 1864.*

frequently change trains where track of one gauge met track of another. (This liability, however, would prove something of an asset later in the war because it delayed the transport of Union troops and supplies with the South.)

*The Construction Corps of the USMRR built this spectacular railroad bridge over Potomac Creek on the right-of-way of the Richmond, Fredericksburg & Potomac Railroad.*

*The Civil War drained army resources from the Great Plains and Far West, leaving no military force to police white–Native American relations. In Minnesota, the result was the so-called Great Santee Sioux Uprising of 1862, which drove some two thousand settlers in terror from their homes. The refugee crisis, as seen here, was dire.*

### The Homestead Act

The other great Western legislation of the war years was the Homestead Act, also signed into law in 1862. It authorized any citizen—or immigrant who intended to become a citizen—to select any surveyed but unclaimed parcel of public land west of the Mississippi up to 160 acres, settle it, improve it, and, by living on it for five years, gain title to it. Alternatively, a homesteader could "preempt" his parcel after living on it for just six months by purchasing it at the bargain price of $1.25 per acre. The law also provided for augmenting the 160-acre claim. The intention of the Homestead Act was to "settle" the West rapidly enough to bolster what was left of the Union by creating an unbroken chain of loyal citizens from sea to shining sea. Like the Pacific Railway Act, the Homestead Act was also a claim on and affirmation of an American national future.

What neither act took into consideration was the future of the Native Americans who also populated the West. Though they were distant from Washington and Richmond, some Indian tribes were affected profoundly by the Civil War. In some parts of the West, especially in Arizona, New Mexico, and southwestern Texas, the withdrawal of federal troops from their western outposts to eastern battlegrounds unleashed an epidemic of Indian raids. In some places, the absence of troops to police the region prompted white settlers to make war on their Indian neighbors. Like the French and Indian War and the American Revolution in the eighteenth century and the War of 1812 early in the nineteenth, the Civil War in the West often blurred into the Indian wars that had begun before 1861 and would not end until the Wounded Knee massacre in December 1890.

# FIGHT AT PEA RIDGE

AS SEEN IN CHAPTER 2, Kansas had been torn by warfare between pro-slavery and antislavery factions before the Civil War began, and its neighbor Missouri was the scene of the first of the war's battles west of the Mississippi. After the impetuous Union captain-turned-general Nathaniel Lyon was defeated by Confederate forces at Wilson's Creek, Missouri, on August 10, 1861 (Chapter 5), his commanding officer, Major General John Charles Frémont, nevertheless acted as if Lyon had won and, on August 30, ostentatiously imposed martial law on Missouri and proclaimed the emancipation of the state's slaves. Predictably, these precipitous acts provoked Confederate-leaning Missourians, who now rushed to the Southern cause. Confederate general Sterling Price took advantage of the pro-Confederate activism to win a sharp, small engagement at Lexington, Missouri, on September 13. Angered by Frémont's reckless acts, President Lincoln removed him from command of the Department of the West and sent him to West Virginia (see Chapter 6).

*Confederate general Sterling Price, as seen in a print from a glass-plate negative.*

In October 1861, a boisterous pro-Southern minority of the Missouri legislature convened at the town of Neosho and voted to secede from the Union. The vote was hardly legitimate, but Jefferson Davis welcomed the state into the Confederacy nevertheless; however, he refused to give General Price the additional troops he asked for to hold Missouri. In contrast to Lincoln, who tended to trust his generals (often to a fault), Davis's instinct was to second-guess them at the very least and to be downright suspicious of them at worst. He knew that Sterling Price had been a close friend of William S. Harney, former commanding officer of the U.S. Army's Department of the West, and, despite Price's recent victories, Davis could not bring himself to trust the man with more of his soldiers. The result was that Price, facing forces under Brigadier General Samuel R. Curtis, who replaced Henry Wager Halleck to become the latest commander of the Department of the West, had to withdraw from Missouri into Arkansas.

In Arkansas, Price linked up with a Texas contingent commanded by Ben McCulloch, a crusty veteran of the Texas War of Independence of 1836 and a charter member of the Texas Rangers. This combined force was then joined to reinforcements under Earl Van Dorn, including several thousand Indians led by the Cherokee Stand Watie, who had been made a brigadier general in the Confederate army. Van

*Texas Ranger and hero of the Texas War of Independence and U.S.-Mexican War, Ben McCulloch fought for the Confederacy and fell at the battle of Pea Ridge, Arkansas, on March 7, 1862.*

Dorn took charge of this impromptu army of seventeen thousand men and set out to strike Curtis, who commanded at most eleven thousand Union troops.

Van Dorn had hoped to multiply his numerical advantage with the element of surprise, but a civilian scout employed by the army (widely but erroneously believed to have been young James Butler "Wild Bill" Hickok) saw the Confederate build-up and gave timely warning to Curtis. Made aware that Van Dorn had the advantage of numbers, Curtis sought the advantage of position and formed his battle line on March 6 at Pea Ridge, the high ground that overlooked Little Sugar Creek.

Van Dorn's skirmishers engaged Curtis's front line near Elkhorn Tavern at dawn on March 7. The crisp air of early spring soon rang with a rising crescendo of musketry as the battle grew hot. Curtis's men held out against the onslaught all day on the seventh. Believing he had weakened the Federals, Van Dorn renewed the attack on March 8, but, to his surprise, Curtis's outnumbered men soon seized the initiative and turned from defense to offense, forcing Van Dorn's motley army into a disordered retreat. Curtis dared not press his luck with a pursuit, and, in any case, orders reached Van Dorn to march to the aid of the Confederate forces that were in the process of losing the Mississippi River to General Grant (Chapter 6). Thus the battle of Pea Ridge ended without a clear victor.

*The battle of Pea Ridge, as depicted by lithographers Kurz & Allison.*

# SCORCHED EARTH

PEA RIDGE WAS THE LAST organized battle in the Arkansas-Missouri region. The Neosho legislature scrambled out of Missouri following it, and the state became the stage for a guerrilla war between pro-Union civilian raiders called "Jayhawkers" (or "Red Legs," after the red leggings some of them wore) and Confederate-sympathizing guerrillas dubbed "Bushwhackers." The most notorious of the latter was William Clarke Quantrill, a schoolmaster's son and onetime teacher himself who had been a vehement abolitionist before the war yet, for reasons never explained, impulsively discarded his former beliefs and joined the Confederate cause. Commissioned a captain in the Confederate army, he and his top lieutenant, William "Bloody Bill" Anderson, preyed on Kansas border patrols as well as Missouri's Union militia. In July 1863, General Thomas Ewing Jr. promulgated General Order No. 10, authorizing the arrest of anyone who aided or abetted Quantrill's raiders. Most of those rounded up were women and children, who were remanded to a number of Kansas City buildings used as makeshift prisons. Among these was a dilapidated warehouse, the top floor of which collapsed on August 13, 1863, killing five women, including "Bloody Bill" Anderson's fourteen-year-old sister. Quantrill had been planning for some time to raid Lawrence, which was a seat of abolitionism before the war and a Union loyalist stronghold during it. The warehouse collapse gave the plan added urgency.

## NUMBERS

### Pea Ridge Toll

Of 11,250 Union troops actively engaged at Pea Ridge, 1,393 were killed, wounded, or missing. About 14,000 of Van Dorn's 17,000-man army were committed to the battle. Approximately 800 were killed and another 200 captured.

*The pro-Union, staunchly abolitionist stronghold of Lawrence, Kansas, was the target of a Confederate guerrilla raid on August 21, 1863.*

On August 21, Quantrill led 450 Bushwhackers in a fierce raid on Lawrence, killing 164 unarmed civilians and razing most of the town.

Predictably, Quantrill's act of reputed vengeance brought swift Union retaliation. General Ewing Jr. promulgated a new "General Order," No. 11, on August 25, 1863, commanding every person who lived within one mile of a Union military post in Jackson, Cass, Bates, and the northern half of Vernon counties to vacate their homes within fifteen days. The order further required these people to deliver all of their grain and hay to the local military post. After the deadline passed, the army would set out to destroy all other crops and foodstuffs. True to the order, soldiers swept through the countryside, burning everything of value they encountered. For many years after the Civil War, this part of Missouri would be called the "Burnt District."

Predictably yet again, General Order No. 11 served only to exacerbate the depredations of Quantrill and his ilk. At Baxter Springs, Kansas, on October 6, 1863, the guerrilla leader and his men put on captured Union uniforms and, thus disguised, lured a detachment of federal troops into a bloody ambush. Of the company of one hundred Union soldiers they fell upon, sixty-five were killed in the initial attack. The rest were taken prisoner, disarmed, and *then* executed. As for Quantrill, he survived the war to a most bitter of bitter ends. On May 10, 1865, he was traveling (he believed) incognito through Kentucky—bound, some have claimed, for Washington, D.C., to carry out a final mission, the assassination of President Abraham Lincoln. Union troops ambushed him near the town of Taylorsville. Shot through the chest, he lingered in agony until June 6.

## FARTHER FRONTIERS

THE CIVIL WAR REACHED BEYOND Arkansas, Kansas, and Missouri to the far Southwest, where Confederate lieutenant colonel John Robert Baylor took advantage of the greatly reduced Union army presence to march through the southern New Mexico

*The legendary outlaws Frank and Jesse James—this 1864 picture shows Jesse posing with the tools of his trade—were violent alumni of Missouri and Kansas guerrilla action in the Civil War.*

Territory, from the Rio Grande to California. After capturing Fort Bliss at El Paso, Texas, in July 1861, he advanced through New Mexico's Mesilla Valley and captured Forts Fillmore and Stanton. Having won these victories, Baylor proclaimed the creation of the Confederate Territory of Arizona, encompassing all of present-day Arizona and New Mexico south of the 34th parallel. Since no one was around to tell him differently, he appointed himself governor of the territory.

*Brigadier General Henry Hopkins Sibley, Confederate States Army.*

During the winter of 1861–62, General Henry Hopkins Sibley (a Confederate who was no relation to Union general Henry *Hastings* Sibley), set out to acquire the rest of New Mexico and also to gain control of Colorado's silver mines, which could feed the ever-famished coffers of the Confederate treasury. Sibley's authorization from President Davis extended to invading southern California, if he could get that far. As Abraham Lincoln sought to tie the northern reaches of the trans-Mississippi West to the Union by means of a transcontinental railroad and the Homestead Act, so Jefferson Davis set out to gain control of as much of the Southwest as he possibly could.

Advancing up the Rio Grande, Sibley intended to capture Fort Union, which presided over the principal thoroughfare of the entire region, the Santa Fe Trail. Fort Union was the headquarters of Colonel Edward R. S. Canby, who commanded the army's Department of New Mexico. Already beleaguered by Navajo raids in the region, Canby was unable to resist Sibley's attack on Valverde, New Mexico, on February 21, 1862. He withdrew, and Sibley took Santa Fe without meeting any resistance. He then headed for Fort Union.

*Major General Edward R. S. Canby, United States Army.*

Both the Union and Confederate forces in the Southwest faced a common enemy in the harsh, hard, dry terrain of the high desert, and, to get to Fort Union, Sibley had to march through Apache Canyon and then the Glorieta Pass at the crest of the Sangre de Cristo Mountains. If Sibley was going to be stopped, Canby understood, he was going to be stopped here. On March 26, 1862, Union troops under

Colonel John Slough, in concert with Colorado volunteers commanded by Major John Milton Chivington, fell upon Sibley's column as it traversed Glorieta. The fighting did not end until March 28, by which time Sibley had lost fifty killed, eighty wounded, and ninety-two captured to fifty-one killed, seventy-eight wounded, fifteen captured, and three wounded for the Union. Beaten, the Confederate withdrew to Texas. It was by no means a battle on the epic scale of those in the war's eastern theater, but some historians have called it the "Gettysburg of the West," because it was here that the western war turned decisively against the Confederates. Fought at an elevation of seventy-five hundred feet, the battle of Glorieta Pass also has the distinction of being the highest encounter of the Civil War.

If Glorieta Pass was the loftiest Civil War fight, the battle of Picacho Peak, fought on April 15, 1862, in Arizona, was the westernmost. Having raised for the Union the 1st California Regiment of Infantry, Colonel James H. Carleton led this unit, dubbed the "California Column," into Arizona territory. His mission was to bring an end to the so-called Confederate Territory of Arizona, and Picacho Peak was the culminating battle in this campaign, which swept the last Confederate holdouts out of the region.

## THE HEART OF TEXAS

FOR THE CONFEDERACY, possession of the far Southwest proved an elusive *aspiration*. Texas, however, was a Confederate *fact*. At the outbreak of the war, Governor Sam Houston, the architect of Texas independence from Mexico in 1836, defied the majority by declaring his loyalty to the Union. When the state legislature nevertheless voted to secede in February 1861, he resigned, and Brigadier General David E. Twiggs, commander of the U.S. Army's Department of Texas, promptly turned over all federal property to the new

*Union brigadier general David E. Twiggs, commanding the U.S. Army's Department of Texas, gave up to the Confederates without a fight, then joined their ranks.*

Confederate government there. He had not fired a single shot, and in fact, a few days later, Twigg defected and was enrolled as a general in the Confederate army.

The Union strategy with regard to Texas was essentially to isolate it. In October 1862, a U.S. Navy expedition captured the port of Galveston, which was occupied by Union troops in December. The Confederates responded by hastily converting two commercial side-wheeler riverboats, the *Neptune* and *Bayou City*, into gunboats. After a four-hour fight on New Year's Day 1863, they succeeded in retaking the town. But it hardly mattered. The U.S. Navy returned to establish a blockade of the port. While the city itself refused to surrender to Union forces until June 2, 1865, a full month after Robert E. Lee yielded at Appomattox, it spent the war in isolation, completely cut off, and played no role in the outcome.

Indeed, before the end of 1863, the Mississippi River was under Union control, and all of Texas was severed from the rest of the Confederacy—but not, strangely enough, from the Union. Like much of the rest of the world, the North needed cotton, and President Lincoln therefore authorized, sometimes officially, sometimes under the table, limited trade with Southern cotton planters. When this policy led to outrageous gouging by Northern speculators, Lincoln ordered General Nathaniel Banks to raid Texas and simply seize whatever cotton the Union required. The result was called the Red River campaign, which spanned from March to May 1864. Its principal objective was to capture Shreveport, Louisiana, possession of which would give the Union control of East Texas and entrée into cotton country.

*The highly capable Confederate general Richard Taylor handed Union commander Nathaniel Banks sharp defeats at Sabine Cross Roads (April 8, 1864) and Pleasant Hill (April 9) during the Red River campaign.*

The Red River campaign did not go according to plan. A combined army-navy operation, intended to position troops for the capture of Shreveport, was delayed by treacherous river currents. This gave Confederate commander Lieutenant General Richard Taylor all the time he needed to outmaneuver Banks's army and set fire to local cotton warehouses rather than let them fall into Union hands. Taylor was then able to turn the tables on Banks, attacking him at Sabine Cross Roads (April 8, 1864) and Pleasant Hill (April 9), forcing his men into a humiliating retreat back onto their river transports. With that ignominy, the Red River campaign ended. Taylor wanted to pursue Banks to total defeat, but his superior officer, General Edmund Kirby Smith, ordered half of Taylor's command to Arkansas, forcing him to break off the pursuit.

FORGOTTEN
FACES

### Cherokee General

Stand Watie (1806–71) was a Cherokee tribal leader of mixed blood who had been educated at a Moravian mission school in Georgia. Watie, a slaveholder, was commissioned a colonel in the First Cherokee Mounted Rifles after Chief John Ross and the Cherokee Council decided that the tribe should support the Confederacy. Soon promoted to brigadier general, he was one of two Indians in the Civil War to achieve general officer rank. (The Union army promoted the Seneca Ely S. Parker to the rank of brigadier.)

At Pea Ridge, Stand Watie's troops captured important Union artillery positions and then served in the rearguard, covering the Confederate retreat. Stand Watie, whose Cherokee name *Degataga* means "stand firm," was the very last Confederate general to surrender his troops at the end of the war, in June 1865.

## A DIFFERENT WAR

DESPITE THE UNION'S HUMILIATING END in the Red River campaign, the Confederacy had lost the war in the West when it gave up New Mexico and Arizona by the end of 1862 and the Mississippi River by mid-1863. Fears persisted among Western supporters of the Union that the Confederates would soon begin recruiting masses of Indian allies and hurl them into combat, but this happened only to a very limited degree. Some among the Caddos, Wichitas, Osages, Shawnees, Delawares, Senecas, Cherokees, Chickasaws, Choctaws, Creeks, and Seminoles did join the Confederate cause, but their numbers were few, and they had little impact on the war. When Indians fought during the Civil War, they generally made no distinction between Union and Confederate, but attacked both sides. The disruptions created by the Civil War created the conditions in which Cochise and others led Apache raids from 1861 to 1863, a paroxysm of violence the army labeled the "Apache Uprising." Friction between soldiers under the command of Edward R. S. Canby and local Navajos ignited war with members of that tribe. In November 1864, John Milton Chivington, the man who had performed so brilliantly against Sibley at Glorieta Pass, led his Colorado volunteers against a peaceful encampment of Cheyenne and Arapaho at Sand Creek, Colorado, on November 29, 1864. Without provocation, Chivington and his men massacred—there is no other word for it—some two hundred Indians in the encampment.

*Colonel John M. Chivington leads the 3rd Colorado Regiment in an attack against peaceful Cheyenne and Arapaho at Sand Creek on November 29, 1864.*

Two-thirds of those killed were women and children. This atrocity served to unite the Southern Sioux, Northern Arapaho, and Cheyenne in costly raids the army called the Cheyenne-Arapaho War of 1864–65.

In south-central Minnesota, the failure of local reservation officials to distribute needed rations and other supplies mandated by treaty to the resident Santee Sioux triggered an Indian siege against the remote immigrant village of New Ulm in August 1862. Thirty-six townspeople were killed, and most of the town was razed. Panic swept the Minnesota plains, sending some two thousand settlers to seek refuge in Mankato. By August 27, the Sioux nation throughout Minnesota was on the warpath.

Rumor—entirely unfounded—claimed that the Confederates were behind the uprising. The cause was neither more nor less than government betrayal and Indian starvation. Yet even though the Santee Sioux Uprising was not a Confederate plot, it did have a significant impact on the Civil War because it forced a long delay in recruiting Minnesota's quota of inductees into the Union army. The terror did not end until September 23, 1862, when the Santee were at last decisively defeated at the battle of Wood Lake.

*Henry August Schwabe, a German-born American artist, painted this vivid scene of the August 19, 1862, attack on New Ulm, Minnesota, during the so-called Santee Sioux Uprising.*

## WHY THE WEST MATTERED

THE AMERICAN WEST IS VAST, but the Civil War armies that fought there were miniscule by comparison with those of the eastern theater. Until the fairly recent appearance of such books as Alvin M. Josephy Jr.'s *Civil War in the American West* (1993), many historians customarily dismissed the western battles as mere sideshows. Certainly far smaller in scale than Shiloh or Antietam or Gettysburg, they were nevertheless hardly peripheral to the war. The West was a source of immediate wealth—gold, silver, abundant crops, and beef—and it was a long-term source of inspiration. The Civil War tore the country along its North-South axis, but *west* was already the dominant direction of the American story. To possess the West was to own the future. To lose it was to concede to another power leadership of the national destiny. The battles were slight, the stakes very great.

**TAKEAWAY**

Although Richmond remained an elusive target for the Union armies, the capture of New Orleans came swiftly. Its loss did irreparable damage to the Confederacy and was the beginning of the end of any hope the seceded states had of possessing the American West. The battles fought beyond the Mississippi did not determine the outcome of the Civil War, but they ensured that whatever future the Confederacy might have, it would be geographically and economically constrained.

# CHAPTER 11

## PROCLAIMED IN BLOOD

### *Limping toward Emancipation*

**A**UDACES FORTUNA IUVAT, THE ROMAN POET VIRGIL WROTE IN HIS *AENEID*. "Fortune favors the bold." How fortune treats the timid, the overcautious, and the fearful is something else entirely.

From the West (Chapter 10), we return to the East and back to the early summer of 1862. Believing himself outnumbered, George Brinton McClellan not only failed to apply the great instrument at his command, the Army of the Potomac, he divided it, sending some twenty-five thousand men, to pursue (futilely, as it turned out) Stonewall Jackson, as that genius seemingly romped throughout the Shenandoah Valley (Chapter 9). This meant that, at the end of June 1862, a quarter of McClellan's army was positioned north of Virginia's Chickahominy River, completely cut off from the other three quarters. By failing to act boldly, McClellan dropped the initiative, which Jackson was quick to take up.

### SEVEN DAYS

It isn't as if McClellan hadn't already experienced what happens when you leave part of your army hanging out to dry. A month before McClellan divided his forces, one of his corps, commanded by Erasmus Darwin Keyes, found itself isolated. Quick to recognize its vulnerability, Joseph E. Johnston struck Keyes on May 31, 1862, at Fair Oaks and Seven Pines. The result would have been much worse for the Union had the attack gone off without a hitch; however, confusion of orders created delays that stretched the fighting out over two days. That was long enough for McClellan to send reinforcements. These were sufficient to prevent defeat but not enough to bring victory, and the battles of Fair Oaks and Seven Pines were drawn, costing the Union 5,031 killed or wounded out of 41,797 troops engaged, and the Confederates 6,134 casualties out of a force of 41,816.

Among the Confederate wounded was General Johnston, hurt badly enough (he had been shot in the shoulder and chest) that he had to withdraw from the war for a time. His replacement was Robert E. Lee. No one on the Confederate side was very happy about this. Lee

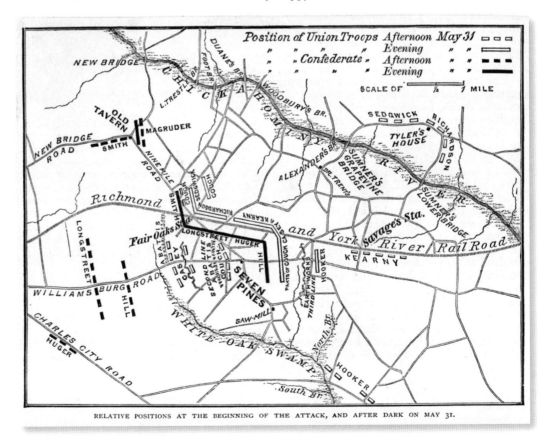

*This map of the battle of Seven Pines shows the positions of Union and Confederate troops at the beginning of the attack and after dark on May 31, 1862.*

# RUNNING RINGS AROUND TARDY GEORGE

One of the greatest of McClellan's string of humiliations came between June 12 and 15, 1862, when James Ewell Brown Stuart—better known as "J. E. B." or just plain "Jeb Stuart"—led his twelve hundred cavalrymen in a daring reconnaissance mission in which they trotted, galloped, and walked a complete circle around all Army of the Potomac positions in Virginia, literally running rings around the Young Napoleon.

The Confederate newspapers ate this up, and Stuart, not yet thirty at the time, made the most of it. Riding at the head of his fellow horsemen, he had adorned himself in a rakish, broad-brimmed hat topped with an ostrich feather, a crimson-lined cape falling from his shoulders, and, at his heels, spurs of real gold. He did not rely on reporters to convey his exploits, but passed his evenings in camp writing up the stories himself and seeing to it that they reached not only the Richmond papers but the London press as well.

Stuart had relied on his daring scout, First Lieutenant John Singleton Mosby, to guide him around the Union army. Mosby's subsequent fame as the "Gray Ghost of the Confederacy"—leader of a

*James Ewell Brown ("Jeb") Stuart was one of the Confederacy's most dashing—and ultimately least reliable—cavalry commanders.*

glamorous guerrilla outfit known as the "Partisan Rangers"—would threaten to eclipse even that of his former commanding officer.

In a war that was mostly about killing on an anonymous mass scale using the weapons of a heartless Industrial Age, the exploits of Stuart and Mosby still make for gratifyingly romantic reading. Doubtless, their chivalric deeds had an impact on morale—casting down the North, raising up the South—but, in the end, it was the dedicated journeymen of modern warfare, the Grants and the Shermans for whom war was a joyless duty, who created victory. In the Civil War, mere glory proved far too small an objective, and, as will be seen in Chapter 14, the flamboyance of Jeb Stuart had strategic and tactical limitations that would carry terrible consequences for his comrades at arms.

*Henry Alexander Ogden, a popular American illustrator of the late nineteenth and early twentieth centuries, specialized in military subjects such as this print: "Gen. J. E. B. Stuart's raid around McClellan, June 1862."*

had stumbled badly in western Virginia (Chapter 9)—and no one who served with him now could forget this. As for McClellan, his attention was neither on Johnston nor Lee, but Jeb Stuart, who had just led twelve hundred Confederate cavalrymen, unscathed, in a ride around the Army of the Potomac. The humiliation came as a cruel kick in the pants, at last prompting McClellan to take action. Unfortunately, the action he took was to split off twenty-five thousand men—a whole corps under Fitz-John Porter—from the rest of his army.

"Tardy" George had habitually and mistakenly believed that he was outnumbered. Acting on this fear, he now created the very situation he most feared. Twenty-five thousand of his soldiers, under Porter, were about to face sixty-five thousand Confederate troops under Lee, who was, to McClellan, a brand-new adversary. While Porter pursued Stonewall Jackson, the rest of the Army of the Potomac moved south of the river. This situation—McClellan on the move, his forces split—triggered a rapid series of hard-fought battles collectively called the "Seven Days."

## Day One

As McClellan's columns marched along the Chickahominy, reaching the hamlet of Oak Grove on June 25, Confederate units intercepted them. In the initial exchange, the Union troops fell back, but McClellan quickly pulled up artillery reinforcements, who blasted the soldiers in gray with deadly canister shot, mowing down anyone caught in the blast.

*This carte de visite ("calling card") portrait of Major General Fitz-John Porter was produced by the studio of Mathew Brady.*

## Day Two

Thanks to the timely arrival of the Union artillery, McClellan blasted through Oak Grove, the first of the Seven Days battles. But Lee had intended that attack to be little more than a distraction to hold McClellan's attention. His principal objective was Fitz-John Porter's corps isolated north of the Chickahominy. Lee planned to leave only a skeleton force to defend Richmond while he brought most of his 65,000-man army to the north bank of the Chickahominy, where he would annihilate Porter's 25,000-man command. Lee well understood that the terrible constant of this war was its numbers. The North had more men (more of everything, really) than the South. Army against army, Lee knew he could not win. But when

*The indefatigable combat artist Alfred R. Waud drew "McClellan recon-noitering the Turnpike to Richmond from the Peach Orchard at Mechanicsville" during the Seven Days.*

an army was divided, for whatever reason, he had a chance. It was known as "defeating the enemy in detail." And that is what he proposed to do now.

The Union had known much heartbreak and disappointment in the first year and more of the Civil War. Now it was the Confederacy's turn. The great Stonewall Jackson, having just tweaked the North and dazzled the South with his Shenandoah Valley campaign, suffered a sudden and unaccountable lapse in military judgment. Instead of leading off the attack on Porter, he chose on June 26 to bivouac—to stop and set up camp. This was bad enough, but when Jackson failed to materialize, the impatient General A. P. Hill decided to launch an attack on his own without orders from Lee. What resulted on the second of the Seven Days was the battle of Mechanicsville, in which Hill was soundly repulsed, and Porter found the time and opportunity to march back to the south bank of the Chickahominy, where he rejoined the rest of the Army of the Potomac.

## Day Three

All of this should have redeemed George McClellan and prompted him to renew his advance on Richmond, which was now only lightly defended, since so many of Lee's soldiers were in the field. Instead, with all the advantages returned to his hands, McClellan yet again gave in to the spectacularly inflated assessments of Confederate strength Detective Allan Pinkerton was handing him.

# MECHANICSVILLE THE DECISIVE BATTLE!?

It is a commonplace of Civil War history to point to all McClellan's failures to act as war-winning opportunities lost. Robert E. Lee, however, is rarely taken to task for *his* failures.

This is understandable. Commanding smaller numbers of often poorly equipped and hungry troops, his failures are far less remarkable than his many successes—triumphs built, after all, upon so very little. Yet had Lee been able to control Stonewall Jackson so that he and Jackson could coordinate an attack on Fitz-John Porter's highly vulnerable corps north of the Chickahominy, Lee might have achieved the strategic end he always hoped for. Had he decimated an entire Union corps—it is possible that the clamor in the North for a negotiated end to the war might have been too boisterous to suppress. When George Washington and the Comte de Rochambeau defeated Lord Cornwallis's army at Yorktown in 1781, the British still controlled all but one major American port and held thirty of the thirteen colonies' most populous cities and towns. But the loss of this army, this one military unit, persuaded a majority of the British Parliament that the war was no longer worth fighting, and, for all practical purposes, the American Revolution was over. What would the loss of an entire corps have meant to the people and politicians of the North in 1862? Could it be that Mechanicsville, one of the lesser-known of an estimated *ten thousand-plus* Civil War armed encounters (ranging from big battles to brief skirmishes), a battle that is rarely mentioned except in connection with the others of the "Seven Days," might have proven the decisive engagement of the entire conflict?

McClellan may also have been intimidated by Lee's aggressive daring at Gaines' Mill on June 27, day three of the Seven Days. The Confederate general tried to force a showdown battle here, but once again Jackson showed up late, and Fitz-John Porter, on whom the brunt of the attack fell, once again received the gift of time sufficient to reinforce his menaced position. Porter could not avoid a battle, and when the fighting came, it was dreadful—the bloodiest of the Seven Days fights. Reinforced, Porter held his line until just before nightfall. By then, Jackson was in place, and Lee was able to launch the coordinated attack he had planned. It came too late to decimate Porter, however, who nevertheless was forced into a costly retreat.

Considering the punishment the Confederates had taken, Gaines' Mill should not have unduly discouraged McClellan. But it did. Instead of punching through to what was now a critically exposed Richmond, he ordered a withdrawal to a new supply base on the James River, south of Richmond. Instead of advancing toward his

## NUMBERS

### A Very Bad Day

The battle of Gaines' Mill, June 27, 1862, cost 893 Union lives; 3,107 men were wounded; and 2,836 reported missing out of a total of 34,214 troops engaged. The Confederates prevailed in that they drove the Union from the field, but their casualties were even heavier: 8,751 killed or wounded.

objective, he ordered a retreat from it. Lee did not declare victory, but McClellan seemed to be proclaiming defeat. Even his most ardently loyal officers protested the idea of withdrawing. But it didn't matter. McClellan was convinced that he was saving his army.

One thing Robert E. Lee possessed above all else was an instinct for weakness in others. When an army retreated from him, Lee never hung back, but, on the contrary, dogged his receding prey all the more ferociously. Thanks to McClellan's disgruntled-but-determined field officers, every corps of the Army of the Potomac fought a highly effective rearguard action, some of which escalated into full-out counterattacks. An army never wins by retreating, but at least McClellan's lieutenants made the retreat costly to Lee.

## Days Four and Five

Seething to renew the attack on the retreating Union army, Lee forced himself to bide his time until he was certain of the direction of McClellan's withdrawal. So he waited through June 28 (day four) and then decided to intercept McClellan at a place called Savage's Station on June 29 (day five).

The attack began late in the day, and while it was vigorous, it was also hobbled by Lee's overly complicated plan. His corps commanders lost control of their units and stumbled over one another. "Prince John" Magruder never even committed all of his brigades to combat. Out of six available, only two and a half actually got into the fight. As for Jackson—he did not arrive until three o'clock in the morning of June 30. So, yet once more, Lee was forced to absorb another round of vicious rearguard actions and counterattacks.

Absorb them he did, however, and it began to look as if the Federals were indeed doomed this time to suffer a major defeat. What saved them was not a brilliant general or a heroic captain but an act of God or nature. A terrific thunderstorm, more terrible than any human battle, suddenly ended the fight, rescuing the Union's rear guard from total annihilation.

### NUMBERS

**Savage Result**

The Union lost 1,590 killed or wounded at Savage's Station; the Confederacy, 626.

*The battle of Savage's Station was fought on June 29, 1862—Day Five of the Seven Days. This steel engraving was made from a sketch by Alfred R. Waud.*

## Day Six

After retreating from Savage's Station, McClellan consolidated his army along a line behind White Oak Swamp extending out of the swamp to a broad ridge of high ground called Malvern Hill. McClellan's purpose in this deployment was to defend Union supply trains bound for Harrison's Landing on the James River—the area to which he intended to withdraw. In this, he was less concerned with destroying the enemy than with preserving his own army.

Lee quickly drew up a new plan to engage the Army of the Potomac with the object of disrupting what he knew McClellan was most intent on protecting: its line of retreat. Once again, however, his subordinate commanders in the field proved incapable of achieving the level of coordination required to make the battle of Frayser's Farm (also called the battle of Glendale) a decisive victory on June 30; nevertheless, it did not go well for McClellan, who was again driven from the field.

## Day Seven

McClellan pulled back from White Oak Swamp and consolidated his entire army at Malvern Hill, a low, broad ridge running along the James. He had managed not to lose the Army of the Potomac, but the significance of this retreat was undeniable. It was a bad end to the Peninsula campaign. On day seven of the Seven Days, the Army of the Potomac had incurred serious losses and was farther away from Richmond, its objective, than when the Peninsula campaign had begun.

Still, the picture was hardly rosy for Robert E. Lee. Although McClellan had been defeated, he had withdrawn to the high ground. Lee could not attack him from the flank or the rear. If he was going to break the back of this army, Lee would have to attack it head-on, whole army against whole army. This happened on the seventh day, July 1. It was the battle of Malvern Hill.

From the start, Lee was again plagued by an absence of coordination among his corps commanders. Worse, the terrain was against him. He could not mass his artillery effectively. This meant that his attacks were

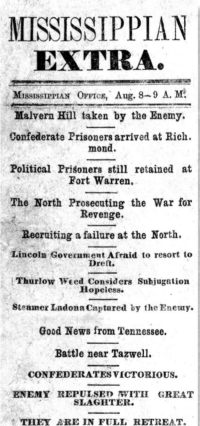

**NUMBERS**

**Lee's Pyrrhic Victory**

Lee defeated McClellan at Frayser's Farm, but lost more men than he: 3,615 killed or wounded to 2,853 on the Union side.

*The* Mississippian *(Jackson, Mississippi) published an "Extra" carrying the news of the Union victory at the battle of Malvern Hill (July 1), the last of the Seven Days battles.*

mere thrusts, sporadic and unfocused. McClellan, in contrast, had thoroughly prepared his defenses on the excellent high ground he occupied. His artillery batteries were arrayed all along Malvern's ridge. In many places, the cannon were practically wheel to wheel, and their fire was deadly.

Lee's attack was turned back so decisively that Porter and another of McClellan's field commanders, Colonel Henry J. Hunt, pleaded with their general to seize the initiative, to use Malvern Hill as a springboard for a surprise counterattack. Instead, McClellan marched his men off Malvern Hill and completed what he had started: the withdrawal to Harrison's Landing.

The Seven Days offered more than enough heartbreak to go around. The battered Army of the Potomac had failed in its mission—or, rather, its commander had failed the Army of the Potomac. Casualties totaled sixteen thousand killed or wounded, most of which incurred while fighting not in advance, but in full retreat. McClellan tried to point out that Lee had actually taken the worst of it. His casualties totaled nearly twenty thousand killed or wounded. That much was true, and, what is more, whereas the Union could afford to replace the men it lost, the Confederacy was hard-pressed to do so. If this war were considered strictly as a contest of numbers, the Confederacy, despite its triumphs, was losing. Yet the war was not all numbers. Morale in the South remained high, while that in the North—understandably—was all but crushed. Without victories, the Union's will to continue the struggle would soon be exhausted. And that, really, is all the Confederacy needed to win.

> "I now pray for time. My men have proved themselves the equals of any troops in the world— but they are worn out. Our losses have been very great. I doubt whether more severe battles have ever been fought—we have failed to win only because overpowered by superior numbers."
>
> *Major General George B. McClellan, telegram to U.S. War Department, July 2, 1862, after the Seven Days battles*

*Major General Daniel Butterfield ordered his bugler to come up with a new call for evening "lights-out." The result was "Taps."*

# HOW TO LOSE FRIENDS AND ALIENATE PEOPLE

On July 14, 1862, Major General John Pope delivered to his new command, the Army of Virginia, what may well be the worst motivational speech any leader has ever offered the men he is supposed to inspire.

Let us understand each other. I have come to you from the West, where we have always seen the backs of our enemies; from an army whose business it has been to seek the adversary and to beat him when he was found; whose policy has been attack and not defense. In but one instance has the enemy been able to place our Western armies in defensive attitude. I presume that I have been called here to pursue the same system and to lead you against the enemy. It is my purpose to do so, and that speedily. I am sure you long for an opportunity to win the distinction you are capable of achieving. That opportunity I shall endeavor to give you . . .

If Pope offended his colleagues, he was even more provocative to his adversaries. He tyrannized over the small portion of Virginia occupied by the Army of Virginia, commandeering food supplies and threatening to hang as traitors civilians and POWs alike. Robert E. Lee, who liked to think of the Union generals he faced as gentlemen, dismissed Pope as a "miscreant" and declared that he "should be suppressed."

## A NEW COMMANDER

NO GENERAL IS PERCHED MORE PRECARIOUSLY than a defeated general, except for a defeated general who asks for more. Huddled with his dispirited army at Harrison's Landing, McClellan moaned that he had been beaten by overwhelming numbers. Lee's army, he said, was nearly two hundred thousand strong (in fact, it amounted to barely sixty-five thousand men), and he now demanded massive reinforcements. Abraham Lincoln responded by summoning Major General John Pope to take command of what would be called the Army of Virginia, to include various forces in and around Virginia that would otherwise have been incorporated into the Army of the Potomac. For McClellan, this action was a much-deserved vote of no confidence; however, the elevation of Pope to this important command was hardly a popular step with the men and officers of the Union army. Pope was as ambitious as he was obnoxious. Although he had shown brilliance as leader of the Army of the Mississippi (Chapter 8), he had a positive genius for alienating practically everyone with whom he served. Instead of attempting to inspire the men of his new command and heal their wounded morale, he upbraided them for their failures under McClellan and other commanders.

## DETAILS, DETAILS
### Sideshows
While Longstreet and Jackson maneuvered into position, a band of Pope's troops hatched a surprise of their own, staging a lightning raid on Jeb Stuart's camp, from which they snatched Stuart's adjutant. Stuart himself got away, but, in the haste of flight, he had left behind his ostrich-plumed hat and crimson-lined cape, which Pope's men purloined as treasured souvenirs. At this loss more than that of his adjutant, Stuart seethed. On August 22, he galloped with a small party into General Pope's headquarters camp at Catlett's Station, took 300 prisoners, "appropriated" $35,000 in Union army payroll money, raided the general's personal baggage (although he failed to recover his own hat and cloak, he took Pope's dress uniform coat), and even found a cache of Pope's battle plans.

As spring turned to summer and summer verged on fall, Henry Wager "Old Brains" Halleck, on whom Lincoln had called to serve as the latest general in chief of the Union armies, gave up any notion that McClellan would ever leave Harrison's Landing. He therefore ordered him to return to northern Virginia, where three corps of his army were taken from him and attached to Pope's new Army of Virginia.

### By the Nose
The whittling away of the Young Napoleon's command took time, and the opportunity of time was something Robert E. Lee was always ready to seize. On August 9, 1862, he sent Stonewall Jackson to attack a portion of the Army of Virginia at Cedar Mountain, near the town of Culpeper. In and of itself, the battle was slight, but it forced Pope to pull back to the northern bank of Rappahannock River, which is just where Lee wanted him. His object was to hit Pope before those three corps of the Army of the Potomac joined the Army of Virginia.

Mediocre commanders violate basic tactical principles out of timidity or panic. Thus McClellan had divided his army on either side of the Chickahominy River. Brilliant commanders break these same rules out of pure military genius. Lee now divided his army in the presence of the enemy, putting half his forces under the command of Major General James "Old Pete" Longstreet, to occupy Pope's front. The other half he sent under Stonewall Jackson, who marched them roundabout to the northwest, so that he could make a surprise attack on the rear of Pope's army. Many years later, in another war in another century, General George S. Patton Jr. would explain his own favorite tactic: "Hold the enemy by the nose and kick him in the ass." This is precisely what Lee now intended to do with Pope—though he was too much the gentleman ever to have used Patton's language to describe it.

Stonewall Jackson struck first. On August 26 he descended upon and destroyed Pope's supply depot at Manassas Junction, Virginia, very close to the site of the Bull Run battle. The loss of supplies was serious, but, even worse, Jackson severed Pope's rail and telegraph lines, leaving him hobbled and unable to communicate quickly. Pope responded by chasing Jackson, but he could not locate him until Jackson chose to be found. On August 28, the Confederate commander turned against a brigade led by Brigadier General Rufus King at Groveton. In the heated exchange that ensued, the commanders of both Confederate divisions

*Edwin Forbes portrayed this scene of Pope's retreat to Groveton—a prelude to the second battle of Bull Run.*

engaged were severely wounded, and King's "Black Hat Brigade" (later called the "Iron Brigade," on account of its heroism) fought with a relentless ferocity that stunned Jackson. King inflicted many casualties, but he also lost one-third of his Black Hat Brigade.

## ANOTHER BULL RUN

ALTHOUGH THE MANASSAS RAID and the subsequent battle of Groveton were Confederate victories, with them, Jackson had sacrificed the element of surprise. Pope now knew where he was and moved to concentrate his forces near Groveton with the object of crushing Stonewall once and for all. Boasting (Pope was nothing if not the most boastful general in the Union army) that he would "bag the whole crowd," he attacked Jackson on August 29.

To give the Union general his due, he acted with aggressive vigor, pounding Jackson's Confederates, who nevertheless managed (at great cost) to repulse each thrust. At day's end, Jackson withdrew, and Pope let himself believe that Stonewall had been whipped. There would be ample time to finish him off the next day.

Pope knew where Jackson was, but he had no idea that the other half of Lee's divided army, the portion under Longstreet, was about to join the fray. Those forces arrived at about eleven o'clock on the morning of August 30, the second day of what history would record as the second battle of Bull Run. Longstreet unleashed all five of his divisions into Pope's fully exposed flank along a sweeping two-mile front. The result was both stunning and catastrophic. Pope's defeat was total, and, once again, the Union army had been humiliated—at Bull Run, no less.

*Brigadier General Rufus King's "Black Hat Brigade" (later known as the "Iron Brigade") fought valiantly against Stonewall Jackson at the battle of Groveton. The unit lost a third of its men.*

*Currier & Ives's depiction of the second battle of Bull Run makes it look like a Union victory. It was, in fact, an unmitigated disaster, in which Major General John Pope suffered a devastating 21 percent casualty rate.*

*In May 1886,* Century Magazine *published Rufus F. Zogbaum's depiction of the Union retreat over Stone Bridge after the second battle of Bull Run.*

## NUMBERS

### Bull Run II

At the second battle of Bull Run, Pope commanded 75,696 Union troops against 48,527 Confederates—a numerical advantage that made his defeat all the more stunning. The Union army suffered a devastating 21 percent casualty rate in this battle: 1,724 killed, 8,372 wounded, and 5,958 missing. However, Confederate losses were almost as bad at 19 percent: 1,481 killed, 7,627 wounded, and 89 missing.

Lee's army, however, had given all it had at Groveton and Bull Run. The men were spent, and Lee in consequence did not order them to pursue Pope. This allowed the Union army, depleted as it was, to retreat in good order. The Army of Virginia left the Second Bull Run deeply wounded, but still an army.

Just three days after the second battle of Bull Run, Pope received orders to go West—*without* what was left of his army. He was exiled to the "Department of the Northwest" and assigned to do battle with the Santee Sioux in Minnesota. His Army of Virginia was disbanded and most of its units incorporated into the Army of the Potomac, including the three corps that had been detached from it earlier.

# "IF I COULD SAVE THE UNION WITHOUT FREEING ANY SLAVE…"

HORACE GREELEY, ABOLITIONIST EDITOR of the *New York Tribune*, wrote an open letter in his paper titled "The Prayer of the Twenty Millions," to Abraham Lincoln on August 19, 1862. Written, Greeley asserted, on behalf of the twenty million citizens of the loyal states, it urged President Lincoln to emancipate the slaves immediately and thereby elevate the Civil War into a struggle to set men free. Lincoln replied just three days later:

> My paramount object in this struggle is to save the Union, and
> is not either to save or destroy Slavery. If I could save the Union
> without freeing any slave, I would do it; and if I could save it
> by freeing all the slaves, I would do it; and if I could save it by
> freeing some and leaving others alone, I would also do that.
> What I do about Slavery and the colored race, I do because I
> believe it helps to save the Union; and what I forbear, I forbear
> because I do not believe it would help to save the Union.

Although personally opposed to slavery, Lincoln had not run for president on an abolitionist platform. Not only did he continue to believe that the Constitution protected slavery where it existed, he also continued to fear that issuing an executive order of emancipation would send the border states running into the arms of Confederacy, would incite new violence in those parts of the Confederacy occupied by Union forces, and would alienate many Northerners, civilians as well as soldiers—people who were willing to fight (as a then-current racist slogan put it) "for Uncle Sam but not for Uncle Sambo." Moreover, Lincoln also worried that the Supreme Court would declare an executive proclamation of universal emancipation unconstitutional, thereby reinforcing the legal protection of slavery and quite possibly ensuring that slavery in the United States would last forever. Yet Lincoln was hardly deaf to the increasing volume of pro-abolitionist sentiment throughout the North,

*James F. Gibson, among the least well known of the significant Civil War photographers, captured this extraordinary image of "contrabands" at Cumberland Landing, Virginia. Slaves subject to confiscation (and consequent emancipation) by Union forces were officially classified as "contraband of war" to avoid the appearance of violating the due process clause of the Fifth Amendment.*

*Benjamin Butler, the same Union general who would make himself obnoxious to New Orleanias when he occupied their city in 1862, declared on May 27, 1861—when he commanded Union forces in Virginia and North Carolina—that slaves who successfully fled to Union lines were "contraband of war" and would not be returned to their Confederate owners. This 1861 print depicts a scene at Fort Monroe, Virginia, in which a plantation owner waves his whip and shouts, "Come back you black rascal." To this the freed slave replies: "Can't come back nohow massa. Dis chile's contraban."*

and, quietly, he began work on an emancipation proclamation that, he hoped, would offend no one unduly and would even pass muster with the courts.

The content of such a proclamation was only one problem. The other issue was one of timing. If Lincoln issued his order following a string of Union defeats—the situation in the summer of 1862—it would look like a toothless act of desperation. In August 1861, Congress had passed an earlier Confiscation Act that classified as "contraband" those slaves who had been employed directly in the war effort. The first act had authorized Union officers to "confiscate" such individuals—in effect emancipating them. Lincoln now encouraged Congress to pass a broader Confiscation Act, which it did on July 17, 1862. The new law declared free any slaves owned by supporters of what it called "the rebellion." With this foundation in place, Lincoln, on July 22, 1862, read to his Cabinet the first draft of the emancipation proclamation he had composed. Secretary of State William H. Seward brought up the issue of timing, warning that an outright proclamation of emancipation would ring hollow following a train of Union defeats.

## TO SAVE THE COUNTRY

NOW, MORE THAN EVER, Lincoln needed a victory. He needed a credible platform from which to proclaim emancipation, thereby giving the Civil War new moral force. With John Pope a failure—the second battle of Bull Run had produced *five times* the Union casualties of the first battle of Bull Run—Lincoln, reasoning that, for all his shortcomings, George B. McClellan at least had the ability to win the confidence and loyalty of troops, once again placed into his hands the entire Army of the Potomac, complete with all the units Pope had led. The Young Napoleon wrote to his wife: "Again I have been called upon to save the country."

*To save the country.* On September 5, 1862, that phrase suddenly took on new urgency. Up to this point, the Confederate strategy had been to fight a defensive war against an "invading" Union army with the objective of making the invasion so costly to the Union that its politicians and people would lose the will to continue the fight and therefore negotiate a favorable peace with the seceded states. Now Robert E. Lee marched across the Potomac into Maryland, a state of the Union. The Confederate States of America was invading the United States of America.

The invading army of about sixty thousand men was hardly an imposing spectacle. The Army of Northern Virginia was tired and tattered. The only commodity scarcer than ammunition was decent shoes. But Lee had decided he could no longer count on winning a war of attrition. He was no longer willing to gamble that the Union's passion to continue fighting would wane before the Confederacy ran out of fighting men. Moreover, the border state of Maryland had many pro-Confederacy citizens. It was low-hanging fruit, and if Lee could grab it, the world (mainly Great Britain and France) would take note, and the North would be thrown into panic and despair. Shortly after he set foot in Maryland, Lee published on September 8 an invitation to secede, claiming that the "government of your chief city has been usurped by armed strangers; your Legislature has been dissolved and by the unlawful arrest of its members; freedom of the press and of speech has been suppressed. . . . Believing that the people of Maryland possess a spirit too lofty to submit to such a government, the people of the South have long wished to aid you in throwing off this foreign yoke, to enable you again to enjoy the inalienable rights of freemen, and restore the independence and sovereignty of your state. . . . It is for you to decide your destiny. . . ."

## IF I CANNOT WHIP BOBBY LEE . . .

DURING THE NINETEENTH CENTURY, the American popular stage was ruled by melodrama, the theatrical genre that gave birth to the adjective *melodramatic* to describe any story with a plot so broadly drawn as to be utterly unbelievable. What happened next in the Civil War was so improbable a twist of plot that it would have made even the most shameless author of melodrama blush.

Lee drew up Special Order No. 191, which spelled out his plan for invading Maryland. He distributed copies to his chief lieutenants, but Stonewall Jackson also personally ordered a set copied for General Daniel Harvey Hill. No one is quite sure why. Hill may have already received the order directly from Lee, but for some reason discarded it. Recent research suggests that the order may have been lost en route to Hill. In any event, on September 13, 1862, Union forces occupied a campground that D. H. Hill had recently vacated. While scrounging for anything of value that the Confederates might have left behind, Union private W. B. Mitchell, 27th Indiana Infantry, spied a real prize. It was a clutch of cigars bundled together in a piece of paper. Understandably, Mitchell's principal interest was in the stogies, not in their wrapper, but he did take the time to examine the paper and, deciding it might be important, passed it to his company commander. Soon, it found its way up to General McClellan.

"Here is a paper with which, if I cannot whip Bobby Lee, I will be willing to go home," the Young Napoleon reportedly exclaimed.

He instantly recognized the great gamble Lee was about to take—how he intended to divide his forces, sending Stonewall Jackson in the direction of Harpers Ferry and "Old Pete" Longstreet toward Hagerstown. Armed with this knowledge, McClellan had a golden opportunity to strike first and defeat Lee in detail. Victory, it seemed, had fallen out of the very heavens and into his hands.

And yet there are some people who, if it were raining soup, would rush outdoors with a fork. McClellan was not only assailed by his habitual belief that he was massively outnumbered by the Confederates, but was also agitated by a possibility "Old Brains" Halleck had suggested to him: The "lost order" was a trick, a lure to ambush and destruction. It was all quite sufficient to hold McClellan back just long enough to cause him to lose the incalculable advantage he had been given. He sent his troops tentatively to probe three gaps in South Mountain on September 14. General Hill's outnumbered Confederates offered stiff resistance, which gave Lee just the time he needed to deploy the main part of his army west of Antietam Creek, near the Maryland hamlet of Sharpsburg.

McClellan's plan was to launch a three-pronged assault, hitting both of Lee's flanks, then using his reserves to attack his center. It was a strategy as old as Hannibal, whose Carthaginians defeated an army of the Roman Republic in 216 BCE at Cannae in southeastern Italy by achieving just such a "double envelopment": hitting the Roman army's

*Special Order No. 191 was Robert E. Lee's detailed plan for the invasion of Maryland. A Union soldier found it lost or discarded in a vacated Confederate camp, and it was given to Major General George B. McClellan, who exclaimed, "Here is a paper with which, if I cannot whip Bobby Lee, I will be willing to go home."*

flanks, and then annihilating its center. The classic battle occupied an honored place in the West Point curriculum.

And it was a very good plan. As usual, however, hesitation, an excess of caution, a case of nerves, and the failures of unit commanders in the field resulted in faulty execution and an absence of coordination when the attack was launched on September 17. Nevertheless, it began well when the Union's irascible Joseph Hooker pushed Stonewall Jackson's corps back so far and so fast that Lee had to call in his reserves to bail him out. Had the other elements of the attack materialized at this point, the Army of Northern Virginia, its reserves now occupied, would have been doomed, but Hill and Longstreet were able to get their men into position in what was called the East and West Woods, patches of greenery in a cornfield belonging to one Farmer Miller and surrounding a little church that was the place of worship for a Christian sect of devout pacifists known as the Dunkards.

### Bloody Lane

McClellan's men fought hard, but the piecemeal nature of the attacks prevented the Union from breaking through. As the day inched toward noon, the fighting became concentrated along a sunken farm road held by General Hill. After a battle of five hours, Union major general Edwin "Bull" Sumner drove the Confederates out of the shallow trench formed by the road. From that moment forward, it would be remembered as "Bloody Lane."

*Major General Ambrose Everett Burnside: popular, earnest, brave, inept, and cursed with as bad a luck as any commander in any war ever had.*

While the fighting raged there, Major General Ambrose Burnside, commanding the entire left wing of the Union army, squandered time and men trying to capture the bridge across Antietam Creek. An affable commander whose generous mutton-chop whiskers would soon lend themselves to an enduring tonsorial style dubbed (by a curious inversion of his name) "sideburns," Burnside was courageous, well-meaning, and had the love and loyalty of his men. But he possessed almost no military imagination at all. As he prodigally spent blood and hours in an effort to force a passage across the stone bridge, it never occurred to him simply to bypass the span and ford the shallow creek.

*Kurz & Allison published this color lithograph of the battle of Antietam c. 1888.*

It was late afternoon before Burnside finally broke through the Confederate line—only to be smartly repulsed by a counterattack from General Ambrose Powell Hill (no relation to Daniel Harvey Hill), whose "Light Division" had just come in from Harpers Ferry.

## A Thousand Bugles

Despite McClellan's fears, despite the piece-meal attack, despite Burnside's tragic delay and subsequent repulse, Confederate Brigadier General John Brown Gordon recalled that, "McClellan's . . . infantry fell upon the left of Lee's lines with the crushing weight of a land-slide." Sheer superiority of numbers (75,500 Union troops versus 39,000 Confederates engaged) made up for many of the errors and other failures of command. Still, as Gordon later reported, even as his lines were being

*An 1862 hand-colored photograph of "Burnside Bridge," the cause of a delay that made Antietam more of a costly draw than a substantial Union victory.*

crushed in a landslide of blue, Robert E. Lee personally rode among his beleaguered troops and "re-formed" them, so that, "with a shout as piercing as the blast of a thousand bugles, [they] rushed in countercharge upon the exulting Federals [and] hurled them back in confusion."

This was the nature of the battle at Antietam Creek. Sheer numbers were pitted against sheer grit, and blood filled the gaps that marred the execution of battle plans. It became what military historians call a "soldier's battle," a battle fought not because men are ordered to fight, and a battle won (for the Union chose to call Antietam a victory) not because of a general's plan, but a battle fought and won because of the muscle, brain, and heart of the soldiers themselves.

"Whether the regiment was thrown into disorder or not, I never knew. I only remember that as we rose and started, all the fire that had been held back so long was loosed. In a second the air was full of the hiss of bullets and the hurtle of grape-shot. The mental strain was so great that I saw at the moment the singular effect mentioned, I think, in the life of Goethe on a similar occasion—the whole landscape for an instant turned slight red."

*Private David Thompson, Company G, 9th New York Volunteers, recalling his experience at Antietam, September 17, 1862*

### POP CULTURE
#### Haunted Span

"Burnside Bridge" still stands, a graceful three-arch stone span across the Antietam at Sharpsburg in what is today the Antietam National Battlefield. It is near State Highway 65. Confederate sharp-shooters under Brigadier General Robert Toombs were positioned on high ground overlooking the narrow bridge and had an easy time picking off those who tried to cross. The needless slaughter went on for three hours before Burnside's men were finally able to make the crossing. Today, many locals claim the span is haunted. There have been reports of "blue orbs" hovering about the structure at night, sometimes to the muffled cadence of martial drums.

Even after his soldiers had driven the Confederates out of Sharpsburg proper, George B. McClellan could not persuade himself that he possessed the field. Lee had invaded Maryland. McClellan's army had pushed him back. The next step should have been a ruthless pursuit and merciless hammering of the invaders before they could recross the Potomac back into Virginia. McClellan, however, gave no such orders, and, yet again, the Army of Northern Virginia retired, battered but intact. Invasion had been defeated, but the Civil War would go on.

## LINCOLN PROCLAIMS

JUDGED TACTICALLY, THE BATTLE of Antietam was a draw. From the strategic point of view, it was a victory for the Union inasmuch as McClellan had driven Lee out of Maryland. Of course—strategically— it could have been much more. Lee's bold gamble carried the very real possibility that his army would be destroyed. McClellan, however, let it go. The enemy who is not killed or captured today fights tomorrow.

GENERAL ORDERS, }     WAR DEPARTMENT,
                             ADJUTANT GENERAL's OFFICE,
     No. 139.  }                *Washington, Sept.* 24, 1862.

The following Proclamation by the President is published for the information and government of the Army and all concerned:

### BY THE PRESIDENT OF THE UNITED STATES OF AMERICA.

#### A PROCLAMATION.

I, ABRAHAM LINCOLN, President of the United States of America, and Commander-in-Chief of the Army and Navy thereof, do hereby proclaim and declare that hereafter, as heretofore, the war will be prosecuted for the object of practically restoring the constitutional relation between the United States and each of the States, and the people thereof, in which States that relation is or may be suspended or disturbed.

That it is my purpose, upon the next meeting of Congress, to again recommend the adoption of a practical measure tendering pecuniary aid to the free acceptance or rejection of all Slave States, so called, the people whereof may not then be in rebellion against the United States, and which States may then have voluntarily adopted, or thereafter may voluntarily adopt, immediate or gradual abolishment of slavery within their respective limits; and that the effort to colonize persons of African descent, with their consent, upon this continent or elsewhere, with the previously obtained consent of the governments existing there, will be continued.

That on the first day of January, in the year of our Lord one thousand eight hundred and sixty-three, all persons held as slaves within any State or designated part of a State, the people whereof shall then be in rebellion against the United States, shall be then, thenceforward, and forever free; and the Executive Government of the United States, including the military and naval authority thereof, will recognise and maintain the freedom of such persons, and will do no act or acts to repress such persons, or any of them, in any efforts they may make for their actual freedom.

That the Executive will, on the first day of January aforesaid, by proclamation, designate the States, and parts of States, if any, in which the people thereof respectively shall then be in rebellion against

*The preliminary Emancipation Proclamation was published to the Union army in General Order No. 139, on September 24, 1862.*

Lincoln, therefore, had yet another heartbreak of disappointment to endure. But he was determined to make of the deeply flawed Antietam all that he could. On September 22, 1862, he explained to his Cabinet:

> Gentlemen, I have, as you are aware, thought a great deal about the relation of this war to Slavery, and you all remember that, several weeks ago, I read to you an Order I had prepared upon the subject, which, on account of objections made by some of you, was not issued. Ever since then my mind has been much occupied with this subject, and I have thought all along that the time for acting on it might probably come. I think the time has come now. I wish it was a better time. I wish that we were in a better condition. The action of the army against the rebels has not been quite what I should have best liked. But they have been driven out of Maryland, and Pennsylvania is no longer in danger of invasion. . . . I have got you together to hear what I have written down. I do not wish your advice about the main matter—for that I have determined for myself. . . . What I have written is that which my reflections have determined me to say. . . .

What he had "written down" was no eloquent liberation of the slaves. In fact the *preliminary* Emancipation Proclamation, issued on September 23, 1862, freed no one at all. It was just a warning to slave owners living in states "still in rebellion on January 1, 1863" that their property would be declared, come that deadline, "forever free." In effect, the September 23 proclamation was a threat to seize the slaves of those who dared continue to fight against the Union. On January 1, Lincoln duly issued the *final* Emancipation Proclamation, which did liberate those slaves in areas still "in rebellion"—but nowhere else.

## The Great Emancipator?

The Emancipation Proclamation earned Abraham Lincoln the historical appellation "the Great Emancipator." In actuality, neither the preliminary nor final proclamations set any slave free. Those living in the parts of the South that were not yet occupied by the Union army were proclaimed free, but precisely because the United States did not control these areas, they could not be freed in fact. Elsewhere, in the

## TAKEAWAY

As a result of the so-called Seven Days battles, George B. McClellan lost yet another chance to take Richmond and begin the definitive destruction of the principal Confederate force, the Army of Northern Virginia. Lincoln looked to the arrogant John Pope to win the victories the Union so desperately needed, but when he lost the *second* battle of Bull Run (at far greater cost than the *first* battle of Bull Run), the president reluctantly turned back to McClellan. He wanted a victory that he could use to redefine the purpose of the Civil War by proclaiming it not only a struggle to save the Union, but a crusade to break the chains of slavery. McClellan delivered a horrifically costly *tactical* draw at Antietam, Maryland, which Lincoln deemed a *strategic* victory sufficient to serve as a platform from which to issue an Emancipation Proclamation.

*This fancifully idealistic print from 1864 shows a Union soldier reading the Emancipation Proclamation by torchlight to a group of slaves.*

border states as well as in the parts of the South that were currently under Union control, slavery continued.

As a moral document, the Emancipation Proclamation had a profound impact, for many transforming the Civil War into a crusade against slavery. This not only rallied the Northern multitudes, reinvigorating the will to continue the fight by injecting it with a noble purpose, it made it all but impossible for foreign powers—especially Great Britain and France—to openly support the Confederacy. After all, they were not about to proclaim themselves defenders of slavery. As a legal document, however, the Emancipation Proclamation was strictly limited in scope and, in any case, impossible to enforce. Nevertheless, it did establish the legal precedent that spurred Congress to bold action. On April 8, 1864, the U.S. Senate passed the Thirteenth Amendment to the Constitution. After a hard fight, the House followed suit on January 31, 1865; it would be ratified by the states on December 18, 1865. Much briefer than the Emancipation Proclamation, the amendment says all it has to say in a single sentence: "Neither slavery nor involuntary servitude, except as a punishment for crime whereof the party shall have been duly convicted, shall exist within the United States, or any place subject to their jurisdiction."

Has any people in any age paid so high a price for thirty-two words? But, then, have any thirty-two words ever had such a profound and far-reaching effect on humanity and its history?

# CHAPTER 12

## THE WASTELANDS

*"My God! My God!"*

To Abraham Lincoln, THE BATTLE OF ANTIETAM WAS BOTH AN opportunity to publish the Emancipation Proclamation and yet another crushing disappointment delivered by George B. McClellan. Lincoln complained that the Army of the Potomac commander suffered from a "bad case of the slows," and his patience was wearing thin. The president had no way of knowing that Antietam, costly and heartbreaking though it was, marked the beginning of the Confederacy's decline. With Great Britain quite possibly on the verge of recognizing the Confederate States of America, Lee had invaded the United States of America. Yet he didn't get very far, and, after Lincoln put the abolition of slavery in the forefront of the reasons for war, the chances that any foreign power would lend legitimacy to the breakaway republic evaporated.

### RELUCTANT GENERALS

As Lincoln saw it, the price paid at Antietam was far too high for the results obtained. Compounding his frustration was the fact that, after the battle, McClellan did nothing. The president traveled to Antietam to speak personally with McClellan and to survey the situation for himself. To a friend who accompanied him, Lincoln pointed to the vast

*McClellan judged the battle of Antietam to have been a glorious victory. President Lincoln evaluated it far more accurately as at best a very narrow win and therefore a profound disappointment. Lincoln is pictured here meeting with McClellan in the general's tent at Antietam.*

encampment of the Army of the Potomac and asked his companion if he knew what lay before them. "It is the Army of the Potomac," the man answered. "So it is called," President Lincoln replied, "but that is a mistake; it is only McClellan's bodyguard."

The president, though embittered, avoided a personal showdown, but as soon as he returned to Washington, on October 6, he wrote an order to McClellan directing him to "cross the Potomac and give battle to the enemy." McClellan replied by doing nothing.

Abraham Lincoln gave him a week before he wrote another letter. *Why had he not crossed the Potomac?* the president demanded. *Why had he failed to attack?* McClellan responded that the horses of his cavalry were exhausted. "Will you pardon me for asking," the president shot back, "what the horses of your army have done since the battle of Antietam that fatigues anything?"

### Another Ride around the Army

President Jefferson Davis had no need to send such sarcasms from the Richmond "White House" to *his* commander. While McClellan waited for his horses to revive, Lee dispatched Jeb Stuart back across the border. His target this time was not a slaveholding border state

[1862, Sept. 2]

*copy*

*The undersigned, who have been honored with your selection, as a part of your confidential advisers, deeply impressed with our great responsibility in the present crisis, do but perform a painful duty in declaring to you our deliberate opinion that, at this time, it is not safe to entrust to Major General George B. McClellan the command of any ~~considerable portion~~ of the armies of the United States.*

*And we hold ourselves ready, at any time to explain to you, in detail, the reasons on which this opinion is founded* (Signed by)

E.M. Stanton, *Sec'y war*
S.P. Chase, *my Treasury*
C.B. Smith, *Sec. Interior*
Edw. Bates, *Att'y Gen'l*

*To the President*
[Delivered Sep.t 2.d 1862]

*Note. Mr. Blair p.m.g.° declined to sign ( no reason given that I heard; but preserving a cautious reticence )*

*Gideon Welles, Sec'y Navy, declined to sign, for some reason of etiquette, but openly declared in Council, his entire want of Confidence in the general*

*W.H. Seward, Sec. of State, absent*

over

*Abraham Lincoln was hardly alone in his despair over George B. McClellan's performance. On September 2, 1862, Secretary of War Edwin M. Stanton, Secretary of the Treasury Salmon P. Chase, Secretary of the Interior Caleb B. Smith, and U.S. Attorney General Edward Bates, all key members of Lincoln's Cabinet, sent a "Remonstrance against General McClellan" to the president, "declaring . . . our deliberate opinion that, at this time, it is not safe to entrust to Major General McClellan the command of any of the armies of the United States."*

with strong Confederate sympathies, but the solid, free, Union commonwealth of Pennsylvania. As if this weren't challenge enough, Stuart reprised his celebrated ride around the Army of the Potomac (Chapter 11), once again pounding around McClellan before he and his men rode into Chambersburg, Pennsylvania, which they looted from October 9 through October 12.

Physically, Stuart did little damage to the town. His men demolished a machine shop, stole five hundred horses, and appropriated a variety of needed supplies. Emotionally, the toll was heavier. Soldiers of the Confederacy occupied and abused a loyal town for four days, and the United States proved powerless to stop them.

HARPER'S WEEKLY.

693

[NOVEMBER 1, 1862.]

THE REBEL FORAY IN PENNSYLVANIA—GENERAL VIEW OF CHAMBERSBURG.—[SKETCHED BY MR. DAVIS.—[SEE PAGE 696.]

THE REBELS EXCHANGING THEIR RAGS FOR U. S. ARMY OVERCOATS AT CHAMBERSBURG, PA.—[SKETCHED BY MR. DAVIS.]

BURNING THE ENGINE HOUSE AND MACHINE SHOPS AT CHAMBERSBURG, PA.—[SKETCHED BY MR. DAVIS.—[SEE PAGE 696.]

*Confederate general Jeb Stuart led his cavalry in a second "ride around" McClellan, pounding through Chambersburg, Pennsylvania, which his men looted from October 9–12, 1862. These three wood engravings are "General view of Chambersburg; The Rebels exchanging their rags for overcoats at Chambersburg, Pa.; [and] Burning the engine house and machine shops at Chambersburg, Pa."*

## A New Commander

McClellan let a fortnight elapse before he roused his army into a slow-motion advance toward Warrenton, Virginia, on October 26. It was a dawdling stroll more than a march, and Lee had no trouble getting his Army of Northern Virginia advantageously positioned between the approaching Army of the Potomac and Richmond. Nor was the Confederate commander the only one eyeing the stately progress of the Young Napoleon. The next communication McClellan received came from the president via Henry Wager Halleck, the Union's general-in-chief, on November 7, 1862. "General," the telegram began. "On receipt of the order of the President, sent herewith, you will immediately turn over your command to Major-General Burnside. . . ."

Like McClellan, Ambrose Everett Burnside was much beloved by the troops who served under him. Beyond this, the two generals had nothing in common. Whereas McClellan suffered from "the slows," Burnside had shown himself to be an aggressive, if unimaginative, commander. More important, whereas McClellan had promised Lincoln that he "could do it all," Burnside was all too conscious of his own limitations. He was brave and earnest, and he wanted to serve his country, but twice he turned away Lincoln's offer of command of the Army of the Potomac, protesting quite frankly that he was just not up to the job.

"The order depriving me of the command created an immense deal of deep feeling in the army—so much so that many were in favor of my refusing to obey the order, and of marching upon Washington to take possession of the government. My chief purpose in remaining in the army as long as I did after being relieved was to calm this feeling, in which I succeeded."

*Major General George B. McClellan,*
McClellan's Own Story, 1887

The president was well aware that Burnside's stubborn blundering at the Antietam stone bridge had cost many lives in that battle, but, as he saw it, no better candidate for command presented himself, and he was willing to let a man outlive a mistake. When he sent an envoy to offer him for the *third* time the Army of the Potomac command, he added an additional incentive. The reluctant general was told that, if he declined the position, it would be given to Joseph Hooker. Now, Ambrose Burnside was affable to a fault (perhaps his most egregious shortcoming as a commander was his hapless eagerness to please everyone in everything all the time), and one would have to look far and wide to find a single brother officer for whom he had no affection. Hooker was that officer, however, and everyone knew it. There was no personal enmity between the two generals, but Burnside was convinced that Hooker, crude, full of empty boasts, and almost congenitally disloyal to his superiors, was unfit for major command. Presented with this ultimatum, Burnside reluctantly accepted command of the Union army's flagship force.

## Burnside in Command

The *Memoirs* of Ulysses S. Grant is notable for two qualities. It is a literary masterpiece, truly a monument among American historical writing. And it is also a document of great generosity, in which the aged, ailing, and impoverished Grant—he would succumb to throat cancer just four days after proofreading the galleys of his book in July 1885—acknowledged the contributions and sacrifices of many officers and men. Yet in all his carefully crafted assessments of the character of his commanders, he never evaded the truth. Burnside, he wrote, was "an officer who was generally liked and respected. He was not, however, fitted to command an army," adding (quite accurately), "No one knew this better than himself."

Burnside's reign of error began even before he took the Army of the Potomac into combat. He decided to simplify the organization of the army, reducing its structure to three huge "Grand Divisions," each consisting of two corps. This made for a magnificent paper chart, but, in the field, it created problems of communication and logistics that impeded rather than streamlined the progress from order to execution and compounded the already formidable difficulties of efficiently maneuvering a huge force. Nevertheless, having completed his reorganization, Burnside (to Lincoln's infinite relief and satisfaction) got the army on the move, completing in early November what McClellan had only begun, the advance to Warrenton. There he deployed his forces on the north bank of the Rappahannock River.

*As usual, artist Alfred R. Waud was on hand to record a momentous battle—in this case the blood-drenched catastrophe of Fredericksburg.*

Lee's Army of Northern Virginia was within his reach and consisted of just two corps, which were separated from each other. The logical thing for Burnside would have been to attack between these corps, slicing between them like a thick wedge, and then striking out at the flanks of both. Given the superiority in numbers the Army of the Potomac enjoyed, this tactic would have given Burnside an opportunity to defeat Lee's army in detail, not one corps at a time, but simultaneously.

*The Army of the Potomac belatedly crosses the Rappahannock on the fatally delayed pontoon bridges. This print was published in 1888 by Kurz & Allison.*

But Burnside did no such thing. If he lacked talent as a tactician, let alone genius, he possessed in great abundance a desire to please, and what the political leaders in Washington wanted—no, *demanded*—was their idea of absolute victory. This meant attacking and taking Richmond, period. Eager to oblige, Burnside passed up Lee's divided and vulnerable main force, and advanced well to the south of Warrenton to attack Fredericksburg.

## FREDERICKSBURG

THE TWO-CORPS GRAND DIVISION of Major General Edwin V. Sumner was the first portion of the Army of the Potomac to get into position before Fredericksburg, on November 17. Sumner's men were separated from the town by the broad Rappahannock. Because Sumner had managed to reach the river before General James Longstreet's Confederate corps arrived—it would not get there until November 18—Burnside should have seized the moment to order the Grand Division to cross the river immediately. Instead, he directed Sumner to await the arrival of five pontoon bridges, which (predictably) were delayed. It was a fatal blunder. Sumner obediently bivouacked his men on the north bank of the Rappahannock, thereby giving Longstreet ample time not only to reach Fredericksburg, but to dig into the hills overlooking the town from the south and west.

It was bad enough that, before a shot was fired, Burnside had yielded the high ground to the enemy, but when the errant pontoon bridges failed to materialize day after day, Lee had all the time in the world to

**ALTERNATE TAKE**
**A Matter of Priorities**
In an age when political policy and military strategy were still formulated under the long shadow of Napoleonic history, most politicians and military leaders defined victory in terms of territory occupied and towns taken. This drove Burnside's decision to march south of Lee to attack Fredericksburg. Had he possessed sufficient imagination to see beyond military doctrine, Burnside would have seized on the opportunity to attack Lee's dangerously divided army. Had such an attack succeeded, it would have dealt the Army of Northern Virginia a blow from which it probably could not have recovered. Almost certainly, the Civil War would have been significantly shortened, and Burnside, instead of being reviled by military historians as the worst general of the Civil War, would have been ranked among the conflict's heroes. But it would be March 12, 1864, before the Union army had a general in chief who could see that the first priority in any war was to kill the enemy, not take territory.

bring virtually his entire available army into high-ground positions and to fortify them elaborately. By December 11, more than seventy thousand Confederates were dug in just south of Fredericksburg—the town wedged between them and the south bank of the Rappahannock. It was on this day that the Union's pontoon bridges were finally in place, and Burnside ordered his men to begin crossing the river. And it was on this day that he also ordered a massive artillery barrage against the town.

## "Kill 'em All"

The question was and remains: *Why did Burnside open fire on Fredericksburg?*

Historians have assumed the massive barrage was intended to suppress sniper fire that emanated from the town, but employing cannons against snipers is like using the proverbial elephant gun to kill the proverbial fly. Whatever the motive, the cannonade did nothing to suppress enemy fire, but it did destroy much of Fredericksburg, and when Burnside's troops began entering the town—or what was left of it—they swarmed over the ruins in search of anything sufficiently intact to loot.

To the Confederates who watched from the hills, the Yankees looked like so many blue insects picking over the corpse of what had been a fine old Virginia settlement. After the battle—which was about to begin in earnest—Stonewall Jackson would look in disbelief at the needless devastation Burnside's men had wrought. He was a profoundly religious man, but his inclination toward Christian charity was more than balanced by an allegiance to the Old Testament ethos of an eye for an eye. A just war was one thing, wanton destruction another. Standing beside the general, an aide shook his head. *What*, he mused aloud, *should be done about all this?*

"Kill 'em," Jackson replied. "Kill 'em all."

The real killing started south of town at 8:30 in the morning, when Major General William Franklin, another of Burnside's Grand Division commanders, pushed through a gap in the Confederate defenses. It was a promising start, but Burnside, anxious to coax the battle to its crisis, began a series of headlong charges against what were essentially unassailable positions dug into the hills. In this, there was an utter absence of strategy and no discernible tactic, except to charge straight ahead, directly into the guns of the enemy.

Burnside was nothing if not determined. He saw his blue-clad soldiers, dead men now, falling on top of one another, a berm of corpses accumulating before a stone wall that ran along a sunken road just beneath the Confederates' strongest position at a place the locals called Marye's Heights. Even as the bodies piled higher and spread wider, Burnside continued to order one wave after another to charge. Burnside's men loved him, and he more than returned their affection, lending them money sometimes, visiting them in the hospital when they were sick or wounded. But the sight of their ruined bodies falling in rows and heaps did not deter him. On and on, he sent one doomed wave after another, assault after forlorn assault.

This is "murder, not warfare," a Union officer remarked, and one of Longstreet's artillerists, perched on Marye's Heights, opined that "a chicken could not live on that field" once his guns had opened up on it.

*Had Burnside not ordered Major General Edwin Vose Sumner to delay crossing the Rappahannock with his two-corps Grand Division, the battle of Fredericksburg would almost surely have ended as a Union victory.*

"Men bred as soldiers have no fancy for orders
that carry want of faith on their face."

Lieutenant General James A. Longstreet,
on Ambrose Burnside's orders at Fredericksburg,
December 13, 1862

*The battle of Fredericksburg: As usual, the Northern-based printmakers Currier & Ives gave a terrible Union defeat the look of a glorious victory.*

## NUMBERS

The history of the United States Army is a proud one, but the battle of Fredericksburg remains one of its deadliest defeats. Ambrose Burnside threw some 106,000 soldiers into the battle. Of these, approximately 12,700 were killed or wounded. Confederate casualties were less than half this number: 5,300 killed or wounded out of about 72,500 engaged.

By dusk, Burnside judged that he had time for one more charge before darkness made battle impossible. By dusk, he had already ordered fourteen separate assaults on the heights. With tears in his eyes, he announced that, this time, he would lead the charge personally. That is when the officers around him counseled that the Army of the Potomac had done all it could. Another charge would produce nothing but more casualties. In the failing light, Ambrose Burnside finally saw reason in this assessment. He ordered his army's buglers to call Retreat.

What he would always remember of that day were the dead, of course. But even more painful to him was the undying echo of the silence as he rode slowly past his defeated army. His aide-de-camp, riding beside him, called to them for the traditional three cheers, *Hip, hip. . . .* The call produced nothing but silence.

## MUD MARCH

"To THE BRAVE OFFICERS AND SOLDIERS . . . I owe everything," General Burnside wrote to Henry Wager Halleck in his after-action report on Fredericksburg. "For the failure in the attack I am responsible. . . ." He went on to offer all that he could offer: to "the families and friends of the dead," his "heartfelt sympathy"; to the wounded, his "earnest prayers for their comfortable and final recovery."

But to Halleck, he offered a fresh proposal: to recross the Rappahannock and launch a new attack against Lee. At the time, he was unaware that, in a violation of the chain of command as shocking as it is understandable, a group of Burnside's subordinate commanders had conveyed directly to President Lincoln the gist of the new plan. Appalled, the chief executive immediately stayed Burnside's hand, and so the battered Army of the Potomac, surely the most misused major force in American military history, was idled once again and settled into winter quarters.

*Battlefield artist Arthur Lumley sketched General Burnside—bald head, mutton-chop whiskers, and trademark sideburns prominently featured—ordering Major General William B. Franklin to evacuate his position at Fredericksburg.*

To his credit, Ambrose Burnside refused to yield to despair. On January 20, 1863, he began execution of what looked to be yet another tactical plan, and a pretty good one at that. Instead of striking out at Lee head-on, as he had done with such catastrophic results at Fredericksburg, he decided to envelop the Army of Northern Virginia by advancing into position across the Rappahannock at a more distant crossing, Banks's Ford. This required a long march, however, and, Burnside, as often the victim of bad luck as of his own bad ideas, was pounded by two days of heavy sleet that churned the hard ground into a quagmire. Burnside's advance was transformed into the infamous "Mud March."

One has only to read anything Abraham Lincoln wrote to recognize the man's poetic sensibilities. Perhaps it was the intense symbolism of the Army of the Potomac struggling through the mud that moved him on January 26, 1863, to relieve Ambrose Burnside as that army's commander and replace him with Joseph "Fighting Joe" Hooker. On this occasion, Lincoln addressed a personal letter to Hooker enumerating his reasons for having chosen him to assume command of the Army of the Potomac. To these reasons, he added a frank statement of his reservations. He criticized his nominee for having failed to support Burnside (Hooker was indeed notoriously disloyal), and he expressed particular displeasure over Hooker's widely quoted opinion that, in the current crisis, "both the Army and the Government needed a dictator." The president gently turned the remark against him, in effect advising the general to put up or shut up: "Only those generals who gain success can set up dictators. What I now ask of you is military success, and I will risk the dictatorship. . . . Beware of rashness, but with energy and sleepless vigilance go forward and give us victories."

## FIGHTING JOE

JOSEPH HOOKER WAS A WEST POINT MAN (class of 1837) who had served in the Second Seminole War and the U.S.-Mexican War. A lapse in loyalty (it was the first of many) during the Mexican War turned his commanding officer, Winfield Scott, sour on Hooker, so that, at the commencement of the Civil War, Scott gave him no official assignment. Taking the hint, Hooker resigned his commission and thereby became just one of the throng of civilian spectators to the first battle of Bull Run. This experience prompted him to write President Lincoln: "I was at . . . Bull Run . . . and it is neither vanity nor boasting in me to declare

**"FIGHTING JOE HOOKER."**

O, fighting Joe Hooker the brave,
  The nation so proudly admires;
His country and Flag he will save,
  From rebels and ruthless vampires.
He will humble the haughty foe,
  And scatter their columns of might;
In their ranks spread havoc and woe,
  And put the vile dastards to flight.

Great chieftain of honor and fame,

*General Hooker may have come upon his nom de guerre "Fighting Joe" by way of a careless editor's newspaper headline, but the sobriquet stuck and even became the basis of a song.*

*Major General Joseph P. Hooker, as pictured in a carte de visite photograph from the studio of Mathew Brady.*

that I am a damned sight better general than you, sir, had on that field." That was true enough, and the commander-in-chief responded by commissioning Hooker a brigadier general of volunteers. If his letter to Lincoln had been unseemly (though effective), his outspoken assessment of George B. McClellan, under whom he now served, was downright insolent. He called him an "infant among soldiers." Who, therefore, can blame Hooker's fellow officers for being unhappy about his appointment to command the Army of the Potomac?

Hooker might not have been embraced by the officer corps, but the common soldier took to him instantly. To his credit, he worked hard to restore the shattered morale of the Army of the Potomac. He saw to it that clothing, shelter, and rations were upgraded. He replaced the much-despised hardtack (the inedible, not to say infrangible, crackers the soldiers christened "tooth dullers") with freshly baked bread. Hooker also undid Burnside's cumbersome structural organization and restored efficient manageability to the army. He rode his commissary officers hard, ensuring that their corrupt ways came to an end. Tactically, Hooker was a forward thinker. Union cavalry had been underutilized, misused, and generally badly used throughout the first year and a half of the war. Hooker now began employing it as it was meant to be: for advance reconnaissance. Indeed, so determined was Hooker to get battlefield intelligence that he even hired civilian balloonists as artillery spotters, perching them in tethered balloons instead of laboriously constructed observation towers. A telegraph wire was run along the tether, so that the spotter could transmit his observations in real time.

By the early spring of 1863, Hooker felt entitled to boast that his was the "finest army on the planet," for which reason, he vowed, "May God have mercy on General Lee, for I will have none." Restored to its maximum strength of 130,000 men, it certainly was once again a formidable instrument of war, and, whereas McClellan had been reluctant to employ it and Burnside had employed it with tragic ineptitude, Hooker resolved to use it to hit Lee both aggressively and effectively. He knew that Lee had a total of just sixty thousand at Fredericksburg, and, unlike

*As he had earlier replaced McClellan with Burnside, Lincoln now replaced Burnside with Joseph "Fighting Joe" Hooker. The president's ambivalence toward his latest choice as commander of the Army of the Potomac is evident in the letter he wrote him on January 26, 1863, chastising Hooker for disloyalty to his predecessor, cautioning him to "beware of rashness," and charging him to "go forward and give us victories."*

## POP CULTURE

### A New Name for the Oldest Profession?

Here's the story. Under General Hooker, the Army of the Potomac was camped in a disreputable quarter of Washington, D.C., that bristled with brothels. Locals dubbed the district "Hooker's Division," and the ladies of the evening therein became known as "hookers." Nice story; however, "hooker" was a familiar British and American term for a prostitute long before the Civil War. It is true that by 1862, the army's presence created high times for hookers. D.C. officials estimated 7,500 full-time prostitutes working in 450 bordellos. (It's believed that Richmond was home to similar numbers.)

As for Hooker's own nickname, "Fighting Joe," the general had neither sought nor earned it. It had been conferred upon him through the carelessness of newspaper proofreaders. Covering the Seven Days battles (Chapter 11), the Associated Press issued a story headed "Fighting—Joe Hooker." Almost all the nation's newspapers that picked up the story printed the headline *without* the dash that punctuated the original.

McClellan, Hooker accepted the reality of his own numerical advantage. He was also determined not to repeat Burnside's great tactical error. Instead of ramming his army head-on into formidably defended Fredericksburg defenses, he sent Major General John Sedgwick with a third of the army to cross the Rappahannock above the Confederates' Fredericksburg entrenchments and there stage a diversionary attack. While Lee was occupied defending against this, he, Hooker, would personally lead a third of the army up along the river, and then wheel around to descend on Lee's left flank and rear. The remaining third of the army he would hold in reserve at nearby Chancellorsville, where it could be dispatched to reinforce either Sedgwick or Hooker as required. As for the cavalry, Brigadier General George Stoneman led ten thousand troopers in hit-and-run raids on Lee's lines of communication to Richmond.

## HOOKER VS. LEE

UP TO THIS POINT, ROBERT E. LEE had been the beneficiary of the failings and errors of his Union adversaries. But Hooker's plan was a very good one. Its only defect was that Lee instantly grasped it. Possessed of a powerful military imagination, the Confederate general had an uncanny ability to put himself in the mind of his opposite number.

To begin with, he did not take the bait offered by Stoneman's cavalry. Instead of parrying its thrusts, he largely ignored them, employing his own cavalry, under the redoubtable Jeb Stuart, to seize control of the roads in and out of Chancellorsville, which by April 30 was where Hooker had established an encampment of about seventy thousand men. Disabled by Stuart from sending out patrols, Hooker was deprived of his eyes and ears. Suddenly unable to tell where the Confederates were, he panicked and cast his plan aside. Instead of marching to the battlefield he had carefully identified a dozen miles east of town, Hooker remained hunkered down in Chancellorsville. He thus relinquished the initiative before a single shot was fired, swapping a sound offensive plan for a desperate defensive one.

If Hooker had been blinded, Lee's eyesight was sharper than ever. Stuart's reconnaissance revealed that the men of the Army of the Potomac who were not tied down at Chancellorsville were preparing to attack the flank and rear of the Army of Northern Virginia via a dense patch of growth known as "the Wilderness." To delay this

# SHODDY TREATMENT

The soldiers of the Civil War were poorly fed and poorly equipped. Both Billy Yank and Johnnie Reb subsisted on meager and unwholesome rations. In the case of the Confederate soldier, this was chiefly due to the government's lack of resources. The Union warrior, however, was routinely the victim of corruption and war profiteering. The U.S. Army contracted with suppliers who often furnished old or improperly preserved meat, including meat that had been condemned as unfit for human consumption.

Ill-fed, the troops were also ill-clothed. Again, in the South, this was typically the result of the government's poverty. In the North, many contractors turned to a material called *shoddy* to make the required handsome blue uniforms. Instead of being woven cloth, shoddy was an amalgam of waste fabric felted and glued together. When new, shoddy uniforms were perfectly passable. Let them get wet, however, and they fell apart, disintegrating as the glue dissolved. Soldiers marching to battle suddenly found themselves clothed in rags and tatters.

In the North, war profiteering was not confined to unscrupulous merchants and manufacturers. Lincoln's first secretary of war, Simon Cameron, was knee-deep in dirty deals with military contractors. After the U.S. House of Representatives voted a resolution of censure against Cameron, President Lincoln replaced him with the highly capable Edwin M. Stanton and, in January 1862, sent Cameron as far away from the war as he could by naming him minister to Russia. Learning of the appointment, a senator who knew Cameron all too well let out a guttural *ugh!* and advised sending advance "word to the czar to bring in his things at night."

*On both sides, many young men joined the fight in search of glory and adventure. Mostly what they found was the squalor and bad food of camp life. This is the surviving half of a stereograph depicting "Camp of 71st New Vols. Cook house Soldiers getting dinner ready."*

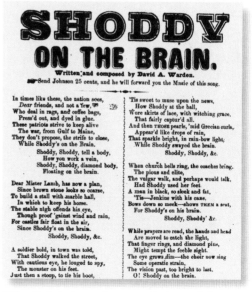

*"Shoddy" cloth, as these song lyrics explain, was made of "rags, and coffee bags, / Press'd out, and dyed in glue."*

movement, Lee sent Jubal Early with ten thousand men to resist the Union advance through the Wilderness. Lee intended to use the delay to make a preemptive attack on Chancellorsville.

It was a good idea, but, on further reflection, Lee deemed it too conventional. Around midnight on May 2, he summoned Stonewall Jackson to his headquarters. The two generals pulled up a pair of cracker barrels and sat down to hammer out a new plan. Lee decided once again to employ the same radical, high-risk tactic he had used against Pope at the second battle of Bull Run (Chapter 11), dividing his army in the face of the enemy. He would detail a force of twenty-six thousand men to Jackson, who would lead them in a surprise attack through the Wilderness and smack into Hooker's flank. While Hooker was thus engaged on his flank, Lee, with seventeen thousand men, would occupy his front. In the meantime, Early would continue to fight a holding action to pin down the

# ORIGINS OF THE U.S. AIR FORCE

Immediately after the fall of Fort Sumter, commercial balloonists, who made a precarious living giving people thrill rides, did their best to interest the U.S. Army in their services. The army did buy a single balloon for use as an observation platform at the first battle of Bull Run, but it was wrecked before it arrived at the battlefield. Still, the idea of balloon-borne observation was sufficiently appealing that, by January 1862, the Union army had a fleet of seven balloons, which constituted the first American air force.

Most generals, North and South, scoffed at the balloons, which were indeed cumbersome and dangerous. They could be filled with coal gas obtained by tapping into city gas mains, or they could be lofted by means of hydrogen, which was generated on site in a wagon-mounted apparatus that mixed acid and zinc to produce the explosive gas. Unlike his colleagues, Hooker was a balloon enthusiast, eager to use the technology not only for reconnaissance and artillery spotting (aiming of cannon), but for directing battles from aloft. Perhaps with this purpose in mind, he became the only Civil War general ever to make an ascent himself.

*A photographer was present at the battle of Fair Oaks to capture Professor Thaddeus Lowe's ascension in the observation balloon he had invented. General Hooker was quick to see the reconnaissance value of this earliest of military aircraft.*

rest of the Army of the Potomac at Fredericksburg and keep them from coming to Hooker's aid.

Jackson's mission was daunting. He had to lead twenty-six thousand Confederate soldiers to within two-and-a-half miles of the Union front and do so undetected—a very tall order, even with Jeb Stuart controlling the roads in and out of Chancellorsville. As it happened, pickets of the Union XI Corps saw the movement and reported it; however, corps commander O. O. Howard dismissed it as insignificant, as did Hooker, so that, two hours before sunset on May 2, when Jackson attacked Howard, who commanded Hooker's right flank, he caught the Union troops entirely unawares. Some were eating, some passing the time with cards—almost no one was holding a rifle. These weapons were neatly stacked outside of every tent.

Jackson descended, one bluecoat later recalled, "like a clap of thunderstorm from a cloudless sky." And that storm was relentless. An entire corps dissolved under the initial onslaught, routed in terror, thereby forcing Hooker to abandon his own well-prepared Chancellorsville defenses in an effort to maneuver and avoid destruction. This put his army precisely where Lee wanted it—out in the

*Alfred R. Waud depicted the men of II Corps, under Major General Darius N. Couch, "forming line of battle in the fields at Chancellorsville to cover the retreat of XI Corps disgracefully running away." Major General O. O. Howard, commanding XI Corps, had blundered by failing to heed warnings of the approaching attack of Stonewall Jackson. Unprepared, Howard's men were in no position to respond effectively to what was a fierce and brilliantly executed assault.*

open—and Jackson exploited the opportunity to the maximum. The battle raged for two days, ending late on May 4. Throughout it, Hooker was unable to receive reinforcements from the other wings of his divided army and therefore gave away his own great advantage: superior numbers. As May 4 ended, Hooker could do nothing more than withdraw north of the Rappahannock.

*The distinguished Civil War photographer Andrew J. Russell produced this image of the 110th Pennsylvania Infantry Regiment at Falmouth, Virginia, on April 24, 1863. As the caption to the photograph notes, the regiment was "nearly annihilated at battle of Chancellorsville."*

> "The rebel army is now the legitimate property of the Army of the Potomac. . . . The enemy is now in my power, and God Almighty cannot deprive me of them."
>
> *Major General Joseph Hooker, May 1, 1863, on the eve of the battle of Chancellorsville*

## THE COST OF COMBAT

FIGHTING JOE HOOKER'S DEFEAT at Chancellorsville was a horrifying bookend to Burnside's debacle at Fredericksburg. Hooker's army was more than twice the size of Lee's, yet Lee defeated him—albeit at a terrible cost to his own army. Whereas the Army of the Potomac suffered 17 percent casualties and was forced into retreat, Lee, though victorious, lost a quarter of the Army of Northern Virginia, killed or wounded.

The numbers, terrible though they were, did not represent the full extent of the Confederate losses. Having opened his assault on Hooker late in the day on May 2, Jackson had to break off the action before he had completed the operation to his satisfaction. In preparation for resuming the attack the next day, he and his staff quietly probed the Wilderness in search of ground through which to make a hazardous night attack. As he returned to his own lines from this reconnaissance, an entire line of North Carolina infantry opened fire on him and his staff.

Those of Jackson's aides who managed to survive the friendly fire attack were relieved that the bullets had found nothing vital. The general's right hand, left wrist and hand, and left arm had been penetrated. He had a chance. He had a very good chance against the initial wound—thanks to a timely amputation—but not against the almost inevitable infection that followed. Fever was succeeded by pneumonia; on May 9, according to Dr. Hunter McGuire, the surgeon who attended him, Jackson's "mind . . . began to . . . wander, and he frequently talked as if in command upon the field. . . ." Dr. McGuire leveled with his patient, doubtless looking into the otherworldly blue of his eyes at 1:30 in the morning of May 10 when he told him that he had perhaps only two hours to live.

"Very good; it is all right," came the reply, feeble but firm. But as the final hour approached, the general drifted into delirium: "Order A. P. Hill to prepare for action! Pass the infantry to the front rapidly. Tell Major Hawks—" He trailed off, smiled, and "said quietly, and with an expression as if of relief," according to McGuire, "'Let us pass over the river and rest under the shade of the trees.'" They were Stonewall Jackson's final words.

*Kurz & Allison's late nineteenth-century lithograph depicts, among other actions, the mortal wounding of Stonewall Jackson (which actually occurred in a quiet interval between the first and second day of fighting).*

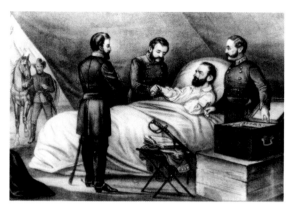

*This somewhat primitive Currier & Ives lithograph presents the death of Stonewall Jackson. Note the dying man's amputated arm.*

"I have lost my right arm," Lee said of Jackson's death. As for Lincoln, contemplating Hooker's terrible defeat hard on the heels of Burnside's, he could do no more than gasp in disbelief: "My God! My God! What will the country say? What will the country say?" Hitherto brash and boastful, Hooker (some have reported) analyzed the cause of the disaster with unaccustomed humility: "Well, to tell the truth, I just lost confidence in Joe Hooker."

## LEE'S NEW STRATEGY

JEFFERSON DAVIS AND MUCH OF THE CONFEDERATE NATION hailed Chancellorsville as a great triumph, but Robert E. Lee's own appraisal was far more ambivalent. The cost of victory had been so high that, to the extent that the outcome of the war would be a matter of numbers, that victory was really a defeat. But Lee also knew that the outcome was *not* all about numbers. It was also about morale and will—and these, he knew, had by Chancellorsville been brought low in the Union. He believed that *now* was the moment to capitalize on this sentiment and amplify it. If he could build on what the North saw as a disaster in Chancellorsville by staging a new invasion of the United States, it was quite possible that the Union's will to fight on would be smashed.

It was a terrific gamble. Fighting defensively on Southern soil had great advantages. Men defending their homeland were highly motivated, supplies were far more readily available on friendly soil, and it is easier to defend against a larger force than it is to attack a larger force with a smaller one. Yet no war is ever won by defensive action alone, and Lee understood that attrition, while it might wear down the Yankee will to fight, reduced his own available manpower far more quickly than that of the Union. Moreover, unlike many other commanders, who looked only at their own slice of the war, Lee also looked west and appreciated the meaning of all that Grant was achieving along the Mississippi (Chapter 6). Clearly, Vicksburg, the last great Confederate Mississippi River fortress town, could not hold out forever against Grant (Chapter 13). Once the Union gained complete control in the western theater, a huge number of troops would be freed up to return east for duty against the Army of Northern Virginia.

## NUMBERS

### Chancellorsville Toll

Hooker lost some 17,000 killed or wounded at Chancellorsville. This was 17 percent of those engaged. Lee's casualties numbered 13,000, but accounted for nearly a quarter of his significantly smaller army.

This was the strategic picture as Robert E. Lee saw it in June 1863. It prompted him to move north.

Dividing the Army of Northern Virginia into three corps, he assigned James Longstreet to command the lead corps—even though "Old Pete" (sometimes called "Gloomy Pete") counseled Lee that an invasion was a bad mistake. He proposed instead staging smaller offensives within Virginia, while giving Braxton Bragg sufficient reinforcements to hold Chattanooga, Tennessee, and while also sending more troops west to counter Grant. But, a good soldier who was loyal to his commander, Longstreet followed the orders he was given. He advanced as far as Culpeper Court House, Virginia, and (per orders) paused.

The second of the three corps, commanded by Richard S. "Old Baldy" Ewell, struck out against Union forces scattered throughout the lower Shenandoah Valley. The third corps, under A. P. Hill, lingered at Fredericksburg to keep the Yankees busy there.

Shaken as he had been by Chancellorsville, Joe Hooker had a bold proposal for responding to Lee's northward movement: ignore it. He wanted instead to concentrate on attacking Richmond, which was now very poorly defended. This would not only menace and perhaps even conquer the Confederate capital, but would force Lee to cut short his incursion into the North and force him to return to Richmond's defense. Lincoln, however, was unwilling to use Washington or the towns of Pennsylvania as pawns in a massive gambit. Besides, he had little confidence in anything Hooker proposed; therefore, he instructed him to do nothing more than follow Lee, fighting defensively as required.

## Shadowing Lee

Hooker raised no protest, but grimly followed orders. On June 5, he dispatched a reconnaissance mission under John Sedgwick to determine whether the Confederates had left Fredericksburg. This blew up into a skirmish at Franklin's Crossing, Virginia, which prompted Hooker to send Alfred Pleasonton with a large cavalry contingent to make a deeper penetration in order to discover the full extent of Lee's movements. Jeb Stuart responded to Pleasonton's move on June 9, and the clash that resulted was the battle of Brandy Station, the war's first major battle of cavalry against cavalry and the biggest cavalry battle ever fought in North America, with twenty thousand horsemen engaged for a dozen hours of charging and countercharging.

Pleasonton was bested by Stuart, but he and his troopers had acquitted themselves spectacularly nevertheless; and although Stuart had prevailed, he had also come close to defeat. His legend of invincibility was not shattered, but it was cracked, and the fickle Confederate press showered him with criticism bordering on scorn. Yet Brandy Station did provide a distinct advantage to Lee. Before the battle, he had been unaware that Hooker was so closely shadowing him. As a result of the battle, he now knew. His assumption was that Hooker would now advance on Richmond. (Lee had no way of knowing or even guessing that Lincoln and the Union high command had already vetoed this.) Therefore, on June 10, Lee ordered Ewell to attack all the Union garrisons still in the Shenandoah Valley. He believed this would compel Lincoln to order the Army of the Potomac to come to the defense of Washington.

No such thing happened, of course, because Hooker was not about to advance against Richmond. Instead, there were inconclusive skirmishes at Berryville (June 13) and Martinsburg (June 14), Virginia, and a major attack by Ewell on the Union garrison at Winchester during June 13–15, in which the Confederate captured 4,058 Union troops and killed or wounded 443 for a loss, killed or wounded, of just 269 of his own.

*A thrilling (and highly imaginative) depiction by Edwin Forbes of the clash at Brandy Station, the biggest cavalry battle ever fought on the North American continent.*

## The Invasion Begins

On June 15, 1863, the Army of Northern Virginia began its second invasion of the United States. While Lee's units crossed the Potomac into Maryland, Jeb Stuart's cavalry kept Pleasonton's Union cavalry occupied, thereby screening Lee's movements. This meant that Hooker was unable to determine whether Lee intended to invade Pennsylvania or attack Washington. Pleasonton attempted to pierce Stuart's screen at Aldie, Virginia (June 17), then again at Middleburg (June 19) and Upperville (June 21)—all inconclusive cavalry skirmishes.

For his part, Stuart was determined to restore his aura of invincibility, which had been dimmed at Brandy Station. Lee's brief to Stuart was to be his eyes, always reporting Hooker's whereabouts. The quickest way to get into position to accomplish this mission was simply to ride across the Potomac. Stuart proposed to Lee that he instead be permitted to ride all the way around Hooker's rear and flank. He justified this by asserting that it would enable him to raid Hooker's supply depots and lines of communication. Lee allowed himself to be talked into what was clearly Stuart's bid for glory. He had already made two "rides around" the Army of the Potomac. This one would be even more spectacular.

## The Price of Glory

Historians call it "Stuart's Gettysburg Raid," and it was indeed magnificent. Stuart disrupted Hooker's supply lines, captured 125 supply wagons at Rockville, Maryland, and came out on top in skirmishes at Fairfax Courthouse, Virginia (June 27); Westminster, Maryland (June 29); Hanover, Pennsylvania (June 30); and Carlisle, Pennsylvania (July 1).

But this ride for glory came at a terribly high price. Neither Stuart nor Lee had imagined how widely distributed the Army of the Potomac was. As a result, Stuart's "ride around" consumed far more time than either he or his commander had predicted. For ten full days, Stuart was out of contact with Lee. For ten full days, Lee had neither eyes nor ears. Unlike Hooker, who, blinded, had hunkered down, Lee, sightless and deaf, continued his advance into Pennsylvania, unaware that what lay ahead was a crossroads town in which he would have to fight, quite by accident, the war's greatest crossroads battle.

---

**TAKEAWAY**

When George B. McClellan, restored to command of the full Army of the Potomac, continued to avoid decisive battle, Abraham Lincoln replaced him with a reluctant Ambrose Burnside, who obediently led the army into a major battle at Fredericksburg, Virginia, and there suffered one of the worst defeats in U.S. military history. In his turn, Burnside was replaced by the boastful but aggressive "Fighting Joe" Hooker, who led the Army of the Potomac into another catastrophic defeat at Chancellorsville, Virginia. Buoyed by these victories, which were nevertheless also costly to the Confederacy, Robert E. Lee led his Army of Northern Virginia on a second invasion of the United States.

# PART FIVE

# THESE
# HONORED
# DEAD

# CHAPTER 13

## VICKSBURG EPIC

### The Fight for the "Gibraltar of the West"

THE EASIEST TALES TO TELL ARE THOSE WITH BUT A SINGLE STORYLINE that begins at a beginning and does not stop until the end. They are like an unaccompanied melody—a tune you can whistle all the way through. The story of the Civil War, however, is no simple song, but a fugue worthy of Johann Sebastian Bach, its many lines reeling out at the same time, here entwining with one another, there diverging, spiraling out onto their own courses, always moving, always changing, and always simultaneously.

The cataclysmic combat in the Atlantic seaboard states is mostly a single narrative, one melodic line, however discordant, always propelling us ahead. As with any good story or catchy tune, we are driven to get to wherever it will take us, to discover how it all ends. Anything else seems so much sideshow and distraction. Even during the war itself, Americans had difficulty paying attention to every simultaneous turn in the vast counterpoint of the struggle. Most fixed their minds and imaginations on the unfolding drama east of the Appalachian chain. But a more perceptive minority—Lincoln and Lee were among them—also harkened to the plot unfolding in the western theater.

To understand the Civil War as they did, we must likewise turn from the big Eastern tune—for the moment leaving Lee's Army of Northern Virginia on the verge of Pennsylvania—and face the counterpoint that played out along the Mississippi and the far reaches of its broad valley.

# ON TO CORINTH

WE MUST ALSO STEP BACK IN TIME, from the summer of 1863 to that of 1862. After Grant had captured Forts Donelson and Henry on the Mississippi, Confederate major general Edmund Kirby Smith pulled out of Knoxville, Tennessee, and on August 14, 1862, invaded the border state of Kentucky. Two weeks later, he received reinforcements from Braxton Bragg, who had withdrawn from Chattanooga. At this point, on August 30, 1862, the Union's Don Carlos Buell sent forces in pursuit. They took the hamlet of Munfordville, Kentucky, after a surprisingly hot skirmish. On September 14, Confederates made an ill-advised attempt to retake the town, but suffered a bloody repulse. Even as more Union troops marched into Munfordville, Bragg launched a larger attack under General Simon Bolivar Buckner. After surrounding the Union garrison on September 16, Buckner demanded its surrender.

War is always a serious matter and, more often than not, a tragic one as well. In this case, however, it verged on comedy. The U.S. Army had entrusted the 4,133 men of Munfordville's garrison to a Colonel J. T. Wilder, an Indiana factory owner, prominent in his community but lacking even a modicum of military experience. He knew enough to understand that surrender was never a desirable outcome, but he knew too little to figure out an alternative. As a businessman accustomed to speaking frankly with other businessmen, he answered Buckner's surrender demand by calling on the enemy commander with a flag of truce. He explained his problem to him: that, being quite ignorant of matters military, he needed some frank advice. Wilder told Buckner that he believed him to be both an officer and a gentleman, and, as such, he was confident that he would not be the victim of deception. With this understanding, he asked Buckner whether or not he really should surrender.

Precisely because he considered himself an officer and a gentleman, Buckner demurred, explaining that it was very bad form for a commander to give surrender advice to his enemy. Undaunted, Wilder replied that he understood Buckner's reservations but asked if he might be permitted to count Buckner's cannon. The Confederate commander agreed and conducted Wilder on a tour of his front.

"I believe I'll surrender," the Union colonel announced at the conclusion of the tour.

*Colonel J. T. Wilder, commanding the 4,133-man Union garrison at Munfordville, Kentucky, was so inexperienced that he felt compelled to ask Simon Bolivar Buckner, the Confederate general who demanded his surrender, whether or not he should comply.*

**PREVIOUS SPREAD:** *David McConaughy, a prominent attorney living in Gettysburg, commissioned the Pennsylvania artist Peter F. Rothermel to create a massive oil painting of the battle of Gettysburg. Completed in 1871, it hangs today in the State Museum of Pennsylvania. Reproduced here is a popular engraving made after the painting. The action is probably intended to be Pickett's Charge.*

# THE MOST DIFFICULT GENERAL

Casual Civil War buffs pay little attention to Braxton Bragg these days, but among hard-core armchair generals and professional historians, he is one of the most controversial commanders of the conflict.

Union general James McPherson classed him among the "bumblers . . . who lost the West" for the Confederacy, and practically no one who knew or served under him liked him. He was dour, perpetually pessimistic, and eager to dish out blame to anyone handy. He was, however, a skilled organizer who managed to keep his army together under the most difficult of circumstances at the western fringes of the Confederacy, and, unlike many other Confederate generals, he managed to work effectively with Jefferson Davis throughout much of the war.

Born in 1817 in Warrenton, North Carolina, he graduated fifth in the fifty-member West Point class of 1837 and served with distinction in the Second Seminole War and the U.S.-Mexican War, in which he received rapid promotions for bravery. Yet his reputation for orneriness became legendary.

Like Grant, Sherman, and so many others, Bragg resigned his commission in the 1850s because of the limited opportunities offered by the peacetime army, but joined the Confederate cause at the outbreak of the war. Despite his indifferent performance as a corps commander at the battle of Shiloh, Bragg was promoted to general on April 12 (retroactive to the sixth), 1862, largely because of his reputation as an effective disciplinarian—one of few officers capable of transforming the ragtag forces typical of much of the Confederate military into something of a genuine army. Bragg was one of only seven Confederate officers promoted to the rank of full general.

Bragg led the invasion of Kentucky in August 1862 and won a narrow victory against Don Carlos Buell at Perryville, Kentucky, on October 8, but declined to pursue Buell and instead withdrew to Knoxville—probably in reaction to the defeat of Earl Van Dorn and Sterling Price at Corinth. This action may well have saved his army, but it drew the scorn of the Confederate press, and from this point forward, it seemed that Bragg could do no right. He became a scapegoat for the failure of the invasion of Kentucky and other reverses, and many subordinates sought transfer out of his army. Bragg might have redeemed himself with his costly victory against William S. Rosecrans at Chickamauga (Chapter 16), but his refusal to capitalize on the victory by attempting to drive the Union army out of Chattanooga prompted a number of prominent generals to petition Jefferson Davis for his removal from command. Davis defended Bragg, who went on to defeat at Chattanooga (Chapter 16), whereupon the Confederate president accepted his resignation. He ended the Civil War as a military adviser to Jefferson Davis and as a subordinate field officer. After the war, he served as the superintendent of the New Orleans waterworks and subsequently, as chief engineer for the state of Alabama, designed harbor improvements at Mobile. He ended his career and his life in Texas as a railroad inspector, literally dropping dead on September 27, 1876, while strolling down a Galveston street.

*By the time of the Civil War, Braxton Bragg was already legendary for his inclination to dispute anything with anyone—even himself.*

The comical fall of Munfordville had serious consequences. It cut Buell's lines of communication with the Union stronghold of Louisville. Fortunately for Buell, however, Bragg, an unimaginative and unaggressive officer, failed to exploit the opportunity this presented. Determined to build up his force, he wanted to avoid a fight until the arrival of Kirby Smith's men, and he also intended to recruit troops from among the Confederate-leaning faction of the state's citizenry. Moreover, an inveterate organizer, he decided it was important to set up supply dumps before doing anything else. Only after all of this preparation would he be ready for combat.

On September 19, Confederate general Sterling Price suffered a sharp defeat at the hands of William S. Rosecrans, one of Grant's subordinates, at Iuka, Mississippi. Driven southward, Price linked up with General Earl Van Dorn to attack Corinth, Mississippi, formerly held by Confederates and now—according to Van Dorn's intelligence—held by a small Union force. He therefore struck the town on October 3, only to discover that Rosecrans had twenty-three thousand men encamped there, hardly a small force. The combined strength of Van Dorn and Price was outnumbered by a thousand men, but the Confederates fought hard—withdrawing on October 4, after receiving an alert that Grant had dispatched reinforcements to Rosecrans.

## KENTUCKY LIBERATED

FROM CORINTH, VAN DORN AND PRICE limped to Holly Springs, Mississippi, leaving Braxton Bragg isolated in Kentucky without any realistic hope of receiving reinforcements. The Union's Buell was uncharacteristically quick to pounce. He closed in on Bragg, forcing him to a stand at the Kentucky village of Perryville on October 8.

Buell had every reason to anticipate a smashing victory. It was all a matter of numbers. He had nearly thirty-seven thousand men under his command, whereas Bragg, cut off by Van Dorn's defeat, could muster less than half that number: about sixteen thousand troops. But it is one thing to have bigger numbers on paper and quite another to get them all in the right place at the right time. Buell was never able to muster his full complement into the firing line. Bragg is usually credited with having achieved a narrow tactical victory at

**NUMBERS**

**Bloody Corinth**
Union and Confederate forces were almost evenly matched at Corinth—23,000 versus 22,000—but the repulse of the Confederate attack was decisive. Rosecrans lost 2,520 killed, wounded, or missing, whereas the losses of Price and Van Dorn amounted to 4,233 killed, wounded, or missing.

*Currier & Ives celebrated the battle of Corinth, Mississippi, in this 1862 chromolithograph print.*

## REALITY CHECK

### The Cost of Conventional Thinking

Few who had graduated from West Point in the decades before the Civil War would have thought to criticize Henry Wager Halleck's strategy of deploying the 100,000 men available in the western theater broadly over a wide area rather than consolidating and concentrating the force. At the time, the chief business of an invading army was seen as taking and holding territory, and that meant dispersing the available manpower. Yet had Halleck dared to think outside of the antebellum box, concentrated his forces, and identified as his chief objective the enemy's army rather than the enemy's territory, he would not have yielded the initiative to the Confederates by assuming what was essentially a defensive posture. Using 100,000 men to attack each of the smaller forces arrayed against him, Halleck might well have crushed much of the Confederate military west of the Appalachians. Had he succeeded in this, the Civil War would have been shortened significantly.

Perryville, although both he and Kirby Smith withdrew clean out of Kentucky. As for Buell, he was unable to organize a pursuit of their forces into eastern Tennessee, and this prompted Union high command to replace Buell as commander of the Department of the Ohio with William S. Rosecrans.

Buell's failure to achieve decisive victories was part of a much larger pattern of Union command. General in chief "Old Brains" Halleck had created the pattern in the western theater by dispersing his forces widely so as to occupy territory instead of concentrating and consolidating for the purpose of killing the enemy. Grant's earlier victories against the Confederate Mississippi River forts had proven the effectiveness of building up a large force in one place, using it hard, fast, and violently, then moving on to the next enemy position. Grant's conception of war was quick, nimble, mobile, and deadly. It was the essence of modern warfare. Halleck, however, belonged to an earlier generation raised on the tradition of Napoleonic conquest. For him, the measure of victory was the occupation of space that had formerly belonged to the enemy. Whereas Grant embraced dynamic strategy, Halleck was stuck in an outmoded concept of static war.

Despite the limitations of Halleck's static strategy, he did bring to an end the Confederate invasion of Kentucky by the middle of October 1862. With Kentucky secured, Ulysses Grant was free to return to his advance down the Mississippi. He and Halleck differed radically in strategy and temperament, to be sure, but they were agreed on the importance of possessing the mighty Mississippi. As Halleck put it, "the opening of the Mississippi River will be to us more advantage than the capture of forty Richmonds." Operating from this assumption, Grant understood that the final step toward controlling the river was the capture of Vicksburg. Unfortunately for him, Confederate high command possessed precisely the same understanding.

"Vicksburg was the only channel . . . connecting parts of the Confederacy divided by the Mississippi. So long as it was held by the enemy, the free navigation of the river was prevented. Hence its importance."

*Ulysses S. Grant, Personal Memoirs, 1885*

Vicksburg possessed a combination of natural and artificial features that made it a most forbidding fortress of a town. It occupied a steep bluff overlooking the Mississippi and was also ringed by a six-and-a-half-mile defensive line, which included the entire repertoire of nineteenth-century fortification architecture, ranging from firing holes and trenches to strong points known as "redoubts," crescent-shaped fortifications called "lunettes," and a number of full-blown forts. The very names of the fortifications seemed to cry out with impregnability: Fort Hill, Square Fort, South Fort, Stockade Redan, 3rd Louisiana Redan, and the Great Redoubt. These built fortifications were artfully integrated into a formidable natural terrain of hills and knobs, which would certainly retard the progress of any attacker, thereby exposing him to annihilation. As for a riverborne naval assault, the guns of Vicksburg were set to rake the Mississippi, transforming its bend at Vicksburg into a watery killing field. Although Grant commanded 35,000 men in December 1862 (with access to many more) when he began the long Vicksburg campaign, and Confederate lieutenant general John C. Pemberton had at most 18,500, the position and fixed defenses of Vicksburg multiplied the effectiveness of Pemberton's limited manpower many, many fold.

*Union mapmaker Robert Knox Sneden drew this view of "the rebel position at Vicksburg, Miss., May 1863."*

## ULYSSES SISYPHUS GRANT

GENERAL GRANT HAD PROVEN HIMSELF an aggressive commander as willing to inflict casualties as he was to absorb them, but he was a far cry from the likes of Ambrose Burnside. Assigned to take Vicksburg, Burnside would doubtless have made any number of suicidal frontal assaults to no avail. Grant understood that he would have to find another way to capture Vicksburg, and he also understood that it would take much time and preparation. Accordingly, in December 1862, he scratched out an advance base at Holly Springs, Mississippi. His intention was to rally forces here and load them—some forty thousand troops—onto rail cars for transportation down the tracks of the Mississippi Central Railroad to a rendezvous with William Tecumseh Sherman's thirty-two thousand troops arriving on riverboats. Confederate general Earl Van Dorn was determined to stop Grant before he could get under way.

On December 20, Van Dorn led a lightning cavalry attack against the 8th Wisconsin Regiment, whose members were slumbering in their tents. The raiders stormed into the town of Holly Springs proper and there destroyed a 1.5 million-dollar cache of supplies. Riding the momentum of this successful hit, Van Dorn struck one Union outpost after another. Simultaneously, Nathan Bedford Forrest, whom Sherman called "the very devil" (and, strictly in military terms, intended that as a compliment), led another cavalry unit in an attack on the Mississippi Central, tearing up more than sixty miles of track.

The Confederate cavalry was far superior to that of the Union, but most of its mounted raids made a greater impact on morale than on strategy. The raids of Van Dorn and Forrest were different, however. Between them, they stopped Grant cold, and that meant that he could not link up with Sherman, who had been assigned to attack the Confederate position at Chickasaw Bluffs, several miles north of Vicksburg. Though undermanned, Sherman did his best from December 27 to December 29 to take his assigned objective. His terse report of the action seems to invert Julius Caesar's famed *Veni, vidi, vici*: "I reached Vicksburg at the time appointed, landed, assaulted, and failed."

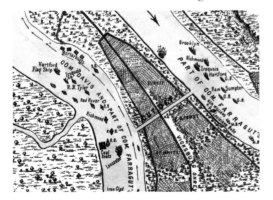

*Seen on a map, "Grant's Canal," which was excavated during the siege of Vicksburg, looks like simplicity itself. The actual task proved Herculean and the result ultimately unsatisfactory.*

Not one to be stymied, Grant tried an entirely different approach. Recalling how John Pope had evaded the formidable Confederate guns of Island No. 10 in a sharp bend of the Mississippi by digging a canal that cut across the bend and thereby bypassed the fortress (Chapter 8), he commenced digging a canal of his own to get around the guns of Vicksburg and thereby allow a naval assault on the town. This inspiration was the start of a series of labors that bring to mind not so much the mythical figure of Hercules as that of Sisyphus, who slaved under a curse, perpetually compelled to roll an enormous boulder up a hill only to have to watch it roll back down.

In January 1863, Grant decided to build on the so-called Williams Canal across DeSoto Point, which had been started in July 1862 under Benjamin Butler's orders, only to be abandoned. Grant thought it possible to complete the canal in a way that would bypass the Vicksburg guns and therefore ordered William Tecumseh Sherman to expand its width ten times, from six to sixty feet, and to dredge out another foot of depth, taking it from six to seven feet. Sherman hated the idea, and whereas the rest of the army referred to the project politely as "Grant's Canal," he christened it "Butler's Ditch." A combination of Confederate artillery fire and torrential rains forced abandonment of the work by February.

Grant next ordered Brigadier General James B. McPherson to dredge a canal from the Mississippi to Lake Providence, northwest of Vicksburg, by which transports could gain entry to the city. The canal would allow passage to Bayous Baxter and Macon and, via these, to the Tensas River and Black River, which fed into the broad Red River. This would allow Grant's men to link up with those of Brigadier General Nathaniel Banks on the Red River. Although McPherson completed the work on March 18, the complex of waterways proved navigable only by small, shallow-draft boats, which lacked the capacity to transport a sufficient number of men quickly enough to have a significant strategic effect.

Even before abandoning "Butler's Ditch" and McPherson's canal project, Grant ordered the demolition of a Mississippi River levee located near Moon Lake (in the vicinity of Helena, Arkansas), a full 150 miles above Vicksburg. This flooded the so-called Yazoo Pass from Yazoo City, Mississippi, to Memphis, Tennessee, which would allow troop transport via the swollen Coldwater and Tallahatchie Rivers into the Yazoo River at Greenwood, Mississippi. From here, troops could gain the high bluffs northeast of Vicksburg. The operation, dubbed the "Yazoo Pass Expedition," began with the demolition of the levees on February 3, 1863, but was soon foiled by thick growth and fallen trees— many chopped down by the Confederates—which blocked the passage of gunboats. By early April, the Yazoo Pass Expedition joined the other abandoned operations in strategic oblivion.

By March, it was clear to the U.S. Navy's Admiral David Dixon Porter that the Yazoo operation was headed for failure. On March 16, therefore, he made a stab at traversing the Yazoo Delta via Steele's Bayou a short distance north of Vicksburg. His objective was to get gunboats and troops to Deer Creek, where they would be in position

## REALITY CHECK
### Red-Faced Author
The entire canal-digging debacle was apparently so embarrassing to Grant that he attempted in his *Memoirs* to write off the nearly four futile months of labor-intensive projects as nothing more than make-work intended all along to accomplish no more than occupy his men in order to enforce discipline during long weeks of idleness in winter and early spring. This may well be the single whopper in a personal account of the Civil War otherwise remarkable for its unblinking adherence to unvarnished truth.

*The lithographic firm of Middleton, Strobridge & Co. published "Battle of Jackson, Mississippi— Gallant charge of the 17th Iowa, 80th Ohio and 10th Missouri, supported by the first and third brigades of the seventh division" in 1863.*

to make a flanking attack on Fort Pemberton, a major Confederate fortification at Greenwood, Mississippi. With this fort neutralized, troops could be landed between Vicksburg and Yazoo City.

On a map, it looked like a good idea. In the water, however, the gunboats and their crews soon found themselves tangled in willow reeds and fallen trees, again mostly deliberately felled by Confederates. As the gunboats bogged down, Confederate troops menaced them from shore, forcing Sherman to send reinforcements. It was all quite enough to prompt the abandonment of this waterborne route to Vicksburg.

Grant began digging another canal, this one from Duckport Landing to Walnut Bayou, in the knowledge that only very light, shallow craft would be able to navigate it past Vicksburg. He hoped this would be enough, but the canal was only approaching completion in early April when water levels became so low that nothing but the most modest of flatboats could get through. The project was therefore useless.

## DEADLY HILL

AFTER HIS ATTEMPT TO LINK UP with Nathaniel Banks for a joint assault on Port Hudson, Louisiana, came to nothing, Grant sent two corps under generals McPherson and Sherman to attack and capture Jackson, Mississippi, which he had identified as a rallying point for Confederate reinforcements. The attack succeeded on May 14, 1863, and led to another engagement, at Champion's Hill, just two days later. This proved to be the hardest-fought battle of the entire Vicksburg campaign, and although the Union emerged victorious, the cost was sufficiently great to prompt Halleck and others to question Grant's strategy. He moved from objective to objective, apparently willing to attack whatever concentration of enemy troops happened to present itself. While Grant's superiors and fellow commanders might have questioned what appeared to be an absence of overall plan, Grant, in fact, never deviated from his single-minded intention of taking Vicksburg. It was just that he believed the way to accomplish this was by an unremitting offensive. Unlike George McClellan and most of the other Union commanders, Grant was unwilling ever to idle his troops. He fought at every opportunity. *That* was his plan.

## UNDER SIEGE

As Grant viewed what modern commanders would call the Vicksburg "battlespace," it seemed to him that he was now in as good a position as he would likely get for an assault on the fortress city itself. On May 19, he unleashed a frontal assault on the city, which, predictably, was repulsed. Regrouping, he mounted a second foray on May 22. This time, the Federals suffered crushing casualties: some thirty-two hundred killed and wounded.

No commander enjoys siege warfare. It is tedious, erodes morale, invites disease, and consumes time. It is also oddly inglorious. But, for all his stubborn willingness to spend lives where necessary, Grant was not about to repeat Burnside's cataclysmic error at Fredericksburg. After two attempts, he was convinced that he could not take Vicksburg by storm, and so he dug in and, from late May through the beginning of July, continuously pounded the fortress town with shells from more than two hundred cannon and siege mortars.

"The capture of Vicksburg has proved a bigger thing than I supposed it would. . . . Since crossing the Miss. River an army of (60,000) sixty thousand men has, in the various battles been killed, wounded, captured, and scattered so as to be lost to the Confederacy, and an armament for an army of (100,000) one hundred thousand men has departed from their forever."

*Major General Ulysses S. Grant, dispatch to the adjutant general of the U.S. Army, July 11, 1863*

> ### NUMBERS
> #### Champion Hill Combat
> A total of 29,373 Union troops fought at Champion's Hill, of whom 410 were killed, 1,844 wounded, and 187 went missing. Outnumbered, the 20,000 Confederates engaged lost 381 killed and an estimated 1,800 wounded, while 1,670 went missing or were captured.

## EYEWITNESS

A woman—her name is unknown, but she was clearly a Northerner who had the misfortune of living in Vicksburg during the war—wrote in her diary on May 28, 1863:

*We are utterly cut off from the world, surrounded by a circle of fire. . . . The fiery shower of shells goes on day and night. . . . People do nothing but eat what they can get, sleep when they can, and dodge the shells . . . . I watched the soldiers cooking on the green opposite. The half-spent balls . . . were flying so thick that they were obliged to dodge at every turn. At all the caves . . . people were sitting, eating their poor suppers at the cave doors, ready to plunge in again. As the first shell again flew they dived, and not a human being was visible. . . . I think all the dogs and rats must be killed or starved: we don't see any more pitiful animals prowling around.*

Confederate leaders called Vicksburg their "Gibraltar of the West," but like the original Gibraltar, it was both fortress and city, with a population of some five thousand civilian men, women, and children, all of whom endured the terrible hardships of siege warfare. Under unremitting bombardment, they abandoned their homes and clawed cave-like shelters into the hills of yellow clay. Many brought with them into these shelters their furniture, which provided a pathetic modicum of domestic comfort among dark, dank, dirty chambers infested by insects, rodents, and snakes. Although the people could find some refuge from bombardment, there was no evading the specter of starvation as the Union siege lines tightened around the town. Dogs, mules, horses, rats—all were jealously eyed as means of subsistence.

*Born in Bavaria, Adalbert J. Volck was a dentist by profession and a political cartoonist by avocation. He came to the United States sometime before the Civil War and served as personal courier to Jefferson Davis. He was in Vicksburg during the siege, and, while there, sketched this portrayal of life in one of the caves in which residents took shelter from incessant Union bombardment.*

# INDEPENDENCE DAY

UNDER SIEGE AND BOMBARDMENT since May, Vicksburg surrendered on July 4, 1863—one day after Lee fled in defeat from Gettysburg (Chapter 14). The Pennsylvania victory overshadowed the one at Vicksburg. Gettysburg, after all, was in the East, Vicksburg was in the West; Gettysburg was a battle between armies in the field and could be called glorious, but Vicksburg was the strangulation and battery of a city by an army, and it summoned up any number of adjectives other than *glorious*. Yet the Vicksburg result was every bit as important as that produced at Gettysburg. It seized the Mississippi River from the Confederacy and delivered it to the Union, so that the forces of the Union now controlled the northern and the western borderlands of the Confederacy, leaving Confederate Texas isolated and impotent, and the entire South without a vital avenue of supply and communication. True, the South had not yet lost the war, but, hemmed in on the north and the west, it could go nowhere to escape it. No wonder that, for more than eight decades after July 4, 1863, the people of Vicksburg defiantly declined to join the American nation in celebrating Independence Day.

## TAKEAWAY

Grant's Vicksburg campaign, the culmination of the struggle to control the Mississippi River and its vast valley, ended on July 4, 1863, with the fall of the Confederate fortress city of Vicksburg to the Union. Overshadowed by the Federal victory at the battle of Gettysburg, won one day earlier, the fall of Vicksburg was, with Gettysburg, the turning point of the Civil War. Although the costliest battles had yet to be fought, the Confederacy's prospect of victory vanished, and all that could be hoped for was a negotiated peace with the North that might win for the seceded states some degree of autonomy and honor.

*Kurz & Allison published this romanticized view of the siege of Vicksburg in the 1880s.*

# CHAPTER 14

## AN ACCIDENTAL BATTLE

*"... These Dead Shall Not Have Died in Vain"*

FROM HIS HARD TRIUMPH AT CHANCELLORSVILLE, A VICTORY HE BOUGHT with the lives of 1,665 Army of Northern Virginia men, paramount among them Thomas J. "Stonewall" Jackson, Lee rode off determined to break Northern morale by invading Pennsylvania (Chapter 12). He knew he was making an all-or-nothing wager, but at least he could count on the redoubtable cavalryman Jeb Stuart to be his eyes in the field, and that would give him an edge sufficient to hedge his bet. He needed Stuart's reconnaissance, and he counted on having it. But Stuart failed him, his "ride around" the Army of the Potomac taking ten mortal days, far longer than anyone thought possible. And so Robert E. Lee led the principal army of the Confederacy into the country of its enemy quite blind.

Still, he *was* Lee, and what he lacked in factual reconnaissance he sought to make up for with an exercise of his brilliant military imagination. Putting himself in Hooker's place, a commander almost prostrated by total defeat, Lee assumed that Hooker had not yet led the Army of the Potomac across the Potomac. He therefore felt reasonably safe in stringing his own army out in a long line, the better to gather the needed intelligence that Stuart was not feeding him. As June turned to July, the rear of Lee's army was at Chambersburg, Pennsylvania, and the front some fifty miles to the east, at York.

## PRESSED FOR TIME

FOR ONCE, LEE FAILED TO OUTTHINK his opposite number. Hooker *had* managed to cross the Potomac during June 25–26—a fact Lee did not discover until June 28, when he learned that the enemy was deployed in the vicinity of Frederick, Maryland, due south of the elongated flank of his army. If Hooker chose to strike immediately, Lee knew, the Army of Northern Virginia would have a hard time delivering a repulse. But then Lee also found out that Fighting Joe Hooker was no longer in command. President Lincoln had just replaced him at the head of the Army of the Potomac with Major General George Gordon Meade.

Lee was happy enough to hear this. Meade was certainly competent. Like Lee himself, he had been assigned as an engineer after graduating from West Point, and Lee would later comment to his staff that "General Meade will commit no blunder in my front, and if I make one he will make haste to take advantage of it." But that was the best he could say of him. Meade was an unimaginative soldier, dull and predictable, not to mention ill-tempered. The Confederate commander well knew that Lincoln could have chosen better, and he was glad that he hadn't.

Hooker's defeat at Chancellorsville had been one in a long, dreary string, and discontent was heavy in the North. Down South, during this same period, the public complaints had very little to do with generals. The issue was hunger. As more ships were added to Winfield Scott's once-derided Anaconda, it became increasingly effective. The loss of major ports, especially New Orleans, put a stranglehold on the Confederacy, and although neither McClellan, Burnside, nor Hooker had come even close to overrunning Richmond, almost all of the big battles had been fought where the farms and the farm roads were. Crops were therefore unplanted or unharvested, cattle unslaughtered, food undelivered. General Lee was intent on snapping the North's will to continue the fight, but he was also aware that civilian morale was eroding, maybe even more rapidly, all over the South. On

*George Gordon Meade replaced Joseph Hooker as commander of the Army of the Potomac just three days before the battle of Gettysburg. Robert E. Lee knew him to be an unimaginative but highly competent general, whom he said would "commit no blunder in my front, and if I make one he will make haste to take advantage of it."*

April 2, 1863, a gaggle of usually courteous southern belles transformed themselves into riotous mob. Shouting "*Bread! Bread!*" they looted the principal shopping streets of Richmond, shattering windows and diving after baked goods, groceries, and pork—not to mention clothes, jewelry, and other finery. The mayor did not scruple to call out the militia against them, giving the troops leave to open fire on the ladies if the ladies would not behave and go home.

In the end, the great Richmond "Bread Riot," as the city's histories call it, was personally ended by Jefferson Davis—at least that's what his wife, Varina, records. Clambering atop a wagon, the president of the Confederacy shamed the women for snatching at jewels even as they cried out for bread. "You say you are hungry and have no money—here is all I have!"

He thrust his hands into his pockets and withdrew two fistfuls of coins and currency, throwing it all into the crowd. This done, he reached next into his vest pocket, pulled out his watch, glanced at it, and matter-of-factly announced his intention to order the militia to start shooting—five minutes from *now*—at anyone lingering in the street.

*Frank Leslie's Illustrated Newspaper, a popular Northern weekly, gleefully depicted the Richmond "Bread Riot" with an engraving that transformed the opulent Southern belles of the Confederate capital into gaunt harpies, hungry and desperate.*

SOUTHERN WOMEN FEELING THE EFFECTS OF REBELLION, AND CREATING BREAD RIOTS.

No end of armchair generals have condemned Robert E. Lee for failing to heed James Longstreet's advice to refrain from invading the North. Lee, however, was driven by his awareness that the Confederacy was running out of time and that dramatic action was the only chance to end the war with anything other than abject surrender. But his more immediate problem was to discover the whereabouts of the enemy before the enemy discovered his. With Stuart out of touch, Lee relied on advance elements of his army, such as A. P. Hill's division, for timely reports of enemy contact. Besides performing reconnaissance on the afternoon of June 30, 1863, a detachment under Brigadier General Henry Heth was also foraging—not for food, but for shoes. If a

# CONFEDERATE CRISIS

During the war, the Confederate states suffered severe shortages, which produced massive price inflation. A Richmond newspaper published in 1863 estimated that the cost of feeding a small family in the city was $68.25 per week, whereas in 1862, the cost had been a mere $6.55.

Consider that a manual laborer or factory worker earned no more than a dollar a day and the hardships created by the war are apparent. What is worse, the paper's estimates were based on U.S. dollars, whereas Confederate currency was plummeting in value by the day.

The Richmond government had sought to finance the war through the sale of bonds, which promised 8 percent interest yearly. Before the end of 1861, however, inflation in the seceded states was in excess of 12 percent every month. With tax revenues decreasing, the Confederate treasury resorted to printing large numbers of treasury notes to defray the costs of the war. A Confederate paper dollar was valued at 82.7 cents in 1862, 29 cents in 1863, and 1.7 cents in 1865.

*The fifteen Confederate dollars pictured here, worth $12.41 in 1862, would be valued at 26 cents in 1865.*

Confederate soldier was usually hungry, he was also frequently shoeless, and Heth's men hoped they could turn up some badly needed footgear in the prosperous Pennsylvania crossroads town of Gettysburg.

## CONTACT

AS IT TURNED OUT, THE TROOPS of Heth's detachment found no shoes in town, but they did observe some Union cavalry nearby, and Heth sent a messenger to Hill for permission to march into Gettysburg with a brigade to clear the enemy cavalry out. Neither Heth nor Hill guessed that these Yankees, troopers of a division commanded by Brigadier General John Buford, were the advance guard of the *entire* Army of the Potomac. Lee, however, had an inkling. With Stuart out of communication, General Longstreet had hired a civilian spy named Henry Thomas Harrison. Beyond this, just four things are known about him: he was a Mississippian, had a full beard, pale hazel eyes, and, by profession, was an actor. Longstreet summoned Harrison to report to him and General Lee. The spy said this: Soldiers of the Army of the Potomac were on the march, closing in, and moving fast. What Harrison could not say was just how much of the army was nearby.

*Brigadier General Henry Heth, CSA, led a foraging detachment that made first contact with federal troops at Gettysburg on June 30, 1863.*

*A tough, determined, and combat-savvy cavalryman, Union brigadier general John Buford led the advance guard of the Army of the Potomac and was the first to clash with the Confederates at Gettysburg. He is pictured, seated, with his aides.*

Lee had not intended to fight a major battle in Pennsylvania. His purpose was mainly to raise hell, jangle nerves, destroy public confidence, and menace Washington, but he believed that battle was being forced upon him, and he resolved to make the most of it. Convinced—quite correctly—that Meade was unaware of his presence, he thought he had surprise on his side. Now, he had defeated the Army of the Potomac twice before, at Fredericksburg and at Chancellorsville. They were decisive, even horrific victories, but they were won on *Confederate* soil. If he now seized the opportunity fortune had presented to him and concentrated his army at Gettysburg, he could defeat the Army of the Potomac a third time—and, this time, in the United States of America. It could, he believed, be the turning point of the war. The people of the North might continue to support their generals and their president even if Pennsylvania fell victim to a Confederate raid, but Lee doubted that even Lincoln could maintain his countrymen's will to continue the struggle after the biggest and most powerful army of the Union armies had been beaten on the soil of its own country, especially if its defeat opened the door to an attack on Washington.

Of all his generals, Lee loved and respected none more than "Old Pete" Longstreet. Though Longstreet was fourteen years younger than he, Lee affectionately called him "My Old War Horse" and frequently sought his counsel. But Lee had turned a deaf ear when Longstreet tried to talk him out of the Pennsylvania adventure, and he refused now to heed his advice to shun battle with the Army of the Potomac at Gettysburg.

Lee conceded that the Army of Northern Virginia was outnumbered; he didn't know by how much, but he assumed, as Longstreet argued, that the disparity was significant (in fact, the Army of Northern Virginia deployed 70,226 at Gettysburg, the Army of the Potomac, 88,289). Lee also admitted Longstreet's contention that the town occupied no particularly important strategic point. But, with the sands rapidly running through the hourglass of the Confederacy, he insisted that battle here and now was an opportunity that the army could not afford to miss. The enemy was spread out. Concentrate the army rapidly at Gettysburg, and there was a fair chance of destroying the Union force in detail as its far-flung elements straggled in. Even if this didn't bring about the instantaneous collapse of the Union's war will, it would certainly discredit the Lincoln administration, thereby clearing the way for a candidate of the Democratic Party—which favored an immediate negotiated end to the war—to defeat Lincoln when he ran for reelection in 1864. Besides, Lee reflected, his army was in much the same situation as Meade's: spread out. If he did not concentrate at Gettysburg, there was a good chance that Meade, seeing the Army of Northern Virginia strung out over fifty miles, would seize the initiative and attack him, defeating him in detail. Speaking to Longstreet, Lee concluded his case for a showdown battle by arguing that he really had no choice and so it was best to make the most of it.

"At 3 P. M. we began to meet wounded men coming to the rear, and the number of these soon increased most rapidly, some hobbling alone, others on stretchers carried by the ambulance corps, and others in the ambulance wagons. Many of the latter were stripped nearly naked, and displayed very bad wounds. This spectacle, so revolting to a person unaccustomed to such sights, produced no impression whatever upon the advancing troops, who certainly go under fire with the most perfect nonchalance. They show no enthusiasm or excitement, but the most complete indifference. This is the effect of two years' almost uninterrupted fighting."

*Lieutenant Colonel James Freemantle,*
*British observer attached to the Confederate Army of Northern*
*Virginia, Gettysburg, July 1, 1863*

## A CONTEST FOR THE HIGH GROUND

AS A KENTUCKIAN, Major General John Buford might easily have declared himself a Confederate at the start of the war, but, perhaps because he had spent most of his life in Illinois, he chose to fight for the Union. And that was the Union's very good fortune. He had served in Texas and the Southwest before the war, molding himself into a superb cavalryman and cavalry commander. Fighting Indians had given him expertise in reading a landscape with a combatant's eye, and, at Gettysburg on July 1, 1863, he immediately and instinctively took in the problem. There was high ground—McPherson's Ridge, it was called—on the western edge of town. That, he knew, was what he'd have to occupy and hold; if he let it fall to the incoming Confederates—well, he had fought at Fredericksburg, where the enemy owned the heights and, from them, brought slaughter to the Army of the Potomac.

His troopers would have to dismount and hold the ridge until more of the army arrived. That might be hours or longer, and he knew he would be badly outnumbered, but he also knew that his men would be on the high ground and, as cavalry troopers, they carried not the infantry-issue muzzle-loading rifle-muskets, but breech-loading cavalry repeating carbines. They would be able to shoot and reload considerably faster than the Confederates. Maybe that would be edge enough, at least for a little while.

Buford had little enough time to deploy his men. By nine that morning, the fighting was under way. His dismounted cavalry repulsed the initial Confederate waves, and he was relieved by the arrival of the first elements of Major General John Reynolds's I Corps as early as 10:30. Reynolds carried the news that O. O. Howard was also on the way, with XI Corps. Yet the Confederates were forming up, rapidly building superior strength. As keenly aware of the stakes as Buford was, Reynolds assumed personal command of the first of his units to get into position,

*The Gettysburg battle-field as depicted in a fine chromolithograph published by Endicott & Co. of New York City.*

*A terrible moment for the Union at Gettysburg: "The Fall of Reynolds," depicted by Alfred R. Waud.*

*The appearance on the field of Major General John F. Reynolds, I Corps commander, inspired the Union soldiers around him with confidence of victory. Before he could lead his men out of the woods and into the battle, a Confederate bullet pierced his neck, toppling him from the saddle and killing him before he hit the ground.*

the eighteen hundred men of the already legendary "Black Hats," or "Iron Brigade." He was determined to prevent a breakthrough and formed up the brigade in McPherson's Woods, just west of the ridge.

I Corps loved their commander, and no I Corps unit loved him more than the Iron Brigade, whose iconic black hat Reynolds proudly wore. They would follow him, to a man, into hell, if that's where he led them; however, before he could even lead them out of the woods, a Confederate bullet pierced John Reynolds's neck, toppling him from his saddle, dead. Amid stricken, stony faces, command was passed to Reynolds's senior division commander, Major General Abner Doubleday, but the men of the Iron Brigade were stunned to the point of paralysis by the sudden loss of their leader, and their confusion quickly spread throughout I Corps. By the time O. O. Howard appeared with the bulk of XI Corps, he found the battlefield a chaos. As Doubleday's senior, he took over from him command of both I Corps and XI Corps and set about restoring order among the troops. He scrambled to consolidate the still-outnumbered Union forces by attempting to fuse a division under Major General Carl Schurz to the two corps, but he was unable to form up effectively on the contested McPherson's Ridge and adjacent ground. Driven by what seemed an unstoppable momentum, the Confederates, under generals Robert Rodes, Jubal Early, and A. P. Hill, finally pushed the bluecoats out of position, sending them off the ridge and out of every position they had held to the west and the north of town.

The line of the Union retreat was down from McPherson's Ridge and into Gettysburg proper. It had been a tidy, somnolent academy town, home of Pennsylvania College, but now its few simple streets were jammed with troops. Fighting was house to house and hand to hand. The superior Confederate numbers and the momentum of their onslaught proved irresistible. The Federals withdrew through the town, then poured onto the Baltimore Pike, the principal artery flowing to the southeast. Receiving word of the deteriorating situation, General Meade dispatched Winfield Scott Hancock, a highly respected officer Meade regarded as his right hand, to rally and regroup the defense. He hardly converted defeat into victory that first day of battle, but Hancock did stem the general Union rout. At the end of the day, the high ground of McPherson's Ridge was lost, and that was a bad blow. Nevertheless, the Union army still clung to East Cemetery Hill, Cemetery Ridge, and Culp's Hill, together forming a high-ground position that ran south then southeast of the town. By nightfall of July 1, the main portions of the two armies engaged occupied ridges and hills southwest and south of town. The Confederate infantry division under the insatiably aggressive twenty-nine-year-old Major General William Dorsey Pender (he had been wounded at Frayser's Farm in the Seven Days battles, at the second Bull Run, twice at Fredericksburg, and would suffer a mortal wound at Gettysburg) was strongly deployed on Seminary Ridge, the southwestern high ground, while Jubal Early's understrength infantry division was at the southeastern edge of town, hovering dangerously near the northern-most flank of the Union position, Howard's XI Corps and Doubleday's I Corps, which were arrayed from northeast to southwest along Cemetery Ridge just below Gettysburg. About a mile and a half south of these corps were two more Union divisions, holding positions north of two hills, Round Top and Little Round Top. Between the principal forces—Pender's Confederates and the Union troops under Howard and Doubleday—lay a mile-wide expanse of open fields and clumps of woods.

Though he had won the day, Lee was not pleased with the static situation of two opposing forces facing off but doing nothing. It is not the way he'd wanted to end July 1. He had directed Major General

# PLAY BALL!?

The one thing almost everyone claims to know about Abner Doubleday (1819–93) was that he invented baseball in a Cooperstown, New York, cow pasture. In 1907 an official commission ratified this assertion as gospel truth, but, in recent years, a consensus has formed among historians that Doubleday did no such thing. Certainly, *he* never claimed credit for the sport.

He was, however, a man of many parts. A career army officer who graduated in the middle of his 1842 West Point class (note that he was a cadet at West Point in 1839, when he was said to have invented baseball), he served in the U.S.-Mexican War and against the Seminoles from 1856 to 1858. He was second in command under Major Robert Anderson at the fall of Fort Sumter and rightfully claimed credit for firing the first shot in reply to the Confederate bombardment. Thus he fired the Union's first shot of the Civil War.

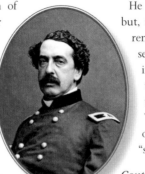

He was a journeyman officer at best, but, unlike many of his colleagues, he remained in the army after the war, serving until 1873. Before he left, he invented a cable car railway system that is still used in San Francisco, he then practiced law, and he became a Theosophist—a leading member of an organization dedicated to the "search for Truth." He died in 1893.

*Contrary to popular myth, Union brigadier general Abner Doubleday did not "invent" baseball, but he did fire the Union's first shot in the Civil War, at Fort Sumter.*

Richard Stoddert Ewell to exploit the initial rout of the Union army, "if he found it practicable." The phrase was typical of Lee. A gentleman officer speaking to other gentlemen officers, he was loath simply to order anyone to do anything, and Ewell chose to interpret Lee's concluding phrase as license to give his hard-worked men a rest, if that's what he thought they needed.

## A NEW DAY

SICKNESS ACCOUNTED FOR SOMEWHAT more than a third of all Civil War casualties. A fully manned regiment might show a thousand soldiers on its muster roll, but it typically went into combat with about six hundred due to sickness and noncombat injury. Officer or enlisted man, no one was immune, and when the sun rose over Gettysburg on July 2, 1863, Robert E. Lee was wracked by diarrhea and exhaustion. Both were endemic to camp life, with its filthy conditions, bad food, and water sources that often served as both fountain and toilet.

Lee did his best to shake off the effects of illness and summoned his corps commanders early to lay out what he intended to be an all-out effort to destroy the Army of the Potomac. He knew that the enemy army was massing, but, because of Stuart's failure to provide reconnaissance, he could only guess at how quickly. His belief was that he had to strike now, hard, before many more Federals arrived in Gettysburg. Longstreet, predictably, disagreed. His guess was that virtually all of the Army of the Potomac would arrive before the day was over. If this happened, it could well be the Army of Northern Virginia, not the Federal force, that would be crushed. Absent reliable intelligence about the enemy, Longstreet advised adopting what he called "strategic offense" tempered by "tactical defense." Instead of forcing a showdown here at Gettysburg, he thought that Lee should withdraw (this was "tactical defense"), pulling the enemy along with him, thereby forcing the Army of the Potomac farther from its lines of supply and reinforcement. Then, when the enemy was in a disadvantaged position, he should turn to counterattack (the "strategic offense"). Longstreet pointed out that something very like this approach had resulted in victory at the two Bull Runs and at Fredericksburg, and that it had exacted a heavy cost on the Union forces at Antietam as well. Specifically, Longstreet advised withdrawal back into Virginia, then a move against the rear of Meade's army.

*The all-important high ground: Culp's Hill as seen from Cemetery Hill, in a 1923 stereo-graph published by Keystone, purveyor of newsreels and his-torical still images.*

It was a reasonable proposal, but Lee responded that he could not bring himself to order his officers and men to withdraw after having won the day on July 1. This affront to martial honor would both demoralize the army and squander time the suffering Confederacy no longer had. No, Lee insisted firmly, today was the day for the showdown fight. With that, he laid out the choreography of the victory he planned.

Lee—and practically everyone else who has looked at a map of Gettysburg as the situation stood early on July 2, 1863—saw that the main Union line was deployed on its high ground in the shape of an inverted fishhook, with the curve of the hook at the northeastern end, around the top of Cemetery Hill (defended by I Corps), and, east and slightly south of this, its barb, consisting of most of XI Corps, on Culp's Hill. The shaft extended southwest along Cemetery Ridge, occupied by II Corps, just joined by III Corps at its flank. The "tie end" of this shaft was just short of the two hills south of town known as Little Round Top and Big Round Top.

Lee ordered Longstreet to attack the shaft all along Cemetery Ridge and ending at the Round Tops. This constituted the Union's left flank. Lee intended to poise his own corps northwest of the fishhook to attack where its curve joined the shaft at Cemetery Hill, and he assigned Ewell—whose corps was due north of Cemetery Hill, above the curve of the hook—to swing down swiftly and hit the Union's right hard. Thus every yard of the Union line would be hit in rapid succession, if not simultaneously, and once the line began to break, there would no way for the Federals to maintain possession of Cemetery Ridge and the adjacent high ground. Orderly withdrawal from these rugged positions would also be impossible, and the Union army would surely be routed.

## ROUND TOP AND DEVIL'S DEN

IF GEORGE GORDON MEADE HAD BEEN SHAKEN by the rebuff Union forces had suffered on the first day of battle, he concealed it thoroughly. An aide described his manner on the morning of July 2 as "quick" and his mood as "bold, cheerful, and hopeful."

But did he have any reason to feel this way? After all, the Union fishhook was encircled on three sides—along the entire length of the shaft, above the curve of the hook, and to the east of the barb. Everyone, Union and Confederate, knew Meade to be a conventional, even plodding officer; nevertheless, he was an engineer, and he viewed

---

**REALITY CHECK**

**"If I had Stonewall Jackson . . ."**
Only years after the war did Lee publicly criticize Ewell's deficiency of initiative, declaring, "If I had Stonewall Jackson at Gettysburg, I would have won that fight." The usually modest, frank, and self-critical Lee uncharacteristically let himself off too easily here. Jackson died before Gettysburg. That was a fact beyond Lee's control. Nor could anything Lee might have done convert an Ewell into a Jackson. What Lee might have managed more effectively was his own command style. Had he issued a firm and absolute order instead of a polite request, Ewell would have followed it, or at least tried to. Lee should never have empowered a journeyman commander like Ewell to make a decision as to whether or not to pursue the retreating enemy. The failure, a lapse in leadership, was Lee's, and its result was the first stroke of the Confederacy's death knell.

# SICK DAY

No commander in American military history is more widely respected than Robert E. Lee, but some authorities suggest that admiring historians have attempted to ascribe Lee's defeat at Gettysburg to ill health rather than admit his fallibility. The truth is that Lee took bold gambles at Gettysburg and made some bad decisions, but there is also ample evidence that his medical condition during the battle was poor. He almost certainly suffered from heart disease by this time, although, on July 2, he may have also been laid low by overindulgence in fresh fruit, especially cherries, which his men picked abundantly in Pennsylvania.

It is known that late in March 1863, Lee suffered a severe sore throat, which, according to his physician, caused a rheumatic inflammation of the pericardial sac (which today would be labeled acute pericarditis secondary to a throat infection). This diagnosis was based on Lee's complaints of paroxysmal chest, back, and arm pain, which suggests angina pectoris. During the final two years of his life, 1869–70, he complained that any exertion produced chest pain and shortness of breath, which suggests a longstanding cardiac disorder, probably heart failure. Moreover, Lee was frequently described as "florid" in complexion, a condition that may have been produced by long-term hypertension associated with arteriosclerosis. In short, during the single most important battle of the Civil War, the commanding officer of the Army of Northern Virginia was probably quite ill, afflicted by a combination of the diarrhea endemic to camp life and a chronic, worsening cardiac condition.

*Political connections got Dan Sickles the rank of major general, and he performed far better than most nonprofessional commanders, but his impetuosity on day two of Gettysburg nearly lost the battle for the Union.*

the situation that morning not in the two dimensions of a flat map, but in the three dimensions of the actual battle space. Yes, I and XI Corps were surrounded, but they occupied magnificent high ground at every point. This meant that any Confederate attack would have to be made from below and only after traversing clear fields of observation and fire. What looked to be a Confederate advantage when viewed in two dimensions could well be interpreted as a Union advantage when seen in three. Besides, by this time nearly ninety thousand soldiers of the Army of the Potomac were gathered and positioned at Gettysburg. Total Confederate strength was at most seventy-five thousand, and that was strung out along a wide encirclement, whereas the Federals were mostly concentrated on Cemetery Ridge, Cemetery Hill, and Culp's Hill—all more or less contiguous high ground.

On the morning of July 2, at the southwest ("tie-end") of the fish-hook, was the newly arrived III Corps of Major General Daniel Sickles. Its position, at the very end of the Union line, was critical. Fighting front to front, one enemy line against another, is hard fighting indeed; but manage to smash into the end of the enemy's line,

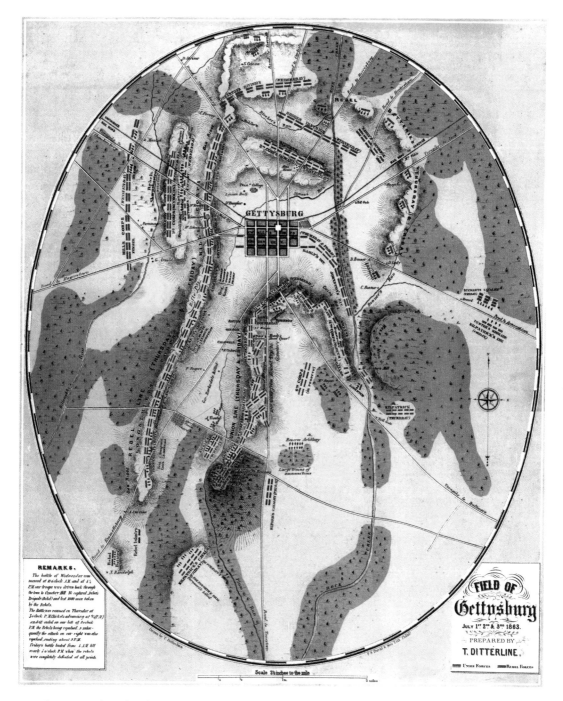

*Popular mapmaker Theodore Ditterline sketched the "Field of Gettysburg, July 1st, 2nd & 3rd, 1863" for inclusion in a twenty-four-page pamphlet devoted to the battle, published later that year.*

*Federal dead,
Gettysburg, at the
end of day one,
July 1, 1863.*

bringing your front against his flank, and you have a tremendous advantage. Whereas you can bring many guns to bear, the enemy can reply with but few. It is like the maneuver known as "crossing the T" in an old-fashioned sea battle in the age of sail, when one man o' war maneuvers its broadside, with its double row of cannon, to front the enemy at his bow, where he has no guns (the position of the attacking ship is perpendicular to the victim, as the horizontal stroke of a capital T is perpendicular to the vertical stroke). If Sickles faltered, there was nothing to stop the Confederate forces from rolling up the whole Union line.

Now, Dan Sickles had compiled a decent record of command at the Seven Days, Antietam, Fredericksburg, and Chancellorsville, but he was undeniably a "political general," having received his commission and his command on the strength of his formidable power and influence in the Republican Party and not on account of any military qualifications. In fact, he had a reputation as one of Washington's more dissolute social lions and carried a heavy freight of scandal compounded of sexual intrigue and murder. When President Lincoln, who was both a political and personal friend, had nominated him as a brigadier general back in September 1861, the Senate, charged with the constitutional duty of advice and consent, withheld its consent and only by calling in a lot of favors did the president push the nomination through the second time around.

Despite a decent, even admirable, battle record, Sickles never shed his reputation as a loose cannon, and what he did that July 2 suddenly and shockingly justified the popular view of him. Without any order from Meade, Sickles led III Corps out of its all-important position, which anchored the Union line, advancing to a point just over a half-mile west of that line. In doing this, he not only isolated his corps, exposing it to the prospect of defeat in detail, but laid bare before General Longstreet the flank of virtually the entire Union force assembled at Gettysburg.

Yet "Old Pete" Longstreet was not also called "Gloomy Pete" for nothing. He had entered the second day of Gettysburg in deep disagreement with what Lee was doing. If Sickles was a loose cannon, erratic and impulsive, Longstreet was a rock, deliberative to a fault. He could not bring himself to believe that Sickles had advanced out of place without very good reason, most likely to draw him into an enveloping attack of some sort, and so Longstreet debated with himself until four in the afternoon before finally deciding to attack.

He sent Major General John Bell Hood, his most aggressive division commander, to hit the Union III Corps where it was now deployed, in an area called the Peach Orchard, which was northwest of the Round Tops. Sickles's men reeled under the onslaught, falling back toward Little Round Top via an ugly patch of boulder-strewn land soon to be hallowed by Hood's soldiers as the Devil's Den on account of the unexpectedly fierce resistance that met them there.

Lee had predicted that Meade, dull though he might be, would make no mistakes. Yet putting the likes of Sickles in so important a position along the line of battle was a spectacular blunder. If the battle of Gettysburg had been a chess match, this would have been the losing move.

But no battle is a game. Chance and character have a way of intervening in combat, sometimes ruining good plans and other times redeeming even the worst mistakes. Very shortly before Hood had begun his attack on III Corps, Brigadier General Gouverneur K. Warren, chief engineer of the Army of the Potomac, noticed something that had escaped the attention of Meade and every other Union commander. Little Round Top, just below the tie end of the Union fishhook, was unoccupied, save for a few wig-wag men (signalmen who communicated in semaphore fashion using flags). In a flash, Warren pictured the disaster to come. Hood's division would run up the side of Little Round Top, concentrate on that high ground, and then descend from it to crash into the Union's defenseless flank. Assuming Hood could maintain the momentum of that attack, there would be nothing to stop him from rolling right up the fishhook shaft, thus adding the battle of Gettysburg to the dismal litany of Army of the Potomac defeats at the hands of Robert E. Lee and the Army of Northern Virginia.

*Aggressive, valiant, and abundantly courageous, John Bell Hood was a favorite general of Jefferson Davis, despite his shortcomings as a strategist and tactician, which would later contribute to the Confederacy's loss of Atlanta.*

*Artist Alfred R. Waud sketched Union brigadier general Gouverneur K. Warren "on Hill Top" at Gettysburg. Chief engineer for the Army of the Potomac, Warren ordered the occupation of Little Round Top in the proverbial nick of time. His action proved critical to the outcome of Gettysburg on day two of the battle.*

Warren hastily dispatched a staff officer to Colonel Strong Vincent with orders that he immediately lead a brigade into position on Little Round Top. Vincent was killed in the ensuing fight against Hood's advance, but his brigade bought time for another brigade, under Brigadier General Stephen Weed, to get into position as well. At the extreme southern end of this brigade—and, therefore, at the very end of the Army of the Potomac—was the 20th Maine Regiment. It was a tired, haggard, depleted outfit, having been reduced by battle to less than half strength, just five hundred men (including a number of captured deserters the regiment had been assigned to guard), all under the command not of some West Point officer, but Colonel Joshua Lawrence Chamberlain, until the year before a gentle professor of rhetoric at Maine's Bowdoin College. Upon this battered, tattered half regiment commanded by a schoolteacher depended, at least for one afternoon, the course of the battle and, quite possibly, the outcome of the Civil War.

Alabama men, fresh and in superior numbers, hammered against the 20th Maine. Chamberlain and his troops found the grit to hold on, but when word reached the colonel that the regiment's ammunition was all but used up, he chose not to do what was expected in such a situation—give up—but instead ordered his men to fix their bayonets on their empty rifle muskets and attack.

## DETAILS, DETAILS

### Colonel Emeritus

Joshua Lawrence Chamberlain would be wounded before the battle of Gettysburg was over, and he would be wounded in subsequent battles on three more occasions, but his deed at Little Round Top was not forgotten. Mindful of it, General Grant accorded him the honor of receiving the Confederate surrender at Appomattox Court House on April 9, 1865, and, belatedly, in 1893, Congress conveyed the thanks of the nation by awarding him the Medal of Honor.

> "Desperate as the chances were, there was nothing for it, but to take the offensive. I stepped to the colors. The men turned towards me. One word was enough,— 'BAYONET!'—It caught like fire, and swept along the ranks."

*Colonel Joshua L. Chamberlain, on the bayonet charge of his 20th Maine at Little Round Top, Gettysburg, July 2, 1863*

They had one advantage on their side: the force of gravity. The 20th Maine, including the deserters under guard, charged down the slope of Little Round Top, driving the enemy before them, at the points of their bayonets. Some of the proud Alabamans ran, while others threw down their muskets and threw up their hands in instantaneous surrender. The Bowdoin professor had saved the Union flank.

# SCANDAL MAN

Professedly strait-laced Victorian America loved a juicy scandal, and Dan Sickles provided the juiciest. Two years before the fall of Fort Sumter, Sickles, at the time a Democratic congressman (he would cross to the other side later) already infamous for having left his pregnant wife in New York while he toured England with a prostitute, strolled into Washington's Lafayette Park, withdrew a pistol, and shot dead Philip Barton Key, district attorney of the District of Columbia and the son of Francis Scott Key, author of "The Star-Spangled Banner." Sickles had just learned that Key had been carrying on an affair with his wife.

The congressman turned himself in and was tried for a murder he could not deny having committed. Future secretary of war Edwin M. Stanton, the best lawyer in Washington, boldly pleaded his client not guilty, for the first time in legal history basing that plea on what Stanton called "temporary insanity," his wife's infidelity having caused him to lose his mind, at least long enough to kill Key.

*Washingtonians were scandalized less by the fact that Sickles gunned down his wife's lover and that he was subsequently acquitted of murder on the novel grounds of "temporary insanity" than they were by the fact that Sickles not only forgave her, but took her back to his home, his hearth, and his bed.*

*In broad daylight on February 27, 1859, across the street from the White House, Daniel Sickles, at the time a U.S. representative, shot and killed Philip Barton Key, the son of the man who wrote "The Star-Spangled Banner" and the lover of Mrs. Daniel Sickles.*

The public was riveted to newspaper coverage of the trial, and, in Washington, the courtroom gallery was packed, with a throng always gathered outside as well. A friendly press depicted Sickles as a hero, Key as a rogue, and, when it came, they hailed the jury's verdict of acquittal as a vindication of the sanctity of the marital bed. Nevertheless, the public was scandalized once again when Sickles forgave his errant wife and took her back into his home and his bed.

## The Approach of Twilight

Chamberlain hadn't won the battle, but he kept the Union from losing it. Despite this, Hood's men had taken and, by the end of the day, held the Devil's Den at the foot of Little Round Top. From the cover of boulders in this rugged patch, they poured fire up against the Union men who clung fiercely to the hill. Simultaneously, battle raged in the Peach Orchard, northwest of Little Round Top, and also in the adjacent

Wheatfield, where Hood mounted a half dozen attacks, each successfully repulsed by Union counterattacks.

In the end, having hesitated so long to exploit Sickles's blunder, Longstreet launched a devastating offensive, but was unable to achieve the coordination required to make it decisive. By sundown, Winfield Scott Hancock, now in operational command of both II and III Corps, filled the gaps Sickles had left in the Union line and was thereby able to repulse each of Longstreet's attempts to break through. The final assaults fell upon Cemetery, East Cemetery, and Culp's Hills. By this time, the Union lines were so solid that all the attacks were turned back, save that against Culp's Hill.

## THE FINAL DAY

THAT THE MOMENTUM OF BATTLE had shifted from the Confederate side to the Union was made apparent early on the morning of July 3, when Federal forces launched an attack on Culp's Hill, retaking it after seven fierce hours of combat. Yet Lee believed the Union was living on borrowed time at Gettysburg. On the first day, he had gained much. On the second, he had failed to bring the battle to a close, but, as he saw it, he had worn down the Union defenders. Yes, they clung to their high ground, but, he believed, only by their very fingernails. This day, July 3, 1863, would finish them, provided he could mount an overwhelming final assault.

As usual, Longstreet, like the doomsaying Cassandra of Greek myth, objected, warning that the Union men were fighting like devils, were strongly positioned, enjoyed superior numbers, and were all very much aware of what was at stake. They did not intend to lose.

Lee's counter to this argument was not so much that victory was clearly in his grasp

*Jeb Stuart's brigade renews the Confederate attack on Culp's Hill on July 3, in an unsuccessful effort to retake it from the Union.*

as it was that too much blood had already been spent to abandon the field now. He ordered a massive infantry charge, head-on. Of this Longstreet later wrote, "My heart was heavy. I could see the desperate and hopeless nature of the charge and the hopeless slaughter it would cause. That day at Gettysburg was one of the saddest of my life."

*Swedish-born American illustrator Thure de Thulstrup (1848–1930) painted this depiction of Pickett's Charge.*

It would be called "Pickett's Charge," though Major General George Pickett led but three of the nine brigades Lee committed to it. Generals James Johnston Pettigrew and Isaac Ridgeway Trimble led the other six brigades, taking three each. Against the background roar of relentless musketry, Pickett and the others formed their ranks as if for a parade. And a parade it would be, clear across the mile of open field separating the principal Confederate lines from the Union soldiers occupying Cemetery Ridge.

One hundred and fifty Confederate Napoleons opened up against the ridge in a bid to soften resistance there. Instead, the salvos succeeded only in eliciting even heavier return fire from the Union artillery. The war had occasioned plenty of artillery exchanges before, but never had there been such a massive and sustained antiphonal duel, each side replying to the other, the replies overlapping in a grotesque babble of detonation, whoosh, impact, explosion, and the cries of the wounded and the dying.

At 1:45, the Confederate guns fell silent, and nine Confederate brigades, 12,500 men, rank on gray rank, marched forward, first at a walk and then, on closer approach to the enemy, at a trot. Suddenly there arose from this multitude the now-familiar keening of the "rebel yell" that was first heard at the first battle of Bull Run. At this signal, the trot became a run.

*Artist Edwin Forbes was behind the breastworks of the Union position at Culp's Hill on July 3, 1863. Union rifle and artillery fire from this and other positions decimated Pickett's Charge, General Lee's doomed effort to turn the tide at Gettysburg.*

Up and down the rows of Union cannoneers, the order was passed to exchange solid shot for canister, the deadly antipersonnel ammunition that sprayed grape-sized iron shot and jagged shrapnel across the field of fire. Aligned wheel to wheel, the Federal guns transformed the space below Cemetery Ridge into a plain swept by metallic missiles.

"Over on Cemetery Ridge the Federals beheld a scene which has never previously been enacted," George Pickett wrote to his fiancée the night after the charge, "an army forming in line of battle in full view. . . ."

They watched it form, and they watched it advance, each wave seeming to break as men fell under the canisters' deadly impact. But still, the advance continued, and when the first ranks approached too close for artillery fire, the Union men opened up with their rifle muskets, shooting from high-ground cover.

One Union soldier later described the approach of Pickett's Charge as "an overwhelming relentless tide of an ocean of armed men sweeping upon us! On the move, as with one soul in perfect order . . . magnificent, grim, irresistible." Pickett himself wrote that night: "My brave boys were so full of hope and confident of victory as I led them forth!" He painted for his distant sweetheart a picture of them "charging across a space nearly a mile in length, pride and glory soon to be crushed by an overwhelming heartbreak," only to trail off in an epistolary murmur. "Well, it is all over now. The awful rain of shot and shell was a sob—a gasp."

It was over now, but, even as Pickett wrote his letter he could "still hear them cheering as I gave the order, 'Forward!' the thrill of their joyous voices as they called out, 'We'll follow you, Marse George, we'll follow you!' On, how faithfully they followed me on—on—to their death, and I led them on—on—on—Oh God!"

To his sweetheart, Pickett apologized that he could not "write . . . a love letter today," telling her that, but for her, he "would rather, a million times rather, sleep in an unmarked grave." That was the very fate that met two of three brigadier generals leading the charge on the afternoon of July 3. The third brigadier was severely wounded, and every regimental commander—fifteen in all—were likewise killed or wounded. Of the 12,500 soldiers who began Pickett's Charge, five thousand returned from it. There was a place on Cemetery Ridge, it was known as the Angle, at which a hundred fifty men with Brigadier General Lewis Armistead at their head broke through to plant the Confederate colors. The flag waved briefly over the Union-held position before Armistead was killed, all his men killed or captured, and the flag torn down.

*Confederate victims of Union artillery fire from the Round Top batteries: "Well, it is all over now," George Pickett wrote to his fiancée of the Confederate infantry charge history has named after him. "The awful rain of shot and shell was a sob—a gasp."*

## NUMBERS

### These Honored Dead

A total of 88,289 Union soldiers fought at Gettysburg; 3,155 of them were killed, 14,529 were wounded, mortally wounded, or captured; and 5,365 went missing. Of an estimated 70,226 Confederates engaged, 3,903 were killed, 18,735 wounded, and 5,425 reported missing or captured.

# "ALL MY FAULT"

NEARLY TWO-THIRDS OF THE MEN in Pickett's Charge lay dead on a Pennsylvania field. "It was all my fault," Lee said to Longstreet, and, having said that, he continued: "Get together, and let us do the best we can toward saving which is left us."

> "On the Fourth—far from a glorious Fourth to us or to any with love for his fellowmen—I wrote you just a line of heartbreak. The sacrifice of life on that bloodsoaked field on the fatal 3rd was too awful for the heralding of victory, even for our victorious foe, who, I think, believe as we do, that it decided the fate of our cause. No words can picture the anguish of that roll call—the breathless waits between the responses. The 'Here' of those who, by God's mercy, had miraculously escaped the awful rain of shot and shell was a sob—a gasp—a knell—for the unanswered name of his comrade called before his. There was no tone of thankfulness for having been spared to answer to their names, but rather a toll and an unvoiced wish that they, too, had been among the missing."

*George E. Pickett, letter to his fiancée, July 6, 1863*

So the retreat began and, with it, the withdrawal of any rational hope for a Confederate victory in the Civil War. Meade and his commanders had turned back an invasion of the United States, had prevented an attack on Washington, and had preserved the administration of Abraham Lincoln, together with his intention to fight the war through to victory. That was a momentous achievement, but if Meade had been Grant, he would doubtless have achieved far more—or tried to.

The three days of Gettysburg took such a horrific toll on the Army of the Potomac that Meade thought he had no choice but to rest his men. In doing so, he allowed the Army of Northern Virginia to limp back into Virginia, depleted but intact. At news of this, Abraham Lincoln could only exclaim: "My God, is that all?"

# CHAPTER 15

## A NEW BIRTH OF FREEDOM?

*Issues of Race and Resolve*

FEW HISTORIES FAIL TO IDENTIFY THE UNION VICTORY AT GETTYSBURG, in combination with that at Vicksburg the following day, as the turning point of the Civil War, yet, in the summer of 1863, the news of these victories did not have a decisively dramatic impact on the public. In the South, the economy and morale continued to decline, perhaps somewhat more sharply than before, even as the hardships of daily life continued to multiply. In the North, there were still many people who agitated for an immediate end to the war through a negotiated settlement with the South. Ideas concerning the nature of such a settlement ranged from inviting the seceded states back into the Union with explicit constitutional protection for slavery to ratifying the legality of secession by cordially agreeing to let the Confederacy exist. The polite name for those who favored ending the war through negotiation was "Peace Democrat," but most pro-Union Northerners referred to them more bluntly as "Copperheads," picking up a term first printed in the *New York Tribune* on July 21, 1861, in which the Peace Democrats were compared to those venomous snakes in the grass, especially abundant in the South, which strike without warning.

THE COPPERHEAD PARTY.—IN FAVOR OF A VIGOROUS PROSECUTION OF PEACE!

*Members of the "Copperhead party," who favored a negotiated settlement with the Confederacy—are depicted menacing "Columbia," symbolizing the United States, who defends herself with a sword and the shield of "Union."*

The point was this: Union victories at Gettysburg and Vicksburg may have somewhat accelerated the decline of morale in the South, but they did not dramatically invigorate the war will of the North. The Civil War pitted the Confederacy against the Union, but even within both regions, there was significant dissonance and dissent. Neither "nation" was truly unified.

## ARMIES OF THE UNWILLING

DESPITE HIGH-FLOWN CLAIMS OF PATRIOTISM, by 1863 Confederate soldiers were deserting in ever larger numbers. In July of that year, after Vicksburg and Gettysburg, an estimated fifty to one hundred thousand of them walked away, though desertion rates had been quite high from the beginning of the war and continued so through to the end. On October 6, 1864, for instance, the Richmond *Enquirer* reported that President Davis had announced that "two-thirds of the Army are absent from the ranks." If this was true, Confederate deserters had come to outnumber Confederate soldiers.

Critically short of manpower, the Confederacy, which had broken with the Union in a declared protest of federal tyranny, enacted a conscription law on April 16, 1862, nearly a year before the Union would do the same. The law obliged all white males ages eighteen to thirty-five to give three years of service. Before the end of the year, the upper age limit was advanced to forty-five, and in February 1864, to fifty, while the lower limit was rolled back to age seventeen. None of the Confederate draft laws made an attempt to be equitable. Like those later enacted in the North, they provided two alternatives to service—for anyone with the means to pay for them. A draftee could stay out of the army by paying the government a commutation fee or by hiring an acceptable substitute to serve in his place. In the Confederacy, men who either owned or oversaw twenty slaves or more were also automatically exempt.

The Union enacted a conscription law on March 3, 1863. Like the Confederate law, it gave the well-to-do a way of avoiding service, either by hiring a substitute or by paying a $300 commutation fee—this at a

*A recruitment poster for a New Jersey regiment, published in the summer of 1863. Each state had a monthly quota of volunteers it was expected to deliver into the federal service.*

THE VOLUNTARY MANNER IN WHICH SOME OF THE SOUTHERN VOLUNTEERS ENLIST.

*The lithographic firm of Currier & Ives, best known for quaint decorative prints, also published elaborate social and political cartoons, such as this one lampooning "The voluntary manner in which some of the Southern volunteers enlist." Bayonets in the rear and plenty of whiskey up front, the cartoon implies, were the essential ingredients of Confederate volunteerism.*

time when a common laborer earned approximately a dollar a day. It should be noted that the Union army, which enlisted a total of 2,778,304 men during the war, remained overwhelmingly a volunteer force. Just 52,068 conscripts were actually held to service during the entire war; an additional 86,724 conscripted men paid the $300 commutation fee to receive exemption, and 42,581 hired substitutes. Nevertheless, passage of the conscription laws, widely and accurately perceived as unjustly exploiting the ordinary working man, touched off demonstrations, even riots, in New York, Iowa, Illinois, Indiana, and Ohio.

> "In giving freedom to the slave, we assure freedom to the *free*—honorable alike in what we give, and what we preserve. We shall nobly save or meanly lose the last, best hope of earth."
>
> Abraham Lincoln, annual message to Congress,
> December 1, 1862

## New York Riots

The worst was the New York City Draft Riots, which began on Monday, July 13, 1863, in response to the commencement of the draft in the city and within days of the victories at Gettysburg and Vicksburg. A newspaper reporter, Joel T. Headley, described how "a ragged, coatless, heterogeneously weaponed army" of rioters "heaved tumultuously along toward Third Avenue," tearing down telegraph poles as they crossed the Harlem & New Haven Railroad track, then surging "angrily up around the building where the drafting was going on." They broke into the draft office, seized the draft lottery wheel, and destroyed whatever books, papers, and lists they encountered. Finding a safe, some of the rioters attempted to break into it. When this failed, they put the building to the torch and then stormed the Second Avenue armory, looted it, and proceeded to ransack a variety of Third Avenue stores, including jewelry and liquor establishments.

And then the riot took a new turn, both terrible and revelatory, as marauding gangs broke off from the principal mob and ran down those African Americans unfortunate enough to be out and about that afternoon. Some they beat, some they beat to death, and some they hanged from lampposts.

The majority of rioters were immigrants, many of them recently arrived from the desperate poverty of Ireland, almost all of them the commonest of common laborers, who barely scratched out a living at the bottom of the socioeconomic ladder. They believed the draft treated them unfairly, that it required them to risk their lives in a war to free slaves who would grab the jobs right out from under them. They believed they were being called to fight a war to take the bread from the very mouths of their families, and they turned their rage not against the lawmakers but against members of a race they feared

Frank Leslie's Illustrated Newspaper *published this New York City recruiting scene on March 19, 1864. In both the North and the South, most soldiers voluntarily enlisted—moved by patriotism, a thirst for adventure, the lure of an enlistment bonus, peer pressure, or some combination of these motives.*

and hated. On Monday afternoon, a mob set fire to Manhattan's Colored Orphan Asylum, then stood back to cheer the blaze and the screams of those burning within. It rained on Tuesday, but on Wednesday, rioters roamed the black neighborhoods, wrecking the clapboard houses, tearing many down with their bare hands.

On Wednesday evening, a large contingent of Union troops marched into New York City. They had come from Gettysburg, and they were in no mood to treat the rioters any way but harshly. They fired canister shot into the mob, one witness recalling that the streets "were swept again and again" by artillery that had so recently been used against the Confederates who charged Cemetery Ridge. The troops stormed houses "at the point of a bayonet," he reported, and "rioters were picked off by sharpshooters as they fired on the troops from housetops; men were hurled, dying or dead, into the streets." It did not take Meade's battle-hardened veterans long to suppress the New York City Draft Riots, though spasms of violence continued to shake nearby Brooklyn, Jamaica, Staten Island, Jersey City, Newark, and, more distantly, Albany and Troy, New York; Boston; Portsmouth, New Hampshire; and portions of Kentucky and Wisconsin. Two Pennsylvania counties near Philadelphia also saw violence, the cause of which one newspaper editor summed up under an ugly headline:

*The "Draft Riots" of July 1863 were driven by a powerful racial component. Some members of the working class, struggling immigrants mostly, were outraged by the prospect of fighting to free slaves, who, they feared, would migrate to the North and take their jobs.*

WILLING TO FIGHT FOR UNCLE SAM
BUT NOT FOR UNCLE SAMBO

In New York and elsewhere, draft riots were race riots.

## CONSPIRACY THEORY

THE HISTORIAN SAMUEL ELIOT MORISON has called the destruction done in New York the "equivalent of a Confederate victory" in battle, and, indeed, many Northerners believed the riots had not erupted spontaneously but were the result of deliberate provocation engineered by undercover Confederate agents and Copperheads. The latter, it is true, made no secret of their fear that Union victory in the Civil

### NUMBERS
**The Cost of Riot**
The distinguished modern Civil War historian James M. McPherson puts the death toll of the New York Draft Riots at 120 and estimates that some 2,000 persons were injured. Property damage amounted to a million 1863 dollars, with fifty buildings a total loss.

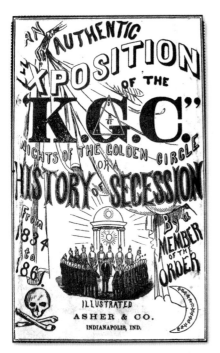

*Copperhead groups often organized them-selves into secret societies, the largest of which was the Knights of the Golden Circle, most popular in Indiana and Ohio.*

War would bring about a nation "swarming" with "free negroes," and they further believed (with con-siderable justification) that Republican extremists, the so-called Radical Republicans, intended to use the war as an excuse to permanently dismantle the Democratic Party and thereby impose one-party rule on the United States. In some places, especially the Midwest, Copperheads organized themselves into secret societies with such names as Knights of the Golden Circle and the Sons of Liberty.

Most of these groups were toothless gatherings of gripers and racists, but Indiana governor Oliver Morton was so fearful of Copperhead activity in his state that he persuaded Secretary of War Edwin Stanton to send Brigadier General Henry B. Carrington to Indianapolis to organize an undercover counter-insurgency to infiltrate the secret societies. Little of a truly sinister nature was discovered, except that some Copperheads were clearly aiding and abetting one John Hunt Morgan, the Confederate leader of Morgan's Raiders, who, among other operations,

*Harper's Weekly (August 15, 1863) published this etching of John Hunt Morgan's raid on Washington, Ohio. Terrifying, daring, and thrilling, Morgan's raids had no strategic impact on the war.*

# FORGOTTEN FACES: A MAN CALLED MORGAN

John Hunt Morgan (1825–64) was a native of Huntsville, Alabama, whose family moved to Lexington, Kentucky, after his father's pharmacy failed and he lost the family home. Young Morgan enrolled in Transylvania College, only to be suspended in his sophomore year for dueling. He enlisted in the U.S. Army in 1846 as a cavalry private during the U.S.-Mexican War, then went into business, but never lost his interest in military matters. He raised a militia artillery battery in 1852, then a private infantry company, the "Lexington Rifles," in 1857.

**M**organ did not initially support secession, and even believed Lincoln would prove to be a good president, but soon came to feel that the Union was victimizing the Southern states, and in July 1861, Morgan took his militia company to Tennessee and there joined the Confederate army. He raised the 2nd Kentucky Cavalry Regiment, becoming its colonel and leading it at the battle of Shiloh. He soon discovered, however, that his real talents lay in what was called "irregular warfare" and conducted highly disruptive raids throughout Kentucky.

*This idealized portrait remains the most widely known image of John Hunt Morgan. It first appeared years after the Civil War and contributed to the spread of an enduring fame that is grossly out of proportion to his actual role in the course of the conflict.*

Promoted to brigadier general on December 11, 1862, he received the formal thanks of the Confederate Congress on May 1, 1863. That summer, he led his men across the Ohio River to raid southern Indiana and Ohio. Most of his raiders were captured on July 19, 1863, at Buffington Island, Ohio, and Morgan, with the rest of his men, also surrendered in Ohio eight days later.

Lodged in the Ohio Penitentiary, Morgan and a half dozen of his top officers tunneled out of their cells and made good their escape. Aided by Copperheads, they returned to Confederate territory. Although the Indiana-Ohio raid terrorized the region, the capture of the raiders deprived the Confederacy of their most skillful light cavalrymen. Morgan organized a new unit of raiders and once again invaded Kentucky. The new men, however, behaved more like bandits than soldiers, and the Confederate military establishment was contemplating Morgan's removal from command when he was killed on September 4, 1864, by Union forces raiding Greeneville, Tennessee.

*"Morgan's Men" pose comfortably in the Western Penitentiary, where they were imprisoned. Left to right: Captain William E. Curry, Lieutenant Andrew J. Church, Lieutenant Leeland Hathaway, Lieutenant Henry D. Brown, and Lieutenant William Hays. Morgan himself was not photographed with this group.*

staged the longest cavalry raid of the war. From July 2 to July 26, 1863, Morgan and his men covered seven hundred miles and terrorized parts of Indiana and Ohio, plundering homes and businesses, wrecking railroads and bridges, and looting whatever wasn't nailed down tight. Morgan was captured at Lisbon, Ohio, on July 26, but managed to escape from the Ohio State Penitentiary. It was said that he was an agent of a "Great Northwest Conspiracy" intended to foment revolution in Ohio, Indiana, Kentucky, and Illinois. If so, it came to nothing, though the discontented and disturbing talk continued throughout the war.

## STANDING UP

IF MANY WHITE NORTHERNERS objected to fighting a "war for the Negro," a growing number of African Americans, including fugitive slaves, freed slaves, and Northerners who had never been slaves, were no longer content to see *their* freedom defended exclusively by white men. In August 1861, Frederick Douglass, a former slave, self-educated, whose extraordinary autobiography had catapulted him to the forefront of the abolition movement before the war, made eloquent public pleas for the enlistment of black soldiers, as did other prominent figures, white and black. At every turn, such pleas met with resistance. Some whites, both military and civilian, simply could not tolerate the thought of an African American in the uniform of the United States Army. Others believed the "African race" was inherently inferior to the white race and claimed that, through no fault of their own, black men were cowardly and untrainable. Still others feared arming former slaves, who might turn indiscriminately against all whites, Union and Confederate. And even some well-meaning white officers predicted that, far from aiding the war effort, the presence of African American soldiers in the Union army would enrage and rally Southerners, lifting the morale and the resolve of the Confederate armies. Even Abraham Lincoln worried that recruiting black soldiers might send the border states into the Confederate fold.

*"Make way for liberty!" was part of an illustrated album titled "The Slave in 1863," published in Philadelphia that year. The image of an African American soldier attacking a Confederate with a bayonet was intended to lay to rest widespread doubts about the martial prowess of the "colored race."*

" MAKE WAY FOR LIBERTY!"

> "Neither confiscation of property, political execution of persons, territorial organization of States, or forcible abolition of slavery, should be contemplated for a moment.... Military power should not be allowed to interfere with the relations of servitude either by supporting or impairing the authority of the master, except for repressing disorder."

> *Major General George B. McClellan,*
> *letter to President Abraham Lincoln, July 7, 1862*

Despite the resistance, during the spring of 1862, Major General David Hunter raised an African American regiment, consisting of volunteers as well as men he drafted, to help garrison the Union-occupied Sea Islands of South Carolina. When the War Department objected, Hunter disbanded the regiment, save for a single company. That summer, in August, Major General Benjamin Butler took it upon himself to recruit three black regiments as the Louisiana Native Guard, or Corps d'Afrique, to help garrison New Orleans. They began active service in November, even though the War Department declined to muster them in officially. In Kansas, militia officer James H. Lane raised two regiments of fugitive slaves and free blacks, which were committed to combat before the War Department recognized them in 1863.

*The "Band of the 107th U.S. Colored Infantry" was photographed in November 1865 by William M. Smith. Civil War photographs of black soldiers are remarkably rare.*

**NUMBERS**

**Black Roll Call**

Although all U.S. Army "colored" formations were commanded by white officers, a small number of African Americans (fewer than 100) were commissioned before the war ended. The highest rank any held was major, which was conferred on 8 African American army surgeons. On the day the war ended, U.S. Army muster rolls listed 178,985 African Americans serving in 166 segregated regiments. Some 37,300 black soldiers died in the Civil War, and 16 African American soldiers and sailors received the Medal of Honor.

With the Second Confiscation Act of July 17, 1862, Congress began to catch up with field commanders who were already recruiting African Americans. The law authorized the president to "employ as many persons of African descent as he might deem necessary and proper for the suppression of the rebellion." The following month, on August 25, the War Department officially authorized the military governor of the South Carolina Sea Islands to raise five regiments of "colored" troops, and on November 7 these were formed up as the First South Carolina Volunteers. Following the final Emancipation Proclamation of January 1, 1863, President Lincoln personally called for four black regiments, and by war's end, 10 percent of the Union army was African American.'

"Thair is a great controversy out hear about the nigger Question . . . . If they go to Sending them out hear to fight they will get Enough of it for it Will raise a rebellion in the army that all the abolitionist this side of Hell could not stop. The Southern People are rebels to government but they are White and God never intended a nigger to put White People down."

*Sergeant Enoch T. Baker, U.S. Army, 1863*

*African Americans served in the U.S. Navy long before the army accepted "colored troops." During the Civil War, 15 percent of naval personnel were African Americans.*

All African American soldiers were strictly segregated into "colored" regiments commanded by white officers. Typically, black troops were less well clothed, less well fed, and were armed with weapons often deemed too old or obsolescent for white soldiers to use. For much of the war, they were paid at a lower rate than their white counterparts. Although black soldiers fought and died in combat—the troops of the 54th Massachusetts Regiment under Colonel Robert Gould Shaw, for example, became legendary—most were restricted to duty as laborers.

Treated shabbily by the country they served, African American soldiers faced even greater dangers than whites. On May 1, 1863, the Confederate Congress authorized President Davis to "put to death or . . . otherwise [punish]" any black soldiers captured as prisoners of war. The same fate was promised to white officers found in command of black troops. This law prompted President Lincoln to respond on July 30 with an executive order warning that "for every soldier of the United States killed in violation of the laws of war, a Rebel soldier shall be executed; and for every one enslaved by the enemy or sold into Slavery, a Rebel soldier shall be placed at hard labor on public works."

Even as President Jefferson Davis vowed to execute black troops captured in the Union service, with Confederate white manpower dwindling, the Richmond Congress authorized in February 1864 conscription of free blacks as well as slaves for "auxiliary" (noncombat) military service in the Confederate army. On March 13, 1865, that Congress passed a Negro Soldier Law, which allowed the recruitment, but not conscription, of slaves as combat soldiers. Service did not automatically bring freedom. Only with the "consent of the owners and of the States" could volunteers be emancipated. Although a handful of African American Confederate troops were enlisted, none took the field before the war ended, and recent claims that slaves actually fought for the Confederacy are false.

*The 54th Massachusetts Regiment under Colonel Robert Gould Shaw became legendary for its courage after its doomed assault on July 18, 1863, against Fort Wagner on the South Carolina coast.*

## POP CULTURE
### Glory

In 1897, a superb bronze bas-relief sculpture by Augustus Saint-Gaudens was dedicated on Boston Common to memorialize the heroism of Robert Gould Shaw and the men of the 54th Massachusetts Regiment. In 1989, *Glory*, one of the best in a long line of movie depictions of the Civil War, brought an awareness of Shaw and the 54th to a new generation. The film culminates in the regiment's magnificent but doomed assault on Fort Fisher's Battery Wagner on the South Carolina coast, in which 281 of the 600 men engaged, including Shaw, were killed. Seeking to dishonor the white colonel, the Confederates threw his body into a mass grave with those of his African American soldiers. Learning of this, Shaw's father spoke on behalf of his family: "We can imagine no holier place than in which he lies."

*Lincoln delivers his Gettysburg Address at the dedication of the Soldiers' National Cemetery on November 19, 1863. This early twentieth-century illustration is entirely fanciful; Lincoln's nearly comical oratorical stance is out of character both with himself and his message.*

## LINCOLN DEFINES GETTYSBURG

THE VICTORIES AT GETTYSBURG AND VICKSBURG lifted great weight from Abraham Lincoln's heart, but failed to spontaneously galvanize the national resolve to fight through to victory. Doubtless, the president hoped that the dedication of the Soldiers' National Cemetery at Gettysburg on November 19, 1863, would help the country to accept the terrible cost of victory. He hadn't, however, planned on speaking personally at the dedication and was invited to do so only at the last minute to add no more than a grace note to the featured speech of Edward Everett, generally regarded as the nation's

*The "Nicolay Copy," preserved by President Lincoln's secretary and biographer, John Nicolay, is believed to be the earliest copy of the Gettysburg Address and may even have been the very document from which the president read on November 19, 1863.*

Executive Mansion,

Washington,                    , 186

Four score and seven years ago our fathers brought forth, upon this continent, a new nation, conceived in liberty, and dedicated to the proposition that "all men are created equal"

Now we are engaged in a great civil war, testing whether that nation, or any nation so conceived and so dedicated, can long endure. We are met on a great battle field of that war. We have come to dedicate a portion of it, as a final resting place for those who died here, that the nation might live. This we may, in all propriety do. But, in a larger sense, we can not dedicate— we can not consecrate— we can not hallow, this ground— The brave men, living and dead, who struggled here, have hallowed it, far above our poor power to add or detract. The world will little note, nor long remember what we say here; while it can never forget what they did here.

It is rather for us, the living, to stand here,

greatest orator. Everett spoke for two hours, Lincoln for two minutes, but it is Lincoln's "Gettysburg Address" that the nation and the world remembers. Lincoln's speech concentrated as no pronouncement before or since the meaning of the war as a test of whether a nation "conceived in Liberty, and dedicated to the proposition that all men are created equal . . . can long endure." The men who gave their lives to pass this test, Lincoln said, had challenged "us the living . . . to be dedicated here to [their] unfinished work." He called on the nation to take "from these honored dead . . . increased devotion to that cause for which they gave the last full measure of devotion" and to "highly resolve that these dead shall not have died in vain—that this nation, under God, shall have a new birth of freedom—and that government of the people, by the people, for the people, shall not perish from the earth."

*The real thing: This photograph is the only confirmed image of the president at the dedication of the Soldiers' National Cemetery, November 19, 1863. Blurred by movement, Lincoln, hatless, is visible roughly four rows from the top and approximately fourth to the right of the furled flag.*

## TAKEAWAY

Despite the turning-point Union victories at Gettysburg and Vicksburg, the Confederacy grimly fought on, and the Union remained deeply divided between those determined to prosecute the war to absolute victory and those who wanted to negotiate with the Confederacy an immediate end. In the North, the most divisive issue was race. While many Northerners had embraced the Emancipation Proclamation as the moral core of the conflict, many others were outraged at being called on to fight a "war to free the slaves" or a "war for the Negro." This sentiment ignited draft riots and incited at least some Northern aid to Confederate insurgents. At the dedication of the Soldiers' National Cemetery at Gettysburg on November 19, 1863, Abraham Lincoln delivered his most famous speech, the Gettysburg Address, which sought to unify the Union's resolve to carry the heartbreaking struggle through to final victory.

PART SIX

# TOTAL WAR

# CHAPTER 16

## MUD AND CLOUDS

*Chattanooga to Chickamauga to Chattanooga*

I N MOST WARS, TURNING-POINT BATTLES TRIGGER A RAPID SERIES OF INTENSE events, clearly pushing toward the conflict's final decision. Not so in the Civil War. After Vicksburg and Gettysburg, except for the spasms of violence on the Union home front ignited by the commencement of the draft and the panic caused by Morgan's nearly month-long raid in Indiana and Ohio (Chapter 15), the war slipped into the somnambulism of exhaustion.

America's warriors had reason to be tired. Meade could not bring himself to lead his battered Army of the Potomac in pursuit of Lee, who, encountering a Potomac swollen with floods, lingered tantalizingly in Maryland before crossing to Virginia, ordering his Gettysburg veterans to dig in at Williamsport. Even given this opportunity, Meade refrained from attack, thereby allowing Lee to slip his forces into Virginia on July 14, with Major General Harry Heth fighting a rearguard action against Union cavalry pursuers at Falling Waters, Maryland. The Confederates lost a brigadier in the battle, James J. Pettigrew, mortally wounded, but the cavalry could do only so much in the absence of determined support from Meade, and although Federal commanders did their best to puff up the significance of the exchange, the battle of Falling Waters quickly receded into deserved historical obscurity.

## A CHANGE OF SCENE

LIKE THE ARMY OF THE POTOMAC, the Union's Army of the Tennessee had ample cause for fatigue, but its commanding general, Ulysses S. Grant, was made of different stuff from George Gordon Meade. Grant understood that if *he* and *his* men were tired, the enemy must be nearly spent, and so he proposed advancing deep into southern Mississippi and Alabama to do his best to do them in. He wanted most of all to capture Mobile, Alabama, not just because it was a major port city (blockaded though it was by Scott's Anaconda), but because doing so would force Braxton Bragg to leave Chattanooga to defend it. This would give Grant an opportunity to defeat more of Bragg's army at Mobile while also forcing the Confederates to weaken Chattanooga, thereby yielding the city that controlled passage along the Tennessee River. For Grant, taking territory was always less about seizing land than it was about disrupting supply and communication and pushing the enemy into the very place you wanted him to be.

Thus, the principal scene of war began a shift from the eastern theater to central Tennessee and northern Georgia, but, thanks to Union general in chief Henry Halleck, it did so very, very slowly. Clinging to the outworn doctrine of passively holding territory at all costs, "Old Brains" insisted on widely dispersing and therefore diluting Grant's army. Instead of allowing him to consolidate and move against the enemy army, Halleck had Grant planting men in Louisiana, Missouri, Arkansas, and in idle garrison units in Union-occupied Tennessee and Mississippi.

Frank Leslie's Illustrated Newspaper *(August 8, 1863) included an illustration of the 6th Michigan Cavalry making a "gallant charge . . . over the enemy's breastworks" at Falling Waters, Maryland, July 14, 1863, during the battle of Williamsport.*

**PREVIOUS SPREAD:** *Sherman vowed to "make Georgia howl" with his "March to the Sea," depicted here by F. O. C. Darley, the dean of nineteenth-century American book illustrators, better known for embellishing the books of Cooper, Hawthorne, Irving, and Dickens than commemorating the ravages of war.*

*Major General
William S. "Old Rosy"
Rosecrans, compe-
tent if phlegmatic,
was destined for dis-
grace at the battle of
Chickamauga.*

# OLD ROSY MOVES

AGAINST GRANT'S WILL, his Army of the Tennessee was broadcast over much of the middle South, leaving the Army of the Cumberland, under William Starke "Old Rosy" Rosecrans, to do battle alone with Braxton Bragg and his Confederate Army of Tennessee. The two commanders had been trading punches since the end of October 1862, and, at the battle of Stones River, Tennessee (December 30, 1862–January 3, 1863), Old Rosy narrowly avoided a serious defeat. Grant wanted to help him take Chattanooga, then launch him back east to Knoxville, thereby seizing control of the eastern half of a Confederate state harboring so much Union support that it would probably rejoin the Union if its two principal cities were taken.

Even while Grant was still occupied at Vicksburg (Chapter 13), Rosecrans felt upon the back of his neck the impatient breath of Abraham Lincoln. The president had had his fill of McClellan and his ilk and was in no mood for excuses about having to delay action against Chattanooga. Old Rosy was enough of a big-picture strategist to understand that once Grant crossed the Mississippi below Vicksburg on May 1, 1863, Bragg would almost certainly feel compelled to send reinforcements to the imperiled Mississippi River fortress. Rosecrans and Grant agreed that the Army of the Cumberland would move to block Bragg and prevent this reinforcement. True, it took Rosecrans until June to finally get the Army of the Cumberland on the move, but once it was moving, he out-generaled Bragg with it, pushing him south of the Tennessee River. Then, through seventeen days of early summer rains, Rosecrans maneuvered the Army of the Cumberland into position behind Bragg's right flank near Tullahoma, Tennessee.

Through skillful pursuit, Rosecrans pushed and shoved Bragg in such a way that he kept him many miles from Vicksburg. That was his mission, but once it was accomplished, he did not let up. On July 4, the very day Vicksburg fell to Grant, Rosecrans executed another brilliant flanking movement, which forced the outnumbered Bragg to withdraw from Tullahoma and fall back on Chattanooga.

And this is just where Old Rosy wanted Bragg. More important, it is where Abraham Lincoln wanted his general to put him. Yet Rosecrans's pleas for reinforcements sufficient to capture Chattanooga fell on Halleck's deaf ears, and so Old Rosy kept his army marching and maneuvering, at least forcing Bragg into a confusion of anticipation—until, all of a sudden, Rosecrans crossed the Army of the Cumberland over the Tennessee River thirty miles west of Chattanooga.

When Ambrose Burnside felt the insistent push of Abraham Lincoln as he and the Army of the Potomac stood before Fredericksburg, he made fourteen suicidal frontal assaults on that well-prepared Confederate stronghold (Chapter 12). To Rosecrans's credit, much as he wanted to please Lincoln (he rightly felt his continuance in command depended on doing so), he refused to be goaded into a frontal assault. Instead, he continued the marching and maneuvering that had served him so well and advanced through a complex of gaps in Lookout Mountain. More an elongated ridge than a mountain, it runs south-southwest of Chattanooga, commanding—when not mysteriously enshrouded by mist and fog—a breathtaking view of the city. But Rosecrans's purpose was not to bombard Chattanooga from these heights. Instead, he aimed at the tracks of the Western and Atlantic Railroad, which traversed a Lookout Mountain gap, constituting Bragg's only line of supply and communications with Atlanta. It was the carotid artery of Chattanooga and thus also of the Army of Tennessee. By severing it, Rosecrans gave Bragg no alternative but to pull out of the city.

In a war characterized by so many tragic missteps and missed opportunities, each almost always drowned in blood, it was a brilliant achievement. Practically without firing a shot, Old Rosy had won a great strategic prize on the Moccasin Bend of the Tennessee.

## IGNORANT ARMIES

ROSECRANS HAD BEEN SLOW to begin his campaign, but once it was under way, he marched and marched and marched. Having taken Chattanooga, he should have stayed there, consolidating his forces and awaiting the reinforcements from Grant that even the shortsighted Halleck was sure to release to him by and by. Perhaps still feeling the less-than-gentle hand of Lincoln at his back, or all too aware that most of his fellow commanders had been quite rightly faulted for standing still too often and too long, or maybe because he sensed greater glory to be won on the horizon, the usually slow and deliberate Rosecrans

> **DETAILS, DETAILS**
> **The Definite Article**
> Recall that both the Union and the Confederacy named their field armies geographically, the Union after the nearest principal river (Army of *the* Tennessee) and the Confederacy after a state or portion of a state (Army of Tennessee). This can lead to confusion for a reader who fails to look out for the *the* or its absence. Take care.

*An early twentieth-century view of the Tennessee River's Moccasin Bend as seen from Lookout Mountain.*

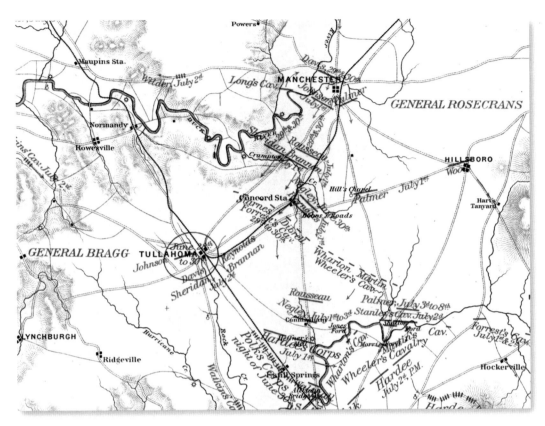

*This 1891 publication was created directly from a U.S. Army map of the Middle Tennessee and Chattanooga campaigns of June–September 1863.*

acted against his own nature and flogged the three tired corps of the Army of the Cumberland into continuing the active offensive against a retreating Bragg.

This strategy could have worked if Rosecrans had nothing but plains and gently rolling hills ahead of him. But getting out of Chattanooga required leading his sixty-thousand men through rugged mountain passes. In these, the units of the Army of the Cumberland soon became separated, their bewilderment heaped upon the exhaustion of months of long marches. As for Bragg, he had stopped at LaFayette, Georgia, twenty-five miles south of Chattanooga, where he rendezvoused with reinforcements, among them two full divisions under the command of James Longstreet. It would now be Bragg and Longstreet's turn to give Old Rosy his comeuppance. They prepared to counterattack the straggling, footsore columns of the Army of the Cumberland at a place of twisted, swampy growth along the passage of Chickamauga Creek into Georgia, less than a dozen miles south of Chattanooga.

Ten years before the Civil War began, the British poet Matthew Arnold stood on Dover's shore along the English Channel, gazed upon the twilit beach, and wrote of feeling as if he stood "on a darkling plain / Swept with confused alarms of struggle and flight, / Where ignorant armies clash by night." On the night of September 18, 1863, Rosecrans, Bragg, Longstreet, and their officers and men would have understood these lines all too well. In the dark, commanders on both sides were vaguely aware of one another's presence but of precise location, strength, and disposition, profoundly ignorant. Both sides moved troops through the moonless, muddy tangle, hoping to jockey for the most advantageous position. But in those thick Georgia woods, lightless, neither side really knew where the other was, and, what is even worse, amid all the movements, no commander was even fully aware of the disposition of his own troops. It was blind man's bluff about to be played by 125,000 men—60,000 Union, 65,000 Confederate—each man armed to the teeth.

*Union brigadier general John Brannan led a reconnaissance force that made first contact with the Confederate forces of Nathan Bedford Forrest on the banks of the Chickamauga near Lee and Gordon's Mill. This was the commencement of the battle of Chickamauga.*

## BATTLE AT CHICKAMAUGA

AT SUNUP ON SEPTEMBER 19, Union general George Henry Thomas sent Brigadier General John Brannan with a reconnaissance force to probe the banks of the Chickamauga. Near Lee and Gordon's Mill, a dirty, white, two-story clapboard structure on the creek, Brannan's men encountered the dismounted cavalry of Confederate Nathan Bedford Forrest. In the initial skirmish, Forrest and his men, apparently beaten back, withdrew, doubtless to the accompaniment of Yankee *huzzah!*s.

But Forrest did not withdraw far—just far enough to round up adjacent infantry and assemble a counterattack, which exploded into a titanic battle. Within hours, every Confederate unit, but for two divisions purposely held in reserve,

*Lee and Gordon's Mill, where the battle of Chickamauga began.*

was engaged, as was every division of Rosecrans's three corps. The opposing sides traded a pounding of the most primitive sort: two armies, not arrayed in battle formation on some "field of glory," but firing on each other wildly from the cover of tree trunks, fallen logs, mounds of earth, whatever promised even the prayer of cover, often barely able to see the men whom they targeted.

> "What a terrible day it has been! Night approaches. What horrors will it bring forth? Surely if my comrades cannot help me I must die; and I must die here, with no friend to soothe my last moments or tell the story of my death to the loved ones at home. . . . Fever is in my veins, and I am perishing from thirst."
>
> *Union Private Arthur van Lisle,*
> *wounded at Chickamauga, September 19, 1863*

By nightfall, neither side had gained a clear advantage, and the confusion of the commanders—especially Rosecrans—had only increased. The Cumberland men dug in where they stood or lay, frantically scooping out impromptu trenches and rifle pits from earth that had been churned to soupy mud by incessant rain. Bragg, in the meantime, did his best to position reinforcements from Longstreet's division, feeling his way more than seeing it.

It was the Confederates who seized the initiative the next morning, Sunday, September 20, hitting the Federals hard for two hours, from nine to eleven. While the fight raged, Rosecrans strained every sense in the labor of getting his arms around the bewildering situation. Try as he might, the Union commander could not form the battle picture in his head; however, based on fragmentary reports that trickled in, he concluded that, whatever else was happening, a gap had opened up in his right flank. Through that morning, the gap, a gaping wound in his side, became the epicenter of his thoughts. A general should—and will—do anything to keep from being flanked, and so Rosecrans ordered troops from what he believed was his left wing to plug the gap he believed was on his right.

The "fog of war," the German military theorist Carl von Clausewitz had called it. He defined it as an inevitable companion of combat. Confusion, according to Clausewitz, was the rule, not the exception. Even the best commanders got lost in it. The fog of war fell now on the Union general. Not only was the supposed "gap" a figment, entirely nonexistent, the Chickamauga thicket worked upon Old Rosy's mind as if it were some cursedly enchanted ground out of a dark fairy tale. The place had literally bewildered him. There was no gap, and, believing that he was moving troops from his left wing to his right, he had actually moved them from the right to the left, thereby creating the very gap he had thought to fill.

And Longstreet saw him do it.

Unlike what had happened at Gettysburg when Dan Sickles inexplicably moved his III Corps out of position, exposing the Union flank (Chapter 14), Longstreet did not hesitate now. At 11:30, he sent everything he had into the freshly made hole in the Union line of battle, striking out at divisions under the command of Major General Philip Sheridan and Brigadier General Jefferson Columbus Davis (no relation to the Confederate president). Hit where they were most vulnerable,

*Published around 1890, this Kurz & Allison lithograph portrays Chickamauga as a glorious clash of gallant armies on an open field of battle. It was, in fact, a confused, dark, and bloody night-and-day fight in what was mostly a dense tangle of old-growth Georgia and Tennessee forest.*

## POP CULTURE
### River of Death

For years, both Civil War and local Georgia and Tennessee historians have pointed out the cruel symbolism of the name *Chickamauga*, which, they say, is a Cherokee word meaning "River of Death." Popular culture is always eager to embrace those episodes of history in which life seems to follow art, yet students of the Cherokee language have pointed out that *chickamauga*, though certainly of Cherokee origin, seems to have no definitive meaning. It may once have meant "river of death" (either because some long-forgotten inter- or intra-tribal battle was fought here, or because the creek was associated with one of the epidemics of smallpox that more than once swept through the Cherokee Nation), but others have suggested that it once meant something else, their translations ranging from "good country" to "stagnant water"—in addition to no discoverable meaning at all.

these divisions simply broke apart, creating what is to an army the equivalent of the collapse of a very tall building. As story falls into story, so man fell into man, the Union right smashing down hard into the Union left, a big part of the Army of the Cumberland imploding.

It was a terrible thing to see, to hear, and to feel. As there is only one outcome possible when one floor of a building falls into another, the result of one flank of an army driven into the other is also virtually certain: total collapse. Rosecrans and two of his corps commanders, Thomas Leonidas Crittenden (son of the Kentucky senator whose proposed compromise had failed to avert the war in 1861) and Alexander McDowell McCook, shouted orders in what they quickly came to judge a doomed effort to rally the troops. But a retreat—no, a rout—was already under way, and, believing the Army of the Cumberland was in the throes of its destruction, Rosecrans, Crittenden, and McCook joined the exodus of officers and men who were falling back on Chattanooga.

*Major General George H. Thomas, USA—the "Rock of Chickamauga."*

> "I have never seen the Federal dead lie so thickly on the ground, save in front of the sunken wall at Fredericksburg."
>
> *General Daniel Harvey Hill, Confederate States Army, describing the results of the Union rout at Chickamauga, September 20, 1863*

## THE ROCK

TWO OF THREE ARMY OF THE CUMBERLAND corps commanders were on the run, along with the army's commanding general. Only one commander and his corps refused to join them. Major General George Henry Thomas quickly rallied brigades under brigadier generals Thomas John Wood and John Brannan, throwing them southward, fast, in order to block Longstreet's advance there and prevent his further exploitation of the catastrophic breakthrough he had already achieved.

By this point in the battle, Bragg had committed everything he had, including the divisions initially held in reserve. There was nobody close enough to help Longstreet capitalize on his breakthrough, and, thanks to the timely arrival of Wood's and Brannan's

# THE HUMANITY OF WAR

Arthur van Lisle, a Union private who had been wounded in the first day's fighting, languished in thirsty agony, his cheek pressed to the Chickamauga mud. "The day is waning," he later recalled in a journal. "What a terrible day it has been! Night approaches. What horrors will it bring forth? Surely if my comrades cannot help me I must die; and I must die here, with no friend to soothe my last moments or tell the story of my death to the loved ones at home."

He was conscious of "growing weaker and weaker from the loss of blood," which was "drying upon my body and stiffening my clothing." He felt a parching fever course through his veins.

"Oh for a drink! Water, water, WATER!" It is not clear from van Lisle's recollection whether these words were only thought or actually spoken, but soon he saw a Confederate soldier standing over him. "Seeing my bloody side and parched lips, [he] stooped down and, throwing the strap of his canteen over his head, put the nozzle to my mouth, saying as he did so, 'Drink, Yank, I reckon you're powerful dry.'" Private Arthur van Lisle drank and drank deeply, then stretched out his arm to return the canteen. "'Jest you keep it,' I heard him shout as he retired, loading his gun."

men, the Confederate advance bogged down. General Thomas knew, however, that Longstreet's momentum had hardly been spent and that the two brigades engaging him now could not hold out indefinitely. Fortunately, the Army of the Cumberland had another brigadier possessed of extraordinary initiative. Gordon Granger had orders from Rosecrans to protect the army's flank at all costs. But Rosecrans was gone along with most of the army, and so Granger led his two brigades out of their flanking positions and, following the roar of musketry, to the aid of General Thomas. Reinforced, Thomas held the field until the fighting ended that night and Longstreet and Bragg disengaged. Thomas, his brigadiers, and their men had saved what was left of the Army of the Cumberland, and this earned for George Thomas the epithet of "Rock of Chickamauga."

## THE GOOD DOG BRAGG

AFTER ROSECRANS SUCCESSFULLY REPULSED Bragg at the battle of Stones River on December 31, 1862, he had remarked: "Bragg's a good dog, but Hold Fast's a better." *Hold Fast*—the self-bestowed name never stuck to Rosecrans, but after he joined in the partial rout at Chickamauga, it became a badge of unintended self-mockery. A total of 3,969 men, Union and Confederate, were killed in battle during

## NUMBERS

### Bragg's Costly Victory

The Army of the Cumberland fielded 58,222 men at Chickamauga, of whom 1,657 were killed, 9,756 wounded, and 4,757 went missing. Bragg and Longstreet suffered heavier casualties—2,312 killed, 14,674 wounded, and 1,468 missing out of 66,326 engaged— but achieved a tactical victory by sending Rosecrans packing back to Chattanooga. In terms of casualties on both sides, Chickamauga was the most destructive battle of the Civil War's western theater.

September 18–20, 1863, as were the reputations of Rosecrans and his subordinates, generals McCook and Crittenden. On the Confederate side, Bragg was appalled by the Pyrrhic victory his commanders had given him, purchased in blood at a greater price than the Union had paid. He fired three of his subordinate generals, Leonidas Polk, Daniel Harvey Hill, and Thomas C. Hindman, all of whom Jefferson Davis later reinstated after Braxton Bragg was himself relieved as Army of Tennessee commanding general late in December 1863.

In the meantime, though, Braxton Bragg was still in charge, and he laid siege to the Army of the Cumberland, which was holed up at Chattanooga. It was a desperate situation. The fate of an entire Union army hung in the balance. But perhaps such dire straits were exactly what Washington and General Halleck both needed. Union political and military leaders suddenly put their minds and hearts into the work of saving the Army of the Cumberland by addressing a theater of the war that had been too long neglected.

Fighting Joe Hooker was detached from the Army of the Potomac at the head of two corps, which were carried by train from the banks of the Rappahannock River in eastern Virginia to Bridgeport, Alabama, in just eight days, arriving on October 2. No other movement in the Civil War more dramatically demonstrated the importance of railroads in modern combat operations. From the west, Halleck at last released both William T. Sherman and Ulysses S. Grant. Sherman led a portion of the Army of the Tennessee east from Memphis, and Grant was given a vastly enlarged command, now called the Military Division of the Mississippi, encompassing the armies of the Ohio, the Cumberland, and the Tennessee—in effect virtually all major Union army operations west of the Alleghenies. No longer would he be the unwilling vassal of Henry Wager Halleck (who still served as the Union army's general-in-chief, but was now obliged to give Grant wide strategic latitude).

As Grant defined the crux of combat as the killing of the enemy, so he now focused on the crux issue of an army under siege: the urgent need for sustenance and supply. He planned and executed a rapid succession of operations that overran a Confederate outpost on the Tennessee River just west of Lookout Mountain and, through this, carved out a supply route to Chattanooga. By this time, the disgraced Rosecrans had been relieved as commanding officer of the Army of the Cumberland, replaced by none other than the Rock of Chickamauga, George Henry Thomas. He and his hungry men gratefully dubbed the source of supply Grant had given them the "Cracker Line." It was a logistical wonder, an unbroken sixty-mile chain of steamboats, flat-bottomed scows, a pontoon bridge, and wagons, all operating, without interruption, in enemy-held territory.

The Cracker Line having foiled his plan to starve out the Army of the Cumberland, Bragg sent raiders to disrupt it and other Union lines of communication. Both Wheeler's Raid (October 1–9) and Roddey's Raid (October 7–14) were indeed disruptive, but hardly decisive, and as Bragg's siege dragged on, those laying the siege grew hungrier than the Cracker Line–fed Federals enduring it.

*Confederate forces did everything they could to impede the movement of the Union armies, including burning key railway bridges, such as this one over the Rappahannock River in eastern Virginia. The sketch is by Alfred R. Waud.*

## LOOKOUT MOUNTAIN

SHERMAN WAS DELAYED IN REACHING the Union assembly point at Bridgeport, Alabama, until November 15. His problem hadn't been the enemy, but Old Brains Halleck, who ordered him to pause long enough to repair the rail lines into Nashville. Grant had also been delayed, not by man but by nature, in the form of torrential rains. At last, however, the day of battle was appointed: November 24, 1863.

As it dawned in thick clouds and dense fog, Grant ordered Major General Joseph Hooker to capture Lookout Mountain. Fighting Joe was bound and determined to redeem the disaster of Chancellorsville, but his mission was daunting. Lookout Mountain rose to an elevation of eighteen hundred feet above Chattanooga, necessitating a fight that would literally be uphill, every inch of it.

Hooker began at eight in the morning and did not stop until after midnight. When day broke on November 25, troops from the 8th Kentucky Regiment lurched ahead of the rest of Hooker's forces, scaled Lookout's summit, and pitched Old Glory on the knife edge of a ridge. At eighteen hundred feet, the sun was just showing over the horizon. War correspondents who had accompanied Hooker and now gazed up from their perches on the slope of the mountain struggled to find

*Union soldiers show the Stars and Stripes on Point Lookout at Lookout Mountain, above Chattanooga.*

words to describe the sight of the Stars and Stripes made translucent by the morning light. They did not call it the battle of Lookout Mountain in the news stories they filed, but, rather, the "Battle above the Clouds." The same war that had taken a good general like Old Rosy Rosecrans and cast him into disgrace now elevated Hooker, a general broken by hard defeat, to new heroism.

## BATTLE OF MISSIONARY RIDGE

SHERMAN WAS NOT AS LUCKY this time as Hooker. Against the Confederate right wing outside of Chattanooga he made little impact, prompting Grant to order General Thomas to assist him on the afternoon of November 25 by making an assault on the Confederate rifle pits that had been carved out at the base of Missionary Ridge to the east of Lookout Mountain and south of Chattanooga. Grant's aim was to force Bragg to transfer troops from Sherman's front to reinforce the rifle pits, thereby giving Sherman the edge that might allow him to break through Bragg's right and end the threat to Chattanooga. Thomas gave the mission to Major General Granger and his IV Corps.

The men of the Army of the Cumberland had been cooped up in and around Chattanooga for a long time. The soldiers of Hooker and Sherman, who had come to their rescue, derided them for having run away from the fight at Chickamauga. It was one thing to be held under siege by Braxton Bragg, but quite another to be mocked by the soldiers of a rival Union army. The Cumberland men had had enough. They lurched forward in fine order and swarmed over the Confederate rifle pits they had been assigned to take. This put them at the foot of Missionary Ridge. What they did next they did without orders from Thomas or Grant.

Having accomplished their mission, they refused to stop fighting. Advancing beyond the rifle pits, they shot their way up the forbidding slope of Missionary Ridge, brushing aside all resistance before them and breaking through Bragg's line not where it was thinnest but at its very strongest part, along the heights of the ridge. "The Yankees were cutting and slashing, and the [Confederate] cannoneers were running in every direction," a soldier in Bragg's army later related. "I saw [one Confederate] brigade throw down their guns and break like quarter horses. Bragg was trying to rally them. I heard him say, 'Here is your commander,' and the soldiers hallooed back, 'Here is your mule.'"

Grant observed it all from a distance: men in blue scrambling up the ridge, men in gray and butternut (in the western theater, by 1863, many Confederate "uniforms" were improvised homespun and colored not gray but yellow-tan with dyes made from nuts) breaking before them.

"By whose order are those troops going up the hill?" Grant demanded of Thomas. The Rock of Chickamauga calmly replied that they were probably going up on their own. Grant replied that, "It was all right if it turned out all right." Then he continued: "If not, someone would suffer."

It turned out "all right." The advance broke Bragg's line, sending his army into retreat. At this, a newspaper correspondent eavesdropped on an exchange between Gordon Granger and some of his IV Corps men.

"You ought to be court-martialed, every man of you," he thundered in a counterfeit rage. "I ordered you to take the rifle pits, and you scaled the mountain!" The reporter noted that his cheeks, as he said this, "were wet with tears as honest as the blood that reddened all the route."

*As was the firm's custom, Kurz & Allison created an image of the Union assault up Lookout Mountain on November 24, 1863, compounded more of myth than of reality.*

"The strength of the rebellion in the center is broken . . . And another victory is added to the chapter of 'Unconditional Surrender Grant.'"

*Quartermaster General Montgomery C. Meigs, U.S. Army, report to Secretary of War Edwin Stanton on the victory at Chattanooga, November 25, 1863*

## WALLED IN

THE LOSS OF THE TRANS-MISSISSIPPI WEST, the Mississippi Valley, and the Tennessee Valley gutted the Confederacy, and the loss of the Mississippi and Tennessee Rivers walled in what was left of the would-be Southern republic. Military maneuver was now severely limited, as were sources of food and the transport of everything. If the Confederates were to fight on, they would have to do so in the East, where the war had begun, and what had started as a sweeping rebellion, which took in the expanse of nearly half of a broken nation, was now compressed into less than a quarter of it. No longer a grand revolution, the Civil War had taken on the character of a last stand.

"The year closes more satisfactorily than it commenced," Union navy secretary Gideon Welles, a quiet, thoughtful man Lincoln affectionately called "my Neptune," entered into his diary on December 31, 1863. "There have been in some instances errors and misfortunes. But the heart of the nation is sounder and its hopes brighter."

*Private Henry McCollum, Company B, 78th Pennsylvania Infantry Regiment, poses with three of his regimental comrades (their names unknown) on Point Lookout following the battles of Lookout Mountain and Missionary Ridge. Ohio photographer Royan M. Linn took care to pose the quartet with triumphant nonchalance.*

# CHAPTER 17

## "AND FIGHTIN' MEANS KILLIN'"

### *War without Mercy*

NONE OF THEM WERE BAD MEN, AND EACH OF THEM WAS A PROFESSIONAL soldier who had received the best training the military establishment of the United States could offer. George B. McClellan, with such high hopes tapped to replace the superannuated Winfield Scott, had graduated near the top of his West Point class. Ambrose Burnside was also a West Point man, as was his successor, Fighting Joe Hooker. Other highly placed commanders, including Irwin McDowell, John Pope, and Henry Wager Halleck, were also respected West Point graduates—and, even more, Halleck was considered one of the finest military minds of his age.

Of all the commanders of the Army of the Potomac, George Meade was the most competent, and he did preside over the Gettysburg victory, having assumed command from Hooker only days before the battle. Yet even he lacked the fire in the belly that would have moved him to drive his army, no matter how spent after Gettysburg, in pursuit of Lee and his even more depleted Army of Northern Virginia. History remembers Meade less as the victor of Gettysburg than as the general who let the Confederate commander slip away.

Year after year, Mr. Lincoln's generals, well meaning, well trained, failed him and the nation. All that while, Ulysses Grant was producing remarkable results in the western theater, but, year after year, he was passed over for the highest command.

## LINCOLN FINDS HIS GENERAL

FOR MUCH OF THE WAR, Grant was held back by three things. First was his commanding officer, Henry W. Halleck, who never had sufficient confidence in him to make full use of his aggressive talent. Second was his own scruffy personal appearance and slovenly habits, which included at least partially substantiated rumors of heavy drinking (Chapter 6). Third was his lack of influence outside of the army. The Civil War was the era of the "political general," the man who achieved high command strictly on the strength of his civilian political connections. Even for professional soldiers, however, including West Point graduates, possessing political savvy and politically influential friends was a golden key to advancement. Grant had neither the savvy nor the friends.

And then there was the nature of the victories Grant did produce. His triumphs at Fort Henry and Fort Donelson were both magnificent and important, but, because they took place in the western theater, they did not command the popular attention that they merited. People and politicians *did* take note of his victory at Shiloh (Chapter 8), but chiefly to recoil at its cost: more than thirteen thousand boys in blue killed, wounded, or missing. The president had even been inundated by calls for his relief. Although Lincoln stoutly resisted, Grant himself came close to resigning. His insight into warfare was not taught at West Point and was not promoted in novels or news-

*President Lincoln was often confronted with rumors concerning General Grant's drinking. Ohio newspaperman Murat Halstead wrote this letter to Secretary of the Treasury Salmon P. Chase, warning that Grant was "most of the time more than half drunk, and much of the time idiotically drunk." Lincoln investigated and discovered that Grant did indeed drink—as did most other men in the 1860s, generals, privates, and civilians included—but concluded that his drinking never affected his performance as a military commander.*

papers. He understood war to be all about killing and dying. Glory, honor, conquest, winning, losing—for Grant, these things clung to war like a mist, but they were not its substance, and if the politicians and people could not accept this, then, he thought, there is no reason for him to continue to ply what he knew to be his stock in trade.

Fortunately for the Union, Abraham Lincoln understood that men died under Grant's command because Grant used them aggressively to kill the enemy. Called on to fire Grant, the president did not reply that he couldn't do it because Grant was a great strategist or a great leader of troops but because "he fights." As Lincoln saw it, Grant possessed in abundance what his other generals lacked: sheer aggression.

> "A military life had no charms for me, and I had not the faintest idea of staying in the army even if I should be graduate, which I did not expect."
>
> Ulysses S. Grant, recalling his state of mind
> while a West Point cadet, in Personal Memoirs (1885)

The president's assessment was partly right; however, Grant's aggressiveness did not come from a warrior spirit or some inner reserve of savagery. It came, rather, from an understanding of war in general and the Civil War in particular. That war is always about killing Grant took as a given. *This* war between the North and the South, however, was shaped by two irresistible, irreducible facts.

First: the weapons, long arms and artillery, were unprecedented in their industrially mass-produced volume and, individually, in their destructiveness. Additionally, such innovations to warfare as the railroad and the telegraph meant that masses of men could bring these weapons to bear more quickly and over greater distances than ever before. A war fought with such products of science, invention, and industry could be nothing other than terrible, even beyond most people's imagining.

Second: The North had more industrial capacity, more railroads, more telegraph wire, and more weapons than the South; it also had many more men to produce and to use these weapons. The South could ill afford to lose what little it had, whereas the North could afford to lose more of everything, especially soldiers.

**REALITY CHECK**
**From Understudy to Star**
Grant was a courageous general who understood that war meant inflicting and absorbing casualties. He was also a highly competent strategist and tactician—something for which he is not always given the full credit due him. And he had one other advantage. Precisely because he spent the first part of the war in the western theater, he was not subjected to the same degree of scrutiny from the public, the press, and the politicians who always second guessed and threatened to stifle principal commanders in the East. Grant had the time and space to mature as a commander, to make mistakes and to learn from them. That was the upside of what most historians interpret as his unduly long western exile.

While the first fact guaranteed that war would be deadly, the second fact, as Grant saw it, meant that the North would inevitably prevail as long as it chose to keep fighting. That was the simple, terrible math of the thing—an equation scrawled in blood and gore. Grant would strive for victories, but if he could not always win, he was determined to lose in ways that would exact a heavy cost on the enemy, a cost the South could not afford to pay, even in victory.

## A FRESH START

ON MARCH 9, 1864, Ulysses Grant was summoned to Washington, D.C., to be commissioned as the only lieutenant general in the United States Army. The next highest-ranking officers were major generals; there had not been a full, four-star general in the U.S. Army since George Washington. Along with his exalted rank came an appointment as chief of all the Union armies.

Grant was the first Union commander who brought to his job a radically new doctrine. Up to this point, each new commander, whether of all the armies or only the Army of the Potomac, had been a conventional American military officer. With each new man, Lincoln's hope was that he had found a commander with more skill, a more aggressive nature, and maybe more luck than his predecessor. What he should have been looking for was a general with a new idea. That is what he found in Grant. This commander's purpose would be to fight and to keep fighting with the sole objective of destroying the Confederate armies. Like his predecessors, he would attack cities, but only to force the enemy to fight and to die in the city's defense. Possession of the place in question was beside the point, a mere byproduct of the enemy's destruction.

By this point in the war, just two principal Confederate armies really mattered. These were Robert E. Lee's Army of Northern Virginia and the Army of Tennessee, which had been commanded by Braxton Bragg until he lost Chattanooga and was now under the command of Joseph E. Johnston. There were other armies, but these were west of the Mississippi River, completely cut off by Grant's western victories. Unable to move east, they were all but irrelevant. Eliminate Lee and Johnston, and the war would be over—unless diehard Confederates decided to fight as guerrillas, as some were doing now in the North Carolina mountains and, like Quantrill and

Bloody Bill Anderson (Chapter 10), on the western plains. But there would be time to deal with the guerrillas later, if it came to that.

Grant inherited a very good army, and he enjoyed an advantage that had been denied to most of his predecessors: After three years of war, it was an army that included in its ranks a great many seasoned veterans. Grant ensured that these men were thoroughly sown among the ranks of the raw recruits. They would augment training, and they would put some iron in the newcomers' spines.

As William Tecumseh Sherman had succeeded Grant to command the Army of the Tennessee when Grant was assigned command of the Military Division of the Mississippi under Halleck, so Grant now turned over the division to Sherman. A commander of great sophistication, Sherman nevertheless avoided Halleck's error of habitually over-intellectualizing military problems. On the contrary, he approached them as a finely honed razor, cutting to the heart in a stroke. He summed up his understanding of his assignment in a single terse sentence: "I was to go for Joe Johnston." This meant that he would march down the right-of-way of the Western and Atlantic Railroad with the objective of taking Atlanta, which would serve the dual purpose of neutralizing the South's major rail junction and one of its most important centers of manufacturing and supply while also luring Johnston into open battle. For just as Grant targeted Richmond to draw out the Army of Northern Virginia so that he could fight it and kill it, Sherman drew a bead on Atlanta, knowing that the Army of Tennessee would march east to its defense.

*Joseph E. Johnston was a skilled Confederate commander who relied heavily on strategic retreat—far too heavily to please President Jefferson Davis, who, midway in the defense of Atlanta relieved him of command of the Army of Tennessee and replaced him with the aggressive but impulsively reckless John Bell Hood.*

*Atlanta was first and foremost a Southern rail transportation hub. This photograph by George N. Barnard shows the ruins of a roundhouse, with locomotives and rolling stock still in place amid the collapsed stone walls.*

## DETAILS, DETAILS

### Terminus

Unlike most of the world's important cities, Atlanta was not built on the shore of an ocean or lake or along some great river, but rather as a place for a rail line, the Western and Atlantic Railroad, to end in 1837. Fittingly, the brand-new town was named "Terminus." Subsequently renamed "Marthasville," it became "Atlantica-Pacifica" before the name was finally shortened to "Atlanta." Although it quickly grew into a major rail junction—and therefore a center of manufacturing and warehousing—Atlanta was ninety-ninth in population among U.S. cities when the census of 1860 was taken, but, among cities of the Confederacy, it ranked twelfth. Its population of nearly 10,000 more than doubled in the course of the war to about 22,000—and became a mandatory target for Union invasion.

This arrangement still left Grant with one remaining problem of command. While Sherman concentrated on fighting the Army of Tennessee, Grant was determined to lead the final campaign personally—historians call it the "Overland campaign"—in the East. The trouble was that the principal force in this region was the Army of the Potomac, already commanded by George Meade. Since Meade's

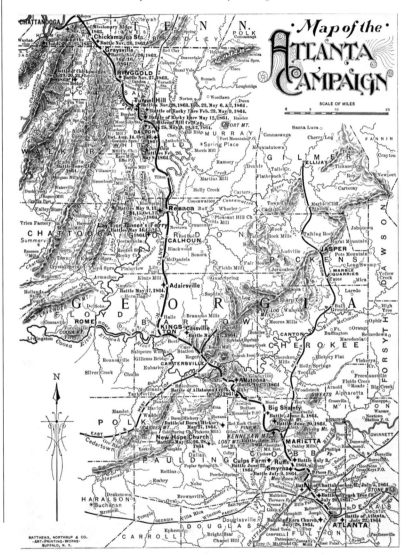

*The Western and Atlantic Railroad published this "Map of the Atlanta Campaign" in 1887 and distributed it free of charge to tourists interested in surveying the scenes of the momentous campaigns of the Civil War.*

army was Grant's most important instrument, Meade found himself in the depressing position of being something of a commander in name only, rather like the captain of a vessel that the admiral has chosen as his flagship. Fortunately, Meade respected Grant and was willing to play the role that had been thrust upon him. For all practical purposes, therefore, the long endgame of the Civil War was played out between Lee and Johnston on the Confederate side and Grant and Sherman for the Union.

## The Rest of Grant's Plan

There was one more top commander to add to the lineup under Grant. The Union cavalry had always been inferior to that of the Confederacy, and it had rarely been used to full effectiveness. Grant wanted to put his West Point classmate and trusted friend, Major General William B. Franklin, at the head of the Army of the Potomac's Cavalry Corps, but Henry Wager Halleck enthusiastically recommended Philip Sheridan, who had served under him in the western theater. Grant had ample reason to hold a grudge against Halleck, who had continually suppressed him when he was his commanding officer. It is a measure of Grant's character and judgment, however, that he not only recognized where Halleck's true talents lay by appointing him to serve as his chief of staff, a complex and demanding administrative position, but also heeded his advice by summoning Sheridan to the East. Unfortunately, whereas Grant successfully navigated the potential pitfalls of what was essentially the shared command of the Army of the Potomac, Sheridan initially had a great deal of difficulty with George Gordon Meade. Grant had encouraged Sheridan to use the cavalry to its utmost, the way Confederate commanders did—especially for hit-and-run raiding. Meade, however, who was Sheridan's immediate superior, insisted on employing the Cavalry Corps as it had always been used: for reconnaissance, for screening larger forces from enemy reconnaissance, and for guarding rear-echelon areas such as railheads and the like. It was not until well into the Overland campaign that Grant intervened, sending Sheridan on a raid toward Richmond, during May 9–24, 1864, which we will look at in Chapter 18. Despite the conflict between him and Meade, Sheridan was adored by his troopers, who affectionately called their dapper, if short and scrappy, commanding officer "Little Phil."

*German-born Union general Franz Sigel was popular with the large German American population and therefore a valuable officer. Despite having been trained at the Karlsruhe Military Academy, however, he was a hopelessly inept tactician.*

The two biggest armies of the Union, Sherman's Army of the Tennessee and Meade's Army of the Potomac, would do the heaviest lifting—Sherman against Johnston, Grant against Lee, but Grant also had two smaller forces to point toward Richmond: the Army of the James, thirty-three thousand men led by the politically influential but militarily inept Benjamin Butler, and the men of the newly created Department of West Virginia, commanded by Franz Sigel a better general than Butler—bold and aggressive where Butler was blustering yet hesitant—but also a military asset of questionable value.

Despite the two weak independent commanders who were poorly integrated into the Overland campaign, Grant had put in place the elements of the first strategically coordinated campaign of the Civil War. Sherman would target Atlanta and Johnston simultaneously with Grant's operations against Lee and Richmond.

## THE END OF PAROLE

GRANT WAS DEAD SERIOUS about changing the way the Civil War was being fought. On April 17, 1864, shortly after he was appointed as the Union's top military commander, he ordered an end to the prisoner of war exchange policy that had been in effect officially since 1862 and, unofficially, even before that.

It was a controversial step that revived the invective formerly hurled at Grant. The fact is that by the time of the Civil War, most "civilized" Western nations routinely made credible shows of treating prisoners of war humanely. In a few instances, warring powers signed treaties—usually called "cartels"—agreeing mutually to uphold certain standards of decent treatment. Of course, the most humane treatment an army can afford an enemy prisoner is to release him. No army wanted the trouble of maintaining large POW camps, which were not only expensive, but tied down manpower that could otherwise be used in active combat; therefore, most belligerents agreed to prisoner exchanges. Theoretically, these operated on a one-to-one basis—you release one of mine, I'll release one of yours. However, in practice, officer prisoners were typically regarded as worth more than one private or corporal, and the higher the rank of the prisoner to be exchanged, the greater the "cost" in enlisted men to be exchanged for him.

Abraham Lincoln, the Great Emancipator, had a reputation for ample humanity, but he adamantly refused to make a cartel or anything

# "I'M GOING TO FIGHT MIT SIGEL"

Born in Germany in 1824, Franz Sigel graduated from the Karlsruhe Military Academy, served in the army of Baden, and fought in the German revolution of 1848—on the side of the revolutionaries. The Prussian army defeated him, and after serving as commander in chief and secretary of war during the brief existence of the revolutionary government in Baden, Sigel fled a Prussian invasion, settling in Switzerland and then England before immigrating to the United States in 1852. He settled, as did many other Germans, in St. Louis, where he became a schoolteacher and a professor before gaining election to the post of director of the city's public schools.

Sigel was active and influential in Missouri politics, and when the Civil War broke out, Lincoln made him a brigadier general in the hope that doing so would draw many German Americans to the Union cause. It did, but Sigel soon earned a mostly deserved reputation for ineptitude (except at Pea Ridge, March 8, 1862; Chapter 10) and was later relieved of command of the Army of the Potomac's XI Corps early in 1863. Despite his unpopularity with his superiors, Sigel's men in XI Corps adored him. Most were recent German immigrants who knew but one sentence of hybrid English: "I'm going to fight mit Sigel."

Sidestepping then general in chief Henry W. Halleck, who wanted to cashier Sigel altogether, Lincoln ordered his secretary of war, Edwin Stanton, to create a Department of West Virginia and to install the politically valuable Sigel as its commanding officer. Under Grant, during the Overland campaign, Sigel commanded the men of the department in the Shenandoah Valley, where Major General John C. Breckinridge dealt him a stunning defeat at the battle of New Market (May 15, 1864), a beating made the more humiliating because teenage cadets rounded up from nearby Virginia Military Institute were instrumental in it. After an indecisive exchange with Jubal Early at Harpers Ferry, Sigel was at last removed from command. The official reason for his relief, "lack of aggression," was one with which Lincoln chose not to argue, and Sigel sat out the rest of the war.

After formally resigning his commission on May 4, 1865, Sigel became a newspaper reporter in Baltimore, then an editor in New York City. In 1869, he unsuccessfully ran for secretary of state of New York, but in 1887, President Grover Cleveland appointed him pension agent for the city of New York. He died in 1902.

Many a proud German American marched off to war proclaiming "I'm going to fight mit Sigel"— a fact this song (to be sung to the tune of "The Girl I Left Behind Me") celebrates in the appropriate dialect: "Un now I gets mine sojer clothes, / I'm going to fight mit Sigel."

else resembling a treaty with the Confederacy. To do so, he believed, would be to concede, however tacitly, legitimate sovereign status to the states in rebellion. After all, nations make treaties with other nations, not with mobs and certainly not with traitors. Notwithstanding this reservation, the president gave his generals permission to make informal prisoner exchanges from time to time under flags of truce. This ad hoc arrangement was formalized by the Dix-Hill Cartel of July 22, 1862, which was concluded not between one government and another, but between the opposing armies. As such, Lincoln allowed it, and from then on, the object was to exchange prisoners within ten days of capture: private for private, two privates for one "noncom" (noncommissioned officer), and so on up the ladder of rank. (A lieutenant general was to be exchanged for no fewer than sixty privates.)

The Dix-Hill Cartel was a noble idea, but never a very practical one, given the high volume of prisoners each side routinely took. In practice, hundreds and then thousands of prisoners accumulated in improvised military stockades or grossly overburdened civilian prisons, all awaiting exchange. Because the provost (guard and prison) systems of each side's armies had been designed with exchange in mind, POW facilities, including sanitation, shelter, and food, were never adequate. In search of an alternative, military authorities on both sides devised a "parole" system whereby POWs awaiting exchange were returned to their units on their solemn word not to return to duty until they had been officially exchanged. General Grant had had firsthand experience with the parole concept following his victory at Vicksburg (Chapter 13). A staggering thirty-one thousand Confederate soldiers became his prisoners, and there was no practical way to transport, let alone feed, shelter, and guard them. Grant therefore paroled them all.

*The noted American illustrator Arthur Lumley created this delicate sketch of "Union & rebel officers taking the last drink after signing the papers of parole & exchange of prisoners" and before bidding one another "goodbye." Determined to deprive the Confederacy of fighting men, Grant ordered an end to the gentlemanly practice of parole in March 1864.*

*The railroad depot at Chattanooga served as a makeshift holding yard for Confederates captured during the battles in this vicinity. The next step was to load them into trains headed to POW camps in the North, which were every bit as miserable and inhumane as those the Confederates operated in the South.*

Some five months later, fighting the Chattanooga campaign (Chapter 16), Grant was chagrined by the volume of reports he received revealing that a great many of the prisoners he was taking at Chattanooga were men he had paroled at Vicksburg.

Pressed for manpower, the Confederacy routinely violated parole and put released POWs immediately back into the ranks. Grant was no longer willing to tolerate spending blood and treasure to capture prisoners, only to release them to fight again. That was his principal stated motive for ending prisoner exchange. He also made public his disgust at the refusal of Confederate commanders to exchange black POWs and their white officers. Yet he had a deeper, unstated motive for ending exchange, and it was all about the numbers. The Confederacy desperately needed the return of its captured soldiers, whereas the Union could get along without the men it lost to enemy captivity. Prisoner exchange therefore served the Confederate war effort far more than it did that of the Union. As Grant saw it, it unduly slowed Confederate attrition.

"July 19. There is no such thing as delicacy here. Nine out of ten would as soon eat with a corpse for a table as any other way. In the middle of last night I was awakened by being kicked by a dying man. He was soon dead.... Got up and moved the body off a few feet, and again went to sleep to dream of hideous sights."

John L. Ransom, Andersonville Diary (1883)

## HELL ON EARTH

VIOLATIONS OF PAROLE and the inequality of the benefits of prisoner exchange were ample reasons to end prisoner exchange, but Grant also believed that having to cope with prisoners put a severe burden on a Confederate government that was already struggling to feed and clothe its own soldiers and, for that matter, its own civilian population. Of course, this assumed that the Confederate authorities were making a genuine effort to provide for the basic needs of their POWs. In truth, Grant—and everyone else—knew this was not the case. Escaped prisoners told vivid horror stories of conditions in Confederate POW camps, of which Camp Sumter, better known by the name of the adjacent town, Andersonville, ten miles northeast of Americus, Georgia, was only the most infamous.

Georgia in summer is a hot place, and Andersonville was at the very core of the furnace. It was little more than a rude stockade, sixteen and a half acres open to the sun and to the rain, tents providing the only shelter. Never intended to hold more than ten thousand prisoners, it accepted at times as many as four hundred a day, so that, in August 1864, thirty-three thousand men jammed a facility without medicine or medical care, subsisting on starvation rations, and fetching their water from a miserable trickle dubbed Stockade Creek, which doubled as a common latrine.

Andersonville's commandant was Captain Henry Wirz, who had taken over from the camp's founder, Confederate

*The front page of* Frank Leslie's Illustrated Newspaper *shocked the Northern public with these images of emaciated Union prisoners released at the end of the war. Engraved from photographs, the images seem to anticipate the genocidal horrors of twentieth-century warfare.*

army provost marshal Brigadier General John Henry Winder, after he was transferred to Richmond. Winder graduated from West Point in 1820, but he served in the army for just four years before resigning his commission to manage his family's Maryland plantation, which he proceeded to ruin. Seeking a new living, he was reinstated into the army and taught for a year at West Point but was dismissed for venting his impatient rage on a cadet. After joining the Confederate cause, he was given a rear-echelon appointment as provost marshal. Because of the Confederacy's critically pinched resources, the job would have taxed a man of the greatest ability. Winder, however, was an incompetent, far more concerned with his expensively tailored uniforms than with the all-but-hopeless job he was failing to perform.

If Winder was a feckless failure, Wirz, a physician in civilian life, earned a reputation as a zealous sadist. One inmate reported overhearing the Swiss immigrant (he had been born in Zurich) boast that he "was killing more damned Yankees with his treatment than they were with powder and lead in the army." Hauled before a U.S. Army tribunal after the war, accused of causing at least ten thousand prisoner deaths (the actual death toll was much higher), Wirz denied purposely killing prisoners, whether through mistreatment or deliberate neglect, but he was unable to deny having drawn a perimeter within the Andersonville stockade he called the "dead line." His guards had orders to shoot, without warning, any prisoner who strayed over the line.

*Taken on August 17, 1864, this photograph, a southwest view of the Andersonville stockade, clearly shows the so-called dead line, running from the bottom of the photograph toward the upper right. Prisoners attempting to cross this line were shot without warning.*

# DELIBERATE ATROCITY OR UNAVOIDABLE COST OF WAR?

Most Northerners greeted the conviction and execution of Henry Wirz—the only Confederate soldier or officer tried for his wartime actions—as just, but the trial, which certainly did not meet constitutional standards of due process of law, created its share of controversy. Southerners in particular argued that the prisoner deaths at Andersonville were caused by two things: General Grant's policy prohibiting prisoner exchange (which created an intolerable burden on Confederate POW camps) and unavoidable food shortages everywhere in the wartime South, the result of the Union's inhumane blockade. Moreover, they pointed out, the death rate among Southern POWs in Northern camps had been similar to that at Andersonville.

**M**ost of the controversy died out shortly after Wirz's execution, but the United Daughters of the Confederacy, a heritage association founded in 1894, would not let go of the cause, accusing the federal government of having committed a vengeful "judicial murder." In 1909, the UDC dedicated a memorial to Henry Wirz, which still stands in the town of Andersonville, Georgia. It is the world's only monument to a concentration camp commandant.

Beyond dispute is the fact that, of the 45,000 prisoners housed in the camp during 1864–65, 13,000 were accorded the dignity of burial in marked graves. Almost certainly, others were disposed of in mass burials. Even if only the official death toll is accepted, mortality at Andersonville averaged 29 percent. One other Confederate camp, at Salisbury, North Carolina, housing no more than 10,000 POWs, laid claim to an even higher death rate: 34 percent.

*The death warrant is read to former Andersonville commandant Captain Henry Wirz, on the scaffold, just before his execution by hanging on November 10, 1865, in this photograph by Alexander Gardner.*

After a two-month trial, Wirz was found guilty of conspiracy and eleven counts of murder and was hanged on November 10, 1865, on the site of what is today the U.S. Supreme Court.

Winder, Wirz, and the Confederate government may be condemned for their inhumane treatment of prisoners of war, but their pleas of critical food shortages were not unfounded. In contrast, the Union had plentiful supplies, but also abused its prisoners as a matter of policy. "Hellmira," as the Confederates called the Union stockade at Elmira, New York, held twelve thousand POWs, a quarter of whom died due to a combination of malnutrition and outright starvation and exposure during the harsh upstate New York winter. What is more, instead of acting to increase what everyone agreed were inadequate rations supplied to

Confederate POWs, Secretary of War Edwin Stanton ordered cuts to the level of rations Union wardens gave Confederate prisoners.

## THAT DEVIL FORREST

SPEAKING AT THE COMMENCEMENT ceremonies of the Michigan Military Academy on June 19, 1879, General William Tecumseh Sherman observed, "War is at best barbarism. . . . Its glory is all moonshine. It is only those who have neither fired a shot nor heard the shrieks and groans of the wounded who cry aloud for blood, more vengeance, more desolation. War," Sherman concluded, "is hell." And places like Andersonville and "Hellmira" proved it to the public, though generals like Grant and Sherman himself had known this—and, what is more, had accepted this—all along. They were among the "great" generals of the Civil War, if *great* is defined as the most effective, and if *the most effective* is defined as the most lethally destructive. According to these definitions, add one more general to this duo.

We encountered Nathan Bedford Forrest in Chapter 6, refusing to join generals Simon Bolivar Buckner and Gideon Pillow in the surrender of Fort Donelson on the Mississippi. This bold action not only saved his own command from capture, but the hundreds of additional volunteers he quickly recruited. Forrest was never a man to meekly accept an intolerable status quo. Born to a poor Tennessee family in 1821, he was entirely self-educated and possessed the native intelligence to build a fortune through cotton planting and slave trading before the war. When the war broke out, he turned his back on his own wealth and influence to enlist in Tennessee as a lowly Confederate private. Learning of this, Tennessee governor Isham G. Harris immediately commissioned Forrest a colonel and asked him to raise a cavalry battalion. Forrest went about his assignment with a passion, using his own money and promising his recruits little more than a very good time "killing Yankees." And that, it turned out, was precisely what they wanted. His ranks were soon filled.

Although he had no military training other than what he picked up in his brief tenure as a Confederate private, Forrest soon proved to be a military prodigy. Not only did his men adore him, he himself was credited with personally killing thirty-three of the enemy. Forrest always relished a good fight.

*Although untutored in the military art, Nathan Bedford Forrest was one of the Confederacy's most effective field commanders. William T. Sherman called him a "devil" and considered him the "most dangerous" of the South's generals.*

*Born poor, Forrest made a substantial fortune as a slave dealer operating out of an office in Memphis, Tennessee.*

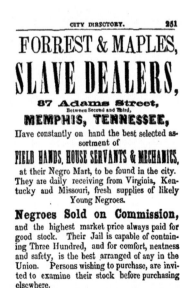

CITY DIRECTORY. 251

**FORREST & MAPLES,**
**SLAVE DEALERS,**
**87 Adams Street,**
Between Second and Third,
**MEMPHIS, TENNESSEE,**
Have constantly on hand the best selected assortment of
**FIELD HANDS, HOUSE SERVANTS & MECHANICS,**
at their Negro Mart, to be found in the city. They are daily receiving from Virginia, Kentucky and Missouri, fresh supplies of likely Young Negroes.

**Negroes Sold on Commission,**
and the highest market price always paid for good stock. Their Jail is capable of containing Three Hundred, and for comfort, neatness and safety, is the best arranged of any in the Union. Persons wishing to purchase, are invited to examine their stock before purchasing elsewhere.

They have on hand at present, Fifty likely young Negroes, comprising Field hands, Mechanics. House and Body Servants, &c.

# A HARD MAN TO ADMIRE

Forrest was a remarkable fighter and a natural military leader. Nevertheless, most historians agree that atrocities were committed at Fort Pillow, either at Forrest's explicit command or with his sanction and compliance. A minority of Southern historians dissent from this view and believe that the massacre story is the product of Northern propaganda.

Forrest survived the war and made a valiant effort to rebuild his fortune, becoming a plantation owner again as well as president of the Selma, Marion, and Memphis Railroad, but, during the nationwide financial Panic of 1873, saw the railroad slip into bankruptcy even as he suffered personal bankruptcy. He spent his last years as warden of a state prison work farm.

If anything, his postwar reputation fared even worse than his finances. His prominent role in the early Ku Klux Klan, which he joined either in 1866 or 1867, has marked him among many as a rabid racist. The purpose of the Klan at this time was to undermine Union Reconstruction efforts by terrorizing freed blacks and discouraging them from voting or running for office. By definition, this was a racist objective, but its motives were less about hatred of African Americans than they were about resentment of the Northern military occupation of the South. Many historians refute the long-held assertion that Forrest served as the KKK's leader, its Grand Wizard. However, it is also true that, in 1875, Forrest, invited to address an organization of Southern blacks called the Jubilee of Pole-Bearers, made a boldly progressive plea for racial reconciliation and for at least the economic integration of African-Americans into white-controlled businesses and professions.

*"Visit of the Ku-Klux," by Frank Bellew, was published in* Harper's Weekly *on February 24, 1872. In the dead of night, a Klansman menaces an innocent, unarmed African American family.*

He was the only Confederate commander who fought well— brilliantly, in fact—at Fort Donelson in February 1862, and, when this and Fort Henry fell, he took command in Nashville, managing the evacuation of irreplaceable gunsmithing machinery, which he was able to remove from the city before Nashville fell to Grant. Without Forrest, the South would have lost most of its already limited capacity to manufacture firearms.

At Shiloh, Forrest commanded a fierce rearguard action that took a substantial toll on Federal forces. Sustaining a pointblank back wound in this battle, he was nearly paralyzed by the minié ball that lodged near his spine. Nevertheless, he recovered to be promoted to brigadier general and led a succession of raids in 1864 throughout Mississippi, Tennessee, and Alabama so devastating that Sherman personally decreed that the "devil Forrest" be "hunted down and killed if it costs ten thousand lives and bankrupts the Federal treasury." The commanding officer of the Army of the Tennessee declared that there "will never be peace in Tennessee till Forrest is dead." It was high praise indeed coming from a warrior like Sherman.

## MASSACRE AT FORT PILLOW

SHERMAN HATED FORREST—saw him as his nemesis—precisely because the two men shared a common vision of war, of "war as hell"—albeit necessarily so. To both men, claims of gallantry and glory were, as Sherman would say after the war, "moonshine." Confederate general Joseph Johnston believed that if Nathan Bedford Forrest "had the advantages of a thorough military education and training, [he] would have been the great central figure of the Civil War." Perhaps. Or perhaps it was his very lack of training—the kind of training that inhibited the likes of McClellan and Halleck—that had made him the remarkable figure he was. His battle doctrine was simple enough to fit into a single sentence: "Get there first with the most men," a precept that his admirers, in an effort to underscore his unlettered state, fictionalized in backwoods dialect as "Git thar fustest with the mostest."

Even more important was another expression of his understanding of war. This time, the Southern dialect was probably genuine. Forrest declared that "War means fightin', and fightin' means killin'." Neither Sherman nor Grant could have put it more eloquently.

Unlike most of the Confederate commanders he faced, men he had known during the war with Mexico or in the peacetime army, Ulysses Grant never met Nathan Forrest—and, after the Civil War, never made any effort to meet him. While the two saw the essence of warfare in much the same way, Grant, though sometimes scorned as a "butcher," always managed to remain a soldier. On at least one infamous occasion, Forrest's killer instincts drove him into another identity.

On April 12, 1864, he dispatched a division commanded by Brigadier General James R. Chalmers to Fort Pillow, a Mississippi River combination military fort and civilian trading post, built mostly of earth on a high bluff above the river not far from the town of Henning. The fort had been established in 1861 by its namesake, Confederate general Gideon Pillow,

*Brigadier General James R. Chalmers commanded the 9th Mississippi Infantry in an attack on Fort Pillow in which members of the Union garrison were cut down after they surrendered. A disproportionate number of the victims were African American troops. Chalmers reputedly took his orders for the Fort Pillow "massacre" directly from General Nathan B. Forrest.*

*This depiction was meant to leave no doubt that the "battle" of Fort Pillow was a massacre and not an honorable military operation. Stabbing and bludgeoning predominate over shooting, and the Confederate army is clothed not in standard-issue uniforms, but in a motley assortment of rough civilian clothing that make them look like highwaymen.*

but, like the other Confederate river strong-points, was now garrisoned by the Union and served to defend Union supply lines. Chalmers's assignment was to retake Fort Pillow, which would thereby render Union logistics vulnerable to raids Forrest intended to lead personally.

Fort Pillow's Union garrison was slim, consisting of 262 African-American soldiers and 295 whites, most of them Tennesseans who were loyal to the Union. Chalmers's attack quickly sent Fort Pillow's pickets retreating into the fort. This accomplished, he laid siege to the garrison and awaited the arrival of Forrest with the main body of his command. Forrest wasted no time. On his arrival, he demanded the surrender of Fort Pillow. When this was refused, he ordered his men to storm the fort.

Both Union and Confederate accounts agree on one thing. Vastly outnumbered, the garrison was quickly overwhelmed and suffered total defeat. Beyond this, memories—or versions—sharply diverge.

Of the 557 members of the garrison, 221 were killed and about 100 wounded; 168 whites and 58 blacks were taken prisoner. Forrest's losses were minimal at 14 killed and 86 wounded. Surviving Union troops later claimed that, once the fort had been penetrated, they tried to surrender, only to be hooted down with cries of "No quarter! No quarter! Kill the damned niggers; shoot them down!" Nor was this the result of a mob's passion. Witnesses claimed that General Forrest personally directed the slaughter, explicitly ordering men who had surrendered to be shot down wherever they stood. Although no one claimed that Forrest specifically ordered more black prisoners to be shot than whites, the fact is that whereas 56 percent of the white garrison was marched out of Fort Pillow as POWs, only 20 percent of the blacks who surrendered were so fortunate. Forrest's version of events, the official Confederate version, was that the garrison's refusal to surrender was responsible for the horrendous death toll.

After the battle—the Union called it a "massacre"—President Lincoln was quick to conclude that Forrest had purposely directed the slaughter against black troops and accordingly issued a stern demand that the Confederacy treat all captured black soldiers—whether free men or fugitive slaves—as soldiers entitled to the protection of the generally accepted conventions of "civilized war." When Confederate authorities spurned the demand with contempt, the U.S. Congress weighed in, its Joint Committee on the Conduct of the War convening hearings that branded Forrest and the men of his command war criminals, guilty of having murdered most of the garrison after it had surrendered. The committee heard gruesome eyewitness testimony of the living burial of some black troops and of Confederates setting fire to tents that sheltered the Union wounded. By the spring of 1864, it seemed, *this* is what the Civil War had come to.

## WILDERNESS

ON MAY 4, 1864, Ulysses Grant led George Meade and the 120,000 men of the Army of the Potomac across the Rapidan River. With this, the Civil War returned to the eastern theater where it had begun. Unlike George McClellan, Grant had no fear of being outnumbered. He knew Lee's Army of Northern Virginia was vastly overmatched, and he believed—accurately, as it turned out—that the Confederate commander could no longer field more than sixty-six thousand men. Eager to kill this army, to overwhelm it with superior numbers, Grant intended to force Lee into open ground, which gave the Union infantry plenty of room to maneuver and clear fields of fire for Union artillery.

But Lee was not about to cede to Grant the choice of battlefield. His defeat at Gettysburg was so terrible that it should have destroyed the will, spirit, and self-confidence of any general. But Lee was not "any general." Instead of surrendering or digging in defensively, he attacked Grant's approaching columns as boldly as he had made war against the Army of the Potomac in Pennsylvania. He understood that Grant wanted him out in the open, and so he seized the initiative to attack Grant first and to hit his army when and where it was most vulnerable, while marching through the densely forested region known as the "Wilderness," the very ground that had brought Joseph Hooker to ruin at Chancellorsville nearly a year to the day before (Chapter 12).

*The exchange of musket and artillery fire was so intense in the Wilderness that, in some places, the woods were set ablaze, claiming many lives on both sides.* Harper's Weekly *published this engraving of "Our wounded escaping from the fires in the Wilderness" on June 4, 1864.*

## NUMBERS

### Wilderness Toll

Grant and Meade committed 101,895 soldiers of the Army of the Potomac to the battle of the Wilderness, a battle neither man had wanted to fight. Of this number, 17,666 became casualties: 2,246 killed, 12,037 wounded, the rest missing. An army that incurs a casualty rate of 10 percent is generally deemed to have suffered a catastrophe. At 17 percent, Grant's losses also included the deaths of two generals, the wounding of two more, and the capture of another two. Confederate losses are harder to gauge, but it is believed that, of 61,025 troops engaged, 11,125 were killed, wounded, or missing, an 18 percent casualty rate. Lee also lost three generals killed; four others, including Longstreet, were wounded. Indeed, Longstreet was the victim of friendly fire, shot at virtually the same spot where Stonewall Jackson had been mortally wounded, also by friendly fire, just a year earlier.

A conventional general would have avoided battle in the Wilderness because it was "bad ground," entirely unsuited to combat as it was conventionally fought in the mid-nineteenth century. Cavalry was all but useless in woods overgrown with underbrush and veined with waterways ranging from broad rivers to deep ravines. This meant that reconnaissance, the cavalry's stock in trade, was all but impossible. As for artillery, always the great advantage of the heavily industrialized North, there were few positions from which it could be effectively brought to bear against the enemy, and the scarcity of roads made it almost impossible to transport the Napoleons, let alone the heavier guns. Outnumbered nearly two to one, Lee saw the "bad ground" of the Wilderness as a much-needed ally, a means of evening the formidable odds stacked against his much-depleted Army of Northern Virginia.

"Will was standing by my side, but in the open. He, with a groan, doubled up and dropped on the ground at my feet. He looked up at me. His face was pale. He gasped for breath a few times, and then said faintly: 'That ends me. I am shot through the bowels.'"

*Union private Frank Wilkeson on the death of a fellow soldier in the battle of the Wilderness, in his* Recollections of a Private Soldier in the Army of the Potomac *(1886)*

The battle of the Wilderness began on May 5 and would continue through the next day. Perhaps out of an excess of consideration for the difficult position of George Meade, Grant relied on him to manage the tactical situation, but Meade quickly found himself out-generaled by Lee. The confusion in the Wilderness was, if anything, even worse than what had prevailed at Shiloh (Chapter 8) and Chickamauga (Chapter 16). It was hard on both sides, but hardest by far on the Army of the Potomac. Combat on day one was horrific but indecisive. Day two of the battle saw the arrival of James Longstreet and his corps, which were more than sufficient to envelop Meade's faulty deployment and thereby drive in the two flanks of the Union army, one into the other. As night fell, Grant ordered Meade to begin a fighting withdrawal.

The retreat was conducted under gunfire so intense that many brush fires were ignited. Before long, the night was torn by flame. Everywhere, the Wilderness was ablaze, and an estimated two hundred men, Confederate as well as Union, burned to death or were overcome by smoke and carbon monoxide during the night of May 7/8.

## GRANT IN DEFEAT

THE BATTLE OF THE WILDERNESS was a terrible way to begin the Overland campaign. In his *Memoirs,* written two decades after the battle, Grant observed simply: "Our losses in the Wilderness were very severe. Those of the Confederates must have been even more so, but I have no means of speaking with accuracy upon this point." Doubtless this was the thought that sustained him after the battle: The Union could afford to lose men; the Confederacy could not. Driven by this equation, as simple as it was terrible, Grant proved himself as unconventional a commander as Lee. Defeated, a general is supposed to retreat. Defeated, Grant, ordered the Army of the Potomac not to retreat but to advance. Sidestepping Lee's position, he led the men of the Overland campaign southward to a courthouse at a Virginia crossroads town called Spotsylvania. It was squarely on the road to Richmond, a fact Robert E. Lee understood all too well.

### TAKEAWAY

Named to command of the Union armies, Grant brought a new doctrine to the war. Instead of setting out to capture territory, cities, and towns, he targeted the enemy army, focusing the war effort on destroying the Confederate military, man by man, with the knowledge that the Union had the population to replace its casualties, whereas the Confederacy was starved for manpower. The new doctrine removed from the war all illusion of glory, reducing it to the formula Confederate general Nathan Bedford Forrest had offered: "War means fightin', and fightin' means killin'."

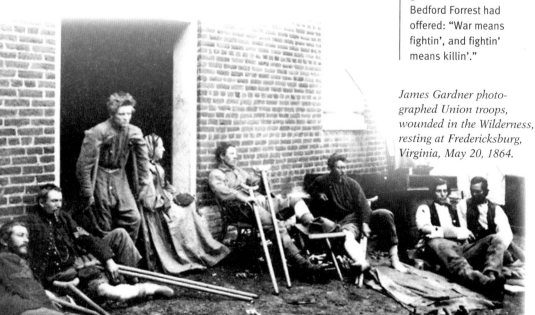

*James Gardner photographed Union troops, wounded in the Wilderness, resting at Fredericksburg, Virginia, May 20, 1864.*

# CHAPTER 18

## "On This Line"

### Testing the Limits of Endurance

HEN JOSEPH HOOKER TOOK OVER THE ARMY OF THE POTOMAC from Ambrose Burnside, he formulated a new plan to hit Lee at Fredericksburg (Chapter 12). Unlike the crude frontal assault that had brought catastrophe under Burnside, Hooker plotted out an enveloping attack right out of the West Point textbook. Trouble was that Lee had read that same textbook and had read it harder and better. He grasped Hooker's intended strategy almost before Hooker did.

Ulysses S. Grant was not Joseph Hooker. His plans did not come from textbooks. If anything, he fought around the books or despite them. He was an unconventional general. But, then, so was Robert E. Lee. Although he was surprised and dismayed by Grant's response to defeat at the Wilderness—advance instead of retreat—his prodigious military imagination did not desert him. He understood what Grant was doing, and, harnessing the momentum of his army's Wilderness victory (despite the heavy losses, the spirits of his men were high) he outran the Army of the Potomac, reaching Spotsylvania before the Union commander.

# LEE: A STRATEGY OF HOLDING ON

THE MOST TERRIBLE OF STORMS rarely burst upon us. They begin with a subtle increase of wind, a barely perceptible drop in temperature, a splash of rain. And so Spotsylvania, a battle of twelve days, began on May 8, 1864, with a skirmish between elements of Lee's army—Jeb Stuart's cavalry and I Corps commanded by Richard H. Anderson (in place of Longstreet, who was recovering from wounds)—and the Union's V Corps under Major General Gouverneur K. Warren.

As Lee had anticipated Grant's immediate tactic—his intention to advance on Spotsylvania—so he fully grasped his larger strategy: to attack Richmond, force a showdown, destroy the Army of Northern Virginia, and thereby extinguish the Confederate States of America. Lee was prepared—and he prepared his entire army—for the climactic campaign of the Civil War. His purpose, however, was not to make some glorious last stand. Lee and the Confederacy clung to one final hope. In November 1864 Abraham Lincoln would stand for reelection. He would be opposed by a Democrat, probably George B. McClellan, whose intention to bring the long and terrible war to an immediate end with a negotiated settlement was widely spoken of (if not necessarily true). If Lee could exact a sufficiently terrible cost on Grant, Lincoln would likely lose the election, making way for a president willing to settle for something far more advantageous to the South than unconditional surrender. The question was: Could the Army of Northern Virginia—and the people of the Confederacy—outlast the Union's waning will to continue the fight?

*L. Prang & Co., a publisher of deluxe chromolithographs, created this commemoration of the battle of Spotsylvania in 1887.*

## HASTY DEFENSE

THE BATTLE UNFOLDED IN A COMBINATION of bitter struggle—some of the most desperate fighting of the war—and daring maneuver. Unlike previous Union commanders, who either withdrew or stood fast, Grant pursued the always dangerous tactic of maneuvering in the midst of combat. He repeatedly shifted his principal line to his left, continually jabbing, thrusting in search of vulnerability in Lee's flank. For his part, Lee remained sufficiently nimble to cover his flank. His troops labored mightily to scratch out of the Virginia soil what a later generation of American soldiers would call a "hasty defense," nothing more, really, than holes in the ground—rifle pits—quick cover from which they might more effectively resist the enemy's relentless blows. This agile defense took a terrible toll on Grant's men, but his continual sidestepping forced Lee to extend his already undermanned defensive line to meet the onslaught. The old style of combat, the Napoleonic doctrine taught at West Point, involved maneuver, to be sure, but ultimately came down to a confrontation in which opposing lines stood still and pounded each other. The side that could pour more fire more rapidly on the other side won. Grant departed from this outworn doctrine. An attacker was supposed to attack the enemy until the enemy submits. Instead, Grant combined attack with maneuver. Instead of massing against Lee at some one point, he forced Lee to stretch and stretch some more. The only question was: Whose line would snap first?

*The cartoonist Joseph E. Baker put his plea for an immediate end to the war into the mouth of the personification of America, Columbia, who demands, "Mr. Lincoln, give me back my 500,000 sons!!!" The president, at his feet a signed proclamation calling for five hundred thousand troops, responds by starting to tell a joke: "Well the fact is—by the way that reminds me of a STORY!!!" Baker was responding to a false rumor that Lincoln had cracked a joke while visiting the Antietam battlefield.*

**COLUMBIA DEMANDS HER CHILDREN !**

## SHERIDAN'S MARCH

PICTURE A PAIR OF WRESTLERS. Each looks for an opening that will permit the pinning move. To the spectator of the match, it is a contest of grasping arms and thrusting legs, hardly static, yet the two antagonists are locked together nevertheless. That was the situation when Grant

# TYRANNUS?

As everyone knows, the actor turned assassin John Wilkes Booth addressed the audience at Ford's Theatre the night he murdered Abraham Lincoln, declaiming the state motto of Virginia: *Sic semper tyrannis*—Thus always to tyrants.

In the twilit retrospect of history, it seems nothing more or less than the declaration of a madman. Lincoln—a tyrant! How could anyone believe this of the author of the Gettysburg Address? And yet there were many rational people, both in the North and the South, who thought just this. Lincoln was the first and (so far) the only president to deliberately suspend habeas corpus. The draft, as many saw it, was likewise the act of a tyrant. His proclamation emancipating at least some slaves was widely seen as a violation of the Fifth Amendment's guarantee against deprivation of property without due process of law.

And just as some objected to what they deemed Lincoln's tyrant ways, others, including such influential members of his Cabinet as Edwin Stanton, believed that he should assume more sweeping dictatorial powers in a time of extraordinary crisis. The seceded states had, after all, broken faith with the Constitution, therefore the Constitution should be held in abeyance until the unconstitutional rebellion had been safely suppressed. Many, perhaps most, in government would have understood and approved had Abraham Lincoln called off or suspended the election of November 1864 rather than risk ushering into the White House an administration that would turn its back on three years of sacrifice to make an easy peace with the Confederacy.

What if Lincoln had done this?

He and many who supported his uncompromising stand on the war would have been relieved of the anxiety of reelection, but the price of this relief would have been to hand the South a moral victory by certifying the chief grievance it presented to its people and to the world: that the region was, collectively, the victim of another region's tyranny. The rebellion might still have been suppressed, but its suppression would not have been a triumph of constitutional democracy.

Lincoln was a pragmatist willing to take some extraordinary measures to end the rebellion, but he believed it ultimately impossible to divide means from ends. The victory he envisioned had to be unambiguously and transparently a triumph of democracy and law over oppression and error. Such could be claimed only if that victory were achieved by wholly democratic means. As he faced reelection, Lincoln calculated a strong possibility that he would lose, and yet he believed even more strongly that the law was more important than he, a mere man. By holding the election as prescribed by the Constitution, Lincoln believed he was affirming the principles of the Union over and above the usurping anarchy of Jefferson Davis—a president appointed, not elected—and his Confederacy.

liberated Phil Sheridan from the conventional clutches of George Meade. Sheridan proposed to lead the 10,000-man cavalry corps of the Army of the Potomac in a breakout toward Richmond, Grant agreed to the proposal and overruled Meade. The Union general in chief embraced Little Phil's confident pledge that he would "whip Stuart out of his boots." Grant believed that menacing Richmond would compel Stuart—whose forty-five hundred horsemen were outnumbered better than two to one—to fight and to die. This would pry open a passage to Richmond, forcing Lee to break off at Spotsylvania, thereby permitting the whole Army of the Potomac to lurch closer to the Confederate capital, hastening the destruction of the Army of Northern Virginia.

The size of Sheridan's cavalry corps was an advantage, of course, but it also created a problem. No matter how skillfully he deployed his troopers, Little Phil could not conceal their movement from the keen eyes of Jeb Stuart. The column, four riders abreast, was strung out along some thirteen miles! The Confederate commander looked at a map, found a place called "Yellow Tavern," a disused inn just six miles north of Richmond, and planted his forty-five hundred troopers there to block Sheridan's advance.

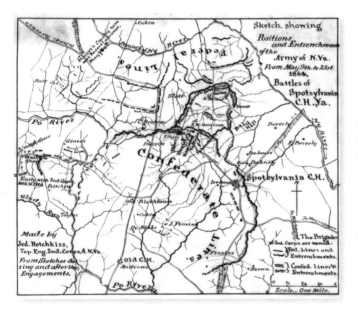

Stuart had the advantage of a solid defensive position, and his troopers, every one of them, were well aware that they and they alone stood between Lincoln's soldiers and the capital of their country. The front of Sheridan's column engaged Stuart at Yellow Tavern for some three hours, then withdrew—though not before one of Little Phil's troopers, seeing an ostentatiously uniformed rebel officer just thirty feet in the distance, leveled his carbine and squeezed off a round. Jeb Stuart fell from his saddle and died the next day. No one took his loss harder than Robert E. Lee. First Jackson (Chapter 12), now Stuart. From head to tail, he was losing his army.

*Jedediah Hotchkiss, a "topographical engineer" attached to II Corps, Army of the Potomac, produced this map of the battle of Spotsylvania "showing positions and entrenchments" of Lee's Army of Northern Virginia.*

"General Lee . . . hoped—perhaps I may say he was almost convinced—that if we could keep the Confederate army between General Grant and Richmond, checking him for a few months longer, . . . public opinion in the North might induce the authorities at Washington to let the Southern States go, rather than force their retention in the Union at so heavy a cost."

*Confederate general John B. Gordon, reporting an after-battle conversation with Robert E. Lee, May 7, 1864*

## MULE SHOE: THE BLOODY ANGLE

AFTER DAYS OF THRUSTING into Lee's side, only to be repulsed each time, Grant believed he had found a weak spot and sent Major General Winfield Scott Hancock with twenty thousand men against Confederate general Richard Ewell's corps. The Confederate line here was deployed in a salient, a curved entrenchment bulging outward like an inverted U and intended to give the defenders a 180-degree field of fire. To the Union men who attacked the position, the upside-down U looked more like a Mule Shoe—and that's what they called their objective, at least until a day of close-quarters fighting called for a new name: "Bloody Angle."

Grant had chosen his man well. Hancock had shown himself to be a valiant and aggressive leader at Gettysburg, and, on May 12, he poured his heart and soul against Mule Shoe. His attack stepped off at 4:30 in the morning, a predawn hour in which defenders are most inclined to give in to dread and panic. By quarter to five, Hancock's soldiers were a torrent of blue, flowing through the holes they had punched into Ewell's line. By 6:30, they had collected between two and four thousand prisoners—accounts vary widely—among them a brace of generals, along with some twenty cannon.

*Edwin Forbes sketched Union artillery making its way through a storm near Spotsylvania Court House.*

But Ewell did not let the bleeding go on for long. Transferring all he could into the breach, he arrested Hancock's advance by late morning, and for the remainder of May 12, the fighting was primal, hand to hand, not something out of the Industrial Age, but the Dark Ages. General Grant's aide de camp, Horace Porter, believed that Bloody Angle was "probably the most desperate engagement in the history of modern warfare." He saw "opposing flags . . . thrust against each other, and muskets . . . fired with muzzle against muzzle." Men "clubbed" their muskets, that is, grasped their weapons by the barrel and used the heavy wooden stock as a club, crushing skulls, Porter wrote. They thrust their swords and bayonets "between the logs in the parapet which separated the combatants," blindly stabbing the enemy to death. "Wild cheers, savage yells, and frantic shrieks rose above the sighing of the wind and the pattering of the rain"—the rain that had been falling since the day before—the mingled sounds forming "a demoniacal accompaniment to the booming of the guns as they hurled their missiles of death into the contending ranks." The rain grew to a torrential downpour as night fell, but, Porter recorded, even "the darkness of night and the pitiless storm failed to stop the fierce contest, and the deadly strife did not cease till after midnight."

*Robert E. Lee was an officer famed for his physical courage. Anxious to close up gaps in the Confederate line at Mule Shoe, he repeatedly exposed himself to enemy fire, prompting an anguished outcry of "Lee to the rear!" among rank-and-file soldiers terrified by the prospect of losing their commander.*

## THE STRONG AND THE WEAK

MULE SHOE, OR BLOODY ANGLE, created such a crisis in the Confederate lines that Lee defied the pleas of his subordinates and ventured to the front to direct the defense personally. The men fighting at Mule Shoe were so terrified by the prospect of losing Lee that they took up a chant of *"Lee to the rear"* and even refused to advance until he had withdrawn to safety. In the end, Ewell—and Lee—managed to beat back Hancock's assault, but, as before, Grant refused to withdraw. Stymied, he yet again sidestepped Lee and edged closer to Richmond.

The horrific fight at Mule Shoe was the zenith of combat at Spotsylvania and was followed by minor battles and skirmishes through May 21, plus two larger engagements on May 24, at the North Anna River and the Totopotomoy Creek, from May 26 through May 30. Nowhere could Grant achieve the breakthrough he so desperately sought, but every exchange drew Confederate blood, and while each resulted in a repulse against Grant, the Union general always responded by slipping to the side and advancing around whatever flank presented itself. Lee was scoring indecisive victory after indecisive victory, but slowly bleeding to death in the process.

While Hancock and Ewell fought like Titans, Franz Sigel and his West Virginia unit were whipped at New Market in the Shenandoah Valley on May 15 by Major General John C. Breckinridge with the assistance of 247 cadets from the nearby Virginia Military Institute. Benjamin Butler and his Army of the James suffered an even more humiliating—and consequential—defeat in a series of battles fought during late May and collectively known as the Bermuda Hundred campaign. Bermuda Hundred had been established in 1613, just six years after the founding of Jamestown, and was located on the narrow peninsula separating the Appomattox and James Rivers as they approached confluence. In an act of extraordinary stupidity, Butler had encamped his small army—thirty-three thousand men—on the peninsula, much as, during the American Revolution, Lord Cornwallis had made the mistake of planting his army on the tip of the Yorktown peninsula. In both cases,

*Timothy O'Sullivan, one of the most important combat photographers of the war shot this image of Union soldiers occupying breastworks on the north bank of the North Anna River.*

# WAR IS HELL? IT IS HARD

The history of the Civil War is rife with missed opportunity, some of which was due to the incompetence of command and some to plain bad luck. But even when commanders were at their best, as Winfield Scott Hancock and his men were at Mule Shoe, attacks that began with great promise were often blunted by an adversary whose determination was equal to that of the attackers.

It is easy to criticize generals and their soldiers, but the real lesson of the Civil War is the Herculean nature of modern combat, not the shortcomings of those who fought. Hancock "failed" because Ewell did not "fail." The two sides fought to exhaustion and death, whichever came first.

At least 618,000—some estimates top 700,000—died in Civil War combat; yet, strangely, it was quite difficult for soldiers to kill one another. One historian has calculated that, on average, it required nine hundred pounds of lead and four hundred pounds of powder to kill a man, meaning that the vast majority of shots fired in the heat of battle hit nothing. Nevertheless, the sheer numbers who fought ensured that many thousands would die.

the commanders obligingly placed their forces in a cul de sac, which the opposing armies neatly tied off, bagging their foes. In Butler's case, the Confederates quickly erected a stout line of fortified earthworks across the base of the peninsula, sealing it off. This done, there was no need to destroy the Army of the James. Thanks to Butler's ineptitude, it had been neutralized, and Lee was able to transfer valuable resources from this front to throw into the fight against Grant.

## TELEGRAM TO WASHINGTON

ON MAY 11, GRANT TELEGRAPHED the War Department in Washington, unblinkingly reporting his very heavy losses at Spotsylvania, but adding his belief that "the loss of the enemy must be greater." Numerically, this was not actually the case. In proportion to the dwindling manpower of the Confederacy, however, it was an accurate assessment. "I . . . propose," Grant concluded, "to fight it out on this line, if it takes all summer."

The next big fight came on June 1. Lee had beaten Grant to Spotsylvania. Now, by night, Grant rushed to another crossroads, Cold Harbor, just six miles northeast of Richmond. Once again, however, Lee anticipated him, reached Cold Harbor first, and entrenched his forces for a battle that developed shortly after dawn on the first and continued through June 2. During this span, Grant threw his army against the Confederate trenches, losing five thousand killed or wounded by nightfall of the second day.

He shook off his losses. As always, Grant's response to defeat was to fight some more, and at 4:30 on the morning of June 3, he sent better than half the Army of the Potomac, sixty thousand men, against the Confederate positions. Whereas at Mule Shoe the fighting had been hand to hand, here the Union men stormed entrenchments that hid the enemy. Many never saw the Confederate soldiers who killed them. For the first time in the war, Confederate artillery proved to be devastating. Firing from well-prepared positions—Lee, after all, was an engineer—his Napoleons sliced through the Union regiments, which were swallowed up in great gouts of thrown-up earth and rock and bone and flesh.

"I have always regretted that the last assault at Cold Harbor was ever made," Grant wrote in his *Memoirs*. In the first hour of that final assault, seven thousand Union soldiers fell dead or wounded, the majority of them in the first eight minutes of the assault. When it was over, the Overland campaign, to date, had cost the Army of the Potomac fifty thousand casualties, killed, wounded, captured, or missing.

*Union troops hurriedly erect breastworks at the battle of Cold Harbor in this June 1864 illustration by Edwin Forbes.*

The main phase of the battle ended with the June 3 assault. Officially, Grant recorded that his front had "stabilized," but what this really meant was that the men and officers of the Army of the Potomac were no longer capable of renewing the attack. After three more days of desultory combat, at daybreak of June 7, as Pennsylvania infantryman Daniel Chisholm recorded in his diary, "The enemy advanced a white Flag, asking permission to bury their dead, which was granted. We had an armistice of two hours." By this time, those dead were horrible to look at. "We sat on the works and let our legs dangle over the front and watch the Johnnies [Johnny Rebs] carry off their dead comrades in silence, but in a great hurry," Chisholm wrote, noting that the "live Rebel looks bad enough in his old torn, ragged Butternut suit, but a dead Rebel looks horrible all swelled

*Kurz & Allison's postwar depiction of the battle of Cold Harbor, one of the bloodiest of the entire war, appears quite orderly—even pastoral.*

up and black in the face." After the dead had been collected, "there was nothing left but stains of Blood, broken and twisted guns, old hats, canteens, every one of them reminders of the death and carnage that reigned a few short hours before." As for the wounded, by the time of the truce, there were but few alive to rescue. Three days of agony in the field had killed most of them.

## HORRID PIT

COLD HARBOR RENEWED AMONG SOME in the Northern public the outcry for Grant's removal. Like everyone else, Abraham Lincoln was appalled by the fifty thousand men who had died under his new general's command. This represented 41 percent of the force Grant had begun with. But Lincoln did not stop with analyzing Grant's losses. Lee, he learned, had lost some thirty-two thousand killed or wounded. That was 46 percent of his Army of Northern Virginia. Lincoln could rebuild the Army of the Potomac. Jefferson Davis could not do the same for Robert E. Lee. Lincoln urged Grant to fight on.

And so he did, slipping the Army of the Potomac out of Cold Harbor by night and crossing the Chickahominy. Observing this, Lee could reasonably conclude only one thing. Grant was continuing the march to Richmond. The Confederate leader rushed most of his surviving army to defend the outskirts of the capital. But, for the first time in this bloody duel, Lee had mistaken Grant's move. He was bound not for Richmond, but for Petersburg, an Appomattox River port and rail junction. The stage magician dazzles his audience through misdirection, prompting all eyes to focus on the obvious while he performs the subtle, so as to elevate deception to the apparent status of magic. In a stroke of strategic sleight of hand, Grant turned away from the obvious and targeted a town that was poorly defended but that was nevertheless a vital objective. Grab it, and Richmond would be cut off from the Confederacy. Already blocked at the north, the Confederate capital would be severed from the east. Like a plant torn at the root, Richmond would wither and fall.

The first of Grant's army, sixteen thousand men, arrived outside of Petersburg on June 15. Just three thousand Confederates under P. G. T. Beauregard were present to defend it. All that was necessary was to move fast. Tragically—not just for Grant and the Union, but for all the soldiers, Northern and Southern, living now who would die in the coming months of continued fighting—those first arrivals were under the command of one Major General William Farrar "Baldy" Smith, a tired man leading tired men. Instead of driving them into an immediate attack, an attack in

*Major General William F. "Baldy" Smith was photographed (center) with his staff at Cold Harbor. Presented with a golden opportunity to break through the thinly manned Confederate lines at Petersburg, Virginia, Smith instead rested his men, unwittingly giving General P. G. T. Beauregard all the time he needed to reinforce his position. Thanks to this missed chance, instead of a rapid breakthrough, the Union was forced to mount a long, dreary, costly siege that may have prolonged the war by nearly a year.*

which they would surely have rolled over the force they outnumbered more than five to one, Smith rested his troops on the Petersburg front, giving an incredulous Beauregard all the time he needed to reinforce the city's defenses, already a very formidable complex of trenches and fortifications that had been built early in the war by far-seeing commanders who recognized the town's strategic importance.

Grant realized the opportunity that had been lost. Assuming personal command at Petersburg, he nevertheless tried to redeem it by launching two assaults, on the sixteenth and eighteenth. Against the now-reinforced and fortified positions, they were repulsed. Clearly, the only alternative now was to do what had been done at Vicksburg: lay siege, no matter how long it took. Or so it seemed.

Among the commanders assembled at the Petersburg siege lines was Ambrose Burnside. After being relieved of command of the Army of the Potomac following Fredericksburg, Burnside, who sincerely wanted to continue serving the United States, asked to be demoted and assigned to a subordinate command, which he was confident he could handle. He was now one of Meade's corps commanders. Burnside was

*The Confederate defensive works around Petersburg were some of the most formidable and elaborately constructed on any battlefield of the war. Their resemblance to the heavily engineered trenches of World War I is striking.*

approached by Colonel Henry Pleasants, in civilian life a mining engineer who now commanded the 48th Pennsylvania Infantry, a regiment made up almost entirely of coal miners. He had an idea, which he and his brigade commander, Brigadier General Robert Potter, presented.

Pleasants proposed to "mine"—that was the military term for digging a tunnel—from the Union siege lines to the Confederate entrenchments around Petersburg and enlarge the end of the tunnel on the Confederate side, thereby creating "galleries" into which several tons of black powder explosives would be packed. These would be detonated, blowing a large hole and gap in the Confederate defenses, through which elements of the Union army could advance and break through, enfilade the Confederate position (that is, attack along the axis of the entrenchments, instead of head-on), and open up a way for the entire Army of the Potomac to continue the advance all the way into Petersburg. It was a brilliantly promising alternative to a prolonged siege.

Military mining, including "undermining"—the detonation of explosives under an enemy position—was hardly new. In fact, it was as old as the art of fixed fortification, dating back to the Middle Ages and probably even to ancient times; however, what Pleasants and Potter proposed was an extraordinarily long tunnel (at more than five hundred feet, it would be the longest military tunnel ever excavated) that would be dug quickly, the activity totally concealed from the enemy.

At length, Burnside was persuaded of the project's feasibility. Quite probably, he saw it as a golden opportunity to redeem himself and repair his shattered reputation. He spoke with Meade and Grant, who were reluctant and skeptical, but grudgingly willing to allow Pleasants's men to dig. Siege work, after all, involved much idleness, and idleness above all else was inimical to good order and discipline. If the mine proved in the end to have been just so much make-work, so be it. Digging began on June 25 and was completed on July 27. The Pennsylvania miners quietly carried through the tunnel to the galleries some four tons of powder, laid fuse, returned to the Union lines, and packed the Union end of the mine with hundreds of sandbags to absorb any backfire, leaving just enough room for a man to crawl through to light the fuse.

While Pleasants and his miners had been digging, Burnside saw to the special training of a division of

*Although the siege of Petersburg is best remembered for the Union "mine" (military tunnel) that was detonated beneath the Confederate lines at the battle of the Crater, the Confederates defending Petersburg also excavated tunnels in an attempt to undermine Union fortifications. This is the entrance to a mine at Fort Mahone, which was intended to undermine the Union's Fort Sedgwick a few hundred feet away.*

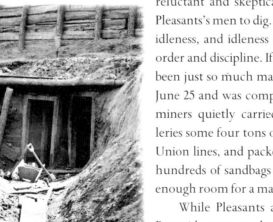

# DRAWING BREATH

At 510.8 feet in length, the Petersburg mine was the longest military tunnel in history. No previous military tunnel had exceeded 400 feet in length because, in a horizontal shaft longer than about 400 feet, the pressure of the surface atmosphere is inadequate to circulate the air essential to the exchange of oxygen for carbon dioxide that surface-dwelling creatures take for granted. The historian of the 48th Pennsylvania explained the ingenious system by which Colonel Pleasants allowed his miners to breathe:

Ventilation was accomplished in a very simple way—after a method quite common in the anthracite coal mines. A perpendicular shaft or hole was made from the mine to the surface at a point inside of the Union rifle pits. A small furnace, or fire-place, was built at the bottom of this hole, or shaft, for the purpose of heating the air, and a fire was kept constantly burning, thus creating a draft. The door made of canvas was placed in the gallery, a little outside of this fire-place, thus shutting it in and shielding it from the outside air at the mouth of the mine. Wooden pipes, extending from the outside of this canvas door, along the gallery to the inner end thereof, conducted the fresh air to the point of operations, which, after supplying the miners with pure air, returned along the gallery toward the entrance of the mine, and, being stopped by the canvas door, the vitiated air moved into the furnace and up the shaft to the surface. By this means a constant current of air circulated through the gallery. As the work advanced, the inside end of the wooden pipe was extended so as to carry good air up to the face of the workings.

*These contemporary diagrams of the Union mine intended to blast through the Confederate defenses around Petersburg suggest the complexity of the engineering required to dig a military tunnel more than 500 feet long.*

762      *THE TRAGEDY OF THE CRATER.*

*Alfred R. Waud's impressionistic sketch of Colonel Henry Pleasants supervising the arrival of black powder in his mine powerfully evokes the eerie subterranean conditions.*

"colored" troops to exploit the gap that would be blasted into the Confederate lines. The most critically important thing was to charge through the enemy entrenchments without getting trapped in the blast crater and without slowing or stopping, lest the attackers get jammed together, pile up on one another, bog down, and make easy targets for the defenders. Ensuring the rapidity of the advance required the division assigned to the initial attack to master a series of complex movements, which were choreographed with the precision of a ballet and rehearsed to perfection.

The day before the blast was set to be detonated and the attack launched, Major General George Meade summoned Burnside to give him new orders. He and Grant had had second thoughts about using African American troops for what was clearly an extraordinarily hazardous mission. Both commanders felt that, if the attackers suffered heavy losses—which was likely—the two of them would be condemned by the public, press, and politicians for having deliberately sacrificed "colored" lives instead of risking white ones. It would appear that Union army high command believed black men were of less value than white. Meade therefore summarily ordered Burnside to find a white division to lead the assault.

Burnside protested, but to no avail. He knew that sending an untrained division into the breach would almost surely mean the failure of the mission. Frustrated and exhausted, however, he did not even bother to make a command decision. Instead, he summoned the commanders of his white divisions, explained the situation, and ordered them to draw straws. The short one fell to Brigadier General James H. Ledlie, quite probably the very worst of the Union's welter of "political generals."

Shortly after midnight on the morning of July 30, Ledlie's division prepared to make the assault. At 3:15 a.m., Colonel Pleasants entered the tunnel, walked through four hundred feet of it, and lit a ninety-eight-foot fuse. This done, he ran out of the tunnel as fast as a man can run at a crouch through a passage barely five feet high.

Forty-five minutes passed without an explosion. Someone had to investigate. Since there was no telling when a fuse, apparently extinguished, might flare into life and set off the blast, it was an extraordinarily hazardous mission. The Irish sergeant who had served as foreman of the excavating party volunteered, ventured into the tunnel, and discovered that the fuse, which had been spliced in many places, had fizzled. After cutting out the failed area of the fuse, he respliced it, relit it, and ran out. Within minutes, 175 feet of Confederate entrenchments exploded. Major William H. Powell, one of Ledlie's staff officers, recalled the "deep shock

# "A DISQUALIFICATION LESS COMMON AMONG SOLDIERS"

Born in Utica, New York, in 1832, James Hewett Ledlie graduated from Union College in Schenectady and became a successful civil engineer, specializing in railroad construction. Political connections secured him an appointment as major of the 19th New York Infantry shortly after the outbreak of the Civil War, and he performed well enough to earn promotions to colonel and to brigadier general, with command of the Artillery Brigade of the Department of North Carolina in December 1862. At first, the Senate failed to confirm the appointment, but, when he was reappointed in October 1863, the Senate gave its confirmation.

Ledlie was assigned mainly to garrison commands with coastal artillery units—postings in which little was demanded of him and in which he could do little harm. He accepted command of a brigade in Burnside's IX Corps and was soon promoted to command the 1st Division in that corps soon after Grant's Overland campaign commenced.

After Ledlie drew the short straw that made his division responsible for the initial attack following the detonation of the Petersburg mine, he was apparently so terrified by the prospect of leading his troops in this perilous assault that he did not even bother to brief them or their commanders in preparation. It may have been this particular item of dereliction that caused them to advance into the blast crater instead of around it. Most of those inside the crater were slaughtered by Confederates defending their lines.

A court of inquiry following the battle of the Crater formally censured Ledlie for failing to lead—or even accompany—his men in the assault, and although he received no judicial punishment, he was removed from all active command by General Meade, acting on Grant's orders. Ledlie voluntarily resigned his commission on January 23, 1865, and took up his railroad career where he had left it. He died in 1882. In his memoirs, Grant, always restrained in his criticism of fellow officers, condemned Ledlie as "inefficient." Used by a commander to describe a subordinate, it is a damning word. Even more damning was the phrase Grant added to his evaluation, remarking that Ledlie possessed a "disqualification less common among soldiers." It was the long way around pronouncing him a coward.

*James Hewitt Ledlie's incompetence and cowardice helped to ensure that the Union attack on the Petersburg lines in the battle of the Crater would end in tragic failure.*

and tremor of the earth and a jar like an earthquake," which was followed by a "heaving and lifting of the [Confederate] fort and the hill on which it stood"—the strongpoint in the Confederate line under which the four tons of powder had been packed. He saw a "monstrous tongue of flame" shoot two hundred feet into the air, followed by "a great spout or fountain of red earth . . . mingled with men and guns, timbers and planks, and every other kind of debris, all ascending, spreading, whirling, scattering and falling with great concussion to the earth once more." The blast buried alive nearly an entire Confederate regiment.

Now was the moment for the attack. Blanching, Ledlie promptly turned over leadership of the charge to a subordinate. Complaining of injury and illness, he retired to a bombproof—a blast shelter—and, while his division ventured out to attack, Ledlie hunkered down, drinking the "medicinal" whisky the surgeon had on hand. This is how he would spend the duration of the attack.

As for Burnside, apparently flabbergasted by Meade's ruinous last-minute order to substitute an untrained white division for the trained black one, he had forgotten to order the preparation of passages through his own fortifications. This meant that the attacking division had to climb out and over the Union's own entrenchments and outer obstacles a few men at a time. From the beginning, therefore, the attack got off to a slow start, and the attackers dribbled into the no-man's land between the Union and Confederate lines piecemeal instead of en masse.

There was worse to come.

Untrained, unrehearsed, and thoroughly confused, the doomed division blindly charged into the crater, which was 175 feet across and 34 feet deep, instead of around it. Because they had not carried siege ladders with them, the men had a great deal of difficulty climbing out of the crater, and they soon piled up within it. Those who did manage to climb out were soon lost in the wreckage of what had been a complex warren of Confederate entrenchments.

### "Put in the dead men."

*Order given to improvise a parapet during the
battle of the Crater (July 30, 1864)*

The Confederate defenders, appalled at the horrific nature of the attack they had suffered, an attack that blew to bits or buried alive hundreds of their comrades, closed in from all sides on the attackers. They killed the men wallowing in the trenches, and they poured into the crater itself musket fire supplemented by rocks and other debris. Some even hurled their empty, bayonet-tipped muskets into the crater, harpoon fashion, skewering the Yankees. Before the struggle ended under a sweltering sun, Union casualties, killed or wounded, topped five thousand.

The so-called battle of the Crater was, Ulysses Grant later observed, "the saddest affair I have witnessed in the war." Because it had failed to achieve a breakthrough, the situation at Petersburg settled into a siege, a miserable siege for the next eight months, in which sickness killed more men on both sides than bullets. The world would not again see trench warfare on this scale and with this squalor for another fifty years, when men fighting the "Great War" would slice into France a six-hundred-mile scar of trench from the English Channel to the border of Switzerland. For now, outside the American town of Petersburg, American armies squatted in opposing ditches, enduring filth, vermin, the relentless sun, snipers' bullets, and artillery bombardment, each man in those miserable armies hoping to avoid death even as he awaited his own orders to kill an enemy whose face, hidden below a filthy lip of earth, he could not see.

*The massive detonation of the Union mine during the Siege of Petersburg and the fighting that followed transformed the fertile, rolling hills of middle Virginia into a scarred and cratered moonscape. This photograph was made in the aftermath of the failed assault.*

## TAKEAWAY

The heaviest fighting of the Overland campaign came at Spotsylvania and Cold Harbor. At both places, Lee's outnumbered Army of Northern Virginia dealt Grant's Army of the Potomac a bloody repulse, inflicting a total of fifty thousand casualties. Yet Grant responded to each defeat by sidestepping Lee and advancing farther south, forcing him to take a new stand and, even in victory, to suffer losses the Confederacy could not support. After Cold Harbor, Grant feinted toward Richmond, his obvious objective, prompting Lee to send the bulk of his army to the defense of the Confederate capital. However, Grant shifted his march to Petersburg, a thinly defended port town and rail junction on the Appomattox River. When the Union army missed an opportunity to storm the town, the Confederates reinforced it. An early attempt to blast through the Confederate defenses was bungled at the highest levels, and the Petersburg campaign became a long, costly, and miserable siege.

# CHAPTER 19

## "WAR IS CRUELTY"

### Atlanta's Fall and the March to the Sea

NOTHING IN THE UNITED STATES MILITARY IS MORE SACROSANCT THAN the chain of command. That is true now, and it was true in 1864. Higher command gives lower command an order and so it goes, down the chain. The upper commander does not tell the lower how to execute the order. He is not expected to. He is not supposed to. So when Grant ordered Sherman ". . . to move against Johnston's army, to break it up, and to get into the interior of the enemy's country as far as you can, inflicting all the damage you can against their war resources," it was up to Sherman to determine how these missions would be carried out. He recorded his understanding of the first part of the order simply by rephrasing it: "I was to go for Johnston." He said even less about the second part, but his execution of it was to prove perhaps the most enduringly controversial phase of the Civil War. The doctrinal and strategic innovation Grant brought to the war was the policy of targeting troops rather than territory, yet in ordering Sherman to inflict all the damage he could against the enemy's "war resources," Grant threw open the door to a much wider war. For as Sherman saw it, "war resources" encompassed just about everything an army needed or might need or might ever think it needed. This took in just about everything the civilian population produced and consumed. As Sherman executed them, Grant's instructions were an order for total war.

## Total War

The cataclysmic world wars of the twentieth century made total war—war directed against civilian populations, not just the enemy army—a horrifically commonplace concept. It hit mid-nineteenth-century Americans as something shocking, however, although it would have been familiar to the generation that lived through the American Revolution or the French and Indian War two decades earlier. Yet, even in the Civil War, Sherman was not the first commander to wage total warfare. "Bleeding Kansas" and guerrilla-ravaged Missouri had experienced total warfare—in the case of Kansas, even before a shot was fired against Fort Sumter (Chapter 2). And while the great armies of Grant and Lee dueled on a scale of bloodshed unprecedented, the Confederacy was deploying against the civilian population of the North bands of what were then called "irregulars" and would today be classed as terrorists.

There are many instances. For example, during the late spring and early summer of 1864, residents of coastal Maine took note of strangers among them, artists, apparently, who engrossed themselves

*A July 1864* Harper's Weekly *article was illustrated with two vignettes from Sherman's march through Georgia: a skirmish at Woodlands; and burning the railroad bridge at Resaca.*

in making sketches of the craggy and picturesque coastline. In actuality, the "artists" were a coterie of no fewer than fifty professional topographers, cartographers, and chart makers, all in the Confederate employ. They meticulously charted Maine's myriad inlets and hidden coves to identify those that might serve as secluded anchorage for a pair of armed steamers, the CSS *Tallahassee* and CSS *Florida*, which were being fitted out for a terrorist assault far into the North. It was one thing for Lee's Army of Northern Virginia to venture across the Confederate-Union border into Maryland and Pennsylvania but quite another for Confederate forces to suddenly materialize in a place so far north and so remote from the war. Insurgent warfare, war brought into the very places the enemy feels safest, is intended to demonstrate a government's inability to protect its own.

Despite the meticulous preparation, word of the intended raids in Maine leaked to the U.S. consul in St. Johns, Quebec—Confederate agents operated extensively in Canada—who duly communicated with the War Department, which in turn notified the local Home Guard. When a handful of insurgents descended upon the Calais (Maine) National Bank—their object was to "liberate" funds for the cash-strapped Confederacy—Home Guardsmen, an array of police officers, and even the marshal of Portland were prepared. Most of the raiders were rounded up, including one Francis Jones, who, as the saying goes, sang like a canary, revealing that he and the others were but the vanguard of a much greater raid to be delivered amphibiously. Jones's information killed the element of surprise, the main phase of the amphibious operation was called off, and Confederate agents were arrested throughout Maine, Massachusetts, New York, Pennsylvania, Maryland, Illinois, Missouri, Kentucky, Tennessee, and Ohio. This counterinsurgency sweep foiled the large-scale plot even as it spread alarm throughout the North.

The Northern fears were largely unfounded. Insurgent acts by Confederates and Confederate sympathizers were for the most part aborted, although, on October 19, 1864, a gang of about twenty did manage to storm three banks in St. Albans, Vermont, near the Canadian border. The raiders made off with nearly a quarter of a million dollars, a spectacular haul in the mid-nineteenth century (less than half was recovered). They also killed one St. Albans man and wounded another. For the first time in the war, the terrorists used an improvised incendiary device known as "Greek fire," which they hurled against several St. Albans buildings, igniting blazes that razed at least one building to the ground.

The St. Albans raiders withdrew into Canada and found refuge there. It was at best a semi-successful operation, yet some insurgent leaders were not satisfied with robbing banks and committing isolated acts of terror. They wanted to visit total war upon the North. A number of would-be insurgents—nobody knows how many—plotted a nationwide terrorist operation simultaneously targeting Chicago and Cincinnati, as well as a number of smaller towns throughout Missouri and Iowa, and, above all, New York City. D-Day was to be November 8, 1864, the Union's election day.

As it turned out, only the New York plot actually went forward—at least part way. The original objective had been to ignite many blazes throughout the city; to seize and raid the United States Sub-Treasury in Manhattan; and to liberate Fort Lafayette, a POW camp located in what is today Bay Ridge, Brooklyn. Thanks to the diligence of Union army counterintelligence officers, the Chicago scheme was exposed well in advance, and with its collapse, the other operations were officially called off. The three principal planners of the New York plot, however, were unwilling to give up entirely. Colonel Robert Martin and Lieutenant John W. Headley—both men formerly officers under the celebrated raider John Hunt Morgan (Chapter 15)—along with an operative known to history only as "Captain Longuemare from Missouri" decided to go it alone.

*Built during the War of 1812 (but not completed until 1818), Fort Lafayette was intended to defend the Narrows of New York Harbor and was used to house Confederate POWs during the Civil War. The historic fort was destroyed in 1960 to make way for the Verrazano-Narrows Bridge.*

## DETAILS, DETAILS
### Greek Fire

Thucydides (460 BCE–395 BCE) is the first military historian to refer to "Greek fire," an incendiary substance deployed through a tube-like weapon that anticipated the modern flamethrower. The name "Greek fire" was applied through much of history to describe any number of chemical-based incendiary weapons, including those used by Confederate terrorists in the Civil War. No complete record of the formula for Civil War–era Greek fire exists, but it was a liquid almost certainly compounded (in part) of sulfur, charcoal, saltpeter, and quicklime. When exposed to oxygen, the mixture spontaneously and violently combusted so it was typically poured into a glass container, which was tightly sealed. When the container was shattered, the sudden exposure to air would initiate the reaction. The flame was intense, although the blaze was not self-sustaining; however, it would ignite any flammable substances it came into contact with. Any competent chemist could create Greek fire using simple household substances.

Their intention was to quickly recruit enough additional men to simultaneously check into nineteen of New York's biggest and most elegant hotels. Each guest would calmly go up to his room, set it ablaze, and just as calmly walk out, close the door, and leave the hotel to burn. The incendiary of choice was Greek fire, and Longuemare happened to know a Greenwich Village chemist who possessed the willingness, knowledge, and supplies to fill an order for 144 four-ounce bottles of the stuff. What the conspirators had failed to work out was just how this highly unstable substance would be transported the eighty or so city blocks from the Village uptown to their safe house near what is today Central Park—at the time, a shantytown on the fringe of the city, which was in the process of being landscaped to create the park. Assigned to pick up the consignment, Headley loaded the bottles into an oversized carpetbag valise, a forty-plus-pound load, which he lugged several blocks to the horsecar tracks. He boarded a northbound car, took a seat behind the conductor, and gingerly tucked the carpetbag between his legs. Despite this precaution, the rough ride up the teeming avenue jostled the bag's contents. Soon, the stench of hydrogen sulfide was unmistakable. Rotten eggs, concentrated.

Doubtless with visions of imminent self-immolation, Headley glanced down at his feet, fearing that he would see an accumulating

puddle of the substance. But, no. Maybe he was safe. As he settled back against the wicker upright of the bench, he noticed a woman sniffing at the air. At length, she called out: "Something smells dead here! Conductor, something smells dead in that man's valise!"

This being New York, no one reacted to her complaint—except for Headley himself, who immediately exited the horsecar many blocks prematurely. He lugged his load the rest of the way on foot, reached the safe house, and shared out the bottles. At seven that evening, November 25, 1864, the conspirators fanned out (nobody knows how many, but certainly fewer than the nineteen the plan called for), entered their assigned hotels, registered, and walked up to their rooms. Headley, who checked into the Astor House, wrote a memoir after the war: "I hung the bedclothes loosely on the headboard and piled the chairs, drawers of the bureau and washstand on the bed. Then stuffed some newspapers about among

*Harper's Weekly (December 17, 1864) imagined this scene of a "Southern Gentleman about to Fire the Hotel."*

the mass and poured a bottle of turpentine over it all." He knew that Greek fire would explode if he hurled the bottles violently against the floor or wall. Instead, therefore, he slowly poured it on a "pile of rubbish. It blazed up instantly and the whole bed seemed to be in flames, before I could get out." He "locked the door and . . . left the key at the office as usual."

Apparently because the three principal conspirators were unable to recruit enough men to set fires in all nineteen planned targets (fewer were actually struck), they each did double or triple duty. Headley walked briskly through the Astor House lobby and set off to register at the City Hotel. He performed his work here, hit a third hotel, then calmly strolled along the West Side waterfront, where he casually hurled Greek fire at several ships tied up there.

Soon, the city was swept by alarms of fire. The streets buzzed with rumors of an imminent rebel invasion. Yet, despite the panic, the fires failed to coalesce into the great conflagration the arsonists had intended to create. To be sure, some serious damage was done. Two entire floors of the Belmont Hotel and the Metropolitan were burned out, and the St. Nicholas Hotel blazed to the ground, as did a nearby dry goods firm. Several ships suffered substantial fire damage. Most spectacular was the blaze at P. T. Barnum's Museum on lower Broadway. The terrified menagerie housed there erupted in roars, from the tigers and lions, and unearthly trumpeting, from the elephants. Almost as disturbing was the sight of Barnum's seven-foot-tall giantess, whose panicked frenzy was quelled only by the intervention of five strong firemen and a double dose of a physician's opiate.

But this was the extent of it. It is not known why the Greek fire performed so poorly. Like all American cities of the period, New York was almost entirely frame built. As the Great Chicago Fire would demonstrate a half-dozen years after the war, the combustion of a single structure could spread rapidly and destroy virtually an entire city. But not this time. It is possible that the Greenwich Village chemist had prepared the Greek fire improperly; after all, an amount of it had spilled in Headley's carpetbag without producing a flame. Some of those who have read Headley's own account closely note his failure to mention having opened a window in the room. Perhaps the quick-burning accelerant rapidly consumed all the oxygen in the closed room and therefore burned out spontaneously before spreading very far. In any event, the three conspirators made haste for Canada and were never apprehended. The New York fires were quickly brought under control, and although Barnum's Museum was a total loss, it was soon rebuilt—only to burn again (by accident) three years later. As for the Confederate insurgency, it died with the city's flames, and the North was never again the target of Southern terror.

## THE ATLANTA CAMPAIGN COMMENCES

BEFORE SHERMAN COULD CARRY OUT *his* mission of total war—and not with a small insurgency, but three armies totaling 100,000 men between them—he had to engage Joe Johnston and his Army of Tennessee. Sherman left Chattanooga, bound for Georgia, on May 4, 1864. Although he was well aware that he outnumbered Johnston, who commanded at the moment somewhat more than fifty thousand troops, he was not about to attempt a main-strength, head-on attack. Instead, he sent Army of the Tennessee commander Major General James Birdseye McPherson with an infantry division and, just ahead of McPherson, a cavalry division under Brigadier General Judson Kilpatrick to hit and turn Johnston's left flank as another division under John M. Schofield (commanding the Army of the Ohio) menaced his right. While these actions were ongoing, a larger force under Major General George Henry Thomas, the redoubtable "Rock of Chickamauga" (now commanding the Army of the Cumberland), would attack the center.

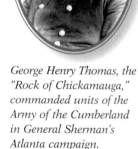

*George Henry Thomas, the "Rock of Chickamauga," commanded units of the Army of the Cumberland in General Sherman's Atlanta campaign.*

It was an excellent plan, which revealed Sherman as the fine tactician that he was. Johnston, however, deftly avoided a major battle, dueling in a skirmish at Rocky Face Ridge during May 7 through 13 before falling back on Resaca, about ten miles down the Western and Atlantic Railroad, which marked Sherman's line of march. At Resaca, Sherman's generals again maneuvered to envelop Johnston, this time from the west. Yet again, Johnston squirmed out of a major battle, although the armies clashed in skirmishes during May 13 through 16. Again, Johnston withdrew southward, following the Western and Atlantic right of way and stopping at Cassville, twenty-five miles south of Resaca. At this place, he decided, he had yielded enough ground to Sherman. Concentrating his army, he decided to counterattack Sherman's forces, which were now widely separated and therefore vulnerable.

*Major General John M. Schofield led a Union division in the Atlanta campaign.*

Johnston's plan was to send generals William J. Hardee and Joseph Wheeler against McPherson and Thomas, and John Bell Hood, his most aggressive but least tactically adept commander, to strike at Schofield. In contrast to Hood, Schofield was an accomplished journeyman, who had positioned his cavalry to foil any counterattack by misleading the attacker. Hood fell for the deception, attacked from the wrong direction, and thereby wrecked any chance Johnston had to coordinate his counterattack effectively. Unable to swing into action, Johnston had no choice but to save his army by withdrawing to Allatoona Pass, thereby yielding another twelve miles of Georgia to Sherman's advance.

For his part, Sherman resisted the temptation to move prematurely. Allatoona Pass was a strong defensive position, and his own army was exhausted from the pursuit. After resting his troops for three days, Sherman marched and skirmished, sparring with his enemy and driving him yet closer to Atlanta.

*In the desperate defense of Atlanta, President Jefferson Davis replaced Joseph Johnston with the far more aggressive—but far less capable—John Bell Hood.*

## ASSAULT ON KENNESAW MOUNTAIN

JOHNSTON AND THE ARMY OF TENNESSEE were perilously close to what they knew to be Sherman's objective. But, for Johnston, this was just the point. He deployed his troops on the twin peaks of Big and Little Kennesaw, and, using tow ropes and brute strength, dragged his artillery to lofty positions overlooking the railroad as well as much of the flat plain that stretched between Kennesaw and Pine and Lost mountains. Under ordinary circumstances, Johnston knew, a savvy general like Sherman would never attack an army dug into a mountain. But this was no ordinary circumstance. Both generals were well aware that Atlanta lay just beyond this point, and Johnston believed that Sherman would be unable to resist attacking in the hope of making a quick breakthrough to his objective.

*This souvenir map, produced after the war by the Western and Atlantic Railroad, shows the town of Marietta in relation to Kennesaw Mountain.*

Johnston's hunch was accurate. On June 19, Sherman deployed his army into positions that would, he hoped, allow him to flank Johnston. This required moving troops south of the Confederate left so that they controlled the Marietta road. Johnston saw what Sherman was trying to do and immediately sent Hood to defend the road. Johnston underscored that Hood's mission was strictly defensive, and he instructed him to take up a blocking position at the farm of the

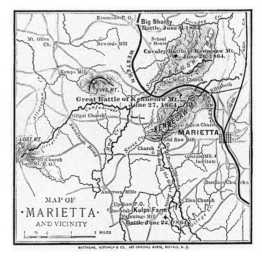

## NUMBERS

### Wasted Lives

Hooker lost 350 killed or wounded at Kolb's Farm, while Hood suffered at least 1,000 casualties. Seeing these lopsided numbers, Sherman vented his displeasure on Hooker for failing to continue the fight to a breakthrough. As it was, Kolb's Farm was a futile encounter.

*The problem with this colorful Kurz & Allison chromolithograph of the battle of Kennesaw Mountain is its failure to reveal Sherman's biggest problem: He attacked uphill, against well-entrenched Confederate forces— a virtually unwinnable proposition.*

widow of a man named Valentine Kolb. Hood did as he was told, and on June 22 successfully repulsed Union forces.

Success encouraged Hood, always impulsive to exceed his orders. Instead of maintaining his blocking position to protect the main part of the Army of Tennessee, he counterattacked. Once out in the open, however, he was outmatched by the Union forces, which fought back—hard. The resulting battle was indecisive but costly to both sides. A furious Johnston rebuked Hood, who replied by criticizing his commanding officer's apparent unwillingness to fight the Yankees, even as they closed on Atlanta. The battle of Kolb's Farm left Sherman angry as well. He criticized Hooker for having relinquished the initiative to Hood. Sherman could not understand why Hooker did not attempt to break through.

As Johnston rode Hood, so the Southern press railed at Johnston for failing to arrest Sherman's advance on Atlanta; and as Sherman berated Hooker, so the Northern press, impatient with a campaign of endless maneuver and futile pursuit, raised doubts about Sherman's willingness to fight. Tempted by the proximity of Atlanta, aware that Lincoln wanted a major victory before the November elections, and feeling the pressure of the press, a frustrated Sherman ordered an all-out frontal assault on Kennesaw Mountain at eight in the morning, June 27. Such an uphill attack was a long shot under the best circumstances, and the twenty-seventh was hardly that. Heavy rains had transformed the slope roads into quagmires and, off the trail, thick undergrowth impeded any advance. The attack failed, and losses were heavy.

Sherman responded to his defeat by waiting for the rains to stop and the roads to dry out. During this time, on June 30, he wrote to his wife, Ellen: "I begin to regard the death and mangling of a couple thousand men as a small affair, a kind of morning dash—and it may be well that we become so hardened." The next day, July 1, Sherman once again began an effort to flank Johnston. Although Johnston had won the day at Kennesaw, he believed he had no choice but to fall back on Atlanta. He took up a position at the Chattahoochee River on the city's outskirts. Here he picked up reinforcements and began deploying his augmented forces in Atlanta's well-prepared and very formidable fortifications.

The truth is that Joe Johnston was a military realist. He believed that his army, even reinforced, would ultimately lose a showdown fight for Atlanta. His only hope was, he thought, also the best hope for the Confederacy. It was to keep his army intact and exact a costly delay on Sherman that would, while bleeding him, prevent his taking Atlanta long enough to cost Lincoln reelection. With a Democrat such as George B. McClellan in the White House, the Confederacy would have a good chance of negotiating a favorable peace.

It was not an attractive strategy. Perhaps it was not even a very good strategy. But it was probably the only realistic strategy available to the Confederacy—short of giving up. Jefferson Davis should have recognized this; however, all he recognized were the footfalls of Sherman's army approaching a city he could not afford to lose. Accordingly, on July 17, 1864, the Confederate president relieved Joseph E. Johnston as commander of the Army of Tennessee and replaced him with one whose willingness to fight, regardless of cost, was never in question: John Bell Hood.

## PEACHTREE CREEK

WILLIAM TECUMSEH SHERMAN was also a military realist. His assault on Kennesaw Mountain was out of character, an aberration, and he was not about to give in to pressure from anyone again. He knew that the enemy army was on the ropes, but he also knew that Atlanta was one of the most formidably defended cities of the Confederacy. To assault the city's concentric rings of defensive earthworks might just beat his army to nothing by the November elections. He needed a different strategy.

*What*, he asked, *was the reason for Atlanta?* The answer was obvious: the railroads. They were the city's reason for existence, they constituted the city's chief importance to the Confederacy, and they were the lifeline serving the city and the Confederate troops garrisoning and defending it. Cut the four rail lines into Atlanta, and there would be no need to take the city by force. Hood would have to show himself for a fight, wither under siege, or retreat and relinquish Atlanta.

*The Confederates labored mightily on fortifications surrounding Atlanta. Note the elaborate entrenchments and the use of chevaux-de-frise, the pointed wooden anti-personnel obstacles arranged crosswise at the lower left of the photograph.*

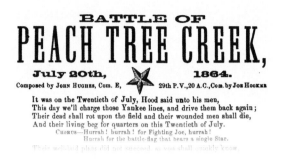

It was a brilliant plan because it used Atlanta's very strengths, its railroad network, against it. Sherman did make an error in executing the plan, however. He deployed McPherson's Army of the Tennessee and Schofield's Army of the Ohio contiguously but left a gap between these forces and Thomas's Army of the Cumberland. Hood noticed. As Schofield and McPherson closed in on Atlanta from

*The Union victory at the battle of Peachtree Creek—then outside of Atlanta, today within a quiet upscale city neighborhood—was celebrated in gloriously gory song.*

the east and Thomas crossed Peachtree Creek, north of the city, Hood attacked Thomas's open flank on July 20. The result was the battle of Peachtree Creek. It was a savage encounter, but Thomas proved himself still to be worthy of his "Rock of Chickamauga" epithet. He withstood and ultimately repulsed the attack.

## THE BATTLE OF ATLANTA

BOTH SHERMAN AND MCPHERSON observed the withdrawal of the Confederates from Atlanta on July 22. In light of the damage General Thomas had done, Sherman believed Hood was whipped and was relinquishing the city. McPherson disagreed. He had been Hood's classmate at West Point. He knew his man. He told Sherman that he believed Hood was maneuvering to attack the Army of the Tennessee on the right as well as the rear. Even as the two Union commanders debated this, four Confederate divisions led by Lieutenant General William J.

*Sherman was relentless and thorough in his destruction of the railroads in and around Atlanta, as this photograph shows.*

Hardee flanked the Union's XVI Corps under Major General Grenville Dodge. McPherson rode out to give instructions to XVII Corps, another unit, when he was intercepted by Confederate pickets.

"Halt!" they yelled.

McPherson responded by raising his hand to his head, as if to doff his hat in salute or acknowledgment of surrender. But—suddenly—he jerked back on the reins, wheeled his mount, and laid spurs into its sides. The Confederates fired a volley, mortally wounding McPherson.

# EYEWITNESS

The most famous fiction writer to emerge from the Civil War was Ambrose Bierce (1842–1914?), whose darkly cynical stories, many drawn from his war experience—including the remarkable "An Occurrence at Owl Creek Bridge," the dream-vision of a Confederate spy about to be hanged—earned him the sobriquet "Bitter Bierce."

At Kennesaw Mountain, Bierce was severely wounded: shot in the head. Bierce was as celebrated for his nonfiction Civil War writing as for his short fiction. In *What I Saw of Shiloh*, he records the horror of war with a chilly detachment, as in this description of the aftermath of a forest fire touched off by artillery:

*Known as "Bitter Bierce," Ambrose Bierce—short-story writer, journalist, and all-around misanthrope—poses in a painting by J. H. E. Partington with what was for him a most appropriate prop.*

*Death had put his sickle into this thicket and fire had gleaned the field. Along a line which was not that of extreme depression, but was at every point significantly equidistant from the heights on either hand, lay the bodies half buried in ashes; some in the unlovely looseness of attitude denoting sudden death by the bullet, but by far the greater number in postures of agony that told of the tormenting flame. Their clothing was half burnt away—their hair and beard entirely; the rain had come too late to save their nails. Some were swollen to double girth; others shriveled to manikins. According to degree of exposure, their faces were bloated and black or yellow and shrunken. The contraction of muscles which had given them claws for hands had cursed each countenance with a hideous grin. Faugh! I cannot catalogue the charms of these gallant gentlemen who had got what they enlisted for.*

Bierce ended a successful career in literature and journalism by slipping into Mexico late in 1913—he was in his seventies at the time—ostensibly to cover the activities of Pancho Villa in the ongoing revolution. He disappeared, as the saying goes, without a trace. Some believe he was a casualty of the revolution; others that he planned the disappearance; still others, that he committed suicide.

The death of McPherson, and the enveloping attack on the Army of the Tennessee that accompanied it, marked the beginning of the battle of Atlanta proper, the culmination of Sherman's Atlanta campaign. Even without its commander, the Army of the Tennessee repulsed the attempt to envelop it, and Sherman succeeded in cutting the rail lines entering Atlanta from the north and the east. Next, he advanced to

### A Friend's Obituary for His Enemy

James McPherson was a fine commander who was universally liked and admired by his army colleagues. This includes the man whose own army had killed him. John Bell Hood wrote: "I will record the death of my classmate and boyhood friend, General James B. McPherson, the announcement of which caused me sincere sorrow. Since we had graduated in 1853, and had each been ordered off on duty in different directions, it has not been our fortune to meet. Neither the years nor the difference of sentiment that had led us to range ourselves on opposite sides in the war had lessened my friendship; indeed the attachment formed in early youth was strengthened by my admiration and gratitude for his conduct toward our people in the vicinity of Vicksburg. His considerate and kind treatment of them stood in bright contrast to the course pursued by many Federal officers."

the southwest, capturing the Macon and Western Railroad. On July 28, Hood renewed the attack on the Army of the Tennessee, now commanded by O. O. Howard, doing battle at Ezra Church, west of the city. Howard beat back the assault, imposing a heavy toll on Hood and putting Atlanta within Sherman's grasp.

## SHERMAN'S GENIUS

IF SHERMAN HAD BEEN A CONVENTIONAL Union general, he would have begun celebrating his victory. But an adherent of Grant's battle doctrine, Sherman understood that victory was not about possession of a city. He had been assigned to kill the Confederate Army of Tennessee, originally under Joe Johnston, now under John Bell Hood. Sherman knew he could beat Hood. He knew Atlanta would become his. But he also knew that Hood would keep fighting as long as he possibly could, and if he could hold out long enough, tying Sherman down at Atlanta, the entire Union rear would be open to attack from none other than Nathan Bedford Forrest, who had already, on July 15, forced Major General A. J. Smith to withdraw from Tupelo, Mississippi.

A conventional general would have kept pounding at Atlanta, no matter how long it took, but Sherman was sufficiently unconventional to know better than to underestimate the highly unconventional Forrest. He therefore made an extraordinary decision. On August 25, 1864, at the seeming verge of victory in the Atlanta campaign, Sherman ordered the bombardment of Hood's Atlanta entrenchments halted. By August 26, most of Sherman's army had departed the field.

Hood concluded what Sherman knew the impulsive Hood would conclude: that he had beaten the Union army, and it had withdrawn.

Actually, Sherman had resumed the execution of his original plan. Instead of continuing to menace Atlanta directly, he wheeled far to the south of the city and cut the Macon and Western Railroad, the city's last rail connection. As for Forrest, he did beat Smith, but the Union commander had managed to occupy the Confederates long enough to keep Forrest from reinforcing Hood. In the meantime, Hood was just beginning to see the light. Sherman had severed Atlanta, at the heart of the Confederacy's rail network, from the rest of the Confederacy. On September 1, Hood evacuated the city, and on September 2, Sherman occupied it.

His first step was to order Atlanta's citizens out of the city. When the mayor and two city councilmen protested, Sherman responded with a letter refusing to rescind the order of evacuation. "Our military plans make it necessary for the inhabitants to go away," he explained, and then went on to concentrate in the rest of his letter everything he held true about the nature of war:

> You cannot qualify war in harsher terms than I will. War is cruelty, and you cannot refine it. And those who brought war into our country deserve all the curses and maledictions a people can pour out. I know I had no hand in making this war, and I know I will make more sacrifices to-day than any of you to secure peace. But you cannot have peace and a division of our country. . . .
>
> You might as well appeal against the thunder-storm as against the terrible hardships of war. They are inevitable, and the only way the people of Atlanta can hope once more to live in peace and quiet at home, is to stop the war. . . .

He closed by assuring the mayor and the councilmen that he wanted peace, but that he believed "it can only be reached through union and war; and I will ever conduct war purely with a view to perfect an early success." And then he promised: "my dear sirs, when peace does come, you may call on me for any thing. Then will I share with you the last cracker, and watch with you to shield your homes and families against danger from every quarter." He bade them "go, and take with you the old and feeble, feed and nurse them, and build for them, in more quiet places, proper habitations to shield them against the weather until the mad passions of men cool down, and allow the Union and peace once more to settle over your old homes at Atlanta."

Despite Sherman's evacuation order, only about half the citizens of Atlanta left. It did not matter. Ignoring them, Sherman set about transforming the Southern city into a Northern fortress, and he mentally inventoried what its conquest meant. First, the Confederacy was without its chief rail hub. Second, President Lincoln was now almost certain to be reelected (though Lincoln himself still had his doubts). Finally, without Atlanta, the Confederacy was all but hollowed out. And this last outcome prompted Sherman to rethink the priorities of his orders from Grant. He was to destroy the army of Johnston (now Hood) *first* and *then* "get into

*Headquarters for General Sherman's occupation of Atlanta was the provost (military police) office he established in a grand Atlanta house. About one-half the population of Atlanta obtained passes from the provost office to leave the city in obedience to Sherman's evacuation order, pictured here.*

# WHO BURNED ATLANTA?

The most widely read piece of Civil War literature was written years after the conflict by the Atlanta novelist Margaret Mitchell, whose *Gone with the Wind,* and the 1939 MGM movie based on it, vividly portray the burning of Atlanta.

No doubt the city burned, but Civil War buffs still debate just who burned it. Some claim Sherman ordered the blaze, whereas others counter that the Confederate army itself burned the city down. The truth is a combination of both interpretations.

After he withdrew from Atlanta, General Hood ordered the demolition of a Confederate ammunition train to keep it out of Union hands. Embers from this blast ignited a massive fire early on the morning of September 1, 1864. This widespread blaze was, however, only the first of two big fires in the city. On November 11, General Sherman ordered the destruction of everything of military significance in Atlanta. Much as Sherman interpreted his orders from Grant very broadly, so Sherman's subordinates took his order as instructions to put to the torch everything that had escaped destruction in September. On November 16, 1864, when Sherman marched out of Atlanta, he left behind a smoldering ruin.

the interior of the enemy's country" to inflict "all the damage [he could] against their war resources." It now occurred to Sherman that the best way to achieve the *first* priority was to begin by addressing the *second*. He proposed to Grant that he would personally lead sixty thousand of his troops—60 percent of his combined armies—out of Atlanta on a "March to the Sea," advancing southeast to Savannah to cut the Confederacy in two, dividing North from South in much the same way as Grant's earlier victories on the Mississippi River had divided East from West. The March to the Sea would put Sherman in position to attack Lee's Army of Northern Virginia from the south even as Grant bore down on it from the north, forcing the beleaguered enemy general into fighting a two-front campaign he could not possibly win. Moreover, in the process of his march, Sherman would burn a swath of ruin that would "make Georgia howl," as he wrote. His army would live off the land, burning whatever they did not need, so as to deprive the Confederate army of these resources and to break the will of the civilian population to continue to support a government that could not protect it or even provide for its most basic needs. In sum, Sherman proposed waging total war on an unprecedented scale.

At the same time, he proposed to send most of the rest of his force west to fight Hood and Forrest, but, Sherman pointed out to Grant, these two generals and their armies could no longer accomplish very much in a Confederacy that was becoming increasingly feeble with each passing day. Grant agreed to the new priorities; however, Sherman decided to take one final stab against Hood. Early in October, he marched out of Atlanta, leaving behind a single corps to hold the city. He tried to run Hood to ground and force him to a finish fight. But Hood kept slipping the noose and marched westward, toward Forrest. He intended to link up with him and, together, overwhelm the thirty thousand men under Major General George Thomas, whom Sherman had detailed to clear the last Confederates out of Tennessee. Confident of Thomas's ability to deal with Hood and Forrest, Sherman turned away from his quarry in November. Now the Confederate and the Union armies marched in opposite directions.

Hood was flabbergasted by this development, but he continued to believe that if he and Forrest could sufficiently menace Thomas, Sherman would be compelled to break off his Georgia raid—maybe even relinquish Atlanta as well—in order to rush to Thomas's aid. Looking forward, Hood even envisioned retaking Tennessee for the Confederacy, then using it as a springboard for an invasion of Kentucky. With that state secured, he could attack Cincinnati and maybe even maneuver toward the rear of the Army of the Potomac, thereby relieving the menace to both Lee and the Confederate capital.

## TENNESSEE SHOWDOWN

GRANDIOSE IN ITS AMBITION, Hood's plan was the product of an impulsive military sensibility and never had any plausible chance of success. Nevertheless, he and Forrest posed a very real threat to Thomas. By early November, the "Rock of Chickamauga" had received reinforcements and now commanded fifty thousand men in and around Nashville. He was well aware that Hood had been advancing against Union general John M. Schofield and had pushed him into a tight spot at Spring Hill, Tennessee, on November 29. Had Hood possessed more tactical skill or just plain good luck, he might have succeeded in cutting off Schofield's path of retreat from Columbia, Tennessee, to Franklin,

*George N. Barnard's photograph reveals the bleak landscape of the Union army's outer line outside of Nashville on December 16, 1864.*

a town just south of Nashville. But Schofield slipped through his fingers and reached Franklin. There, on November 30, Hood, his patience exhausted, threw his forces against Schofield's very well-prepared defenses. It was an assault so reckless that some have suggested Hood's judgment had been compromised by the opiates he liberally dosed himself with to ease the pain of battle wounds. Perhaps. But Hood had already shown himself to be a commander whose aggressive nature far outpaced good judgment. He had 26,897 men at the battle of Franklin, committing at least 18,000 of them, of which he lost 6,252 killed, wounded, captured, or missing.

After beating off Hood, Schofield wisely resumed his withdrawal to Nashville, where he linked up with Thomas. The combined Union forces now outnumbered Hood better than two to one. Yet Thomas refused to be lulled into overconfidence by his numbers. He developed his position preparatory to the battle of Nashville slowly and deliberately—so much so that Grant worried that Thomas would allow Hood to escape with his army intact. When a sudden ice storm imposed a further delay, Grant actually cut an order relieving Thomas of command and, on December 15, was about to transmit it when word reached him that Thomas had finally launched his offensive. By the next day, Hood had suffered a defeat so decisive that the Confederate Army of Tennessee, though saved from total destruction by valiant rearguard work led by Forrest, was finished as a strategically significant fighting force.

> "Until we can repopulate Georgia, it is useless for
> us to occupy it; but the utter destruction of its roads,
> houses and people will cripple their military resources.
> I can make this march, and make Georgia howl."

*Major General William Tecumseh Sherman, message
to General Grant, September 9, 1864*

## MARCH TO THE SEA

WHILE THOMAS FINISHED OFF the Army of Tennessee, Sherman visited boundless destruction on Georgia, encouraging his men—"bummers," they proudly called themselves—not only to forage with gusto, but to destroy with abandon. His army entered Savannah on December 22, 1864, the terrified city surrendering without a shot, whereupon Sherman dispatched a telegram to a freshly reelected Abraham Lincoln: "I beg to present you, as a Christmas gift, the city of Savannah, with one hundred and fifty heavy guns and plenty of ammunition; also about twenty-five thousand bales of cotton."

Just before Sherman's army departed Savannah to invade South Carolina, a fire broke out in the city. Unlike the two Atlanta fires, it seems to have been totally accidental in origin, but it quickly spread to a Confederate arsenal, the explosion of which ignited an inferno that swept through much of the beautiful old port town. Union troops labored shoulder to shoulder with Savannah residents and their newly freed slaves to put the fires out. Despite this, much of the city was destroyed.

Having vowed to "make Georgia howl," Sherman promised next to "punish South Carolina as she deserves." He made no secret of the fact that his "whole army is burning with an insatiable desire to wreck vengeance upon" the state that had begun the Civil War. "I almost tremble for her fate."

The Union army reached the outskirts of Columbia, the capital, on February 16, 1865. The mayor surrendered the city on the next day. Once again, Sherman's occupation was accompanied by terrible fires

*A jubilant William Tecumseh Sherman telegraphed President Lincoln on December 22, 1864: "I beg to present you as a Christmas gift the City of Savannah with 150 heavy guns & plenty of ammunition & also about 25,000 bales of cotton."*

*Columbia, capital of South Carolina—the first state to secede from the Union—burns.*

Tasked by General Grant to eliminate Joseph Johnston's (later John Bell Hood's) Army of Tennessee and to destroy anything of military value throughout Georgia and South Carolina, William Tecumseh Sherman transformed the Civil War into "total war" (warfare waged against civilians as well as soldiers) on a scale that would be exceeded only by the world wars of the twentieth century, although Confederate terrorists had already attempted or executed several total war operations on a small insurgent scale. Sherman's Atlanta campaign broke the back of the Confederacy's transportation network and served as the springboard to his infamously destructive scorched-earth "March to the Sea" by which Sherman kept his vow to "make Georgia howl."

of obscure origin. After the war, in 1866, former Confederate general Wade Hampton sent a letter to the United States Senate, accusing the Union commander of having ordered arson. Sherman retorted that the fires were the work of Confederates, who were intent on destroying warehoused cotton rather than let it fall into Northern hands. What is beyond dispute is that half the town was burned to the ground.

## FULL CIRCLE

COLUMBIA WAS OCCUPIED BY UNION FORCES on February 17. The very next day, the Confederate garrison of Fort Sumter decamped. Charleston, which had held out against repeated assaults from the sea, meekly surrendered to Sherman, and, on February 22, the Stars and Bars were lowered and replaced by the Stars and Stripes over the fort in the city's harbor.

Sherman did not pause to make a ceremony of it, but pressed northward, headed toward the rear of the Army of Northern Virginia. A more ceremonial flag raising over Fort Sumter was postponed until April 14, 1865. On that day, Robert Anderson, a major in 1861 and now holding the rank of major general, personally presided over the hoisting of the very flag he had lowered four years and a day before. It was a glorious moment, but a fleeting one, wholly eclipsed by the murder of President Abraham Lincoln hours later.

*Ruins in Charleston, South Carolina. Fortunately, most of the historic and graceful old city came through the Civil War intact.*

# CHAPTER 20

## PIRATES AND SUBMARINERS

### *The Civil War at Sea*

At the outbreak of the Civil War, the battle fleet of the United States Navy consisted of approximately ninety ships, of which forty-two were seaworthy at the time (the rest were laid up in dry dock for long-term repairs and maintenance). By 1865, the fleet had expanded to 671 vessels—dramatic evidence of the financial and industrial superiority of the Northern states over the Southern. Although Jefferson Davis installed a secretary of the navy in his first cabinet at the outbreak of the war, that man, former Florida senator Stephen R. Mallory, had no navy over which to preside. His first act was to scrape together about thirty ships, only fourteen of which were seaworthy. As for personnel, thirty-two captains, fifty-four commanders, seventy-six lieutenants, and 2,011 enlisted sailors resigned from the U.S. Navy to join the Confederate service. Even after this defection, the Union navy mustered seventy-five hundred officers and sailors at the start of the war, a number that rapidly grew to more than twenty-two thousand, who answered an enlistment call.

*Crew members of the USS* Monitor *relax on deck. The all-iron ship's revolutionary rotating gun turret (which profoundly changed naval weapons technology) is clearly visible behind them.*

It was clear to Mallory, to Jefferson Davis, and to other Confederate military planners that a Confederate States Navy would never be able to compete directly with the U.S. Navy. Fortunately for the Confederates, most civil war is by nature principally land war; but the would-be nation nevertheless had to find ways to prosecute the war at sea, hopelessly overmatched as its sea power was. Astoundingly, the Confederacy did find those ways.

## BLOCKADE RUNNERS AND PRIVATEERS

JOB ONE FOR THE CONFEDERACY AT SEA was to penetrate Winfield Scott's "Anaconda," the naval blockade of Southern ports (Chapter 5). In the beginning, this was not very difficult. With few warships available, the blockade was extremely porous early in the war, and enterprising skippers willing to risk their cargoes, passengers, ships, and themselves could readily find ways of slipping through the blockade undetected, putting in not at the principal Southern ports, but in any number of secluded coves and inlets. Although blockade running became increasingly risky and costly as the U.S. Navy expanded its fleet and more ships were dispatched to blockade duty, the odds continued to favor skillful and daring blockade runners up to the end of the war.

Blockade runners were civilian merchant mariners, not Confederate naval personnel. Doubtless, some deemed themselves patriots, but they were also well compensated, usually in hard currency, silver, or gold. It was civilians who filled the yawning gulf that existed between the navies of the United States and the Confederacy, not only by manning the vessels that evaded the U.S. Navy and its blockade, but also by engaging in daring offensive action. In the Civil War, naval warfare was first and foremost a war on commerce, but whereas the Northern strategy was to blockade the South in an effort to strangle its import and export trade, the Southern strategy was to attack Northern commerce not at its ports, but on the high seas.

On April 17, 1861, President Jefferson Davis promulgated a "proclamation, inviting all those who may desire by service in private armed vessels on the high seas to aid this Government in resisting so wanton and wicked an aggression, to make application for commissions or letters of marque and reprisal, to be issued under the seal of these Confederate States." *Letters of marque and reprisal.* If the phrase had a distinctly antique ring about it, that was because the concept of state-sanctioned piracy—"privateering," it was called—was very old. Queen Elizabeth I's favorite seadog, the redoubtable Sir Francis Drake (1540–96), was a privateer in Her Majesty's service, who wreaked havoc on the naval forces of the Spanish empire toward the close of the sixteenth century, and some of history's most celebrated "pirates," such as Sir John Hawkins (1532–95) and Sir Henry "Captain" Morgan (1635–88), were really privateers. During the War of 1812, the fledgling U.S. Navy was dwarfed by the Royal Navy, and the government of President James Madison made extensive use of privateers, including the skipper and sailors of the merchantman *Yankee*, who set a record for the war by seizing or destroying some five million dollars' worth of English property and merchandise.

With ample precedent to back him, Davis had few qualms about the legality of privateering. He was concerned, however, that the Confederate constitution did not explicitly give the executive the authority to issue letters of marque and reprisal, so he prevailed upon the Confederate Congress to grant him the authority. This the legislators did by passing two acts, one "concerning letters of marque, prizes, and prize goods," on May 6, 1861, and another "regulating the sale of prizes and distribution thereof," passed on May 14. Neither act was radically innovative; both embodied policies already on the books of the United States and other nations. Although the Declaration of Paris of 1856 had abolished privateering, the only major signatories to the declaration were Britain and France. The United States, along with several other European powers, declined to sign on. President Lincoln did not dispute the legality of privateering, but he did not

## EYEWITNESS

John Wilkinson, a Confederate blockade runner, wrote this account in 1877:

*. . . A blockade-runner did not often pass through the fleet without receiving one or more shots, but these were always preceded by the flash of a calcium light, or by a blue light; and immediately followed by two rockets thrown in the direction of the blockade-runner. The signals were probably concerted each day for the ensuing night, as they appeared to be constantly changed; but the rockets were invariably sent up. I ordered a lot of rockets from New York. Whenever all hands were called to run through the fleet, an officer was stationed alongside of me on the bridge with the rockets. One or two minutes after our immediate pursuer had sent up his rockets,*

*I would direct ours to be discharged at a right angle to our course. The whole fleet would be misled, for even if the vessel which had discovered us were not deceived, the rest of the fleet would be baffled . . .*

*Published on October 10, 1861, "The Song of the Privateer"—by a lyricist calling himself "Quien Sabe?" (Who Knows?) — romanticizes the exploits of the Confederate-sanctioned pirates who ventured "Away o'er the boundless sea, / With steady hearts and free," hoping to serve their cause while earning big prize money.*

recognize the Confederate States of America as a sovereign nation, and therefore declared that any so-called privateers would be treated as pirates if captured and would be subject to hanging. The Davis government responded by promising to hang Union POWs by way of retaliation for any execution upon a privateer, and the Union ultimately hanged none.

Initially, Southern ships' masters, as well as some Northern mercenaries, responded in such volume to Davis's call for privateers that the Confederate government scrambled to cloak the enterprise in a mantle of legality by passing strict regulations, which demanded the posting of a substantial bond and issued letters of marque only to actual ship owners, not their skippers. This reduced the number of applicants, since relatively few mariners could afford to post the required bond. Nevertheless, privateers were sufficiently numerous and active to make an impact on Northern commerce and to affect the Union's naval strategy. Activity was so intense off Cape Hatteras, North Carolina, that most Union ship owners either curtailed or even abandoned their Caribbean routes or went to the expense of "reflagging" their vessels by transferring registry from the United States to Great Britain. (The last thing a Confederate privateer wanted to do was molest a British ship.) In a mostly successful effort to suppress privateering in this area, the Union launched an amphibious operation to capture the two Confederate-held forts defending Hatteras Inlet.

*Combined Union naval and army forces scored an early victory against the Confederate-held forts at Hatteras Inlet, North Carolina, on August 27, 1861.*

The resulting battle of Hatteras Inlet Batteries (August 28–29, 1861) forced the Confederates out of the forts, thereby making them the first seceded territory to be retaken by the Union.

The battle of Hatteras Inlet Batteries did nothing to inhibit the privateers who preyed upon Northern shipping off the coasts of Charleston, Savannah, and New Orleans; however, most ship owners soon dropped out of the privateering business, because, thanks largely to the Confederate government's own increasingly burdensome regulations, the rewards were insufficient to justify the risks.

## The *Alabama*'s Long Run

Even at the height of privateering, the Davis government realized that it could not rest the fate of the Confederate cause at sea on legalized piracy alone. With limited industrial capacity and almost no ability to build its own warships, the Confederate government clandestinely commissioned ships from British builders. The most famous of these vessels was CSS *Alabama,* the building of which, by the Laird Shipyards, was negotiated in 1861 by a Confederate agent named James D. Bulloch. His activities were closely monitored by very capable United States minister plenipotentiary to Great Britain, Charles Francis Adams, who lodged a vehement protest with Her Majesty's government. Despite British neutrality laws, which unequivocally forbade building warships for either the Confederacy or the United States, many powerful members of Parliament were eager to resume the profitable cotton trade with the American South and therefore winked at the clear violation of the law. As Adams protested in vain, the *Alabama* was launched—as a merchant vessel innocently christened *Enrica*—on July 29, 1862.

Adams refused to accept defeat. All that Laird had launched was essentially a decked hull. It still had to be towed from the Laird yards at Birkenhead to a Liverpool dry dock for fitting out with masts, boiler, and steam engine. Adams consulted Robert R. Collier, Britain's most celebrated barrister, and secured a legal opinion, which he presented to Britain's foreign secretary Lord Russell, arguing that releasing the *Enrica* would expose Her Majesty's government to liability for whatever damage the ship, under Confederate command, might do. Duly impressed, Lord Russell called on the Queen's Law Officer—the government's chief attorney—Sir John Harding and demanded from him an immediate legal opinion.

**DETAILS, DETAILS**
**Marque and Reprisal**
A "letter of marque" is a government warrant or commission that authorizes the holder of the letter to search, seize, or destroy property, assets, and even personnel belonging to a foreign power or foreign party. A letter of marque may be issued against a foreign party that has committed a specific offense, or it may be used to authorize the raiding of merchant shipping in a time of war. When a letter of marque is used in the context of war, it is usually referred to as a "letter of marque and reprisal." It should be noted that the acts passed by the Confederate Congress deviated from accepted international law in one important respect. They extended the reach of privateering by inviting masters to attack warships as well as commercial vessels, offering prize money for capturing or sinking U.S. Navy ships. No Confederate privateer actually ever attempted this, however.

*Charles Francis Adams, U.S. ambassador to Her Majesty's government of Great Britain.*

Adams was amply justified in feeling himself on the verge of foiling a major Confederate plot, but history is created moment to moment by human beings, and human beings are subject, moment to moment, to myriad forces, foibles, and disorders. In the case of Harding, he was in the throes of what Victorians called "nervous collapse," but his wife had covered for him so thoroughly that no one in the Law Offices had an inkling of his condition. Neither Lord Russell nor anyone else could understand why Harding kept putting off his response to the demand for a legal opinion, and as the bewilderment increased and the delay lengthened, someone in the British government let Bulloch know that *Enrica* was in peril of seizure. Bulloch acted immediately, announcing that the ship was to undergo immediate "sea trials," then return to Liverpool to complete her fitting-out. She sailed on July 29, but, of course, never returned to Liverpool.

# PIRACY PRECEDENT

On June 2, 1861, the Confederate privateer *Savannah,* having already captured the brig *Joseph* off the Charleston coast, targeted another vessel only to discover—too late—that it was the USS *Perry*, a well-armed U.S. Navy warship. The two vessels exchanged several volleys before the *Savannah*'s skipper gave up.

Taken into custody, he and his crew of twelve were tried in a regular civilian court, the U.S. Circuit Court for the Southern District of New York, beginning on October 23, 1861. The charge was piracy; the penalty, death by hanging.

In response to the trial, the Davis government published by name a list of Union prisoners of war who would be summarily executed in retaliation for any execution of the *Savannah* crew. This threat was sufficient to deadlock the jury, a mistrial was declared, and the prisoners, denied bail, were returned to jail to await a second trial. Also fearing retaliation, the U.S. government declined a new prosecution, and the *Savannah* crew members were all reclassified as prisoners of war. The decision was controversial, and—at least in theory—its ramifications profound. While reprisal against Union POWs had been avoided, the U.S. government had been put in the position of effectively acknowledging the pirates as agents of a legitimate belligerent power. By implication, this could be interpreted as a concession of sovereignty to the Confederate States of America—precisely what President Lincoln most assiduously sought to avoid.

*The Confederate privateer* Savannah *was captured on June 2, 1861, by the USS* Perry*, a warship the Savannah's hapless skipper mistook for an unarmed commercial vessel.*

Quietly, *Enrica* put into a secluded port on the Welsh coast. Bulloch's plan was to board her there, sail her out of English waters and far beyond the reach of Adams or any other diplomat. Although British authorities turned a blind eye toward the illegal building of ships for the Confederacy, they drew the line at actually arming them. Arm a ship, and there was no credible way of pretending that you were

*A fine pencil-and-ink-wash sketch of CSS* Alabama, *the South's most celebrated commerce raider, engaging one of its victims, the* Brilliante.

building nothing more than an innocent merchant vessel. Therefore, commerce raiders were sailed to distant ports for the installation of guns. Bulloch intended to take the *Enrica* to the Azores, receive her cannon, and then personally assume command. At this juncture of Bulloch's brilliant evasion, Confederate navy secretary Mallory intervened. He ordered Bulloch to rendezvous with a commercial vessel called the *Agrippina* and take aboard one Captain Raphael Semmes. *He* would become the *Alabama*'s skipper.

En route to the rendezvous, *Enrica* gave a U.S. Navy sloop the slip and barreled through a harrowing storm on the always tumultuous Irish Sea. Semmes boarded his new command, his figure unmistakable: a large head atop a slight body; huge, intelligent eyes deep set under full brows; a long, aquiline nose, below which was an exuberant handlebar moustache, the ends of which were twisted and waxed into a shape that called to mind a Texas longhorn; below the lip, hardly balancing the florid moustache, Semmes sported a diminutive "Imperial," the chin-whisker style favored by Napoleon III and widely emulated by the military men of the Union as well as the Confederacy. Maryland born and a longtime resident of Alabama—it was he who gave *Enrica* her nom de guerre, *Alabama*—Semmes was fifty-one years old in February 1861, when he resigned his commission as a commander in the U.S. Navy to join the Confederate service as a foreign arms purchaser. This was necessarily a covert position; officially, Semmes was named to head the Confederate Lighthouse Bureau. Soon, however, he sought and was given active service in the Confederate navy. He took command of the cruiser *Sumter*, which had been converted for combat from the *Habana*, a Philadelphia-built commercial steamer that, at the outbreak of the war, happened to be in the port of New Orleans and was purchased by the Confederate government. Semmes quickly earned a reputation as a remarkable seaman for

*Raphael Semmes was the daring, highly skilled, and extraordinarily successful skipper of CSS* Alabama.

*The Confederate blockade runner* Sumter *eludes USS* Brooklyn *at Pass à l'Outre, Louisiana, on June 30, 1861.*

the ease with which he broke through the Anaconda, which was an especially heavy presence around New Orleans. He then sailed his new command for six months, claiming during that period no fewer than eighteen "prizes," as captured ships were called, before leaving the CSS *Sumter* in Gibraltar, climbing aboard the *Agrippina*, and, as ordered, meeting up with *Enrica/Alabama*.

A six-month scourge in command of the *Sumter*, Semmes now embarked on a career of positive terror. Officially commissioned by the Confederate navy on August 24, 1862, *Alabama* prowled all the important shipping lanes from September of that year to June 1864. Captain Semmes seized or sank sixty-five (some sources report sixty-nine) ships during that period, a run that not only took a significant toll on Union commerce and Northern maritime insurers, but, even more important, necessitated removing many Federal ships from blockade duty so that they might search for and pursue CSS *Alabama*. While the authorities agree that Semmes took at least sixty-five prizes, it is impossible even to guess how many blockade runners evaded the Anaconda because of his long raiding campaign.

## DAY OF RECKONING

ONE OF THE SHIPS SUMMONED AWAY from the blockade was the USS *Kearsarge*, a handsome steam sloop displacing 1,083 tons and mounting seven guns. She was riding at anchor off the Dutch coast on Sunday, June 12, 1864, when her skipper, Captain John A. Winslow, received a report that the *Alabama*, quarry he had been pursuing now for nearly a year, had just steamed into the French port of Cherbourg to unload prisoners and to fill her empty bunkers with coal. At fifty-two, Winslow had been sailing with the navy since 1827. Born in Wilmington, North Carolina, he might well have chosen, like Semmes, to resign his commission and join the Confederate service; but the call of his New England ancestors—he traced his lineage to the *Mayflower* and was a descendent of Plymouth Colony governor Edward Winslow—was overwhelming. He remained loyal to the Union.

Winslow weighed anchor and poured on the steam, reaching the vicinity of Cherbourg in just two days. In the nineteenth century, international maritime law set a three-mile limit to any nation's territorial waters. France was a neutral with respect to the Civil War, and Winslow knew that he could not venture closer to Cherbourg than the three-mile limit. He therefore took up a station at the southern mouth of the English Channel, waited, and watched.

Semmes had a choice. He could attempt to wait Winslow out, or he could try to fight his way out. There were two strikes against the first option. First: Winslow had been pursuing him for nearly a year. Doubtless, Semmes figured, he was prepared to wait a very long time now. Second: Just by bottling him up in port, Winslow had won because he was preventing *Alabama* from doing her job. The only viable option, therefore, was to fight. Semmes knew he had seamanship on his side, but he also knew that Winslow had a pair of eleven-inch smoothbore Dahlgren guns—the very latest in naval ordnance—as well as another advanced weapon, a 30-pounder Parrott rifle, plus four conventional 32-pounder cannons, whereas he had six conventional 32 pounders, a 110 pounder, and a 68 pounder, none of which could outgun a Dahlgren or a Parrott.

Semmes slipped the *Alabama* out of port at 9:45 on Sunday morning, June 19. By that time, word of the impending high seas duel had spread throughout Cherbourg and beyond. Not only were the dockside and shore jammed with French locals, the town's hotels were filled to overflowing with the curious who had come from afar. As for Captain Winslow, he left the watching to his lookout while he went about his usual Sunday morning routine of reading the Sabbath service to his crew.

"She's coming out," the lookout suddenly cried out. Winslow stopped reading. "And she's headed straight for us!"

Winslow announced the end of the service, bidding the crew to "go in peace," then, as if in direct contradiction of this injunction, ordered "beat

*John Ancrum Winslow, captain of the USS* Kearsarge, *the ship that finally ended the career of the* Alabama.

*The* Kearsarge *versus the* Alabama, *as imagined by L. Prang & Co., lithographers.*

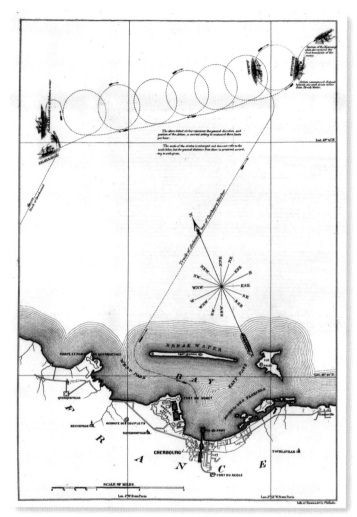

*This extraordinary chart of the battle between USS* Kearsarge *and CSS* Alabama *on June 19, 1864, off the coast of Cherbourg, France, was published by order of the U.S. secretary of the navy in December 1864.*

to quarters," the summons of all hands to battle stations. Assuming his command position on the quarterdeck, Winslow rang up all-ahead flank on the *Kearsarge*'s engine-order telegraph and made haste out of the Channel and into open waters. Not only did he want maneuvering room, he was anxious to prevent his quarry from finding refuge in some cove or inlet. Winslow knew that he would have to bring to bear his superior firepower as accurately as possible, because *Alabama* was faster—it could make thirteen knots to *Kearsarge*'s eleven. On the other hand, although *Alabama* was lighter than *Kearsarge* by five hundred tons, it had a deeper draft, nearly eighteen feet, which meant that she rode four feet lower in the water than the Union sloop. *Kearsarge* might just have the edge on maneuverability.

At three minutes before eleven, the adversaries were no more than a mile apart and *Alabama* initiated combat by firing her heaviest gun, the 100-pounder. It was just what Winslow had anticipated, because it is just what he would have done in Semmes's place. Knowing that the big gun was capable of the greatest range, Winslow resisted the temptation to attempt evasion or to put distance between him and his quarry. Instead, he continued to bear down on *Alabama*, straight ahead and with all the speed he could muster. Semmes ordered his guns to fire and to keep firing, but Winslow was closing so rapidly that every shot was too long and too high. The Confederate gunners could not re-lay (adjust the elevation of the guns) quickly enough to draw a good bead on their target.

With practiced calm, Winslow withheld his fire until he had closed to within half a mile. Then he ordered a methodical barrage, cautioning his gunners to make every shot count. Whereas *Alabama* hurled some 400 volleys in little more than an hour, Winslow fired (by his careful calculation) just 173, many more of them finding their mark than those loosed by the *Alabama.* And that made all the difference. Both ships sustained damage. That was the nature of naval combat at mid century. But by noon, CSS *Alabama* was taking on water faster than its pumps could bail it out. She was sinking, and fast.

"No one who is not a seaman can realize the blow which falls upon the human heart of a commander, upon the sinking of his ship. It is not merely the loss of a battle—it is the overwhelming of his household. . . . The *Alabama* had not only been my battle-field, but my home, in which I had lived for two long years . . ."

*Confederate rear admiral Raphael Semmes,*
Memoirs of Service Afloat (1868)

As soon as he saw the Confederate crew begin to abandon ship, Winslow ordered his smallboats to be launched—only to discover that all but two had been blown to bits. They would never accommodate all of the *Alabama*'s survivors. Winslow turned to a British yacht that, with other pleasure craft, had ventured out to observe the duel.

"For God's sake," he bellowed through a megaphone, "do what you can to save them!"

Within little more than twenty minutes from the order to abandon ship, at 12:24 precisely, CSS *Alabama* slipped under the waves. *Kearsarge* fished seventy survivors out of the water, while French boats recovered twelve more. Semmes and forty of his crew were rescued by the yacht *Deerhound*, to whom Winslow had appealed for aid. Because the British were neutral, they were not obliged to surrender Semmes or the others to Winslow. Thus the Confederate captain remained free and, after a leisurely indulgence in the Grand Tour—a continental vacation—he sailed back to the Confederacy, successfully ran the coastal blockade, and assumed command of the James River squadron.

# COMBAT SHIFTS TO THE COURTROOM

Captain Winslow wrote the final chapter of the *Alabama*'s military career, but there was a sequel to its story nevertheless. Hard feelings set in between Britain and the United States after the war, in large part because of the British role in turning the *Alabama* loose upon the U.S. commercial fleet.

The American government demanded reparations. For years, the Crown refused, but finally agreed to the appointment of a joint high commission to adjudicate the "*Alabama* Claims" and other reparations issues. The commission drew up the Treaty of Washington, which, signed by the United States and Britain on May 8, 1871, created a system of arbitration, which included a tribunal consisting of five representatives each from the United States, England, Italy, Switzerland, and Brazil. The American government demanded payment of $19,021,000 for damages caused by eleven Confederate craft, including the *Alabama*, that had been built in British yards in contravention of the nation's declared neutrality. On September 14, 1872, the tribunal ordered the Crown to pay to the United States $15,500,000 in gold. The debt was duly discharged early the following year.

## REBIRTH OF AN OLD IDEA

MALLORY AND HIS CONFEDERATE NAVY eagerly embraced the unconventional. It was their only hope. Privateering, commerce raiding, and, as we saw in Chapter 7, ironclad warships, were all employed against the far stronger Union navy. The submarine was hardly a new concept at the time of the Civil War—it had been sketched out as a possibility in 1578 by the British mathematician and naval architect William Bourne and was transformed into a prototype in 1620 by Cornelius Drebbel, a Dutch inventor in the employ of the British Royal Navy. He built a wooden frame, greased some leather hides to render them waterproof, stretched them over the frame, submerged himself, and actually maneuvered underwater. Drebbel built a total of three submarines, culminating in one that accommodated sixteen passengers—including, on one occasion, King James I. More famously, David Bushnell, a student at Yale College, tried his hand at building a military submarine for the Continental Navy during the American Revolution. His celebrated one-man *Turtle* worked, insofar as it managed to submerge and resurface, but proved useless as a weapon. Steamboat pioneer Robert Fulton built a submarine christened the *Nautilus* in 1800, tried unsuccessfully to interest Napoleon in it, but did subsequently extract some research and development funding from the U.S. Congress. His death in 1815 came before he had built a prototype.

Born in Tennessee in 1823, Horace Lawson Hunley was practicing law in New Orleans when the Civil War began but had been trained as a naval architect. With two other Confederates, James R. McClintock and Baxter Watson, he decided to resurrect the submarine idea and, this time, build one that would serve as a practical weapon, specifically a means of conquering the Union blockade. The partners' first effort was christened the *Pioneer*, which was scuttled in 1862, before it was ever tried in combat, to prevent its capture by approaching Union forces. The three men ponied up financing for another vessel, the *American Diver*, which proved unseaworthy and sank—without resurfacing—during tests in Mobile Bay. The third boat was completed in July 1863. A number of names were applied to it, including the descriptive if unimaginative *Fish Boat*, but Hunley himself gave it the name by which it would enter history: his own.

Harper's Weekly *reported on November 2, 1861, the rumored existence of a Confederate "Submarine Infernal machine intended to destroy the [USS] 'Minnesota.'" There was, in fact, no such manned submarine at the time, but in July 1863, the submarine* H. L. Hunley *was completed and would succeed in sinking* USS Housatonic, *albeit at the cost of its own sinking with the loss of all men on board.*

*H. L. Hunley* was built to Hunley's specifications by a boilermaker and, at just forty feet long, it looked, not surprisingly, like an oversized steam boiler, except that it was tapered, wedge-like, both fore and aft. Construction consisted of wrought-iron plates, curved to create a cylinder, to which were fitted key features of a modern submarine, including a conning tower (actually, two) and a set of moveable dive planes, which gave it vertical maneuverability under water. Propulsion was a major issue in a submarine. Sails were out, for the obvious reason that there is no wind underwater, but so was steam power, since combustion requires air. The *Hunley* was therefore powered by human muscle. A crankshaft ran the length of the vessel. Seven to eight crewmembers stood facing the shaft along its length, and each grasped a part of the shaft, turning it in unison. The shaft end was attached to a single screw, or propeller. The boat's commander doubled as its helmsman, steering the vessel by means of rods and cables linked to a rudder and controlling depth with a lever attached to the dive planes. At the same time, he also operated a hand pump to take in or expel ballast water, depending on whether he wanted to dive or surface.

*The* Hunley *emulated the design and construction of a large steam boiler. This 1902 drawing was based on a painting by an artist who may or may not have actually seen the submarine. It was not until August 8, 2000, when the* Hunley *was salvaged from the ocean floor, that researchers were able to view the actual boat—for the first time in nearly 140 years.*

The great limiting factor in all submarine designs is the availability of breathable air. Without some means of drawing fresh air into the submarine and evacuating carbon dioxide, submersion time would have to be fairly brief. For eight crewmembers and their captain, this meant no more than two hours, after which unconsciousness ensued and death quickly followed. The *Hunley* included a bellows and snorkel system intended to bring in fresh air from the surface, but no one was ever able to make it work properly, and so captain and crew accepted the two-hour operational limit as a fact of life (or death).

The *Hunley* carried just one weapon. It was a so-called spar torpedo, nothing more than a waterproof torpedo-shaped container into which ninety pounds of black powder was tightly packed. A lanyard was attached to a detonator. The torpedo itself was affixed to a long spar projecting out from the bow. An attack was supposed to go like this: The submarine would sight its target, submerge, and head for the broadside of the target's hull. The crew would crank the crankshaft for all they were worth, building up as much ramming speed as possible so as to hit the target ship below its waterline, piercing the hull with the spar torpedo. This done, the crew would crank in reverse, leaving the torpedo, separated from the spar, embedded in the hull. The lanyard attached to the torpedo's detonator ran back to the submarine. When they reached the limit of the lanyard, about two hundred feet, a crewman would yank it, detonating the black powder and blasting a gaping hole in the target's hull, sending it to the bottom.

## THE ULTIMATE WEAPON?

REPLICAS OF THE *HUNLEY* COULD BE BUILT cheaply and quickly. The Confederate hope was to launch as many of them as possible against the Union blockading fleet, sinking its constituent ships with impunity. But first, of course, the prototype vessel required testing. For this purpose, it was loaded on a railroad flatcar and transported to Charleston, South Carolina.

The *Hunley* dived beautifully, but returning to the surface proved much harder. Once the boat did manage to resurface, she showed herself to be only marginally seaworthy at best and was easily swamped. During one trial, *Hunley* was floating with her hatches open when a steamer glided by, creating a wake that washed over the submarine's deck and into the open hatches. The intake of water was more than enough to send Hunley to the bottom, with captain and seven crewmen aboard. The skipper and two of his crew bobbed to the surface; the other five went down with the boat and were drowned.

After *Hunley* was refloated, H. L. Hunley decided to assume personal command in order to perfect the dive-and-surfacing routine. He took her down on October 15, 1863. Those watching from shore saw a frantic burst of air bubbles. When the submarine failed to surface, grappling hooks were lowered and the vessel retrieved from the bottom for the second time in her career. As the salvage crew opened her hatches, they discovered that the seal on one of them was faulty. The boat had flooded.

General P. G. T. Beauregard, commanding officer at Charleston, observed as *Hunley*'s hatches were open. For the rest of his life, this general who had seen many men killed in battle—and who would see many more before the war ended—was haunted by the vision of (in his words) men "contorted into all sorts of horrible attitudes; some clutching candles . . . others lying in the bottom tightly grappled together." He instantly cut an order banning any further tests.

*Hunley* skipper Lieutenant George Dixon, who had not accompanied the inventor in the fatal practice dive, appealed to Beauregard not to abandon the submarine. He proposed to the general that the vessel be employed, partially submerged only, its deck barely awash, in a nighttime attack. The darkness would render it invisible, and its spar torpedo would ride low enough beneath the surface to penetrate a hull below its waterline. Beauregard reluctantly gave his permission, and at 8:45 on the night of February 17, 1864, the partially submerged *Hunley* rammed the USS *Housatonic*, a nine-gun sloop-of-war on blockade duty in Charleston Harbor.

Members of the ship's company had reported a dark object in the water, but it appeared to them to be a barrel, plank, or other debris—anything but a watercraft. The attack and the explosion that followed were therefore a complete surprise. The *Hunley*'s spar torpedo, piercing the *Housatonic*'s hull, had entered the ship's powder magazine, which instantly exploded. The stricken ship listed to port and then quickly went down by the head. She was a total loss, and five of her crew, two

## POP CULTURE
### *Hunley* Lives

After it was raised, CSS *Hunley* was transported to the privately financed Warren Lasch Conservation Center located at Charleston Navy Yard in Charleston, South Carolina. As of 2011, the vessel is still undergoing conservation, but many artifacts associated with it are on display, and the Lasch facility is open to the public on weekends only; during the week, it is occupied by marine archaeologists. Admission costs help to finance their conservation efforts. Yet to be answered is the cause of the *Hunley*'s loss. One plausible explanation is that the *Housatonic* explosion had created enough of a sufficient shockwave to damage the submarine. Some have further speculated that whoever sent the mysterious lantern signal may have failed to properly secure the hatch from which the signal had been displayed. Swamped by a wave, the *Hunley* might have gone to the bottom.

officers and three sailors, died. The rest of the crew, however, either piled into two of the ship's boats or simply climbed the masts and rigging. Charleston Harbor was so shallow that much of each mast remained well above the surface as the hull settled on the bottom. The crew of the *Hunley* did not fare as well.

> "GENERAL: . . . I am of the opinion that the torpedoes being placed at the bow of the boat, she went into the hole made in the *Housatonic* by explosion of torpedoes and did not have sufficient power to back out, consequently sunk with her."
>
> *Report by M. M. Gray, Captain in Charge of Torpedoes to Confederate major general Dabney H. Maury, April 29, 1864, on the loss of the submarine* Hunley

Eyewitnesses observing from the stricken *Housatonic* agreed that the *Hunley* withdrew after the explosion. That much they all saw. But what happened after that, no one could tell. At the time, it was assumed that the submarine had been damaged by the blast and sank nearby. Assumptions, however, do not satisfy historians, especially when one scholar ran across a naval record that reported an exchange of lantern signals between shore and "some object" at sea. A notation on the record indicates that the exchange took place shortly after the *Housatonic* exploded.

The site of the *Housatonic* wreck was well known, and yet nothing of the *Hunley* was ever found close by. This fact, combined with the exchange of lantern signals, prompted numerous investigators over the years to speculate that the *Hunley* and its crew may have survived the attack, only to be lost somewhere else.

The mystery began to unravel in August 1994, when a research expedition detected a metal object whose dimensions were consistent with what was known about the *Hunley*. It was located more than a thousand feet southeast of the *Housatonic*'s boiler, which still lay on the floor of Charleston Harbor, off Sullivan's Island. In May 1995, divers confirmed the wreckage as that of CSS *Hunley* and, on August 8, 2000, a complex salvage operation raised the submarine.

# THE ASSAULT ON MOBILE BAY

WHILE THE DARING OF HER INVENTOR and the others who sailed CSS *Hunley* is undeniable, the submarine was an impractical weapon that had no effect on the course of the Civil War. It did, however, presage a vessel type that would be of profound importance in two world wars, the Cold War, and beyond. At least one naval action after the *Hunley* episode, equally daring, did have significant impact on the outcome of the Civil War. Rear Admiral David Farragut achieved a spectacular victory at Mobile Bay that not only deprived the Confederacy of its only remaining Gulf port—New Orleans having been captured in 1862— but, in conjunction with the capture of Atlanta, virtually assured the reelection of Abraham Lincoln and, therefore, the Union's determination to continue fighting to absolute victory.

Mobile Bay was the single most formidable naval objective in the Confederacy, defended by no fewer than three forts, which were supplemented by a trio of gunboats and the CSS *Tennessee*, an ironclad ram built not abroad but in Selma, Alabama, and commissioned on February 16, 1864. As a ram, she was purpose-built for destructive collision with other ships. In addition, the Confederates had sown the channel into the bay with mines: wooden kegs—called "torpedoes," because of their elongated shape—anchored to the channel bottom by tethers, so that they bobbed barely at the surface of the water. Each torpedo was packed with black powder and rigged to a detonator that was actuated by contact with a passing vessel.

Farragut decided that Mobile Bay would not yield to clever tactics, but required a combination of main strength and sheer guts. He assembled a task force consisting of four monitors—iron ships patterned after USS *Monitor* (Chapter 7)— and fourteen vessels of conventional wooden construction. The wooden ships he lashed together in pairs to better the odds of their surviving the pounding they would surely get from the artillery mounted in the Confederate forts. The objective was not maneuvering. It was simply to survive the gauntlet and attack the bay.

From his flagship USS *Hartford*, Farragut led the flotilla out at six in the morning on August 5, 1864. As the enemy's fire intensified, Farragut, sixty-three at the time, clambered up a ratline and ordered a deckhand to lash him to the mast. He expected to be wounded, and he did not want to fall. Soon, however, the smoke of a hundred or more guns became so

*Farragut ordered his men to lash him to the mast of his flagship (some accounts report that he was lashed to the shrouds, the heavy guy-ropes steadying the mast) so that he would not fall if he was wounded as he directed the assault on Mobile Bay.*

*Franklin Buchanan, skipper of CSS* Virginia *(ex-*Merrimack*) in its historic Hampton Roads duel with USS* Monitor, *later commanded the Confederate ram* Tennessee *in the battle of Mobile Bay.*

thick that he could no longer see to direct the battle. Untying himself, he climbed higher, then once again lashed himself to the rigging.

The battle went well—that is, the flotilla continued its advance through the storm of iron and fire—until, suddenly, USS *Tecumseh*, a monitor and therefore considered all but indestructible, exploded. It had struck a torpedo. The iron ship, once broken, sank with frightening speed. In response, the captains of the other ships slowed down in an effort to avoid the torpedoes. In slowing, however, they presented to the Confederate gunners far easier targets. Farragut grasped the situation immediately. Determined to set an example of high speed, he turned to Percival Drayton, his flag captain. "Damn the torpedoes!" he shouted. "Full speed ahead, Drayton!" The *Hartford* raced ahead, and that was enough to kick the rest of the flotilla forward. In rapid succession, one of the Confederate gunboats was captured, and Farragut's relentless fire wrecked the two others. The big ram *Tennessee*, under the command of Franklin Buchanan, the very man who had skippered the CSS *Virginia* (ex-*Merrimack*) in its epic duel with the USS *Monitor*, was the only Confederate warship still in action.

If ever there was a time for bold action, Buchanan decided, now was that time. Ordering flank speed, he aimed the *Tennessee*'s solid iron ram at the *Hartford*. Farragut and his crew braced for impact—only to

*L. Prang & Co. published this exciting bird's-eye view of the battle of Mobile Bay c. 1886, long after the Civil War had ended.*

be met by anticlimax. The collision was stunning precisely because it produced remarkably little effect. Buchanan's chagrin can only be imagined as USS *Monongahela* and *Lackawanna*, together with the *Hartford*, swarmed in on him. By turn, at intervals of precisely five minutes, the three Union ships rammed the *Tennessee*. Buchanan's ironclad remained afloat and maneuverable under this pounding, even as the captains of the three Union warships became confused. The elaborate choreography of alternating impacts soon fell apart, and USS *Lackawanna* suddenly plowed into the fantail of the admiral's flagship, its bow making contact almost precisely where Farragut stood directing the action. He narrowly escaped death.

When the ramming proved ineffectual, Farragut ordered his ironclads to turn their turrets upon the *Tennessee*. That finished it. The ship's captain, James D. Johnston, witnessed the impact of a shell hitting "the edge of the [gun]port cover, immediately over the spot where [a] machinist [was repairing the jammed gun port so that the cannon could be brought into action]. His remains had to be taken up with a shovel, placed in a bucket, and thrown overboard. Iron splinters . . . killed a seaman . . . and broke the admiral's leg below the knee."

Johnston summoned Fleet Surgeon D. B. Conrad to attend to the injured admiral. "All of the gun's crew and the admiral were covered from head to foot with [the machinist's] blood, flesh, and viscera," the surgeon later reported. He asked: "Admiral, are you badly hurt?" "Don't know," Buchanan answered. But Dr. Conrad could see that "one of his legs [was] crushed up under his body." The surgeon carried him on his back down the ladder to the cockpit below, noting that "his broken leg slap[ed] against me as we moved slowly along." Conrad bandaged the ruined limb as best he could, and Buchanan, sitting on the deck, propped himself up against a bulkhead as he received reports. Finally, he called for Captain Johnston: "Well, Johnston, they have got me again. You'll have to look out for her now; it is your fight." "All right. I'll do the best I know how."

But the *Tennessee*, which had endured pounding from the wooden ships, could not live long under fire from the Union monitors. By 10:00, the vessel was out of control, and Johnston, out of options, struck her colors. Over the next two days, two of the bay's forts fell, and the third, Fort Morgan, gave up on August 23. Mobile Bay was in Union hands. One by one, the doors were closing on the Confederate States of America.

## TAKEAWAY

Although the Civil War was mostly fought on land, both sides waged naval warfare directed against each other's commerce. The Union tried to enforce a blockade, and the Confederacy, relying heavily on civilians, did its best to penetrate the blockade while also striking out at Northern commercial shipping through a combination of privateers (state-sanctioned pirates) and high-seas commerce raiders, such as the CSS *Alabama*. Well aware that a Confederate navy could never become as large or as powerful as the United States Navy, Jefferson Davis's secretary of the navy, Stephen R. Mallory, embraced novel technologies, including ironclads and the submarine *Hunley*, in an effort to even the odds. In the end, it was the Union navy's sheer superiority of numbers, as well as the daring of such leaders as David Farragut, that won the naval war. Farragut's successful assault on Mobile Bay deprived the Confederacy of its last Gulf port and, along with the fall of Atlanta, signaled its doom.

## PART SEVEN

# LAST CASUALTIES

# CHAPTER 21

## "WAKE UP, WE ARE COMING"

### Climax and Collapse

T HE UNION'S SINGLE BIGGEST ARMY, THE ARMY OF THE POTOMAC, was locked in siege against Lee at Petersburg, Virginia, during the summer of 1864, while three smaller Union armies, gathered under the command of William T. Sherman, took Atlanta, marched through Georgia to the sea, invaded South Carolina, and began rolling through North Carolina toward the rear of the Army of Northern Virginia.

It was these forces that fought the central struggle of the Civil War's climax, but the stage of the conflict remained large and crowded. While Grant wrestled Lee, and as Sherman battled through the South, Jubal Anderson Early, a grizzled graybeard, his slender six-foot frame badly bent by the arthritis that was his legacy from the war with Mexico, broke into Maryland with ten or twelve thousand infantrymen and a band of four thousand cavalry troopers. It would be the Confederacy's final invasion of the United States.

### MY BAD OLD MAN

THE LATE, LAMENTED STONEWALL JACKSON (under whom Early had served) was by any measure an unusual man, but his pious zealotry put him squarely in the

Southern fundamentalist tradition, whereas Early was that rarity in nineteenth-century America and almost unique in the South: an outspoken atheist, whom Lee lovingly dubbed "my bad old man." Early not only disavowed religion, but, in common with the commander of the Army of Northern Virginia, he also disapproved of secession. Yet, like Lee, he could not bring himself to renounce his loyalty to his "country," which was Virginia.

Early was a West Point man, class of 1837, but he served only briefly, against the Seminoles, before resigning his commission in 1838 to practice law, which he did brilliantly. He then rejoined the army just long enough to serve in the U.S.-Mexican War of 1846–48. His affection for strong drink was increased by his arthritic pain, and only the threat to Virginia could bring him back into the saddle. Bent, thin to the point of emaciation, he appeared to one Confederate trooper who served under him like "a plain farmer-looking man," yet "every inch a soldier." As the war turned increasingly against the Confederacy, the former antisecessionist became hard set against the Union. After the war, he would summarily declare, "I cannot live under the same Government with the Yankee" and made haste for Mexico and then Canada. Early remained an expatriate until 1869, when he would return to Virginia, resume his law practice, and espouse the Confederate point of view as cofounder and president of the Southern Historical Society. He was soon identified with the so-called Lost Cause, the idea that the Confederacy fought nobly and well against federal oppression but was doomed by the economic, demographic, and industrial superiority of the North. Perhaps it was a prelude to this sentiment that motivated Early's daring Valley campaign, which began on June 27, 1864, the day he led his men out of the Shenandoah town of Staunton, Virginia, and into the valley.

*Jubal Anderson Early led the final Confederate incursion into the North, which was more terrorist raid than full-scale invasion.*

"The conditions of domestic slavery, as it existed in the South, had not only resulted in a great improvement in the moral and physical condition of the negro race, but had furnished a class of laborers as happy and contented as any in the world."

Jubal A. Early, A Memoir of the Last Year of the War for Independence in the Confederate States of America (1867)

*PREVIOUS SPREAD:*
*The fall of Richmond, as pictured by Currier & Ives.*

*Alfred R. Waud sketched the troops of Philip Sheridan "following Early up the Valley of the Shenandoah."*

*Major General Lew Wallace failed to stop Early at Monocacy, but he did delay him long enough for the defenses of Washington to be adequately reinforced against his attack. After the war, Wallace became the territorial governor of New Mexico, the U.S. minister to the Ottoman Empire, and the author of several novels, most notably the bestseller* Ben-Hur: A Tale of the Christ *(1880).*

At first, no one on the Union side—not Grant, not Halleck—took what seemed an old man's Quixotic expedition very seriously. But by July 6, it became clear that Early's small army, as it advanced through the Shenandoah Valley—which both sides considered Washington's "backyard"—posed a real threat to the capital. Grant began scrambling to reinforce Washington, which is just what Early had calculated that he would have to do. Maybe victory was indeed a "lost cause," but if he could force Grant to dilute the Army of the Potomac on the Petersburg front in order to defend the Union capital, maybe Lincoln would fail to win reelection, and maybe, just maybe, the North would be moved to treat honorably with the South.

On July 6, Grant detached two brigades from the Petersburg front, about five thousand men, to reinforce the only Federal troops standing between Jubal Early and Washington: just twenty-three hundred soldiers under Major General Lew Wallace. These were mostly so-called Hundred Days Men, short-term volunteers who were used as rear-echelon and garrison troops. Very few had been in combat. On Saturday, July 9, the reinforcements Grant sent linked up with Wallace's men, and the combined force took up a blocking position along the National Road where it crossed Monocacy Creek in Maryland, about forty miles northwest of Washington.

Stiffened by the veterans from Petersburg, Wallace's rear-line men fought with unexpected heroism, as if they were fully aware that they were defending their nation's capital. But they could not work miracles. The roughly fifty-eight hundred Union troops who were engaged at Monocacy could not hold off some fourteen thousand Confederates forever. Early inflicted nearly thirteen hundred casualties against Wallace, sustaining seven to nine hundred losses—killed or wounded—himself before opening the road to Washington.

He could have pursued the Federal troops as they fell back on Baltimore; however, he did not want to burden his raiders with POWs, and, although he detached a cavalry brigade to harry

# THE "LOST CAUSE"

After a four-year sojourn in Mexico and Canada, Jubal Early returned to his native Virginia to practice law and to craft *his* history of the Civil War. He was one of the founders of the Southern Historical Society, serving as its president from 1873 until his death in 1894, and he published extensively in the *Southern Historical Society Papers*. Thanks to Early and others of similar sentiments, the Civil War was fought and refought in the public imagination. Early did not deliberately distort history, but he was zealous in his efforts to slant it. His accounts of battle elevated Robert E. Lee from a richly warranted reputation as a superb tactician to something approaching martial sainthood—often at the cost of the reputations of his subordinate commanders.

The portrait Early painted was of a general who could do no wrong but who was sometimes poorly served by the men under him. Early demonized General James Longstreet, on whom he heaped the blame for Lee's defeat at Gettysburg. But Early's most important and lasting contribution to Civil War historiography was the so-called Lost Cause thesis, which held that secession had been an honorable response to the Northern-based tyranny of the federal government. This view suppresses the role of slavery as a precipitating issue of the war and identifies instead states' rights and the defense of the Constitution.

Having accepted the fact that the South had lost the Civil War, Early immediately took up the battle to win control of the popular memory of that war. His provocatively titled *A Memoir of the Last Year of the War for Independence, in the Confederate States of America* (1867) was the very first Civil War memoir by a general in that conflict, and his posthumously published *Autobiographical Sketch and Narrative of the War between the States* was long popular, especially in the South.

Baltimore, Early continued his advance on the capital with the main body of his force, but it was already too late for such haste. As Grant commented years later in his *Memoirs*, "General Wallace contributed . . . by the defeat of the troops under him a greater benefit to the cause than often falls to the lot of a commander of an equal force to render by means of a victory." He had bought time for the reinforcement of Washington.

Grant dispatched more Army of the Potomac soldiers to the capital's defense. In addition, Washington-based administrative troops and even civilian Washingtonians rushed to help garrison the city's ring of forts. But Lincoln wanted even more. He asked—though did not order—General Grant to return to Washington to direct defense operations in person. Grant understood that this was precisely the objective of Early's raid, to relieve the pressure on Petersburg, and he was determined to do no such thing. Lincoln was worried, but not panicked. He understood Grant's argument and, however reluctantly, accepted it. His general in chief would remain on the Petersburg front.

Still, the situation was terrifying. Early approached the Washington forts on July 11. By this time, the War Department had assembled every man it could lay hands on, including retirees from the Soldiers' Home outside of the city and disabled veterans still enrolled in the Invalid Corps, whose members were usually called on to do nothing more than clerical work. In the proverbial nick of time, VI Corps of the Army of the Potomac drew up on Early just as he was about to order a general attack against the capital. The corps clashed with his men just beyond the outermost line of the defensive forts. On July 12, President and Mrs. Lincoln, together with a contingent of political dignitaries, paid a visit to Fort Stevens in northwest Washington. While they were there, an exchange erupted with some of Early's sharpshooters. Eager for a better look, the president mounted a firing step in order to peer over the parapet of the fort's wall. Lincoln was both horrified and fascinated by combat, and he seemed to take no notice that both his head and chest were exposed to the enemy's fire. An army surgeon who stood beside the president fell back, wounded. This drew the attention of a young officer nearby.

"Get down, you damn fool!" he shouted, recognizing only that a man in civilian dress was idiot enough to expose himself needlessly. Lincoln responded by crouching down. The officer who had issued the timely if abrupt warning was a Massachusetts man, Captain Oliver Wendell Holmes, Jr., future associate justice of the United States Supreme Court.

By the end of the day on July 12, Early was persuaded that he would never be able to penetrate Washington's defenses, and he began his withdrawal that night, falling back on the Shenandoah Valley.

## Ruin in the Valley

Jubal Early did not go quietly. His Washington foray had been turned back, and he had withdrawn from Maryland, but during the first week of August, his men repeatedly tweaked the small Union detachments broadcast widely throughout the Shenandoah Valley. Although he was loath to dilute the Petersburg front, Grant once again called on his cavalry chief, Phil Sheridan, and sent him

# IF WASHINGTON FELL

**Both sides targeted the enemy's capital city for invasion, with two purposes. One was to force the other side to weaken its offensive operations by drawing men for the defense of Richmond or Washington. The other was an assumption that, if the enemy capital fell, general surrender would soon follow.**

The assumption does seem a product of common sense, but like many common sense notions, it is not necessarily correct. In fact, the nation's own history hardly suggests that the fall of a capital ends the war. The British captured and occupied Philadelphia, seat of the Continental Congress and the revolutionary government of the United States, and yet the patriots fought the American Revolution to victory and independence. Moreover, garrisoning Philadelphia proved burdensome to the British army, which ultimately walked away from its hard-won prize.

The zeal to capture the enemy's capital was born of the outworn military doctrine that defined victory in terms of the conquest of territory rather than the total defeat of the opposing army. Had George McClellan succeeded in taking Richmond early in the war, it is quite probable that the Confederacy would have fought on, provided that Jefferson Davis did not compel Lee and his other generals to fight to the death in defense of the city. Likewise, had Early succeeded in breaching Washington's defenses, he would probably have gained little enough. His gamble was that this would cause the people to turn against Lincoln and to elect a president and Congress willing to negotiate peace with the Confederacy on more or less favorable terms. It is just as likely, however, that the occupation of Washington—which would have been short lived—would have galvanized the Union's resolve to redeem the national honor by fighting through to complete victory. In the end, the only strategic benefit the Confederacy could have hoped to derive from a successful assault on Washington was the temporary weakening of the Union's siege against Petersburg.

with forty-eight thousand men to scour the Shenandoah Valley, assigning him not only to rid the valley of Early, but to eliminate the region as a source of trouble once and for all. Grant was determined never again to allow a menace to Washington to divert him from what he considered the single war-winning objective of destroying Lee's army. Moreover, Sherman's actions in Georgia were teaching Grant an important lesson about total war. There was more than one way to kill an enemy army. You could shoot it, or you could starve it. Sheridan's assignment was not only to reclaim Washington's "backyard," but also to ravage what the Confederacy had been jealously guarding as the breadbasket for its armies. Grant ordered Sheridan to transform the lush and verdant Shenandoah into a place so barren that "a crow flying across the Valley would have to carry its own rations."

## NUMBERS
### Valley Toll

Sheridan suffered more casualties than Early at Winchester—5,020 killed or wounded versus 3,610—but he outnumbered Early, committing some 40,000 of his troops against Early's 12,000. Early took a stand at Fisher's Hill and suffered a defeat that cost him 1,234 killed, wounded, or taken prisoner, whereas Sheridan suffered 528 killed or wounded.

## NUMBERS
### Cedar Creek Attack and Counterattack

The battle of Cedar Creek began with a Union rout and ended with a successful Union counterattack. The cost to Sheridan was 5,665 men killed, wounded, or missing, out of 30,829 engaged in the battle. Early committed 18,410 men, the largest force he had ever commanded in the Shenandoah Valley. Of these, 2,910 were killed, wounded, or missing. What finished Early, however, was the catastrophic loss of supplies—the Confederate commander could no longer feed his army, and the forty-three cannon he lost to Sheridan he could not replace.

"Wherever the enemy goes,
let our troops go also."

*General Ulysses S. Grant to Major General Henry W. Halleck regarding Sheridan's mission in the Shenandoah Valley, August 1, 1864*

The Union cavalryman took up his assignment with gusto. As he relentlessly pursued Early up the valley, he burned everything in his path: crops, barns, and even cattle. Guerrillas harried and ambushed his columns. The most celebrated of these was the remarkable Colonel John Singleton Mosby, leader of the Partisan Rangers and a figure celebrated even in his own day as the "Gray Ghost of the Confederacy." But neither Mosby nor any other Confederate leader was powerful enough to deter Sheridan. On September 19, 1864, he ran Early to ground at Winchester, dealing him a sharp defeat (this third battle of Winchester is sometimes called the battle of Opequon), and when Early fell back on Fisher's Hill, Sheridan was there to fight him again on September 22.

Despite his losses, come the dawn of October 19, Jubal Early mounted an attack against Sheridan at Cedar Creek, Virginia. Surprise was complete, and Sheridan's veterans, having allowed themselves to become complacent in their superiority of numbers, panicked, broke, and ran. At the time, General Sheridan was just returning from a meeting in Washington. Word of the rout in progress reached him at Winchester. Mounting a fresh horse, he pointed it toward Cedar Creek, spurred it to a full gallop, and set about personally rallying his troops. The sight and sound of "Little Phil" was all they needed. By four o'clock that afternoon, Sheridan was sufficiently confident in the restored fighting spirit of his men that he organized them not in a last-ditch defense, but a full-out counterattack. It was now Early's turn to taste the bitterness of rout. He yielded the Shenandoah Valley to the Union.

## "Let Us Strive to Finish"

Sherman's conquest of Atlanta (Chapter 19), Farragut's capture of Mobile Bay (Chapter 20), the collapse of Early's Valley campaign, and the failure of his assault on Washington all contributed to Abraham Lincoln's reelection in November 1864 with 55 percent of the popular vote over George B. McClellan's 45 percent and 212 electoral votes to McClellan's 21. But if the people who returned Lincoln to office expected him to wreak vengeance on the South, they must have been disappointed by the message he delivered in his second inaugural address on March 4, 1865. "With malice toward none, with charity for all, with firmness in the right as God gives us to see the right," he implored his countrymen, "let us strive to finish the work we are in, to bind up the nation's wounds, to care for him who shall have borne the battle and for his widow and his orphan, to do all which may achieve and cherish a just and a lasting peace among ourselves and with all nations." It was a message of conciliation intended to

*This detail from the photo of Lincoln's Second Inaugural Address shows the man many historians believe to be John Wilkes Booth—who became the president's assassin on the night of April 14.*

be heard not only by those loyal to the Union, but, even more clearly, perhaps, by the people of the South. It was an entreaty. It was a promise of forgiveness. But insofar as it was a request for forgiveness in return, the people of the South turned to it with a stony deafness. They did not want to hear of an absence of malice from the commander in chief of an army that had burned their chief cities, destroyed their croplands, and stolen their property, whether of brick and mortar or flesh and blood.

## No More Than Annoy

All the armies of the Confederacy fought on. At this point, however, the continued existence of the Confederate States of America depended entirely on Lee and his Army of Northern Virginia, almost all of which was locked in siege warfare against the Army of the Potomac in the trenches at Petersburg. Both of those armies were miserable. Misery was the way of siege warfare. But the 125,000 or so Union men arrayed against half that number under Lee were reasonably well fed and well clothed, whereas the Army of Northern Virginia had been reduced to squalor and semi-starvation.

Lee had to contend not only with Ulysses Grant, but also Jefferson Davis and Davis's insistence that Richmond had to be defended at all costs, which meant, obviously, that Lee could move no one out of the Petersburg entrenchments. Lee countered that the only hope of avoiding total defeat and unconditional surrender lay in the Army of Northern Virginia's breaking out from the Petersburg siege and withdrawing south-

# AS THE SAYING GOES . . .

American elections have produced some memorable campaign slogans, including "Tippecanoe and Tyler too" (William Henry Harrison, 1840), "He kept us out of war" (Woodrow Wilson's reelection, 1916), "Keep cool with Coolidge" (Calvin Coolidge, 1924), "Yes we can" (Barack Obama, 2008), and the one Lincoln used to help get himself reelected in 1864: "Do not change horses in the middle of the stream."

The line was not original with Lincoln, but a familiar proverb. Candidate Lincoln seems to have first used it in informal remarks he made to a National Union League delegation who had called to offer their congratulations on his renomination on June 9, 1864. "I do not allow myself to suppose that either the Convention or the League have concluded to decide that I am either the greatest or the best man in America," he said, "but rather they have concluded it is not best to swap horses while crossing the river, and have further concluded that I am not so poor a horse that they might not make a botch of it in trying to swap." The saying is often cited as "Don't swap horses in midstream."

Democratic challenger George B. McClellan might have chosen to give voters a reason to swap. It had been generally assumed that he would toe the party line by campaigning on a pledge to negotiate immediate peace with the Confederacy—whereas Lincoln was committed to continuing the fight to total victory, no matter how costly. Instead, McClellan, more patriot than opportunist, decided against running on a peace platform. Doing so may have ensured his defeat.

east to link up with the pitiable remains of the Army of Tennessee, no more than thirty thousand men. As of February 22, 1865, that force had been returned to the command of Joseph Johnston, who was now using it to fight Sherman in North Carolina. "I can do no more than annoy him," Johnston said of his mission against Sherman, but Lee believed that this might just be enough to salvage something that could be taken to a negotiation with the Lincoln government. Johnston could "annoy" Sherman long enough to allow the Army of Northern Virginia to consolidate with the Army of Tennessee. Together, they could cause enough hurt to Sherman and Grant that the people of the North, though they had reelected Lincoln, might clamor for him to honor his second inaugural address and make a peace truly without malice. The cost of buying this negotiating position would certainly be the loss of Richmond sooner instead of later, but, Lee believed, it was better to sacrifice the capital for some good purpose than to lose it and gain nothing in return.

In the meantime, Confederate secretary of state Judah P. Benjamin renewed his government's appeals to both France and England for recognition as a sovereign nation, promising in return to abolish slavery in the Confederate States of America. It was an incredible offer. Though many—foremost among them Jubal Early—would argue after the war that the fight had been about states' rights and against federal tyranny, the stubborn fact was that had the Confederacy renounced slavery, there would have been no Civil War. Now Benjamin was offering to renounce the very cause of the war in order to win support for the war. His government was willing to abolish the institution it had sought to preserve. It was, of course, much too late for that. The French and British governments rejected Benjamin's proposal. Almost certainly, both he and President Davis knew that they would. Perhaps they hoped to gain nothing more than a fragment of moral high ground. Perhaps they did not want the Confederacy to suffer defeat in the defense of slavery.

In January 1865, Jefferson Davis himself met in Richmond with Francis P. Blair Sr., the father of Lincoln's former postmaster general, Montgomery Blair, and of Francis P. Blair Jr., who commanded one of Sherman's corps. President Lincoln not only knew of the meeting, he approved it. He wanted to gauge the state of Davis's mind.

The picture Blair brought back to Washington suggested that the Confederate president's mind was no longer balanced. Davis did indeed embrace the prospect of negotiations to effect a reunion of the states—but only to propose, perhaps at Blair's suggestion, that the reconstructed United States maintain its armies in the field and use them jointly to invade Mexico for the purpose of ousting the French-supported regime of Emperor Maximilian. Lincoln overlooked the manifestly bizarre, not to say irrelevant, nature of this proposal and approved a quasi-official peace conference, which was convened on February 3, 1865, aboard a U.S. Navy ship riding at anchor in Hampton Roads, Virginia. Both President Abraham Lincoln and his secretary of state, William Seward, attended, whereas Jefferson Davis sent in his stead Vice President Alexander Stephens and two others. Nothing came of the conference, almost certainly because Lincoln

*Francis P. Blair Sr., a friend of Lincoln's, visited Jefferson Davis in January 1865, listened to his peace proposal, and reported to Lincoln his opinion that the man's mind was no longer balanced.*

had nothing to offer the Confederacy save a demand that it lay down its arms at once and acknowledge the supreme authority of the government of the United States.

## ATTACK AND COUNTERATTACK

HAVING FINALLY EXTRACTED Jefferson Davis's permission to attempt to disengage from Grant and break out of the Petersburg entrenchments, Lee ordered Major General John Brown Gordon to send twelve thousand men in an assault against Fort Stedman, a hardened redoubt in the Union siege line just 150 yards from the Confederate trenches. By hitting Fort Stedman, Lee hoped to force Grant to contract his lines to cover the fort, thereby creating a new breach through which Lee could squeeze some part of the Army of Northern Virginia and get in on the march to North Carolina.

Sometime after midnight on March 25, 1865, Gordon sent sappers—men with axes and other tools—to stealthily dismantle some of the obstacles arrayed before Fort Stedman.

"Who goes there?" a Union picket, hearing the activity, called into the darkness. "Never mind, Yank," a voice drawled in return. "We are just gathering a little corn."

"All right, Johnny," the guard shouted back. "I'll not shoot at you while you are drawing your rations."

Such was the brotherhood of soldiers, even those sworn to kill one another. But it cut both ways. When General Gordon, at four in the morning, ordered the very soldier who had spoken to the Union picket to fire a shot signaling the commencement of the Fort Stedman assault, the young man hesitated. Gordon repeated his order. The soldier pointed his musket to the sky and covered the trigger. "Hello, Yank!" he yelled. "Wake up. We are coming." And with this warning given, he fired the signal.

Under the onslaught, Fort Stedman folded, yielding to Gordon a thousand Union prisoners, including one stunned general. Following this conquest, Gordon was supposed to go on to take as quickly as possible the succession of smaller forts that lay behind Stedman. But his first objective had fallen so quickly that his reinforcements, essential to his farther advance, had not yet arrived. In addition, having

*On January 18, 1865, in a letter to Blair, Lincoln responded to a peace feeler from Jefferson Davis. The letter ends: ". . . our one common country." The last four words are most significant because they pointedly refuse to recognize the existence of a "Confederacy" separate from the United States.*

# A CONFEDERATE NAMED JUDAH

Judah Philip Benjamin served the government of the Confederacy as its first attorney general (February 25–September 17, 1861), second secretary of war (September 17, 1861–March 24, 1862), and third (and last) secretary of state (March 18, 1862–May 10, 1865). Except for Secretary of the Navy Stephen Mallory, Benjamin was the only truly effective member of Jefferson Davis's Cabinet. He was also the only Jew to hold high Confederate office; indeed, he was the first Jewish Cabinet member in any North American government.

Before the war, he had been the first Jew considered for appointment to the U.S. Supreme Court (by presidents Millard Fillmore and Franklin Pierce; he declined both offers of nomination) and was the second Jew elected to the U.S. Senate (the first, if one discounts Florida's David Levy Yulee, who converted to Presbyterianism before his election in 1845).

Benjamin was born a British subject in St. Croix (now one of the U.S. Virgin Islands), moved with his family to the Carolinas, attended Yale Law School (but did not graduate), then settled in New Orleans, where he completed his legal studies and went into private practice. After marrying a wealthy Creole woman in 1833, Benjamin became a slave-owning planter in Belle Chasse, Louisiana, became a state legislator in 1842, and a U.S. senator in 1853. During his freshman year, a dispute on the Senate floor moved him to challenge a senator from Mississippi to a duel. That man, Jefferson Davis, apologized, thereby avoiding the necessity of a duel and beginning one of the few close friendships of the prickly Davis's life. When abolitionist Senator Benjamin Wade of Ohio criticized the slave-owning Senator Benjamin as a "Hebrew with Egyptian principles," Benjamin replied not with another challenge, but an insult: "When my ancestors were receiving their Ten Commandments from the immediate Deity, amidst the thundering and lightnings of Mt. Sinai, the ancestors of my opponent were herding swine in the forests of Great Britain." Benjamin resigned his Senate seat on February 4, 1861, when Louisiana seceded.

An enthusiastic Confederate, he became President Davis's close adviser and earned a reputation as the "brains of the Confederacy." He performed poorly as secretary of war, but did his best as secretary of state to win support and recognition from France and Great Britain and was a passionate advocate of emancipating slaves who enlisted in the Confederate army. After the war, Benjamin fled to England, where he became a prominent barrister and, in 1872, was appointed Queen's Counsel. He died during a stay in Paris in 1884.

*The portrait on this two-dollar bill issued by the Confederate States of America is of Judah P. Benjamin, by far the most competent (and remarkable) member of the Jefferson Davis Cabinet.*

*A "bomb-proof" (shelter against artillery bombardment) at Fort Stedman in the Union siege lines at Petersburg, Virginia.*

taken Fort Stedman, Gordon now found himself and his men in the very midst of extremely well-fortified Union entrenchments. Where should he go? Where could he go? Having gotten so far so fast, Gordon was bewildered, and because he was stuck, his men—all twelve thousand of them—were stranded, marooned in a gathering sea of blue.

By first light, Union reinforcements were rushing in, a tidal wave. In short order, they drove Gordon's men back into Fort Stedman. Observing the sudden reversal, Lee, at eight in the morning, ordered a general retreat. But it was already too late. The Federal artillery already had the range on the Confederate line of retreat and was raking it mercilessly. To withdraw was to be killed. To remain in place was also to be killed. Of Gordon's twelve-thousand-man force, nearly five thousand were killed, wounded, or captured.

## NORTH AMERICAN WATERLOO

THE PETERSBURG SIEGE was a highly deceptive operation. To all appearances, especially as seen through the impatient eyes of the people of the North, it was a contest of attrition, all but stalemated. As Grant saw it, however, it was a slow war of maneuver. Throughout the entire period of the siege, Grant had been extending his entrenchments relentlessly westward. His object was either to flank Lee, getting around his front, or to force him to extend his own entrenchments to prevent them from being flanked. Grant gave his adversary no other choice: either stretch his lines or suffer a devastating flanking attack. Sooner or later, Grant knew, the line was bound to snap. The ease with which he was able to retake Fort Stedman showed him that the breaking point had been reached.

Grant's first effort was a drive around Lee's right, but the Confederate general remained nimble enough to repulse the attempt. At this juncture, General Sheridan came back from his wrathful ride through the Shenandoah Valley, and so, on March 31, Grant pointed him, at the head of twelve thousand cavalry troopers, toward Five Forks, the place where the White Oak Road, Scott's Road, Ford's (also called Church) Road, and Dinwiddie Court House Road all met. If the Union took Five Forks, Lee would be unable to make his move to North Carolina, and his line of supply to his present position outside of Petersburg would be severed. Lose Five Forks, and the Army of Northern Virginia would be permanently and hopelessly cut off from the Army of Tennessee. Without supplies, Lee would have to relinquish both Petersburg and Richmond—and gain nothing for the sacrifice. Lose Five Forks, and Lee would have no good place to go and no good option to take. Accordingly, he sent a dispatch to George Pickett, whose men—estimates of his strength vary wildly, from ten to nineteen thousand—occupied the junction: "Hold Five Forks at all hazards. Protect road to Ford's Depot and prevent Union forces from striking the Southside Railroad."

Sheridan targeted Five Forks with his twelve thousand cavalry troopers backed by an entire infantry corps. Not only was Pickett massively outnumbered, he—a tactician of modest ability at best—was roundly out-generaled. Sheridan quickly flanked his position, and then routed it. In a matter of minutes, five thousand Confederates became Sheridan's prisoners. Those who escaped capture or death simply fled, making then and there a "separate peace." Though many Confederate soldiers fought to the bitterest of bitter ends, the closing weeks of the Civil War saw a flood of desertion.

> "This is a sad business, colonel. . . . It has happened
> as I told them in Richmond it would happen.
> The line has been stretched until it is broken."
>
> General Robert E. Lee to an aide, April 1, 1865,
> after the collapse of the Petersburg defenses

Five Forks brought to mind nothing more vividly than the defeat of Napoleon at Waterloo. The difference was that the 1815 contest between the Duke of Wellington and Napoleon had been, in Wellington's memorable words, "the nearest run thing you ever saw in your life, by God!" The "Waterloo of the Confederacy," however, was a complete collapse, long in coming but terribly sudden and one-sided in its culmination. Now, at Petersburg, after nine months of digging, inching entrenchments ever west, Grant suddenly smashed through Lee's lines in an assault on April 2, which killed, among many others, Confederate general Ambrose Powell Hill. Lee fell back on the

## TAKEAWAY

While the Union's Army of the Potomac and the Confederacy's Army of Northern Virginia continued their standoff before Petersburg, Confederate Jubal Early raided the Shenandoah Valley, invaded Maryland, and aimed an abortive but frightening assault against Washington, D.C. Robert E. Lee persuaded Jefferson Davis to allow him to sacrifice both Petersburg and Richmond in an effort to join the Army of Northern Virginia with Joe Johnston's Army of Tennessee in the hope of prolonging the war beyond the North's will to continue the fight, thereby prompting the Union to offer something more favorable than a demand for unconditional surrender. Union cavalry chief Philip Sheridan's successful attack on Five Forks cut Lee off from any easy route to Johnston and his army. The stage was set for the Army of the Potomac's final battle with the Army of Northern Virginia.

city of Petersburg, quickly evacuated it, and then retreated at full speed toward Amelia Court House, a railroad stop where he hoped to be resupplied and perhaps find quick escape to North Carolina and the Army of Tennessee.

That—a little food and the slim prospect of joining with another general and his army—was the best left to Lee. Jefferson Davis had even less to hope for.

April 2 was a Sunday. As on every Sunday morning, President Davis was seated in his customary pew at St. Paul's Church. At approximately eleven, the scrape of a War Department messenger's boots was heard shuffling along the aisle. The soldier halted by Davis's side and handed him a telegram from Robert E. Lee. He advised Davis to make "all preparation . . . for leaving Richmond tonight."

Politicians are generally well practiced in the art of concealment, maintaining a poker face regardless of the hand dealt them. But one man seated near the Confederate president, who saw him unfold the telegram, smooth it with his bony fingers, and read it silently, remarked how a "gray pallor" stole "over his face." Jefferson Davis rose, walked out of the church and into the War Office nearby. Here he dictated an order for the evacuation of the government of the Confederate States of America.

*After the Confederate lines finally broke at Petersburg on April 2, 1865—depicted in this lithograph from Currier & Ives—Lee led the tattered remnant of the Army of Northern Virginia in a desperate march toward Amelia Court House, where he believed he could secure supplies and an escape route to North Carolina, the location of Johnston's Army of Tennessee.*

# CHAPTER 22

## A WRAITH OF MORNING MIST

### Toward Appomattox and Beyond

O N SUNDAY NIGHT, APRIL 2, 1865, JEFFERSON DAVIS SENT WORD TO THE Treasury to gather up every piece of gold and silver it had, coins as well as ingots, box it all up, take it to the depot, and load it on a special train bound for Danville, a little Virginia town just above the North Carolina state line. In the meantime, he convened his Cabinet for their last meeting in Richmond. He instructed them to board the train for Danville, explaining that it was the new capital of the Confederacy. As for the cargo that accompanied them, the total value of the Confederate nation's ready cash was exactly $528,000.

Davis and his government weren't the only Richmond residents headed out of town. Writing for the paper he edited, the *Richmond Examiner*, Edward Pollard described the city's streets as "thronged with fugitives making their way to the railroad depots; pale women and little shoeless children struggled in the crowd; oaths and blasphemous shouts smote the air." Pollard reported that two militia regiments were deployed to keep order, and "every drop of liquor in the warehouses and stores" was ordered destroyed. "But the militia ran through the fingers of their officers . . . and in a short while the whole city was plunged into mad confusion and indescribable horrors." The night of April 2/3, after the Confederate government had decamped, "was an extraordinary night; disorder, pillage, shouts, mad revelry of confusion. . . . The gutters ran with a liquor freshet, and the fumes filled the air." Straggling soldiers got drunk, "sidewalks were encumbered with broken glass; stores were entered at pleasure and stripped from top to bottom; yells of drunken men, shouts of roving pillagers, wild cries of distress filled the air, and made night hideous."

And the morning? It "broke on a scene never to be forgotten. . . . The smoke and glare of fire mingled with the golden beams of the rising sun. . . . The fire was reaching to whole blocks of buildings. . . . Pillagers were busy at their vocation, and in the hot breath of the fire were figures as of demons contending for prey."

*Currier & Ives portray the fall of Richmond. By this point, the loss of the Confederate capital was anticlimactic, more symbolic than an actual end to the war.*

## "THANK GOD I HAVE LIVED TO SEE THIS"

ON APRIL 3, MAJOR GENERAL GODFREY WEITZEL led the Army of the Potomac's XXV Corps into Richmond, the smoke of the blazing city acrid in the soldiers' nostrils. The general located the house that had been occupied up to the day before by Jefferson Davis and his family. This became his headquarters. From it, Weitzel sent his chief of staff, Johnston de Peyster, to climb to the roof of the former Confederate capitol and raise over it the Stars and Stripes.

While XXV Corps set up the occupation of the Confederate capital, Abraham Lincoln was already in Petersburg, where he met General Grant, whose hand he shook (in the recollection of the general's aide) "for some time . . . pouring out his thanks and congratulations with all the fervor of a heart that seemed overflowing with its fullness of joy." Lincoln's secretary of war, Edwin Stanton, sent the president a telegram, which was forwarded to him in Petersburg. It warned him to "consider whether you ought to expose the nation to the consequences of any disaster to yourself" by visiting the town. Lincoln dashed off a reply: "Yours received. Thanks for your caution, but I have already been to Petersburg, stayed with Gen. Grant an hour & a half, and returned here [to Grant's headquarters at City Point]." Then he continued with news he was sure would upset the worry-prone Stanton even more: "It is certain now that Richmond is in our hands, and I think I will go there tomorrow," adding "I will take care of myself."

*The abandoned "Confederate White House" in Richmond was one of the first places Abraham Lincoln visited when he landed in the captured Southern capital on April 4, 1865.*

On April 4, the president boarded Admiral David Porter's flagship *Malvern*, which raised steam for Richmond. "Thank God I have lived to see this," Lincoln said to Porter. "It seems to me that I have been dreaming a horrid dream for four years, and now the nightmare is gone."

Stanton was right to worry, of course. If Lincoln risked assassination in Petersburg, he took an even greater chance in walking the streets of the Confederate capital. A guard who accompanied him remarked that "wherever it was possible for a human being to gain a foothold there was some man or woman or boy straining his eyes after the President." The man noted that "every window was crowned with heads. Men were hanging from tree-boxes and telegraph poles," and yet Lincoln's guard marveled at the silence of the crowd—"thousands of watchers, without a sound either of welcome or of hatred."

The stillness characterized the *white* citizens of Richmond. As for the black residents of the city, their greetings were very different.

"Bless the Lord! The great Messiah!" a white-haired slave, now free for the first time in a long life, called out. "I knowed him as soon as I seed him. He's been in my heart four long years. Come to free his children from bondage. Glory, hallelujah!" When he threw himself down at Lincoln's feet, as did others nearby, the president gently chided: "Don't kneel to me. That is not right. You must kneel to God only, and thank Him for the liberty you will enjoy hereafter."

One of General Weitzel's staff officers, Thomas Thatcher Graves, recalled the president "walking with his usual long, careless stride, and looking about with an interested air and taking in everything." When Graves saluted him, Lincoln asked, "Is it far to President Davis's house?" It was not, and Graves led him right to it. Inside, he was ushered into a reception room, which the housekeeper had identified as Davis's office. Lincoln seated himself, remarking (according to Graves), "'This must have been President Davis's chair,' and, crossing his legs, he looked far off

## REALITY CHECK
### Fires of Richmond

Fire was the bright shadow of Union occupation. Atlanta, Georgia; Columbia, South Carolina; Savannah, Georgia; and Richmond, Virginia, all suffered extensive blazes. In each city, Union and Confederate men pointed to each other as the source of conflagration. There really could be no controversy in Richmond, however. On April 2, Confederate naval officers ordered the demolition of ironclads docked along the James River to keep them out of Union hands. The explosions hurled embers and blazing debris onto the roofs of wharfside warehouses, including several used to store and dry tobacco. The fires ignited in these spread to large sections of Richmond before burning out late in the night of April 3.

with a serious, dreamy expression. At length he asked me if the house-keeper was in the house. Upon learning that she had left he jumped up and said, with a boyish manner, 'Come, let's look at the house!' We went pretty much over it; I retailed all that the housekeeper had told me, and he seemed interested in everything."

Graves and the president descended a staircase and, at its foot, ran into General Weitzel. "At once President Lincoln's face lost its boyish expression as he realized that duty must be resumed." Lincoln met with a few Confederate military officers and other locals Weitzel ushered to him, then the general took him to visit two infamous POW facilities, Libby Prison and Castle Thunder. What, he asked the president, should he "do in regard to the conquered people"? Graves recalled that Lincoln demurred, explaining that he "did not wish to give any orders on that subject, but, as he expressed it, 'If I were in your place I'd let 'em up easy, let 'em up easy.'"

Frank Leslie's Illustrated Newspaper *published this wood engraving of Abraham Lincoln riding through the fallen Confederate capital. His aides had great fear for his life as he passed through the streets of Richmond. Most white people, however, were silently polite, though some cheered, none threatened. African Americans were generally exuberant, some falling to their knees at the president's approach.*

## FROM HOPE TO DUTY

THE FALL OF PETERSBURG was like the defeat of Cornwallis at Yorktown in 1781. In any meaningful military sense, it was the end of the war. Yet, just as the American Revolution continued after Cornwallis surrendered, so the Civil War went on as Lee marched what was left of the Army of Northern Virginia, not quite fifty thousand men, out of the Petersburg line and to the west. Tactically, it was still his intention to link up with Johnston's Army of Tennessee in North Carolina, which required that he reach the town of Amelia Court House, where he believed he would be able to feed his hungry troops and connect with the Richmond and Danville Railroad for transport south. Strategically, Lee no longer had any hope of avoiding defeat. Hope was lost. What he still held onto was duty, and he felt that if he could continue to do his duty, his men would continue to do theirs: duty—and, with it, honor. That was all he could give his army now. Perhaps it would be enough to persuade the Northern negotiators to treat the soldiers and the people of the Confederacy with a modicum of goodwill. For this objective, Lee believed, it was worth continuing to spill blood in a war he knew he could not win.

### Custer vs. Two Lees

*Duty, honor, glory.* Lee believed these still had value. Thousands had died for these words, and thousands more had risked their lives for them. Among the latter was George Armstrong Custer, who had graduated dead last in the West Point class of 1861 then distinguished himself in the Civil War with one exuberant display of reckless gallantry under fire after another so that, on June 28, 1863, three days before the commencement of Gettysburg, his commanding officer, Major General Alfred Pleasonton, jumped him from the rank of regular army first lieutenant to brigadier general of volunteers, making him, at twenty-three, one of the youngest general officers in U.S. Army history.

*George Armstrong Custer was just a lieutenant when this 1862 photograph was made during McClellan's Peninsula campaign. On June 28, 1863, three days before Gettysburg, his consistently reckless bravery got him jumped from captain to brigadier general of volunteers. Just twenty-three years old, he was dubbed "the boy general."*

Directly after Five Forks (Chapter 21), Custer, now holding the rank of major general in the regular army, led a brigade of his division in pursuit of Confederate cavalry under Robert E. Lee's nephew Fitzhugh Lee. Custer fought Fitzhugh Lee to a stand at Willicomack Creek, but the Confederates wriggled away until they were run down again at Namozine Church. Here, Fitzhugh Lee wheeled his men around to make a spirited counterattack, which Custer skillfully parried, prompting Fitzhugh Lee to divide his forces. Part of his brigade followed another Lee, William Henry Fitzhugh Lee (the second-eldest son of Robert E. Lee, who called him Rooney) toward Bevill's Bridge across the Appomattox River. Simultaneously, Fitzhugh Lee led the others directly toward Amelia Court House, where, by April 5, most of Robert E. Lee's army was already gathered.

## "HALF OUR ARMY IS DESTROYED"

AMELIA COURT HOUSE was thirty miles west of Petersburg. Custer and other commanders under Sheridan were determined that Lee would get no farther, and Custer positioned his division to block the Richmond and Danville Railroad so as to prevent a breakout.

Bottled up at Amelia Court House, the Army of Northern Virginia was also starving. Lee had anticipated drawing rations for his men here, but in the chaos attending the fall of Richmond, no one in the quartermaster department had dispatched the promised rations. Well aware of the enemy army's desperate condition, Sheridan sent a brigade to reconnoiter back in the direction of Lee's retreat. At Amelia Springs, in the rear of the Army of

*Robert E. Lee's nephew Fitzhugh Lee battled with General Custer as the final curtain began to fall on the Civil War.*

Northern Virginia, the Federals found a wagon train. The Union troops attacked, seized 320 white prisoners and as many black teamsters, then put two hundred wagons to the torch. These had carried the pitiful remnant of the Confederate army's supplies, as well as most of Lee's papers.

Unable to push past Amelia Court House and now completely without supplies, Lee turned his army to the southwest and set out for Rice Station, another opportunity to obtain provisions and set out toward North Carolina. But Grant would not let up. His pursuing forces hit the rear of the Army of Northern Virginia, provoking Richard S. Ewell to counterattack at Little Sayler's Creek. The Federals were stunned by the ferocity of the counterpunch. How could a defeated army have so much left to deal out?

Ewell managed to push back the Union's center at Little Sayler's Creek, but his troops were soon checked by the arrival of Federal reinforcements. Worse for Ewell, Grant kept pouring on the men until there were enough to execute a double envelopment of the Confederate's vastly outnumbered command. Three of Ewell's subordinate commanders, Richard H. Anderson, Bushrod Johnson, and George Pickett, were able to extricate themselves and the bulk of their units as Ewell remained behind to fight a rearguard action. Combat was hand-to-hand, and, again, the Union troops were amazed and dismayed by the strength of hungry men clothed in butternut tatters, some, lacking even shoes, fighting barefoot.

Not that Ewell had any hope of prevailing. He and his warriors were swamped by the enemy. Ewell, together with five other Confederate commanders, among them Lee's eldest son, George Washington Custis Lee, were taken prisoner. His father saw it all. In the flat tone with which he customarily stated a fact, Robert E. Lee remarked to a subordinate, "that half of our army is destroyed."

## "NOT YET"

LEE HAD OVERESTIMATED THE LOSSES at Little Sayler's Creek. A third, not a half, of the Army of Northern Virginia was no more. The troops under General John Brown Gordon, though they had taken severe casualties, were still a viable force after the battle, and Gordon managed to push them farther west, to High Bridge, a majestic railway span atop sixty-foot piers thrown across the Appomattox at Farmville. As Fitzhugh Lee fought a rearguard action, Gordon linked up with Longstreet's men and withdrew across High Bridge.

It was a magnificent action, but not without tragic error. William "Little Billy" Mahone, who commanded a division fighting to cover Gordon's withdrawal, was supposed to demolish High Bridge after the Confederates had safely crossed it. This would have greatly slowed the Union pursuit. But it is difficult to destroy the monuments of one's own homeland, and Mahone, trained as an engineer and, before the war, president of the Southside Railroad, which had built High Bridge, could not bring himself to order its demolition. By the time his omission had been realized, the Confederate skirmishers sent to put the bridge to the torch fell under such intense fire that they were unable to burn down the span. Mahone's emotional attachment to High Bridge meant that Union forces were able to continue to close in on what remained of the Army of Northern Virginia.

*If Confederate general William "Little Billy" Mahone had followed orders to destroy High Bridge, across the Appomattox, Union forces would have been delayed in their pursuit of the Army of Northern Virginia.*

Yet Gordon had managed to get to Farmville, where the famished army finally found some refreshment. Lee also paused here long enough to receive a message from Grant calling upon him to surrender the Army of Northern Virginia. Wordlessly, the Confederate commander passed the paper to James Longstreet. If anyone were likely to advise Lee to comply with Grant's request, it was "Old Pete," who had tried in vain to persuade Lee against invading Maryland and against launching Pickett's Charge at Gettysburg. Instead of making the expected recommendation, however, Longstreet handed the note back to Lee.

"Not yet," he said.

And so, on April 8, 1865, Robert E. Lee deployed between Appomattox Station (along the railroad tracks) and Appomattox Court House (a few miles northeast of the station) all that was left of his army.

Custer led his division against Appomattox Station, smashing into a pair of Lee's divisions, which withdrew, but not before Custer had seized their supply train, along with twenty-five to thirty cannon. From here, he advanced toward Appomattox Court House, then drew up his lines opposite the Confederate defenses southwest of town. Custer's commanding officer, Phil Sheridan, caught up with him here and deployed the main body of the Union cavalry. The two men made ready to launch an attack the next day.

To the very last, Robert E. Lee seized the initiative. Instead of waiting for Sheridan and Custer to attack, he ordered, at five o'clock on the morning of April 9, John Brown Gordon and Fitzhugh Lee to make an assault on the defenses the Union men had hastily scratched out from the earth. It was a sharp, preemptive slap, and it stung, but it served only to trigger the culminating battle. Union cavalry and infantry advanced from Appomattox Court House, which was northeast of Gordon and Fitzhugh Lee's position, crossed the Confederate line of march, then closed in on the entire Army of Northern Virginia from the southwest, Appomattox Station.

Lee's army—no more than thirty thousand men now, only half of them even armed—were in the jaws of a vise. There was no way forward. There was no way back. To a staff officer, Lee said, "There is nothing left me but to go and see General Grant, and I had rather die a thousand deaths."

> "How easily I could be rid of this [life] and be at rest! I have only to ride along the line and all will be over. But it is our duty to live. What will become of the women and children of the South if we are not here to protect them?"
>
> *Robert E. Lee, pondering surrender, quoted in* A. L. Long, Memoirs of Robert E. Lee, 1886.

## A WHITE FLAG EARNESTLY BORNE

JOSHUA LAWRENCE CHAMBERLAIN, at Gettysburg a regimental colonel who saved the Army of the Potomac, months before that a professor of rhetoric at Maine's Bowdoin College, and now a brevet major general waiting for the order to attack, once again found himself at precisely the place where opposing armies met. The morning was still misty as he watched the enemy's line, watched and waited. He wrote about it later—how suddenly there "rose to sight . . . a soldierly young figure, a Confederate staff officer undoubtedly. Now I see the white flag earnestly borne, and its possible purport sweeps before my inner vision like a wraith of morning mist."

The young man, wrote Chamberlain, "comes steadily on, the mysterious form in gray, my mood so whimsically sensitive that I could even smile at the material of the flag—wondering where in either army was found a towel, and one so white." He drew near and dismounted, "with graceful salutation and hardly suppressed emotion [delivering] his message" to Chamberlain: "Sir, I am from General Gordon. General Lee desires a cessation of hostilities until he can hear from General Grant as to the proposed surrender."

The brevet major general answered as best he could: "Sir, that matter exceeds my authority. I will send to my superior. General Lee is right. He can do no more."

While Lee awaited Grant's response, he instructed an aide, Colonel Charles Marshall, to find a house where he could meet General Grant. Marshall later recalled that the very first man he encountered on his search was one Wilmer McLean, "who used to live on the first battle field of Manassas, at a house about a mile from Manassas Junction. He didn't like the war, and having seen the first battle of Manassas, he thought he would get away where there wouldn't be any more fighting, so he moved to Appomattox Court House." Now Marshall asked him to point out a house where the generals could meet.

*Young General Custer received the first flag of surrender offered by a unit of the Army of Northern Virginia— an event recorded by Alfred R. Waud.*

The first place McLean showed him was a gutted shell of a place, whatever furniture it might once have held long gone. Marshall rejected it. McClean brightened. "Maybe my house will do!"

In his *Memoirs* of 1885, Grant himself left the fullest account of Lee's surrender. He recalled that when he had left camp that morning he "had not expected so soon the result that was then taking place, and consequently was in rough garb."

> I was without a sword, as I usually was when on horseback on the field, and wore a soldier's blouse for a coat, with the shoulder straps of my rank to indicate to the army who I was. When I went into the house I found General Lee. We greeted each other, and after shaking hands took our seats. I had my staff with me, a good portion of whom were in the room during the whole of the interview.
>
> What General Lee's feelings were I do not know. As he was a man of much dignity, with an impassable face, it was impossible to say whether he felt inwardly glad that the end had finally come, or felt sad over the result, and was too manly to show it. Whatever his feelings, they were entirely concealed from my observation; but my own feelings, which

had been quite jubilant on the receipt of his letter [offering surrender], were sad and depressed. I felt like anything rather than rejoicing at the downfall of a foe who had fought so long and valiantly, and had suffered so much for a cause, though that cause was, I believe, one of the worst for which a people ever fought.

Grant felt painfully self-conscious in Lee's presence, dressed, as the Confederate commander was, "in a full uniform which was entirely new, and . . . wearing a sword of considerable value, very likely the sword which had been presented by the State of Virginia. . . . In my rough traveling suit, the uniform of a private with the straps of a lieutenant-general, I must have contrasted very strangely with a man so handsomely dressed, six feet high and of faultless form."

But soon the embarrassment melted as the two "fell into a conversation about old army times." The "conversation grew so pleasant that I almost forgot the object of our meeting." It was Lee who "called my attention to the object of our meeting, and said that he had asked for this interview for the purpose of getting from me the terms I proposed to give his army."

In victory, Grant could have thundered, could have threatened, could have lectured, and could have demanded—almost anything.

*This sardonic "death certificate" for the "Southern Confederacy" commemorated Lee's surrender at Appomattox Court House on April 9, 1865.*

Instead: "I said that I meant merely that his army should lay down their arms, not to take them up again during the continuance of the war unless duly and properly exchanged." At this, Lee suggested that, "the terms I proposed to give his army ought to be written out," and so Grant sat down to do just that.

Grant, whose abolition of prisoner exchange earlier in the war had brought into being such POW hellholes as Andersonville and "Hellmira" (Chapter 17), proposed to take no prisoners now, but rather accept the word of officers and men to lay down arms "until properly exchanged." The fact was that although the biggest and most important Confederate army had surrendered, the war was not over. Nevertheless, Grant gave permission for Confederate officers to retain their sidearms and allowed all personnel to keep their horses and personal property. He specified that everyone would be "allowed to return to their homes, not to be disturbed by United States authority so long as they observe their paroles."

After the surrender letter had been drafted and signed, Lee lingered before leaving the McLean house. According to Grant's *Memoirs*, Lee explained to Grant that his army "was in a very bad condition for want of food, and . . . had been living for some days on parched corn exclusively." To Lee's request "for rations and forage," Grant answered "certainly," and asked for how many men he wanted rations. Lee's answer was "about twenty-five thousand"; and Grant "authorized him to send his own commissary and quartermaster to Appomattox Station . . . where he could have, out of the trains we had stopped, all the provisions wanted."

Now it was Lee's turn to take up the pen. On April 10, 1865, he wrote General Order No. 9, his last to the Army of Northern Virginia:

*The McLean House, Appomattox County, Virginia: site of Lee's surrender to Grant.*

*Robert E. Lee, at about the time of his surrender to Ulysses S. Grant.*

> After four years of arduous service, marked by unsurpassed courage and fortitude, the Army of Northern Virginia has been compelled to yield to overwhelming numbers and resources.
>
> I need not tell the brave survivors of so many hard fought battles who have remained steadfast to the last, that I have consented to this result from no distrust of them. But feeling that valor and devotion could accomplish nothing that could compensate for the loss that must have attended the continuance of the contest, I determined to avoid the useless sacrifice of those whose past services have endeared them to their countrymen.
>
> By the terms of the agreement, officers and men can return to their homes and remain there until exchanged. You will take with you the satisfaction that proceeds from the consciousness of duty faithfully performed and I earnestly pray that a Merciful God will extend to you his blessing and protection.
>
> With an unceasing admiration of your constancy and devotion to your Country, and a grateful remembrance of your kind and generous consideration for myself, I bid you all an affectionate farewell.

# PARTING SHOTS

THE CIVIL WAR HAD NOT ENDED, but Grant nevertheless remarked to Lee that he "thought this would be about the last battle of the war," and that was why he specified that the soldiers should keep their horses. "The whole country had been so raided by the two armies that it was doubtful whether [the men] would be able to put in a crop to carry themselves and their families through the next winter without the aid of the horses they were then riding."

Horses to make winter's sustenance possible, food for the desperately hungry now. There was no ceremony. No cheers. No lowering of one flag and hoisting of another. The surrender of Lee to Grant consisted only of practical matters, matters of survival and of decency, matters decided between two officers who had once served in the same army.

Grant was not quite right about Appomattox being the last battle, unless we put the emphasis on his qualifying adjective, "*about* the last." On April 12, Union cavalry under James H. Wilson took Montgomery, Alabama, and, on the same day, the city of Mobile—its bay having long since fallen to Admiral Farragut (Chapter 20)—surrendered to occupying land forces. General Sherman occupied Raleigh, North Carolina, on the next day, and, during April 17–18, he sought to emulate Grant by hammering out an armistice with Joseph E. Johnston. Sherman, however, overstepped Grant in two respects. First, he asked for and received Johnston's sword as a token of his absolute surrender, and, second, he drew up with him an armistice so inclusive as to constitute a general treaty of peace, which included an amnesty

## REALITY CHECK

### Purest Romance

Those who later wrote of the surrender at Appomattox portrayed the gallant Lee offering his sword to the gallant Grant, who promptly handed it back. In his *Memoirs*, Grant explained that the "much talked of surrendering of Lee's sword and my handing it back, this and much more that has been said about it is the purest romance. The word sword or side arms was not mentioned by either of us until I wrote it in the terms. There was no premeditation, and it did not occur to me until the moment I wrote it down."

*Currier & Ives's depiction of Joseph E. Johnston's surrender to William T. Sherman, which took place on April 17/18, 1865. The terms of surrender were then repudiated by President Andrew Johnson on April 21 and had to be renegotiated on April 26.*

extended to soldiers and civilians alike. Andrew Johnson, who had become president upon the death of Abraham Lincoln (Chapter 23), repudiated Sherman's peace on April 21, prompting him to return to Johnston with terms identical to those Grant had concluded with Lee. The Confederate general accepted these on April 26, the very day that the Confederate Cabinet held its final meeting, in Charlotte, North Carolina, after which its members resigned one by one. Except for Judah P. Benjamin, who fled the country, the other Cabinet members and Jefferson Davis returned to their homes—or attempted to. The repudiation of the original Sherman-Johnston armistice meant that none of them enjoyed amnesty, and they were, in fact, fugitives subject to arrest and trial for high treason.

> "As to the charge of want of loyalty, or zeal in the war, I assert, from as much opportunity for observation as any individual had, that no people ever displayed so much, under such circumstances, and with so little flagging, for so long a time continuously. . . . And this spirit continued not only after all hope of success had died, but after the final confession of defeat by their military commanders."

*General Joseph E. Johnston, Narrative, 1874*

On May 8, Confederate lieutenant general Richard Taylor—the son of Zachary Taylor, hero of the U.S-Mexican War and twelfth president of the United States—surrendered the last major Confederate military formation, the Department of East Louisiana, Mississippi, and Alabama, to Major General Edwin R. S. Canby at Citronelle, Alabama. Two days later, on May 10, 1865, President Andrew Johnson declared armed resistance "virtually at an end." Nevertheless, on May 13, a skirmish broke out between Confederate troops under John Salmon "Rip" Ford and Union forces at Palmito Ranch, near Brownsville, Texas. This last armed exchange of the war ended in a Confederate victory. Notwithstanding this, Ford's commanding officer, General Edmund Kirby Smith, surrendered to General Canby on May 26.

## TAKEAWAY

The fall of Petersburg effectively ended the Civil War in any meaningful military sense. Nevertheless, Robert E. Lee, driven by his understanding of duty and honor, continued to fight in an effort to link up with Joseph Johnston and his Army of Tennessee. It was a hopeless enterprise and, as such, soon ended. After a pursuit west from Petersburg some thirty miles, troops under Philip Sheridan, including Major General George Armstrong Custer, forced Lee to a stand between Appomattox Station and Appomattox Court House. Trapped, the Confederate commander surrendered the Army of Northern Virginia to Ulysses S. Grant. The remaining military formations of the Confederate States of America soon followed, and the Confederacy itself dissolved.

# CHAPTER 23

## "Sic Semper Tyrannis!"

### Assassination, Impeachment, Reconstruction, Revenge, and Recovery

ABRAHAM LINCOLN'S DESK WAS FULL OF PIGEONHOLES, ONE OF WHICH HIS secretary, John Hay, designated a "special pigeonhole." It was here that the president kept what Hay described as a "bulging folder" in which he had collected during the past four years approximately eighty letters, every one of them a death threat. It was by no means a complete collection. Lincoln apparently saved only those threats he took seriously; although Elizabeth Keckley, Mary Todd Lincoln's seamstress, a woman from whom the president's wife kept no secrets, later remarked that Mr. Lincoln treated *all* the threats lightly. No one, he said, would be silly enough to write a letter announcing his plan to kill the president.

Still, he could not banish the fear from the deepest recesses of his mind. On Tuesday evening, April 11, 1865, Mrs. Lincoln, the president's close friend Ward Hill Lamon, Iowa senator James Harlan, and a handful of others were enjoying a social evening in the Red Room of the White House. Suddenly, Lincoln began relating a dream. It was a nightmare, really.

He spoke of "a deathlike stillness about me. Then I heard subdued sobs, as if a number of people were weeping." But the "mourners were invisible. I went from room to room. No living person was in sight." Still, it "was light in all the rooms; every object was familiar to me, but where were all the people who were grieving as if their hearts would break?"

In his dream, the president searched the Pennsylvania Avenue executive mansion that had been his uneasy home for four years of bloodshed, disappointment, and heartbreak relieved, at last, by the glow of victory. He searched every room, then entered the East Room.

"Before me was a catafalque, on which rested a corpse in funeral vestments. Around it were stationed soldiers who were acting as guards: and there was a throng of people, some gazing mournfully upon the corpse, whose face was covered, others weeping pitifully. 'Who is dead in the White House?' I demanded of one of the soldiers. 'The President,' was his answer. 'He was killed by an assassin.'"

## AN ACTOR'S PRIVATE WAR

THEY ARE THE THREE MOST INFAMOUS syllables in American history. John Wilkes Booth.

He was a child of a border state, born in 1838 near Bel Air, Maryland, the ninth of ten children of the most famous actor in the United States, Junius Brutus Booth. John Wilkes was blessed with dark, brooding good looks, the very picture of a matinee idol, yet he enjoyed little success on the Baltimore or Philadelphia stages. Richmond was where his breakthrough came, and it came just before the Civil War. Whereas Northern audiences had been lukewarm, Southern audiences loved him. And Southern women adored him. Below the Mason-Dixon Line, he was showered with cash, acclaim, and feminine favors.

And Southern menfolk thought Booth was all right, too. They were energized by his eloquence, especially when he was in his cups (and he *was* fond of his drink), on the subjects of states' rights, Northern aggression, and white supremacy. He was not a military man, to be sure, but when the call went out for militia volunteers to keep order at the public hanging of John Brown on December 2, 1859, Booth was at the very front of the line.

He was not a military man, and he did not join the Confederate army. Nevertheless, late in 1864, when the tide had turned irreversibly against the South, Booth began to ponder some deed of arms he might perform in the Confederate cause. It had to be spectacular, though the little band of conspirators he managed to pull together

*Contrary to popular mythology, which paints him as a besotted "failed actor," John Wilkes Booth was a prosperous matinee idol, adored in particular by theater-going Southern belles. The photograph dates from shortly before the war.*

was a handful of misfits who hardly presaged great things. There were Michael O'Laughlen (often spelled by others as O'Laughlin) and Sam Arnold, friends from his Maryland boyhood; George A. Atzerodt, a Maryland carriage maker; and David Herold, who worked as a drugstore clerk and, though he was twenty-three, possessed a child's intellect and a lapdog's eagerness to please. The most promising of the conspirators was John Surratt, whose credentials included covert employment as a courier in the Confederate "Secret Service." Booth and these men gathered periodically in the Washington boardinghouse run by Surratt's mother, Mary. Among much talk there emerged a scheme to abduct Lincoln and hold him for ransom in the form of the immediate liberation of all Confederate prisoners of war. There was more talk. Time passed, and the war ground on. Booth's scheme faded, only to reemerge as a plan to snatch the president from his box at Ford's Theatre on January 18, 1865. This time Booth really laid it all out. The actor knew Ford's very well. (He was one of the first actors to appear when the theater opened late in 1863, and Lincoln saw him in a then-popular play about the artist Raphael, *The Marble Heart*, by Charles Selby.) Booth was able to lead his most capable conspirator, John Surratt, to the master gas valve beneath the stage. Booth's plan was to station him at the valve; at a signal, Surratt would turn it, cutting off the gas, and plunging the theater into total darkness. At this point, Booth would enter the presidential box, hold a gun to Lincoln's head, gag him, bind him, tie a rope to him, and lower him from the box onto the stage. Booth would climb down that very rope, bundle the president into a waiting wagon, and drive like the devil for Richmond via Maryland. Just how Booth proposed to do all this with his own two hands he apparently did not say. In any case, Lincoln chose not to attend the theater that evening.

*John Surratt is seen here in the uniform of a Pontifical Zouave. After the Lincoln assassination, he fled to Canada and then to Rome, where he joined the Pope's palace guard. Arrested in the Vatican on November 7, 1866, he managed to escape and flee to Alexandria, Egypt, where U.S. officials seized him on November 23. Sent back to the United States under arrest, he was tried by a Maryland court, only to be released after a hung jury created a mistrial. Never retried, Surratt made a living as a teacher and then as an executive with a steamship company. He died of pneumonia in 1916, at the age of seventy-two.*

Crestfallen by the anticlimax, Booth nevertheless persisted. By February a new man had signed on to the conspiracy. He was a square-shouldered, powerfully built ex-Confederate soldier who called himself Lewis Paine, but whose real name was Lewis Thornton Powell. He would provide the muscle for Booth's latest idea, which was to capture Lincoln on his way to attend a matinee performance of *Still Waters Run Deep* to be given at a local army medical facility, Campbell Hospital, north of the capital. The idea was to storm the president's carriage, remove Lincoln from it, and ransom him for the Confederate POWs. On the appointed day, Booth, Surratt, Powell, Atzerodt, Arnold, and O'Laughlen lay in ambush. The carriage approached. Their hearts quickened. Spurring their ponies, Booth and Surratt galloped out of hiding to overtake the carriage, but when they drew abreast of it and looked through the windows, the president was nowhere to be seen.

This second failure plunged Booth into depression and, according to possibly biased reports, drink. Weeks passed. April came. Richmond fell. Washington celebrated. Lee surrendered. Washington celebrated even more. If the Civil War was a play, the curtain was descending—and Booth had yet even to appear onstage. Kidnap Lincoln? There was no longer any point. All that was left was to kill him. In any case, it was less complicated to kill than to kidnap a man.

> "It is a good face. I am glad the war
> is over at last."
>
> Abraham Lincoln, to his son Robert,
> who had just presented his father with a photograph of
> Robert E. Lee, on the morning of April 14, 1865

*This photograph of Ford's Theatre, scene of the Lincoln assassination, was made after the event in 1865. Note the mourning crepe adorning the windows of the theater and the adjoining building.*

## NIGHT OF THE ASSASSINS

BY THE TIME BOOTH WAS READY to murder Abraham Lincoln, O'Laughlen, Arnold, and John Surratt had dropped out of his circle, leaving to the conspiracy only Powell, Herold, and Atzerodt. Atzerodt's assignment was to kill Vice President Andrew Johnson while Powell and Herold assassinated Secretary of State William H. Seward. Booth would personally shoot the president.

Through his close contact with the Ford family, he knew that Lincoln planned to attend a performance of the popular comedy *Our American Cousin* at their theater on Good

*Famed Civil War photographer Alexander Gardner photographed Lewis Thornton Powell (a.k.a. Lewis Paine or Payne) on board either the USS* Montauk *or* Saugus, *moored at the Washington Navy Yard, where the conspirators were temporarily held after their arrest.*

Friday evening, April 14. Because Booth knew both the theater and its management so well, he'd have the run of the place and little trouble gaining access to the president's box. As for Johnson and Seward, they would have to be murdered in their homes. In the case of Seward, this would be especially easy, since the sixty-four-year-old old man was helpless, laid up with serious injuries he had sustained in a carriage accident. Critical to the entire plot was hitting all three targets simultaneously so as to create the maximum degree of panic.

What Booth hadn't counted on was Atzerodt's backing out at the last minute. He spent the night of April 14, 1865, drinking and never even got close to Johnson. Powell, however, went through with his assignment and made a gory mess of it.

As Herold held his horse on the street outside, Powell knocked at Seward's door, announcing that he had a package of medicine that was to be administered to the secretary immediately. The servant who answered the door explained that the secretary was asleep and could not be disturbed. He offered to carry the medicine to him. Unable to come up with a persuasive reply, Powell pushed past the servant and mounted the stairs, on which he was met by Seward's thirty-four-year-old son Frederick. Powell pulled a pistol, placed it against Frederick Seward's head, squeezed the trigger, and produced nothing but a misfire. Turning the gun in his big hand, he brought its butt down on the young man's skull several times, knocking him unconscious.

Now aware that his sidearm was a no-go, Powell drew a bowie knife from the package he carried and climbed the stairs to Secretary Seward's darkened bedroom. In the room were Seward's daughter, Fanny, and a male army nurse, George T. Robinson. Robinson caught the gleam of the blade through the darkness, sprung up from his chair, and rushed Powell. The big man slashed Robinson across the forehead, then knocked him to the floor. He turned next on Fanny Seward, striking hard enough to knock her out cold. His path to Seward clear, he hurled himself upon the old man as he lay abed and stabbed him repeatedly and wildly, tearing a hole through his cheek.

Either from the force of the attack or under his own power, Secretary Seward rolled off the bed and under it, even as Robinson shook off the effects of the initial attack and threw himself once again against Powell. The would-be assassin plunged his knife into Robinson just as another of Seward's sons, Major Augustus Seward, burst into the room. Still wielding the knife, Powell slashed at the major, slicing into his forehead and his hand. This done, he blew past the stunned man and ran full tilt down the stairs just as a State Department messenger was entering the house. Powell slashed him and ran out the door bellowing, "I'm mad! I'm mad!"

## Performance of a Lifetime

John Wilkes Booth was aware of none of this. Some say he had been drinking steadily in the days leading up to Good Friday. Others believe he was immersed in planning out his own moves. In either case, on the evening of the fourteenth, he was stone sober and acutely focused. At about ten, he walked quietly up the carpeted stairs to Lincoln's box. The lock, he knew, was broken and had been so for days. With his right hand, he withdrew a diminutive single-shot derringer from his coat pocket. With his left, he turned the doorknob.

He knew the script of *Our American Cousin* backward and forward. Professional actor that he was, Booth timed his entrance with aplomb. He approached the president from the rear. Just as the male lead, Harry Hawk, began drawling in backwoods dialect the line that always drew the biggest laugh, Booth leveled his weapon between Lincoln's left ear and spine.

"Wal," Hawk declaimed to the leading lady, the popular comedienne Laura Keene, "I guess I know enough to turn you inside out, you sockdologizing old mantrap."

And amid the inevitable burst of laughter, Booth squeezed off his single shot.

> **DETAILS, DETAILS**
> **Mayhem's Aftermath**
> For all the blood Powell drew, he succeeded in killing no one. Every one of his victims made a full recovery, including Seward, who would continue to serve as secretary of state in the Cabinet of Andrew Johnson and, in 1867, would negotiate from the czar of all the Russias the purchase of Alaska, a transaction contemporary pundits derided as "Seward's Folly," unable as they were to see any value in possessing a vast "icebox."

*This depiction of the assassination, one of many such images, was published by E. R. & E. C. Kellogg, of Hartford, Connecticut, in 1865.*

*Booth used a diminutive single-shot .44-caliber derringer to murder the president. He fired into the back of Lincoln's head at point-blank range.*

*Booth leaps from the presidential box to the stage after shooting the president and stabbing Major Henry Rathbone in the arm. The print is clearly not the work of an eyewitness. It mistakenly depicts the box as almost level with the stage (in reality, Booth leaped from a significant height) and shows Lincoln on his feet (the president was rendered unconscious immediately and slumped in his chair). The artist has taken care, however, to show Booth's spur, which caught on the Treasury Regiment banner, ultimately causing him to break his leg.*

Ford's Theatre was sold out that night, packed with 1,675 men and women who, like the president, sought a few hours' relief from the war, even as it drew to its conclusion. No one, it seemed, heard the pop of the little gun or, if they did, paid much attention. Mrs. Lincoln, seated next to her husband, and their guests in the box, Major Henry Rathbone and his fiancée, Clara Harris, surely heard the gun's report but were not alarmed by it.

The president slumped forward. Still, it took time for the crime to register, even for those closest to it. Rathbone did rise from his seat. He lunged toward Booth, who had by now grabbed hold of the broad-bladed bowie knife he carried. This he plunged into the major's arm. Reflexively, Rathbone released his grip. Booth mounted the rail at the front of the box and leaped for the stage, which was still occupied by the two actors. But the spur on his right boot caught the heavy fabric of the U.S. Treasury Regiment flag that festooned the presidential box. It yanked his leg up, hard, forcing his other leg, the left one, to absorb the full force of his impact on the stage. A bone snapped just above the actor's instep.

The show must go on.

Turning to the audience, Booth delivered his only line of the evening: "Sic semper tyrannis!" It was the defiant state motto of Virginia: *Thus ever to tyrants.*

The actor assassin limped toward the wings, misstepped, fell, recovered himself, and lurched as best he could offstage, then backstage, and out the stage door, into the alley—Baptist Alley, it was called—where a Ford's Theatre gofer and peanut vendor named Joseph Burroughs (a.k.a. "Peanut John" or "Johnny Peanut") was waiting with Booth's horse, as the actor had told him to. Burroughs dozed on a carpenter's bench, the reins looped around his fingers.

Booth brought the heavy handle of his bowie knife down hard on Burroughs's thick skull, and, roused, the man released the reins to Booth, who rode off into the Washington night. Not a soul gave chase.

## "Now He Belongs to the Ages"

Booth had been upstaged by his victim. In Ford's Theatre, all attention turned to the stricken president, while the leading man, his assassin, save for his injury, made a clean escape.

Dr. Charles Augustus Leale, a twenty-three-year-old army surgeon, was in the audience and was the first medical man to reach Lincoln. A civilian physician, Dr. Albert F. A. King, and another army doctor, Charles Sabin Taft, were soon by his side. They labored intensely over their patient.

"I can't save him," Leale sobbed to Taft. "His wound is mortal. It is impossible for him to recover."

No one even noticed the arrival of Laura Keene in the president's box. Responding to a call for water, she had grabbed a pitcher from the backstage green room, ran up a set of back stairs, and entered with the water.

"While we were waiting for Mr. Lincoln to regain strength," Leale later recalled, "Laura Keene appealed to me to allow her to hold the President's head. I granted the request, and she sat on the floor of the box and held his head in her lap." (The actress would preserve, lifelong, the dress stained with Lincoln's blood.)

Discussion now turned to whether the president should be moved to the White House. Leale and the two other doctors agreed that the seven-block trip would probably kill him. When someone ran next door to inquire if Lincoln might be brought to Taltavull's Saloon, Mr. Taltavull replied that it "would not be right" for the president to die in a saloon. Leale therefore decided that his patient should be taken to the nearest available house across the street, which was owned by a German tailor named William Petersen. The president was carried up to a bedroom, but his six-foot-four frame could be accommodated only by laying him diagonally across the bed.

Through the night of April 14 and into the morning, a clutch of quiet men, plus Mrs. Lincoln, moved in and out of the bedroom in the Petersen house. There was no thought of saving the president. It was a death watch, and at 7:22 on the morning of April 15, it ended, the doctors pronouncing Abraham Lincoln dead.

# FLIGHT OF THE ASSASSIN

For eleven days after he shot the president, John Wilkes Booth eluded the small army of soldiers, policemen, and detectives in search of him. On April 26, shortly after midnight, a cavalry detachment cornered Booth and David Herold hiding in a tobacco barn on a farm near Port Royal, Virginia. Herold immediately gave himself up, but Booth was bent on a shootout. Deciding to smoke Booth out, the troopers set fire to the barn.

**W**hat happened next has never been entirely clear. The generally accepted account is that Sergeant Boston Corbett, seeing Booth silhouetted in flame, leaning on a crutch and carrying a carbine, took it upon himself to fire his revolver into the barn. The round passed through the actor's neck, and he crumpled to the floor. The soldiers retrieved him from the burning structure. He was totally paralyzed, and he may (or may not) have uttered, "I thought I did for the best," then, asking that his lifeless hands be lifted so that he might see them, stared, and gasped out "Useless, useless," and, with these words, died.

That Sergeant Corbett had acted without orders has generated the same kinds of conspiracy theories that have been built upon the murder of accused JFK assassin Lee Harvey Oswald by Jack Ruby. Some believe that the man shot and killed in the tobacco barn was not Booth, who (they say) got away and died years later of natural causes.

There is no compelling evidence for this theory and much against it. Booth was a famous actor, whose face was well known. All those of the 16th New York Cavalry who saw the wounded man believed it was indeed Booth, and Herold confirmed it. The body was transported by the monitor USS *Montauk* to Washington Navy Yard, where it was autopsied.

More than ten people personally acquainted with Booth identified him there. Also noted was a "JWB" tattoo on his left hand and a known scar on his neck. Booth was hurriedly buried in what has been described as a "storage room" of the Old Penitentiary. In 1869, the body was reburied in an unmarked grave at Green Mount Cemetery in Baltimore.

*Philadelphia lithographer J. L. Magee imagined the scene of Booth's fatal wounding in "The Murderers [sic] doom. Miserable death of J. Wilkes Booth, the assassin of President Lincoln. Shot through the head by Sergeant Boston Corbett in a barn on Garrett's Farm, near Port Royal, near Rappahannock, April 25, 1865." (Note that the actual date of Booth's shooting and death was April 26.) While Booth's co-conspirator, David Herold, surrendered to the soldiers surrounding the barn, Booth remained inside, despite efforts to burn him out. Sergeant Corbett took an unauthorized shot at Booth, hitting him in the neck, not the head.*

Secretary of War Edwin Stanton solemnly raised his hand, put his hat on his head, then just as solemnly removed it. Taking charge as he often did, he addressed Lincoln's pastor. "Doctor," he asked—or commanded—"lead us in prayer." After the requisite words were spoken, Stanton looked about, went to one window after another, and drew the curtains across each of them.

"Now he belongs to the ages," he said. At least that is what it sounded like to most of those who heard it. But the secretary of war now spoke so softly, as if to himself, that some thought they heard the word *angels* instead.

## A TAILOR IN THE WHITE HOUSE

"Useless, useless"? Booth's last words should have been "Senseless, senseless." The man he murdered in the name of the South was the South's best hope for a "Reconstruction" (as the process of reintegrating the seceded states into the Union was called) with "malice toward none." Although Lincoln had prosecuted the war with an uncompromising determination to fight through to absolute victory, he was by no means in the camp of the "Radical Republicans," the legislators bent on seeing the South punished and, in particular, its political and military leaders purged, rounded up, and tried as traitors. In contrast to this faction, Lincoln wanted to extend a wide amnesty in an effort to (as he said in his second inaugural address) "bind up the nation's wounds."

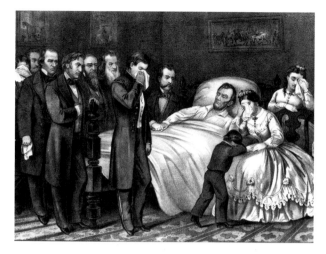

*This Currier & Ives scene of Abraham Lincoln's death was one of many published shortly after the assassination. Although this image depicts otherwise, Edwin Stanton, who took charge of the bedroom of the Petersen rooming house in which Lincoln died, banished the hysterically grieving Mary Todd Lincoln from the room. The bed on which the comatose president lay was far too small to accommodate his lanky frame, so he had to be laid across it on an awkward diagonal.*

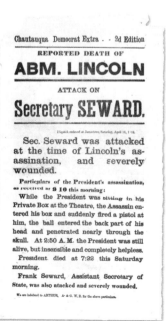

*A typical example of the news reports that swept across the nation after Lincoln's death.*

Chautauqua Democrat Extra - - 2d Edition

**REPORTED DEATH OF**

# ABM. LINCOLN

ATTACK ON

## Secretary SEWARD.

Dispatch received at Jamestown, Saturday, April 15, 1-65.

Sec. Seward was attacked at the time of Lincoln's assassination, and severely wounded.

Particulars of the President's assassination, as received at **9 10** this morning:

While the President was sitting in his Private Box at the Theatre, the Assassin entered his box and suddenly fired a pistol at him, the ball entered the back part of his head and penetrated nearly through the skull. At 2:50 A. M. the President was still alive, but insensible and completely helpless. President died at 7:22 this Saturday morning.

Frank Seward, Assistant Secretary of State, was also atacked and severely wounded.

We are indebted to ARTHUR, A- & G. W. R. for the above particulars.

*Crude, graceless, and hard-drinking, President Andrew Johnson lacked the political skill and personal charisma to lead Reconstruction effectively.*

The Radical Republicans believed they had righteousness on their side (less nobly, many also looked forward to the opportunity to dismantle or at least permanently cripple the Democratic Party), but they were also savvy politicians. In 1864, fearful of frightening off the moderate voters needed for victory, they did not insist that Lincoln stand for reelection with a running mate drawn from the Radical ranks, but, quite the contrary, approved his selection of Andrew Johnson, a *Democrat,* and even countenanced a new name for the ticket on which they ran. It was neither the Democratic nor the Republican party, but the "National Union Party."

Andrew Johnson was born in North Carolina in 1808, but, at sixteen or seventeen, moved to Tennessee. A self-educated tailor by trade and a politician by inclination, he served as a mayor, a state legislator, a U.S. representative, governor of Tennessee, and a U.S. senator. He rarely deviated from the Democratic party line until 1860, when he took a bold stand against secession. When Tennessee seceded in June 1861, he was the only Southern senator who refused to join the Confederacy and who retained his Senate seat. President Lincoln rewarded his loyalty by appointing him military governor of Union-occupied Tennessee in March 1862. Thus Johnson's demonstrated allegiance to the Union made him a desirable choice for running mate in 1864. Besides, in the nineteenth century, the vice presidency was largely a ceremonial office whose occupant enjoyed little influence and less power. Putting Johnson on the ticket seemed a perfectly safe gesture with little downside. At fifty-five, Abraham Lincoln was relatively young, after all, and while both Lincoln and Stanton seemed to have feared the possibility of assassination, such a crime had never occurred before. True, a disgruntled individual had made an attempt against Andrew Jackson in 1835, but his pistols misfired and Old Hickory beat off his assailant with his walking stick.

Nobody, it seems, had even thought to tell Vice President Johnson that the president had been shot, and it was some hours after Lincoln died that Senator Solomon Foot of Vermont escorted Chief Justice Salmon P. Chase to Johnson's house.

Admitted into the residence, the senator and chief justice were shown to the vice president's bedroom. The door was closed. Senator

On the morning of April 15, 1865, Abraham Lincoln's body was enfolded in an American flag and escorted by Union officers from the Petersen house, across the street from Ford's Theatre, to the White House. There the body lay in state until it was put aboard a special train bound for Lincoln's hometown of Springfield, Illinois, which would be his final resting place. The train took a slow, circuitous 1,654-mile route, passing through large cities and small towns, where millions gathered along the right-of-way to see and salute the crepe-and-flag-festooned train. In some of the larger cities and towns—including New York, shown here—Lincoln's casket was removed from the train and conducted through the streets in a solemn procession. The train finally arrived in Springfield on May 3.

Foot rapped sharply on it and, at length, Johnson, hair tousled, feet unshod, breath heavy with whiskey (according to Foot, a possibly biased Radical Republican), opened the door, admitted the men, then slumped into a chair.

"The president has been assassinated," Chief Justice Chase announced. "He died this morning, and I have come to administer the oath of office to you."

Lifting himself from his chair, Johnson faced Chase, raised his right hand, and muttered thickly, "I'm ready."

Andrew Johnson is sworn in as the seventeenth president of the United States by Salmon P. Chase, whom Lincoln had just appointed chief justice of the Supreme Court. The oath was administered in the "small parlor" of the Kirkwood House, the Washington hotel in which the vice president lodged.

Lincoln's eldest son, Robert Todd, accompanied his father. The exhumed remains of another son, William Wallace Lincoln, known as Willie, who had died in 1862 at age eleven, were also placed on the train, to be permanently interred in Springfield. Mary Todd Lincoln, prostrated with grief, did not return to Illinois until a month later.

# HISTORY'S DEMONS

Over the 150 years since the Civil War, both the Radical Republicans on the one hand and Andrew Johnson on the other have been subject to a degree of oversimplification that can only be described as demonization. The Radical Republicans have been depicted as self-righteous opportunists, determined to humiliate the South even as they destroyed the Democratic Party.

There is an element of truth to this, but the Radical Republicans were also men who were and had always been absolutely opposed to slavery and believed that freed men were entitled to all the rights of any other American citizens. They were morally upright idealists whose idealism trumped their willingness to make even useful compromises and whose motives were not always pure.

As for Johnson, while some have depicted him as a put-upon torchbearer of Lincoln's lenient Reconstruction policy as well as a defender of constitutional separation of powers—in particular, the authority of the executive branch versus the legislative—he was undeniably a white supremacist, a racist even by the standards of his day. In the message that accompanied his veto of the Civil Rights Act, Johnson declared his belief that blacks were not qualified for citizenship, and he further believed that the act would "operate in favor of the colored and against the white race."

## CONGRESS TAKES OVER RECONSTRUCTION

THE RADICAL REPUBLICANS REFUSED to lose heart. They had believed Johnson to be weak and therefore pliable—probably easier to deal with than Lincoln—but Johnson quickly demonstrated his determination to carry out what he understood as Lincoln's intended policy of Reconstruction built on reconciliation. The slain president had already set elements of the policy into motion, approving new governments for Louisiana, Tennessee, and Arkansas, all of which were under Union control at the time of his assassination. And maybe Lincoln could have pulled it off, despite the hard line of the Radicals in his own party. Eloquent and inspiring, he invited trust. Johnson was earnest in his desire to build on the Lincoln legacy, but he was also driven by an intense racism (he did not believe blacks should be slaves, but he believed even less that they should be regarded as the equal of whites), and he lacked virtually every personal quality his predecessor had had in abundance. Often publicly intoxicated, Johnson was loutish, abrasive, dour, and—most unusual in a successful politician—misanthropic. No matter what he chose to advocate, it is likely that Johnson the man would have met with bitter opposition.

Even before Lincoln's death, the Radical Republicans who controlled Congress rejected the governments Lincoln had approved for Louisiana, Tennessee, and Arkansas and passed the Wade-Davis Bill (the work of Radical Republican senators Benjamin F. Wade and Henry W. Davis), which installed provisional military governments and governors in all the seceded states. The act specified that a state could convene a new constitutional convention only after a simple majority of its white citizens had sworn an oath of allegiance to the Union; moreover, the new state constitution was required to explicitly abolish slavery, repudiate secession as illegal, and forbid any former official of the Confederacy to hold office or even to vote. The act laid down additional stringent requirements for voting, requiring every voter registrant to swear an oath that he had never voluntarily aided the Confederacy. This amounted to disenfranchisement of the majority of Southern males (the only gender federally eligible to vote in the North or the South), since many had served in the Confederate army and almost everyone else had in some way supported the Confederate government, even if it was only by paying taxes.

Lincoln had responded to passage of the Wade-Davis Bill by exercising a so-called pocket veto. The Constitution requires the president either to sign or to veto a bill within ten days of its being presented to him. If Congress adjourns before the passage of those ten days, and the president has "pocketed" instead of signed the bill, it does not become law and must be reintroduced when Congress reconvenes.

On the death of Lincoln, the Radical Republicans advised Johnson to purge the Cabinet of all Lincoln loyalists and replace them with bona fide Radicals. Johnson defiantly retained the entire Cabinet and then deliberately chose not to call the recessed Congress into special session. This meant that, from April until December, when Congress was regularly scheduled to reconvene, Johnson conducted Reconstruction on his own by means of executive proclamations. He sought to preempt reintroduction of the Wade-Davis Bill by issuing an executive order granting full amnesty to those who pledged their loyalty to the Union hence forward, thereby discounting any prior loyalty to the Confederacy. Johnson further stipulated that the creation of a new state constitution was not contingent on the majority of the state's adult male population taking the loyalty oath. He did require, however, that each state ratify the newly enacted Thirteenth Amendment, abolishing slavery; that each state constitution explicitly forbid slavery; and that each state repudiate all debts incurred during the rebellion, thereby relieving the federal government of any obligation to discharge them. Finally, each state constitution was required to declare secession null and void. Every former Confederate state, save Texas, rushed to comply by the end of 1865, and even the Texas holdouts were outvoted by the following year.

When Congress reconvened in December, a majority—Radicals and moderates alike—was outraged by what it considered Johnson's usurpation of legislative authority and his apparent determination to prevent the elevation of the former slaves to their full rights as citizens. Congress responded by passing in 1866 the Freedmen's Bureau Act, which created a federal agency to provide food, clothing, medical care, and rudimentary education to the former slaves to assist them in making the transition to their new lives.

Johnson vetoed the bill—which was supported by moderates and Radicals alike—thereby signaling his opposition to any compromise whatsoever. Now virtually *all* of the Congress turned against the president, who further poisoned the political climate by vetoing a Civil Rights Act that explicitly declared African Americans citizens, affirmed their right to make legal contracts, to sue and to bear witness in courts of law, to own property, and to receive equal protection of the law. As with the Freedmen's Bureau veto, Congress readily overrode the veto of the Civil Rights Act, in the process effectively seizing control over Reconstruction from the executive branch.

Having wrested the Reconstruction initiative from Andrew Johnson, Congress next passed another constitutional amendment, the Fourteenth, section 1 of which explicitly extended citizenship to everyone "born or naturalized in the United States," barred states from

*The congressional resolution creating the Thirteenth Amendment, which forever ended slavery in the United States.*

# MALICE TOWARD SOME

As mentioned in Chapter 17, the United States prosecuted only one Confederate soldier for war crimes, Andersonville commandant Henry Wirz, and, equally remarkable, no Confederate civilian was ever brought to trial for treason, although some were summarily stripped of their citizenship.

It is true that Union soldiers captured Jefferson Davis on May 10, 1865, near Irwinville, Georgia, and that he was immediately remanded to prison, at Fort Monroe on the Virginia coast. He remained behind bars for a year before he was finally indicted for treason, and then awaited trial for another year until prominent citizens from the North and the South raised bail money, securing Davis's release in May 1867. He moved to Canada to await the trial.

The government, in the meantime, lost its stomach for a prosecution. Although a federal court rejected a motion to nullify the indictment, prosecutors dropped all charges on December 25, 1868; Davis was set free, and became president of a Memphis-based insurance company until his retirement in 1877 to a modest estate near Biloxi, Mississippi. There he died in 1889.

As for Robert E. Lee, he accepted in September 1865 an offer of the presidency of Washington College (today called Washington and Lee University) in Lexington, Virginia. He died on October 12, 1870. In 1975, Congress posthumously restored Lee's U.S. citizenship.

Those implicated in Lincoln's assassination did not escape judicial retribution. Booth had been shot and killed, all of those associated with him, with the exception of John Surratt, were quickly arrested and tried. Powell, Herold, Atzerodt, and Mary Surratt were convicted, sentenced to death, and, on July 7, 1865, were hanged together. Three other conspirators, Michael O'Laughlen, Sam Arnold, and Dr. Samuel Mudd, a Maryland physician who treated Booth's broken leg, were sentenced to life imprisonment at Fort Jefferson in the Dry Tortugas. In 1868, President Andrew Johnson pardoned Mudd in recognition of his life-saving ministrations to guards and inmates during a yellow fever epidemic that swept the prison. O'Laughlen died in 1867, during the epidemic, but Arnold was paroled in 1869. Edward Spangler, a Ford's Theatre carpenter found guilty of having assisted Booth, served six years.

John Surratt fled to Canada immediately after the assassination, then set sail for Europe, ending up in Italy, where he found employment among the Papal Zouaves, mercenaries who guarded the Pope. After another Zouave identified him to authorities, Surratt was arrested on November 8, 1866, but managed to escape and fled to Egypt. He was found, arrested, and returned to the United States on June 10, 1867. The popular climate having cooled, Surratt, who disclaimed any involvement in the plot, was acquitted.

Stranger and more tragic was the fate of Major Henry Rathbone, the guest in the Ford's Theatre presidential box whom Booth overcame. He married Clara Harris, with whom he had attended *Our American Cousin*, but murdered her in 1883 out of jealousy, he said, for her love of their two children. He spent the remainder of his life in an asylum for the criminally insane. His final words, when he died in 1911, reportedly were "The man with the knife! I can't stop him! I can't stop him!"

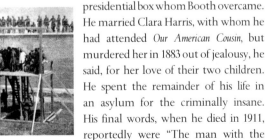

*A view (by Alexander Gardner) of the execution of the Lincoln assassination conspirators, July 7, 1865. Mary Surratt, Lewis Powell, David Herold, and George Atzerodt were hanged simultaneously from a scaffold erected in the courtyard of the Washington Arsenal.*

enacting laws "which shall abridge the privileges or immunities of citizens of the United States," and guaranteed the voting rights of all citizens. Section 2 stipulated that if any state prohibited any part of the adult male population from voting, its representation in Congress would be proportionately decreased.

Who could argue with the rightness and noble purpose of the first two sections of the Fourteenth Amendment? Section 3, however, demonstrated that even the noblest of congressional Reconstruction purposes was subject to contamination by motives of naked vengeance. This provision barred former Confederates from holding federal or state office, unless individually pardoned by a two-thirds vote of Congress. Section 4 seemed to demonstrate the willingness of Congress to violate the very Constitution it amended. This provision repudiated debts incurred by the former Confederate government, but it also barred compensation for "the loss or emancipation of any slave." Slaves had been constitutionally protected property, and now (as many Southerners saw it) Congress was enacting, *ex post facto*, an amendment that justified that seizure with neither compensation nor due process of law.

The former Confederate states were willing to accept a constitutional amendment abolishing slavery (Thirteenth Amendment), but the Fourteenth ignited something of a new rebellion. Of all the seceded states, only Tennessee ratified the amendment. This provoked from Congress a series of punitively harsh Reconstruction Acts, which transformed Reconstruction from the healing process Lincoln had envisioned into a combination of noble intentions, political opportunism, and outright tyranny that would perpetuate regional hostility in the United States for years to come and, even worse, ensure that life for the South's African American citizens would be hard, frequently humiliating, and often dangerous.

In "We Accept the Situation," the satirical cartoonist Thomas Nast contrasts the Reconstruction enfranchisement of an African American with the disenfranchisement of a former Confederate.

By act of Congress on March 2, 1867, every Southern state except Tennessee was put under military government. The only way out for a state was ratification of the Fourteenth Amendment and the drafting and ratification of a state constitution that enfranchised African Americans and disenfranchised ex-Confederates. Next, Congress authorized the federal military government in each state to use armed troops to ensure the registration of all eligible voters and to supervise the election of delegates to the state constitutional conventions. The white majority in each state responded by registering to vote but refraining from voting, so that the constitutions, while drafted, could not be ratified. Congress sought to sidestep this act of defiance by changing the requirement for ratification from a majority of registered voters to a majority of those who actually cast ballots—no matter how few. Outmaneuvered, the former Confederate states resentfully complied, Arkansas becoming the first to be readmitted to the Union in June 1868 and Georgia, readmitted in July 1870, the last.

## The Unmaking of a President

WHILE CONGRESS JOUSTED WITH THE STATES of the former Confederacy, it also battled the president of the United States. Andrew Johnson had used the congressional recess to seize control of Reconstruction. Upon its return to session, Congress undid most of Johnson's handiwork and retook control of Reconstruction.

On March 2, 1867, Congress passed, over President Johnson's veto, the Tenure of Office Act. The Constitution required major presidential appointments to be made with the "advice and consent" of the Senate, but was silent concerning the authority of the president to remove such appointees from office. Nevertheless, every president had assumed removal was exclusively an executive prerogative, and Congress went along. The new Tenure of Office Act, however, required the president to obtain senatorial approval prior to the removal of any civil office holder who had been appointed with senatorial consent. The act was clearly part of an effort to transfer to Congress as many executive prerogatives as possible, but its passage had been specifically motivated to prevent Johnson from removing Secretary of War Edwin Stanton, a powerful Radical Republican. When President Johnson defied the law in 1868 by removing Stanton without obtaining the Senate's consent—his intention was to test the constitutionality of the law in the Supreme Court—the House of Representatives voted to impeach him.

Johnson was tried by the Senate in a proceeding that stretched from March to May 1868. The key votes on the articles of impeachment, May 16 and 26, 1868, came up just one vote shy of the two-thirds majority

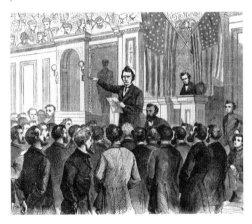

*Thaddeus Stevens, Radical Republican representative from Pennsylvania, made the impassioned final speech on March 2, 1868, that closed the House debate on the resolution to impeach Andrew Johnson. The impeachment trial began in the Senate on March 13.*

*George T. Brown, sergeant at arms of the U.S. Senate, serves President Andrew Johnson with a summons to his impeachment trial.*

required to remove a president from office. Although the entire impeachment was partisan in its motivation, seven Republicans knowingly destroyed their political careers by yielding to the dictates of conscience and voting to acquit. Thus Johnson remained in office, but stymied by a Republican legislative majority, he was effectively stripped of power. More fiercely determined than ever, the Radical Republican Congress imposed on the South laws that brought to pass many great reforms, including the establishment of state-supported free public schools and more equitably apportioned taxes, but also levied universally heavy taxes and created conditions that led to widespread local corruption. Former slaves, most of them illiterate and certainly unprepared to govern, were arbitrarily given important offices in state and local government. If the object of this was to humiliate the former masters, the result was a combination of chaos and bitter resentment that made life hazardous for any person of color as well as any white who sought to help him or her.

The mass enfranchisement of former slaves brought into the South hordes of Northern politicians and financial adventurers itching to exploit the inexperienced and pliable freedmen to obtain political office, make a quick buck, or both. These "carpetbaggers"—unwelcome guests who brought nothing with them except what their "carpetbag" satchels could hold—were aided and abetted by "scalawags," Southerners who sold out to the interlopers in what many saw as the rape and ruin of their homeland.

"Our legislature was composed of a majority of Negroes, most of whom could neither read nor write. They were the easy dupes and tools of as dirty a band of vampires and robbers as ever preyed upon a prostrate people.... Life ceased to be worth having on the terms under which we were living, and in desperation we determined to take the government away from the Negroes..."

*Senator Ben Tillman of South Carolina, giving the Southern view of Reconstruction, in the Congressional Record, January 21, 1907*

Throughout the South, whites looked for ways resist Reconstruction. In 1866, in Pulaski, Tennessee, a group of Confederate veterans banded together in a fraternal order they dubbed the Ku Klux—probably a corruption of the classical Greek word for circle, *kyklos*—Klan. It was one of several newly emerged secret societies intended to reclaim the South for the white race. When the KKK held its first big meeting in Nashville in 1867, its members styled themselves the "Invisible Empire of the South." It is positively known that former Confederate general Nathan Bedford Forrest joined the early KKK, and it is generally believed (though disputed by some) that he was elevated to the post of "Grand Wizard," or leader. True to their grandiose self-characterization, the Klan operated as a shadow government, acting both as a vigilante posse (the postwar South was torn by lawlessness) and a terrorist mob dedicated to intimidating blacks, discouraging them from voting or claiming the other rights recently given them by law. At first, Klansmen clothed themselves in sheets and hoods to disguise themselves from federal and military authorities and also to frighten the former slaves; soon, however, scare tactics escalated into "night rides," violent nocturnal raids against black communities,

*Thomas Nast portrays the evil of the KKK in "The Union as it was. The Lost Cause, worse than slavery."*

black families, and even against individuals. Buildings were burned, and men were beaten, whipped, or lynched—usually by hanging from the nearest convenient tree limb. Ratification of the Fifteenth Amendment in March 1870, which explicitly barred states from denying the vote on the basis of "race, color, or previous condition of servitude," served only to amplify the influence and popularity of the KKK. By this time, however, Forrest himself had come to believe that the Klan had become nothing more than a brutal mob, and officially disclaimed any connection to the organization and even tried to persuade the Klan to disband. It was too late. Local branches—called "klaverns"—ignored Forrest and continued on their own authority to terrorize the Southern countryside. Congress responded with the Force Act of 1870 and the Ku Klux Klan Act of 1871, which gave the president extraordinary authority to suppress domestic terrorist organizations, including the power to suspend *habeas corpus*.

# KKK: DEATH AND RESURRECTION

By the 1880s, with the end of Reconstruction and the institutionalization of racist law throughout the South, the Ku Klux Klan, having lost its reason for being, faded away. During the second decade of the twentieth century, when Southerners (and some in other regions) felt threatened by the influx of immigrants into the United States, a new Ku Klux Klan appeared, organized in 1915 by Colonel William J. Simmons, an inveterate joiner of fraternal organizations (his military title was really his rank in the Woodmen of the World, a popular fraternal order), who had been inspired by the heroic depiction of the Klan offered in D. W. Griffith's epic Civil War movie, *The Birth of a Nation*.

The Ku Klux Klan was born in the immediate aftermath of the Civil War and, in many parts of the Reconstruction-era South, functioned as both a terrorist organization and a shadow government. The new Klan still targeted blacks, especially those bold enough to assert themselves and their rights, but it also sought to suppress immigrants, Jews, Catholics, and "Bolsheviks," all perceived as threats to "true" American values.

The height of the new KKK activity came in the 1920s, when the organization claimed more than four million members. The Great Depression brought a decline in membership, and the national KKK even officially disbanded itself in 1944, during World War II. When the civil rights movement rose to its zenith in the early 1960s, the Klan was again revived, and its members were often implicated in bombings, arsons, beatings, and lynchings, mainly in the South. Today, the KKK is loosely organized at best and is overshadowed by other right-wing extremist groups, including various manifestations of the neo-Nazi movement.

*The KKK faded with the end of Reconstruction, but reemerged during the 1920s, not just in the South, but in the Midwest and even in the Northeast, largely in response to an influx of immigrants and the migration of rural African Americans into industrial Northern cities. In many parts of the country, the new Klan became a powerful political and commercial force, and members made bold to march in the open, even in the nation's capital, as in this photograph from September 13, 1926.*

## TOWARD THE STOLEN ELECTION OF 1876

THE POWER OF THE KU KLUX KLAN was diminished somewhat under the new federal laws, but it and similar terrorist organizations would not be fully suppressed until Reconstruction was completely ended in the South.

After Andrew Johnson's term came to a close in 1869, Republican Ulysses S. Grant assumed office. A great general, Grant proved to be an inept president, under whom the political and financial corruption rampant in the postwar South spread throughout the corridors of power in Washington, Wall Street, and the nation generally.

Although the Grant administration vigorously used the Force Act and the Ku Klux Klan Act to suppress terror groups in the South, it did nothing about the more general defiance of Reconstruction, the Fourteenth and Fifteenth Amendments, and other federal laws intended to protect civil rights. A so-called redeemer movement developed through which Southern white activists promoted passage of state laws that variously sanctioned the social, legal, and economic subjugation of blacks. Collectively, such legislation was referred to as "Jim Crow" laws, a name taken from a racially demeaning song and dance routine that was a staple of the blackface minstrel shows popular in the North and South alike.

The political influence of the Southern redeemers grew rapidly, and by the end of Grant's second term, it had become national in scope. In the general election of 1876, Democrat Samuel J. Tilden easily captured the Southern vote and, nationally, outpolled Republican presidential candidate Rutherford B. Hayes by a margin of a quarter-million votes. Using Reconstruction laws, Republican politicians managed to reverse the tally in three Southern states, arguing that African American voters had been intimidated, coerced, and terrorized to keep them from the polls. These results, combined with a challenge to the neck-and-neck outcome of the polling in Oregon, sent the presidential contest to the House of Representatives. With

*Republicans contested Tilden's electoral victory over their candidate, Rutherford B. Hayes, thereby throwing the election of 1876 into the House of Representatives. (Tilden is pictured here on the sheet music of his campaign song.)*

*Rutherford B. Hayes and William A. Wheeler, the Republican nominees for president and vice president, in 1876.*

Frank Leslie's Illustrated Newspaper *published this depiction of the congressional Electoral Commission holding a secret session by candlelight to resolve the disputed election of 1876.*

Inauguration Day—at the time, March 4—looming, the House was stalemated. Not only were legislators considering the appointment of the current secretary of state as interim chief executive (an improvisation not provided for in the Constitution), some Southern politicians were throwing about the word *secession.*

On March 2, Congress created a bipartisan Electoral Commission even as legislators frantically hammered out a backroom bargain. It was this: Southern Democrats would make it possible for Hayes to become president in return for the Republican Party's pledge that Reconstruction would end immediately and absolutely and, what is more, that no Republican administration would ever again interfere in the states' rights of the South. This was tacitly understood to include the "right" to continue to pass laws institutionalizing racism, racial segregation, and racial discrimination.

## HEALING POSTPONED

THE INSTALLATION (it cannot properly be called the election) of Rutherford B. Hayes abruptly ended Reconstruction, both the bad of it and the good of it. For the next seventy-five years, until the modern civil rights movement began in the mid-1950s, institutionalized racism and racial segregation gripped the South, not only casting African Americans in the role of a permanent underclass, but retarding the post–Civil War economic recovery of the entire South, black as well as white, and ensuring that the region would lag behind the North well into the twentieth century.

The truth was that racism poisoned both North and South, but in the South it had the force of law, and when that law fell short some enacted their own brand of "lynch law." Between 1882 (the first year for which reliable statistics exist) and 1968 (when counting stopped), 4,743 persons were murdered by lynching, of whom 3,446 were African Americans. Terrorism, whether overt in the form of lynching or more subtle in the form of discrimination, eventually drove a national civil rights movement, and laws slowly changed. On July 26, 1948, President Harry S. Truman issued an executive order officially desegregating for the first time in American history the U.S. armed forces. On May 17, 1954, the U.S. Supreme Court, in its ruling on *Brown v. The Board of Education of Topeka*, found public school segregation unconstitutional. The very next year, in Montgomery, Alabama, an African American seamstress named Rosa Parks defied a city segregation ordinance by refusing to yield her bus seat to a white passenger. Her arrest triggered a black boycott of Montgomery's city buses and brought national attention to the issue of civil rights in the South. From this incident, the modern civil rights movement, led by Dr. Martin Luther King, Jr., and others, grew. President Dwight D. Eisenhower federalized the National Guard to enforce integration of schools in Little Rock, Arkansas in 1959, and in 1964, under President Lyndon B. Johnson, a landmark Civil Rights Act was passed and was followed the next year by the Voting Rights Act. By the 1970s, the South, which had resisted change for more than a hundred years, found itself the beneficiary of growing economic opportunities as corporations and individuals began moving to a region that no longer strove to make racial injustice legal.

## Beyond Appomattox

The causes of the Civil War were many and complex, but at their core was one overriding issue: human rights in the form of racial justice versus racial injustice. The Civil War continues to fascinate Americans. It is, to borrow the title of Charles P. Roland's classic history of the subject, our "American Iliad." Its outcome is the ratification of the United States as a true nation, one and indivisible, not a mere "confederacy" of separate states. It is also proof that Americans will fight for what they believe in. So, understandably, many Americans avidly read fiction and history about the Civil War; watch movies and television programs based on it; and some even don the blue, the gray, and the butternut to reenact it.

But the Civil War is not just fodder for a good story. Nor is it simply history. To the degree that racial justice has triumphed over racial injustice in the United States, the Civil War is over and done and can be considered the stuff of history. To the degree that human rights remain an issue unresolved, the Civil War has yet to end.

**TAKEAWAY**

The assassination of Abraham Lincoln deprived America of the one man who stood a good chance of making Reconstruction a process of national healing instead of regional alienation. The fight between President Andrew Johnson and the Radical Republican Congress created a poisonous social and political climate, which damaged race relations, the cause of social justice, and even the national economy for nearly a century after the war ended.

# CIVIL WAR TIMELINE

## 1860

**NOVEMBER 6:** Lincoln elected.

**DECEMBER 20:** South Carolina is first state to secede.

**DECEMBER 26:** Federal garrison at Fort Moultrie, South Carolina, moves to Fort Sumter in Charleston Harbor.

## 1861

**JANUARY 9:** Mississippi secedes. Confederates turn back the steamer *Star of the West* carrying supplies to Fort Sumter.

**JANUARY 10:** Florida secedes.

**JANUARY 11:** Alabama secedes.

**JANUARY 19:** Georgia secedes.

**JANUARY 26:** Louisiana secedes.

**JANUARY 29:** Kansas admitted to the Union as a free state.

**FEBRUARY 4:** The Provisional Confederate Congress convenes at Montgomery, Alabama.

**FEBRUARY 9:** The Provisional Confederate Congress names Jefferson Davis provisional president of the Confederate States of America.

**FEBRUARY 23:** Texas secedes.

**MARCH 4:** Lincoln inaugurated as sixteenth U.S. president.

**APRIL 12/13:** Fort Sumter endures a thirty-four-hour bombardment before commandant Major Robert Anderson, United States Army, surrenders to Confederate general P. G. T. Beauregard.

**APRIL 17:** Virginia secedes.

**APRIL 19:** Baltimore rioters attack 6th Massachusetts Regiment; Lincoln orders blockade of Southern coast.

**APRIL 29:** Border state Maryland rejects secession.

**MAY 6:** Arkansas secedes.

**MAY 10:** Union forces capture Camp Jackson, St. Louis, igniting a prosecession riot.

**MAY 13:** United States Army troops occupy Baltimore.

**MAY 20:** North Carolina secedes.

**MAY 24:** Union troops seize Alexandria, Virginia.

**JUNE 3:** Union wins the battle of Philippi, western Virginia (present-day West Virginia).

**JUNE 8:** Tennessee secedes.

**JUNE 10:** Confederates win the battle of Big Bethel, Virginia.

**JUNE 17:** Union wins the battle of Booneville, Missouri.

**JULY 5:** Pro-Confederate Missouri State Guard defeats Union forces at the battle of Carthage, Missouri.

**JULY 11:** Union wins the battle of Rich Mountain, western Virginia (present-day West Virginia).

**JULY 13:** Union wins the battle of Carrick's Ford, western Virginia (present-day West Virginia).

**JULY 18:** Confederates win the battle of Blackburn's Ford, Virginia.

**JULY 21:** Confederates win the first battle of Bull Run, Virginia, stunning the North.

**AUGUST 10:** Pro-Confederate Missouri State Guard defeats Union forces at the battle of Wilson's Creek, Missouri.

**AUGUST 27:** Union captures Fort Clark, North Carolina.

**AUGUST 28:** Union captures Fort Hatteras, North Carolina.

**SEPTEMBER 3:** Confederates invade Kentucky, forcing an end to the border state's declared neutrality.

**SEPTEMBER 6:** Union troops capture Paducah, Kentucky.

**SEPTEMBER 10:** Union wins the battle of Carnifex Ferry, Virginia.

**SEPTEMBER 12–15:** Union wins the prolonged battle of Cheat Mountain, western Virginia (present-day West Virginia).

**SEPTEMBER 12–20:** After a siege, Union forces at Lexington, Missouri, surrender to the pro-Confederate Missouri State Guard.

**OCTOBER 21:** Confederates win the battle of Ball's Bluff, Virginia, in which Union colonel and U.S. senator Edward D. Baker is killed.

**NOVEMBER 6:** Jefferson Davis is elected as regular (not provisional) Confederate president.

**NOVEMBER 7:** Union forces capture Belmont, Missouri, and Port Royal, South Carolina.

**NOVEMBER 8:** USS *San Jacinto* intercepts British ship *Trent*, seizing Europe-bound Confederate diplomats James Mason and John Slidell.

**NOVEMBER 28:** Confederate Congress admits Missouri to the Confederacy, even though the state has not seceded.

**DECEMBER 13:** The battle of Camp Alleghany, western Virginia (present-day West Virginia), proves inconclusive.

**DECEMBER 20:** Union wins a minor victory at the battle of Dranesville, Virginia.

# 1862

**JANUARY 19:** Union wins the battle of Mill Springs (a.k.a.: Fishing Creek and Logan's Crossroads), Kentucky.

**FEBRUARY 6:** Confederate Fort Henry, on the Tennessee River, falls to a Union assault.

**FEBRUARY 8:** Union wins the battle of Roanoke Island, North Carolina.

**FEBRUARY 12–16:** Confederate Fort Donelson, on the Cumberland River, falls to a Union assault.

**FEBRUARY 21:** Confederates win the battle of Valverde, New Mexico Territory.

**MARCH 6–8:** Union wins the battle of Pea Ridge (Elkhorn Tavern), Arkansas.

**MARCH 8–9:** The battle of Hampton Roads, Virginia, pits USS *Monitor* against CSS *Virginia* (ex-USS *Merrimack*); both sides claim victory.

**MARCH 14:** In separate actions, Union forces capture New Madrid, Missouri, and New Bern, North Carolina.

**MARCH 23:** Union forces defeat Stonewall Jackson at the battle of Kernstown, in the Shenandoah Valley of Virginia.

**MARCH 26:** Union forces win a closely fought strategic victory at the battle of Apache Canyon, New Mexico Territory.

**MARCH 28:** The Union's strategic victory at the battle of Glorieta Pass, New Mexico Territory, turns the tide against the Confederates in the far Southwest.

**APRIL 5–MAY 4:** Union general George B. McClellan wins an empty victory at the siege of Yorktown, Virginia.

**APRIL 6–7:** Ulysses S. Grant wins a narrow, very costly victory at the battle of Shiloh, Tennessee.

**APRIL 7:** Union forces capture Island No. 10, Missouri.

**APRIL 11:** Union forces capture Fort Pulaski, Georgia.

**APRIL 25:** In separate actions, Union forces capture Fort Macon, North Carolina, and capture and occupy New Orleans, Louisiana.

**APRIL 29–MAY 30:** Union general H. W. Halleck lays cautious siege to Corinth, Mississippi, capturing it, but allowing Confederate forces to withdraw intact.

**MAY 5:** The battle of Williamsburg, Virginia, proves inconclusive.

**MAY 8:** Confederates win the battle of McDowell, West Virginia.

**MAY 10:** Union forces occupy Norfolk, Virginia.

**MAY 15:** Confederates win the battle of Drewry's Bluff, Virginia.

**MAY 23:** Confederates under Stonewall Jackson win the battle of Front Royal, Virginia.

**MAY 25:** Confederates under Stonewall Jackson win the first battle of Winchester, Virginia.

**MAY 31–JUNE 1:** The battle of Seven Pines (a.k.a. Fair Oaks), Virginia, is fought to a draw.

**JUNE 5:** Confederates abandon Fort Pillow, Tennessee.

**JUNE 6:** Union wins the battle of Memphis, Tennessee.

**JUNE 8:** Confederates win the battle of Cross Keys, Virginia.

**JUNE 9:** Confederates win the battle of Port Republic, Virginia.

**JUNE 16:** Confederates win the battle of Secessionville, South Carolina.

**JUNE 26:** Union general McClellan wins a tactical victory at Beaver Dam Creek (Mechanicsville), Virginia, during the Seven Days battles.

**JUNE 27:** Confederates win the battle of Gaines' Mill, Virginia (Seven Days battles).

**JUNE 29:** The battle of Savage's Station, Virginia (Seven Days battles), ends in a draw.

**JUNE 30:** The battle of Frayser's Farm (Glendale), Virginia (Seven Days battles), ends inconclusively

and is followed by the battle of White Oak Swamp, also a draw.

**JULY 1:** Union wins the battle of Malvern Hill (Seven Days battles).

**AUGUST 5:** Union wins the battle of Baton Rouge, Louisiana.

**AUGUST 9:** Confederates win the battle of Cedar (Slaughter's) Mountain, Virginia.

**AUGUST 17–SEPTEMBER 23:** The Santee Sioux uprising disrupts the raising of Union troops in Minnesota.

**AUGUST 28–30:** Confederates win a stunning victory at the second battle of Bull Run, Virginia.

**AUGUST 30:** Confederates win the battle of Richmond, Kentucky.

**SEPTEMBER 1:** Confederates win a strategic victory at the battle of Chantilly (Ox Hill), Virginia.

**SEPTEMBER 14:** Union wins the battles of South Mountain and Crampton's Gap, Maryland.

**SEPTEMBER 15:** Confederates capture Harpers Ferry, West Virginia.

**SEPTEMBER 17:** Union wins a narrow victory at the battle of Antietam, Maryland; on the same day, Confederates win the battle of Munfordville, Kentucky.

**SEPTEMBER 19:** Union wins the battle of Iuka, Mississippi.

**SEPTEMBER 22:** Spurred by the victory at Antietam, President Lincoln issues the Preliminary Emancipation Proclamation.

**OCTOBER 3–4:** Union wins the second battle of Corinth, Mississippi.

**OCTOBER 8:** The battle of Perryville, Kentucky, yields mixed results, the Confederates winning a tactical victory, while conceding strategic victory to the Union.

**DECEMBER 7:** Union forces make strategic gains at the battle of Prairie Grove, Arkansas.

**DECEMBER 13:** The Union's Army of the Potomac suffers crushing defeat at the battle of Fredericksburg, Virginia.

**DECEMBER 20:** Confederates raid Holly Springs, Mississippi.

**DECEMBER 29:** Confederates win the battle of Chickasaw Bayou, Mississippi.

**DECEMBER 31, 1862–JANUARY 2, 1863:** Union wins the battle of Murfreesboro, Tennessee.

# 1863

**JANUARY 1:** Final Emancipation Proclamation takes effect. In Texas, the battle of Galveston Harbor results in Confederate evacuation.

**JANUARY 11:** Union captures Arkansas Post, Arkansas.

**JANUARY 19–22:** Ambrose Burnside's attempt to commence a post-Fredericksburg winter offensive mires the Army of the Potomac in a "Mud March," which precipitates Burnside's replacement by Joseph Hooker.

**MARCH 11:** During the Vicksburg campaign, Ulysses S. Grant's Yazoo Pass Expedition is blocked at Fort Pemberton, Mississippi.

**MARCH 17:** Confederates win the battle of Kelly's Ford, Virginia.

**APRIL 7:** Confederates beat back a Union naval assault at the first battle of Charleston Harbor, South Carolina.

**MAY 1:** In the Vicksburg campaign, Union forces win the battle of Port Gibson, Mississippi.

**MAY 1–4:** At the battle of Chancellorsville, Virginia, the Army of the Potomac, now under Joseph Hooker, suffers another catastrophic defeat against Robert E. Lee's Army of Northern Virginia; however, Thomas "Stonewall" Jackson, Lee's greatest general, is mortally wounded by friendly fire.

**MAY 12:** In the Vicksburg campaign, Union wins the battle of Raymond, Mississippi.

**MAY 14:** In the Vicksburg campaign, Union wins the battle of Jackson, Mississippi.

**MAY 16:** In the Vicksburg campaign, Union wins the battle of Champion Hill, Mississippi.

**MAY 17:** In the Vicksburg campaign, Union wins the battle of Big Black River Bridge, Mississippi.

**MAY 18–JULY 4:** The Vicksburg campaign culminates in the siege of Vicksburg, Mississippi, which ends in the fall of that fortress city to Grant's Union forces.

**MAY 21–JULY 8:** The Union prevails in the siege of Port Hudson, Louisiana.

**JUNE 7:** Union wins the battle of Milliken's Bend, Louisiana.

**JUNE 9:** The largest cavalry engagement of the Civil War, the battle of Brandy Station, Virginia, ends inconclusively.

**JUNE 14:** Confederates win the second battle of Winchester, Virginia.

**JUNE 23–JULY 7:** In the brilliantly executed Tullahoma campaign, Union general William S. Rosecrans drives Confederate Braxton Bragg's Army of Tennessee out of middle Tennessee.

**JULY 1–3:** In winning the battle of Gettysburg, Pennsylvania, the Union turns the tide irreversibly against Lee's Army of Northern Virginia and the Southern cause.

**JULY 8–26:** Confederate guerrilla John Hunt Morgan conducts his spectacular Ohio Raid.

**JULY 10–SEPTEMBER 6:** Union forces lay siege of Battery Wagner, Charleston Harbor; the Confederates abandon the fort on September 6.

**JULY 13–15:** Deadly "draft riots" sweep New York City.

**AUGUST 21:** Quantrill's infamous Confederate raiders sack Lawrence, Kansas.

**SEPTEMBER 10:** Union forces capture Little Rock, Arkansas.

**SEPTEMBER 19–20:** Confederates win the battle of Chickamauga, Georgia.

**OCTOBER 14:** Union wins the battle of Bristoe Station, Virginia.

**NOVEMBER 7:** Union wins the second battle of Rappahannock Station, Virginia.

**NOVEMBER 23–25:** Union wins the battle of Chattanooga, Tennessee.

**NOVEMBER 29:** Union wins the battle of Fort Sanders (Knoxville), Tennessee.

# 1864

**FEBRUARY 14–20:** Union wins the battle of Meridian, Mississippi.

**FEBRUARY 20:** Confederates win the battle of Olustee, Florida.

**FEBRUARY 22:** Confederates win the battle of Okolona, Mississippi.

**MARCH 10–MAY 22:** Confederates prevail against Union major general Nathaniel P. Banks's Red River campaign, Louisiana.

**APRIL 8:** Confederates win the battle of Mansfield (Sabine Crossroads; Pleasant Grove) Louisiana.

**APRIL 9:** The battle of Pleasant Hill, Louisiana, yields mixed results, with the Union scoring a tactical victory, but the Confederates a strategic win.

**APRIL 12:** Confederate troops under Nathan Bedford Forrest target African-American troops in the infamous "Fort Pillow Massacre," Tennessee.

**APRIL 12–13:** Union wins the battle of Blair's Landing, Louisiana.

**APRIL 17–20:** Confederates win the battle of Plymouth, North Carolina.

**APRIL 30:** While retreating during the failed Red River campaign, Union forces score a victory at the battle of Jenkins' Ferry, Arkansas.

**MAY 5–6:** Confederates win a tactical victory at the battle of the Wilderness, Virginia, but fail to stop Grant's advance toward Richmond.

**MAY 6–7:** Union wins the battle of Port Walthall Junction, Virginia.

**MAY 7–SEPTEMBER 2:** Union major general William Tecumseh Sherman leads the Atlanta campaign, first against Joseph E. Johnston and then William Bell Hood.

**MAY 8–21:** Confederates win a tactical victory at the battle of Spotsylvania Virginia, but again fail to halt Grant's advance toward Richmond.

**MAY 11:** Confederate cavalry win a tactical victory battle of Yellow Tavern, Virginia, but suffer strategic defeat at the hands of Philip Sheridan; Confederate cavalry genius Jeb Stuart is killed in combat.

**MAY 13–15:** The battle of Resaca, Georgia, part of the Atlanta campaign, ends in a draw.

**MAY 15:** Confederates win the battle of New Market, Virginia.

**MAY 16:** Confederates win the battle of Drewry's Bluff, Virginia.

**MAY 23–26:** The battle of the North Anna, Virginia, part of Grant's costly Overland campaign, ends inconclusively.

**MAY 25–JUNE 4:** Confederates win the battle of New Hope Church, Georgia, during Sherman's Atlanta campaign.

**MAY 30–JUNE 3:** The battle of Totopotomoy Creek (Bethesda Church), Virginia, part of Grant's Overland campaign, ends in a bloody draw.

**JUNE 1–3:** Confederates win the battle of Cold Harbor, Virginia, but fail to stop Grant's continuing southward advance.

**JUNE 10:** Confederates win the battle of Brice's Crossroads, Mississippi.

**JUNE 11:** Confederates win the battle of Trevilian Station, Virginia.

JUNE 18, 1864–APRIL 2, 1865: Grant uses the Army of the Potomac to lay siege against strongly defended Petersburg, Virginia.

JUNE 19: USS *Kearsarge* sinks the infamous Confederate commerce raider CSS *Alabama* near Cherbourg off the French coast.

JUNE 27: Confederates win the battle of Kennesaw Mountain, Georgia, during Sherman's Atlanta campaign.

JULY 9: Confederates win a tactical victory at the battle of Monocacy, Maryland, but Union forces delay Jubal Early's advance on Washington and therefore score a strategic win.

JULY 11: Union defenders of Washington, D.C., repel Jubal Early's forces at the battle of Fort Stevens, D.C.

JULY 14: Union wins the battle of Tupelo, Mississippi.

JULY 20: Union wins the battle of Peachtree Creek during Sherman's Atlanta campaign.

JULY 22: Union wins the battle of Atlanta during Sherman's Atlanta campaign.

JULY 28: Union wins the battle of Ezra Church during Sherman's Atlanta campaign.

JULY 30: A Union effort to break through Confederate defensive fortification at Petersburg fails in the bloody battle of the Crater, Virginia.

AUGUST 5: Union wins the battle of Mobile Bay, Alabama.

AUGUST 25: Confederates win the battle of Ream's Station, Virginia.

AUGUST 31–SEPTEMBER 1: Union wins the battle of Jonesboro, Georgia.

SEPTEMBER 2: Sherman's Atlanta campaign ends with the Union occupation of Atlanta, Georgia.

SEPTEMBER 19: Union wins the third battle of Winchester (battle of Opequou), Virginia.

SEPTEMBER 22: Union wins the battle of Fisher's Hill, Virginia.

SEPTEMBER 29–30: Union wins the battle of Chaffin's Farm and New Market Heights, Virginia

SEPTEMBER 30–OCTOBER 2: Union wins the battle of Peebles' Farm (Poplar Springs Church), Virginia.

OCTOBER 5: Union wins the battle of Allatoona (Allatoona Pass), Georgia.

OCTOBER 9: Union wins the battle of Tom's Brook, Virginia.

OCTOBER 19: Union wins the battle of Cedar Creek, Virginia.

OCTOBER 23: Union wins the battle of Westport, Missouri, ending the last significant Confederate operation west of the Mississippi River.

OCTOBER 27: The battle of Burgess Mill (Boydton Plank Road), Virginia, ends inconclusively and thereby fails to cut off supplies to besieged Petersburg.

NOVEMBER 8: Abraham Lincoln is reelected, ensuring that the Union will settle for nothing short of absolute victory.

NOVEMBER 16–DECEMBER 21: Sherman conducts his "March to the Sea."

NOVEMBER 29: Union wins the battle of Spring Hill, Tennessee.

NOVEMBER 30: Union wins the battle of Franklin, Tennessee.

DECEMBER 15–16: Union wins the battle of Nashville, Tennessee, breaking the back of John Bell Hood's Army of Tennessee.

DECEMBER 21: Sherman's Union forces occupy Savannah, Georgia.

DECEMBER 19–APRIL 26: Sherman conducts his Carolinas campaign against the remainder of the Confederate Army of Tennessee, now commanded by Joseph E. Johnston; the campaign ends with Johnston's surrender and, along with the defeat of

Lee's Army of Northern Virginia, is the culminating campaign of the Civil War.

# 1865

**February 5–7:** Union wins the battle of Hatcher's Run, Virginia.

**March 2:** Union wins the battle of Waynesboro, Virginia, essentially destroying the forces led by Jubal Early.

**March 8–10:** Union wins the battle of Kinston, North Carolina.

**March 19–21:** Sherman's victory at the battle of Bentonville, North Carolina, was his last major battle with Joseph E. Johnston.

**March 22–24:** In Wilson's Raid, into Alabama and Georgia, Union brigadier general James H. Wilson destroyed remaining manufacturing facilities in the region.

**March 25:** In the battle of Fort Stedman, Union forces repulsed a Confederate attempt to break through the siege lines at Petersburg, Virginia.

**March 31:** Confederates win the battle of Dinwiddie Court House, Virginia, during the Appomattox campaign.

**April 1:** Philip H. Sheridan's victory against Confederate forces under George Pickett at the battle of Five Forks, Virginia, prompts Lee to abandon his defense of Petersburg and soon leads to his surrender at Appomattox Court House.

**April 3:** Union forces occupy Richmond and Petersburg, Virginia.

**April 6:** In the Appomattox campaign, Union forces win the battle of Sayler's Creek, Virginia.

**April 7:** In the Appomattox campaign, the battle of High Bridge, Virginia, ends inconclusively—though with substantial Union losses.

**April 9:** In the Appomattox campaign, Robert E. Lee, defeated at the battle of Appomattox, surrenders the Army of Northern Virginia to Ulysses S. Grant at the McLean house at Appomattox Court House.

**April 9:** Union wins the battle of Fort Blakely, Alabama.

**April 12:** Mobile, Alabama, formally surrenders to Union forces.

**April 14:** John Wilkes Booth, actor and Confederate sympathizer, shoots President Abraham Lincoln at Ford's Theatre, Washington, D.C.

**April 15:** The wounded president dies at 7:22 a.m. Vice President Andrew Johnson becomes the seventeenth president of the United States.

**April 16:** Some consider the battle of Columbus, Georgia, a Union victory, to be the final battle of the Civil War; others believe the final engagement was the battle of Palmito Ranch, a Confederate victory, on May 13.

**April 26:** General Joseph E. Johnston surrenders to William T. Sherman in North Carolina.

**May 13:** Some consider the battle of Palmito Ranch, Cameron County, Texas, to be the final battle of the Civil War; ironically, it ends in Confederate victory.

**May 26:** General Edmund Kirby Smith surrenders to Major General E. R. S. Canby, west of the Mississippi River; this was the final surrender of a significant Confederate force.

**June 23:** Following the postwar battle of Doaksville, Brigadier General Stand Watie, a Cherokee, is officially the last Confederate general to surrender, at Fort Towson, Indian Territory (modern Oklahoma).

# LIVE AND IN PERSON

## ABRAHAM LINCOLN BIRTHPLACE
2995 Lincoln Farm Road
Hodgenville, KY 42748
270-358-3137
www.nps.gov/abli

## ANDERSONVILLE NATIONAL HISTORIC SITE
496 Cemetery Road
Andersonville, GA 31711
229-924-0343
www.nps.gov/ande

*Located on GA 49, ten miles northeast of Americus, Georgia. This is the most infamous POW camp of the Civil War.*

## ANDREW JOHNSON NATIONAL HISTORIC SITE
101 North College Street
Greeneville, TN 37743
423-638-3551
www.nps.gov/anjo

## ANTIETAM NATIONAL BATTLEFIELD AND NATIONAL CEMETERY
P.O. Box 158
Sharpsburg, MD 21782
301-432-5124
www.nps.gov/ancm

*Located on MD 65 and MD 34, immediately to the north and northeast of Sharpsburg, Maryland. The Union's narrow victory here served as the springboard for the Emancipation Proclamation. Antietam was the bloodiest day of the war.*

## APPOMATTOX COURT HOUSE NATIONAL HISTORICAL PARK
Highway 24, P.O. Box 218
Appomattox, VA 24522
434-352-8987, ext. 26
www.nps.gov/apco

*Lee surrendered his Army of Northern Virginia to Grant at the McLean house.*

## ATLANTA CAMPAIGN
### ATLANTA CYCLORAMA
800 Cherokee Avenue, SE
Atlanta, GA 30315
404-658-7625
www.atlantacyclorama.org

*The cyclorama of the battle of Atlanta is the largest painting in the world; combining two- and three-dimensional elements.*

## BOSTON AFRICAN AMERICAN NATIONAL HISTORIC SITE
14 Beacon Street, Suite 401
Boston, MA 02108
617-742-5415
www.nps.gov/boaf

*This collection of roughly two dozen sites along the Black Heritage Trail relates to the abolition movement and to the organization of the "colored" 54th Massachusetts Regiment.*

## FIRST AND SECOND BATTLES OF BULL RUN
## MANASSAS NATIONAL BATTLEFIELD PARK
12521 Lee Highway
Manassas, Virginia 20109
703-361-1339
www.nps.gov/mana

*Located at VA 234 off I-66. The defeat at the first battle of Bull Run stunned the Union, and the losses at the second battle of Bull Run were even worse.*

## CHANCELLORSVILLE BATTLEFIELD UNIT
### FREDERICKSBURG AND SPOTSYLVANIA COUNTY BATTLEFIELDS MEMORIAL NATIONAL MILITARY PARK
120 Chatham Lane
Fredericksburg, Virginia 22405
540-786-2880
www.nps.gov/frsp

*For GPS users: Use 9001 Plank Road, Fredericksburg, VA 22405. The Confederate victory at Chancellorsville is considered "Lee's masterpiece."*

## CHICKAMAUGA BATTLEFIELD AND CHATTANOOGA CAMPAIGN
### CHICKAMAUGA AND CHATTANOOGA NATIONAL MILITARY PARK
P.O. Box 2128
Fort Oglethorpe, GA 30742
706-866-9241
www.nps.gov/chch

*Although closely associated, these two battlefields are dramatically different—the one a tangled lowland, the other a so-called battle above the Clouds.*

## FORD'S THEATRE AND THE PETERSEN HOUSE

### FORD'S THEATRE NATIONAL HISTORIC SITE

511 Tenth Street NW
Washington, DC 20004
202-426-6924
www.nps.gov/foth

*Site of Lincoln's assassination.*

### THE PETERSON HOUSE

516 Tenth Street NW
Washington, DC 20004
202-426-6924
www.nps.gov/foth

*Site of Lincoln's death.*

## FORT SUMTER

1214 Middle Street
Sullivan's Island, SC 29482
843-883-3123
www.nps.gov/fosu

*This is where the Civil War began.*

## FREDERICKSBURG, SPOTSYLVANIA, AND WILDERNESS BATTLES

### FREDERICKSBURG AND SPOTSYLVANIA COUNTY BATTLEFIELDS MEMORIAL NATIONAL MILITARY PARK

120 Chatham Lane
Fredericksburg, VA 22405
540-373-6122
www.nps.gov/frsp

*For GPS users: Fredericksburg's address is 1013 Lafayette Boulevard, Fredericksburg, VA 22405.*
*For Spotsylvania, it's 9550 Grant Drive West, Spotsylvania, VA 22553.*
*For Wilderness Battles, it's 35347 Constitution Highway, Locust Grove, VA 22508.*

*These are the sites of some of the Civil War's costliest battles.*

## GETTYSBURG NATIONAL MILITARY PARK

### VISITOR'S CENTER

97 Taneytown Road
Gettysburg, PA 17325
717-334-1124, ext. 8023
www.nps.gov/gett

*Along with Vicksburg, the battle of Gettysburg is considered the turning point of the Civil War—the end of the Confederacy's chance for victory. Gettysburg was also the biggest battle fought in the Americas.*

## HARPERS FERRY NATIONAL HISTORICAL PARK

P.O. Box 65
Harpers Ferry, WV 25425
304-535-6029
www.nps.gov/hafe

*This was not only the scene of John Brown's 1859 raid, a prelude to the war, but an important battlefield during the war.*

## KENNESAW MOUNTAIN NATIONAL BATTLEFIELD PARK

900 Kennesaw Mountain Drive
Kennesaw, GA 30152
770-427-4686, ext. 0
www.nps.gov/kemo

*From I-75 take exit 116, Barrett Parkway, and follow signs to the park. This beautiful park highlights a Confederate victory in the battles of the Atlanta campaign.*

## CSS VIRGINIA (EX-USS MERRIMACK)

### THE PORTSMOUTH NAVAL SHIPYARD MUSEUM

2 High Street
Portsmouth, VA 23704
757-393-8591
www.portsnavalmuseums.com

## THE HAMPTON ROADS NAVAL MUSEUM

333 Waterside Drive
Norfolk, VA 23510
757-322-2987
www.hrnm.navy.mil

*These facilities house important artifacts relating to the Confederate navy's great ironclad.*

## USS MONITOR

### THE MARINERS' MUSEUM

100 Museum Drive
Newport News, VA 23606
757-596-2222
www.marinersmuseum.org

*The museum houses artifacts relating to the Monitor as well as other Monitor-class ships and ironclads.*

## MONOCACY NATIONAL BATTLEFIELD

4801 Urbana Pike
Frederick, MD 21704
301-662-3515
www.nps.gov/mono

*Less famous than many other Civil War battles, Jubal Early's victory at Monocacy brought his raiders to the very edge of Washington, D.C.*

## PEA RIDGE NATIONAL MILITARY PARK

15930 E. Highway 2
Garfield, AR 72732
479-451-8122, ext. 227
www.nps.gov/peri

*The Union victory at Pea Ridge ensured that Missouri would not become a Confederate state.*

## PETERSBURG NATIONAL BATTLEFIELD

5001 Siege Road
Petersburg, VA 23803
804-732-3531
www.nps.gov.pete

*This is the site of Grant's nine-month siege of Petersburg and the explosive battle of the Crater.*

## RICHMOND NATIONAL BATTLEFIELD PARK

3215 East Broad Street
Richmond, VA 23223
804-226-1981, ext. 23
www.nps.gov/rich

*The park is dedicated to the battles for the capital of the Confederacy.*

## SHILOH NATIONAL MILITARY PARK

1055 Pittsburg Landing Road
Shiloh, TN 38376
731-689-5696
www.nps.gov/shil

*On TN 22, twenty-two miles northeast of Corinth, Mississippi. After the battle of Shiloh, some Northerners called for Grant's relief, condemning him as a "butcher."*

## VICKSBURG NATIONAL MILITARY PARK

3201 Clay Street
Vicksburg, MI 39183
601-636-0583
www.nps.gov/vick

*A spectacular site that shows the critical importance of Grant's victory here.*

# READ MORE, SEE MORE

## BOOKS

Axelrod, Alan. *The War between the Spies: A History of Espionage During the American Civil War.* New York: Atlantic Monthly Press, 1992.

Billings, John D. *Hard Tack & Coffee: The Unwritten Story of Army Life.* 1887; reprinted, Lincoln: University of Nebraska Press/Bison Books, 1993.

Boritt, Gabor S. *Lincoln's Generals.* Lincoln: University of Nebraska Press/Bison Books, 2010.

Catton, Bruce. *The Coming Fury.* Garden City, NY: Doubleday, 1961; reprinted, New York: Phoenix Press, 2001.

———. *Glory Road.* Garden City, NY: Doubleday, 1952; reprinted, New York: Anchor Books, 1990.

———. *Mr. Lincoln's Army.* Garden City, NY: Doubleday, 1951; reprinted, New York: Anchor Books, 1990.

———. *Never Call Retreat.* Garden City, NY: Doubleday, 1965; reprinted, New York: Phoenix Press, 2001.

———. *A Stillness at Appomattox.* Garden City, NY: Doubleday, 1953; reprinted, New York: Anchor Books, 1990.

———. *Terrible Swift Sword.* Garden City, NY: Doubleday, 1963; reprinted, New York: Fall River Press, 2009.

———. *This Hallowed Ground.* Garden City, NY: Doubleday, 1955.

Cornish, Dudley Taylor. *The Sable Arm: Black Troops in the Union Army, 1861–1865.* Lawrence: University of Kansas Press, 1987.

Current, Richard N., Paul D. Escott, Lawrence N. Powell, James I. Robertson Jr., and Emory M. Thomas, eds. *Encyclopedia of the Confederacy.* New York: Simon & Schuster, 1993.

Davis, Burke. *Sherman's March.* New York: Random House, 1980; reprinted, New York: Vintage, 1988.

Davis, William C. *The Commanders of the Civil War.* New York: Salamander Books, 1990.

———. *Jefferson Davis: The Man and His Hour.* New York: HarperCollins, 1991.

Donald, David Herbert. *Lincoln.* New York: Simon & Schuster, 1995.

Douglass, Frederick. *Narrative of the Life of Frederick Douglass: An American Slave.* 1845; reprinted New York: Signet Books, 1968.

Dyer, Frederick H. *A Compendium of the War of the Rebellion: From Official Records of the Union and Confederate Armies, Reports of the Adjutant Generals of the Several States, the Army Registers, and Other Reliable Documents and Sources.* 1911; reprint ed., New York: T. Yoseloff, 1959.

Eicher, David J. *The Civil War in Books.* Champaign-Urbana: University of Illinois Press, 1997.

Foote, Shelby. *The Civil War: A Narrative, Vol. 1, Fort Sumter to Perryville.* New York: Random House, 1958. Vol. 2, *Fredericksburg to Meridian.* New York: Random House, 1963. Vol. 3, *Red River to Appomattox.* New York: Random House, 1974. All reprinted, New York: Vintage, 1986.

Freeman, Douglas Southall. *Lee.* New York: Scribner, 1934.

Furgurson, Ernest B. *Chancellorsville 1863: The Souls of the Brave.* New York: Knopf, 1992.

Goodwin, Doris Kearns. *Team of Rivals: The Political Genius of Abraham Lincoln.* New York: Simon & Schuster, 2005.

Gragg, Rod. *The Illustrated Confederate Reader.* New York: Harper & Row, 1989; reprinted, New York: Harper Perennial, 1991.

Heidler, David S., and Jeane T. Heidler, eds. *Encyclopedia of the American Civil War: A Political, Social, and Military History.* Santa Barbara, CA: ABC-CLIO, 2000.

Hennessy, John J. *Return to Bull Run: The Campaign and Battle of Second Manassas.* New York: Simon & Schuster, 1993.

Hurst, Jack. *Nathan Bedford Forrest: A Biography.* New York: Knopf, 1993.

Marszalek, John F. *Sherman: A Soldier's Passion for Order.* New York: Free Press, 1993.

McFeely, William S. *Grant: A Biography.* New York: Norton, 1981.

McPherson, James M. *Battle Cry of Freedom.* New York: Oxford University Press, 1988.

———., ed. *The Atlas of the Civil War.* New York: Macmillan, 1994.

Morris, Roy, Jr. *Sheridan: The Life and Wars of General Philip Sheridan.* New York: Crown, 1992.

Nevins, Allan. *Ordeal of the Union.* New York: Scribner's, 1947–1971.

Nolan, Alan T. *Lee Considered: General Robert F. Lee and Civil War History.* Chapel Hill: University of North Carolina Press, 1991.

Oates, Stephen B. *A Woman of Valor: Clara Barton and the Civil War.* New York: Free Press, 1994.

Robertson, James I., Jr. *Soldiers Blue and Gray.* Columbia: University of South Carolina Press, 1988.

———. *Stonewall Jackson: The Man, the Soldier, the Legend.* New York: Macmillan General Reference, 1997.

Sears, Stephen W. *George B. McClellan: The Young Napoleon.* NY: Ticknor & Fields, 1988.

———. *Landscape Turned Red: The Battle of Antietam.* New York: Ticknor and Fields, 1982.

Sifakis, Stewart. *Who Was Who in the Civil War.* New York: Facts on File, 1988.

Stanley, Dorothy, ed. *The Autobiography of Sir Henry Morton Stanley.* Boston and New York: Houghton Mifflin, 1909.

Thomas, Emory M. *Bold Dragoon: The Life of J.E.B. Stuart.* New York: Random House, 1986.

———. *Robert E. Lee: A Biography.* New York: Norton, 1995.

United States War Department. *The War of the Rebellion: A Compilation of the Official Records of the Union and Confederate Armies. Washington, DC:* Government Printing Office, 1880–1901. Also available on CD-ROM from the Guild Press of Indiana, Inc., 10665 Andrade Drive, Zionsville, IN 46077.

Wagner, Margaret, Gary W. Gallagher, and Paul Finkelman. *The Library of Congress Civil War Desk Reference.* New York: Simon & Schuster, 2002.

Warren, Robert Penn. *John Brown: The Making of a Martyr.* Payson & Clarke, 1929; reprinted, Nashville: J. F. Sanders, 1993.

Watkins, Sam R. *"Co. Aytch": A Side Show of the Big Show.* New York: Macmillan, 1962.

Wertz, Jay, and Edwin C. Bearss. *Smithsonian's Great Battles and Battlefields of the Civil War.* New York: Morrow, 1997.

Wheeler, Richard. *Voices of the Civil War.* New York: Crowell, 1976; reprinted, New York: Meridian. 1990.

Wiley, Bell Irvin. *The Life of Billy Yank: The Common Soldier of the Union.* 1953; reprinted, Baton Rouge: Louisiana State University Press, 1978.

———. *The Life of Johnny Reb: The Common Soldier of the Confederacy.* 1943; reprinted, Baton Rouge: Louisiana State University Press, 1978.

Williams, T. Harry. *Lincoln and His Generals.* New York: Knopf, 1952.

Wills, Garry. *Lincoln at Gettysburg: The Words That Remade America.* New York: Simon & Schuster, 1992.

# Websites and Blogs

People interested in the Civil War tend to be *really* interested in the Civil War—and they think and talk a lot about it. In the Internet Age, this has given birth to hundreds of websites devoted to the subject. Soldierstudies.org, which maintains one of the very best sites, also ranks the "Top 100" sites. Begin your cyber journey through the Civil War by checking out www.civilwar.soldierstudies.org/top100. If you want a more exhaustive guide to Civil War resources on the Internet, go to: www.civilwarroster.com.

Here are ten more must-not-miss sites and blogs:

### Civil War Books and Authors
www.cwba.blogspot.com
You'll find news and reviews as well as interviews.

### Civil War Interactive
www.civilwarinteractive.com
The site's subtitle says it all: "The Daily Newspaper of the Civil War Since 1996."

### Civil War Virtual Tours
www.civilwarvirtualtours.com
Using high-quality maps and impressive digital graphics, this site aims to provide in cyberspace a virtual alternative to touring key battlefields on foot. Fascinating.

### Civil War Women
www.civilwarwomen.blogspot.com
The site presents biographies and other stories of women of the Civil War era.

### Confederate Digest
www.confederatedigest.com
The Civil War from a Confederate perspective.

### Lincoln Studies
www.lincolnstudies.com
A site dedicated to Lincoln and the Civil War.

### Seeing the Elephant
www.recreatedelephant.blogspot.com
During the Civil War "to see the elephant" was to experience combat firsthand. This blog will introduce you to the hobby/obsession of Civil War re-creation.

### Soldier Studies Letter Archives
www.soldierstudies.org
Civil War soldiers and their families wrote a great many letters, which are now a primary source for history and, equally important, a means of gaining an intimate sense of the war. Go to the site and follow the "Letters" links.

### To the Sound of the Guns
www.markerhunter.wordpress.com
This unique blog hunts down and discusses Civil War battlefields (the famous and the obscure) as well as historical markers and other sites.

### TOCWOC—A Civil War Blog
www.brettschulte.net/CWBlog
Bills itself as "The Order of Civil War Obsessively Compulsed—Informed Amateurs Blog the American Civil War."

# Films

### *Andersonville* (1996)
A well-made TV movie of life and death in the Civil War's most notorious POW camp. Directed by John Frankenheimer.

### *The Birth of a Nation* (1915)
This silent classic was Hollywood's first true epic. The film tells the story of the Civil War (beginning with the lead up and taking the story through the assassination of Lincoln) and Reconstruction from the juxtaposed perspectives of a Northern abolitionist family and a traditional Southern family. Film historians are agreed that *The Birth of a Nation* is a masterpiece of filmmaking—it is the source of many of the conventions and techniques of modern movie production—but its glorification of the Ku Klux Klan (based on one of the film's sources, *The Clansman*, by Thomas Dixon, who also participated in the screenplay) has been roundly condemned. Directed by D. W. Griffith.

### *Gettysburg* (1993)
Based on *The Killer Angels* (1974), the extraordinary Gettysburg novel by Michael Shaara (father of Jeff Shaara, who wrote *Gods and Generals*), the film was produced with an eye toward meticulous historical re-creation. It is largely a superbly filmed reenactment of the battle of Gettysburg, filmed at the Gettysburg National Military Park. Directed by Robert F. Maxwell.

### *Glory* (1989)
Perhaps the most moving Civil War film ever made, *Glory* tells the story of the "colored" 54th Massachusetts Regiment and its young white colonel, Robert Shaw. The performances throughout are

universally splendid, especially Matthew Broderick as Shaw and Denzel Washington and Morgan Freeman as 54th Regiment troops. Directed by Edward Zwick.

## Gods and Generals (2003)

This film version of Jeff Shaara's novel reveals the prewar background of the key commanders at Gettysburg. Directed by Ronald F. Maxwell.

## Gone With the Wind (1939)

Adjusting the figures for inflation, no movie has ever made more money than this grandiose epic based on Margaret Mitchell's 1936 bestselling novel. Here is the Civil War from the perspective of the Southern plantation world—centered, in this case, on Scarlett O'Hara, perhaps the most famous heroine in American popular fiction. An icon of popular culture, the film would be worth seeing if only for its spectacular depiction of the burning of Atlanta. Directed by Victor Fleming (with uncredited contributions by George Cukor and Sam Wood).

## North and South (1985)

Produced as a made-for-TV miniseries, it is an engrossing and (at twelve hours) a surprisingly comprehensive and ambitious approach to the Civil War story. The late Patrick Swayze is the leading man, but the miniseries also includes the likes of Forest Whitaker, Robert Mitchum, Elizabeth Taylor, and Johnny Cash (as John Brown). Directed by Richard T. Heffron.

## The Outlaw Josey Wales (1976)

Clint Eastwood stars as Josey Wales, a Missouri farmer who gets caught up in the guerrilla warfare of Civil War–era Kansas and Missouri. Directed by Clint Eastwood.

## The Red Badge of Courage (1951)

A classic American film based on Stephen Crane's short novel. Written in 1894, the book was so realistic that readers assumed Crane was a veteran. Actually, he was born in 1871. As Henry Fleming, the main character, the film stars Audie Murphy, the most decorated combat soldier of World War II. The celebrated combat and political cartoonist Bill Mauldin (creator of World War II's "Willie and Joe") also plays a starring role. Directed by John Huston.

## Ride with the Devil (1999)

The film views the Civil War not as a political or moral or patriotic struggle, but as a species of tribal or clan warfare—which, in Missouri and Kansas (the setting of the film) is what it may well have been. Directed by Ang Lee.

# INDEX

# PICTURE CREDITS

LC-DIG-pga-01844; 236: LC-USZ62-88802; 239: LC-DIG-ppmsca-22378; 240–241: LC-DIG-pga-03266; 243: LC-USZ62-113167; 244: LC-USZC4-7984; 245: LC-USZC4-2086; 250: LC-DIG-pga-02196; 252: LC-USZ62-100070; 253: LC-DIG-pga-01871; 255: LC-DIG-ppmsca-19398; 256: LC-USZ62-42028; 257 (b): LC-DIG-cwpb-07586; 258: LC-DIG-cwpbh-03218; 261 (l): LC-DIG-ppmsca-20161; 261 (r): LC-USZ6-285; 263: LC-DIG-cwpb-04466; 264: LC-USZ62-10164; 266: LC-DIG-cwpb-05563; 268: LC-USZC4-1828; 269 (b): LC-DIG-ppmsca-21353; 271 (t): LC-DIG-ggbain-01096; 271 (b): LC-USZ62-54709; 272: LC-USZ62-44943; 273: LC-DIG-pga-04033; 274: LC-DIG-ppmsca-22569; 275: LC-DIG-stereo-1s02945; 278 (t): LC-USZ62-132749; 279: LC-USZ62-8383; 280: LC-USZ62-93555; 281: LC-USZ62-47037; 283 (t): LC-DIG-ppmsca-22939; 284: LC-USZC4-2519; 285: LC-DIG-ppmsca-02781; 286: LC-DIG-ppmsca-11280; 287: LC-DIG-pga-01949; 289: LC-DIG-cwpb-07639; 290–291: LC-DIG-ppmsca-09326; 293: LC-USZ62-126962; 294: LC-DIG-cwpb-06052; 295: LC-DIG-ppmsca-18199; 297 (t): LC-DIG-cwpb-06831; 297 (b): LC-D4-71768; 299: LC-DIG-pga-01846; 300: LC-DIG-cwpbh-00679; 303: LC-DIG-ppmsca-21139; 304: LC-DIG-ds-00298; 305: LC-DIG-pga-01853; 306: LC-DIG-ppmsca-31695; 311 (b): LC-DIG-ppmsca-18960; 314: LC-DIG-ppmsca-08359; 316: LC-DIG-ppmsca-20782; 317: LC-DIG-cwpb-02114; 318: LC-USZ62-130792; 319: LC-USZ62-122695; 320: LC-DIG-cwpb-04194; 321 (t): LC-DIG-ppmscd-00082; 322: LC-USZ62-127756; 323: LC-DIG-cwpb-07598; 325: LC-USZ61-1122; 327: LC-USZC4-4582; 329: LC-DIG-pga-04038; 330: LC-DIG-ppmsca-15768; 333: LC-DIG-ppmsca-20697; 334: LC-USZ62-46768; 335: LC-DIG-cwpb-01211; 337 (t): LC-DIG-ppmsca-20707; 337 (b): LC-DIG-pga-01881; 338: LC-USZ62-61876;

339: LC-DIG-cwpb-02790; 340: LC-DIG-cwpb-02576; 341: LC-USZ62-64034; 342: LC-DIG-ppmsca-21357; 343: LC-DIG-cwpb-0451; 347: LC-USZ62-104544; 349: LC-USZ62-118283; 352 (b): LC-DIG-cwpb-05934; 354: LC-DIG-pga-01850; 355: LC-DIG-cwpb-03414; 356 (b): LC-DIG-stereo-1s02515; 357: LC-USZ62-20182; 359: LC-USZ62-105256; 361: LC-DIG-cwpb-02087; 363 (b): LC-USZ62; 364: LC-DIG-cwpb-03049; 366: LC-DIG-cwpb-01061; 368 (b): LC-USZ62-1984; 370 (t): LC-USZ62-46426; 370 (b): LC-USZC4-13450; 371 (t): LC-DIG-ppmsca-22823; 371 (b): LC-USZC4-2385; 372: LC-USZC4-4177; 373 (b): LC-DIG-pga-04041; 377: LC-USZ62-127603; 381: LC-DIG-pga-02396; 382 (t): LC-USZ62-62747; 382 (b): LC-DIG-pga-04035; 384–385: LC-DIG-pga-03629; 387: LC-DIG-cwpb-07033; 388 (t): LC-DIG-ppmsca-21001; 388 (b): LC-DIG-cwpb-00934; 390: LC-DIG-npcc-30374; 391: LC-DIG-ppmsca-21296; 392: LC-DIG-ppmsca-21132; 393: LC-USA7-16837; 395: LC-DIG-cwpbh-00036; 398: LC-DIG-cwpb-02853; 400: LC-USZ62-1963; 402: LC-USZC2-2298; 403: LC-D4-43165; 404: LC-USZ62-6931; 405 (t): LC-DIG-cwpb-01553; 405 (b): LC-DIG-cwpbh-03894; 407: LC-DIG-cwpb-01299; 409: LC-DIG-ppmsca-21449; 411 (b): LC-DIG-cwpb-04406; 412: LC-USZC4-1321; 415: LC-USZ62-25166; 416: LC-DIG-cwpbh-00483; 417: LC-DIG-ppmsca-23872; 418: LC-DIG-cwpb-04208; 420 (t): LC-DIG-highsm-04710; 423 (t): LC-DIG-ppmsca-19484; 424: LC-B8184-10690; 425 (t): LC-DIG-stereo-1s01771; 425 (b): LC-USZ62-10122; 429: LC-DIG-stereo-1s02931; 430: LC-USZ62-131562; 431: LC-USZ62-106848; 432: LC-USZ62-106849; 433: LC-USZ62-128619; 434: LC-USZ62-96154; 435 (t): LC-USZ62-89311; 435 (b): LC-USZ62-10354; 436: LC-USZ62-97512

*Rare Book, Manuscript, and Special Collections Library, Duke University*
155: Conf. Music #61

*Rare Book and Special Collections Division*
28: lprbscsm scsm0318; 33: hc0015d; 40: lprbscsm scsm0237; 49: lprbscsm scsm0375; 166: cw105420; 201: lprbscsm scsm0232; 214: lprbscsm scsm1015; 228 (t): cw101730; 229: lprbscsm scsm0601; 231 (r): cw105130; 315: cw102670; 356 (t): cw100490; 368 (t): as112880; 410: lprbscsm scsm0502; 419: lprbscsm scsm0407; 420 (b): lprbscsm scsm0913; 422: lprbscsm scsm0350; 423 (b): lprbscsm scsm0517

**Courtesy of West Point Museum Collection**
257 (t)

**Courtesy of Wikimedia Commons**
58: 1861 Davis Inaugural/ Author: Archibald Crossland McIntyre of Montgomery, Alabama; 71 (l): George-B-Crittenden; 72: Fort Sumter telegram/ Author: Maj. Robert Anderson; 116 (b): Gen. Gideon J. Pillow, C.S.A. – NARA – 528290/ Author: Brady National Photographic Art Gallery; 127 (r): Minie Balls/ Author: Mike Cumpston; 132 (r): Gatlin Gun Drawing; 144: Stanley Founding of Congo Free State H M Stanley/ Author: Henry Morton Stanley; 269 (t): John Bell Hood; 282 (t): Knights of the Golden Circle History of Seccession [sic] book, 1862; 282 (b): Morgan Washington; 283 (b): Morgans [sic] Men POW 1863; 321 (b): Forrest & Maples listing; 324: Battle of Fort Pillow; 345: Petersburg crater aftermath 1865; 353 (t): John Bell Hood; 373: John Ancrum Winslow; 378: Hunley-2

**Naval History and Heritage Command/Washington Navy Yard**
69 (l): NH 51926; 77: NH 49391

**North Wind Pictures Archives**
192: © North Wind Pictures Archives/ Alamy

**Sterling Publishing Co., Inc.**
127 (tl); 127 (bl); 129 (t)